THE ARCHAEOLOGY C
Second Edition

The Archaeology of Britain is the only concise and up-to-date introduction to the archaeological record of Britain from the reoccupation of the landmass by *Homo sapiens* during the later stages of the most recent Ice Age until last century. This fully revised second edition extends its coverage, with greater detail on the first millennium AD beyond the Anglo-Saxon domain, and turning to recent times to look at the archaeology of contemporary society, including the Cold War.

The chapters are written by experts in their respective fields. Each is geared to provide an authoritative but accessible introduction, supported by numerous illustrations of key sites and finds and a selective reference list to aid study in greater depth. It provides a one-stop textbook for the entire archaeology of Britain and reflects the most recent developments in archaeology both as a field subject and as an academic discipline.

No other book provides such comprehensive coverage, with such a wide chronological range, of the archaeology of Britain. This collection is essential reading for undergraduates in archaeology and all those interested in British archaeology, history and geography.

John Hunter is Professor of Ancient History and Archaeology at the University of Birmingham. He specializes in Scottish archaeology, particularly in the Northern and Western Isles. He has published several books, including *Fair Isle, the archaeology of an island community*, and a major excavation monograph on multiperiod excavations on the island of Sanday, Orkney.

Ian Ralston is Professor of Later European Prehistory at the University of Edinburgh. His research interests include Scottish archaeology (notably its later prehistory), the temperate European Iron Age and applied archaeology. His recent books include *Celtic fortifications*, *Angus: archaeology and history* (with Andrew Dunwell) and *Un complexe princier de l'âge du Fer* (with Laurence Augier and Olivier Buchsenschutz).

THE ARCHAEOLOGY OF BRITAIN

An Introduction from Earliest Times to
the Twenty-First Century

Second Edition

Edited by John Hunter and Ian Ralston

Routledge
Taylor & Francis Group

LONDON AND NEW YORK

First published 1999
by Routledge
Reprinted in 1999, 2000, 2001, 2002, 2003, 2005, 2006

This second edition published in 2009
2 Park Square, Milton Park, Abingdon, Oxon OX14 4RN

Simultaneously published in the USA and Canada
by Routledge
270 Madison Ave, New York, NY 10016

Routledge is an imprint of the Taylor & Francis Group, an informa business

© 1999 and 2009 for selection and editorial matter;
individual chapters, their contributors

Typeset in Sabon by
Bookcraft Ltd, Stroud, Gloucestershire
Printed and bound in Great Britain by
Cromwell Press Group, Trowbridge, Wiltshire

All rights reserved. No part of this book may be reprinted or reproduced or utilised in
any form or by any electronic, mechanical, or other means, now known or hereafter
invented, including photocopying and recording, or in any information storage or
retrieval system, without permission in writing from the publishers.

British Library Cataloguing in Publication Data
A catalogue record for this book is available from the British Library

Library of Congress Cataloging in Publication Data
A catalog record for this book has been requested

ISBN 10: 0-415-47716-6 (hbk)
ISBN 10: 0-415-47717-4 (pbk)
ISBN 10: 0-203-86195-7 (ebk)

ISBN 13: 978-0-415-47716-1 (hbk)
ISBN 13: 978-0-415-47717-8 (pbk)
ISBN 13: 978-0-203-86195-0 (ebk)

Contents

Figures

While every effort has been made to trace copyright holders and obtain permission, this has not been possible in all cases. Any omissions brought to our attention will be remedied in future editions.

Tables

Contributors

Nicholas Barton is Professor of Palaeolithic Archaeology at Oxford University and a Fellow of Hertford College. His research interests cover British and north-west European Palaeolithic and Mesolithic archaeology as well as the Palaeolithic of the western Mediterranean. He is currently leading a project on 'Cemeteries and Sedentism' in North Africa involving excavations in the Grotte des Pigeons at Taforalt in Morocco. He specializes in lithic artefact technology.

Eleanor Conlin Casella is a Senior Lecturer in Archaeology at the University of Manchester and has directed fieldwork projects in Australia, North America and north-west England. Her research explores the convergence of industrial, post-medieval and historical archaeologies. Specific topics of interest also include household archaeology, material constructions of social identities, British colonialism and the archaeology of carceral institutions. Her recent books include *The archaeology of institutional confinement* and *The Alderley Sandhills Project: an archaeology of community life in (post) industrial England*.

Timothy Champion is a Professor of Archaeology at the University of Southampton and a past President of the Prehistoric Society. His research interests include the later prehistory of western Europe, the evolution of complex societies, the history of archaeology and the contemporary understanding of the past. Apart from work on prehistoric Britain, recent publications include (as co-editor) *Nationalism and archaeology in Europe* and *The wisdom of Egypt: changing visions through the ages*.

Kate Clark is Director of the Historic Houses Trust of NSW, Australia. She lectured on industrial archaeology at the Ironbridge Institute, collaborating on a major research project, published as *Landscape of Industry*. She then worked with the Council for British Archaeology, English Heritage, the Heritage Lottery Fund and in private consultancy. Her research interests focus on the wider values of heritage and on ideas about the role of significance in managing sites. She has written on conservation (including management planning), social and economic impacts of heritage, sustainable development, and industrial, buildings and landscape archaeology.

Timothy Darvill is Professor of Archaeology and Director of the Centre for Archaeology, Anthropology and Heritage in the School of Conservation Sciences, Bournemouth University. His research interests focus on archaeological resource management and the Neolithic period in northern Europe. He is has recently excavated at Stonehenge, Wiltshire, with Geoff Wainwright and at Billown on the Isle of Man and is Chairman of the Directors of Cotswold Archaeology. His publications include *Ancient Monuments in the Countryside*, *The Concise Oxford dictionary of Archaeology*, and *Stonehenge: the biography of a landscape*.

Stephen T. Driscoll is Professor of Historical Archaeology at the University of Glasgow with main research interests in Scotland's early medieval period, particularly in the Picts and Britons of Strathclyde. He has excavated widely in Scotland, including Edinburgh Castle and Glasgow Cathedral, as well as in Turkey, Jordan and the USA. He is currently co-directing the Strathearn Environs and Royal Forteviot research project, which explores the landscape of a Pictish royal centre.

Simon Esmonde Cleary is Reader in Archaeology at the University of Birmingham. His research focuses on the archaeology of the Roman period in Europe, particularly the later Roman period and the transition to the early medieval period, urban archaeology and material culture. He has conducted fieldwork in Britain and south-west France and his publications include *The ending of Roman Britain* and *Rome in the Pyrenees*.

Roberta Gilchrist is a Professor of Archaeology at the University of Reading. Her research focuses on medieval and social archaeology, with a particular interest in gender. She has published widely on the archaeology of religion, on medieval and early modern burial and on the archaeology of medieval and later standing buildings. Her publications include *Gender and material culture: the archaeology of religious women* and (with B. Sloane) *Requiem: the Medieval Monastic Cemetery in Britain*.

W.S. (Bill) Hanson is Professor of Roman Archaeology and Director of the Centre for Aerial Archaeology at the University of Glasgow, where he has taught for over 30 years. His research interests include Roman Britain, particularly the impact of the conquest on the indigenous population, Roman frontiers and airborne remote sensing. Recent publications include: *Roman Dacia: the making of a provincial society* (co-editor), *Elginhaugh: a Flavian fort and its annexe* and *The army and frontiers of Rome* (editor).

Colin Haselgrove, formerly Professor of Archaeology at the University of Durham, is now Head of the School of Archaeology and Ancient History, University of Leicester. His research interests include the Iron Age in Britain and France, particularly coinage, settlement archaeology and Roman impact on indigenous societies. He has excavated extensively in England, Scotland and France. His publications include *Understanding the British Iron Age: an agenda for action* and *Iron Age coinage and ritual practices*.

Catherine Hills is Senior Lecturer in the Department of Archaeology at the University of Cambridge. Her main interests are Anglo-Saxon archaeology, Europe and Scandinavia in the first millennium AD and the relationship between history and archaeology. She has excavated the Anglo-Saxon cemetery of Spong Hill in Norfolk, the reports on which are published in the series *East Anglian Archaeology*.

John Hunter is Professor of Ancient History and Archaeology at the University of Birmingham. He specializes in Scottish archaeology, particularly in the Northern and Western Isles. He has published several books, including *Fair Isle, the archaeology of an island community*, and a major excavation monograph on multiperiod excavations on the island of Sanday, Orkney. He also has interests in cultural resource management and forensic archaeology which he has helped to develop as a recognized discipline. *Forensic Archaeology: advances in theory and practice* appeared in 2005.

Nicky Milner is a Lecturer at the University of York. Her main research interests span the European Mesolithic and the Mesolithic–Neolithic transition, and she specializes in European shell middens. She has co-directed Mesolithic excavations at Howick, Lough Swilly and currently at Star Carr and elsewhere in the Vale of Pickering. She is editor of *Mesolithic miscellany* and has recently co-edited *Shell middens in Atlantic Europe* and *Mesolithic studies at the beginning of the 21st century*.

Steven Mithen is Professor of Early Prehistory and Dean of the Faculty of Science at the University of Reading. Between 1988 and 1998 he directed the Southern Hebrides Mesolithic Project and since 2003 has been directing the Inner Hebrides Mesolithic Project. He also directs the interdisciplinary Water, Life and Civilisation Project and the WF16 Excavation Project, both involving research in southern Jordan. His books include *The prehistory of the mind* (1996), *After the ice* (2003) and *The singing neanderthals* (2005).

Mike Parker Pearson is a Professor of Archaeology at the University of Sheffield and was previously an Inspector of Ancient Monuments for English Heritage. He directs the Stonehenge Riverside Project, revising knowledge of the site and its surroundings, and the Beaker People Project, recovering patterns of diet, mobility and migration in Britain's Early Bronze Age. His recent books include *Bronze Age Britain*, *The archaeology of death and burial* and (edited) *Food, identity and culture in the Neolithic and Early Bronze Age* and *Warfare, violence and slavery in prehistory*.

Ian Ralston is Professor of Later European Prehistory at the University of Edinburgh. His research interests include Scottish archaeology (notably its later prehistory), the temperate European Iron Age and applied archaeology. His recent books include *Celtic fortifications*, *Angus: archaeology and history* (with Andrew Dunwell) and *Un complexe princier de l'âge du Fer* (with Laurence Augier and Olivier Buchsenschutz); and new editions (with John Hunter) of *Archaeological resource management in the UK* and (with Kevin Edwards) of *Scotland after the Ice Age*.

Julian D. Richards is Professor of Archaeology at the University of York, where he is Head of Department and Director of the Archaeology Data Service. He teaches and researches early medieval archaeology and computer applications. He has excavated Anglo-Scandinavian settlements in the Yorkshire Wolds and the only known Viking cremation cemetery in the British Isles at Heath Wood, Ingleby. He is the author of *Viking Age England* and *The Vikings: a very short introduction*.

John Schofield (Chapter 13) was Curator of Architecture at the Museum of London until 2008. He has been digging in and writing about the City of London since 1974. His main interests are in urban archaeology of all periods and in the relationships between archaeology and documentary history. He has written *The Building of London from the Conquest to the Great Fire*, *Medieval London Houses* and, with Alan Vince, *Medieval Towns*.

John Schofield (Chapter 18) followed a PhD in prehistoric archaeology by turning his archaeological gaze on the contemporary past, the period of close living memory. He has undertaken this research from a position within English Heritage's Characterisation Team, while teaching at the universities of Southampton and Bristol. His research and publications have had a UK focus, but also extend to Malta, Berlin and Nevada. He co-edited *The Heritage Reader* for Routledge and is co-authoring a book on the archaeology of the contemporary past.

Paul Stamper works for English Heritage's Heritage Protection Department. Previously he was on the team writing Shropshire's *Victoria County History*, combining this with excavation on medieval rural sites including Wharram Percy. He has mainly published on medieval and later rural history and archaeology, and on designed landscapes. He is currently President of the Medieval Settlement Research Group and is joint editor of the cross-disciplinary journal *Landscapes*.

Alasdair Whittle is Distinguished Research Professor in the School of History and Archaeology at Cardiff University. He has researched widely on the Neolithic period in Britain, directing fieldwork projects from Shetland to Wessex, and Europe. His major publications include *Europe in the Neolithic*, *An archaeology of people*, *Building memories: the Neolithic Cotswold long barrow at Ascott-under-Wychwood, Oxfordshire* (edited with Don Benson) and *Histories of the dead: building chronologies for five southern British long barrows* (edited with Alex Bayliss).

Ian Whyte taught at University College Swansea and the University of Glasgow before moving to Lancaster, where he is now Professor of Historical Geography. His research interests include landscape and social and economic change in Britain during the post-medieval period with particular focus on upland areas. His recent books include *Landscape and history since 1500* and *World without End? Environmental Disaster and the Collapse of Empire*.

Preface

The idea for the approach taken in the first edition of this book emerged in late 1994 as the editors compared wounds that were the outcome of their previous collaborative editorial effort. Discussion, typical of many then and since, included considering the impacts of rising undergraduate numbers and noting the very different archaeological worlds – both academic and practical – that faced the new intakes of students, compared to that which had been encountered by young archaeologists a generation previously. Talk then turned to the concomitant need to make readily accessible suitable literature for students at the outset of their undergraduate careers, in access classes preparing for university entrance and for those taking A-level and similar courses and for their teachers. The format and contents of this second edition, a further attempt to encapsulate the British archaeological record and its present-day interpretation in an introductory and accessible way, represent the outcome of subsequent thoughts, but honed, improved and extended by anonymous referees, by our contributors and by feedback on the reception of the first edition. Lalle Pursglove and Matthew Gibbons at Routledge have also played a key role in the development of this edition.

No work of this kind could be put together without a team effort, and the contributions of our colleagues, both new and old, who have authored the substance of what follows remain central to the project. As previously, their e-mails and other communications were also of great help in the shaping of the contents. Revising, updating and extending this book (there are two wholly new chapters), and keeping it to a manageable size, was less than straightforward; we offer our grateful thanks to the chapter authors, whose efforts have allowed us to complete this new edition in an acceptable timescale, although not one where some delays did not inevitably occur. We trust they find the final product to their liking, but any deficiencies still present are our responsibility.

Thanks are also due to our partners, Margaret and Sandra, for once more tolerating the trauma of editing during the evenings and weekends and to those of our children still under our roofs for putting up with fathers once again preoccupied with the gestation of this book.

We hope that the following pages encourage and guide new students and interested amateurs in their involvement in British archaeology, and that colleagues across the widening spectrum of archaeological endeavour and beyond find value in the contents.

John Hunter and Ian Ralston
Warwickshire – Kinross-shire
June 2009

1

BRITISH ARCHAEOLOGY SINCE THE END OF THE SECOND WORLD WAR

Ian Ralston and John Hunter

INTRODUCTION

As with so many subjects, archaeology, and in particular British archaeology, has been the subject of greater involvement and awareness than was the case just after the Second World War. Universities teaching archaeology have grown from a mere handful to over 40 today, the subject itself has developed from a traditionally historical or Classical base to include natural, physical, computing, and even forensic sciences, and its scope has expanded to embrace, for example, standing buildings, underwater remains and whole landscapes. By way of a measure, *British Archaeological Abstracts*, first published in 1968, noted fewer than 300 articles that year, while its present successor, *British and Irish Archaeological Bibliography*, averaged over five times as many in the last three years (2005–7). Furthermore, long-established, county-based archaeological societies – the mainstay of the amateur involvement in which British archaeology has its roots – have been joined by an increasing range of special-interest groups whose activities and conferences are recorded in the annual reviews published by *Current Archaeology* and the Council for British Archaeology's (CBA) bi-monthly *British Archaeology*. This amateur involvement became radically 'professionalized' with the appearance of whole new sectors of archaeological endeavour both in local authorities and, most notably, in professional archaeological units, now major archaeological employers. The latter bodies first conducted 'rescue' fieldwork on behalf of state agencies, but now, together with numbers of archaeological companies and consultants, fulfil the needs of a wide range of developers. This is a product of legislative and planning changes by which developers have been required by government to conduct archaeological investigations within the framework of the 'polluter pays' principle (Hunter and Ralston 2006).

The same awareness of heritage has also seen archaeology's remit widening in both scope and detail; its chronological interests lap up against the present, with industrial archaeology (its history is sketched in Chapter 17) now including redundant plant of all kinds reflecting

the quantum leaps of twentieth-century and today's technologies in methods of energy generation, transportation and bulk processing. Moreover, a more recent field of enquiry susceptible
to archaeological approaches covers other aspects of the twentieth, and soon the twenty-first,
centuries, where memory as well as material remains provide a new stimulus to archaeological
endeavours not fully evident when the first edition was published (Chapter 18). Among these
are military monuments and landscapes; thus the remaining tank-traps and other defensive
installations on the beaches of Britain around which today's later-career archaeologists played
as children are now a focus of academic attention and heritage interest (Figure 1.1). Some
are Scheduled Ancient Monuments. In sum, archaeology is defined more broadly, and the
archaeological community that researches, manages and monitors this resource is substantially larger and more diverse than it was a generation ago. Even though many archaeological
jobs remain precarious, far more individuals earn their living from British archaeology in one
of its many guises than was the case in 1950, or indeed 1999, when the first edition of this
book appeared. The most recent analysis available (Aitchison and Edwards 2008) suggests
that the total British archaeological workforce in 2007/8 comprised around 7,000 individuals
compared with fewer than 4,500 10 years earlier.

DEVELOPING SCIENCES

There have also been radical changes in the development and sophistication of scientific
methods and in the intellectual climate in which archaeology has been conducted since the
end of the 1940s. New techniques and their routine application have made significant contributions, for example to the understanding of previous environments and subsistence regimes,
to sourcing the raw materials from which artefacts were made and to providing absolute
dates for archaeological materials. Many techniques are now exercised routinely, and archaeology continues to draw extensively on other areas of expertise, often in the creation of sub-
disciplines that have now evolved in their own right, such as palaeobotany, osteoarchaeology,
bioarchaeology (including DNA studies) and geographical information systems (GIS). These
new approaches and developments are not in themselves a principal concern in this volume
and can be pursued as individual features in the general literature on archaeology as a discipline (e.g. Renfrew and Bahn 2008). They do, however, reflect archaeology's holistic nature
and their results are incorporated in many ways in the following chapters.

Dating

The issue of obtaining dates may stand as particularly symptomatic of the scale and radical
nature of changes since the 1940s. The fixing of chronology has always been an archaeological preoccupation, and many standard archaeological methods – from site stratigraphies
to artefact typologies – contain amongst their primary purposes the establishment of relative chronologies, i.e. the demonstration that building A precedes building B, or that grave

Figure 1.1 The recording of military monuments. Remains from the Second World War now fall within the recognized scope of archaeology. Military remains at Brockhill, Redditch, Worcestershire.
Source: Birmingham University Field Archaeology Unit

C is later than grave D. However, the approaches available for providing absolute dates for archaeological materials immediately after the Second World War were little changed since the nineteenth century and ultimately involved correlations with documentary sources. These historical connections become possible from the Romano-British period onwards, with early chronicles, hagiographies and other components of the emerging written record (see Chapters 9 and 10); and, more reliably, with the later histories, accounts and documents of the Middle Ages. However, for pre-Roman times, chronology could still be established only in relative terms; it was interpreted on the basis of perceived analogies between artefacts or founded on the premises of diffusionist theory, often based on the clumsy 'three-age' sequence of technological progression from stone through bronze to iron. Alternatively, cross-dating was possible, ultimately with literate civilizations, but only intermittently and only as far back at most as the emergence of Middle Eastern civilizations some five millennia ago.

Major advances followed in biological, physico-chemical and geological sciences, particularly with Willard Libby's 1949 discovery of radiocarbon dating which depended on measuring the decay rate of the radioactive isotope of carbon in organic materials. Although the hypotheses on which the technique was developed have required modification, notably in the 'radiocarbon revolution' of the 1970s, when the need for major correction factors was recognized, the measurement of thousands of absolute dates has been of primordial importance in securing and modifying the chronology of prehistory. Radiocarbon measurement from archaeological materials requires adjustment or calibration according to the derived dates of sequences of tree-rings (dendrochronology), which mirror inconsistencies in the amount of radiocarbon in the atmosphere through time.

The effects of these calibrated dates have been both to push back in time the start dates for various innovations and to lengthen the timespans of various segments into which the archaeological record is traditionally sub-divided. Thus, in the mid-1950s, the Neolithic period in Britain was considered on the best evidence then available to have endured for several centuries either side of 2000 BC; early radiocarbon dates pushed its beginnings back to around 3000 BC; while recent calibrated dates place the British Earlier Neolithic even earlier – towards the start of the fourth millennium BC – and have also called into question the nature of the Mesolithic/Neolithic transition (see Chapters 3 and 4). Radiocarbon dates have also been instrumental in demonstrating that the initial interpretations of some elements in the archaeological record were awry (e.g. Fairweather and Ralston 1993). In recent years, the application of Bayesian statistics to radiocarbon datasets holds the promise of considerably greater precision in dating than previously seemed possible (see especially Chapter 4). Dendrochronology is also valuable in its own right, although its scope is restricted by the need for suitable preservation of wood in archaeological contexts, usually buildings and especially churches. Sequences of tree-rings matched between individual samples can provide dates correct to the nearest year; they have a particular role to play in post-Roman periods, where structural timbers may more commonly survive and when radiocarbon dates generally become of decreasing value. Among other techniques increasingly being deployed where suitable sediments are encountered is luminescence dating (Duller 2008).

Other technical innovations

Other techniques, too, have made important contributions to the refocusing of research agenda. Developments of the aqualung and the drysuit, for example, have physically extended the scope of British archaeology into lakes and shallow coastal waters, as witness work on the *Mary Rose* and on Scottish crannogs; moreover, opportunities to examine the archaeological consequences of sea-level changes, for example in the North Sea, have led to the modelling of submerged archaeological landscapes using drilling data derived from exploration on behalf of the oil industry (e.g. Gaffney *et al.* 2007). The widespread application of aerial photography (Wilson 2000) has had a major impact on the numbers of sites now recorded. New categories of archaeological site have also been identified from the air, particularly revealed as cropmarks in free-draining soils in the agricultural lowlands (as far north as the Moray Firth) of eastern and southern Britain (Figure 1.2). The technique has become more refined and versatile, and it currently underpins most regional sites and monuments records (Bewley 2006). Through the identification of former field and land boundaries, aerial imagery has been able to illustrate the vast extent of some systems of earlier settlement and land use; it has been in part responsible for the shift away from the study of individual monuments and their associated artefacts to the investigation of whole landscapes and of their cultural infrastructure through time (Darvill

Figure 1.2   Aerial photography has been a major factor both in increasing the number of known sites and in emphasizing the importance of landscape study. Oblique aerial view over the lowlands of Moray near Pitgaveny House, showing a cemetery of square barrows of probably Early Historic date amongst geomorphological and agricultural marks.
Source: Aberdeen Archaeological Services

et al. 1993). In its turn this has had a direct influence in matters of heritage management. The finer archaeological detail within such zones has been recognized through the refinement of fieldwork strategies, supported by sophisticated three-dimensional software and, most recently, by the application of geographical information systems (GIS), which allow landscapes and monuments to be investigated in terms of their physical and spatial relationships. Moreover, the use of advanced airborne imagery (notably LIDAR: light detection and ranging, a laser-based technology) has provided an interface between aerial and terrestrial surveying and allows landscape or monument contours to be mapped electronically in great detail. In the uplands and other zones where above-ground survival of monuments and landscapes is optimum, the use of electronic distance measuring equipment (EDMs) has long since simplified the task of mapping multiperiod features. Now more sophisticated EDMs, integrated with global positioning systems (GPS), have been developed in both automated and reflectorless modes allowing the generation of three-dimensional 'point cloud' images involving minimal manual input. The outcome is a radical change in the inputs required to acquire data and the scale and precision with which extensive suites of features – archaeological landscapes – can be studied.

Not least of these relationships amongst features distributed across the landscape is the time/depth dimension, which, given the importance attached to non-invasive strategies in fieldwork, is becoming increasingly pursued by geophysical means. Geophysical survey technology in part derives from mid-twentieth-century military developments and quickly became adapted as an archaeological technique in its own right. Its history and applications are well documented (e.g. Gaffney and Gater 2003), with magnetometry and resistivity methods being most commonly used on archaeological sites for both research and commercial evaluation, but with an interest developing rapidly in ground-penetrating radar (GPR). Some recent advances have centred on the determination of depth (e.g. using pseudosections), but in common with aerial and other remote sensing techniques, the effectiveness of geophysical survey is determined by the specific character and condition of the buried remains. This in turn biases understanding of period culture, in that some periods are likely to be more 'visible' than others, a factor especially relevant in sampling on applied archaeological projects related to proposed infrastructure or other developments (Hey and Lacy 2001).

Similarly, some periods or environmental settings are more favoured by taphonomic process than others, such as wetlands or those that simply have more to offer through deep stratification. Some of the following chapters are characterized by archaeological remains that are fragile; in others there are solid walls and durable materials. We can study only what survives or what we are able to locate, and our knowledge of the different periods is skewed accordingly.

The environmental dimension

The degree to which the land and environments of Britain have been shaped and reshaped by previous human communities across millennia is becoming increasingly apparent through the investigation of some components of these landscape palimpsests, in concert with parallel, sometimes integrated, studies by palaeoenvironmentalists. Many approaches are now available, and many sub-disciplines – including the study of sub-fossil midges, beetles, pollen, diatoms and plant macrorests and aspects of geomorphology – contribute; dendrochronology, as well as furnishing absolute chronology, is important also for studies of climate change. A substantial literature has been generated and is summarized in numerous works (e.g. Simmons 2001; Dark 2000; Evans 1999; for Scotland, Edwards and Ralston 2003). The integration of environmental and archaeological studies has been taken further for prehistory than for subsequent periods, but exceptions to this rule are becoming ever more frequent, notably in the analysis of urban deposits. Because of the enhanced possibilities of preservation they offer, and the particular scope for the integration of archaeological and environmental studies, threatened examples of Britain's wetlands have been particular targets for archaeological study (Barber *et al.* 2007 for a recent overview). These include more especially lowland peat mosses and estuarine and other inter-tidal zones. Particularly influential work, such as that undertaken in the Somerset Levels and at Flag Fen, near Peterborough, is mentioned in the succeeding chapters.

CHANGING PERSPECTIVES

Equally relevant are the various ways by which archaeologists have believed the past can be studied. These have implications for the way in which archaeology is conducted in the field (Lucas 2001), and there have been a number of reassessments of what archaeological approaches to the physical record bequeathed by earlier communities may be able to achieve. Intellectual fashions have changed, not only as some archaeologists have absorbed theoretical developments in neighbouring disciplines in the social sciences and elsewhere, but also as they reconsider the nature and potential meanings of the structures and materials contained within the evolving archaeological record. This focus on changing perspectives has been especially prominent in the study of prehistory, most recently using phenomenological approaches which identify the different ways by which we engage with ancient landscapes (e.g. Bender *et al.* 2008).

For later periods, these radical shifts in theoretical stance met greater resistance, partly in view of traditional approaches based on artefact typology, and partly through the presence of written records of a variety of types which enabled the material past to be somewhat artificially compartmentalized into narratives provided by neighbouring disciplines. Also, the more recent the period under consideration, the shorter, in general, has been the tradition of independent archaeological research devoted to it. An indication of this is offered by the foundation dates for the major period-based societies in Britain, those for medieval, postmedieval and industrial archaeology being amongst the most recent, whereas the prehistoric has (along with the Roman) been one of the periods with the longest traditions of archaeological study and investigation. Chapter 18, which is new to this second edition, reflects the extent to which such theoretical developments now underpin our study of even the most modern of cultural remains, as archaeological approaches to these periods have grown in confidence and sophistication.

Culture history and its successors

In the 1950s, the dominant framework for prehistoric studies was provided by the cultural-historical approach, most usually associated in Britain with Vere Gordon Childe, Abercromby Professor of Prehistoric Archaeology at Edinburgh from 1927 and subsequently Director of the Institute of Archaeology at the University of London. This perspective prevailed until the late 1960s; its great achievements included the fuller recognition and ordering of archaeological assemblages, in part through the results of more extensive and systematic excavation.

The latter was a legacy of, amongst others, Mortimer Wheeler and Gerhard Bersu. Bersu's excavations, most celebratedly at Little Woodbury, Wiltshire (discussed in Chapter 7), allowed the import of the best of contemporary continental practice, including techniques appropriate to the recovery of the stances of former earthfast timber structures, as well as furnishing new interpretations. Wheeler's campaigns at Maiden Castle, Dorset, published mid-way through the Second World War (1943), were a demonstration of other technical innovations in fieldwork and provided the archaeological support for Wheeler's vision of British Iron Age developments, as well as showing the potential for public involvement in what was then a distinctly minority interest. In the 1950s, larger-scale open-area excavations, as at Yeavering, Northumberland (Hope-Taylor 1977), became feasible and, particularly in subsequent decades, were much more numerous in the countryside. The mechanization of topsoil removal from archaeological sites, unglamorous but essential, using increasingly sophisticated 360-degree mechanical excavators, enabled the routine stripping and planning of much more extensive areas than had previously been achievable. Some sites were excavated on a scale that made them 'laboratories' for their own period of use, such as West Heslerton or Wharram Percy in North Yorkshire (see Chapters 10 and 15 respectively); others, like Jarlshof in Shetland (Hamilton 1956), became used as a regional control for predicting structural changes in multiperiod settlements. Much of the best field archaeology was avowedly multidisciplinary, as the potential contribution of physical and biological scientists was increasingly recognized. Grahame Clark's promptly published project at Star Carr, Yorkshire, considered in Chapter 3, was particularly influential in this regard.

Much of the pattern of cultural developments recognized, described and refined during this period has survived into later usage. What have since changed, in some instances substantially, are the modes of explanation favoured to account for changes seen in the archaeological record. Until quite well into the second half of last century, the use of 'invasion theory' found much favour, particularly in periods involving recorded Germanic or Scandinavian movement. Although still important for some horizons and periods, its use as the primary means to account for cultural change came under sustained, and often successful, attack (Clark 1966).

From the late 1960s, a change in emphasis marked the way in which the archaeological record was interpreted by a number of influential figures in the discipline. Radiocarbon dating had already pointed towards errors in the chronology of British prehistory as that was traditionally presented, and for some of the new generation of archaeologists the writing of culture history was no longer the primary focus. Archaeology, in some views at least, 'lost its innocence' (Clarke 1973) during this period, but as with the other realignments noted here, the new agenda and approaches were far from universally accepted. Important manifestos, like David L. Clarke's *Analytical archaeology* (1968), drew on other disciplines where traditional perspectives were being challenged (such as the 'New Geography') and on American practice more closely to link archaeological interpretation to dominant perspectives within cultural anthropology, borrowing its vocabulary in the process. Primary aims now included the study of archaeologically recognizable changes in cultural systems, often interpreted from changing spatial patterns in the data. Attention was paid especially to those sub-systems considered most detectable from physical archaeological evidence. Particular targets were subsistence economics and the recognition of social change; as a result, the recovery and analyses of appropriate datasets immediately became of high priority. A distinctly positivist attitude to reading the archaeological record is characteristic of some writing, often called the 'New Archaeology', during this period (Malone and Stoddart 1998).

The period since 1980 has seen major developments in the consideration of fresh ways of approaching the archaeological record and of conveying its meanings. In contradistinction to the New Archaeology of the 1960s and 1970s, frequently termed 'processual', subsequent archaeological theorizing can be labelled 'post-processual' – a term that obscures a burgeoning range of post-modern theoretical stances and agendas. Included amongst external strands that have contributed are social theory, phenomenology, ethnoarchaeological studies, certain kinds of historical practice (particularly that concerned with long-term evolutionary rhythms and often associated with the *Annales* school in France), feminism and gender studies, and attempts to analyse material culture recovered archaeologically as encoded messages, akin to literary texts (e.g. Hodder and Hudson 2003; Shanks and Tilley 1992; Tilley 1994). These approaches have undoubtedly influenced the writing of some of the contributors here; this gives some indication of the competing theoretical approaches to the subject matter and the degree to which these vary according to the data and traditions of the periods under study. Not all branches of archaeological study within Britain have been impacted to the same degree by these more recent theoretical approaches, with some sub-disciplines, perhaps particularly in environmental and scientific archaeology, less radically affected.

Archaeology in the field

In terms of fieldwork, the period dominated in interpretative terms by these processual approaches was broadly coeval with the upsurge in rescue archaeology, a development spurred by the recognition by some archaeologists of the deleterious impact of government and private sector attempts to renew Britain's infrastructure on the archaeological record as it then survived and was understood. Although individual government projects – such as the wartime building of Heathrow airport and the creation of a rocket range on the Outer Hebrides in the 1950s – had been preceded by systematic salvage excavation, archaeological projects of this kind were the exception rather than the rule. Urban renewal projects, especially in the cores of London and some historic cities in England, and the building of the motorway network were major spurs to the case being accepted for increased state support for preliminary archaeological work, and many large-scale, as well as smaller, field projects were undertaken because of such perceived threats. The archaeological resource in the landscapes of Britain is subject to continuing attrition (e.g. Darvill and Fulton 1998), but the nature of the threats and their severity have varied over time. It is arguable for example that the scale of change in the urban cores of many British towns and cities that characterized the post-Second World War decades is unlikely to be repeated for many years into the future, with concomitant effects on the range of opportunities for urban archaeology (Figure 1.3). Much of what we know of medieval towns stems from the opportunity presented by this urban regeneration (see Chapter 13). Much new information was generated, but its assimilation into wider syntheses was not, in many instances, accorded high priority.

The restructuring of field archaeology a generation ago to counter the increasing erosion of the archaeological record occurred differently in the constituent parts of the country; its

Figure 1.3   Urban archaeology developed rapidly under the 'rescue' banner of the 1970s and early
1980s and provided the basis for much of our knowledge of medieval towns. Excavation
at Long Causeway, Peterborough.
Source: Birmingham University Field Archaeology Unit

development was *ad hoc* and inconsistent, and archaeologists today are still burdened by its
legacy. Some parts of Britain received greater archaeological attention and resources than others,
based on local demands and opportunities at the time, not on a rational analysis of longer-term
need. Only Wales developed a coherent, fully nationwide system, whilst funding (tied to present-
day population sizes rather than to archaeological resources or the scale of the threats to them)
was most generous in England (see Chapter 19). This biasing is inevitably reflected in the work
carried out and in the distribution of data recovered. The unevenness of the record emerges too
in the chapters that follow; but it afflicts some periods more than others and is also as much a
measure of the frameworks within which research has taken place as it is of regional disparity
of resources. For example, at chronological extremes, studies of Mesolithic hunter-gatherers
have for long drawn on evidence from across Britain, whereas innovation and change in the
Industrial Revolution is characterized as much in south Wales and west-central Scotland as in
some parts of England. Contrastingly, the existence of a first-millennium AD Anglo-Saxon zone
of Germanic influence in central and eastern England and broadly Celtic influences in contemporary northern and western zones of Britain have contributed to traditions of relatively independent archaeological study (as can be seen from Chapters 10 and 11 here). In some areas, too,
the integration of archaeological information into regional or national overviews developed late:
the first-ever synthesis of medieval Scotland from an archaeological perspective (Yeoman 1995)
appeared only while the first edition of this volume was in preparation. For some chronological
periods, archaeological overviews at the scale of Great Britain have never appeared.

The period since 1980 has also seen substantial alterations in the way in which the practice of field archaeology is structured; and many current archaeologists face new kinds of problems, not always of an 'academic' kind, in examining the record (Hunter and Ralston 2006; Chapter 19 here). Some initially railed against these changes, essentially a by-product of the 'polluter pays' ethos whereby developers are required to mitigate the damage to the archaeological record occasioned by their developments, seeing the outcome as one in which British archaeology 'finds itself in a curious position of self-doubt and indecision' (Biddle 1994, 16). Changes have included a significant trend away from large-scale excavation in favour of small field evaluation exercises, designed in part to test for archaeological remains with a view to protecting them *in situ* rather than excavating them. The driving force was initially the enactment of European Union directives in regulations across Britain, the publication of new advice on archaeology in relation to planning matters by central government and a growing awareness that the archaeological resource should possess a wide, rather than a narrow, social and community relevance (e.g. DCMS and DTLGR 2001). Archaeological remains in Britain are now recognized as a finite, non-renewable resource (Darvill and Fulton 1998) for protection for future elucidation by active sustainable management rather than benign neglect. Reflecting this has been the move towards Historic Landscape Characterisation (HLC) and its equivalents, which view the local archaeological environment in its totality in time and space for public enjoyment and education and much less as an exploitable raw material for the nourishment of archaeological research.

DISSEMINATING THE RECORD

The diverse development of British archaeology has undoubtedly benefited from the publication of overviews, and several of the following chapters make reference to key texts that have served as markers of particular approaches or as 'snapshots in time'. Several of these are either major period-based syntheses or studies of longer timespans (e.g. Renfrew 1974; Megaw and Simpson 1979; Bradley 2007; Pryor 2004). These, and others written for more specialist readerships (e.g. Pollard 2008), have enabled archaeologists both to take stock and to formulate new hypotheses, and allow students to assimilate information and perspectives that are normally diffused through a wide range of publication outlets. This is a continuing process, and recent years have seen in particular important series of introductory accounts, either period-based or framed around major sites, emerging from English Heritage and Historic Scotland (e.g. Armit 2005), some of which are noted in the following chapters.

The gap in currently available overviews that this book was designed to address was of a single volume that provided a panorama of the archaeology of Britain from the Stone Age through to the most recent period to which archaeological approaches had been applied. This was devised as a team effort to reflect the number of fields of expertise now essential to the study of British archaeology. No single archaeologist could realistically hope to master the entirety of the record to be considered, and the volume additionally demonstrates the range of sub-disciplines involved, the approaches taken and the results obtained, both regionally and by period, by environmentalists, documentary historians and other specialists in their areas of major interest. The book also provides the opportunity for archaeologists to achieve the necessary awareness of data types, problems and approaches taken in periods and geographical areas other than those on which their own interests are focused.

Any overview also requires some definition of the word 'British' in its title, particularly given concerns on the impacts of nationalism and imperialism, as experienced in Britain during the time of archaeology's evolution, on the discipline's form and the way in which its discourses are framed (e.g. Champion 1996). This volume is intended to address the record for Britain as a geographical region, rather than as the 'archaeology of a nation'. In some respects this aim also runs counter to differences in the practices and approaches of the various state agencies concerned with archaeological matters, despite the fact that the primary archaeological legislation, the Ancient Monuments and Archaeological Areas Act 1979, applies universally. At the time this second edition was being compiled a new Heritage Act for England was under process of consultation. Not only did this new Act promise to subsume the 1979 Act, but its advocates saw it as an opportunity to draw together legislation and directives embracing both standing and buried historic environments, as well as harmonizing central and local government responsibilities towards managing the past. In the event, political circumstances conspired to stop its progress; but what is also clear is that one outcome of the internal political devolution within Britain is that any legislative change in this domain is likely henceforth to affect only part of the territory here considered.

The emphasis of this book is on Britain (rather than on England, but excluding Ireland) and on a definition of archaeology that spans the full range of contemporary studies: in this second edition Chapter 2 has been extended back in time to outline significant recent discoveries (e.g. within the gravel pits at Boxgrove, West Sussex) long preceding the arrival of *Homo sapiens*, and has been expanded forwards in time to include more modern periods for which a substantial (albeit incomplete) historical record is also available (Chapter 18). Ireland, too, has its own traditions of archaeological research, often and logically embracing both Eire and the counties of Ulster. For some periods, Irish comparanda demonstrate that links across the Irish Sea, or along the western seaways to both Britain and Ireland, were important; and selective instances of such features are mentioned here. A multiperiod archaeological account of the British Isles in their north-west European setting remains a task for the future; perhaps the current work, and recent syntheses of Irish material (e.g. Waddell 2000), will encourage such a development, which was made easier by the inclusion from 1997 of Irish literature in what is now *British and Irish Archaeological Bibliography*.

This volume is intended as a readable introduction to British archaeology written by contributors who not only have a formidable grasp of their own subject areas, but who also have first-hand experience of teaching students and developing teaching from their personal research and that of their colleagues. Their brief was to provide an attractive, readable volume rather than a clinical textbook, one that would reflect their own enthusiasms and not be overburdened with methodological debates and considerations of techniques. They are also all familiar with the changes that have occurred in, and continue to impact on, teaching practices and learning strategies in higher education, and with pressure on library resources, the need for suitable basic texts and the declining purchasing power of current students, particularly those entering the tertiary system later in life.

Moreover, the developments in information technology since the first edition of this volume have also played as much a part in disseminating information as in its collection and processing. Vast quantities of digital field data are collected on a daily basis, catalogued and stored by individual organizations. Increasingly, this material, which includes 'grey' literature from commercial operations undertaken by the applied archaeological companies, is now stored on-line through the Archaeology Data Service (ADS) based at the University of York. The CBA continues to provide a gateway to various relevant data sources (www.britarch.ac.uk) and there are several initiatives which aim to identify appropriate archaeological websites for teaching, research and general digestion (e.g. www.humbul. ac.uk). Of particular interest in this respect is the CANMORE database of Scottish sites developed by the Royal Commission on the Ancient and Historical Monuments of Scotland (RCAHMS; www.rcahms.gov.uk/search.html#canmore). Overall and inevitably, the collection, organization, storage and dissemination of archaeological data is becoming increasingly computer-dependent. A number of excavation reports are now made available on-line only, for example Scottish Archaeological Internet Reports (SAIR; www.sair.org.uk), a method of dissemination which, its advocates argue, is less time-consuming, more efficient and more easily accessible to a wider public. Internet provision also provides challenges to the excavator, for example in the publication of sites in *Internet Archaeology* (http://intarch.ac.uk/), where the 'reader' can explore the excavation report at various levels, from synthesis to primary record and raw data.

The substantial rise in student numbers in university departments over recent years has increased the demand for books but has also caused a shift in the types of book required. Student-centred learning and, more recently, enquiry-based learning, together with competing demands on academic staff time, have brought about the need for students to acquire underpinning knowledge on which academic staff can confidently build and on which perceptions and hypotheses can be based. In some senses, this volume is a practical reaction to the requirements of higher education in the early twenty-first century – the need to draw together and make accessible basic themes and to provide opportunities for students to obtain and begin to question current views.

The text is divided into chronologically linked chapters, each of which is designed to stand in its own right, but with overall chronology running in a single calendrical sequence, avoiding as far as is feasible the admixture of uncalibrated radiocarbon dates and calendrical dates obtained from historical sources that students, plunged into the discipline for the first time, tend to find confusing. Throughout, these chapters are framed in terms of chronologies in calendrical years, from whatever source (including radiocarbon) the dates were originally obtained. The sole exceptions are the remotest periods of prehistory, where dating depends substantially on isotopic determinations of other kinds and for which levels of precision are somewhat lower.

This is a wide-ranging volume, which breaks new ground in the chronological span of its coverage for the geographical area under consideration. Fifty years ago, its scope, dependent on the breadth and depth of archaeological research that underpin its contributions, would not have seemed either appropriate or achievable to many of the archaeologists of the time. Ten years ago in the first edition, the chapters read very differently and the available range of archaeological data for some chapters has since increased significantly. The central difficulty faced by all the contributors has lain in determining how to wrestle with the expansion of knowledge, the changing interpretations and the wealth of data in order to convey the key significances of their period in a condensed form. As a result, the chapter structures were specifically engineered to make this possible. Individual contributors were asked to address, as far as possible, specific elements within their own specialisms, namely principal chronological sub-divisions; major and typical data types; changing perceptions since the Second World War; relevant advances in archaeological science; key sites and assemblages; current perceptions; and the British evidence in a wider geographical framework. The aim was to encourage a degree of consistency throughout the volume in regard to the subject matter, but not in the least to force authors to approach this from any particular theoretical perspective. This standardization of content but not of approach, discussed briefly above in relation to recent developments in archaeological theory, has been allowed neither to smooth out the characteristics of individual periods nor seriously to impinge on individuals' perceptions of what they considered important to lay before the reader.

There are inevitably some differences in the way in which contributions to this book sit within a much wider geographical framework. In those dealing with early prehistory, southern connections are uppermost, not least because Britain was in remote times a north-western peninsula of the continental landmass, whereas later periods have European links of different strengths, and from different directions, from western continental coastlands in the Later Bronze Age to Norse Scandinavia. In the Roman period, contrastingly, Britain was an outlying province of a continental-scale empire. During the periods considered in the final chapters, the influences are even wider and the context, latterly that of British imperial expansion and of the World Wars, almost global.

There is no common database that can supply a consistent set of material for all periods. The archaeological records for most periods exhibit idiosyncratic or high-profile remains that in some instances drew early antiquarians to them – such as stone circles, villas, brochs – and started the process of cultural definition that provides the near-inescapable framework for the chapter sub-divisions employed here. Much of the way in which archaeologists define culture periods still reflects the traditional responses initially attributable to early antiquarians and to historians' sub-divisions for more recent periods. Whilst the development of a much securer chronological framework through radiocarbon dating and new perspectives derived from archaeological approaches to, for example, social change might have permitted a radical alternative framework to be devised, this can be left to others, on another occasion. The primary purpose here is to present a guide to current archaeological interpretations of the sites in Britain's landscapes and the artefacts in its museums.

Despite the breadth of coverage, each chapter has been deliberately restricted in its bibliography. Each has two levels of bibliography: a set of some five key titles that encapsulate the evidence of, and approaches to, the period under consideration; and a further set of about twenty-five to thirty titles that allows for greater detail or specialization. The criteria set were that all citations should be to works likely to be readily accessible in university libraries. This, it is anticipated, should assist students to embark on their own research for essay writing and other practical course requirements. It will also give more highly motivated students opportunities to begin to consider particular approaches or periods that are absent or less stressed in the particular academic environments in which they are studying.

In another context, John Updike wrote that 'the fate of all monuments is to become ... a riddle'. Whilst their interpretation undoubtedly poses challenges, the following chapters represent something of the range of archaeological approaches to the physical fabric left by earlier societies that is now being attempted. Medieval monasteries, for example, once viewed primarily as building layouts and as repositories for the study of the development of architectural styles, are now frequently approached as constituent parts of economic landscapes and as arenas for evolving ritual practices. Similarly, castles, formerly considered essentially as fortifications and as keys to changing military tactics and equipment, may now be viewed as symbols of elite power and as central elements in organized economic hinterlands from which they drew resources. Comparable changes are evident for artefactual studies, where some archaeologists are now much more readily prepared to hypothesize on social and ritual roles than was the case in the years immediately after the Second World War. Medieval artefacts, for example, viewed solely as fodder for art historical studies, have in recent decades been increasingly studied as keys to technology, as products of exchange and trade and as indicators of social relations and stratification.

As archaeological evidence accumulates, the very diverse characteristics of different places, sites and objects, conventionally described in the same way, are writ large. This is a book that encapsulates archaeological change in many forms – a 'snapshot' of how we have been thinking, excavating and learning in the first part of the twenty-first century.

Bibliography

Aitchison, K. and Edwards, R., 2008. *Archaeological labour market intelligence: profiling the profession 2007/8*. Reading: Institute of Field Archaeologists.

Armit, I., 2005. *Celtic Scotland*. London: Batsford / Historic Scotland. New edn.

Barber, J., Clark, C., Cressey, M., Crone, A., Hale, A., Henderson, J., Housley, R., Sands, R. and Sheridan, A. (eds) 2007. *Archaeology from the wetlands: recent perspectives*. Edinburgh: Society of Antiquaries of Scotland (= Wetland Archaeology Research Project Occasional Paper 18).

Bender, B., Hamilton, S. and Tilley, C., 2008. *Stone worlds. Narrative and reflexivity in landscape Archaeology.* Walnut Creek, California: Left Coast Press.

Bewley, R., 2006. 'Aerial surveying for archaeology', in Hunter and Ralston, 276–91.

Biddle, M., 1994. *What future for British archaeology?* Oxford: Oxbow (= Oxbow Lecture 1).

Bradley, R.J., 2007. *The prehistory of Britain and Ireland.* Cambridge: Cambridge University Press.

Champion, T.C., 1996. 'Three nations or one? Britain and the national use of the past', in Díaz-Andreu, M. and Champion, T.C. (eds) *Nationalism and Archaeology in Europe.* London: UCL Press, 119–45.

Clark, J.G.D., 1966. 'The invasion hypothesis in British archaeology', *Antiquity* 40, 172–89.

Clarke, D.L., 1968. *Analytical archaeology.* London: Methuen.

Clarke, D.L., 1973. 'Archaeology: the loss of innocence', *Antiquity* 47, 6–18.

DCMS and DTLGR (= Department for Culture, Media and Sport and Department of Transport, Local Government and the Regions) 2001. *The historic environment: a force for our future.* London: DCMS. www.culture.gov.uk/heritage.

Dark, P., 2000. *The environment of Britain in the first millennium AD.* London: Duckworth.

Darvill, T. C. and Fulton, A. 1998. *The Monuments at Risk survey of England 1995. Main report.* Bournemouth: School of Conservation Sciences, Bournemouth University and London: English Heritage.

Darvill, T. C., Gerrard, C. and Startin, B., 1993. 'Identifying and protecting historic landscapes', *Antiquity* 67, 563–74.

Duller, G.A.T., 2008. *Luminescence dating: guidelines on using luminescence dating in archaeology.* Swindon: English Heritage.

Edwards, K. J. and Ralston, I.B.M. (eds) 2003. *Scotland after the Ice Age.* Edinburgh: Edinburgh University Press.

Evans, J.G., 1999. *Land and archaeology. Histories of human environment in the British Isles.* Stroud: Tempus.

Fairweather, A.D. and Ralston, I.B.M., 1993. 'The Neolithic timber hall at Balbridie, Grampian Region, Scotland: the building, the date, the plant macrofossils', *Antiquity* 67, 313–23.

Gaffney, C.F. and Gater, J. 2003. *Revealing the buried past: geophysics for archaeologists.* Stroud: Tempus.

Gaffney, V., Thomson, K. and Fitch, S. (eds) 2007. *Mapping Doggerland: the Mesolithic landscapes of the southern North Sea.* Oxford: Archaeopress 31.

Hamilton, J.R.C., 1956. *Excavations at Jarlshof, Shetland.* Edinburgh: HMSO.

Hey, G. and Lacey, M., 2001. *Evaluation of archaeological decision making processes and sampling strategies.* London: English Heritage and IFA.

Hodder, I. and Hudson, S., 2003. *Reading the past: current approaches to interpretation in archaeology.* Cambridge: Cambridge University Press. 3 edn.

Hope-Taylor, B.K., 1977. *Yeavering: an Anglo-British centre of early Northumbria.* London: HMSO (= Department of the Environment Research Report 7).

Hunter, J.R. and Ralston, I.B.M. (eds) 2006. *Archaeological resource management in the UK: an introduction.* Stroud: Sutton Publishing. 2 edn.

Lucas, G., 2001. *Critical approaches to fieldwork.* London: Routledge.

Malone, C. and Stoddart, S. (eds) 1998. 'Special section: David Clarke's "Archaeology: the loss of innocence" 25 years after', *Antiquity* 72, 676–702.

Megaw, J.V.S. and Simpson, D.D.A. (eds) 1979. *An introduction to British prehistory from the arrival of Homo sapiens to the Claudian invasion.* Leicester: Leicester University Press.

Pollard, J. (ed.) 2008. *Prehistoric Britain.* Oxford: Blackwell.

Pryor, F., 2004. *Britain BC.* London: HarperCollins.

Renfrew, A.C. (ed.) 1974. *British prehistory: a new outline.* London: Duckworth.

Renfrew, A.C. and Bahn, P., 2008. *Archaeology; theories, methods and practice.* London: Thames and Hudson. 5 edn.

Shanks, M. and Tilley, C., 1992. *Re-constructing archaeology: theory and practice.* London: Routledge. 2 edn.

Simmons, I.G., 2001. *An environmental history of Great Britain: from 10,000 years ago to the present.* Edinburgh: Edinburgh University Press.

Tilley, C., 1994. *A phenomenology of landscape: places, paths and monuments.* Oxford: Berg.

Waddell, J., 2000. *The prehistoric archaeology of Ireland.* Dublin: Wordwell. 2 edn.

Wheeler, R.E.M., 1943. *Maiden Castle, Dorset.* London: Reports of the Research Committee of the Society of Antiquaries 12.

Wilson, D.R., 2000. *Air photography interpretation for archaeologists.* Stroud: Tempus.

Yeoman, P.A., 1995. *Medieval Scotland.* London: Batsford / Historic Scotland.

2

THE LATEGLACIAL OR LATEST PALAEOLITHIC OCCUPATION OF BRITAIN

Nicholas Barton

EARLIER PALAEOLITHIC BACKGROUND

In its broadest sense, the Palaeolithic can be described as the first and by far the longest period of human existence, covering a timespan of more than 2.5 million years. The Palaeolithic is defined largely on the basis of the presence of stone artefacts (hence the derivation of the term 'Old Stone Age') which in turn can be typed and classified according to subdivisions for this period. In Britain and northern Europe such tool-making traditions can be traced back to at least 0.7 million years ago (in the Pleistocene or 'Recent' geological epoch) and continued until the end of the last Ice Age approximately 11,500 years ago.

Historically, ideas concerning the deep antiquity of humans only gained widespread acceptance in the late nineteenth century. Undoubtedly one of the defining moments in this respect came on 6 June 1859 (the same year as the publication of Darwin's *On the Origin of Species*), when John Evans and Joseph Prestwich visited Boucher de Perthes in his home near Amiens in northern France. Here they were shown the bones of extinct animals including mammoth and rhinoceros that had been found in the same gravel beds as stone (hand)axes. After a sumptuous *déjeuner à la fourchette*, Evans records in a letter that they travelled together to the now famous gravel pit 'where sure enough the edge of an axe was visible in an entirely undisturbed bed of gravel and eleven feet from the surface'. The auspicious scene was captured in a photograph which was surely the first occasion on which such a means of verification had been used. Accounts of these discoveries were published soon afterwards in the Royal Society and Society of Antiquaries journals, providing vital scientific proof that ancestral humans with advanced tool-making skills lived cheek by jowl with large extinct animals.

Of course we now know much more about the sequence and dating of gravels in the Somme Valley and elsewhere. This is based on new scientific dating techniques and biostratigraphic indicators (e.g. the presence of distinctive faunal or floral groupings in each of the different archaeological layers). These inform us about past environments, while further evidence for reconstructing earlier climatic conditions and change comes from deep marine cores and long ice records that provide highly accurate measures of successive global warming and cooling episodes. The information derives from ice chemistry and growth patterns, while tiny forams (marine micro-organisms) that settle on the ocean floor can tell us a great deal about former sea temperatures and ocean circulation. Combining all of these sources of information provides a reasonably clear picture of climatic and environmental change throughout the Palaeolithic. In Britain we refer to warm and cold stages by their type names and with reference to global Marine Isotope Stages (MIS; see Table 2.1).

Today, we see Britain as occupying a geographically isolated position on the extreme north-west periphery of Europe. but it should be remembered that for long stretches of the last 1.8 million years (the Pleistocene) Britain was connected to Europe by a substantial land-bridge. As a result we share many of the same rich biological fossil records, since animal (including human) and plant communities were able to move freely across the land-locked connection. Even during warm periods when global sea-levels rose to their present high position, it appears that a wide chalk isthmus existed across the Dover Strait (Stringer 2006). Although the land-link was breached around 450 ka BP (in MIS 12), Britain rarely became fully cut off from the Continent except for brief periods in the warmest phases of interglacials, most notably at around 130 ka BP (in MIS 5e).

The earliest Lower Palaeolithic occupation of Britain

Until recently, any suggestion that Britain (or northern Europe) could have been peopled prior to 500 ka BP (thousand years ago) would have been met with considerable scepticism. These doubts arose from a highly influential model put forward by Roebroeks and van Kolfshoten (1994) that favoured a 'short chronology' of human presence in Europe. They proposed that none of the stringent criteria for authenticating sites in a primary geological context could be matched in examples more than half a million years old. However, in applying the same set of strict criteria, members of the AHOB team (the Ancient Human Occupation of Britain Leverhulme project) have now uncovered finds from a number of sites in East Anglia which push back the dating frontier beyond 700 ka BP. Principal amongst these is the site of Pakefield (Suffolk), where in 2005 indisputable flakes and a core were located in undisturbed (primary) contexts (Parfitt et al. 2005). The lithic industry is considered to be a simple flake-pebble core assemblage (termed Mode 1). Palaeoenvironmental evidence from Pakefield indicates that early people had probably migrated into Britain from the south under warm, Mediterranean-like conditions. This is evidenced by fossil insect remains that reveal average summer temperatures of 18–23°C, while the bones of hippopotamus and straight-tusked elephant confirm frost-free conditions like those in southern Europe today.

Table 2.1 Palaeolithic chronology and lithic technologies.

Approx. age (years)	Marine Isotope Stage	British stage	Sites	Technology
	2	Devensian		Upper Palaeolithic
60,000	3		Lyndford	Mousterian
	4			
130,000	5	Ipswichian IG		
	6			
	7	Aveley IG	Crayford	Levallois blades
230,000			Pontnewydd	Handaxes and Levallois
	8			
320,000	9	Purfleet IG	Purfleet	Levallois Prepared Core
	10			
400,000	11	Hoxnian IG	Swanscombe	Handaxes
			Beeches Pit	Handaxes – Fire
			Barnham	Flake tools – Handaxes
			Clacton	Flake tools
450,000	12	Anglian G		
500,000	13		Boxgrove	Handaxes
			Happisburgh	Handaxes
		Cromerian Complex IG	Kent's Cavern	Handaxes
	? 15		Westbury-sub-Mendip	Flake tools
700,000	15 or 17		Pakefield	Flake tools

It is interesting that the first evidence of human presence in Britain should be signalled by simple flake industries. Suggestions that these were the work of early forms of *Homo* (possibly *Homo antecessor*) are supported by similar finds in northern Spain dating back to about 1.2 million years ago. According to Dennell (2003), these might represent short-lived and rather modest early dispersal events rather than permanent occupation. Such occurrences would have been climatically controlled and would have allowed dispersal into temperate latitudes only during the warmest part of interglacials. In this view longer-term settlement and recolonization probably only became possible after about 500 ka BP, when humans became more independent and were able to cope with a wider range of environmental conditions. No very convincing explanations have yet been put forward for this change in behaviour, but one plausible suggestion is that these later migrations were by a new human type (*Homo heidelbergensis*) who carried with them a technology of handaxes and flake tools. Finds of these types are known from a number of sites in Britain, most notably at Boxgrove (West Sussex). Here there is direct evidence for *Homo heidelbergensis* in the form of fossil teeth and a shin bone, and tools occur at various different levels indicating an adaptation to late temperate as well as fully interglacial conditions of MIS 13. Handaxes, sometimes called bifaces, are typical of the Mode 2 or Acheulian tradition. These teardrop-shaped tools are believed to be all-purpose and highly portable implements. At Boxgrove their presence in conjunction with beautifully preserved cut-marked bones of animals such as wild horse and rhinoceros shows that they were probably often used as butchery tools, and equally, that the people who made them were already expert big-game hunters. One of the reasons for accepting this hunting hypothesis is the positioning of incisions on the meat bones which proves that humans were gaining primary access to the carcasses and no doubt therefore were responsible for hunting as well. Other broadly contemporary sites in Britain include Happisburgh (Norfolk), Kent's Cavern (Devon) and Westbury-sub-Mendip (Somerset), where cut-marked bone also attests to the activities of meat-eating humans.

The early appearance of handaxes in the British and European records seems to mark a fundamental shift in human behavioural and social development (McNabb 2007). Although it takes only a short time for an experienced flint knapper to make a handaxe (which has given rise to the term 'fifteen-minute culture'), the novel appearance of these items implies greater levels of sophistication in the humans that made and used them. This included an improved memory capacity (assuming 50 or more flake removals in making a handaxe), an ability to plan ahead and subordinate immediate goals to long-term objectives, the adoption of special-purpose knapping tools such as antler hammers to finish handaxes, and above all the means to transmit learned behaviour to other members of the group. In particular, many have noted the bi-lateral symmetry of handaxes as evidence of this new complexity, as well as other means of elaborating shape that went beyond functional necessity. Examples of this kind include the elegantly twisted profiles seen in some of the Swanscombe handaxes or the deliberately flattened plano-convex sections of the handaxes in the Wolvercote group. Why this was so can only be surmised. One ingenious suggestion is that these extra touches were an overt signal to attract potential mating partners: the better the handaxe, the greater the skill, prowess and mating fitness of the maker. It is of course difficult to evaluate such claims except in general terms, but they do provide a constant reminder that tools belong within a cultural setting and reflect social relations between individuals of the group (Gamble 2007).

One further curiosity that deserves mention is the existence in the British Lower Palaeo-lithic of two apparently different and quite distinct lithic industries. As observed above, these are often referred to as Modes 1 (flake-pebble type) and 2 (with handaxes). There is much debate over whether they represent contemporary elements of a flexible technology or belonged to two populations with different tool-making traditions. Both modes were present in Britain during the early part of the Hoxnian Interglacial (Table 2.1). At Barnham (Norfolk) it has been suggested by the excavators that the two industries were fully contem-porary, with a few simple handaxes found in one area of the site away from a larger concen-tration of flake artefacts that may have been knapped for some immediate task (McNabb

2007). At Swanscombe (Kent), however, the industries are separated stratigraphically (with the 'Clactonian' Mode 1 industry below the 'Acheulian' Mode 2 levels). The third suggestion that there was an ecological separation in these traditions, with handaxes more common in open habitats and pebble tools limited to small isolated human groups living in forested environments, seems less likely given the known existence of flake-pebble tools in open situations (as at Southfleet Road, Ebbsfleet, Kent) and vice versa.

In addition to the lithic inventories of Modes 1 and 2, wood and other organic materials must have been routinely used in tool-making but because of the fragility of preservation these hardly ever survive. One rare exception is the tip of a sharpened yew-wood stave from Clacton-on-Sea (Essex) in interglacial sediments. The possibility that this was the remains of a fire-hardened spear alerts us that the controlled use of fire must have been a key adaptation in the early settlement of northern temperate environments. The importance of this technology cannot be overestimated, because not only did it afford a regular and reliable source of heat, lighting and protection but it allowed people to cook their meat, thereby neutralizing harmful parasites, as well as improving the digestible quality of various calorie-rich foods such as roots and other plants. Owing to their ephemeral nature, small campfires hardly ever survive in the open, but one important case has recently been described at Beeches Pit (Suffolk). It can be dated to the Hoxnian Interglacial (Table 2.1), broadly the same age as the Clacton artefact and eight wooden spears, some up to 2 m long and made of white spruce, from Schöningen in Germany.

The Mode 3 technology is characterized by the Levallois or prepared core technique. According to conventional wisdom, an early version of this technology can be found at sites like Cagny-la-Garenne in northern France dating to around 420 ka BP (late MIS 12). Curiously, however, it remains unknown in Britain until 100,000 years later during MIS 9, when it can be recognized at Purfleet (Essex). Its significance is due to the fact that the size and thickness of flakes are premeditated. This is achieved by careful shaping of a core, usually by detaching smaller flakes around its circumference, and ending with a flake removal from the upper surface of the core. The end product or Levallois flake, identified by its platform and negative scars on its dorsal surface, was then sometimes further transformed into tools such as side scrapers or points. Why this technique became prevalent is unknown, but it may be linked with the increased use of hafting methods. Certainly, a flake of predetermined shape would have been easier to replace in a wooden handle or spear shaft. The technique also suggests a higher degree of skill and mental capacity on the part of its makers, believed to be the forerunners of Neanderthals.

Neanderthals and the Middle Palaeolithic

The precise timespan and ancestry of the Neanderthals (*Homo neanderthalensis*) have been much discussed. Biologically, some of the physical features attested to Neanderthals (occipital crest at the rear of the skull, enlarged tooth pulp cavity and unusual root shape) were already present in European populations of *Homo heidelbergensis* around 400,000 years ago – as for example in the Swanscombe skull. Likewise, teeth of five individuals, including three children, found at the site of Pontnewydd Cave in north Wales and dating to about 230 ka BP have identifiably Neanderthal characteristics (Stringer 2006). The archaeological finds from the same layers of this site include over 50 small pointed handaxes together with evidence of Levallois cores and flakes. Faunal remains indicate that occupation took place against a background of open woodland conditions in an early part of MIS 7. Following this warm stage a major contraction of human populations is signalled all over northern Europe, presumably as a result of the exceptionally cold conditions of MIS 6. Information on the presence of humans in Britain is extremely limited thereafter until around 60,000 years ago (the beginning of MIS 3), marking a possible break in settlement of over 100,000 years! On the European mainland fully developed Neanderthals are recorded from interglacial sites of MIS 5e, but it appears unlikely that they penetrated into Britain during this period because of the isolation of these islands by high sea-levels.

Throughout Europe the lithic industries commonly associated with the Neanderthals are grouped under the term Mousterian (a Middle Palaeolithic or Mode 3 tradition). In Britain, the majority of Mousterian finds probably belong to the last glaciation and were introduced during the cool, dry conditions of MIS 3. This is when more tundra-like landscapes gave way to rich arid grasslands (known as 'Mammoth steppe'), allowing communities of herbivores such as mammoth, woolly rhino and horse to expand their range into Britain. The resourcefulness of Neanderthal hunters who migrated in at the same time can be seen at sites like Lynford (Norfolk), where portable tools including small flat-butted handaxes were found alongside the tusks and bones of woolly mammoth. Whether this was a kill site remains doubtful because there are few obvious signs of interference with the mammoth bones, but it is conceivable that Neanderthals were exploiting the meat of frozen carcasses that had become trapped in small natural lakes.

In terms of diet, animal bones at sites indicate that Neanderthals processed large amounts of meat, a rich and necessary source of protein especially in cold climates. It has been estimated that their short, powerful physique would have required something in the region of 3,300 to 4,500 kcal per day (modern equivalents in males would be closer to 2,900 kcal per day), but this does not take into account any clothes or other protection worn to buffer against the cold. Some support for a highly carnivorous diet, at least in northern habitats, comes from chemical studies of Neanderthal bones which show signatures similar to those of top-level carnivores such as wolves and hyenas. Such methods unfortunately cannot tell us about the contribution of plant foods in the diet, and thus our view of what Neanderthals ate is somewhat biased.

Evidence that Neanderthals had active lifestyles and were highly mobile comes from stone tools themselves. These show that transfers of lithic raw material were not uncommon and could sometimes involve long-distance movements, as in the case of translucent flint from southern Britain transported around 150 km into the Creswell Crags area of the Midlands.

At Pin Hole Cave (Derbyshire), handaxe flakes of non-local flint occur in combination with cores and flakes of local Bunter quartzite and imply that toolkits were made up of highly portable elements such as handaxes and these were supplemented by local lithic sources for immediate tasks. Similar situational responses have been noted at Coygan Cave (Carmarthenshire) and Ash Tree Cave (near Creswell), where flat-based handaxes and bifacial axe-trimming flakes of non-local rocks have been found, respectively.

The transition to the Upper Palaeolithic

One of the most intriguing problems facing archaeologists is how to interpret relatively abrupt changes in the cultural record (Gamble 2007). Such is the case of the Middle to Upper Palaeolithic transition, covering the timespan from roughly 40 to 30 ka BP when Neanderthals became extinct across Europe and were replaced by modern human populations who apparently introduced totally new technologies. Ancient mitochondrial DNA studies from a total of 15 Neanderthals suggest that they formed a genetically separate lineage from our own; however, in very few cases do we have any direct evidence of the identity of the makers of early Upper Palaeolithic technologies nor whether these toolkits could have emerged from the local Middle Palaeolithic (Mousterian). Relevant examples are the so-called 'leaf point' industries that are found across northern Europe from Poland to Britain. Unifacial leaf points of the kind that occur in the Polish Jerzmanovician occur at a number of sites in southern Britain, most notably at Beedings (Sussex) but also extending further west to Bench Quarry (Devon) and Paviland Cave (South Wales). Dating of these finds has proved difficult except at Badger Hole (Somerset) and Bench Quarry (Brixham, Devon), where stratigraphically associated faunal remains provide ages in the range 38–36 ka BP, using improved methods of ^{14}C (radiocarbon) dating. Similar leaf points from Kent's Cavern (Devon) may have been retrieved from the same level as a human adult upper-jaw fragment but not in the same area of the cave. The jaw has now been redated to around 37–35 ka BP, opening new questions over its taxonomic status and whether it should be reclassified as a Neanderthal (Pettitt 2008).

Although the timing of the initial Upper Palaeolithic and its human associations remain unclear, better indications of a possible sequence are beginning to emerge at Paviland Cave (also known as Goat's Hole). Here reassessment of the dating evidence (Jacobi and Higham 2008) has revealed that the famous 'Red Lady' burial can probably be attributed to an Early Gravettian phase 29–28 ka BP. This is interesting, because the adult young male is very definitely modern *Homo sapiens* and was buried together with artefacts of shaped mammoth ivory consisting of rods and rings, as well as perforated periwinkle shells (*Littorina littorea*). The bones were stained with red ochre. Such representations are typical of the highly symbolic Upper Palaeolithic burials known elsewhere in Europe from this period, and suggest that communities of hunter-gatherers were paying regular visits from the continental mainland. Earlier trips to the cave in the Upper Palaeolithic are marked by Aurignacian lithic artefacts and seem to indicate that the cave was first used by the living and then after a gap of several thousand years as a place for the dead. Dated Aurignacian finds are still comparatively rare in Britain (for a recent discussion see Pettitt 2008), though a typical lozenge-shaped point from Uphill Quarry (Somerset) with an age of 32–31 ka BP provides endorsement that modern human hunters were present in Britain not long after the demise of the Neanderthals.

THE LATEGLACIAL PERIOD

Much greater detail is available for the younger part of the Palaeolithic record covering the Lateglacial Interstadial. This is partly due to taphonomic factors of site representation and survival but also to long-term multidisciplinary research programmes that have been running over the last 20 years as well as progressive improvements in the radiocarbon methodologies that now provide a high-precision calibrated dating record that extends back to 26,000 cal BP.

LATE UPPER PALAEOLITHIC: CRESWELLIAN

Environmental background

The earliest evidence for reoccupation of Britain after the Last Glacial Maximum is currently provided by a series of dates on modified bones of wild horse (*Equus ferus*) and red deer (*Cervus elaphus*) from caves in south-west Britain, dating to around 12,600 ^{14}C yr BP (or about 14,950–14,750 cal BP). This is slightly younger than previously suggested and means that humans were present only from the beginning of the Lateglacial Interstadial. At a global scale such events can be tied in with the onset of rapid warming reflected in ice cores by Greenland Interstadial 1 (GI-1: Table 2.2).

According to annual laminae in the Greenland ice cores and the climatic signal derived from British fossil beetle faunas, the beginning of the Interstadial saw an extremely rapid warming, with mean July temperatures rising by 9–10°C to a maximum of 17°C (Figure 2.1; Lowe *et al.* 1995; Atkinson *et al.* 1987). Based on radiocarbon-dated coleopteran finds from Llanilid in Glamorgan it has been proposed that that the interstadial warming began earlier in western Britain than in Greenland, perhaps around 15,500 cal BP (Walker *et al.* 2003). Leaving this detail to one side, it is generally accepted that although conditions were probably slightly warmer than at present, there was greater continentality in the climate as implied by reconstructed winter temperatures of around 1°C. Evidence from pollen sources shows a considerable time lag in the botanical response to the initial temperature rise. A reflection of the slower vegetational recovery can be found in pollen spectra from the beginning of this period, which show disturbed open-ground species such as *Artemisia* (wormwood/mugwort) only gradually being replaced by low juniper (*Juniperus communis*) scrub.

Table 2.2 British and European sub-divisions of the Lateglacial.

^{14}C years BP	Calibrated ^{14}C years BP	Pollen zones	NW European chronozones	NW European climatostratigraphic units	British biozones	Ice core chronology Greenland Interstadials and stadials
10,000	11,500	IV	PREBOREAL Friesland/Rammelbeek oscillation	FLANDRIAN INTERGLACIAL	FLANDRIAN INTERGLACIAL	
				Transition		
	12,600	III	YOUNGER DRYAS	YOUNGER DRYAS STADIAL	LOCH LOMOND STADIAL	GS-1
11,000		II	ALLERØD	Transition		GI-1a
11,800		Ic	OLDER DRYAS			
12,000	13,900	Ib	BØLLING	LATEGLACIAL INTERSTADIAL	WINDERMERE INTERSTADIAL	
				Transition		
13,000	14,700	Ia	MIDDLE WEICHSELIAN	LATE DEVENSIAN/ STADIAL	DIMLINGTON STADIAL	GI-1e

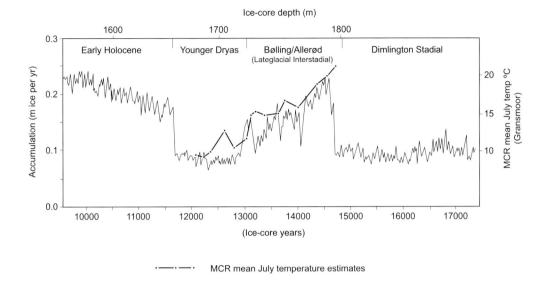

Figure 2.1 Comparison of ice accumulation rates from GISP-2, Greenland, and palaeotemperature
data from Gransmoor, England.
Source: Lowe *et al.* 1995

The beginning of the decline in the peak of these open herb-dominated communities is documented at Llanilid (Walker and Harkness 1990), and was followed by a gradual increase in
birch (*Betula* sp.) pollen leading to the main expansion of woodland from around 12,900
cal BP. Thus the warmest part of the Interstadial was associated with an open vegetation
dominated by herbs, sedges and grasses and only minimal forest development.

Material culture and technology

Typological descriptions of artefacts enable comparisons to be made between individual
tools or groups of artefacts (assemblages/industries). Many of the terms used today were
originally coined by European prehistorians, and in consequence the following descriptions
will include both French or German (in italics) and English forms. Complementing typological studies are those that concern the dynamic processes making up the various stages
of the artefact 'life-cycle'. This concept is often referred to as the *chaîne opératoire*, in one
sense a chain of events that links a succession of conceptual and practical actions, from the
earliest stages of manufacture to the uses and final discard of artefacts.

The first clearly Late Upper Palaeolithic industry present in Britain appears to have been the
Creswellian. The term was adopted by Dorothy Garrod (1926), who recognized it as a regional
variant of a broader grouping of Late Magdalenian technologies in north-west Europe. Today,
the terms Creswellian and Late Magdalenian are largely regarded as synonymous, though for
historical and comparative reasons it is useful to retain the British name here. Descriptions of the

Creswellian lithic industry are provided in a number of publications (e.g. Barton *et al.* 2003; Jacobi and Higham 2009). It is characterized by bitruncated trapezoidal backed blades (Cheddar points) and single truncation examples (Creswell points). Amongst other typical forms are end-scrapers on long, straight blades, the lateral edges often also being modified by retouch. Other tools include piercers, burins, *becs* (some of them true *Zinken*), blades with scalar edge modification, truncated blades with heavily worn or rounded ends (*lames tronquées et usées*) and splintered pieces (*pièces esquillées*). A representative selection is shown in Figure 2.2. To date, 24 or so findspots with characteristic Cheddar points have been identified in England and Wales. Although a single arte-fact of this type has been reported from Fairnington, near Kelso in southern Scotland (Saville in Saville 2004), none is so far known in Ireland (Figure 2.3). A new discovery at Howburn, Lanark-shire, with Havelte points, *Zinken* and blades with éperon butts, resembles Lateglacial finds from southern Scandinavia and northern Germany and suggests contacts with these areas.

Other features of the Creswellian stone industry are equally distinctive. The debitage (waste) is typified by well-made blades and bladelets, detached from cores with a single preferred flaking direction. The butts on the blades are often carefully prepared, and include a special technique that leaves a distinct faceted butt known as a *talon en éperon* (Figure 2.2). Flat, diffuse bulbs on the proximal ends of blades indicate a production method using either soft stone or antler hammers.

A fairly wide range of organic artefacts have been recorded in Creswellian contexts. These are made in a variety of materials including animal teeth, bone, antler and mammoth ivory. Rare examples of artefacts made on mammoth products comprise double-bevelled ivory rods (*sagaies*) from Gough's Cave (Somerset) and Kent's Cavern (Devon). Reindeer antler was used to make batons (*batons percés*) at Gough's Cave (Figure 2.4) and scooped-end rods (also *sagaies*) at Fox Hole (Derbyshire) and Church Hole (Creswell Crags, Derbyshire). Products on reindeer antler include parts of three barbed harpoons from Kent's Cavern, while leg bones of arctic hare (*Lepus timidus*) modified for use as pointed awls (*poinçons*) have been recovered at Gough's Cave and Robin Hood Cave (Creswell Crags, Derbyshire). Other organic items include bone needles at Gough's Cave, Church Hole and Kent's Cavern, plus an awl – though not of hare bone – from the latter site. Several fox tooth beads have also been found at Gough's Cave.

Evidence for the method of working antler is restricted to a single fragment from Gough's Cave that shows groove and splinter modification. Grooves and cuts on the bones of Whooper swan (*Cygnus cygnus*) from Gough's Cave show how needles were manufactured from bone cores.

Radiocarbon dating

Since the 1980s AMS (Accelerator Mass Spectrometry) radiocarbon dating has been used routinely for dating the Lateglacial. The rich archive of available dates is based mainly on high-precision measurements on directly dated human bone and on cut-marked animal bone and teeth, as well as modified bone, antler and ivory objects. The method relies on very small samples of less than 1 g and is therefore minimally destructive. Despite these advances, recent improve-

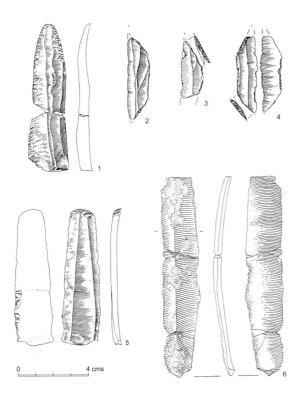

Figure 2.2 Creswellian artefacts from Three Holes Cave and Kent's Cavern, Devon: 1. End-scraper on a blade with scalariform retouch along its lateral margins; 2–4. Trapezoidal-backed blades (Cheddar points); 5. End-scraper on a blade; 6. Blade with 'spur' (*en éperon*) butt preparation.

Sources: Illustrations 1, 5–6 by Karen Hughes, courtesy of the British Museum; 2–4 by Hazel Martingell (from Barton *et al.* 2003)

ments in the methods of screening and the pre-treatment of collagen in specimens have produced better age controls and revealed significant discrepancies with the results of earlier accelerator dating (Jacobi and Higham 2009). This has led to a major project of systematically redating specimens of bones, teeth, ivory and antler using the ultrafiltration method for obtaining very pure samples of collagen (gelatin). The new results are only just beginning to appear, but their impact is already producing a profound effect on our understanding of the dating for this period.

AMS radiocarbon dates using ultrafiltered gelatin are presented (Figure 2.5) for a selection of sites for which reliable associations with Creswellian artefacts exist (Jacobi and Higham 2009). One of the most surprising observations can be seen in relation to the dating of Gough's Cave (Somerset). This site, discussed in more detail below, was previously thought to have included a long period of occupation of up to 1,800 radiocarbon years. Such a view was constructed using the previously available dataset. The new assessment provides a very different picture. Using a combination of Bayesian statistical modelling and comparing the results against the Greenland CICC05 $\delta^{18}O$ ice record, the new dates now indicate with a high degree of probability (68.2 per cent) that the cave was occupied for a maximum of 217 years. The occupation period might of course have been considerably shorter, perhaps no more than two or three human generations (Jacobi and Higham 2009). This completely overturns our ideas about the occupation of the site. Taken as a whole, the newly obtained AMS dates have

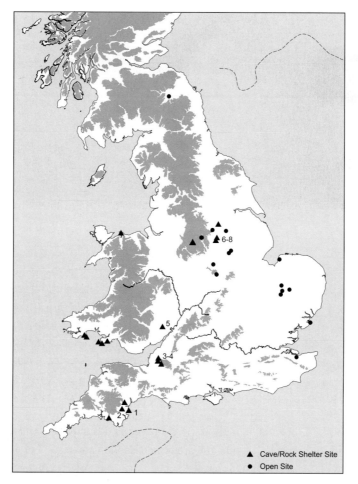

Figure 2.3 Distribution of Late Upper Palaeolithic Creswellian findspots: 1. Kent's Cavern; 2. Three
Holes Cave; 3. Sun Hole; 4. Gough's Cave; 5. King Arthur's Cave; 6. Robin Hood Cave;
7. Pin Hole; 8. Church Hole. Approximate position of European land-bridge connection
is marked by broken line.
Source: Barton 2005 with additions.

helped to show that human presence in Britain probably lagged 500 radiocarbon years or
more behind the main phase of Magdalenian resettlement of the Paris Basin and the Belgian
Ardennes, and in turn this may explain the absence of certain lithic components, such as
microlithic backed bladelets, in the British assemblages (Barton *et al.* 2003).

Raw material and mobility

The 35 findspots with Creswellian activity (defined by the presence of points and/or characteristic blade debitage) consist mainly of collections from cave sites in the west and mid-
central limestone areas of England and Wales, with lesser activity denoted by open-air finds

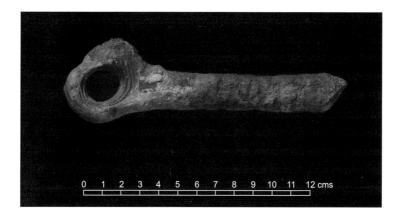

Figure 2.4   Reindeer baton from Gough's Cave (Cheddar Gorge, Somerset).
   Source: Courtesy of the Natural History Museum

locations in the east of the country (Figure 2.3). In cases where evidence is available, the preferred raw material seems to have been good quality flint capable of producing long, straight blades, rather than local rocks of mixed or unpredictable quality.

The use of imported flint is nowhere more apparent than in western Britain, where instances of geologically *in situ* sources of flint are rare. Finds from Kent's Cavern and Three Holes Cave (Devon) include well-made flint blades and tools on long blade blanks. Significantly, although good flint sources are available at Beer (Devon), the only local material employed at Three Holes Cave seems to have been Greensand chert, which occurs at the site almost exclusively in the form of retouched tools (Barton and Roberts 1996). The low quantities of flint debitage with cortication and primary blade waste recorded at both sites further imply that many of the tools and blades were imported as finished items rather than being knapped on the spot. A similar situation has also been described for Gough's Cave (Somerset), where translucent flints appear to have been carried in from sources no nearer than the Vale of Pewsey, on the northern edge of Salisbury Plain (Wiltshire), 60 km to the east (Jacobi 2004). This may also be the source of the flint found in the Devon caves, a minimum distance of 160 km, supporting the contention that Creswellian groups engaged in long-distance movements with correspondingly high residential mobility.

The view that Creswellian groups were highly mobile is strengthened by finds at Gough's Cave of non-local seashells and pieces of Baltic amber, the nearest known source of which is the North Sea coast. Similarly, comparison of individual artefacts and raw materials from sites as far apart as Kent's Cavern and Robin Hood Cave in the Midlands has shown such striking resemblances as to suggest that they were made by a single group (Jacobi in Barton *et al.* 1991). If this is correct, it could give an approximation of the potential size and geography of the annual range exploited by these people.

Interestingly, observations concerning the procurement of non-local rocks for tool-making closely match patterns recorded in the continental Late Magdalenian (Arts and Deeben 1987), where long-distance movements of materials have been correlated with greater mobility of

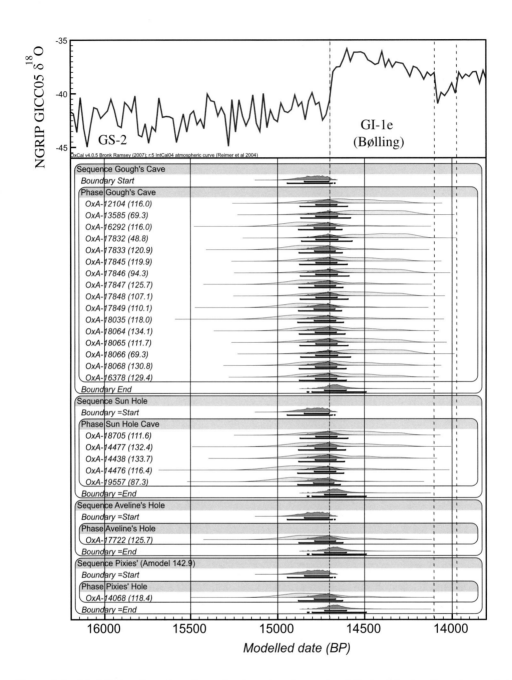

Figure 2.5 Modelled radiocarbon determinations based on redated finds and using Bayesian statistics from the sites of Gough's Cave, Aveline's Hole, Sun Hole and Pixie's Hole. Dates in cal BP. Their relation to NGRIP Greenland Ice Core chronology is shown in the top register.

Source: Jacobi and Higham 2009

hunter-gatherer groups. Amongst various explanations put forward is that either raw materials were exchanged between groups from different territories or that expeditions were deliberately mounted to obtain them. In such instances, the reduction of nodules into more manageable blade forms would make sense as an economizing measure designed to reduce the weight of pieces carried to a more manageable level. The transportability of these toolkits is further emphasized by the fact that the imported implements may show signs of especially heavy use and resharpening. This would certainly appear to be the case at some Creswellian sites.

In terms of landscape use, one of the strongest patterns to emerge is the correlation between the location of Creswellian sites and the edges of the upland margins of western and central Britain (Barton *et al.* 2003). This is a feature that is also apparent in the continental Magdalenian, where sites do not extend very far (if at all) on to the plains and seem to favour distinct regions of upland landscape. Admittedly, such a picture may begin to dilute with the increasing discoveries of new sites, especially in the east of Britain, but nevertheless our model suggests that occupying the upland edge allowed the exploitation of a number of resources, which would have included not just wild horse but a broadening spectrum of other animals such as red deer and wild cattle. It may also be significant that Creswellian sites include some that form clusters along major river catchment systems (Pettitt 2008).

Seasonality and subsistence

Evidence linking the exploitation of mammal faunas and human activity is preserved in the form of cut-marks and other modification to bones, antler and ivory found at Creswellian sites. Species known to have been exploited for meat, raw materials and artefacts included wild horse (*Equus ferus*), red deer (*Cervus elaphus*), arctic hare (*Lepus timidus*), reindeer (*Rangifer tarandus*), mammoth (*Mammuthus primigenius*), Saiga antelope (*Saiga tatarica*), wild cattle (*Bos primigenius*), brown bear (*Ursus arctos*) and lynx (*Lynx lynx*). To this list can probably be added arctic fox (*Alopex lagopus*) and red fox (*Vulpes vulpes*), although no cut-marks have yet been recorded on Lateglacial specimens of these species. Interestingly, for the first time animals sharing the same skeletal morphology as domestic dogs (*Canis* cf. *familiaris*) are recorded at Kent's Cavern and Gough's Cave (Jacobi and Higham 2009).

The food species dominantly represented at Creswellian sites is the wild horse. Although wild horses are now extinct, behavioural studies on semi-feral populations in Mongolia reveal that they live in small herds and move constantly between grazing grounds. Today they are adapted to dry, open grassland habitats, but the main restriction on their distribution is the availability of drinking water. The only limitation to their ceaseless mobility is when young foals are present during the spring and early summer. From April to late June, herds may be highly vulnerable to attack because of frequent resting, as attested by the accumulation of tell-tale piles of dung in these places. The habits of travelling in single file and of mares deliberately isolating themselves during foaling might have made them equally vulnerable to human predation, especially if hunters were accompanied by dogs.

Evidence that wild horse was hunted for meat is well documented at Gough's Cave (Parkin *et al.* 1986). Skeletal elements of the head and limb extremities recorded near the entrance of the cave are heavily cut-marked, showing that carcasses were probably dismembered and butchered there with the use of flint knives. Further into the cave, long-bone flakes and rib fragments imply different activities, perhaps connected with the smashing of bone to extract marrow juice and fat. The very thorough method of butchery and filleting suggests that the occupants of the cave were well used to dealing with horse. Once the meat was stripped from the bone, it is apparent that many elements such as the jaws were fractured longitudinally for marrow extraction purposes. Often meat-poor elements like the head were carefully dissected to remove the brain and the tongue, which may have been considered great delicacies! The stripping-down of the animals also included the removal of the tendons at the back of the legs (for sinew) and of the hooves (possibly for reducing to glue). One curiosity is the relative scarcity of burnt bone. Although this could indicate the eating of raw flesh it may suggest alternative methods of preparation such as meat smoking.

The other numerically common predated species represented in the Gough's Cave fauna are red deer, which seem to have been treated in much the same way as horses, with cut-marks and breakages in identical places on many bones. Opportunities for hunting both these species appear to have been helped by the topography of the gorge, which beyond the cave becomes a narrow winding canyon suitable for driving or corralling animals. Dental evidence provides contradictory indications of the seasonal use of the cave: deer tooth eruption patterns suggest occupation in winter or early spring, whereas incremental banding visible on both deer and wild horse teeth implies that some animals were killed in summer. It thus seems possible that selective hunting took place at various times of year.

In addition to these two large vertebrates, smaller mammals such as the arctic hare were also exploited, but probably less for their lean meat than for their pelts and leg bones that were used for tool-making. Bone awls made on hare tibias have been found at a number of Creswellian locations throughout the country (Figure 2.3), including Gough's Cave. At Robin Hood Cave, the particularly high numbers of cut-marked hare bones have led to the suggestion that the animals were being processed for their thick winter pelts (Charles and Jacobi 1994).

The use of reindeer bone and antler and mammoth ivory is also attested in the Lateglacial of western and central-midland Britain. It is not known whether either of these animals formed part of the contemporary local fauna. At Gough's Cave, three reindeer antler batons have been recovered (Figure 2.4). Spiral grooving inside the pierced holes may indicate a special function linked with controlling rope movement (e.g. in climbing or for lassoing animals). Such items could have been curated and stored or made on naturally shed antler and need not imply local presence or hunting of the species. Similarly, finds of mammoth ivory *baguettes* at Gough's Cave and Kent's Cavern, and reindeer antler *sagaies* at Church Hole and Fox Hole (Derbyshire), prove only that these materials were brought in by humans and possibly left for some future purpose. Apart from these rare objects, there is in fact very little convincing evidence for caching or storage associated with Creswellian sites. However, some activities involving the drying and storing of meat and fat would not have left many archaeologically visible traces.

The absence of cut-marked reindeer bone (as opposed to artefacts) from sites dating to the first phase of the Interstadial is an interesting phenomenon. According to Bratlund (in Larsson 1996), contemporary Late Upper Palaeolithic sites in north-west Europe (Hamburgian, Later Magdalenian) invariably contain evidence of either horse or reindeer, but rarely both. When horse dominates the fauna, the seasonal evidence tends to favour summer and winter hunting, whilst reindeer seems to have been trapped predominantly in the autumn and spring. Accordingly, it is theoretically possible that Creswellian sites represent summer and/or winter hunting locations, rather than those used during the intervening seasons. Alternatively, a climatic explanation might be sought for the absence of reindeer in Britain during the warmest part of the Interstadial (Jacobi and Higham 2009).

Whether the British Creswellian cave sites like Gough's Cave or Kent's Cavern served as 'task locations' or seasonal residential units is difficult to determine on present evidence. Certainly, more than fleeting use of these caves is indicated by the presence of items for sewing and needle-making, as well as hide-working and the rendering down of fat and marrow from animal carcasses. At the same time, it may be significant that tools like micropiercers (*microperçoirs*), delicate enough for engraving small incisions in bone or antler, are found at Gough's Cave, one of the few British sites where there is direct evidence for such activity (see below).

Burials

Although human remains have been recorded at a number of Creswellian sites, very few can be proven by AMS dating to be of Lateglacial age. Amongst the examples definitely attributable to this period are a small collection of finds including an ulna from Sun Hole (Cheddar Gorge, Somerset) and a larger group of individuals from Gough's Cave. The latter site also has a later inhumation ('Cheddar Man') of Mesolithic age.

While the few bones and teeth from Sun Hole offer only equivocal evidence of burial, no such doubt exists over the Gough's Cave finds, which represent a remarkable collection of skeletal material intentionally deposited within the cave. The remains consist of a minimum of five individuals: a young child age three, two adolescents and two adults, probably a male and female (Humphrey and Stringer 2002).

Although precise details are lacking on some of the original finds, more recent work in 1987 uncovered further human material in a narrow fissure just inside the entrance. Convincing evidence that this is probably part of the original burial is provided by a series of refits between bones in the new and old collections. From the associations and fresh condition of the bones, it was also clear that they had not been subject to any major natural disturbance. However, even though the bones of the individuals appeared to be closely grouped within the cave, there is no guarantee that they represented a single collective inhumation, as they were mixed in with what seems to be a midden of occupation debris.

Despite these uncertainties, there is extensive evidence that the skeletons had been treated in an extraordinary way prior to deposition.

From microscopic analysis of the surfaces of the crania, jaws and bones it is apparent that many bear the traces of cut-marks and breakages that must have happened after death. Particularly interesting are marks which indicate scalping (Figure 2.6) and disarticulation of the lower jaw from the skull. In one case, the incisions made on the inside of the chin leave no doubt that the tongue was removed. From the appearance of the cut marks it is clear that soon after death all of the cadavers had been expertly skinned with flint knives and the bodies dismembered in a highly systematic way. In another curious twist, study of the remains showed that limb bones had been smashed and treated little differently from animal bones assumed to have been food debris and found in the same layers (Andrews and Fernandez-Jalvo 2003).

Naturally, today, we would regard such activities as extremely macabre, but need this be interpretable as proof of cannibalism? Examples of two-stage burial practices involving redeposition and secondary reburial are not uncommon in the prehistoric record. Indeed, the evidence from Gough's Cave is not inconsistent with the idea that the bodies had been deliberately reduced to manageable packages which might have been transported to the cave for burial (Stringer 2006). Doubts about nutritional cannibalism can also be raised because of the profusion of wild horse and red deer bones that confirm that animal meat was in plentiful supply. On the other hand, the evidence does not rule out the possibility of ritual consumption of some of the softer human tissues, as a mark of respect to the dead, a practice known ethnographically amongst tribes in

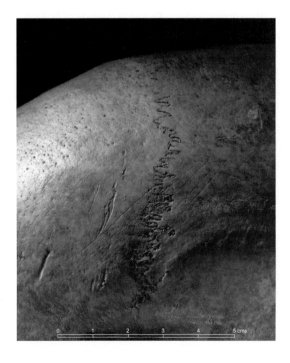

Figure 2.6 Cut-marks on a human skull from Gough's Cave (Cheddar Gorge, Somerset).

Source: Courtesy of the Natural History Museum

Papua New Guinea. Whatever explanation is eventually accepted, it is nevertheless clear that the Gough's Cave humans provide an interesting insight into the great diversity of methods (and no doubt rituals) concerning the disposal of the dead.

The human remains from Gough's Cave have also been subjected to isotopic analyses. These can provide important clues about diet through the presence of characteristic carbon and nitrogen signatures recorded in bone. The Gough's Cave bones indeed confirm that humans were consuming meat, but surprisingly, given its strong presence, horse does not seem to have provided a main source of animal protein. Instead, it appears that deer, bovids and even some carnivores were routinely eaten. There is also the perhaps not entirely serious suggestion that the regular eating of human flesh may have significantly affected the isotopic measurements (Stringer 2006).

Art

Until recently there were no serious claims for the existence of Palaeolithic cave art in Britain. At the same time many, including myself, regarded this as a historical anomaly, especially since convincing Upper Palaeolithic engravings were already known from the interior walls of Gouy Cave, near Rouen, merely 160 km or so from the southern English coast. However, in April 2003 a team of archaeologists investigating Creswell Crags identified engravings of animals and other figures at Church Hole Cave that now amount to some 90 examples. Some of these are very close to the entrance of the cave but remained more or less invisible high above the excavated level of the cave floor and were sometimes partly hidden beneath modern graffiti. The depictions include horse, deer, bison, bear, birds and abstract forms. Even though some were found within the weathering zone of the cave mouth, a willingness to accept them as genuine has been strengthened by uranium series dating of flowstone partly covering a red deer engraving and giving a date of over 13,000 years ago (Pettitt *et al.* 2007). Abstract engravings towards the back of the cave have been interpreted as akin to stylized engraved female figurines from the Magdalenian of the Rhine Basin, implying distant human links with the European mainland.

Examples of mobiliary (portable) art objects are known from several Lateglacial localities. These include non-figurative abstract engravings on stone, bone and ivory from Gough's Cave, Robin Hood Cave, Pin Hole and, possibly, Mother Grundy's Parlour (Creswell Crags, Derbyshire). Church Hole has a unique example of a notched bone object. Regularly spaced groups of delicate incisions on hare tibia awls and on a section of bovid rib from Gough's Cave resemble the gradations on a ruler: these items have been variously interpreted as counting tallies, lunar calendars, spacers, message sticks or simply as gaming pieces. Comparable notations have been recorded on pieces of mammoth ivory from the same cave. An example of figurative art connected with the Creswellian is the engraving of a horse on a rib fragment from Robin Hood Cave, discovered in 1876. A similar example of an engraved horse from Sherbourne (Dorset) has been discredited as a forgery (Stringer *et al.* 1995).

FINAL UPPER PALAEOLITHIC: *FEDERMESSER* GROUPS

Environmental background

In the second half of the Interstadial (equivalent to the Allerød, 13.95–12.9 ka cal BP), many British pollen profiles show a major expansion of birch (*Betula* sp.) (Walker *et al.* 2003). In western Britain, closed birch woodland seems to have developed against a background of gradual cooling in climate (Atkinson *et al.* 1987).

The two trends are not necessarily in conflict: the spread of birch may have been favoured by lower summer temperatures combined with the prevailing moister and less windy but cooler weather conditions (Walker *et al.* 1993). According to proxy data from beetle faunas, mean July temperatures fell by up to 2°C (Coope and Lemdahl 1995). Overall there may have been greater climatic instability in this period as signalled by a short interruption in the birch curve of pollen cores and a minor increase in juniper. This episode and other similar short-term events are also reflected in ice-core records (Figure 2.1).

The second phase of the Lateglacial Interstadial thus appears to have been characterized by the development of a woodland landscape of birch and willow and a mosaic of herbaceous shrub and open grassland species. The presence of birch woodland in northern Britain is indicated at Poulton-le-Fylde (Lancashire) by twigs and leaves preserved in peat and in association with hunted elk (*Alces alces*) remains, showing that this animal and its human predators were in this area during the early part of the Allerød. Despite these vegetational changes, no great turnover of animal species is indicated. The second half of the Interstadial nevertheless saw the final disappearance of open steppe species such as mammoth (*Mammuthus primigenius*), which may have become extinct in other parts of western Europe at about the same time (Street 1998). Amongst the large vertebrates found in Britain dating to this period are red deer (*Cervus elaphus*), elk (*Alces alces*), a large wild bovid (*Bos* sp.) and roe deer (*Capreolus capreolus*). Wild horse (*Equus ferus*) became less common, while reindeer (*Rangifer tarandus*), if it occurred at all, would doubtless have been confined to more open conditions in the northern uplands.

Material culture and technology

Lithic tool assemblages of this period are typologically much more diverse than in the Creswellian and this would be consistent with the suggestion that they also occupied a longer timespan (Barton *et al.* 2003). The term Final Upper Palaeolithic has been used generically to describe these industries, but in fact there is a great deal of similarity with the *Federmesser-gruppen* (Schwabedissen 1954; Taute 1968) of Germany and the Netherlands and it is now also used interchangeably with the term *Azilian* for technologies in some parts of France. One of its main defining characteristics is the presence of a variety of curve-backed points. Subtle differences in the types and combinations of these point forms may be of temporal significance and indicate sub-divisions along chronological lines. For example, based on European analogies curve-backed pieces pointed at both ends (*bi-pointes à dos courbé*) seem to predate those dominated by curved pieces pointed at one end, also known as mono-points (Coudret and Fagnart 2006). Another variant is represented by the presence of straight-backed blades and bladelets (*lames et lamelles à dos*) in association with shouldered points (*pointes à cran*) and angle-backed points (*pointes à dos anguleux*). In northern France these can be shown to belong early in the second half of the Interstadial (Barton *et al.* 2009).

Fitting the British industries into the continental scheme is at present difficult due to the scarcity of reliable dating evidence, but it appears likely that they originated within a short-lived down-turn in climate, linked with GI-1a–c of the Greenland ice record (Jacobi and Higham 2009). Potentially the oldest examples of this technology can be found at the cave sites of Sun Hole, Gough's Cave and Aveline's Hole (Somerset). Comparisons with the curved bi-points from these sites suggests parallels with France, where such innovations are attributed to an early stage in the process of change from Magdalenian to *Federmesser* industries (Jacobi and Higham 2009).

A second artefact grouping in Britain may be represented by Hengistbury-type assemblages (named after Hengistbury Head near Bournemouth in Dorset), which contain straight-backed pieces and shouldered points again with affinities to industries in northern France (Figure 2.7). Open-air localities with artefacts akin to Hengistbury have been recorded at Nea Farm, La Sagesse Convent (both in Hampshire) and at Brockhill (Surrey). Like Hengistbury, the blades in these assemblages are well made but unlike the Creswellian examples are often straighter and do not include the feature of *talons en éperon*. Amongst the other retouched tools present in these industries are truncations, *becs*, blade end-scrapers, short end-scrapers and burins on truncation. A selection of these tool-types is illustrated in Figure 2.8.

Findspots with assemblages characterized by curve-backed forms known as penknife points may constitute a third significant Final Upper Palaeolithic grouping. These types are generally absent in the other two industries, the curve-backed mono-points characteristically have additional basal retouch (Figure 2.9). In western Britain such finds have been made in association with small blades of local raw materials, mainly gravel flint and cherts (e.g. Greensand chert). The blades in such assemblages tend to display wide, lipped butts and their ventral surface features are often consistent with a soft stone hammer mode of percussion. Sites where these have been found include Broken Cavern, Three Holes Cave (Devon) (Barton and Roberts 1996) and Symonds Yat East (Gloucestershire) (Barton 1996). The limited dating evidence available suggests that these artefact types may have become more common in the later part of the Allerød oscillation.

The most common bone and antler artefacts from this period are represented by items of hunting equipment. Bone and antler barbed points that were either leister prongs or projectile heads are known from a number of localities across England. Those with barbs closely set against the shaft and separated by simple criss-cross cutting are generally made of bone and include examples from Royston (Cambridgeshire), Hornsea and Skipsea, Brandesburton, and Fosse Hill (all Yorkshire), Sproughton (Suffolk) and from the Leman

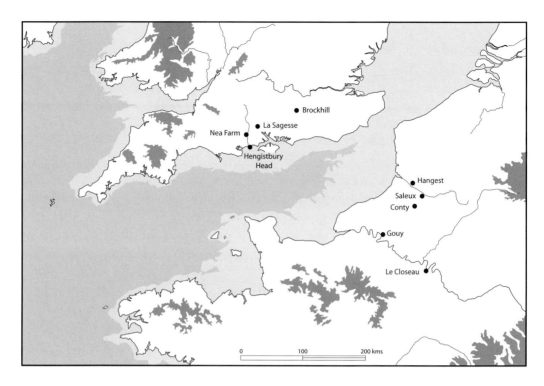

Figure 2.7   Distribution of *Federmesser* sites with affinities to Hengistbury Head.
Source: Barton *et al.* 2009

and Ower banks off the Norfolk coast (Jacobi *et al.* 2009). Dating of the Leman and Ower point and the recent redating of the bone point from Sproughton indicate an Allerød age (Jacobi *et al.* 2009). Other uniserial barbed points, though of slightly different form, come from Poulton-le-Fylde (Lancashire) and Conistone Dib (Yorkshire). The presence of similar artefacts lodged in an elk skeleton at Poulton-le-Fylde demonstrates their effectiveness as projectiles. Finds from Victoria Cave (Yorkshire) include a bilaterally barbed harpoon, though current AMS dating suggests either a very late Interstadial or slightly younger age for this artefact.

Raw materials and mobility

The quality and sources of lithic raw materials vary a great deal in the Final Upper Palaeolithic. This is not altogether surprising given the fact that *Federmesser* findspots can be mapped over a wide area of Britain (Figure 2.10). Predictably, there is a strong relationship between the occurrence of large, well-made flint blades and good sources of primary flint. This can be clearly shown in relation to findspots in eastern and southern England, from Seamer Carr (North Yorkshire; Conneller 2007) to Hengistbury Head (Dorset) in the

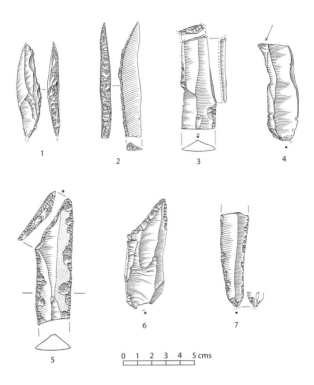

Figure 2.8 Retouched tools from Nea Farm (Hampshire): 1. Curve-backed bi-point; 2. Curve-backed point with a straight proximal truncation; 3. Burin on truncation with 'rounding' on facet and truncated end; 4. Burin on a break; 5–6. *Becs*; 7. Blade with scalar retouch and 'rubbed end'.
Source: Illustrations by Hazel Martingell (from Barton *et al.* 2009)

south (Barton 1992). At Hengistbury, high-quality nodular flint was plentifully available in Cretaceous chalk deposits within 12 km of the site. Further north, but in the same river catchment, blades knapped at Nea Farm probably originated from outcrops at Fording-bridge about 5–6 km away. These two sites also provide some interesting evidence for the circulation of artefacts. At Nea Farm it is clear that mixed in with blades of local flint were tools made of a distinctive striped flint (Barton *et al.* 2009). It is likely these were introduced as ready-made items because no cores or other debitage of this material were recovered in the excavations. Similar striped flint has been observed at Hengistbury and it is plausible that this comes from the same flint source. Both sites are situated in the same river catch-ment and are no more than 26 km apart, so it is conceivable that material was transferred from one location to the other by the same people. This pattern is consistent with the model described for the Vale of Pickering, where there is evidence for the exploitation of local flint sources (to replenish blades and replace broken equipment) but where tools made in till flint were brought in from some distance away (Conneller 2007).

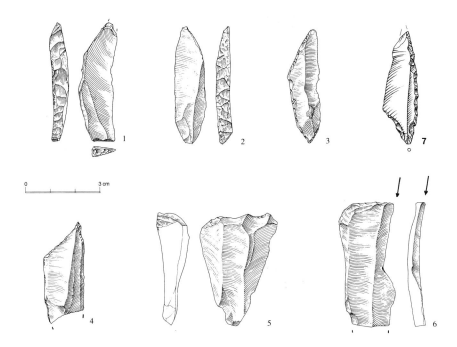

Figure 2.9 Final Upper Palaeolithic *Federmesser* artefacts: 1. Curve-backed point with straight proximal truncation; 2. Curve-backed point; 3. Angle-backed point with oblique basal truncation; 4. Piercer; 5. Short end-scraper; 6. Burin on straight truncation; 7. Curve-backed point with additional basal retouch ('penknife point'). 1–6. Pixie's Hole; 7. Symonds Yat East Rockshelter.

Source: Illustrations by Karen Hughes, courtesy of the British Museum; and Hazel Martingell

In other areas, the lithic *chaîne opératoire* seems to have been organized differently, possibly also reflecting a focus on local amenities. For example, in western Britain outside the main chalk flint-bearing areas, lithic materials such as pebble flint and chert were preferred, with no obvious evidence for the transfer of lithics over long distances. For example at Three Holes Cave (upper hearth) and Broken Cavern (both Devon), short blades of up to 5 cm were knapped from small cobbles of flint and chert that were probably imported from no more than 16 km away. The backed tools at these sites are all on short blades, reflecting the small size of the locally available raw material. In other cases where movement of materials over greater distances (up to 50 km) can be inferred, as at Symonds Yat Rockshelter (Gloucestershire), it is clear that primary reduction of the small nodules appears to have taken place on site rather than at the point of procurement. It suggests that artefacts were 'stored' in cobbles rather than being transported as ready-made forms. Overall the impression is that hunter-gatherers were no less mobile than in the early part of the Lateglacial Interstadial but raw material studies suggest there was greater variability in the home range size of *Federmesser* groups.

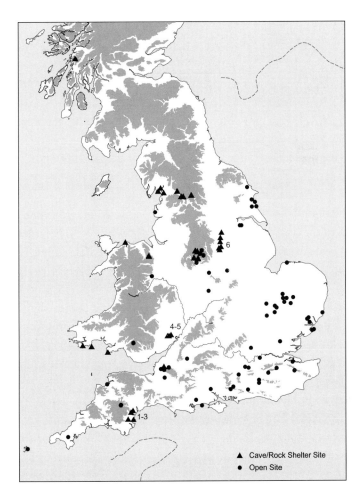

Figure 2.10 Distribution of Final Upper Palaeolithic *Federmesser* findspots: 1. Pixie's Hole; 2. Broken Cavern; 3. Three Holes Cave; 4–5. King Arthur's Cave and Symonds Yat East; 6. Mother Grundy's Parlour. Approximate position of European land-bridge connection is marked by broken line.

Source: Barton 2005 with additions

Geographic distribution and subsistence economy

It has already been noted that the later findspots are more widely distributed than those of the Creswellian. Besides being numerically superior, they include a higher percentage of open-air sites and the area covered by their distribution now extended from as far north as Scotland (Saville in Saville 2004) to the Scillies (Berridge and Roberts 1986), probably already isolated islands by then. The increase in the spread of birch woodland after about 12.9 ka cal BP and the general shift away from more open environments must have exerted a major influence on the distribution and availability of the main prey species for humans. Apart from the addition of elk (*Alces alces*) and giant deer (*Megaloceros giganteus*), other species such as red deer

(*Cervus elaphus*), wild cattle (*Bos primigenius*) and, to a very minor extent, wild horse (*Equus ferus*) continued to be present in the second half of the Interstadial. The visibility and distribution of these animals in the landscape would have been important factors in the type of hunting strategies employed by contemporary human populations. For example, whereas elk are known to be solitary and migrate over long distances, wild cattle probably lived in small herds and were relatively sedentary. According to some specialists, the introduction of new archery technology may have coincided with the period of woodland development. Certainly, the curve-backed and penknife points would have made useful additions to the barbed bone and antler weaponry, and the presence of 'impact fractures' on the tips of some of the lithic points lends further weight to the idea that they were used as projectiles.

Often omitted from lists of Palaeolithic food sources are edible fruits and plants that must have contributed to the human diet, at least seasonally. Amongst the natural flora available would have been wild berries, fruits, seeds and a range of edible fungi, but unfortunately such evidence rarely survives in the record and none so far has been recovered from a British site of this period. One further interesting observation is that Boreal woodland ecosystems are not as productive in terms of plant biomass as open steppe grasslands. They are also characterized by a less stable food chain, with plant (and consequently animal) communities being susceptible to cyclical fluctuations and, sometimes, even catastrophic failures. Thus it is likely that a broad range of different plants and animals was exploited, rather than wholesale reliance being placed on a few select species.

Other information on the human economy can be drawn from artefact spatial analyses. Most of the British Final Upper Palaeolithic sites appear to be quite small by European standards. Exceptions are sites K and C at Seamer Carr (Conneller 2007) and Hengistbury Head (Barton 1992). At Hengistbury close to 16,000 artefacts have been recorded and the main scatter covers an area of roughly 36 square metres. This is not dissimilar in size to some of the smaller *Federmesser* sites in northern France, such as Saleux, where concentrations of lithic material are of broadly similar shape and size and include the presence of hearth combustion zones (Coudret and Fagnart 2006). Hengistbury also has evidence of combustion zones (inferred from burnt artefacts) and like Saleux has a high proportion of broken-backed blades probably mainly the result of manufacturing accidents, though at Hengistbury there were also examples with damage consistent with impact breaks. Another interesting feature at Hengistbury was the presence of red ochre including a worked 'crayon' in a zone rich in end-scrapers and probably marking an area for processing animal hides. Elsewhere, in western Britain, small concentrations of heavily smashed and fragmented bones have been recorded at Three Holes Cave and Symonds Yat East Rockshelter that may indicate systematic splitting of bones and cancellous tissue to extract fat and marrow juice. The presence of a cut-marked bovid scapula at Pixie's Hole (Devon) (Barton and Roberts 1996) certainly confirms that processing of these animals took place at camp-sites.

Burials

Human skeletal material is only rarely preserved, but there is one example of deliberate mortuary behaviour from Kendrick's Cave (Gwynedd). Here, human bones were recovered from what was probably a burial accompanied by grave goods. Five engraved and ochre-stained bone tallies have been recorded from the site and one of these and the human bone can be directly dated to the Allerød. The intermixture of material of more recent age is however indicated by a perforated wild cattle tooth which has been dated to the Holocene. The famous decorated horse maxilla from this site has been dated to around 10,000 BP so may too belong to a later context rather than the burial. Interestingly, the human bone from Kendrick's Cave lacks any of the modifications present on the Gough's Cave individuals (Jacobi and Higham 2009), highlighting diverse funerary traditions in the Lateglacial.

A supplementary source of information on dietary behaviour comes from isotopic studies of the human bone from Kendrick's Cave. The analyses reveal that humans at this site not only hunted inland but exploited marine mammals either from the shore or in boats. The site is located close to the north Welsh coast, which explains why around 30 per cent of dietary protein was made up from marine resources, most probably sea mammals such as seal or dolphin (Richards *et al.* 2005). While this may be unsurprising in itself, it is a reminder that the now submerged Lateglacial shorelines of Britain offered rich habitats for human populations to exploit seasonally or even throughout the year.

Art

Apart from the bone tallies mentioned above there are very few items of non-figurative art that can be directly dated to the second half of the Interstadial. One exception might be an abstract engraving on the cortex of a flint core from Hengistbury Head (Barton 1992) which has continental parallels.

THE END OF THE LAST GLACIATION

Younger Dryas

A return to much colder conditions is marked from 10,800 to 10,000 radiocarbon yr BP (or about 12,650 to 11,500 cal bp) by a dramatic fall of 5–7°C in mean annual sea temperatures in the North Atlantic. Further evidence of climatic deterioration is indicated by the southern limit of winter sea ice which migrated from a position close to Iceland (near where it is today) to a point off the north coast of Iberia. This, coupled with potentially stronger cyclonic activity in the North Atlantic and a northerly wind flow, appears to have provided the right conditions for increased precipitation, much of it probably in the form of snow, feeding local glaciers in the Scottish Highlands and north Wales. According to the ice-core data, the sharp fall in temperatures and the return to a more glacial climate seem to have occurred extremely rapidly, perhaps within as little as a few centuries (Alley *et al.* 1993).

These climatic changes are reflected in the pollen record by evidence for the disruption of birch parkland and increased frequencies of plant communities typical of open tundra. A similar climatic signal is given by the fossil beetle faunas, which show that, if anything, temperatures in Britain were slightly cooler than those of western Europe. The latter observation is consistent with the deflection of the warm Gulf Stream currents away from the western European seaboard. The return to more open tundra-like conditions is also indicated by the reappearance of reindeer and small mammals such as steppe pika (*Ochotona pusilla*) and collared lemming (*Dicrostonyx torquatus*). Directly dated examples of these faunas, in levels with no associated archaeology, are known from a number of caves in western Britain including King Arthur's Cave (Herefordshire). The possibility that the climate became progressively drier in the later part of the Younger Dryas is implied by the occurrence of several different species of *Artemisia*. Such increases in aridity may also have stimulated the growth of wild grasses, creating grazing conditions especially favourable for wild horse and reindeer.

Human settlement and the question of continuity of occupation

Recent reviews have drawn attention to the very sparse evidence for humans in Britain during the Younger Dryas (Barton and Roberts in Saville 2004; Jacobi and Higham 2009). Towards the end of the stadial (GS-1), more pronounced signs of human presence are found in the form of 'long blade' flint industries (Barton 1989). Lithic assemblages of this kind are characterized by large, well-made blades (>12 cm) and opposed platform blade cores more than 10 cm in length. Included in the blades are heavily edge-damaged artefacts, known as 'bruised blades' or *lames mâchurées*. The damage on them has been variously interpreted as resulting from the repair of sandstone hammers or in shaping materials made of wood or antler. Although dominated by blades, these assemblages also include a few formal tools such as end-scrapers and burins, sometimes on the ends of large flakes or blades, as well as microliths.

Assemblages combining long blades and blades with bruised edges are known from 28 findspots mainly in south-eastern Britain (Figure 2.11). Their location is partly determined by the close proximity of good quality flint sources, but it is also clear that many occur in floodplains or on low river valley terraces in situations well placed to intercept migrating herds of animals. The notable absence of hearths or many burnt artefacts at these sites implies that they were occupied for only short periods and leaves open the question whether larger contemporary residential units existed elsewhere. An example of the latter may be Swaffham Prior (Suffolk), which produced higher percentages of retouched tools to waste products than noted at other sites (where typically they form less than 2 per cent of the assemblage). Another possibility is that hunter-gatherers in the Younger Dryas travelled long distances and frequently changed

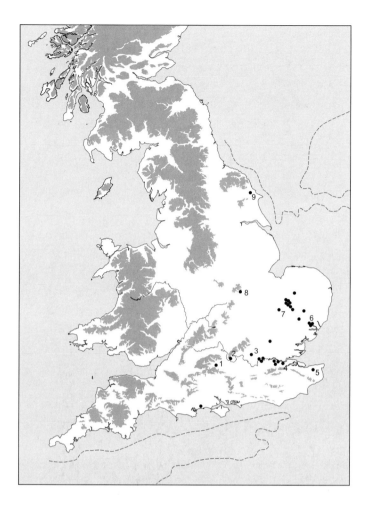

Figure 2.11 Distribution of 'long blade' findspots with bruised blades (*lames mâchurées*): 1. Avington VI; 2. Gatehampton Farm; 3. Three Ways Wharf; 4. Springhead; 5. Riverdale; 6. Sproughton; 7. Swaffham Prior; 8. Launde; 9. Seamer Carr. Approximate position of European land-bridge connection is marked by broken line.
Source: Barton 2005 with additions

location in pursuit of migrating animals (Conneller 2007). Rare cases of sites as far north as the Vale of Pickering suggest distant forays of this kind, perhaps assisted by dogs.

Interesting parallels for the British 'long blade' assemblages can be found in the Eggstedt–Stellmoor group of sites in northern Germany, including the type-locality of Stellmoor itself, which comprised a major reindeer kill on the edge of one of the tunnel valleys typical of this area. The flint projectile tips recovered in association with pinewood arrowshafts at this site were small tanged points of a type so far only recognized at one stratified British site (Avington VI, Berkshire). Small tanged points are also noticeably absent in northern France, where 'long blade' assemblages (known as *industries à pièces mâchurées*) have also been described. At

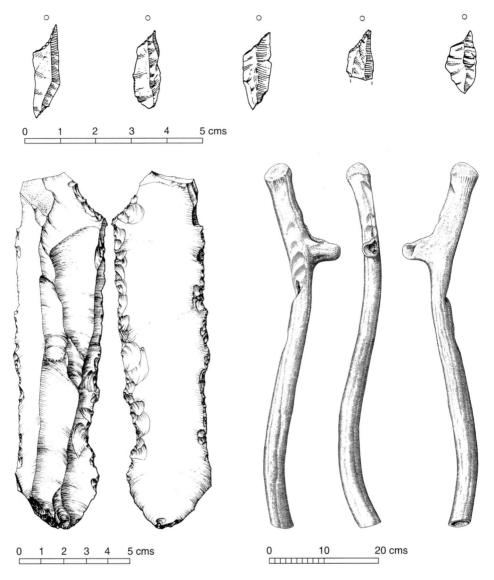

Figure 2.12 'Long blade' artefacts. Top line: microliths with concave truncation from Scatter 'A', Three Ways Wharf (Uxbridge, Greater London); bruised blade from Riverdale (Canterbury, Kent) and reindeer antler Lyngby axe from Earl's Barton (Northamptonshire).
Sources: Barton *et al.* 1991 and Cook and Jacobi 1994

these sites the bones of wild horse and bovids, rather than reindeer, are preserved. Amongst the microliths found at Three Ways Wharf, Uxbridge (west London) and Launde (Leicestershire) (Cooper 2006) are simple oblique points with concavely retouched tips (Figure 2.12) that exhibit striking parallels with those from the Epi-Ahrensburgian sites of Oudehaske and Gramsbergen I in the Netherlands (Barton and Roberts in Saville 2004). Similarities in these microlith types could imply the existence of distant links and geographically extensive social networks stretching from eastern Britain into the northern Netherlands in this period.

Despite the widespread recognition of the 'long blade' technology, there is still very little direct dating evidence for this grouping. This is partly due to an almost total lack of preservation of associated faunal remains but also to the existence of a plateau in the radiocarbon record around 10,000 ^{14}C years bp. The latter gives rise to a compression in the apparent radiocarbon ages that in reality may cover several centuries of true calendrical time. In addition there are other questions relating to contamination of samples. Several bone and antler objects were originally believed on radiocarbon dating evidence to belong to this period. They included a 'Lyngby' axe, from Earl's Barton (Northamptonshire) (Cook and Jacobi 1994) and an enigmatic horse jaw incised with a chevron (zigzag) design from Kendrick's Cavern (Gwynedd). The redating of the reindeer axe (Figure 2.12) using ultrafiltration techniques now suggests an age no earlier than the end of the Younger Dryas, while there are good reasons for suspecting that the date of the horse jaw is erroneous. A reappraisal of two barbed points from Sproughton (though unassociated with the long blade site) now places the uniserial bone artefact within the Allerød stage of the Lateglacial Interstadial, whilst the antler specimen can be shown to belong to an earlier part of the Younger Dryas (Jacobi *et al.* 2009).

The end of the Younger Dryas cold stadial is signalled by an episode of intense climatic warming across Britain and western Europe (Table 2.2, Figure 2.1). The rate of most rapid change may have occurred over a period of less than fifty years (Alley *et al.* 1993; Bell and Walker 2005). The phase at the end of the glaciation is also marked by the Friesland–Rammelbeek oscillation, immediately prior to the Pre-Boreal, in which temperatures fluctuated widely before reaching levels as high as or even higher than those of the present day (Barton in Barton *et al.* 1991). It is feasible that the latest long blade sites with evidence of horse and reindeer (e.g. Three Ways Wharf) belong to the cooler part of the oscillation. By contrast, the appearance of Mesolithic industries containing microliths and items of wood-working equipment (axes and adzes) appears to be linked with increased forestation soon after the beginning of the Holocene. It is noteworthy that non-geometric microlith projectiles present in the Early Mesolithic are similar to types found in the 'long blade' industries (Barton in Barton *et al.* 1991), suggesting some degree of cultural continuity across the Pleistocene–Holocene boundary. In sum, therefore, if there is an argument for a cultural break in human settlement in the Lateglacial it may have occurred during a colder early part of the Younger Dryas. Similarities in material culture suggest there is little to separate the latest glacial 'long blade' industries from the Pre-Boreal Early Mesolithic.

Acknowledgements

I am indebted to Simon Parfitt for his advice on the earlier Palaeolithic section and to Alison Roberts for her help on the Latest Palaeolithic sections of this chapter. Thanks are also due to Alison 'Floss' Wilkins for producing the figures and to Tom Higham and Roger Jacobi for permission to reproduce Figure 2.5.

Key texts

Barton, N., 2005. *Ice Age Britain*. London: Batsford.

Barton, R.N.E., Roberts, A.J. and Roe, D.A. (eds) 1991. *The Late Glacial in north-west Europe*. London: Council for British Archaeology Research Report 77.

Bell, M. and Walker, M., 2005. *Late Quaternary environmental change: physical and human perspectives*. Harlow: Pearson Education. 2 edn.

Gamble, C., 2007. *Origins and revolutions. Human identity in earliest prehistory*. Cambridge: Cambridge University Press.

Jacobi, R.M., 2004. 'The Later Upper Palaeolithic lithic collection from Gough's Cave, Cheddar, Somerset and human use of the cave', *Proceedings of the Prehistoric Society* 70, 1–92.

McNabb, J., 2007. *The British Lower Palaeolithic. Stones of contention*. London and New York: Routledge.

Stringer, C., 2006. *Homo Britannicus. The incredible story of human life in Britain*. London: Allen Lane.

Bibliography

Alley, R.B., Meese, D.A., Shuman, C.A., Gow, A.J., Taylor, K.C., Grootes, P.M., White, J.W.C., Ram, M., Waddington, E.D., Mayewski, P.A. and Zieginski, G.A., 1993. 'Abrupt increase in Greenland snow accumulation at the end of the Younger Dryas event', *Nature* 362, 527–29.

Andrews, P. and Fernandez-Jalvo, Y., 2003. 'Cannibalism in Britain: taphonomy of the Creswellian (Pleistocene) faunal and human remains from Gough's Cave (Somerset, England)', *Bulletin of the Natural History Museum* 58, 59–81.

Arts, N. and Deeben, J., 1987. 'On the northwestern border of the Late Magdalenian territory: ecology and archaeology of early Late Glacial band societies in Northwestern Europe', in Burdukiewicz, J. and Kobusiewicz, M. (eds) *Late Glacial in central Europe. Culture and environment*. Warsaw: Ossolineum, 25–66.

Atkinson, T.C., Briffa, K.R. and Coope, G.R., 1987. 'Seasonal temperatures in Britain during the past 22,000 years, reconstructed using beetle remains', *Nature* 325, 587–92.

Barton, R.N.E., 1989. 'Long blade technology in Southern Britain', in Bonsall, C. (ed.) *The Mesolithic in Europe. Papers presented at the third international symposium, Edinburgh 1985*. Edinburgh: John Donald, 264–271.

Barton, R.N.E., 1992. *Hengistbury Head Dorset. Volume 2: the Late Upper Palaeolithic and Early Mesolithic sites*. Oxford: Oxford University Committee for Archaeology Monograph Series 34.

Barton, R.N.E., 1996. 'Fourth interim report on the survey and excavations in the Wye Valley, 1996', *Proceedings of the University of Bristol Spelaeological Society* 20.3, 263–73.

Barton, R.N.E. and Roberts, A.J., 1996. 'Reviewing the British Late Upper Palaeolithic: new evidence for chronological patterning in the Lateglacial record', *Oxford Journal of Archaeology* 15, 245–265.

Barton. R.N.E., Jacobi, R.M., Stapert, D. and Street, M., 2003. 'The Lateglacial reoccupation of the British Isles and the Creswellian', *Journal of Quaternary Science* 18, 631–43.

Barton, R.N.E., Ford, S., Collcutt, S.N., Crowther, J., Macphail, R.I, Rhodes, E. and van Gijn, A., 2009. 'A Final Upper Palaeolithic site at Nea Farm, Somerley, Hampshire and some reflections on the occupation of Britain in the Late Glacial Interstadial', *Quartär* 56, 7–35.

Berridge, P. and Roberts, A. 1986. 'The Mesolithic period in Cornwall', *Cornish Archaeology* 25, 7–34.

Charles, R. and Jacobi, R.M., 1994. 'The lateglacial fauna from the Robin Hood Cave, Creswell Crags: a re-assessment', *Oxford Journal of Archaeology* 13, 1–32.

Conneller, C., 2007. 'Inhabiting new landscapes: settlement and mobility in Britain after the Last Glacial Maximum', *Oxford Journal of Archaeology* 26, 215–37.

Cook, J. and Jacobi, R.M., 1994. 'A reindeer antler or "Lyngby" axe from Northamptonshire and its context in the British Late Glacial', *Proceedings of the Prehistoric Society* 60, 75–84.

Coope, G.R. and Lemdahl, G., 1995. 'Regional differences in the Lateglacial climate of northern Europe based on coleopteran analysis', *Journal of Quaternary Science* 10, 391–95.

Cooper, L.P., 2006. 'Launde, a Terminal Palaeolithic camp-site in the English Midlands and its north European context', *Proceedings of the Prehistoric Society* 72, 53–93.

Coudret, P. and Fagnart, J.-P., 2006. 'Données préliminaires sur les habitats des groupes de la tradition *Federmesser* du bassin de la Somme', *Bulletin de la Société Préhistorique Française* 103, 729–40.

Dennell, R.W., 2003. 'Dispersal and colonisation, long and short chronologies: how continuous is the Early Pleistocene record for hominids outside East Africa?', *Journal of Human Evolution* 45, 421–40.

Garrod, D., 1926. *The Upper Palaeolithic Age in Britain*. Oxford: Clarendon.

Humphrey, L. and Stringer, C., 2002. 'The human cranial remains from Gough's Cave (Somerset, England)', *Bulletin of the Natural History Museum* 58, 153–68.

Jacobi, R.M. and Higham, T.F.G., 2008. 'The "Red Lady" ages gracefully: new ultrafiltration AMS determinations from Paviland', *Journal of Human Evolution* 55, 898–907.

Jacobi, R.M. and Higham, T.F.G., 2009. 'The early Lateglacial re-colonization of Britain: new radiocarbon evidence from Gough's Cave, southwest England', *Quaternary Science Reviews* 28, 1895–913.

Jacobi, R.M., Higham, T.F.G. and Lord, T.C., 2009. 'Improving the chronology of the human occupation of Britain during the Late Glacial', in Street, M., Barton, N. and Terberger, T. (eds) *Humans, environment and chronology of the Late Glacial of the North European Plain*. Mainz and Bonn: *Tagungsbänder des Römisch-Germanischen Zentralmuseums Mainz* (= Workshop 14 for Commission XXXII, 15th UISPP Congress, Lisbon, September 2006). In press.

Larsson, L. (ed.) 1996. *The earliest settlement of Scandinavia and its relationship with neighbouring areas*. Lund: *Acta Archaeologica Lundensia* series in 8°, 24.

Lowe, J.J., Coope, G.R., Harkness, D.D., Sheldrick, C. and Walker, M.J.C., 1995. 'Direct comparison of UK temperatures and Greenland snow accumulation rates, 15–12,000 years ago', *Journal of Quaternary Science* 10, 175–80.

Parfitt, S., Barendregt, R., Breda, M., Candy, I., Collins, M., Coope, G.R., Dirbridge, P., Field, M., Lee, J., Lister, A., Mutch, R., Penkman, K., Preece, R., Rose, J., Stringer, C., Symmons, R., Whittaker, J., Wymer, J. and Stuart, A., 2005. 'The earliest record of human activity in Northern Europe', *Nature* 438, 1008–1012.

Parkin, R.A., Rowley-Conwy, P. and Serjeantson, D., 1986. 'Late Palaeolithic exploitation of horse and red deer at Gough's Cave, Cheddar, Somerset', *Proceedings of the University of Bristol Spelaeological Society* 17, 311–30.

Pettitt, P., 2008. 'The British Upper Palaeolithic', in Pollard, J. (ed.), *Prehistoric Britain*. Malden, MA and Oxford: Blackwell Publishing, 18–57.

Pettitt, P., Bahn, P. and Ripoll, S. (eds) 2007. *Palaeolithic cave art at Creswell Crags in European context*. Oxford: Oxford University Press.

Richards, M., Jacobi, R., Cook, J., Pettitt, P.B. and Stringer, C., 2005. 'Isotope evidence for the intensive use of marine foods by Late Upper Palaeolithic humans', *Journal of Human Evolution* 49, 390–94.

Roebroeks, W. and van Kolfshoten, T., 1994. 'The earliest occupation of Europe: a short chronology', *Antiquity* 68, 437–61.

Saville. A. (ed.) 2004. *Mesolithic Scotland and its neighbours: the early Holocene prehistory of Scotland, its British and Irish context, and some northern European perspectives*. Edinburgh: Society of Antiquaries of Scotland.

Schwabedissen, H., 1954. *Die Federmesser-Gruppen des nord-westeuropäischen Flachlandes zur Ausbreitung des Spät-Magdalénien*. Neumünster: Karl Wachholtz Verlag.

Street, M., 1998. 'The archaeology of the Pleistocene-Holocene transition in the Northern Rhineland, Germany', in Eriksen, B. V. and Straus, L. G. (eds) *As the world warmed: human adaptations across the Pleistocene / Holocene Boundary*, 45–67 (= *Quaternary International* 49–50).

Stringer, C.B., D'Errico, F., Williams, C.T., Housley, R. and Hedges, R., 1995. 'Solution for the Sherbourne problem', *Nature* 378, 452.

Taute, W., 1968. *Die Stielspitzen-Gruppen in nordlichen Mitteleuropa: ein Beitrag zur Kenntnis der späten Altsteinzeit.* Cologne: Böhlau (= *Fundamenta* A, 5).

Walker, M.J.C. and Harkness, D.D., 1990. 'Radiocarbon dating the Devensian Lateglacial in Britain: new evidence from Llanilid, South Wales', *Journal of Quaternary Science* 5, 135–44.

Walker, M.J.C., Coope, G.R. and Lowe, J.J., 1993. 'The Devensian (Weichselian) Lateglacial palaeo-environmental record from Gransmoor, East Yorkshire, England', *Quaternary Science Reviews* 12, 659–80.

Walker, M.J.C., Coope, G.R., Sheldrick, C., Turney, C.S.M., Lowe, J.J., Blockley, S.P.E. and Harkness, D.D., 2003. 'Devensian Lateglacial environmental changes in Britain: a multi-proxy environmental record from Llanilid, South Wales, UK', *Quaternary Science Reviews* 22, 475–520.

3

HUNTER-GATHERERS OF THE MESOLITHIC

Nicky Milner and Steven Mithen

The last Ice Age came to an end around 9600 BC. Tundra landscapes that supported reindeer herds were colonized by birch and soon became thick deciduous woodland with dispersed fauna including red deer and pine marten. Except in the far north, relative sea-levels rose so that Britain, formerly a peninsula of Europe, became an island at some point around 7000–6000 BC. In this rapidly changing environment, people continued to live by hunting and gathering for several thousand years until domesticated plants and animals appeared *c.* 4000 BC (Mithen 2003). This period was the Mesolithic (Figure 3.1).

THE ENVIRONMENTAL CONTEXT FOR MESOLITHIC SETTLEMENT

At the end of the last Ice Age, as the climate improved, Lateglacial hunters again came northwards (Chapter 2). Sometime around 9600 BC, the global warming that marks the end of the Pleistocene was established: in a few decades, temperatures rose substantially, causing more ice to melt and the sea-level to rise, and insects, plants and animals began to colonize. The earliest Mesolithic sites, such as Star Carr (Yorkshire) and Thatcham (Berkshire), dating to *c.* the ninth millennium BC, were created in relatively open land-scapes in which birch and pine were the principal trees (Figure 3.2). In wetter areas, alder and willow flourished. As this vegetation became established, so too did new animal communities in which red deer, roe deer and wild pig were dominant among the larger herbivores.

As climate ameliorated further, such woodland was progressively replaced by much denser mixed deciduous woodland, and by *c.* 8000 BC hazel, oak, lime and elm were significant. The arrival of hazel is particularly noteworthy because it provided a ready supply of nuts, found in enormous quantities on many Mesolithic sites.

Figure 3.1 Mesolithic sites referred to in this chapter.

Through the Mesolithic period, relative sea-level also changed. In the first part of the Mesolithic, people could have walked eastwards to what are now the Low Countries and Denmark (Figure 3.3). However, the rising sea flooded this landscape sometime between *c.* 7000 and 6000 BC, separating Britain from the Continent. Rivers that had flowed into the now-submerged land silted up; these drainage changes led to the formation of the East Anglian fens. The rising sea-level established the shorelines of southern England much as they are today, but in the north geographical changes were more complex. There, owing to the removal of the weight of ice, the land was rebounding upwards. By *c.* 5500 BC, this isostatic rebound began to outpace the rise in sea-level, resulting in a fall in relative sea-level. In many areas of northern Britain, raised beaches, often about 10 m above current

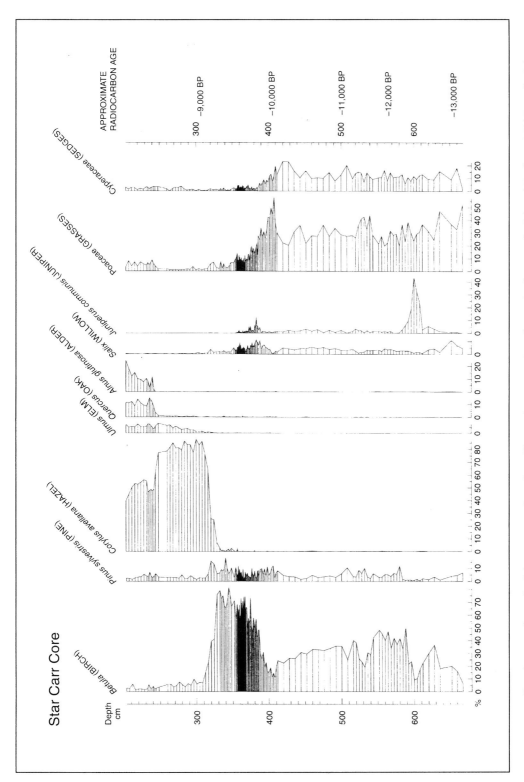

Figure 3.2   Pollen diagram from the lake centre at Star Carr, illustrating vegetation change in the Lateglacial and Early to Mid Postglacial.

Source: Day, P., 1996. 'Devensian late-glacial and early Flandrian environmental history of the Vale of Pickering, Yorkshire, England', *Journal of Quaternary Science* 11, 9–24

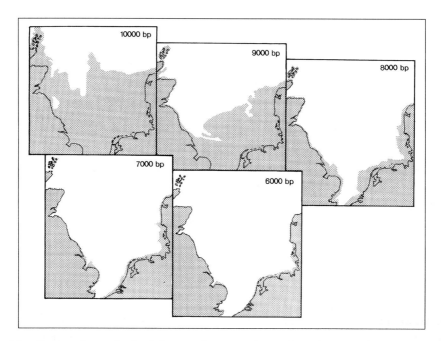

Figure 3.3   Changes in sea-level of the North Sea in the Early Holocene. These maps show how
Britain gradually became detached from the continent, with the flooding of large areas by
the encroaching North Sea leading to the loss of substantial hunting territories.

Source: Verart, L., 1996. 'Fishing for the Mesolithic. The North Sea: a submerged Mesolithic
landscape', in Fischer, A. (ed.) *Man and the sea in the Mesolithic*. Oxford: Oxbow Monograph 53,
291–301

sea-level, mark the Late Mesolithic coastline. As with vegetational changes, however, local
factors played a role: the former location of glaciers and the local geology influenced
local topographic changes. At *c.* 5800 BC there was a tsunami in the North Sea, caused
by an underwater landslide off the coast of Norway. Evidence for this has been found in
northern Britain (Warren 2005).

THE MESOLITHIC RECORD

Scatters of stone tools and the debris from their manufacture are the most abundant feature
of the record. Additionally, middens – large waste heaps of shells, animal bones and artefacts – are known from coastal locations. These two site types constitute the core of the
archaeological record. Both can range from small deposits, suggesting a brief period of
activity, to extensive accumulations reflecting either repeated use of a place or long-term
activity by a large group of people. Caves and rockshelters were also used.

Stray finds generally indicate little other than that Mesolithic people had been present. In
1931, a barbed bone point was brought up by a trawler some 40 km off the Norfolk coast
from a depth of almost 40 m. This findspot on the bed of the North Sea illustrates the major

environmental changes that have taken place since the Early Postglacial. Trails of Meso-lithic footprints found beneath peat on the inter-tidal foreshore of the River Severn are an evocative reminder that the ultimate subjects of study of the Mesolithic are not stone tools, animal bones or pollen cores, but people.

The artefactual record

Chipped stone artefacts dominate the artefactual record. Figure 3.4 shows typical artefacts from an Early and a Later Mesolithic site. The typical artefacts for the period are microliths, small blades, usually of flint, that have been retouched; they occur in a range of shapes and sizes. Microliths are often found in hundreds, and on some sites in thousands. They were probably components of a wide range of tools, including hunting equipment.

Collections including relatively large microliths, either shaped like isosceles triangles or described as 'obliquely blunted points', are referred to as 'broad blade assemblages'. Notable sites include Star Carr and Thatcham. These microliths are very similar to examples found across northern Europe, referred to as the Maglemosian industry.

Late Mesolithic assemblages are usually dominated by much smaller microliths. A wider variety of forms, such as scalene triangles and needle points, as at Kinloch (Rum), are recog-nized. Termed 'narrow blade assemblages', these reflect a cultural development without parallel on the Continent. The period between the appearance of narrow blade assemblages and the Neolithic is referred to as the Late Mesolithic.

This switch in microlith styles remains inadequately explained. It may be the archaeological manifestation of a sequence of changes: the establishment of dense deciduous woodland led to alterations in the behaviour and distribution of game, requiring new hunting strategies that in turn demanded new designs for hunting weapons and consequently new styles of microliths (Myers 1989). Alternatively, the establishment of new cultural traditions of artefact production, which had limited functional significance, may be proposed.

These broad blade assemblages have traditionally been dated to the period before 7500 BC; however, recent dates on sites like Howick (Northumberland), East Barns (East Lothian) and Cramond near Edinburgh are beginning to suggest an earlier start of somewhere between 8500 and 8000 BC for the introduction of narrow blade microliths and there are regional variations emerging in this basic two-stage Mesolithic sequence with overlap in types across Britain (Waddington 2007). In Scotland, the earliest dated site is Cramond, at about 8500 BC (Ashmore in Saville 2004), which also provides the earliest evidence for geometric-style microliths. It remains unclear whether there was Early Mesolithic settlement with a Maglemosian technology in Scotland, although some broad microliths have been found (Woodman 1989).

Maglemosian technology is absent from Ireland: the Early Irish Mesolithic (e.g. Mount Sandel) displays a narrow blade technology. By *c.* 6000 BC, this had been transformed into an industry dominated by large blades, in which microliths are essentially absent. Within England, there

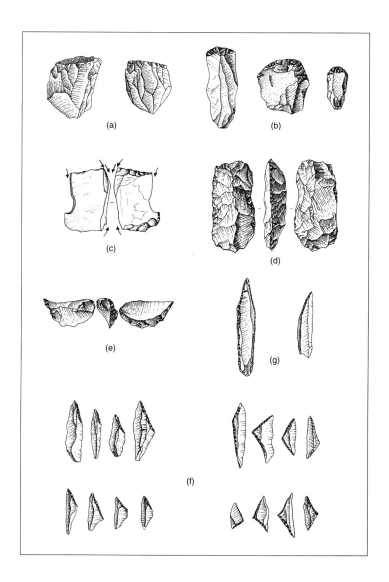

are regional and local variations in microlith forms. For instance, a cluster of Early Mesolithic sites in the Weald produce 'Horsham points', pointed microliths, whose bases have been retouched into a concave form. Elsewhere, certain western sites, such as Cass Ny Hawin (Isle of Man) and Coulererach (Islay), have tanged microliths (Mithen *et al.* in Pollard and Morrison 1996).

While microliths dominate most assemblages, other types of stone tools were important. These include scrapers, burins and awls, known from hunter-gatherer toolkits throughout early prehistory. Flint axes, and their resharpening flakes, are also found and were no doubt used to acquire wood for bows and huts, and perhaps to make forest clearings. Their absence from Scottish assemblages is probably a reflection of the smallness of available nodules. From coastal areas in particular, many sites have tools made from coarse types of

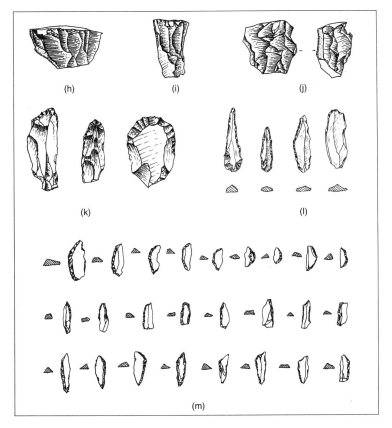

Figure 3.4 *previous page and above* Chipped stone artefacts from Star Carr (a)–(g) and Farm Fields,
Kinloch, Rum (h)–(m). (a) Blade core; (b) Scrapers; (c) Burin; (d) Adze sharpening flake;
(f) Microliths; (g) Borer; (h) Conical platform core; (i) Blade core; (j) Double platform
core; (k) Scrapers; (l) Borers; (m) Microliths (top row, crescents; middle row, backed
bladelets; bottom row, scalene triangles). Scales: (a)–(g) 1:2, (h)–(l) 2:3, (m) 3:4.
Sources: (a)–(g) after Clark 1954; (h)–(m) after Wickham-Jones 1990

stone. Often these are minimally altered beach pebbles and are likely to have been used for
detaching or processing shellfish or processing seal skins.

Tools made from organic materials are very rare (Figure 3.5). Only Star Carr and a set of
middens on the tiny Hebridean island of Oronsay have produced large quantities, although
a good sample has recently been acquired from An Corran, a rockshelter on Skye. The most
important are barbed points made from red deer antler, and antler mattocks. Barbed points
comprise two general types: uniserial points, with one line of barbs, are predominantly
found in the Early Mesolithic, while biserial points, often pierced to make harpoon-heads,
tend to be shorter and are recovered from Late Mesolithic coastal sites.

Antler mattocks, perforated for hafting, have a working edge made by an oblique
transverse truncation of the antler beam (Smith in Bonsall 1989). Those from Star Carr

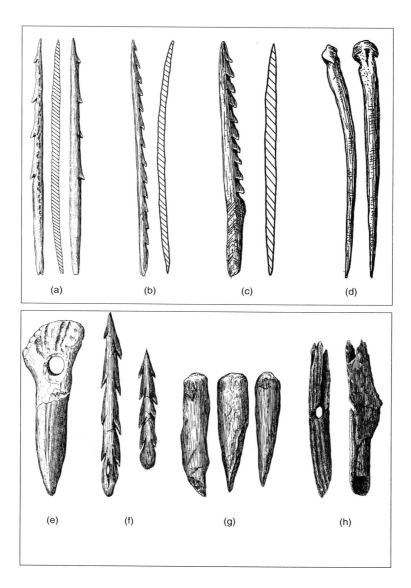

Figure 3.5 Organic and coarse stone artefacts from Mesolithic sites: (a) Barbed antler point from Star Carr (no. 178), *c.* 276 mm; (b) Barbed antler point from Star Carr (no. 145), *c.* 180 mm; (c) Barbed antler point from Star Carr (no. 150), *c.* 138 mm; (d) Bone pin made from the lateral metacarpal bones of elk from Star Carr (no. 160), *c.* 148 mm; (e) Mattock head of elk antler from Star Carr (no. 159), *c.* 262 mm; (f) Bone/antler harpoons from Oronsay middens, *c.* 124 and 81 mm; (g) 'Limpet scoops' made from bone/antler from Caisteal nan Gillean I, Oronsay, *c.*70 mm; (h) Perforated shaped mattock head of red deer antler from Priory Midden, Oronsay, *c.*150 mm.

Sources: (a)–(e) after Clark 1954; (f) after Anderson, J., 1895. 'Notice of a cave recently discovered at Oban, containing human remains, and a refuse-heap of shells and bones of animals, and stone and bone implements', *Proceedings of the Society of Antiquaries of Scotland* 32, 211–230; (g) after Anderson, J., 1898. 'Notes on the contents of a small cave or rock shelter at Druimvargie, Oban; and of three shell mounds in Oronsay', *Proceedings of the Society of Antiquaries of Scotland* 32, 298–311; (h) after Mellars 1987

are of elk antler, while other sites produce examples made from red deer. Wear on their working edges includes lustrous polishes, deep and angular striations and flaking, and is most likely to derive from digging, perhaps to remove roots or raw materials. Three Scottish examples were found associated with whale skeletons, suggesting the removal of blubber.

Non-utilitarian artefacts

Artefacts of a less utilitarian nature are seldom found (Figure 3.6). A small number of beads include shale examples at Nab Head in Dyfed (David in Bonsall 1989) and Star Carr and pierced

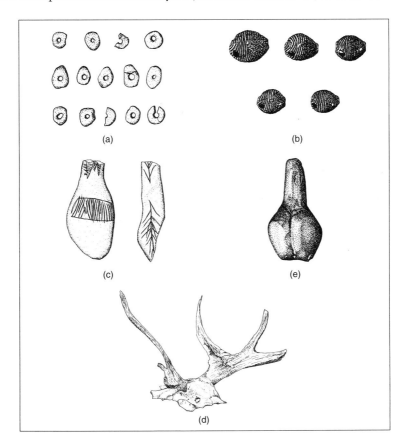

(a)

(b)

(c)

(e)

(d)

Figure 3.6 Non-utilitarian artefacts from Mesolithic sites in Britain: (a) Shale beads from Star Carr; (b) Perforated cowrie shell ornaments from Oronsay; (c) Engraved pebble from Rhuddlan, *c.*86 mm; (d) Red deer antler mask; (e) Shale pebble from Nab Head claimed to represent a phallus, *c.*104 mm.

Sources: (a), (d) after Clark 1954; (b) after Mellars 1987; (c) after Berridge, P. and Roberts, A., 1995. 'The Mesolithic decorated and other pebble artefacts: synthesis', in *Excavations at Rhuddlan, Clwyd, 1969–1973, Mesolithic to Medieval*. York: CBA Research Report 95; (e) Jacobi, R., 1980. 'The Early Holocene settlement of Wales', in Taylor, J.A. (ed.) *Culture and Environment in Prehistoric Wales*. Oxford: BAR British Series 76, 131–206.

cowrie shells from Scottish middens (Simpson in Pollard and Morrison 1996). A unique occurrence of 21 red deer antler frontlets, the bone below the antlers pierced so that they could be worn as masks, occurs at Star Carr. Such artefacts invite speculation: were they worn by shamans or perhaps as part of hunters' disguise? More recent interpretations have suggested that wearing these masks may have made the boundaries between animals and humans ambiguous, transforming people and enabling them to take on animal qualities (Conneller 2004).

Very few decorated objects are known. A shale pebble from Nab Head appears to represent a figurine or a phallus, but this surface find cannot be confidently attributed to the Mesolithic. A piece of red deer antler from Romsey (Hampshire) and a *Bos* bone from the Thames are engraved with chevrons – a design frequent on Mesolithic objects from continental Europe; but, again, neither can be definitely attributed to this period. The site of Rhuddlan (Clwyd) produced incised pebbles with geometric designs: one was in a secure Mesolithic context and, in light of their stylistic unity, all are likely to be Mesolithic. Rock art, consisting of inscribed crosses, has also been recently discovered in the cave site of Aveline's Hole (see below), thought to date to the end of the Ice Age.

Site features: pits, postholes and dwellings

The best-known dwelling structure is from Mount Sandel (Northern Ireland), excavated in the 1970s and discussed below. Substantial structures have also been found more recently at Howick (Waddington 2007), East Barns and Star Carr. The structures at Howick and East Barns are very similar in many respects. They are sub-circular, about 6 m in diameter, cut into the ground and constructed using timber posts. In the centre of the Howick structure there was a sequence of hearths containing large quantities of charred hazelnut shells. A high-resolution dating programme using AMS and Bayesian modelling was undertaken which showed that the structure was initially constructed *c.* 7800 BC and rebuilt or mended several times. The dating indicates that occupation lasted somewhere in the region of 150–200 years, suggesting some form of permanent occupation.

At sites such as Deepcar (Yorkshire) and Morton (Fife: Coles 1971), traces of shelters, perhaps no more than windbreaks, are present. Large depressions on sites including Cass Ny Hawin, Staosnaig (Colonsay: Mithen 2000) and Broom Hill, Hampshire, contain many charred fragments of hazelnut shell, but whether these are the remains of hut floors or specialized features for the processing of plant foods is unclear.

Excavations in the 1980s at Star Carr uncovered part of a timber platform or walkway into the lake. This is constructed of hewn aspen and is the earliest evidence of systematic carpentry in Europe (Mellars and Dark 1998). It is also becoming evident that people in the Mesolithic dug large pits. At Crathes (Aberdeenshire), seven pits in an alignment running over 60 metres have been dated to *c.* 8000–7500 BC. Four pits located in the car park at Stonehenge also date to *c.* 8500–7500 BC, and two pits on Anglesey date to the seventh millennium BC. Unfortunately we cannot determine what these pits were used for, but in addition to the increasing number of hut structures being found, it is clear that Mesolithic people were capable of substantial building and construction. Were these early forms of monuments?

Death and burial

Human bones are exceedingly rare. Aveline's Hole, a cave in the Mendip Hills, may have been a cemetery, containing between 50 and 100 individuals and dating to the second half of the eighth millennium BC (Conneller in Conneller and Warren 2006). Unfortunately, little survives from work carried out here in the nineteenth and early twentieth centuries. The only complete skeleton (a young male) comes from Gough's Cave, also in the Mendips and dating to the same time period. Bryan Sykes of the University of Oxford believes that ancient mtDNA (see Chapter 2) from this skeleton shows a remarkable degree of similarity to modern humans. Elsewhere, human remains consist mainly of isolated bones, usually found in caves, suggesting direct descent, though they are also found deposited in watery contexts and within the Oronsay middens. The disarticulation of human skeletons and deposition of bones in different contexts around the landscape has parallels with the Continent and is a practice which continues into the Neolithic.

Environmental evidence

Environmental evidence can be used to detect Mesolithic activity in areas where Mesolithic sites are unknown (Edwards in Saville 2004). Microscopic charcoal found in soil profiles is sometimes argued to derive from camp fires or the deliberate burning of vegetation, although the possibility remains that the fires were natural occurrences during a more arid period (Tipping in Pollard and Morrison 1996). Pollen analysis can also demonstrate changes in vegetation linked to human presence. Very recently, this hypothesis has been confirmed for Shetland with the discovery of the first Mesolithic site on this archipelago at West Voe: a Late Mesolithic shell midden (Melton and Nicholson 2004).

Animal bones are unfortunately infrequent on Mesolithic sites. Star Carr and shell middens such as Oronsay provide most of the data. However, our understanding of the species present at this time can be supplemented by fossil records: for example, bones found in caves resulting from natural animal deaths (Kitchener *et al.* in Saville 2004). These data can provide us with better understandings of ecological niches and the types of animals which were available for exploitation.

INTERPRETATION

Archaeologists face considerable challenges in interpreting the surviving evidence. While all people during the Mesolithic lived by hunting and gathering, that lifestyle is highly variable.

Hunter-gatherers can live in small, highly mobile egalitarian groups or at semi-permanent sites in societies that display significant social differentiation. Archaeological sites can be small, overnight occupations, camps for specialized activities such as hunting or residential bases; many are likely to be palimpsests from multiple occupations, perhaps each of a different character.

To cope with such complexities in site interpretation, a wide range of methods and techniques is employed. These have changed substantially during the last 50 years, notably with the development of archaeological science.

DEVELOPMENTS IN MESOLITHIC ARCHAEOLOGY: STAR CARR AS A CASE STUDY

Star Carr is located in the Vale of Pickering, Yorkshire. Its excavation (1949–1951), and publication (Clark 1954) ushered in the modern era of Mesolithic studies. This demonstrated the importance of multidisciplinary studies, including contributions from zoologists and botanists. Later, Clark (1972) reinterpreted Star Carr, proposing it as a winter base camp for groups that dispersed into the Pennines or North York Moors during the summer. The season of occupation was determined on the basis of shed antler recovered on site: modern deer shed their antlers between October and March.

Two radical reinterpretations, both founded on Clark's published data, were proposed within a decade. Far from being a winter base camp, Star Carr was, Pitts (1979) argued, a specialized site for working antler and tanning hides. The high frequencies of end-scrapers and awls in the tool assemblage, direct evidence for antler working and the quantities of birch bark and wood recovered, which he believed were tanning agents, were employed in this hypothesis. As tanning requires warmth, Pitts suggested that this took place in the summer months. Shortly thereafter, Andresen and colleagues (1981) proposed that Star Carr had been used for butchery intermittently on short visits through the year, with the assemblages of artefacts and bones taking tens or hundreds of years to accumulate.

The faunal assemblage was reanalysed by Legge and Rowley-Conwy (1988): sex and age distributions by species, seasonality, body-part representation and cut-marks on the surface of bones were considered. They concluded that Star Carr had been a spring/summer hunting camp, dismissing the evidence for winter occupation that had once seemed so critical.

In addition, Dumont (in Bonsall 1989) applied microwear analysis, a method whereby microscopic examination of tool edges may indicate their former use, as different activities such as working wood or hide or cutting meat leave different microscopic traces. This demonstrated that a wide range of tasks had been undertaken, suggesting that arguments for a small set of specialized activities were wrong.

High-resolution pollen and sedimentological analyses were undertaken thereafter on a peat monolith from a new trench at Star Carr. Dark examined pollen frequencies, charcoal fragments and mineral content, thus obtaining a more detailed picture of vegetational history and establishing the extent to which this had been influenced by human activity. New radiocarbon dates were acquired by AMS methods and calibrated: an absolute chronology for the occupation was thus secured (Mellars and Dark 1998). There appear to be two main occupations, the first starting around 8970 cal BC and lasting for roughly 80 years and the second starting around 8790 cal BC and lasting for 130 years (Dark *et al.* 2006). Since the 1970s, further fieldwork has been carried out in the Vale of Pickering around the ancient Lake Flixton, now peat bog (Taylor 2007). In total, 13 Early Mesolithic sites have been investigated, and yet none have produced the material culture assemblage recorded at Star Carr. Shale beads and antler frontlets remain unique to the site and only two fragments of barbed points have been found elsewhere compared with 193 from Star Carr. This uniqueness makes functional interpretations that see Star Carr as a typical site (such as a base camp or butchery site) problematic and has led some researchers to suggest a ritual element to the pattern of artefact deposition (e.g. Conneller and Schadla-Hall 2003).

Since 2004, new fieldwork and excavations have taken place at Star Carr (Milner 2007). These have concentrated on investigating the extent of occupation and the dry-land areas, about which little was known. The results of this work have demonstrated further that Star Carr is much larger than previously imagined: Clark's excavations cover less than 5 per cent of the site and focus only on the lake-edge deposits. This changes interpretations again, and perhaps it can be conceived of as a large aggregation site. The new, dry-land excavations have so far revealed a sub-circular posthole structure, probably some form of a hut, which will provide further insights into the ways in which people were inhabiting the site. In addition, this structure is important more widely as it presently forms the oldest evidence for such a construction in Britain.

OTHER KEY SITES

Thatcham, Berkshire

Thatcham is located in the Kennet Valley. Although discovered in 1920, full-scale excavations were not undertaken until 1958–1961. Radiocarbon dates have since placed this occupation in the ninth millennium BC. It is located in a topographic situation akin to Star Carr on an ancient lake margin and similar ranges of stone artefacts and fauna were recovered. One major difference from Star Carr is the scarcity of wooden and antler artefacts, especially barbed points. Further excavations were undertaken in 1989 (Healy *et al.* 1992). These extended the occupation into the Later Mesolithic. Wear traces on newly excavated artefacts suggest that a wide range of activities, using various raw materials, occurred, implying that Thatcham had been a base camp. Its location in a river valley with easy access to varied land and aquatic resources supports this view. Many other Mesolithic sites are now known in the Kennet Valley.

Oakhanger, Hampshire

Numerous Mesolithic artefact scatters are known at Oakhanger (Jacobi 1981), from sites that span the Early (e.g. Oakhanger II, V, VII, X and XI) and Later (e.g. Oakhanger III, VIII and XX) Mesolithic. Some assemblages are substantial: Oakhanger V provided 85,000 artefacts and site VII 105,678 artefacts; these are in fact parts of a single site now bisected by a road. Most of the material consists of debris from tool-making. The tools are dominated by micro-liths, but truncated blades, burins, core adzes and finely serrated blades occur. The quantities of artefacts imply repeated occupations; at site V, six hearths are evident within the artefact distribution. This array of sites indicates that people had repeatedly returned to this part of their landscape, which must have been a favoured location for hunting and gathering.

Farm Fields, Kinloch, Rum

This, one of the earliest dated sites (Wickham-Jones 1990) in Scotland, dates to the eighth millennium BC. Located at the head of a large bay, the site provided a landing place for people crossing, probably in coracles or canoes, to Rum. The island may have been attractive on account of the locally available 'bloodstone' – a term used for cryptocrystalline silicas that can be flaked much as flint. Farm Fields (Figure 3.7) is typical of many Mesolithic sites in being a palimpsest of many occupations, incorporating numerous small pits of uncertain function. The artefacts, similar to those from contemporary English sites, are dominated by small geometric microliths, particularly scalene triangles.

The Oronsay middens

Oronsay, a tiny island adjacent to the larger Colonsay, lies in the southern Hebrides. It has six Mesolithic shell middens, a remarkable density that remains unexplained. In recent times, however, the island has been a breeding ground for seals, which perhaps provided easy killings for Mesolithic coastal foragers. Our principal understanding comes from work during the 1970s, especially at Cnoc Coig midden (Mellars 1987). Radiocarbon dates show that the middens formed c. 5500–4000 BC. Artefacts from the middens include those probably used for exploiting coastal resources, such as small antler harpoons, and bevel-ended elongated pebbles ('limpet hammers'), employed, perhaps, for detaching limpets from rocks. The middens lack a microlithic industry, as represented at contemporary sites on nearby islands. This absence probably reflects the specific economic activities undertaken on Oronsay, rather than indicating distinct cultural groups with different tool traditions.

Gleann Mor, Islay

This site (Figure 3.8) provides an important contrast to those already described, which are likely to be palimpsests from multiple occupations. Gleann Mor is a small, discrete scatter

Figure 3.7 Excavations at Farm Fields, Rum (Caroline Wickham Jones).

Figure 3.8 Excavations at Gleann Mor, Islay (Steven Mithen).

consisting solely of stone artefacts and manufacturing waste, which probably represents a single occupation event. Excavated as part of a regional study (Mithen 2000), Gleann Mor is set inland within peat moorland, beneath which the artefacts were sealed. When the site was occupied *c.* 6000 BC, hazel-dominated woodland would have surrounded the hunter-gatherers. Apart from thousands of waste chippings, the artefacts are again dominated by microliths, which, like the other tools, are preserved in a fresh condition. Microwear study indicates varied uses, outlined below.

Gleann Mor was probably a small hunting camp, occupied for a short period by a group exploiting the Hebridean islands. Other site types in their settlement system are found nearby. Less than 2 km distant, a much larger and probably contemporary site at Bolsay Farm may have been a residential base. The specialized sites on Oronsay, and that at Staosnaig (Colonsay), are located slightly further away; both have radiocarbon dates that overlap those of Gleann Mor. Thus here archaeologists are gaining insights into how Mesolithic people undertook different economic activities at various locations in the landscape.

Culverwell, Isle of Portland, Dorset

The important site at Culverwell consists of an extensive shell midden, stretching over 300 sq m (Palmer in Bonsall 1989), which seems to have formed in a hollow and derives from the exploitation of a wide range of marine molluscs; the absence of fish bones is puzzling. Evidence of dwelling structures is limited to several hearths, what appears to be a substantial cooking pit and a pavement. The tool assemblage includes an impressive number of picks, made of local Portland chert, perhaps used for removing limpets from rocks or for extracting chert from outcrops.

Mount Sandel, County Antrim

Dated to the eighth millennium BC, this site is located on a 30-m-high bluff overlooking the River Bann (Figure 3.9). Mount Sandel (Woodman 1985) has substantial numbers of microliths dominated by scalene triangles, a narrow blade assemblage contemporary with Howick. Other stone tools include awls, scrapers and axes made on either cores or flakes. The important evidence for structures consists of a large number of postholes that were dug within an enlarged natural hollow. These postholes evidently relate to numerous structures as some intercut or were cut by other features. They seem to represent substantial circular huts, about 5.5 m in diameter, that contained hearths and pits, perhaps for storage.

Goldcliff, Severn estuary

Mesolithic sites have been excavated at Goldcliff on the Severn estuary to the east of a former island (Bell 2007). The Mesolithic occupation dates mainly from the sixth to the

Figure 3.9   Excavations of the hut at Mount Sandel, Northern Ireland (P. Woodman).

fourth millennia BC. Lithics, worked wood and bone artefacts were found. Deer, aurochs and wild boar were the main animals exploited, and there is evidence of fishing, particularly eels. Burning episodes in the now submerged forests and reedswamp are argued to be deliberate activities. Human defecation areas have also been identified through the identification of human intestinal parasites. The site is best known, however, for the remarkably well-preserved human footprints found in the laminated silts, a large proportion of which belong to children. Overall, the evidence has been interpreted as indicative of short-term camps.

TOOLS, SITE ACTIVITIES, MOBILITY AND SETTLEMENT PATTERNS

Stone tools and manufacturing waste provide the largest body of evidence for the British Mesolithic. The basic types comprise microliths, scrapers, burins, axes and adzes. The simple presence of microliths within an assemblage suggests a Mesolithic date – although the possibility that microliths were also made later in prehistory should not be discounted.

Artefact frequencies, site activities and settlement patterns

The relative frequencies of tool types may indicate the activities that were undertaken at a site. In Hampshire, the sites of Iping II and Oakhanger VII have contrasting tool assemblages.

Oakhanger VII has more scrapers, serrated blades and truncated pieces than microliths, while microliths far outnumber these types at Iping. Microburins – quite rare at Oakhanger – are more numerous than microliths at Iping, suggesting that (if microliths are indeed for projectiles) hunting weapons were made there, while processing activities, such as cleaning hides, appear dominant at Oakhanger (Jacobi 1981).

Barton (1992) recognized a correlation between artefact frequencies, topographic locations and the underlying geology in Early Mesolithic assemblages from central-southern England. Sites including Hengistbury (Dorset) and Iping C, which have assemblages that lack tools such as burins, axes and drill bits, are found on high ground and generally occur on sandstone. In contrast, Downton and Thatcham III, on relatively low ground and on silty substrates, have more diverse toolkits. These latter appear to be locations where a wider range of activities was undertaken, compared with the specialized manufacture and use of hunting equipment on the higher sites.

Microwear analysis and tool function

At Gleann Mor, some microliths were employed as projectile points, identifiable from tell-tale striations left on their surfaces. Other microliths here had clearly been used in a circular motion, apparently as bits for awls or drills. While the Star Carr microwear analyses showed that a variety of tasks had been undertaken, few relationships between tool types and specific functions were noted. For instance, 56 scrapers (of 374 from the site) were examined for wear traces: 36 showed signs of use, representing 55 episodes. These were mainly scraping/planing actions, directed principally against hide (40 per cent), bone (22 per cent), antler (22 per cent) and wood (13 per cent). Hints of differences in the morphology of artefacts used on different materials were noted: those used on antler tend to be longer and more curved.

Debitage analysis, site function and site formation

Tools usually constitute only a small fraction of the artefacts from a site. Much more common is the manufacturing waste, or debitage; indeed retouched tools often form as little as 1 per cent of an assemblage. This division between tools and waste needs careful consideration. At Thatcham, for example, a higher percentage of unretouched artefact edges had been used compared to those that exhibited retouch. 'Debitage' thus includes tools that are not retouched.

Mesolithic sites on Islay illustrate how debitage can be studied. The proportions of tools at Coulererach and Bolsay Farm are very similar. At Coulererach, however, the debitage is dominated by large cores and flakes, often the first detached from the raw material; indeed, several discarded flint beach pebbles had just one or two flakes removed. Nodules were tested for quality and the initial stages of flint knapping took place; there was little concern for efficient use of materials. In contrast, at Bolsay Farm most cores are small and debitage is dominated by little flakes characteristic of later stages of knapping. It appears that partially worked cores were carried here, to be worked as efficiently as possible before being discarded. Coulererach lay about 100 m from the Mesolithic coastline, on which flint pebbles are likely to have been abundant, but Bolsay Farm lies 6 km from this source.

When debitage can be refitted, more detailed information about knapping methods is obtainable. At Early Mesolithic Hengistbury Head (Barton 1992), for instance, excavations recovered 35,444 pieces of debitage, a considerable number of which have been refitted. Most cores with opposed platforms here displayed uneven use. Refitting also indicates that most, if not all, of the artefacts were contemporary. This is important, as they were found dispersed vertically through windblown sand deposits. Examples separated vertically by as much as 0.39 m have been rejoined, demonstrating that their separation is due to post-depositional processes such as trampling and bioturbation. Otherwise, this site might have been interpreted as a series of stratified deposits from successive occupations.

Demonstrating contemporaneity between artefacts and features on a single site can occasion difficulties. The artefacts at Oakhanger III covered more than 100 sq m and surrounded four hearths. Are these hearths and artefacts contemporary and indicative of a relatively large social group, or do they simply reflect repeated visits by a small group? Radiocarbon dating cannot necessarily resolve such problems, as the finest resolution appears to be ± 50 years.

The enormous size of the lithic assemblages at many sites indicates that certain locations were repeatedly visited by Mesolithic foragers. While this may be accounted for purely in functional terms – such as access to materials or good hunting – symbolic relationships with specific places and landscape features linked to the inhabitants' cosmology, about which we know nothing, may be invoked.

Raw material sources and mobility patterns

Identifying the sources of raw materials found on sites is important in reconstructing past mobility patterns. For instance, Early Mesolithic sites in the Pennines, both in the eastern foothills, such as Deepcar, and on the summits, have artefacts made from a white flint originating in the north Lincolnshire Wolds 80 km away. The frequency (80–99 per cent) of such artefacts matches that found on sites immediately adjacent to the flint sources. Jacobi (1978) suggested that this may reflect direct procurement by groups that exploited the Pennines in summer and the eastern lowlands in winter. Portland chert, contrastingly, is found in only very small frequencies in assemblages even from sites at distances less than 80 km from its source, such as Oakhanger V and VII. Only one blade of Portland chert was identified in the assemblage of 186,000 artefacts there. Jacobi proposed that the distribution mechanism in this case may have been gift exchange.

The distribution of bloodstone, which has its major source on Rum (Wickham-Jones 1990), is also informative. Assemblages containing bloodstone artefacts come from neighbouring islands, notably Eigg and Skye, and from nearby mainland areas including Ardnamurchan and the shell midden at Risga in Loch Sunart. This pattern may indicate the range over which people from Rum moved during their seasonal cycles.

Further away, on Colonsay and Islay for example, bloodstone is absent from Mesolithic assemblages. These islands may, however, have provided sufficient raw materials, so that bloodstone was not required.

Inferences can be drawn from variations in raw material use through time. During the earlier Mesolithic, northern English assemblages are dominated by white flint; subsequently, there was much greater use of poorer quality chert and translucent flint (Pitts and Jacobi 1979). This change may reflect the exhaustion of high-quality sources, perhaps because of increasing population, or their inaccessibility as a result of rising sea-level or near-impenetrable vegetation. Alternatively, changes in mobility patterns may have been the cause, as later Mesolithic foragers covered smaller distances in the course of their activities and consequently had to rely on local, and poorer quality, raw materials.

THE MESOLITHIC ECONOMY

The subsistence economy has always been one of the key areas of investigation for the Mesolithic period because it can shed light on the way people interacted with the environment and used the resources which would have been available to them. Star Carr provides the best dataset for inland Mesolithic sites thanks to the exceptional preservation conditions. Other sites such as Thatcham, Mount Sandel and Howick have produced additional faunal material, but usually these sorts of sites have unfavourable conditions for organic materials to survive and we have to rely on burnt organic material.

There are also a number of shell middens which provide substantial quantities of faunal remains. The best-known are those on Oronsay, but there is also material from Westward Ho! and Culverwell (south-west England), Morton, An Corran, Ulva Cave (Mull), Sand (near Applecross, Scotland), Polmonthill and Inveravon (near the inner Forth estuary) and Glendhu (Belfast in Ireland).

Palaeodiet

Over the last decade, stable isotope analysis has been an important method for investigating palaeodiet, and much of the available Mesolithic bone has been analysed. This provides direct dietary information through the analysis of human bone. These results have demonstrated that there are very mixed patterns of food consumption right through the period 8500–4000 BC with some highly marine diets on Oronsay, some diets dominated by terrestrial foods, e.g. Aveline's Hole, and some mixed diets (Milner in Conneller and Warren 2006).

The use of terrestrial animals

Star Carr alone has a substantial faunal assemblage and shows that five large species were hunted: red deer, elk, auroch, roe deer and wild boar. It is in the Mesolithic period when the bow and arrow first become extensively used and it is probable that these animals were stalked in thick woodlands, although the possibility that animals were driven into ambushes remains. It is also in the Mesolithic where we have the first evidence for domesticated dog. Domesticated dog was found at Star Carr and at Seamer (a site very close to Star Carr on Lake Flixton) and it is likely that dogs were also used in hunting. Other animals were also exploited, both for food and in some cases fur. Beaver bone has been found at Star Carr and Faraday Road, Thatcham, and in the latter case butchery marks suggest this animal was also eaten. Star Carr also produces evidence for a range of birds living on the lake, and it is likely that these were also included in the diet.

Shell middens and coastal exploitation

The coastal zone is likely to have been the most productive part of Britain during the Mesolithic. It is not surprising that some of the largest sites, including Culverwell, are located there. Access to woodland with its large game, as well as marine mammals and fish and the rich resources of the seashore, including crustaceans, seaweeds and shellfish, would have been easy.

The clearest picture of coastal exploitation comes from western Scotland, notably the middens on Oronsay. Red deer and otter, over 30 types of birds, crabs, seals, shellfish and fish are attested on Oronsay. Over 90 per cent of the fish bones come from saithe and testify to marine fishing, although hooks and nets are absent. Limpets dominate the molluscan remains, but periwinkle and dogwhelk are well represented. On some sites it appears that seaweed was also being gathered: small species of shell have been found which live on seaweed and were probably collected unintentionally.

The use of plants

A contentious aspect of Mesolithic subsistence concerns the importance of plant foods. Clarke (1976) argued that early Postglacial environments would have been rich in plant foods, which are likely to have made a major contribution to diet. Plant remains survive only if normal processes of decay are halted, which in Britain would mean a totally waterlogged site, and even though Star Carr has revealed evidence of plant species, it is presently impossible to be sure which of these were consumed. Charring also preserves plant foods, although the resulting assemblage is biased: charring depends on the proximity of fire, and many plant foods were probably eaten raw. Even when plant remains are preserved, their recovery from sediments requires sieving through very fine-grained mesh or flotation methods that many early, and some recent, excavations have neglected to employ. In consequence, the limited amounts of plant foods known from Mesolithic sites do not reflect their significance in the diet. Raspberry seeds from Newferry and wild pear/apple from Mount Sandel, both in Ulster, offer a glimpse of the range regularly exploited.

Only hazelnuts, usually represented by fragments of their charred shells, have been found in large quantities and on many sites. These were probably roasted to improve their flavour and digestibility or to prepare a paste for ease of transport and storage; in this process, some were burnt. The apparent importance of hazelnuts in Mesolithic diets is likely to be more than a factor of preservation and recovery: as a highly nutritious plant food, they were probably intensively exploited and regularly harvested. At sites such as Broom Hill, Howick and Staosnaig, hundreds of thousands of charred nuts were deposited in large, circular depressions. As these nuts are presumably only a fraction of those roasted, a very intensive exploitation of hazel trees in the vicinity is implied, especially if, as at Staosnaig, such deposits formed over a number of years rather than centuries.

The importance of plant foods in the diet may be indicated by the evidence for environmental manipulation by igniting vegetation, which increases in frequency during the Later Mesolithic. Firing may have been used to encourage plant growth, and been particularly valuable for hazel. Management of plants may also be indicated by artefacts: amongst other purposes, antler mattocks may have been used to break ground or to weed, so that edible wild plants could flourish.

Domesticating the wild?

Apart from the dog, there is no evidence for domestication of animals in Mesolithic Britain. However, the exploitation of animals may have included something approaching management, possibly including the transport of some species to offshore islands. In terms of plants, there are ongoing debates about the beginning of cereal cultivation in Britain. Cereal grain pollen has been identified in some pollen cores for the Late Mesolithic, but these are usually argued to be either contamination by later material or the misidentification of wild grasses. The earliest date for charred cereal grain, which is much more conclusive proof, dates to about 4000–3800 BC, the early stage of the Neolithic.

Palynological evidence shows that Mesolithic foragers fired vegetation, although whether intentionally or accidentally (from uncontrolled campfires) is unclear. Modern Australian Aborigines employ fire with the express aim of encouraging plant growth and attracting game. Perhaps Mesolithic people acted similarly. At North Gill (North York Moors), a high-resolution pollen sequence demonstrated that during the Late Mesolithic or Early Neolithic the tree canopy was opened by the removal of oak, willow and alder, allowing shrubs to flower much better. Evidence for the use of fire is absent, and the decline of these species may indicate the acquisition of foliage for wild game (Simmons and Innes 1996).

SOCIAL ORGANIZATION, IDEOLOGY AND THE HUMAN POPULATION

Little can be stated with confidence about the social organization of Mesolithic hunter-gatherers in Britain. Of course, this does not stop speculation, some of which may be correct. For instance, Jacobi (1978) argued that in northern England during the Earlier Mesolithic, two distinct social groups are represented by assemblages with specific frequencies of particular microlith types and differences in raw material usage. Subtle variations in the retouch of obliquely blunted points, for example, are recognized. Such differences are unlikely to have been functional and, since such equipment is too inconspicuous to have acted as a means of social identification, may reflect largely unconscious social traditions unique to particular human groups. A similar argument may be applicable to other distinctive artefacts, such as Horsham points, found in discrete geographical areas and chronological periods.

Another route into prehistoric social organization is to consider the distribution of prestige goods in order to identify patterns of exchange, but few such items are known. Perhaps the best examples are shale beads, apparently significant artefacts of the Early Mesolithic. At Nab Head over 600 have been found, made from local material. This seems to have been worked there, given the numbers of perforating tools, unperforated shale discs and partially drilled or broken beads recovered. Nab Head may have acted as a production centre for these beads, which were then absorbed into an exchange system, resulting in finds of examples at several inland sites.

Settlement evidence provides few clues as to social organization. The largest sites, such as Culver-well, may represent either a large, semi-sedentary population or many short-term visits, leading to a gradual accumulation of structural features. At present, we do not know which applies, but in future, attempts to look systematically and in detail at the spatial structure of settlements may prove helpful. Estimating the overall population is also fraught with difficulties and impossible to determine with confidence. Recent estimations have suggested a figure of between 4,560 and 20,520 for Britain at any one time (Edwards in Saville 2004). Warren (2005) suggests that communities and the activities which they carried out would have changed according to contexts, places and tasks. In addition, these would have changed significantly over the long term.

OUTSTANDING PROBLEMS

In many ways the Mesolithic record of Britain is seen as impoverished when compared to other periods such as the Neolithic or to other countries such as Denmark. There are relatively few human skeletal remains or cemeteries, a limited faunal dataset and almost no art. However, it has been suggested elsewhere that this is not so much a reflection of what actually survives as a consequence of limited excavation (Bell 2007). Over the last couple of decades this situation has been changing: for example, in Scotland since the 1990s, a number of major fieldwork projects have made important advances and developer-funded rescue work has led to the discovery of sites increasing our knowledge of inland occupation (Saville in Saville 2004). In addition, in the present decade, there has been a significant rise in the number of structures which have been found, particularly dating to the eighth millennium BC, leading to debates about permanence of settlement. Furthermore, new theoretical perspectives are being developed that deal with issues such as ideology and ritual (e.g. Conneller and Warren 2006; Milner and Woodman 2005). Consequently, the Mesolithic should be seen as an exciting period to study: there are plenty of outstanding problems, but a considerable amount of innovative research is underway, and science-based archaeology is having a significant impact.

Acknowledgements

Line drawings are by Margaret Matthews and Kirsty Bambridge.

Key texts

Conneller, C. and Warren, G., 2006. *Mesolithic Britain and Ireland: new approaches*. Stroud: Tempus.

Milner, N. and Woodman, P. (eds) 2005. *Mesolithic studies at the beginning of the 21st century*. Oxford: Oxbow Books.

Mithen, S.J., 2003. *After the ice: a global human history, 20,000–5000 bc*. London: Weidenfeld & Nicolson.

Mithen, S. (ed.) 2000. *Hunter-gatherer landscape archaeology. The Southern Hebrides Mesolithic Project 1988–98*. Cambridge: McDonald Institute Monographs. 2 vols.

Saville, A. (ed.) 2004. *Mesolithic Scotland and its neighbours. The early Holocene prehistory of Scotland, its British and Irish context and some North European perspectives*. Edinburgh: Society of Antiquaries of Scotland.

Bibliography

Andresen, J.M., Byrd, B.F., Elson, M.D., McGuire, R.H., Mendoza, R.G., Staski, E. and White, J.P., 1981. 'The deer hunters: Star Carr reconsidered', *World Archaeology* 13, 31–46.

Barton, R.N.E., 1992. *Hengistbury Head Dorset. Volume 2: the Late Upper Palaeolithic and Early Mesolithic sites*. Oxford: Oxford University Committee for Archaeology Monograph Series 34.

Bell, M.J. (ed.) 2007. *Prehistoric coastal communities: the Mesolithic in western Britain*. York: Council for British Archaeology Research Report 149.

Bonsall, C. (ed.) 1989. *The Mesolithic in Europe*. Edinburgh: John Donald.

Clark, J.G.D., 1954. *Excavations at Star Carr*. Cambridge: Cambridge University Press.

Clark, J.G.D., 1972. *Star Carr: a case study in bioarchaeology*. Reading, MA.: Addison-Wesley Module in Anthropology 10.

Clarke, D.L., 1976. 'Mesolithic Europe: the economic basis', in Sieveking, G. de G., Longworth, I.H. and Wilson, K.E. (eds) *Problems in economic and social archaeology*. London: Duckworth, 449–81.

Coles, J.M., 1971. 'The early settlement of Scotland: excavations at Morton, Fife', *Proceedings of the Prehistoric Society* 37, 284–366.

Conneller, C., 2004. 'Becoming deer: corporeal transformations at Star Carr', *Archaeological Dialogues* 11, 37–56.

Conneller, C. and Schadla-Hall, T., 2003. 'Beyond Star Carr: the Vale of Pickering in the 10th millennium BP', *Proceedings of the Prehistoric Society* 69, 85–105.

Dark, P., Higham, T., Jacobi, R. and Lord, T., 2006. 'New radiocarbon accelerator dates on artefacts from the Early Mesolithic site of Star Carr, North Yorkshire', *Archaeometry* 48, 185–200.

Healy, F., Heaton, M. and Lobb, S.J., 1992. 'Excavation of a Mesolithic site at Thatcham, Berkshire', *Proceedings of the Prehistoric Society* 58, 41–76.

Jacobi, R., 1978. 'Northern England in the eighth millennium BC: an essay', in Mellars, P.A. (ed.) *The early Postglacial settlement of northern Europe*. London: Duckworth, 295–332.

Jacobi, R., 1981. 'The last hunters in Hampshire', in Shennan, S.J. and Schadla-Hall, R.T. (eds) *The archaeology of Hampshire*. Hampshire: Hampshire Field Club and Archaeology Society Monograph 1, 10–25.

Legge, A.J. and Rowley-Conwy, P.A. 1988. *Star Carr revisited: a reanalysis of the large mammals*. London: Centre for Extra-Mural Studies, Birkbeck College.

Mellars, P.A., 1987. *Excavations on Oronsay: prehistoric human ecology on a small island*. Edinburgh: Edinburgh University Press.

Mellars, P. and Dark, P., 1998. *Star Carr in context: new archaeological and palaeoecological investigations at the early Mesolithic site of Star Carr, North Yorkshire*. Cambridge: McDonald Institute for Archaeological Research.

Melton, N.D. and Nicholson, R.A., 2004. 'The Mesolithic in the Northern Isles: the preliminary evaluation of an oyster midden at West Voe, Sumburgh, Shetland, UK', *Antiquity* 78 (on-line project gallery), available online at http://antiquity.ac.uk/ProjGall/nicholson/.

Milner, N., 2007. 'Fading Star', *British Archaeology* 96, 10–14.

Myers, A., 1989. 'Reliable and maintainable technological strategies in the Mesolithic of mainland Britain', in Torrence, R. (ed.) *Time, energy and stone tools*. Cambridge: Cambridge University Press, 78–91.

Pitts, M., 1979. 'Hides and antlers: a new look at the gatherer-hunter site of Star Carr, North Yorkshire, England', *World Archaeology* 11, 32–42.

Pitts, M. and Jacobi, R., 1979. 'Some aspects of change in flaked stone industries of the Mesolithic and Neolithic in southern Britain', *Journal of Archaeological Science* 6, 163–177.

Pollard, T. and Morrison, A. (eds) 1996. *The early prehistory of Scotland*. Edinburgh: Edinburgh University Press.

Simmons, I.G. and Innes, J.B., 1996. 'An episode of prehistoric canopy manipulation at North Gill, N. Yorkshire, England', *Journal of Archaeological Science* 23, 337–42.

Taylor, B., 2007. 'Recent excavations at Star Carr, North Yorkshire', *Mesolithic Miscellany* 18, 12–17.

Waddington, C., 2007. *Mesolithic settlement in the North Sea basin. A case study from Howick, north east England*. Oxford: Oxbow Books.

Warren, G., 2005. *Mesolithic lives in Scotland*. Stroud: Tempus.

Wickham-Jones, C.R., 1990. *Rhum: Mesolithic and later sites at Kinloch. Excavations 1984–86*. Edinburgh: Society of Antiquaries of Scotland Monograph Series 7.

Woodman, P., 1985. *Excavations at Mount Sandel 1973–77*. Belfast: Archaeological Research Monographs 2.

Woodman, P., 1989. 'A review of the Scottish Mesolithic: a plea for normality!', *Proceedings of the Society of Antiquaries of Scotland* 119, 1–32.

4

THE NEOLITHIC PERIOD, *c.* 4000–2400 CAL BC

A changing world

Alasdair Whittle

SETTING THE SCENE: SEQUENCES AND MAIN TRENDS

In the fortieth or thirty-ninth century cal BC, in the Cotswolds at Ascott-under-Wychwood, Oxfordshire, people butchered domesticated animals, used carinated bowl pottery and flint tools, lit fires, dug small pits and made two small timber structures. The material from this occupation was partly scattered about, and partly concentrated in a smaller area, some 14 by 11 m, in what can be called a midden. The area also contained sporadic microliths from Late Mesolithic occupation on the same spot, above the valley of the Evenlode, tributary of the upper Thames, and there were also more abundant traces of earlier Mesolithic use of the place. In the thirty-eighth century cal BC, a trapezoidal long barrow was constructed over these earlier traces, built up of earth, turf and stones, arranged in compartments or bays. Let in from the long sides of the barrow, which were finely revetted in stone, there were two opposed sets of small stone chambers or cists, which contained the remains of some 21 people: male and female, old and young, some deposited as whole bodies, others perhaps partially disarticulated. The barrow was in use for probably three to five generations, ending with final depositions and the closing of the short passage to the cists on the north side probably in the 3640s or 3630s cal BC (Figures 4.1 and 4.2) (Benson and Whittle 2007; Bayliss, Benson *et al.* in Bayliss and Whittle 2007).

This example evokes many of the features of the first part of the Neolithic in southern England and indeed in many other parts of Britain: some degree of continuity at least with the preceding Mesolithic period, in that a particular place in the landscape was reused; innovation in the appearance of domesticated animals (and elsewhere of cereals) and pottery; and further development, on a much more precise timescale thanks to formal modelling of radiocarbon dates in a Bayesian statistical framework (Bayliss and Whittle 2007), in the form of a long barrow, which contained the mortal remains of a relatively small number of

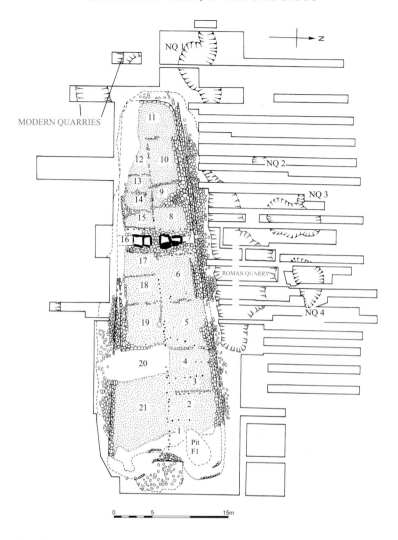

Figure 4.1 Plan of the major features of the Cotswold long barrow at Ascott-under-Wychwood, Oxfordshire.
Source: Benson and Whittle 2007

people from the generations alive during the use of the monument. It has been customary to refer the shape of these barrows to ideas or myths about a much older past, going back to the great timber longhouses of the first continental Neolithic of the sixth and fifth millennia cal BC, but it is possible now to invoke much more recent pasts, and we know of a substantial timber house or hall at Yarnton, in the Upper Thames Valley itself near Oxford, dated to these first centuries of the southern Neolithic (Hey and Barclay in Whittle and Cummings 2007). The Early Neolithic evidence from Yarnton complements that from Ascott-under-Wychwood. The timber structure appears to have been in use for a finite period, and the scale of excavation has established that there were otherwise only pits and small ditched

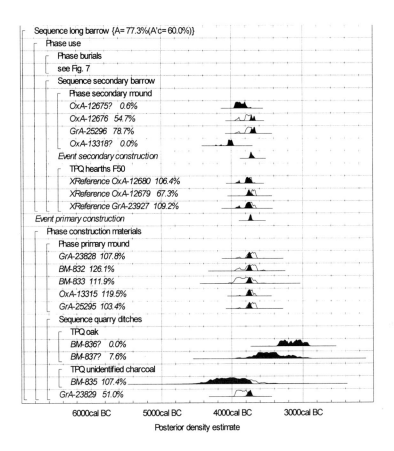

Figure 4.2 Probability distributions of dates relating to the construction and use of the barrow, in the preferred Bayesian model for the chronology of the Ascott-under-Wychwood long barrow. The dates from the human remains within the cists are shown in Bayliss, Benson et al. 2007, Fig. 7. The format of the graph is identical to that of Bayliss, Benson et al. 2007, Fig. 5. The large square brackets down the left-hand side along with the OxCal keywords in Bayliss, Benson et al. 2007, Figs 3 and 5–7 define the overall model exactly. The model was constructed in OxCal v3.10.

Source: Bayliss, Benson et al. in Bayliss and Whittle 2007

features, so that while this was a place where people aggregated and perhaps lived for periods of time, using domesticated animals and cereals, it is hard to characterize the occupation as either a transitory base camp or a substantial permanent settlement.

After the late thirty-seventh century cal BC, very little more was done at the Ascott-under-Wychwood long barrow, and that may apply to many of the other numerous Cotswold long barrows (Darvill 2004). Causewayed enclosures, defining special places for gathering and ritual, to commemorate the dead, to feast and to celebrate the domesticity and sociality of the Neolithic world, began to be built in numbers probably in the thirty-seventh century cal BC (Oswald et al. 2001; Bayliss et al. 2008; Whittle et al. 2008). In the Upper Thames Valley and more sporadically in the Cotswolds these were built in some numbers, but there were none immediately close to Ascott-under-Wychwood or Yarnton. The occupation of Yarnton continued, perhaps episodically, through the fourth and third millennia cal BC, without the place developing into a major settlement (Hey and Barclay in Whittle and Cummings 2007). Linear ditched or cursus monuments came and went in the second half of the fourth millennium cal BC (Barclay and Harding 1999), including numerous examples in the Upper Thames Valley, and in the third millennium cal BC a substantial ditched and banked henge enclosure with internal stone setting, the Devil's Quoits, was built upstream of Yarnton at Stanton Harcourt. Another substantial double-ditched henge was built beside the older cursus monument downstream at Dorchester-on-Thames, but neither the Cotswolds nor the Upper Thames Valley saw the further development of major ceremonial – and perhaps political – complexes on the scale evident more to the south around Avebury, Stonehenge, Cranborne Chase and Dorchester, Dorset (Wainwright 1989; Cleal et al. 1995; Parker Pearson in Larsson and Parker Pearson 2007; Parker Pearson et al. 2009; Gillings et al. 2008), dating from probably the middle part of the third millennium cal BC. But we do not know the third millennium timescales in detail yet, because detailed chronological modelling has barely begun. Do such monuments reflect many generations of continuity and gradual change, or were there again dramatic and concentrated phases of construction?

The essence of the Neolithic seems to lie in a combination of practical and conceptual continuities and changes, but throughout the sequence, there are different schools of thought on key issues. Some archaeologists still favour colonization at the start of the period, for example, while others prefer acculturation (or now a combination of these processes); some deduce political complexity and hierarchy from the great monument complexes of the end of the Neolithic, while others see an overall slower social trajectory through the fourth and third millennia cal BC as a whole.

From this perspective it is probably still useful to distinguish three main phases: *Early Neolithic*, *Middle Neolithic* and *Late Neolithic*.

The *Early Neolithic* (c. 4000–3400/3300 cal BC) appears to display continuity with the Mesolithic in terms of some degree of residential mobility and perhaps some broad-spectrum subsistence, but now involving animal herding (cattle, sheep and pigs) and some cereal cultivation (of wheats and barleys) with accompanying limited clearance of woodland, regional styles of round-based pottery and axe production and varying circulation (perhaps through gift exchange). Isotope analysis in western coastal areas may suggest an overall dietary shift from marine to terrestrial resources, though the pattern is mixed (summarized by Schulting in Pollard 2008; and see Chapter 3), and lipid analysis of pottery indicates the use of dairy products (e.g. Copley and Evershed in Benson and Whittle 2007). At the middle Thames occupation at Runnymede, cattle seem numerically dominant, but appear to have been processed in different ways from pigs and sheep, suggesting a possible use in feasting (Serjeantson and Field 2006); causewayed enclosures also emphasize cattle. There is sporadic evidence for scratch ploughs or ards, including the marks preserved under the

South Street long barrow, Wiltshire. The first tombs and shrines, in a variety of regional types of barrow and cairn, with internal structures of wood and stone, were erected; and within this phase the first causewayed enclosures were built.

Bayesian modelling of the dates of southern long barrows and causewayed enclosures indicates that the former were probably in use from *c*. 3800 cal BC and the latter only from *c*. 3700 cal BC (Bayliss and Whittle 2007; Bayliss *et al.* 2008; Whittle *et al.* in prep.). The same methodology is beginning to offer more differentiation in formal estimates for the date of the start of the Neolithic in southern Britain (Whittle *et al.* 2008, in prep.), and in general must be regarded as the way ahead for establishing a Neolithic divisible not only into centuries, but lifetimes and generations. Dendrochronological dates remain disappointingly scarce, but those for the early Post and Sweet Tracks in the Somerset Levels (in the late thirty-ninth century BC) take on added significance in the emergent new chronological framework.

The *Middle Neolithic* (perhaps 3400/3300–3000/2900 cal BC) is marked by both continuing development of these features and the beginnings of replacement and further change. There is little clear evidence for intensification of cereal cultivation through time (though its scale from the outset has been compared to that of the temperate European *Linearbandkeramik* (LBK) culture: Bogaard and Jones in Whittle and Cummings 2007). Regional sequences are not synchronized, and construction of chambered tombs may have continued in the north-west of Britain after the building of long barrows and chambered tombs in the south had largely ceased. Some at least of the largest and most complex chambered tombs, for example of Maes Howe type on the Orkney Islands, were probably in use, as the largest passage graves in Ireland appear to have been at this time. The linear cursus monuments mostly belong here; in the upper Thames, the causewayed enclosure at Abingdon and the nearby cursus at Drayton may be very close in time, in either the thirty-seventh or thirty-sixth century cal BC (Whittle *et al.* 2008). These may represent in some instances elaborations of ideas to do with pre-existing barrows, probably in the realms of the dead and the circulation of spirits (Tilley 1994). There were some single-circuit circular enclosures, as at Flagstones, Dorchester, Dorset, or the first phase of Stonehenge, and more single or limited-number burials under small barrows or in small ring-ditches date within the Middle Neolithic (though there may not be subsequent continuity of this tradition: Bradley 2007). Round-based pottery styles include the Ebbsfleet variant of the Peterborough tradition, while in the north, flat-based Grooved Ware may have appeared on Orkney by or before the end of the Middle Neolithic, perhaps alongside the round-based Unstan Ware.

To the *Late Neolithic* (*c*. 3000/2900–2400 cal BC) belong the end of the Peterborough pottery tradition and the full development of Grooved Ware, now present over the whole country. On Orkney, the range of subsistence residues in the distinctive small, nucleated Late Neolithic settlements such as Skara Brae does not seem greatly different from that seen in earlier structures at Knap of Howar, Papa Westray; such differences as exist may relate in large part to the nature of group composition and to varying tactics for the intake of new land (Sharples in Sharples and Sheridan 1992; Richards 2005). Even where stone-built, nucleated houses have been examined from these Orkney sites, evidence for extensive agriculture is lacking; a broad-based spectrum of cultivation, gathering, herding, hunting and sea fishing is indicated. Late Neolithic monuments include henges and their internal settings, stone and timber circles. It is not impossible that some cursus monuments date to the start of this phase. Stone rows, some perhaps erected earlier, were incorporated into the layout of ceremonial complexes, such as the West Kennet Avenue attached to Avebury henge in Wiltshire (Gillings *et al.* 2008) or those at Callanish on Lewis. The monumental mound of Silbury Hill appears to be the north Wiltshire equivalent of the developed phases of Stonehenge, and its construction appears to have begun *c.* 2400 cal BC on the basis of formal modelling associated with conservation work on the mound in 2007 (cf. Bayliss *et al.* 2007). Also pre-Beaker are the palisade enclosures of West Kennet (Whittle 1997) and elsewhere. A variety of single burials and cremation areas are also known. The date of introduction of Beaker pottery and associated material culture and practices is still uncertain; the first formal modelling for dates from England and Scotland indicates a date of *c.* 2400 cal BC for the first depositions in graves (Bayliss *et al.* 2007), though that may still leave open the possibility of earlier circulation in other contexts. Likewise it remains unclear if there was any metallurgy before *c.* 2400 cal BC, but evidence, including some from Ireland, may point to a convergence of substantial innovation and change around that date. This horizon is discussed in Chapter 5.

CHANGING PERSPECTIVES IN NEOLITHIC STUDIES

Archaeologists have become more reflective of the ways in which assumptions about the Neolithic period are formed. In terms of dominant theory, Neolithic studies reflect post-war trends rather well, and indeed for some 25 years have been in the forefront of theoretical debate. After the culture-historical model in the 1950s and 1960s, the processual paradigm prevailed in the 1970s and early 1980s. After that came the post-processual challenge, with new emphasis on meaning, symbolism and individuals. But that began over a generation ago, and a much more complicated picture has now emerged. Many post-processual approaches have been absorbed into mainstream thought, though others remain vigorously contested; purposeful deposition of material into pits (e.g. Garrow *et al.* 2005) is widely accepted, for example, but phenomenological approaches to monuments and the experience of being in the landscape (e.g. Tilley 1994) remain controversial (e.g. Fleming 2006). Old debates, especially on the Mesolithic–Neolithic transition, continue (e.g. Whittle and Cummings 2007), with important restatements of the arguments for colonization (e.g. Sheridan in Whittle and Cummings 2007; Bradley 2007). New scientific investigations, including isotopic analyses of human and animal bone and teeth, and lipid analyses of the former contents of pottery, have brought fresh insights into diet and provenance. The application of Bayesian chronological modelling has already been stressed. Field research and its publication have remained important, some generated directly by the post-processualist agenda, as in the Stonehenge Riverside Project, but much more in the commercial or developer-funded sector, results from which, however, often remain unpublished (Bradley 2007). Since 1980, there has been proportionately more work in the north, for example on Early Neolithic houses or timber halls in eastern Scotland (Brophy 2007), and recently in north-west Wales, on monuments and monument complexes in eastern Scotland such as Balfarg, Fife, as well as in Orkney and on occupation sites there and in the Western Isles.

Two examples illustrate something of this complexity and the varying scales of analysis now being carried out. The Stonehenge Riverside Project, running since 2003, has set out to demonstrate the validity of the hypothesis that in the Late Neolithic Stonehenge was the domain of the ancestors, while Durrington Walls was firmly in the domain of the living, with the Avon river and the Stonehenge Avenue serving as a conduit for the spirits of the dead (Parker Pearson in Larsson and Parker Pearson 2007; Parker Pearson *et al.* 2007, 2009). New fieldwork has been carried out at Durrington Walls (both within the enclosure and just outside, revealing an avenue or roadway leading to the river), neighbouring Woodhenge, the major Stonehenge cursus, at Stonehenge itself (one of the Aubrey Holes) and elsewhere. Among many other results, animal bones from Durrington Walls suggest a concentration on mid-winter, and preliminary isotopic analyses indicate the movement of animals to the site from far afield; cremations from the first phase of Stonehenge have been dated to the first half of the third millennium cal BC, and it is claimed that these could represent some kind of pre-eminent social grouping or dynasty (Parker Pearson *et al.* 2009; and see Chapter 5). Precise dating of both Stonehenge and Durrington Walls is still awaited. Another project has concentrated on the source area in the Preseli hills of south-west Wales of the bluestones used in Stonehenge, and proposed healing properties for them (Darvill 2007). At a rather different scale, isotopic analysis of an adult woman and three children buried in a shaft within a pit circle, quite close to the great Dorset cursus on the chalkland of Cranborne Chase, and probably dating to the second half of the fourth millennium cal BC, suggests a complicated pattern of movement through the course of even brief lives. The woman (perhaps 30 years old) may have been born in the Mendips, 80 km away; a young girl (perhaps a five-year-old and probably her daughter) was born off the chalk, while the other two children (slightly older, boy and girl, perhaps siblings but not certainly the children of the woman) were born or raised on the chalk, but subsequently moved off it before returning to be buried in Dorset (Budd *et al.* 2000). One of the key challenges for the future will be to unite this sense of individual lives and lifetime movements with the great events and processes seen at the major monument complexes.

SOME KEY CONTEXTS AND SITES

The Mesolithic–Neolithic transition

Debate on this issue has, if anything, intensified over recent years. It often takes the form of two radically opposed and mutually exclusive alternatives. On the one hand, the scale and range of changes in terms of subsistence, material culture, especially pottery, and monument building are seen as requiring new population from the adjacent Continent, with which it is claimed there was little or no contact in the later parts of the Mesolithic; some areas, such as lowland eastern Scotland, may have had very low Late Mesolithic populations (reviewed in Bradley 2007). A similar view has often been proposed for Ireland. This kind of view has been reinforced by the apparent shift seen in isotopic analyses (principally from coastal areas of western Britain, especially Scotland) from a mainly marine dietary signature in the Late Mesolithic to a strongly terrestrial one in the Early Neolithic (summarized by Schulting in Pollard 2008; variation in the pattern of results is stressed in Chapter 3). The most detailed view proposes different sources and phases of contact and colonization: contact initially in the later fifth millennium cal BC with south-west Ireland, reflected in the non-indigenous cattle bones from Ferriter's Cove, Co. Kerry; then movement from Brittany as far as western Scotland around 4000 cal BC, on the basis of the claimed resemblances of decorated bowl pottery from a cairn at Achnacreebeag, Argyll; then movement from northernmost France or southern Belgium, very soon after 4000 cal BC, the result of expansion of the Michelsberg culture, bringing people with carinated bowl pottery widely into eastern Britain and beyond; and finally, perhaps in the first quarter of the fourth millennium cal BC, further movement from Brittany and Normandy into south-west England, resulting in the establishment of the south-western bowl pottery style (Sheridan in Whittle and Cummings 2007).

The other view sees Early Neolithic assemblages on this side of the Channel and North Sea as bearing only general resemblances to their contemporaries on the other. This proposes that the indigenous Mesolithic population became Neolithic by adopting new material culture, incorporating new subsistence staples and refining its world-view or developing a new one (Thomas in Whittle and Cummings 2007; Thomas in Pollard 2008). One version suggests that the motivation was economic, demographic or both, leading to a recasting of lifestyle to alleviate pressure on resources; another focuses on social competition as the spur to changes in lifestyle; and a third variant sees a kind of cultural convergence or realignment. None of these have really examined why changes came when they did, and a turning point at around 4000 cal BC is normally cited.

We are hampered in this debate by several factors. We do not know as much as we would like about Late Mesolithic developments (Chapter 3), though the general impression is not, however, of packed Late Mesolithic coastal communities, as in say parts of the Baltic; large areas of inland Britain, such as the chalklands, may have been little frequented on a regular basis. There are still no sites that give a clear picture of the Mesolithic–Neolithic transition: no detailed stratigraphic sequences that cover the period in question, no reused features. The situation at Ascott-under-Wychwood already noted is not untypical, nor is the succession of Late Mesolithic and then Early Neolithic material in the natural infilling of the shaft at Fir Tree Field, Cranborne Chase. Some continuities can be suggested. There is evidence for Mesolithic woodland clearance; some clearings may have persisted until, or been reused in, the Neolithic; and Mesolithic people may have been used to tending plants. A few other Neolithic monuments overlie Mesolithic occupation or activity, such as at Hazleton on the Cotswolds (Saville 1990) or at Raunds in the Nene Valley (Harding and Healy 2007), which could imply a closer connection. That may have consisted not of direct residential continuity, but of the maintenance of landscapes with named places, crossed by paths and framed by significant points; in south-west Wales, Neolithic monuments pick out parts of the coastal landscape already containing Mesolithic camps (Tilley 1994). Some population overspill from Neolithic communities in adjacent parts of Europe remains envisageable, and an integrationist or fusion model may emerge as the most plausible explanation at the present time, varying region by region. What has *not* been achieved so far is rigorous examination of the timescales involved. The first formal modelling (Whittle *et al.* 2008), for southern Britain, has suggested significant variations in the date of the first appearance of Neolithic practices, from 4000 cal BC onwards, and it can confidently be predicted that the process will prove to have been more complicated than either of the two currently dominant models allows.

Occupations: settlement, residences and structures

Various built structures are known from the Neolithic as a whole, generally consisting of rectangular settings of postholes, rarely longer than 10 m (Thomas 1999). Larger Early Neolithic buildings have been found, such as at Yarnton and White Horse Stone in the Medway Valley, Kent. An important Early Neolithic series has been established in eastern Scotland, Balbridie in the Dee Valley now joined by its near-neighbour at Warren Field, Crathes, and Claish in Stirlingshire (Brophy 2007). In the far north, stone footings, occasionally walling, define a range of structures, from rectangular and squarish to oval and near-circular. In Ireland, contract archaeology has produced much more numerous rectangular timber structures. It is a curious record. Absent are the great timber longhouses of the first Neolithic of central and western Europe, the LBK culture tradition of the mid-sixth millennium cal BC onward. Such British structures as have been found largely occur singly; there is little to indicate that they become more frequent in later phases. They are generally interpreted as houses, and many may indeed have been residences, but they are not normally associated with large accumulations of rubbish or with ancillary structures. At best, these would have been used for short periods of time, or at irregular intervals, and they have also been seen as halls or meeting houses. There is clear evidence that the eastern Scottish examples were burnt down, perhaps deliberately. Loch Olabhat, North Uist, illustrates the ambiguities (Armit in Sharples and Sheridan 1992) (Figure 4.3). A succession of rectangular stone footings and middens defines the repeated but probably episodic reuse of a chosen locale. The structures may have been covered by light wooden frames or perhaps only by skin tents. Their use, in a waterside location prone to flooding, may have been seasonal.

Some archaeologists consider that more houses will be detected as more fieldwork is undertaken, as has been the case in Ireland, and that more would have been found were it not for the destructive effects of subsequent land use. Until now, however, post-built structures have remained rare as research has increased. Exceptions have indeed been located, as recently at Horton in the middle Thames or in north-west Wales, but the scale of contract archaeology has

86

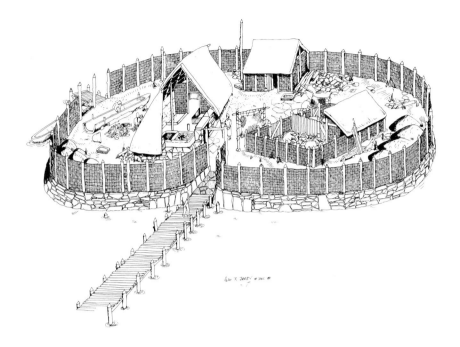

Figure 4.3 Reconstruction of one of the phases of occupation at Loch Olabhat, North Uist (Alan Braby).

been such as to give increased confidence that such buildings were generally rare in the Early Neolithic landscape (Bradley 2007); none have been reported from the gas pipeline laid in 2007 between Milford Haven and Gloucester. The staple fare of the settlement record are artefact scatters, often existing only in the top- or plough-soils, and pits, postholes, stakeholes and other features dug into the subsoil. Hurst Fen (Suffolk) is a larger example of a group of pits, while Peacock's Farm (Cambridgeshire), set beside a small river, has lithic scatters on a sand ridge, with small spills of rubbish down its side. These presumably represent camps or bases, of varying duration in any one episode, though in these cases certainly for repeat visits. Shelter might have consisted of skin tents or other light structures that have left little or no subsoil trace; but we have to be careful here, because fairly substantial dwellings can be built without earthfast posts.

This is the kind of context to which the Coneybury (Wiltshire) pit belongs. Here, in the earlier fourth millennium cal BC, in woodland near the River Avon, people dug a large pit and deposited in it food remains and artefacts: the bones from several cattle and roe deer and at least one pig and two red deer; a few beaver and trout bones; some carbonized cereal grains, probably emmer wheat; flint tools and waste; and many broken sherds from about 40 pots (J. Richards 1990). At Kilverstone, Norfolk, a large number of Early Neolithic pits were arranged in smaller clusters, and patterns and connections among the apparently deliberately deposited material in them (including potsherds, flints, cereal grains and hazelnuts) could suggest a cycle of coming and going rather than prolonged occupation (Garrow *et al.* 2005).

The Neolithic inhabitants of Britain perhaps moved repeatedly through woodland, making clearings and abandoning them, following cattle herds in particular, and tending – but not all of them always on permanent watch over – stands of cereals. Settlement appears to have been based on some kind of pattern of structured movement, or at most on short-term sedentism, or local and regional combinations of the two, which we do not yet really understand. Monuments were important parts of the landscape. The wooden trackways of the Somerset Levels indicate how movement may have been structured. The Sweet Track, for example, was built just before 3800 BC (Coles and Coles 1986). It runs for at least 2 km across wet fen, to take people and perhaps animals out to a small island of dry land. The carefully built single-plank walkway would have needed much timber, but could have been constructed quite quickly by a small group of people. Its significance seems to have been marked, even consecrated, by the deliberate deposition of a rare jadeitite axehead beside it, now of proven origin in the western Italian Alps. The Sweet Track was preceded by another version, the Post Track, and may have been in use for a relatively short time before being covered by peat growth. It was not directly replaced, though several other hurdle trackways succeed it after a while in the vicinity. This pattern seems to mirror the settlement record as a whole: particular structures and features each of short duration, related to occupation, set within a framework of monuments and other places.

There are interesting changes in the character of lithic scatters during the period. Earlier flint knapping involved careful, planned use of raw material, a trait that later working, when a wider range of materials was employed, generally lacks (Edmonds 1995). In some areas, as around Stonehenge and Avebury (J. Richards 1990; Thomas 1999), the density and size of Later Neolithic scatters increased compared with earlier examples. This may represent more people staying in these locales for longer periods, but whether as part of a general trend towards increasing sedentism or in connection with the demands of the ritual cycle it is hard to say.

Later Neolithic Orkney is one important exception to the general trend. Several sites, including Skara Brae, Rinyo, Links of Noltland, Barnhouse and now Ness of Brogar, have stone-walled structures, nucleated to varying degrees and preserved to impressive height at Skara Brae. At Barnhouse in the middle of Mainland, near the elaborate chambered tomb of Maes Howe and the henges with stone settings at Stenness and Ring of Brogar (C. Richards 2005), smaller, squarish houses are succeeded by a more varied range, some with carefully arranged doorways, central hearths and wall recesses that echo the layouts of chambered tombs. The Barnhouse houses may have been permanent residences, part of a strategy for taking in the interior of the islands by larger social groups. Their architecture may still reflect structured patterns of movement and behaviour and also enshrine a cosmology that united people in their daily lives with nature, through a sense of orientation and elements like fire, and with the past, through reference to ancestral tombs and shrines (C. Richards 2005). The largest structure at Barnhouse, no. 8, was set within an outer wall and may represent some kind of communal building. Survey has since shown the area of Barnhouse to extend considerably, and a similar new complex has been found directly across the loch at Ness of Brogar (Card *et al.* in Larsson and Parker Pearson 2007).

The discovery of small rectangular structures or houses at Durrington Walls, with carefully laid floors and hearths (Figure 4.4) (Parker Pearson in Larsson and Parker Pearson 2007), suggests that concentrations of people, probably exceeding the scale seen even in the middle of the Orkneys, took place in the Late Neolithic in southern Britain. Whether these were for prolonged or seasonal or ritual gatherings remains to be established, and it remains to be seen whether similar presences can be found at other major monument complexes and elsewhere.

Axe production sites

Stone and flint axeheads figure prominently in the Neolithic record. Some, perhaps many, were mounted in wooden hafts. The oak planks of the Sweet Track bear their marks; so do various human skulls from long barrows and cairns (Schulting and Wysocki 2005). These may have been the all-purpose heavy-duty tool (and perhaps weapon) of the Neolithic, but it is clear that the axehead itself carried special significance. One was deposited beside the Sweet Track, and

Figure 4.4   House 547 outside the south entrance to Durrington Walls (Mike Parker Pearson).

others occur in the ditches of causewayed enclosures, as well as in a range of other contexts (Edmonds 1995). Many axeheads are found far from their place of origin and must have circulated by various means, including direct acquisition, direct and indirect exchange and perhaps directed trade. Many are isolated discoveries and appear to have been deliberately deposited in the ground. The axe may have stood for several ideas important in the Neolithic world-view: independence or prowess in the realm of subsistence; personal (perhaps gender-related) or group identity; the ability to participate in gift exchange and other social interaction and to acquire exotic material from far away; a willingness to give away to other people and to nature rather than to accumulate; and borrowing of the very material of the earth. And we should not forget that the textures, colours and finishes of axeheads, like much bowl pottery highly polished and smoothed, were perhaps regarded as sensuous and desirable.

Sources of good stone and flint were comparatively limited, with the best stone occurring in the older geologies of the west and north and the best flint coming from southern English chalk deposits (Edmonds 1995). Numbers of stone and flint sources are known. Some of the former can be traced to actual extraction areas, and in some cases shafts were dug through chalk to exploit good seams of flint. Such 'quarries' and 'mines' were often in places remote from usual settlement zones, even in a mobile system. Group VI axes were made from a volcanic tuff quarried from outcrops high in the Langdale hills of the Cumbrian Lake District. Flint mines in Sussex (exploited early on) and in the East Anglian breckland at Grime's Graves (principally used at the end of the Neolithic) may also have been comparatively distant from other settlement. The scale of working seems disproportionate to the needs of everyday existence, though excavation at the Group VI workfaces shows that extraction could be small-scale and episodic (Edmonds 1995).

Graves, shrines and tombs: the remembered dead and other pasts

Formal single burials are relatively rare in the Early Neolithic. Under the back of the outer bank of the Windmill Hill causewayed enclosure (Wiltshire), an adult man was buried in flexed position in an oval pit. He had no grave goods, and the grave pit may have been open for some time. From the Middle or Late Neolithic, some single burials, under small mounds or in small enclosures, are encountered in certain regions. At Radley (Oxfordshire), a man and a woman were buried flexed in a pit within a ditched rectangle, which may have bounded a low barrow; they were accompanied by a shale or jet belt-slider and a partially polished flint knife respectively (Bradley 2007) (Figure 4.5). At Duggleby Howe, Yorkshire, single burials include successive inhumations within a deep grave pit, which was capped by a round barrow. Cremations are found at intervals throughout the Neolithic, from within the Etton causewayed enclosure (Cambridgeshire) to the first phase of Stonehenge.

Human remains occur in other contexts, including the ditches and pits of causewayed enclosures, and later in henges. The excavated portions of the ditches of the Hambledon Hill (Dorset) causewayed enclosure complex, for example, revealed the remains of some 70

Figure 4.5 The primary burials in the Radley oval barrow, Oxfordshire (Richard Bradley).

people, and there could have originally been many more (Mercer and Healy 2008). These included both whole skeletons and incomplete remains (some weathered and dog-gnawed), including skulls lacking lower jaws and one truncated torso. In general, some of the dead may have been exposed, or buried then excarnated, before being redeposited in significant places or circulated among the living, as tokens of indissoluble links with their past.

Rites at long barrows and chambered tombs were very varied, and funerals as such may have formed only part of them. In many instances they certainly began with fleshed, recognizable individuals: witness the complete skeleton of an adult man inside the entrance of the north passage of Hazleton (Saville 1990). In others, corpses or partial remains of them may have been deposited singly or together within the monuments, after initial treatment elsewhere. The end result was collective deposits of varying size, generally comprising the disarticulated and skeletally incomplete remains of a few or tens of people (and exceptionally more, as at Quanterness on Orkney). Monuments may not have been final resting places for all these remains. Some of the incompleteness (for example, too few skulls and longbones) may be accounted for by the circulation of defleshed remains within such monuments and even their subsequent removal from them (Thomas 1999). In some instances, the emphasis seems to have been on the accumulation, perhaps by successive rites and depositions, of an anonymous mass of intermingled white bone, representing the collectivity of the dead. In others, for example in transepted chambered tombs in the Cotswold–Severn area, as at West Kennet long barrow (Figure 4.6), or some of the Orca-

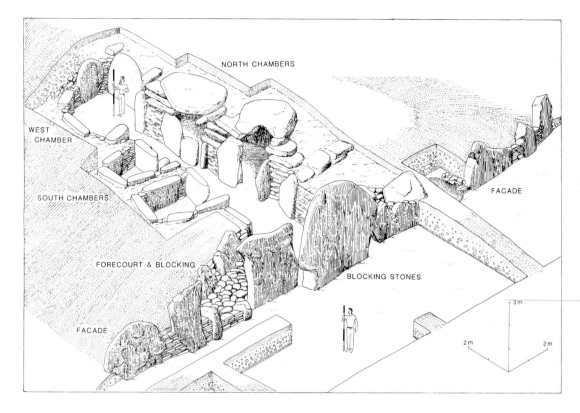

Figure 4.6   The chambers of the West Kennet long barrow, Wiltshire.
Modified from: Piggott, S., 1962. *The West Kennet long barrow excavations*. London: HMSO

dian stalled cairns, including Midhowe, attention was certainly given to the placing of individual remains. At West Kennet, the basis of arrangement seems to have been gender and age: males in the end chamber; a predominance of adult males and females in the inner pair of opposed chambers; and principally the old and young in the outer pair (Thomas 1999).

Much more precise timescales have been modelled for five southern long barrows, suggesting rapid construction and phases of primary use not longer than five generations (at 25 years to a generation) and often fewer. The primary use of the West Kennet long barrow, for example, may have lasted a generation or less, in the later thirty-seventh century cal BC. There is little evidence of old bone being used in these deposits, and in that sense the emphasis from the outset appears to have been rather more on the recent or remembered dead, subject to various treatments and transformations, than on anonymous ancestors (Bayliss and Whittle 2007). The same work throws up the possibility that few long barrows were constructed before *c.* 3800 cal BC, so that a clearer sense of change through time has begun to emerge, and this could be repeated in many other regions.

The structures in which these remains were temporarily or permanently stored may have stood for other ideas and associations than with the dead alone; some had only token human deposits or none at all. All these monuments comprise a mound, cairn or platform, either housing or supporting roofed structures of wood or stone. The actual constructions from region to region and indeed within regions were very varied. Portal dolmens around the Irish Sea had large, stone, box-like chambers, some surrounded by low stone platforms. Court cairns in Ireland, and Clyde cairns in western Scotland, in essence elaborate this form, with larger cairns and divided chambers. Stone chambers set in the ends and sides of long barrows and long cairns occur in many areas, from southern England to the north of Scotland. Round cairns were a mainly northern form, with some in the west and some round barrows in Yorkshire. Many internal chambers or structures were single and approached directly from outside the monument. In other instances, there was a connecting passage, with the chamber housed well within the mound. Internal spatial complexity characterizes the transepted monuments of the Cotswold–Severn group, some west Scottish monuments and the developed stalled cairns and Maes Howe round cairns of Orkney (Bradley 2007; Cummings in Pollard 2008; Sharples in Sharples and Sheridan 1992; Thomas 1999).

Many individual monuments show a sequence of development, and architectural forms were not static through time. Monuments that ended as long barrows or cairns could begin more simply. At Street House, Cleveland, a high wooden façade concealed two small structures connected with the disposal of human remains; only later, when the façade had been burnt down, was the ensemble covered by a low cairn (Vyner 1984) (Figure 4.7). The first monument at Wayland's Smithy was a short, oval barrow, flanked by ditches. It contained, and may have been preceded by, a banked, probably roofed structure with massive split posts at either end, housing a collective deposit of human remains (probably formed in a decade, in the early thirty-sixth century cal BC: Bayliss and Whittle 2007). The Haddenham long barrow, Cambridgeshire, has preserved a massive wooden box or mortuary structure (Evans and Hodder 2006). Subsequently, the first monument at Wayland's Smithy was completely incorporated within a larger, trapezoidal mound, with terminal transepted stone chambers and façade (probably built in the thirty-fifth century cal BC, two centuries after the architecturally very similar West Kennet long barrow, and thus probably in a consciously old style). The trend through time seems often to have been to greater structural complexity and size. West Kennet long barrow, for example, with its very long mound and transepted chamber space, may post-date less impressive and elaborate constructions in its area. On Orkney, the larger stalled cairns and the Maes Howe cairns, with their passages and central and side chambers, and connections to the largest Irish passage graves, seem to follow short stalled cairns and simpler chambered types.

These architecturally varied monuments stood for ideas, associations and memories. Their forms could encapsulate memories of earlier or contemporary structures. Long mounds and cairns, for example, have often been referred to the great timber longhouses of the

Figure 4.7 Reconstructions of two phases of the Street House long barrow, Cleveland.
Modified from: Vyner 1984

continental LBK, but the timescales now apparent may rather suggest a link with the dwellings and houses of the insular Early Neolithic itself. In the former case, they represented a concept of the past, perhaps of an ancestral social order fixed for all time; in the latter case, they may have been part of an intense debate about links between the dead and the living, brought into focus by the adoption of a whole range of new practices (Jones in Pollard 2008). Their construction brought numbers of people together, and the results were not only highly visible, but enduring. Their locales commemorated and sanctified places perhaps already of long significance, providing conspicuous points of reference in the landscape.

Such powerful symbols were open to contestation. Some of the dismantlings, burnings and rebuildings identified could have resulted from hostile activity. Some monuments may have been the focus for inter- or intra-group rivalry. One trend suggested for Orkney is from dispersed small monuments, with modest accumulations of human remains, which served scattered communities, to the grander monuments, more centrally placed, in which the idea of a larger community was expressed by very considerable deposits of bone, some perhaps even robbed from earlier structures (Sharples in Sharples and Sheridan 1992).

Causewayed enclosures, cursus monuments and henges: defining the world

When the first enclosures came to be built, from the thirty-seventh century cal BC onwards (Whittle *et al.* 2008; an ambitious dating programme is nearing completion), their impact, both physical and conceptual, must have been considerable. The outer circuit of the causewayed enclosure on Windmill Hill, for example, had a diameter of some 350 m (Figure 4.8); the three circuits there were built probably successively in the later thirty-seventh century BC. The evidence indicates that this enclosure was set in open woodland or scrub. Moreover, encircling a place with ditches and embankments was a new idea, since earlier monuments here took the form of barrows and related structures. Its source may have lain in similar ditched and palisaded enclosures of the continental Michelsberg and northern Chassey cultures, and the new practice may have stood, in a general way, for older concepts of community and ancestral order, but perhaps more specifically for affiliation with contemporary networks of social interaction.

As with other monuments, there are variations and unities in the use of causewayed enclosures (Oswald *et al.* 2001), which seem to be a mainly southern British phenomenon. They consist of circuits of interrupted ditch, with internal banks, generally low and informal; some ditches are backed by palisades, as at Orsett, Essex, or Haddenham, Cambridgeshire. Circuits range from one to four, and there are regional variations in spacing of circuits and enclosed areas. Some sites have seemingly incomplete circuits and others ones that link natural features such as streams and the sides of promontories. On the chalklands, many are set on hilltops or scarps, but there are numerous examples in southern and Midland river valleys and near the fen-edge of East Anglia. Stone-walled enclosures in the south-west, such as Carn Brea, Cornwall, appear to be an equivalent form. Formal modelling of radiocarbon dates suggests both longer and shorter histories for these sites (Whittle *et al.* 2008).

Figure 4.8   Excavation of bone deposits in the middle ditch of the causewayed enclosure at Windmill Hill (Alasdair Whittle).

Causewayed enclosures do not seem on the whole to have been settlements, though some had restricted occupation within them, perhaps intensifying in later phases of use. They do not generally appear defensive, though the second-phase, more continuous circuit of Crickley Hill, on the western Cotswold scarp, and the Stepleton outworks on Hambledon Hill may have been so designed. Rather, they too stood for a series of ideas and were the focus for intense participatory ceremonialism which marked key aspects of the Early Neolithic lifestyle.

Causewayed enclosures, like barrows, may have evoked the past, but above all they brought people together in their construction, enhanced attachment to place and seem to have celebrated relations among the living, near and far. Their layouts presented a potentially complex and ambiguous symbolism, playing on ideas of inside and outside, access and restriction, belonging and exclusion. There are only limited signs of internal occupation, though artefact scatters and pits do occur and perhaps even some structures. Within the inner circuit of Hambledon Hill, selected and separate groups of artefacts, including stone axeheads and red deer antler, were deposited in pits. At Etton in Cambridgeshire, deliberately placed deposits including human cremations were found in one internal zone, while occupation traces were recorded in the other; placed deposits in the ditches seem approximately to repeat this zonation.

Such internal deposits were apparently part of a broader use that encompassed the surrounding ditches. In these, there are frequently numerous and varied finds: lithic artefacts and pottery, some human remains, charcoal, some charred plant remains and, above all, animal bones, especially those of cattle. Few of these categories are regularly represented by whole finds. There are sherds rather than whole pots, and pieces of human skeleton (some complete child burials occur); animal bone deposits often consist of selected parts of more than one animal of more than one species. Such material may have been middened or stored elsewhere before its deposition. It must come from gatherings, rites and feasting, sometimes involving the large-scale slaughter of animals. Such deposits seem to celebrate various dimensions of the social world: subsistence, eating, sharing, gift giving, relations with neighbours and others and dealings with the dead.

The quantities and character of this material vary from site to site. They can also change from primary to secondary levels within their ditches. They also vary spatially in some enclosures, as already noted at Etton and Hambledon Hill. At Windmill Hill, there is varying emphasis in the three-ditch circuits on different deposits and treatment; there are greater quantities of material and more highly processed bone in the innermost circuit, while the outermost has more unusual deposits, including infant burials. The arena of bounded space may have served, either from the outset or as the outcome of repeated deposition, to map major conceptual concerns.

Cursus monuments were an innovation of the Middle Neolithic. Part of one overlies the causewayed enclosure at Etton, and Drayton in the upper Thames probably dates to the thirty-seventh or thirty-sixth century cal BC (Whittle *et al.* 2008). Ditched and banked linear enclosures, these often appear to have been constructed in stages, and some at least appear unfinished, with open terminals. They range from hundreds of metres upwards in length.

Figure 4.9 The Dorset cursus on Gussage Down, seen from the air (Martin Green).

The longest, the Dorset cursus on Cranborne Chase, runs for almost 10 km (Figure 4.9). Many have been detected on river gravels, and their distribution extends further north than causewayed enclosures (for example, in the complex at Rudston on the Yorkshire Wolds). A related monument in Perthshire, the Cleaven Dyke, has a central mound or bank as well as flanking ditches. Some cursus monuments enclose timber and other settings, though these may normally be later additions. The Dorset cursus incorporates pre-existing long barrows in its layout, and that at Dorchester-on-Thames subsumes earlier and smaller ditched features, interpreted as mortuary enclosures. The roles of cursus monuments may have varied. They may have acted as boundary markers, actual or symbolic; they presumably signify woodland clearance. Their form suggests procession, perhaps already a feature of gatherings and rites, now formalized and made permanent. One connection may have been with the ancestral dead, and there may be some interest in the risings and settings of the sun and moon. It has been suggested that the Dorset cursus was designed to be experienced from north-east to south-west, towards the great 'death island' formed by the Hambledon Hill causewayed enclosure, a few kilometres away (Tilley 1994) – and now demonstrably older.

Stone rows or avenues, early stone circles and early henges may have overlapped with the use of cursus monuments, but focused dating programmes are needed. One of the Thornborough henges in the Vale of York directly overlies a cursus. The simple enclosures of Flagstones (Dorset) and the first phase of Stonehenge belong to the turn of the third millennium cal BC. Both draw on the earlier tradition of interrupted ditches (and Stonehenge has old-style deposits in its primary ditch layers), but have circular or near-circular layouts. This formalization is enhanced in Stonehenge I, the primary monument, by a ring of internal pits (the Aubrey Holes), with cremations deposited subsequently, and probably central timber settings; excavation in 2008 has suggested that a heavy stone, speculatively a bluestone, had been placed in the base of Aubrey Hole 7 (Parker Pearson *et al.* 2009).

The enclosure tradition in the Late Neolithic encompasses various elements: henges, with their internal features including stone and timber settings and stone circles; freestanding stone circles and settings; and circular and oval timber palisades. Their distributions are much wider. The Ring of Brogar and Stones of Stenness on Orkney, with ditches, banks and stone circles, mark the northern limit; there are related sites in Ireland. Nearly everywhere formalization is apparent, indicated by concerns for ordering the approach to, entrance into and movement around these bounded spaces, as well as with their orientations and outward views to horizons and other natural features. While some henges appear as the first large monuments in their areas, others were added to landscapes long sanctified by older exemplars. Most of the very large henges, such as at Avebury and Mount Pleasant in central-southern England, occur within such established complexes (Figure 4.10). The explanation of this has often been sought purely in terms of political power, but the strength of the sacred traditions of long-lived holy areas should not be underestimated.

Figure 4.10 Excavations on Site IV, a vast post-setting circled by a ditch, within the henge at Mount Pleasant, Dorset (Geoffrey Wainwright).

Henges generally have ditches inside their earthwork banks. Their sizes vary considerably, attaining considerable diameters (350 m up to nearly 500 m) at Avebury, Mount Pleasant, Durrington Walls and Marden (Wainwright 1989). The smaller henges generally have one entrance, the larger two, and exceptionally more. These exhibit the general concern for setting, approach and entrance. At Avebury, the approach from the south was by the double stone row of the West Kennet Avenue. A massive stone circle inside the ditch provides the first division of internal space, with exceptionally large stones flanking the southern entrance. Two large inner stone circles with central stone settings further sub-divided the enclosed space, and there may also have been timber settings, contemporary or earlier. Within Durrington Walls there were certainly timber settings, the South and North Circles, the former about 40 m in diameter and consisting of six rings of timbers; but new evidence suggests that the South Circle predates the henge. Whether these settings were roofed is not entirely clear, but new evidence supports the unroofed version (Thomas in Larsson and Parker Pearson 2007). Deposits of animal bone and artefacts, including sherds of broken Grooved Ware, were made in and adjacent to the South Circle. The general nature of the rites seems to echo much earlier practices, but the setting is more ordered, formalized and restricted, symbolized now by the new evidence for a short avenue approaching the South Circle.

There were other large enclosed monuments, formed by bank and ditch (ditch only at Brogar) or by timber settings (such as Meldon Bridge in the upper Tweed Valley), and other significant monument complexes (such as Balfarg, Callanish and Brogar–Stenness–Maes Howe). In the south, Durrington Walls was a truly monumental earthwork. It too was added to an area long significant, from the period of long barrows and causewayed enclosures, to the cursus monuments and first phase of Stonehenge; a smaller henge was constructed at Coneybury (J. Richards 1990). Immediately adjacent lay Woodhenge, a timber setting within a slightly later henge-style ditch. During the Late Neolithic, according to radiocarbon dates (Cleal *et al.* 1995), Stonehenge was further monumentalized (Parker Pearson *et al.* 2009 (cf. Chapter 5) suggest *c.* 2500 cal BC; compare Bayliss *et al.* 2007). Bluestones from south-west Wales and sarsens from north Wiltshire were assembled to create an eternal version in stone of the timber settings seen at Durrington Walls and elsewhere, fixing the ancestral order for all time, making the past timeless, putting (or attempting to put) the present beyond dispute and uniting people with nature. In north Wiltshire, the even more monumental construction of the Silbury Hill mound (which also joined a long-established local complex of monuments) was erected, perhaps as a symbol of the earth itself, and as an expression of ideas to do with origins, regeneration and ancestral cycles. Such ideas might have driven this society as much as did social or political imperatives, though it may be hard to separate the two dimensions. It is hard not to see Stonehenge and Silbury Hill as in some sense rival projects. Silbury Hill appears to have been started *c.* 2400 cal BC. Given that the sarsens for Stonehenge may well have come from the north Wiltshire area around Silbury, were the people driving the Stonehenge enterprise initially dominant? Was this political power at work, or rivalry between sacred places of pilgrimage, each offering a different vision of how the world began, or both? This is likely to have been a time of much wider change, since the further innovations of the

Beaker complex appear to have started *c.* 2400 cal BC (Chapter 5). The greatest undertakings of the Late Neolithic might have been at one and the same time at the end of a long tradition of insular monumentality and a reaction to changes in the wider contemporary world.

CONTINUITY, CHANGE AND FUTURE RESEARCH

A sense of working with nature and of belonging to a timeless world might have continued from the Mesolithic way of life, as well as traits already mentioned, but there were new ways of doing things, and not simply tending newly introduced cultivated plants and domesticated animals. Above all, novel ways of thinking about the world, in terms of beginnings, marked time and the new relations with nature demanded by domestication, mark this period. To what extent were there subsequent changes? There may have been tensions between social ideals and conceptual schemes: of a cyclical past contrasting with marked time, or working with nature clashing with a world in which people had increased control over animals and plants. Some of the practices writ large in the archaeological record may be related to the playing out of such ambiguities. For example, the near-obsession with cattle bone in causewayed enclosure ditches may reflect attempts to come to terms with the changed status of animals. The fact that animal bone was stored, selected, sorted and redeposited – like the human remains in shrines and tombs – could intimate a concern to treat animals and humans similarly. Improving, more precise timescales for the Early Neolithic allow us to begin to see more dynamic sequences of change, and better chronologies must be a key goal for the period as a whole across the entire country.

What further changes occurred? Late Neolithic society has often been proposed as more differentiated than earlier phases; the language has often been of chiefdoms, 'ritual authority structures', dynasties and the like. The evidence for either economic intensification or major population growth is weak, however, and social reconstruction rests to a large degree on interpretation of monuments and mortuary rites. Some of the beliefs and ideals that created the Neolithic in the first place were probably maintained well into the second millennium cal BC. The Late Neolithic too may have seen a continued play between integration and cooperation on the one hand, and differentiation and hierarchy on the other. This needs, for the future, to be teased out in as many settings as possible, and at the scale of individual life histories as well as in the great monument complexes.

Acknowledgements

I am grateful to Jim Leary for discussion of the dating of Silbury Hill from the recent work there.

Key texts

Bayliss, A. and Whittle, A. (eds) 2007. *Histories of the dead: building chronologies for five southern British long barrows*. Cambridge: *Cambridge Archaeological Journal*, 17.1, supplement.
Bradley, R., 2007. *The prehistory of Britain and Ireland*. Cambridge: Cambridge University Press.

Larsson, L. and Parker Pearson, M. (eds) 2007. *From Stonehenge to the Baltic: living with cultural diversity in the third millennium BC*. Oxford: Archaeopress.

Pollard, J., (ed.) 2008. *Prehistoric Britain*. Oxford: Blackwell.

Thomas, J., 1999. *Understanding the Neolithic*. London: Routledge.

Whittle, A. and Cummings, V. (eds) 2007. *Going over: the Mesolithic–Neolithic transition in north-west Europe*. Oxford: Oxford University Press for the British Academy.

Bibliography

Barclay, A. and Harding, J. (eds) 1999. *Pathways and ceremonies: the cursus monuments of Britain and Ireland*. Oxford: Oxbow.

Bayliss, A., McAvoy, F. and Whittle, A., 2007. 'The world recreated: redating Silbury Hill in its monumental landscape', *Antiquity* 81, 26–53.

Bayliss, A., Whittle, A. and Healy, F., 2008. 'Timing, tempo and temporalities in the Early Neolithic of southern Britain', *Analecta Praehistorica Leidensia* 40, 25–42.

Benson, D. and Whittle, A. (eds) 2007. *Building memories: the Neolithic Cotswold long barrow at Ascott-under-Wychwood. Oxfordshire*. Oxford: Oxbow.

Brophy, K., 2007. 'From big houses to cult houses: Early Neolithic timber halls in Scotland', *Proceedings of the Prehistoric Society* 73, 75–96.

Budd, P., Chenery, C., Montgomery, J. and Evans, J., 2003. 'You are where you ate: isotopic analysis in the reconstruction of prehistoric residency', in Parker Pearson, M. (ed.) *Food, culture and identity in the Neolithic and Early Bronze Age*. Oxford: Archaeopress, 69–78.

Cleal, R.M.J., Walker, K.E. and Montague, R., 1995. *Stonehenge in its landscape: twentieth-century excavations*. London: English Heritage.

Coles, J. and Coles, B., 1986. *Sweet Track to Glastonbury*. London: Thames and Hudson.

Darvill, T., 2004. *Long barrows of the Cotswolds*. Stroud: Tempus.

Darvill, T., 2007. 'Towards the within: Stonehenge and its purpose', in Barrowclough, D. A. and Malone, C. (eds) *Cult in context: reconsidering ritual in archaeology*. Oxford: Oxbow, 148–57.

Edmonds, M., 1995. *Stone tools and society*. London: Batsford.

Evans, C. and Hodder, I., 2006. *A woodland archaeology. The Haddenham project, volume I*. Cambridge: McDonald Institute.

Garrow, D., Beardsmoore, E. and Knight, M., 2005. 'Pit clusters and the temporality of occupation: an earlier Neolithic site at Kilverstone, Thetford, Norfolk', *Proceedings of the Prehistoric Society* 71, 139–57.

Gillings, M., Pollard, J., Wheatley, D. and Peterson, R., 2008. *Landscape of the megaliths: excavation and fieldwork on the Avebury monuments, 1997–2003*. Oxford: Oxbow.

Fleming, A., 2006. 'Post-processual landscape archaeology: a critique', *Cambridge Archaeological Journal* 16, 267–80.

Harding, J. and Healy, F., 2007. *The Raunds Area Project: a Neolithic and Bronze Age landscape in Northamptonshire*. Swindon: English Heritage.

Mercer, R.J. and Healy, F., 2008. *Hambledon Hill, Dorset: excavation and survey of a Neolithic monument complex and its surrounding landscape*. Swindon: English Heritage.

Oswald, A., Dyer, C. and Barber, M., 2001. *The creation of monuments: Neolithic causewayed enclosures in the British Isles*. London: English Heritage.

Parker Pearson, M., Cleal, R., Marshall, P., Needham, S., Pollard, J., Richards, C., Ruggles, C., Sheridan, A., Thomas, J., Tilley, C., Welham, K., Chamberlain, A., Chenery, C., Evans, J., Knüsel, C., Linford, N., Martin, L., Montgomery, J., Payne, A. and Richards, M., 2007. 'The age of Stonehenge', *Antiquity* 81, 617–39.

Parker Pearson, M., Chamberlain, A., Jay, M., Marshall, P., Pollard, J., Richards, C., Thomas, J., Tilley, C. and Welham, K., 2009. 'Who was buried at Stonehenge?', *Antiquity* 83, 23–39.

Richards, C. (ed.) 2005. *Dwelling among the monuments: the Neolithic village of Barnhouse, Maeshowe passage grave and surrounding monuments at Stenness, Orkney*. Cambridge: McDonald Institute.

Richards, J., 1990. *The Stonehenge environs project*. London: English Heritage.

Saville, A., 1990. *Hazleton North: the excavation of a Neolithic long cairn of the Cotswold–Severn group*. London: English Heritage.

Schulting, R. and Wysocki, M., 2005. '"In this chambered tumulus were found cleft skulls ...": an assessment of the evidence for cranial trauma in the British Isles', *Proceedings of the Prehistoric Society* 71, 107–38.

Serjeantson, D. and Field, D. (eds) 2006. *Animals in the Neolithic of Britain and Europe*. Oxford: Oxbow.

Sharples, N.M. and Sheridan, A. (eds) 1992. *Vessels for the ancestors*. Edinburgh: Edinburgh University Press.

Tilley, C., 1994. *A phenomenology of landscape: places, paths and monuments*. Oxford: Berg.

Vyner, B., 1984. 'The excavation of a Neolithic cairn at Street House, Loftus, Cleveland', *Proceedings of the Prehistoric Society* 50, 151–96.

Wainwright, G.J., 1989. *The henge monuments*. London: Thames and Hudson.

Whittle, A., 1997. *Sacred mound, holy rings. Silbury Hill and the West Kennet palisade enclosures: a Later Neolithic complex in north Wiltshire*. Oxford: Oxbow.

Whittle, A., Bayliss, A. and Healy, F., 2008. 'The timing and tempo of change: examples from the fourth millennium cal BC in southern England', *Cambridge Archaeological Journal* 18, 65–70.

Whittle, A., Healy, F. and Bayliss, A., in preparation. *Gathering time: dating the Early Neolithic enclosures of southern Britain and Ireland*.

5

THE EARLIER BRONZE AGE

Mike Parker Pearson

INTRODUCTION

The transition from stone to metal technology occurred considerably later in Britain than in other parts of the Old World. Whereas central and southern Europe had a lengthy Copper Age or Chalcolithic period, copper metallurgy was adopted in Britain only two or three centuries before bronze. Conventionally, the arrival of copper in Britain is dated to *c.* 2450/2400 BC but there is circumstantial evidence that copper tools were in use by 2500 BC. Bronze, produced by alloying tin with copper, was adopted in Britain around 2300/2200 BC.

'The Early Bronze Age' is, by and large, a handy shorthand for a specific chronological range (2500–1400 BC) and for a group of associated artefacts – certain styles of pots, houses, lithic assemblages, burials, stone monuments and metalwork. Whilst the British Bronze Age can be divided into a tripartite scheme (Early (2500–1500 BC), Middle (1500–1100 BC) and Late (1100–700 BC)), it is divided here into two: the Earlier (2500–1400 BC) and Later Bronze Age (1400–750 BC). Few archaeologists would still accept the technological determinism which led Vere Gordon Childe in his 1930 study, *The Bronze Age*, to see technical innovation (in this case the use of bronze) as driving social change, and thus providing the chronological framework for prehistory.

The Earlier Bronze Age has been a crucial period for many of the most important questions and debates in British and European prehistory. Was the arrival of Beaker pottery due to the immigration of 'Beaker folk' or was it more the diffusion of an ideological package? Was the great stone monument of Stonehenge built by architects from beyond Britain or by indigenous groups unaware of architectural innovations elsewhere? Was the change from communal to individual burial indicative of changing notions of individuality? Do the monuments and rich graves of Wessex indicate the emergence of elites who controlled chiefdoms? Did Bronze Age metallurgy initiate freedom of production from political constraint and thereby instil core values of freedom and innovation in Western society?

There are many recent books about the British Early Bronze Age and its surrounding centuries (Barber 2003; Barrett 1994; Burgess 1980; Clarke *et al.* 1985; Parker Pearson 2005), written from different theoretical and empirical perspectives and with different emphases and audiences. This is a brief outline of the various types of evidence and the ways in which archaeologists have used them to understand and write about the lives of these vanished and anonymous people. It adopts the methodology of a contextual analysis, examining the various threads of evidence independently and also weaving them together.

METALLURGY, METAL AND STONE TOOLS AND ORNAMENTS

The earliest metal artefacts in Britain were copper axes, knives, rings and awls. These have been found in Beaker-accompanied burials of the period 2400–1900 BC. The same items, together with daggers and halberds (dagger-shaped blades hafted like axes) were later made in bronze after 2300 BC. A bronze axe, associated with a radiocarbon date of *c.* 2300 BC, was found just above the primary silts of the Late Neolithic henge at Mount Pleasant, Dorchester. Despite its initial lateness in adopting metal, Britain was the first place in Europe to move over to an entirely bronze metallurgical industry around this date (Pare 2000).

The earliest true calendar date for metal tools is 2268–2251 BC, established by dendrochronology on a wooden trackway at Corlea, in Ireland, whose timbers were felled with a metal axe. The introduction of copper, bronze and gold metallurgy to the British Isles has long been considered to be associated with people using Beaker pottery. Yet there are signs that metal items may have arrived earlier. In a hoard of copper axes from Castletown Roche in Ireland was a continental import of a form that may predate the Beaker horizon. Two blocks of chalk rubble from the bank of Durrington Walls henge (2480–2460 BC) have marks which appear to have been made by a metal axe, whilst the near-total absence of stone or flint axes in the large flint assemblage found within the earlier village at Durrington Walls, dating to *c.* 2500 BC, hints at the use of metal axes which would have been carefully recycled rather than discarded.

Various chronological schemes have been proposed for metal artefacts within this period (Burgess 1980; Needham *et al.* 1997) (Figure 5.1). Burgess's broad threefold chronology for the Earlier Bronze Age (1980) defines three periods:

- the *Mount Pleasant phase* (2500–2000 BC), when people used flat axes, Grooved Ware and Beaker pottery. Cremation had been widespread across Britain since 3000 BC and continued until after 2400 BC, when Beaker-accompanied inhumation rites were adopted. At the beginning of this period, Stonehenge's sarsen stone circle and trilithons were erected around 2500 BC (largely what we see today), about 500 years after its first phase of ditch, bank and circle of 56 pits known as Aubrey Holes (which initially held Welsh 'bluestones' and cremation burials in 3000–2935 BC);

- the *Overton phase* (2000–1700 BC), when people used flanged axes, flat-tanged daggers, Food Vessels, Collared Urns and Beakers. Some people were buried under mounds – round barrows – with gold and elaborate grave goods (known as the Wessex I phase). A good example is the man buried under Bush Barrow on Normanton Down, close to Stonehenge;

- the *Bedd Branwen phase* (1700–1400 BC), when pottery styles became increasingly regionalized within Britain. Most people were cremated and there were a few with occasional grave goods, such as daggers, flint tools and ornaments but not of gold (Wessex II burials). New styles of bronze spearheads, rapiers and palstave axes began to appear as single finds or components of bronze hoards. This phase spans the period between the Early Bronze Age and the Middle Bronze Age.

Though backward in terms of the European adoption of metallurgy, Britain and Ireland were rich in deposits of copper and tin. Copper was mined at Ross Island in Killarney, Ireland, from 2400 BC onwards (O'Brien 2004). Earliest dates for mining in Britain are from the Great Orme (Dutton and Fasham 1994) and around 1500 BC at Cwmystwyth in Wales (Blick 1991, 51–9). Similarly, the search continues for Early Bronze Age tin extraction in Cornwall and Devon. The smelting of copper ores can be achieved using bellows in small, charcoal-fired, open bowl furnaces. The molten metal collects in the bottom in the form of a 'cake'. The earliest flat axes of copper were made by melting this cake and pouring the liquid into a single-piece open mould of stone or fired clay. Bronze was made by adding one part tin to eight parts copper. Two-part moulds enabled the casting of more elaborate axe and dagger forms. Decoration was also employed, notably on axes (Figure 5.2).

There were certain changes in flint knapping from the Late Neolithic. Although Early Bronze Age knapping debris, with its relatively short blades, cannot be distinguished from Late Neolithic assemblages, the flintwork includes certain diagnostic items such as thumbnail scrapers, barbed-and-tanged arrowheads and flaked knives and daggers. These daggers and arrowheads are carefully worked and suggest a division between specialist knapping of prestigious pieces and everyday manufacture of ordinary blades and edges (Edmonds

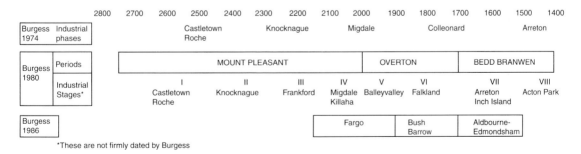

Figure 5.1 Metalwork chronologies for the Earlier Bronze Age.
   Source: M. Hamilton after Burgess 1980

Figure 5.2
Flint axes, such as this example from West Cotton (Northampton-shire), were substituted for metal ones in 'fission horizon' Beaker burials around 2200 BC.
Source: copyright Northamptonshire Archaeology

1995). A similar picture of fine craftsmanship is gained from the polished stone maceheads and battle axes, made of flint or igneous rocks. The flaked daggers were copies of copper prototypes, whilst the battle axes were copies not of copper originals but of stone ones from northern and central Europe. Within this tradition of stone working, we should also consider the quarrying and dressing of large stones, such as the use of crude sarsen mauls and hammer stones to shape the faces of the stones at Stonehenge.

Personal adornment with bead necklaces, boars' tusks, bone pins, stone maceheads and polished axes (for these latter items were as much ornaments as practical items) was already current in the Middle Neolithic from *c.* 3400 BC onwards. It is a major feature of the Earlier Bronze Age, partly because more burial contexts have been investigated and partly because the range of ornamentation increased. Among the most spectacular items are beautiful necklaces of jet or amber beads, especially those from Scotland, the many gold lunulae (crescent-shaped and decorated sheets probably worn as gorgets) from Ireland and southwest England and the gold cape from a burial mound at Mold in north Wales. We also find dress pins, toggles and buttons which, together with awls and needles, indicate that considerable attention was given to clothing, presumably of leather, wool and possibly linen. This increased concern with personal finery and bodily adornment can be interpreted in many different ways. Some see it as the affirmation of individualism, matching the development of individualized funerary rites. Others interpret it as the establishment of visible status gradations necessary in chiefdom-style societies. The 'fancy goods' of Early Bronze Age life form a marked contrast to the pottery and ordinary flintwork which constituted the materials of everyday routines.

POTTERY

Ever since Lord Abercromby's encyclopaedic study of Bronze Age urns in the early twentieth century, pottery analysis has dominated archaeological research into this period. Subsequent compendia of Beaker pots (Clarke 1970; Gibson 1982), Collared Urns (Longworth 1984), Northern Food Vessels and a mass of regional studies have investigated issues of typology, chronology, decorative variation, regionality, production, distribution, status and deposition.

In many respects, the aim of establishing a finely tuned ceramic chronology (Figure 5.3) for the Earlier Bronze Age has not been realized. Even the seven-step sequence proposed for Dutch Beaker styles has been undermined by comprehensive radiocarbon dating programmes on Beaker-associated materials (Kinnes *et al.* 1991; Sheridan in Larsson and Parker Pearson 2007), although a more simplified British Beaker chronology has been proposed (Needham in Larsson and Parker Pearson 2007). This identifies three stages: low-carinated beakers (2400–2250 BC), beakers of the 'fission horizon' and after (2250–1950 BC), and late beakers (1950–1750 BC).

The notional sequence of Beaker pottery (2400–1750 BC), Food Vessels (2200–1800 BC), Collared Urns (2000–1700 BC) and Biconical Urns (1800–1400 BC) can be viewed either as a series of chronological overlaps or, less likely, as a chest-of-drawers replacement of one style by another, thanks to the relative imprecision of the radiocarbon method (since any single date has a 95 per cent probability of falling anywhere within a range of *c.* 200–400 years in that period; however, Bayesian statistical modelling now provides greater precision for dates from groups of samples in stratigraphic association).

The finely made beakers stand out from an otherwise crude ceramic tradition, indicating that the coarseness of other Early Bronze Age wares was a matter of cultural preference and not one of prehistoric incompetence. Found throughout Europe, beakers are identified by their S-shaped profile of an open mouth, narrow neck and bulge in the middle. They are formally known as Bell Beakers and are often decorated, mainly in a series of horizontal zones of impressed cord, incised line and impressed comb patterns. Many of those found

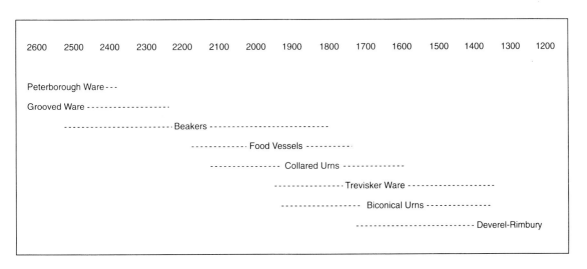

Figure 5.3 Ceramic chronologies for the Late Neolithic, Early Bronze Age and Middle Bronze Age, taking a minimal view of the radiocarbon ranges. Dates are in calibrated years BC.
Source: M. Hamilton

Figure 5.4 A beaker from the Green Low round barrow in Derbyshire.
Source: Sheffield City Museum

in burials (Figure 5.4) may have been made specifically for the grave. Their poorer rock-tempered fabrics and smooth surfaces indicate that perhaps they were to be looked at rather than used (Boast in Kinnes and Varndell 1995). The larger of these funerary vessels often accompany adult male corpses, while small beakers are often found with the bodies of children (Case in Kinnes and Varndell 1995). Their interpretation as a high-status item has been dismissed; they do not take long to produce and were not sought-after trade items. Even the popular notion that they contained an alcoholic beverage such as mead or an unusual cocktail of alcohol and cannabis may be only a small dimension of their use. Pollen in a grave at Ashgrove in Fife may derive from mead or honey spilled from a beaker, though residues from other burials have been reinterpreted as the remains of floral tributes to the dead (Tipping 1994). Beakers from the Durrington Walls settlement were found to contain lipids derived from milk or dairy products (Mukherjee *et al*. 2007).

Within continental Europe, Beaker pots succeeded Corded Ware, and both styles have been interpreted as evidence of invaders or immigrants moving in and replacing indigenous populations. In many parts of Europe, the Beaker formed part of a material culture 'package' (including barbed-and-tanged flint arrowheads, copper or bronze awls, archers' wristguards and metal or flint daggers) which some archaeologists have interpreted as the material manifestation of a religious cult or ideology rather than a movement of people (Burgess and Shennan in Burgess and Miket 1976). Re-examination of the invasionist argument that Neolithic people were dolichocephalic (their skulls were longer than they were wide) and Beaker incomers were brachycephalic (short rounded skulls) has suggested that such changes could result from environmental and genetic changes within an indigenous population (Brodie 1994). Yet the case for Beaker immigration into Britain remains strong. Strontium and oxygen isotope analysis of tooth enamel of the 'Amesbury Archer', buried 3 miles from Stonehenge, indicates that he spent his childhood in the Alpine foothills (Evans *et al.* 2006).

Beaker pottery in Britain is not restricted to burials or ceremonial complexes but regularly turns up in settlements (Gibson 1982). In south-west England, where the geology is suitable for ceramic petrological sourcing, beakers were made locally, deposited within no more than a few miles of their likely places of manufacture (Parker Pearson in Kinnes and Varndell 1995).

Unlike Beaker pots, Food Vessels and Collared Urns are not found on the Continent (Figure 5.5). Food Vessels were used throughout much of the British Isles, predominantly with inhumations (particularly in Yorkshire, Scotland and Ireland) and cremation burials (predominantly in Wales and north-west England), since settlement sites survive so rarely. Where they occur with beakers in burial mounds, they are nearly always placed after them, in secondary associations, yet radiocarbon dates for Beaker pots and Food Vessels indicate a probable chronological overlap of 300–400 years. Food Vessels are narrow-bottomed pots with straight or bowed sides and an out-turned mouth, and are decorated on their upper parts with twisted cord impressions, incised lines, stabmarks, fingermarks and bone impressions. They divide into three overlapping sizes, the largest perhaps for storage, the middle for cooking and the smaller for eating from.

Collared Urns are similar in shape, decoration and size to Food Vessels, except that the rim is in-turned and slopes down to an external, overhanging collar. Their radiocarbon date range indicates that they appeared some centuries after the first Food Vessels but that they also overlapped in time. When they are found in burial mounds with Food Vessels, they are always in secondary or later deposits within the mound. Such differences may have been social rather than simply chronological. Collared Urns are similarly found throughout Britain. In Ireland they are found only in the eastern half of the country.

Cordoned Urns, Encrusted Urns, Biconical Urns and Trevisker pottery are specifically regional styles within the Earlier Bronze Age. Towards the end of the Earlier Bronze Age a variety of cruder, mainly undecorated bucket-shaped styles appeared, notably Deverel–Rimbury wares in southern England and the Green Knowe style in southern Scotland and northern England. Northern Food Vessel Urns can also be considered as a regional variant. Cordoned Urns are found in Ireland and Scotland, Encrusted Urns (broadly a style of encrusted decoration used on enlarged Food Vessels) in Scotland, northern England and Ireland, Biconical Urns in lowland England and Trevisker pottery in south-west England. By the end of the Earlier Bronze Age, the repertoire of vessel sizes and forms had increased from twofold or threefold divisions to complex divisions for Deverel–Rimbury and Biconical assemblages of coarse heavy-duty, coarse everyday, cups/bowls and globular fine wares, and for Trevisker wares of large storage, smaller storage, cooking pots and three types of small vessels (Figure 5.6) (Woodward and Parker Pearson in Kinnes and Varndell 1995). The increasing regionality of ceramics can be paralleled by regional styles of Middle Bronze Age palstave axes (Rowlands 1976), and Ann Woodward has shown how Middle Bronze

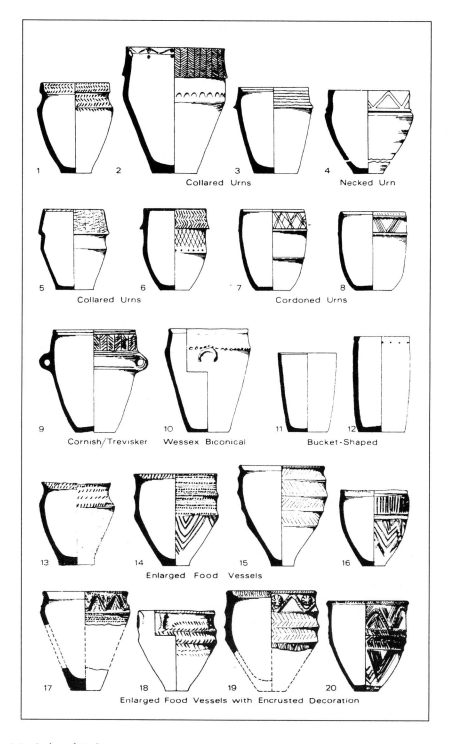

Figure 5.5 Styles of Earlier Bronze Age storage pots used as cremation containers.
Source: Burgess 1980. Copyright Orion Books

Age defended hilltop settlements such as Rams Hill and Norton Fitzwarren in southern Britain lie at the interfaces between these styles, possibly controlling exchange relationships between regions (Ellison 1980). Another interesting interpretation of this growing regionalism from the Late Neolithic to the Middle Bronze Age is that the ceramic repertoires might be considered as 'dialects' in material culture, mirroring or playing off linguistic shifts firstly between Britain and the Continent (Food Vessels and Collared Urns) and latterly within the British Isles (Tomalin in Kinnes and Varndell 1995). In other words, they may be the only surviving traces of growing regional differences in local dialects and customs.

It is in south-west and southern Britain that we get the clearest picture of pottery production and distribution. Food Vessels and Collared Urns in Cornwall were predominantly produced from the high-quality and distinctive gabbroic clays of the Lizard peninsula, indicating a centralized production and distribution pattern very different from Beaker wares. Cornish Trevisker Ware was similarly derived from the Lizard gabbro, though Trevisker pottery in Devon probably came largely from two sources of south Devon clay not far from Dartmoor. Trevisker pots made on the Lizard were even moved by sea along the south coast to Wessex and Kent, and across the Channel to the Pas-de-Calais at Hardelot (Parker Pearson in Kinnes and Varndell 1995). Armorican *vases à anse* came the other way from Brittany to the Isle of Wight and Wessex. Thus the pots support the picture of cross-Channel trade in metalwork (the Salcombe and Dover wreck sites) and seafaring as shown by the recent discovery of a Middle Bronze Age sewn plank boat at Dover (Clark 2004).

Pots are one of the key artefacts, however lowly, in marking social relationships and rites of passage. They accompanied the corpse (or its burnt remains) to the final resting place; they were

Figure 5.6 Assemblage variation within the Trevisker series: (from large to small) the large two-handled storage pot (Style 1); the multiple-lugged storage pot (Style 2); the cooking pot (Styles 3 and 4); and the small serving pot (Style 5).

Source: Peter Dunn

111

involved in the daily rites and routines of food preparation and consumption; and they signalled regional, age, gender and no doubt other social identities. Whilst they were employed in the activities of storage, cooking and serving of food, those essential practices of daily life and relationships, we can only guess at the complexities of the gender and status relationships in which they were used. This is partly due to the paucity of excavated settlements and houses.

HOUSES

There are very few well-preserved Earlier Bronze Age settlements excavated in Europe, and most of the house remains are found in the western regions of Britain. These are very ephemeral and only survive in exceptional circumstances of preservation or where the scarcity of wood has led to their partial construction in stone. The locality with the greatest potential for preservation is the Western Isles of Scotland (the Outer Hebrides), where houses, mostly with stone walls revetted into sand, have been excavated at Northton, Barvas, Dalmore, Allt Chrysal, Cill Donnain and Rosinish (Figure 5.7) (Armit 1996, 88–94; Parker Pearson *et al.* 2004; Simpson *et al.* 2006). Other Earlier Bronze Age stone houses have been excavated in Shetland at Scord of Brouster and Ness of Gruting. A burnt-down round house (4 m diameter) and two other probable houses have been excavated at Stackpole Warren in Dyfed. Post rings of circular houses about 5 m in diameter are known from East Anglia at West Row Fen, Redgate Hill and Sutton Hoo. The supposed houses on the Beaker site at Belle Tout on the chalk downs of Sussex should now be discounted. There are also house remains claimed from a number of different sites of variable preservation and likelihood (Gibson 1982).

These houses vary in shape from round to oval to sub-rectangular, with a central hearth but no preferred axial orientation or place for the doorway. The Northton house (Structure I; Simpson *et al.* 2006) is 7 m long and 4.5 m wide with a hearth positioned centrally, close to its south-west-facing entrance. The relatively sunless location and paucity of faunal remains at Dalmore suggests a specialized and perhaps seasonal use, whereas other settlements may have been occupied all year round. Early Bronze Age houses were different from tombs; they were less symmetrical, smaller and constructed of less permanent materials than the earthen round barrows and cairns in which the dead were placed. Perhaps more effort was invested in funerary structures because people would spend eternity in them, in contrast to their short lives in the houses. At the same time, certain aspects of houses may have been similar to tombs; the central burial or cremation in a barrow may have symbolized the role of the hearth within the house. Such similarities and differences may have served to demarcate the realm of the dead from the living and yet present it as a mirror of life.

There seems to have been a substantial change in domestic architecture towards the end of the Earlier Bronze Age and in the Middle Bronze Age, when houses were constructed more substantially and in larger sizes. Additionally, settlements were increasingly marked by ditched enclosures and were set within laid-out landscapes of field walls and field banks. The large round houses (up to 7 m diameter) at Gwithian (Megaw in Burgess and Miket

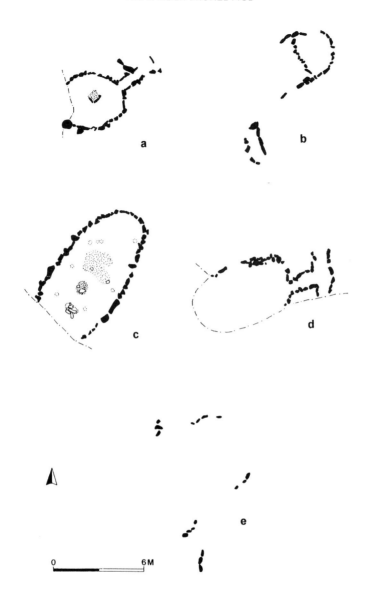

Figure 5.7 Earlier Bronze Age house plans from the Western Isles: (a) Dalmore; (b) Northton Structure 1; (c) Northton Structure 2; (d) Barvas; (e) Cill Donnain.
Sources: After Armit 1996; Burgess and Miket 1976, and with thanks to M. Hamilton and N. Sharples

1976), Trevisker and Trethellan (Nowakowski 1991) in Cornwall, dating from 1800–1200 BC, were solid structures with floor areas in excess of 30 sq m.

In summary, the houses of the British Earlier Bronze Age were not substantial structures except perhaps in the Western and Northern Isles. Nor were they arranged in large settlements, but in small dispersed groups. For much of the Earlier Bronze Age the permanence

113

and solidity of the tombs, standing stones and stone circles expressed levels of group identity much larger than those at the household level. Early Bronze Age identity was undoubtedly layered and complex, but it was probably most strongly fixed around the larger kin groups and lineages who must have come together to attend funerals and construct monuments. By the Middle Bronze Age there appeared a number of settlements enclosed by ditches and palisades such as South Lodge and Down Farm on Cranborne Chase, Dorset (Barrett *et al.* 1991). Not only were houses becoming larger and longer lasting but the household domain was taking on monumental proportions.

BURIALS AND FUNERALS

Since the seventeenth century, Early and Middle Bronze Age round burial mounds and cairns have been dug into and excavated by antiquarians and archaeologists. They have a long history of scholarly research and undoubtedly form the most abundant and perhaps significant remains from this period. Their potential for increasing our understanding of social status, sexual and gender differentiation, exchange and power relations has not been ignored (Barrett 1994; Clarke *et al.*1985; Last 2007; Woodward 2000), and recent theoretical studies have benefited from national and local research programmes of round barrow investigations half a century ago.

There is an extraordinary diversity of Early Bronze Age funerary practices, though this should not surprise us given the long timespan, the likely regionalism and the probable complexity of traditions (Gibson in Larsson and Parker Pearson 2007). Bodies might be inhumed or burnt; some inhumations show signs of prior excarnation (the bones partly jumbled from being left to rot before burial); other burials (such as Eynsham and Cassington, Oxfordshire) seem not to have been buried under mounds; burial deposits might be made in small clearance cairns produced by removing stones from fields (at Shaugh Moor, Dartmoor) rather than formal structures; round barrows come in many shapes, such as bowl, bell, disc and pond (Figure 5.8); burials may be multiple within the same grave (Goldington, Bedford); cremations may be placed within pots, by the side of pots or underneath upturned pots; the mounds may have anything between no and three circular ditches cut around them; mounds may be constructed of subsoil or bedrock or solely of turf (the King Barrows at Stonehenge); some mounds have stake circles; the inhumed corpses may be orientated in a number of different directions. Some of these variations are chronological: there was a broad change from inhumation to cremation after 2000 BC. Others are procedural: male Beaker burials far outnumber female Beaker burials, indicating a gender bias in selection for inhumation. Yet others are regional, such as the wide variety of barrow forms largely confined to the Wessex area. Whilst barrows normally contain burials, certain mounds (such as the Lockington barrow in Leicestershire) have no burial at all, let alone a central burial.

Yet burial under cairns and barrows may not have been the dominant rite. Recent discoveries of human remains in a silted-up channel of the Trent at Langford (Nottinghamshire)

Figure 5.8   Different types of round barrows on Normanton Down, Wiltshire: (from the top left) a
ditched bowl barrow with an outer bank; a disc barrow; a small barrow (left of the track
and partly destroyed by it); a double bell barrow; and a bell barrow.
Source: Courtesy of the Ashmolean Museum

concur with some of the radiocarbon dates for skulls dredged from the Thames to suggest
that Earlier Bronze Age traditions of burial on land may have been only a small part of
funerary rites; it is conceivable that the remains of many, if not most people were deposited
in rivers in this period. At Langford the skulls, bones and partially articulated skeletons
were found in association with animal bones and with timbers, possibly from a depositional
platform, dated by dendrochronology to 2266–2133 BC. It now seems likely that the Earlier
Bronze Age axes, spears, daggers/rapiers and halberds found in rivers were not chance losses
but were depositions related to funerary practices.

With only the final resting place of the dead available to us, what can be gleaned of the
whole sequence of events which made up the funerary rites of passage is problematic (Figure
5.9). Yet certain fortuitous and extraordinary deposits may have important and interesting
implications. Underneath an upturned pot under a barrow at Winterslow G3, in Wiltshire,
were a bronze razor and a small pile of eyebrow hair (Barrett 1994, 123), suggesting that
mourners may have shaved their facial hair as a rite of passage and an act of purification.

At Irthlingborough near Raunds in Northamptonshire (Figure 5.10), buried in alluvial
mud, the top of a burial mound preserved the remains of over 185 cattle skulls and smaller
numbers of cattle mandibles, shoulder blades and pelves. Most of them were from animals
aged around two years, probably bullocks (Davis and Payne 1993). Nearby, at Gayhurst in
Buckinghamshire, the ditches of another round barrow contained remains, mostly leg bones,

from about 300 cattle (Chapman 2007). Such numbers can only have derived in each case either from an enormous herd or more likely from many different herds. Strontium isotope analysis of dental enamel from some of the cattle at both sites indicates that they were brought locally, within about 20 miles, to the burial sites for slaughter. However, some cattle in each burial had originally been brought from western Britain a year or so before each funeral. Together with the Whitby jet buttons, the East Anglian flint dagger and the chalk artefacts found with the body of the adult male in the Irthlingborough burial, they indicate the distances involved in the extensive social contacts of these Bronze Age families.

Yet the Irthlingborough burial is not the most impressive example from the Beaker period. The Amesbury Archer was buried in a grave with no evidence of a mound or any cattle remains, and yet he was accompanied by over 100 grave goods (Fitzpatrick 2002). These included five beakers, three copper knives, two wrist bracers, a pair of gold basket-shaped

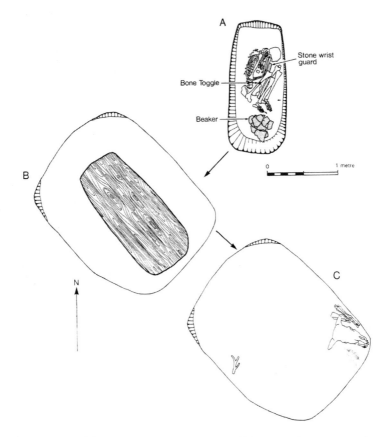

Figure 5.9   The sequence of funerary events at Hemp Knoll barrow: the corpse and grave goods are placed in a treetrunk coffin (A) which may have been covered and lowered into the grave (B), which was backfilled to include an ox head and hooves (either an oxhide cloak or a head-and-hooves offering), an antler pick and charcoal.
Source: Barrett 1994

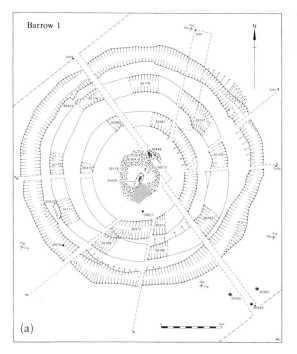

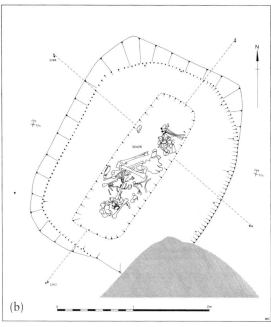

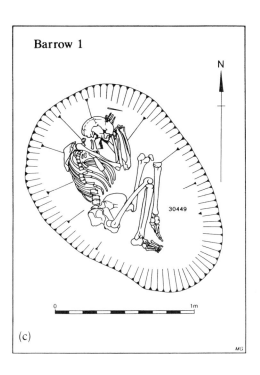

Figure 5.10 (a) A plan of the triple-ditched barrow at Irthlingborough, Raunds, Northamptonshire. Under the stone cairn was a central burial and the remains of a wooden structure. There was a second inhumation to the north-east and five cremation pits to the south (30617 was a Collared Urn containing the ashes of an adult and a teenager, along with a horn-hilted bronze dagger). (b) The crouched adult male skeleton in the central burial was accompanied by a group of grave goods below his feet. These comprised a long-necked beaker, three bone spatulae, five conical jet buttons, an unused flint dagger, a flint arrowhead or point, nine unused flint flakes, an amber ring, two 'sponge-finger' stones (one of chalk and one of Langdale rock), a reused stone wristguard and a boar's tusk. (c) The crouched skeleton of an adult, probably male, north-east of the central grave. The only grave good was a bone needle, placed above the head.

Source: English Heritage

hair-rings and a 'cushion' stone for working sheet metal. His is the most lavishly equipped Bell Beaker grave in Europe, and he was presumably an important individual. His life had not been easy; he had lived for many years with an unhealed injury to his knee. Buried in a second grave close to him was another man, whose surviving grave goods consisted only of a pair of gold hair-rings. In a third grave there was also an unusual multiple burial of seven individuals, known as the 'Boscombe Bowmen'. Isotopic analysis of the three adult males in this burial indicates that they had come from some distance away, most likely Wales or Brittany. The location of these remarkable burials within a few miles of Stonehenge has led to speculation that they were involved in its construction. But the sarsens had already been erected around 2500 BC, before they were born.

A small amount of goldwork has come from a group of burials from 2000–1800 BC mainly from the Wessex area, known as Wessex I (separate from the later Wessex II group of 1700–1500 BC, which is also associated with bronze daggers, stone battle axes and beads of amber and faience but not with gold), first described as the 'Wessex culture' by Piggott in the 1930s. The most impressive of the Wessex I burials are the Normanton Down group, just south of Stonehenge, especially the Bush Barrow with its gold lozenge, stone macehead, three large bronze daggers (one with a pommel inlaid with thousands of tiny gold pins) and bone mounts for the mace's wooden handle, all associated with the corpse of an adult man. Other assemblages containing gold artefacts are known from over 25 locations. They were not always associated with human remains, as is the case with the finds from within round barrows at Clandon in Dorset and Lockington in Leicestershire (a large bronze dagger, two gold armrings and two pots found on the edge of an empty burial mound). There are close similarities between the Wessex I burials and those across the Channel in Brittany such as the Kernonen burial (Clarke et al. 1985, 129–35).

For most archaeologists, these assemblages demonstrate the existence of chiefs (Fleming and Renfrew in Renfrew 1973). Yet the burying of this personal wealth may actually have prevented the accumulation of hereditary power, and funerals such as Irthlingborough and Gayhurst may have acted to disperse and destroy wealth, represented by cattle, in return for personal or family honour and prestige. Perhaps the point was not to keep wealth but to be seen to dispose of it in extravagant gestures at funerals and other ceremonies. Even so, we have to remember that the items that were put into graves may have been only a small proportion of what was kept above ground for economic benefit and displays of status and ownership.

Other inferences about social structure as expressed through funerary deposits can be made from grave goods and from the relative placing of human remains in burial mounds. Some of the grave goods can be divided on gender lines to suggest that there was a certain division of labour between men and women, symbolized in death. Men in Beaker burials were generally laid on their left sides and women on their right sides (Tuckwell 1975). Whilst male graves contain arrowheads, daggers, wristguards, belt rings, amber buttons, flint or stone axes and fire-making tools, female graves are associated with shale and jet beads and the majority of awls and antler picks or hoes; certain items (flint blades, earrings and pebble hammers) are shared equally. Insights into gender and age distinctions can also be gained from the relationship between primary and secondary burials; where adult males are buried first, the later ones may be other adults and children yet where adult females are buried first they are rarely followed by adult males. The pattern closely matches ethnographic observations of societies with patrilineal systems of descent.

The placing of the dead within the landscape was a complex matter, relating to and even reusing earlier monuments and establishing large areas of sacred space. The large barrow cemeteries in south Dorset, Cranborne Chase and the Stonehenge area, either side of the Avon, are far larger than most groups. The western Avon group is built within an area of Neolithic monuments and most mounds are clustered on the edges of an otherwise avoided 'envelope of visibility' around Stonehenge. The Amesbury Archer is one of more than a hundred or so burial sites on the east side of the Avon, all of which are inter-visible with the henge at Durrington Walls. Similar referencing of Late Neolithic henges and stone monuments can be found at Avebury, Irthlingborough and Rudston. The densest grouping of round barrows in Britain was on the Isle of Thanet in Kent. On the chalklands of Wessex the predominant locations chosen are downlands often at a distance from the valley-based settlement areas, suggesting that the dead were buried within areas of pasture. Conversely, in the East Midlands the lighter soils of the river valleys were the principal locations for barrow groups, with each group spaced approximately 10 km along each major river valley. At Irthlingborough, the most intensively investigated of these complexes, the carbonized remains of plants in the pyre debris from one of the excavated barrows derive from grasses which thrive only on land which is not grazed, indicating that animals were kept away from this area.

With the advent of the Middle Bronze Age, cremation was near-universal, and grave goods were largely limited to a single Deverel–Rimbury pot to contain the ashes. The cremated remains were buried in small cemeteries, either of small mounds or within and around an earlier mound, or in unmarked graves, which were located close to settlements. From enclosed settlements like South Lodge and Down Farm on Cranborne Chase, it seems that the dead were placed in the direction away from the entrances thereby maintaining a symbolic distinction between realms of living and dead (Barrett *et al.* 1991). Their unremarkable remains thus marked the land and fields in which the homestead was situated, rooting people in their land and emphasizing identities at the household level rather than the wider kin groups.

ENVIRONMENT AND LAND USE

The landscape of the Earlier Bronze Age was one which was being continuously reworked and remade. It consisted not only of the forests, wastes, pastures and fields but also of the places, monuments and spaces of ancestors and spirits. Neolithic monuments were modified and transformed. For example, in the Western Isles and Orkney many Neolithic chambered tombs seem to have been turned into closed monuments by individual Beaker burials (Armit

1996, 94–5). The entrance to the West Kennet chambered tomb in Wiltshire was blocked with huge stones. Other ancient places were similarly appropriated and transformed. Within the Mount Pleasant henge (Dorset) a palisaded enclosure of enormous dimensions (800 m long) was constructed with large tree trunks forming an impenetrable barrier. Around 2400 BC, the huge mound of Silbury Hill was built between Avebury henge and the West Kennet enclosures (Bayliss *et al.* 2007). Its purpose continues to elude us but it represents the end of an era; one of the last great public works for many centuries to come. Whereas Silbury Hill and, a century earlier, Stonehenge had required labour drawn from many different kin groups, even the largest of the Earlier Bronze Age round barrows could be built by single clans or large kin groups. This may have been a very significant shift in which power relations were decentralized from autocratic rulers to local leaders.

Another indication of how the natural or given landscape was transformed into a social domain is provided by the rock art of cup-and-ring marks found in northern England and Scotland (Bradley 1997). These curious motifs, pounded on to natural rock faces, are problematic to date and perhaps impossible to decipher, yet there is a patterning in their distribution. In certain areas the ring motifs are found at higher elevations than the cup marks which are often found overlooking lowland soils. The larger and more complex designs often overlook the most productive soils in their localities and also are often found in areas with concentrations of henges and ceremonial monuments. In certain stone cist burials within Late Neolithic and Early Bronze Age cairns, some of the stone slabs have been detached from cup-and-ring mark surfaces, and the carvings are generally turned inwards towards the remains of the corpse, perhaps linking the deceased to control of those places.

Barrow groups and cemeteries, as noted, were regularly sited in relation to earlier henges, long barrows, cursuses, stone circles and standing stones. Many of these places of the dead seem to have formed sacred landscapes which were devoid of contemporary settlements, such as the area north-east of Peterborough. Many of these funerary landscapes seem to have been relatively open and suitable for pasture, either on downland or river meadows. The barrow concentrations may well have marked the summer grazing lands for cattle and sheep for different territories, thus embodying the ancestral heartlands of different kin groups. Whilst pastoralism was probably a determining element of Earlier Bronze Age economy, crops of wheat, barley, pulses, oats and flax were grown. Earlier Bronze Age cross-ploughing, presumably with a stone-tipped wooden ard, is known from Gwithian in Cornwall (Megaw in Burgess and Miket 1976) and from Cill Donnain, Cladh Hallan and Rosinish (Shepherd in Burgess and Miket 1976; Parker Pearson *et al.* 2004) in the Western Isles. At Cill Donnain, these ardmarks occur in association with small ditches, possibly forming field boundaries.

Across most of Britain, the lack of houses from this period has fuelled conjecture that people were semi-sedentary, if not nomadic, and thus largely pastoralists, although the archaeologist's-eye view, somewhere below ground level, underestimates the sturdiness and longevity of these small homes. The discovery of seven preserved house floors within the large settlement beneath the henge at Durrington Walls has shown that houses of this period (*c.* 2500 BC) could be perfectly substantial – about 5.5 m × 5.5 m with wattle-and-daub walls and a chalk plaster floor – and yet leave little trace below ground level (Parker Pearson in Larsson and Parker Pearson 2007).

The Earlier Bronze Age was a time of major expansion and clearance. Whereas evidence from land snails indicates that substantial portions of the Avebury, Dorchester and Stonehenge areas were already largely cleared of forest, other areas were now being colonized and cleared (Smith 1984). Beaker-period cultivation was expanding across the chalklands of southern Britain (Allen 2005). In the Midlands, the Millstone Grit of the Peak District was colonized by users of Food Vessels and Collared Urns. Other uplands, such as Dartmoor and Bodmin Moor, were also utilized on a much greater scale than before (Fleming 1988). In these areas, as well as on the chalk downlands and in the river valleys, long linear boundaries established complex and fixed allotments of land from about 1600 BC onwards.

STONEHENGE AND OTHER MONUMENTS

The standing stones, stone rows and stone circles of the British Isles have been the subjects of innumerable books, of which a few of the general surveys can be recommended (Burl 1993; Ruggles and Whittle 1981; Ruggles 1999). Whilst most are thought to date to the Late Neolithic or Early Bronze Age, very few have been properly excavated and closely dated. Some of those whose construction can be dated with certainty to the Early Bronze Age are the recumbent stone circles of Aberdeenshire (Bradley 2005) and the Clava cairns of north-eastern Scotland (Bradley 2000).

Stonehenge spans the Late Neolithic to Early Bronze Age. Recent research by the Stonehenge Riverside Project has reinterpreted its sequence, so previously published syntheses (Cleal *et al.* 1995; Lawson 2007; Richards 2007) are now out of date. Stonehenge was first constructed in the thirtieth century BC (3000–2935 BC) as a bank and ditch enclosing a ring of pits (the Aubrey Holes) which held standing stones (Parker Pearson *et al.* 2009). This initial stone circle was probably composed mainly of Welsh bluestones (mostly Preseli dolerite with smaller numbers of rhyolite, volcanic ash, calcareous ash and sandstone). Cremation burials were inserted into many of the Aubrey Holes, either within the packing for the stones or as secondary burials into or around the holes. The date for the sarsen circle and trilithons has been disputed, but a stratigraphic reanalysis of radiocarbon-dated samples reveals that two antler picks were deposited at the time of their erection (Parker Pearson *et al.* 2007). The picks' combined date of 2620–2480 BC makes it likely that the sarsens were put up around 2500 BC. The sarsens were probably brought from about 20 miles away on the Marlborough Downs, perhaps in the area of Devil's Den (a sarsen trilithon, formerly set upon a mound), where ancient quarry hollows can still be seen today. They were dressed with hand-sized sarsen mauls immediately outside the entrance to Stonehenge.

Stonehenge continued in use as a cremation cemetery until at least 2400 BC, when burials were placed in the outer ditch. With over 60 cremation burials excavated from about half of the monument, this was Britain's largest burial ground during the third millennium BC. Possibly the last of these interments, around 2300 BC, was an inhumation burial, an adult male with multiple arrow wounds indicating that he had been shot from several directions. Whether he was executed or died in some other violent encounter is unknown. Around 2100 BC bluestones were erected in an oval at the centre of Stonehenge over the filled-in pit. About a century later, their plan was altered to form a horseshoe. Two final acts involved the digging of rings of holes around the outside of the sarsen circle, the Z Holes and the Y Holes. Radiocarbon dates indicate that these were constructed centuries apart, the Z Holes around 1800 BC and the Y Holes around 1600 BC. Their purpose is unknown. Stonehenge's avenue was constructed around 2400 BC, after the sarsens were erected. For its first 500 m, it was aligned on the midwinter sunset–midsummer sunrise solstice axis, thereafter curving eastwards and leading to a smaller henge on the bank of the River Avon.

Stonehenge is the subject of a bewildering range of theories concerning ley lines, cosmic energy paths, dowsed underwater stream crossings, crop circles, earth mysteries, ancient computers, astronomical markers of star constellations, megalithic units of measurement and healing properties. What can be empirically demonstrated is Stonehenge's solstitial alignment – the sun sets at midwinter solstice between the uprights of the great trilithon – whereas its associations with lunar movements are less certain (Ruggles in Cunliffe and Renfrew 1997). Recent examination of the geometry of Stonehenge indicates that it was laid out in regular units of a premetric measurement system still known today as 'chainage' (sub-divided into the 'rod, pole or perch' and its base unit of the 'long foot'; Chamberlain and Parker Pearson in Larsson and Parker Pearson 2007). One theory places Stonehenge as one half of a larger complex linked by the River Avon (Parker Pearson and Ramilisonina 1998). Its prediction that the timber circles at Durrington Walls (the Southern Circle, the Northern Circle and Woodhenge) are wooden counterparts associated with the domain of the living as opposed to Stonehenge's association with the dead has now been supported by results from new excavations (Parker Pearson, Pollard, Robinson and Thomas in Larsson and Parker Pearson 2007). The Southern Circle lay at the centre of a large village of small, square houses. This village was probably occupied for a few decades at most (between 2515 and 2480 BC) and probably on a seasonal basis, at least for the midwinter period on the basis of pig-tooth ageing. In addition, a newly found avenue links the Southern Circle to the River Avon. Its alignment on the midsummer solstice sunset, in contrast to the Southern Circle's alignment on the midwinter solstice sunrise, is notable as the opposite of that found at Stonehenge.

There is still a debate amongst geologists as to whether the Stonehenge bluestones were brought to the area by human agency or by earlier glaciers (Williams-Thorpe *et al.* in Cunliffe and Renfrew 1997); if the former, and this seems increasingly likely, then the Preseli Mountains also fit into this elaborate cosmology, perhaps materializing ancestral ties with south-west Wales for the builders of Stonehenge.

OVERVIEW

We find profound changes by the end of the Earlier Bronze Age, indicating new conceptions of territory, land, domesticity and identity. The axe, powerful symbol and tool of Neolithic societies, had been eclipsed by the dagger; by the Middle Bronze Age this form had become elaborated into long bronze rapiers which were effective weapons, along with bronze spearheads. As landscapes changed from zones of movement around sacred monuments and burial mounds to fixed places of occupation and unchangeable blocks of agricultural land, so people became rooted at the centres of their increasingly bounded domains (Barrett 1994). Identities also switched in emphasis from individual variations within a geographically uniform material culture to regional expressions of belonging. Changes in metalwork, with regional styles of palstaves, and in pottery, with the introduction of regional urn styles and Deverel–Rimbury styles, heralded a new regionalism. The increase in size and robustness of houses and the elaboration of food storage, preparation and consumption also point to a new emphasis on the household group and their intimate domestic rituals and routines. Finally, the treatment of the dead was changing from burial or cremation in big groups of large mounds to cremation without grave goods in small cemeteries behind the settlements. The role of the dead had changed from being visibly commemorated ancestral guardians of the wider communities' pastures to local markers of a new sense of place fixed on the homestead. As we move into the Later Bronze Age, people's very nature was changing; personal identities were defined less by lineage and more by territory. Control over land counted as much as control over people.

Acknowledgements

I would like to thank the following for permission to use information and illustrations: John Barrett, Colin Burgess, Mike Hamilton, Jon Humble, Niall Sharples, the Ashmolean Museum, Batsford, Blackwell, English Heritage, Orion Press and Sheffield City Museum. Analytical information on the cattle remains from Irthlingborough and Gayhurst is drawn from Jacqueline Towers's unpublished MSc dissertation, Bradford University.

Key texts

Barber, M., 2003. *Bronze and the Bronze Age: metalwork and society in Britain c. 2500–800 BC*. Stroud: Tempus.
Burgess, C.B., 1980. *The age of Stonehenge*. London: Phoenix. (Published in paperback in 2001.)
Clarke, D.V., Cowie, T. and Foxon, A., 1985. *Symbols of power at the time of Stonehenge*. Edinburgh: National Museum of Antiquities of Scotland.
Larsson, M. and Parker Pearson, M. (eds) 2007. *From Stonehenge to the Baltic: cultural diversity in the third millennium BC*. Oxford: British Archaeological Reports International Series 1692.
Lawson, A.J., 2007. *Chalkland: an archaeology of Stonehenge and its region*. Salisbury: Hobnob Press.
Parker Pearson, M., 2005. *Bronze Age Britain*. London: Batsford / English Heritage.

Bibliography

Allen, M.J., 2005. 'Beaker settlement and environment on the chalk downs of southern England', *Proceedings of the Prehistoric Society* 71, 219–46.

Armit, I., 1996. *The Archaeology of Skye and the Western Isles*. Edinburgh: Edinburgh University Press.

Barrett, J.C., 1994. *Fragments from antiquity: an archaeology of social life in Britain, 2900–1200 BC*. Oxford: Blackwell.

Barrett, J.C., Bradley, R. and Green, M., 1991. *Landscape, monuments and society: the prehistory of Cranborne Chase*. Cambridge: Cambridge University Press.

Bayliss, A., McAvoy, F. and Whittle, A., 2007. 'The world recreated: redating Silbury Hill in its monumental landscape', *Antiquity* 81, 26–53.

Blick, C.R. (ed.) 1991. *Early metallurgical sites in Great Britain BC 2000 to AD 1500*. London: The Institute of Metals.

Bradley, R., 1997. *Rock art and the prehistory of Atlantic Europe: signing the land*. London: Routledge.

Bradley, R., 2000. *The good stones: a new investigation of the Clava Cairns*. Edinburgh: Society of Antiquaries of Scotland.

Bradley, R., 2005. *The moon and the bonfire: an investigation of three stone circles in north-east Scotland*. Edinburgh: Society of Antiquaries of Scotland.

Brodie, N., 1994. *The Neolithic–Bronze Age transition in Britain: a critical review of some archaeological and craniological concepts*. Oxford: British Archaeological Reports 238.

Burgess, C. and Miket, R. (eds) 1976. *Settlement and economy in the third and second millennia BC*. Oxford: British Archaeological Reports 33.

Burl, A., 1993. *From Carnac to Callanish: the prehistoric stone rows and avenues of Britain, Ireland and Brittany*. New Haven: Yale University Press.

Chapman, A., 2007. 'A Bronze Age barrow cemetery and later boundaries, pit alignments and enclosures at Gayhurst Quarry, Newport Pagnell, Buckinghamshire', *Records of Buckinghamshire* 47, 83–211.

Clark, P. (ed.) 2004. *The Dover Bronze Age boat*. London: English Heritage.

Clarke, D.L., 1970. *Beaker pottery of Great Britain and Ireland*. Cambridge: Cambridge University Press.

Cleal, R.M.J., Walker, K.E. and Montague, R., 1995. *Stonehenge in its landscape: twentieth century excavations*. London: English Heritage.

Cunliffe, B. and Renfrew, A.C. (eds) 1997. *Science and Stonehenge*. Oxford: Oxford University Press (= Proceedings of the British Academy 92).

Davis, S. and Payne, S., 1993. 'A barrow full of cattle skulls', *Antiquity* 67, 12–22.

Dutton, A. and Fasham, P.J., 1994. 'Prehistoric copper mining on the Great Orme, Llandudno, Gwynedd', *Proceedings of the Prehistoric Society* 60, 245–86.

Edmonds, M., 1995. *Stone tools and society*. London: Batsford.

Ellison, A., 1980. 'Settlements and regional exchange: a case study', in Barrett, J. and Bradley, R. (eds) *Settlement and society in the British Later Bronze Age*. Oxford: British Archaeological Reports British Series 83, 127–40.

Evans, J., Chenery, C. and Fitzpatrick, A.P., 2006. 'Bronze Age childhood migration of individuals near Stonehenge, revealed by strontium and oxygen isotope tooth enamel analysis', *Archaeometry* 48, 309–21.

Fitzpatrick, A.P., 2002. '"The Amesbury Archer": a well-furnished Early Bronze Age burial in southern England', *Antiquity* 76, 629–30.

Fleming, A., 1988. *The Dartmoor Reaves: investigating prehistoric land divisions*. London: Batsford.

Gibson, A., 1982. *Beaker domestic sites: a study in the domestic pottery of the late third and early second millennia BC in the British Isles*. Oxford: British Archaeological Reports 107.

Kinnes, I. and Varndell, G. (eds) 1995. *'Unbaked urns of rudely shape': essays on British and Irish pottery for Ian Longworth*. London: British Museum.

Kinnes, I., Gibson, A., Ambers, J., Bowman, S., Leese, M. and Boast, R., 1991. 'Radiocarbon dating and British beakers: the British Museum programme', *Scottish Archaeological Review* 8, 35–68.

Last, J. (ed.) 2007. *Beyond the grave: new perspectives on barrows*. Oxford: Oxbow.

Longworth, I.H., 1984. *Collared Urns of the Bronze Age in Great Britain and Ireland*. Cambridge: Cambridge University Press.

Mukherjee, A.J., Berstan, R., Copley, M.S., Gibson, A.M. and Evershed, R.P., 2007. 'Compound-specific stable carbon isotopic detection of pig product processing in British Late Neolithic pottery', *Antiquity* 81, 743–54.

Needham, S.P., Bronk Ramsay, C., Coombs, D., Cartwright, C. and Pettitt, P., 1997. 'An independent chronology for British Bronze Age metalwork: the results of the Oxford Radiocarbon Accelerator Programme', *Archaeological Journal* 154, 55–107.

Nowakowski, J., 1991. 'Trethellan Farm, Newquay: the excavation of a lowland Bronze Age settlement and Iron Age cemetery', *Cornish Archaeology* 30, 5–242.

O'Brien, W., 2004. *Ross Island: mining, metal and society in early Ireland*. Galway: Galway University Press.

Pare, C., 2000. 'Bronze and the Bronze Age', in Pare, C. (ed.) *Metals make the world go round*. Oxford: Oxbow, 1–38.

Parker Pearson, M. and Ramilisonina, 1998. 'Stonehenge for the ancestors: the stones pass on the message', *Antiquity* 72, 308–26.

Parker Pearson, M., Sharples, N. and Symonds, J. with Mulville, J., Raven, J., Smith, H. and Woolf, A., 2004. *South Uist: archaeology and history of a Hebridean island*. Stroud: Tempus.

Parker Pearson, M., Cleal, R., Marshall, P., Needham, S., Pollard, J., Richards, C., Ruggles, C., Sheridan, A., Thomas, J., Tilley, C., Welham, K., Chamberlain, A., Chenery, C., Evans, J., Knüsel, C., Linford, N., Martin, L., Montgomery, J., Payne, A. and Richards, M., 2007. 'The age of Stonehenge', *Antiquity* 81, 617–39.

Parker Pearson, M., Chamberlain, A., Jay, M., Marshall, P., Pollard, J., Richards, C., Thomas, J., Tilley, C. and Welham, K., 2009. 'Who was buried at Stonehenge?' *Antiquity* 82, 23–39.

Renfrew, A.C. (ed.) 1973. *The explanation of culture change: models in prehistory*. London: Duckworth.

Richards, J.C., 2007. *Stonehenge: the story so far*. London: English Heritage.

Rowlands, M. J., 1976. *The organization of Middle Bronze Age metalworking*. Oxford: British Archaeological Reports 31.

Ruggles, C.L.N., 1999. *Astronomy in Prehistoric Britain and Ireland*. New Haven: Yale University Press.

Ruggles, C.L.N. and Whittle, A.W.R., 1981. *Astronomy and society in Britain during the period 4000–1500 BC*. Oxford: British Archaeological Reports 88.

Simpson, D.D.A., Murphy, E.M. and Gregory, R.A., 2006. *Excavations at Northton, Isle of Harris*. Oxford: British Archaeological Reports British Series 408.

Smith, R.W., 1984. 'The ecology of Neolithic farming systems as exemplified by the Avebury region of Wiltshire', *Proceedings of the Prehistoric Society* 50, 99–120.

Tipping, R., 1994. '"Ritual" floral tributes in the Scottish Bronze Age – palynological evidence', *Journal of Archaeological Science* 21, 133–39.

Tuckwell, A., 1975. 'Patterns of burial orientation in the round barrows of east Yorkshire', *Bulletin of the University of London Institute of Archaeology* 12, 95–123.

Woodward, A., 2000. *British barrows: a matter of life and death*. Stroud: Tempus.

6

THE LATER BRONZE AGE

Timothy Champion

INTRODUCTION

The later part of the second millennium BC was a period of major change in Britain and elsewhere in Europe. The earlier period of the Bronze Age had been characterized by evidence for burials and ritual monuments, but both of these cease at this time. The tradition of individual burial in a barrow died out, and in many parts of Britain there is no evidence for human burial for more than a millennium. There is little evidence for any significant activity at the major ceremonial monuments of the Late Neolithic and earlier Bronze Age after the middle of the second millennium BC.

Instead, the focus of archaeological attention turns to the rapidly increasing evidence for human settlement and for the division and exploitation of the agricultural landscape. There was a significant change in the nature and organization of settlement, resulting in more substantial and more visible sites, and traces of them are now found in much greater numbers in many areas of Britain. Settlements, their structures, and related finds, such as pottery and domestic food waste, now form one of the two main sources of information about later Bronze Age societies. The other main source is finds of metalwork, especially bronze: these are rare in the settlements, but single finds or collections of items, called hoards, often without any archaeological context, are very numerous.

The later Bronze Age was a period of radical change in the nature of prehistoric society. We do not need to think of a new population arriving from elsewhere with new ideas, but rather of a fundamental transformation in the culture of Bronze Age society, with the reorganization of the physical landscape and the introduction of new forms of social interaction.

CHRONOLOGY

The cessation of the series of burials containing associations of pottery, metalwork and other items, and the fact that much of the metalwork of the later Bronze Age is found unassociated with other material, mean that chronologies have to be constructed in different ways from previously.

The scheme introduced in Chapter 5 can be extended to one final phase:

- *Knighton Heath* (1400–1250 BC): end of the burial sequence, predominantly cremations with pottery and few other finds; pottery of the Deverel–Rimbury tradition; metalwork of the Taunton phase.

For the later Bronze Age the many finds of bronze metalwork have been used to provide the basis of a chronological scheme, since they can be subjected to careful typological analysis and the hoards offer many examples of associated objects (Burgess 1968; Megaw and Simpson 1979, 242–343; Needham 1996). The characteristic assemblages, named after the findspots of typical hoards, can be dated by comparison with the sequence worked out in continental Europe (O'Connor 1980) and refined by radiocarbon dates (Needham *et al.* 1997); they may overlap somewhat but can be arranged chronologically as follows:

- *Taunton* (1400–1275 BC): palstaves and flanged axes, long rapiers, spearheads; ornaments, including torcs, armlets, bracelets, finger rings and pins; specialist tools for crafts, especially carpentry and metalwork, such as the first socketed axes, socketed hammers, saws, chisels, anvils.
- *Penard* (1275–1140 BC): the first leaf-shaped swords, pegged spearheads.
- *Wilburton* (1140–1020 BC): swords, elaborate spearheads, socketed axes, vehicle and horse trappings, sheet-metal cauldrons (Figure 6.1).
- *Blackmoor* (1020–950 BC): Wilburton types, with early versions of Ewart Park phase objects.
- *Ewart Park* (920–800 BC): swords, regional varieties of spearheads and socketed axes, many types of tools such as knives and gouges, buckets and cauldrons, pins and other ornaments (Figure 6.2).
- *Llyn Fawr* (800–700 BC): the final phase of the Bronze Age industry, overlapping the beginning of the Iron Age: longer swords, heavy socketed axes, horse trappings.

This well-established scheme is of restricted use, however, since finds of metalwork on settlement sites or in association with other material such as pottery are comparatively rare. A parallel sequence based on pottery has also been evolved for southern Britain, using the evidence of typology, associated finds and radiocarbon to give absolute dates. The phases are:

- *Deverel–Rimbury* (named after two sites in Dorset: 1600–1100 BC): regional varieties of coarse-ware bucket urns and fine-ware globular urns; Trevisker pottery is a contemporary tradition in the south-west (Figure 6.3).

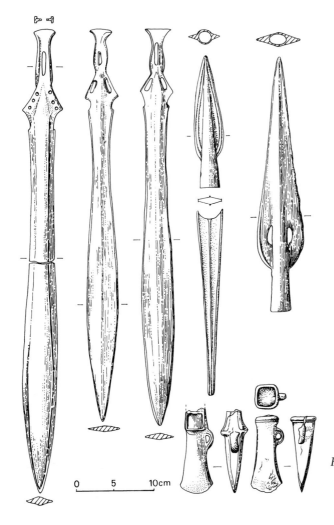

Figure 6.1 Examples of bronzes of the Wilburton assemblage.

Source: Megaw and Simpson, 1979, Fig. 6.27

- *Post-Deverel–Rimbury plain ware* (1100–800 BC): coarse-ware jars undecorated except for finger-tipping, and finer cups (Figure 6.4).
- *Post-Deverel–Rimbury decorated ware* (or Earliest Iron Age) (800–600 BC): similar forms with an increased range of incised and inlaid decoration and applied cordons, overlapping the start of the Iron Age.

CHANGING PERCEPTIONS

Our vision of the later Bronze Age has changed greatly in recent years, and these changes derive from several different sources: reconsideration of old evidence in the light of developing knowledge, especially for the fixing of a correct chronology for the period; new discoveries in the field; the application of new scientific techniques; and the emergence of new theoretical and interpretative approaches to the prehistoric past.

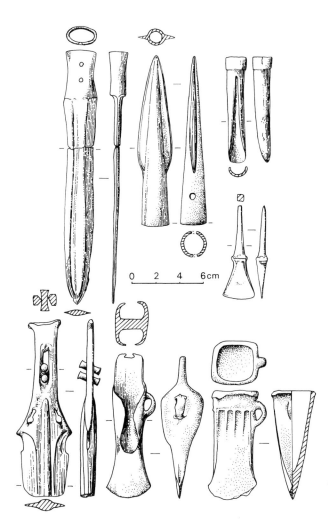

0   2   4   6 cm

Figure 6.2   Examples of bronzes of the
Ewart Park assemblage.
Source: Megaw and Simpson,
1979, Fig. 6.32

Radiocarbon dating has had a very great impact in this period, helped by the absence of the calibration problems that affect its use for the Iron Age. The establishment of a reliable chronology by this means has been fundamental to all research, since it has allowed the integration of the metalwork and the ceramic and settlement chronologies, together with environmental evidence, despite the comparative lack of associated finds. The newly confirmed absolute dates have also proved to be substantially earlier than those previously suggested. The major changes in the archaeological record can now be seen to have started by the middle of the second millennium BC, while the production, circulation and deposition of bronze can be shown to have gone into a rapid decline around 800 BC (Needham 2007).

Other scientific methods have also contributed, especially on questions of climate, environment and agricultural economy, but one set of techniques has been of particular significance. Analysis of

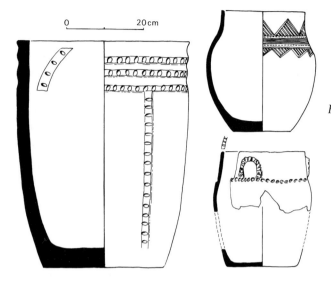

Figure 6.3 Deverel–Rimbury pottery.

Sources: (*left and upper right*) Annable, F.K. and Simpson, D.D.A., 1964. *Guide catalogue of the Neolithic and Bronze Age collections in Devizes Museum*. Devizes: Wiltshire Archaeological and Natural History Society, Figs 576 and 566 respectively. (*lower right*) Dacre, M. and Ellison, A., 1981. 'A Bronze Age urn cemetery at Kimpton, Hampshire', *Proceedings of the Prehistoric Society* 47, 147–203, Fig. 19

metalwork, especially bronze, has allowed different sources of metal to be characterized by their trace elements. In this way the supply and circulation of metal in different regions at different times can be monitored. In some cases the particular types of metal can be identified with specific geological origins, giving important insights into long-distance exchange in prehistory.

One other technical development that has had a significant impact is the availability of cheap and effective metal detectors. One of the commonest types of object found with these devices

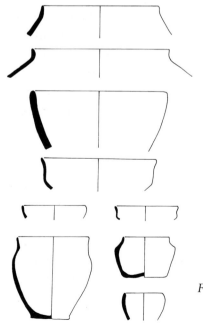

Figure 6.4 Pottery of the Post-Deverel–Rimbury undecorated phase.

Source: Bradley *et al.* 1980, Fig. 11

has been late Bronze Age metalwork; though many finds have not been reported, and others lack good documentation, in some regions the rate of discoveries has been so fast that it has been almost impossible to keep up with the new information. Though it has not fundamentally changed our knowledge of the types of metalwork and their distribution, it has produced a significant change in our perception of the quantity of metal in circulation in the period.

Much new evidence for later Bronze Age settlement and landscape organization was discovered from the 1970s onwards. Many sites of this period have left little or no surface evidence, and even their traces in the subsoil are slight; in many cases, it was the development of methods for stripping large areas that allowed such sites to be recognized for the first time. The proliferation from the 1990s of field investigations funded by developers provided much evidence for the extent and density of later Bronze Age occupation. Other important innovations were large-scale surveys, which focused on the evolution of later prehistoric landscape organization.

Perhaps the most important changes in our perception of the later Bronze Age, however, derive from new theoretical approaches to the understanding of the archaeological record. Greater emphasis has been placed on understanding the patterns in the material record as evidence for the nature of economy and society rather than as an end in itself; recent studies have focused on questions of economy, ritual and settlement organization, and have tended to concentrate on such topics as the changing nature of domestic activities, for example food preparation and consumption as shown by changes in the styles and shapes of pottery; the development of craft production indicated by increasing production of specialist tools; or the meaning and value of material culture such as items of bronze and the social contexts in which they were used.

Particular attention has also been paid to the patterns of deposition that have shaped the archaeological record. It is clear that the burials and other deposits of the late Neolithic and early Bronze Age were carefully selected and deposited in a highly structured way, and that the meaning of these patterns needs interpretation. It would be easy to think that, with the appearance of settlements as one of the major sources of evidence, we were dealing with much simpler and more obvious processes of loss and waste disposal, but it is now clear that these deposits too were carefully structured. Similarly, recent work on bronze finds has focused on the recognition that these finds are more a product of structured and selective deposition than an indication of production.

ENVIRONMENT AND AGRICULTURE

The later Bronze Age was a time of major environmental change. The late Neolithic and earlier Bronze Age had been a period of favourable climate, marginally but significantly warmer and drier than today. The prehistoric people of Britain exploited these conditions to extend their farming into new environments, but this expansion was not sustainable, and by the end of the Bronze Age human occupation had contracted drastically. In part this was due to natural causes, in part to previous human activity. Suggestions that the retreat from some northern uplands was sudden, and attributable to dust-clouds from volcanic activity in Iceland, are not widely accepted (Cowie and Shepherd 2003).

Towards 1000 BC a period of climatic deterioration began. This is seen particularly in the changing rate of growth in peat bogs, and involved a trend to colder and wetter conditions. The growing season for crops was shortened, and existing agricultural practices became increasingly problematic, especially in many upland areas. In some environments, especially those that would become the open upland moors, the increased rainfall, combined with soil changes resulting from human exploitation, produced waterlogging and peat growth. Human over-exploitation also reduced other areas, such as the acid heathlands of the Hampshire–Dorset basin, to their present state. The combination of natural processes and the effects of earlier agriculture resulted in an environment that was increasingly less favourable. All this placed a premium on the soils which were able to withstand more intensive exploitation and sustain their productivity, especially those of the major river valleys and the more fertile lowlands of southern and eastern Britain.

In many parts of Britain, the later Bronze Age shows clear evidence for extensive woodland clearance and the establishment of a predominantly open arable and grassland landscape. Though the Early Neolithic is often regarded as the period when these processes began, it is not until the later second millennium that they culminated in an open and extensively managed environment; the new ways in which this environment was organized, with fields, trackways and other facilities, is discussed below. The agricultural economy also shows other major changes at this time, though their relationship to climatic, environmental or social pressures is not clear. It was a system of mixed agriculture exploiting crops and animals in more complex and more intensive ways than before. In some regions there were changes in the dominant crop species, as new varieties of wheat and barley were adopted, and beans and rye were introduced. Agricultural produce was also treated in new ways, with pits and granaries for grain storage; the salt industry allowed the preservation and transport of meat. Changing attitudes to agriculture and food can also be seen in their increasing involvement in ritual activities. As we will see below, there was a new concern for the preparation and serving of food, much of it concerned with prestige feasting. The growing practice of making special deposits in boundary ditches and storage pits also suggests a focus of ritual very different from that of the earlier Bronze Age. Equally important were new ways of using agriculture for products other than food. Animals were increasingly used for traction, and sheep became for the first time an important source of wool for textiles.

LANDSCAPES AND SETTLEMENTS

The archaeological evidence for the later Bronze Age varies greatly from region to region (Barrett and Bradley 1980; Brück 2001). This variation is mostly due to the very uneven coverage of modern archaeological observation. Some regions, such as Wessex and the Thames Valley, have received much attention, but elsewhere, as in Wales, almost nothing is known of contemporary settlement.

The most striking feature of the archaeological record of this period is the widespread occurrence of organized systems of landscape divisions and fields, often laid out over very large areas. Their form varies considerably in detail, as does their chronology; in some cases fields are overlain by one or more other systems on different orientations. Their functions may also have varied; a common feature is the provision of trackways through the fields in addition to wells and waterholes, indicating livestock management, but in other cases environmental evidence shows a regime of mixed arable and pastoral farming. The increased emphasis on the division of land into field systems or larger territories may have been due to different causes at different times and places; it may indicate the growing importance of land as a scarce resource and changing attitudes to the right to use it or even own it, but it was also a means for its more efficient and intensive exploitation.

Landscape organization of this kind is now well documented in many areas of southern and eastern England (Yates 2007). In some cases extensive modern development has allowed a wider examination of the detailed organization of these systems and their associated settlements, as at Hornchurch, Essex (Guttman and Last 2000) or Heathrow Terminal 5 to the west of London (Framework Archaeology 2006). Elsewhere, remnants of these systems still survive, as on parts of the South Downs or on Salisbury Plain; there, long bank and ditch earthworks were constructed, dividing the land into territories each containing settlements,

Figure 6.5   Simplified plan of Bronze Age land divisions on Dartmoor. Land above 500 m shaded.
    Source: Fleming 2008, Fig. 30

arable and pastoral land (Bradley *et al.* 1994). One of the most striking examples is on Dartmoor (Fleming 2008). This upland block had been occupied earlier in the Bronze Age, but after about 1400 BC the landscape was divided into a pattern of territories which all contained valley land, upland and access to the open moor (Figure 6.5). The unenclosed moorland was separated from the lower land by stone banks, called reaves, and other reaves divided up the territories and defined field systems within them, with settlements scattered through the territories. Similar field systems and settlements are known elsewhere in the south-west, especially in the upland and marginal areas such as Bodmin Moor and Scilly. Further north, in the Midlands, Wales and northern England and Scotland, the evidence is much less clear. In north-east Yorkshire an extensive system of linear earthworks probably dating from around 1000 BC divided the area below the moors into a series of territories or estates with equal access to natural resources (Spratt 1989), and such developments may well have been more common than we currently recognize.

Many of these field systems appear not to have been maintained after the Bronze Age. In some upland zones, such as Dartmoor, the whole area was abandoned, while in lowland zones the fields may still have survived in the form of hedges, but the landscape was exploited in a much less intensive manner. On Salisbury Plain, many of these earthworks went out of use, but at some boundary junctions within this system new enclosures were founded, and these played an important role in the emergence of the Iron Age landscape with hillforts.

Another feature of the changing archaeological record is the proliferation of sites of human occupation. In contrast to earlier periods, settlements are now more permanent, with a greater investment of energy in the building of houses and associated structures. A distinctive tradition of circular structures, whether of timber or stone, was adopted and survived, with much variation, through the Iron Age. Other elements of these sites include small structures interpreted as granaries, and pits for storage or various craft activities. Examples of such sites in

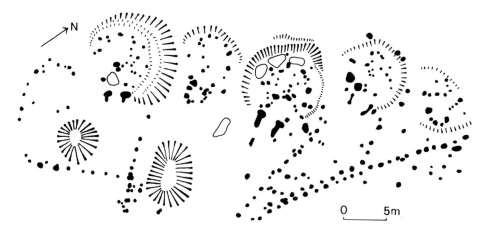

Figure 6.6   Plan of Black Patch Bronze Age settlement.
      Source: Drewett 1982, Fig. 9

the Middle Bronze Age are best known in southern England. At South Lodge, in Cranborne Chase, Dorset (Barrett *et al.* 1991), a small settlement developed in a pre-existing field system. One of the most fully excavated sites is at Black Patch, East Sussex (Drewett 1982), where five circular structures were located on one settlement platform (Figure 6.6). These have been interpreted as a single household cluster, in which different buildings had different functions such as sleeping accommodation for various members of the group, eating, food preparation, craft activities, animal shelter. Small settlements made up of such household clusters may have been typical of this region in the late second millennium, while some fortified sites suggest the emergence of new forms of prestige (Ellison 1981). In the Late Bronze Age a wider range of types of site includes numerous small occupation sites such as Aldermaston Wharf (Bradley *et al.* 1980) or Reading Business Park (Moore and Jennings 1992; Brossler *et al.* 2004); these were unenclosed clusters of round houses and pits, showing evidence for a mixed agricultural economy and craft activity such as textile production, but little metalwork or other wealth.

Evidence from further north is less clear and little is yet known about the sites of this period in the Midlands and the north-west. In the Welsh Marches hilltop sites were being occupied by the end of the Bronze Age (Halstead 2005). Sites at Dinorben, Moel-y-Gaer and the Breiddin (Musson 1991) were all occupied by then, but the construction of defences and their development as hillforts may not have occurred until the beginning of the Iron Age. Sites in northern England consisting of platforms terraced into the hill slope for round houses belong to the early first millennium BC, and these sites extend well into Scotland, where, particularly north of the Forth–Clyde isthmus, there are also many hut circles, penannular dry-stone footings for houses, with associated clearances and field walls, some of which certainly belong to this period (McCullagh and Tipping 1998). Sites in Atlantic Scotland show that a tradition of building substantial round structures in stone had begun (Henderson 2007, 101–103). At Jarlshof, Shetland, a settlement with stone houses has also produced important evidence of Late Bronze Age metalworking.

As well as these settlements, there were other, more distinctive types of site (Brück 2007). One such feature of the settlement evidence of eastern England after 900 BC is a class of defended enclosure, commonest in the region of the lower Thames estuary, but spreading as far north as Thwing, Yorkshire. They were surrounded by impressive defences of timber and earth, with external ditches; some show precisely geometric plans, circular at Mucking North Ring (Bond 1988) and square at Lofts Farm, Essex (Brown 1988) (Figure 6.7). An excavated example at Springfield Lyons, Essex (Buckley and Hedges 1987) shows a carefully organized interior plan with a large circular house, while at Hornchurch a similar site was integrated into a large field system. Such elaborate enclosures may well represent the emergence of new elites towards the end of the Bronze Age, or at least new ways of displaying such status. Another type of site associated with the demonstration of status has been recognized, mainly in north Wiltshire, for example at Potterne (Lawson 2000) and East Chisenbury (McOmish 1996); these are very large middens, with high densities of pottery, animal bone and metalwork. They must represent a regional type of high-status site with an emphasis on the social rituals of feasting.

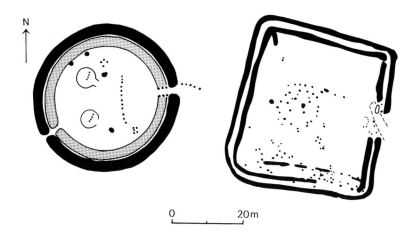

Figure 6.7   Simplified plans of Mucking North Ring (left) and Lofts Farm (right).
Sources: (*left*) Bond 1988, Fig. 3 (*right*) Brown 1988, Fig. 4

More unusual is the site on the Thames at Runnymede Bridge, Surrey (Needham 1991). Here there was a site with a wooden piled waterfront, producing many bronze objects and other imports such as shale and amber, and evidence for metalworking. Sites such as this may have been key links in the exchange system which brought exotic materials into Britain and reworked them and redistributed them into the interior.

The most striking site of the whole British later Bronze Age has been excavated at Flag Fen, Peterborough (Pryor 2001). As the fens grew wetter and formed a shallow inlet, a massive timber platform was constructed about 1000 BC in the open water at the mouth of a bay between areas of dense occupation and field systems. It was linked to the dry land on either side of the bay by an alignment of vertical posts more than a kilometre long. In the peat alongside this alignment were found nearly 300 metal items, together with animal bones and pottery, all originally dropped or carefully placed into the water of the bay. The metal items are mainly bronze, but a few are pure tin; most belong to the later Bronze Age, but some are of Iron Age date. They include many rings, pins and other small items, as well as swords, spears and daggers, and fragments of bronze helmets. This extraordinary site shows a long-lasting tradition of depositing objects in watery places, which can be matched at a number of other sites. One type of site found in many parts of Britain is burnt stone mounds (Buckley 1990). Though best documented in northern Scotland and the Isle of Man, they are being found in increasing numbers as far south as the New Forest, and radiocarbon dates place them mainly in the second and early first millennia BC. They consist of mounds or spreads of stone which has been heated; many of them are near a water supply, and in some excavated examples water troughs are associated with them. Liddle, on South Ronaldsay, Orkney, is a well-excavated example (Hedges 1975). It is assumed that the stone was heated in a fire and placed in the water to boil it, and several functions have been suggested, such as cooking places or sweat lodges (an analogy with ethnographically recorded practices in North America), though some have a possible link with metalworking. Although they are a very common element of the Bronze Age record, their true function is far from clear, and indeed they may derive from many different operations.

CRAFT, TECHNOLOGY AND TRADE

Much of the output of non-agricultural production in the Bronze Age is now lost to us, especially items of organic materials, but scattered evidence of raw material extraction, specialist tools and waste products allows us to form a picture of the developing technology and craft skills of the period.

The flint mines which had been so important a source of raw material in the earlier Bronze Age went out of use. Flint was still used to make tools, but they were simpler and more utilitarian than before; Late Bronze Age flint assemblages are often little more than comparatively crude flakes. The explanation of this change is complex: there may have been an alternative and better source, especially metal, for the many different tools needed; alternatively, an elaborate technology was now unnecessary for stone tools as they were no longer used for symbolically important social roles.

Metal ores were exploited at several locations in western Britain. Deep mines for copper are known from Wales, especially at Great Orme, Llandudno (see also Chapter 4). Analyses of trace elements suggest that a number of western copper sources were used at different times, though copper was also imported from the Continent. Gold, tin and lead were also won, but little is known about their extraction. Other mineral resources exploited include shale from Dorset, used mainly for manufacturing bracelets.

One important new industry was salt-making. At sites along the east and south coasts from Lincolnshire to Dorset seawater was evaporated in fired clay containers to extract the salt, which could then be traded inland. The demand for salt may have arisen from a fashionable taste for salty food, but more probably it was related to a reorganization of food production and a growing need to preserve, store and trade foodstuffs.

Organic materials such as cloth and leather are more problematic. Though no actual examples have survived, they certainly provided finished products that played a critical role in domestic and social life. The best evidence for leather-working is seen in specialized knives first produced in the later Bronze Age, suggesting a new level of craft specialism and an increased importance for non-meat products of cattle. Textiles are best demonstrated by spindle-whorls and loom-weights which become common finds at this point, especially in southern Britain. The main products were presumably clothes. This important new use for sheep as providers of wool would have had a significant effect on their role in the agricultural economy, and textiles would have provided a new medium for decoration and the representation of individual identities.

A little more has survived to demonstrate Bronze Age wood-working skills. A specialized toolkit comprising saws, chisels and gouges made of bronze was produced, as well as the

Figure 6.8 The Dover Bronze Age boat during excavation.

Source: Courtesy of the Canterbury Archaeological Trust

axes which had a variety of functions. The more substantial nature of settlement structures demanded an appropriate level of carpentry, and by the end of the Bronze Age wheeled vehicles were being built. The sewn-plank boats known from Dover (Clark 2004) (Figure 6.8) and elsewhere show us the achievements of Bronze Age skills, and the mass of material from Flag Fen casts much new light on wood-working techniques.

The industries which have left the most evidence are bronze and pottery making. The range of bronze types produced in the later Bronze Age, and the developing technologies required to make them, are discussed in more detail below, but here we can note than the bronze industry needed a supply of copper, tin and lead, all of which were of limited geological distribution and were therefore the focus for long-distance exchange mechanisms; trace element analysis of copper has revealed the use of sources from western Britain, but much of the bronze metalwork of the Wilburton phase in eastern England was made from a distinctive copper which originated in the Alpine region and continued to circulate in later periods, increasingly alloyed with metal from other sources as objects were melted down and recycled (Northover 1982). In the later phases of the Bronze Age large collections of broken bronze items indicate the collection and recycling of scrap metal, in addition to supplies of new metal.

The complexity of the technology, as well as the problems of access to supplies of metal, suggests that bronze working was a specialist skill, and the development of specialized tools such as hammers and anvils supports this. Study of the bronze items themselves suggests

that some types, such as tools, ornaments and small spearheads, were made for comparatively local distribution and use, while other larger or more complex types, such as swords,
were made by a smaller number of more skilled specialists and distributed more widely.

Pottery production also shows a similar pattern. In the Deverel–Rimbury phase, the coarse-
ware jars were made from local materials for local use, while the globular urns and other
finer wares were distributed over a wider area. Less is known about the production of vessels
in the plain-ware phase, but these again seem mostly to have been of local production. The
Deverel–Rimbury and related traditions comprised a very limited range of forms, mainly
large jars and some smaller vessels, mostly in finer wares. In the plain-ware phase (Barrett
1980), there is a greatly expanded range of forms, with more jar types, and especially some
bowls and cups. These smaller vessels were often made in finer wares with careful surface
finishing, and in the final phase were often the object of decoration. These trends indicate
new social uses for pottery, and in particular its role in the serving and consumption of food
and drink.

The evidence for some of these crafts, especially textiles and some pottery making,
suggests that they were widespread domestic activities. That does not mean that every
household practised them, though the majority probably did; it is also likely that such
activities were allocated in some way on the basis of age and gender within the household. Other crafts were certainly more specialized; the complexity of the technology, and
the skills and practical knowledge needed, the production of specialized tools found in
complete toolkits and the quality of some of the finished products all argue for the existence of specialists, though the precise social context in which they worked and their relationship to other groups in society are unclear. Some may have been full-time specialists,
many were also engaged in agricultural production; some may have worked solely for a
particular patron, producing prestige items, others were integrated into a more diverse
network of social relationships.

The corollary of specialist production and craft industries which use rare raw materials
is the need for transport and distribution. Trevisker pottery from Cornwall found in Kent
and shale from Dorset at Flag Fen show how such items could travel; and links extended
overseas, as Alpine copper, Baltic amber and Irish gold show. We have already seen how
metal ores from western Britain and the Continent were used to supply other regions, and
the extensive imitation of fashions, especially in metalwork, suggests that some items were
circulating very widely. Much of this trade is invisible, except through scientific analysis,
but occasionally we can catch a glimpse of it. Two collections of metal objects found off
the coast of southern England, at Dover, Kent, and Salcombe, Devon, are the result of
shipwrecks in the course of such trade; the Dover assemblage consisted mainly of types
from France otherwise unknown in Britain, and would have been melted down to cast
local forms. Finds of sewn-plank boats, as at Dover or North Ferriby, Yorkshire, are good
evidence not only of carpentry and boat-building skills, but also for the importance of
sea-borne trade.

PRODUCTION, USE AND DEPOSITION OF BRONZE

The bronze industry has been intensively studied, not just because bronze objects survive well and are plentiful, but because they contain important evidence for chronology, technology, trade and many other aspects of Bronze Age society. But interpreting this mass of evidence is not easy; there are difficult and interlocking questions relating to supply, production, distribution, use and deposition, many of which are not yet resolved (Barber 2003).

We have already seen that copper and tin sources from the west of Britain were used throughout the later Bronze Age, and that there was major importation of Alpine copper from the eleventh century BC, but the interpretation of this evidence is problematic. Was it a matter of supply and demand, with new sources exploited to meet rising demand for bronze? This is perhaps too modern a view of the prehistoric economy; bronze supply may have been determined by more social or political relationships between south-eastern Britain and the Continent, or a particular significance might have been attached to imported metal simply because it was from far away. Another problem concerns the abundance or scarcity of supply. The volume of bronze objects found can be read as implying a plentiful supply, but there have been no studies of use wear to test how long objects were in use, and the large number of finds from the later phases consisting of scrap for recycling may suggest that there were chronic shortages of raw materials. There can be little doubt that control of access to supplies of metal, as well as control of the technical skills to work it, was an important source of power in the later Bronze Age.

On questions of production, the evidence can be used most clearly for the history of technical progress (Megaw and Simpson 1979, 242–59 and 299–339). The proliferation of socketed spearheads, hammers and axes from the Taunton phase onwards required the use of three-piece moulds to make hollow castings; the replacement of stone and bronze moulds by non-reusable clay ones made larger and more complex castings possible, such as swords. Casting technology was also improved by the addition of a small percentage of lead to the alloy; different alloys were carefully selected for different purposes. The techniques needed to hammer, shape, join, decorate and strengthen large sheet-metal objects were also developed, and impressive new items such as cauldrons, shields and helmets were produced.

Questions about the organization of production are more difficult to answer. Finds of bronze objects are determined by patterns of use and loss or deposition, and they are therefore direct evidence for those activities rather than for production. The limited finds of production debris do not tell us much about the social context of manufacture and usage, and even their location does not always coincide with the distribution of finds of similar finished objects.

Two examples can illustrate some further problems in understanding the production and use of bronze. At Flag Fen, many of the items deposited in the water were of poor quality and unsuitable for functional use; one of the swords was a miniature. Some items were of tin, and there is also nearby evidence for the casting of tin. It is probable that these items were made specially for deposition; their form seems to have been more important than their technical quality, and they had no 'use' except to be deposited. The second example concerns the role of axes in the later Bronze Age. There are many hoards which contain a large number of axes, many of them broken; at the end of the Bronze Age there is a particular type of socketed axe found in considerable quantities in Brittany and southern England. These Armorican axes are highly standardized in size and weight and show little sign of use; some axes are even made of pure lead. They were produced as standard quantities of metal, for their value as a commodity for exchange rather than as functioning axes, and pose the question whether the large numbers of axes found from earlier phases may have been used in the same way. These examples suggest that we should be wary of inferring a utilitarian function from form or assuming modern concepts of quality, and that we should in general be careful in trying to apply concepts derived from modern economies to the Bronze Age.

The major factors influencing the presence of bronzes in the archaeological record are the patterns of prehistoric deposition and modern recovery. One common method of describing them, using terms such as stray finds, settlement or river finds, or hoards, tells us more about how and where the objects were found than about how or why they were deposited. Many items are found on their own, without further archaeological context; little can be said about such 'stray finds', but this may be due mostly to the circumstances of recovery. Finds from settlements are rare, mainly small or broken items, which might be understood as casual losses, but some finds suggest more deliberate deposition. At Springfield Lyons a dump of metalworking material in a ditch terminal was a deliberate ritual act, and the finds of metal from a ditch at Petters Sportsfield, Surrey, may have been a similar ritual deposit associated with the abandonment of the site (Needham 1990). Recent work suggests that hoards may have been more commonly deposited within settlements than was previously thought (Barber 2003, 43–78).

One important locus for deposition was in watery places such as rivers, lakes and bogs (Bradley 1998). These may be called hoards if they are found together, for instance in a dried-up fen or a drained lake, but they were assembled as a result of many individual acts of deposition over a long period, made with the intention that the items should not be retrieved. We have already seen the evidence from Flag Fen, and there are other concentrations of metalwork elsewhere in the Fens; similar practices are well known from major rivers, especially the Thames, which has a long history of dredging and archaeological observation. The material recovered from the river bed spans a very long period, but there are particular concentrations of later Bronze Age metalwork in certain stretches. These are not randomly chosen items, but include especially swords and certain types of spearhead. Human skeletal remains have also been found in the river, and again there is a concentration of dated examples in the later Bronze Age, suggesting a link between the deposition of metalwork and of other classes of objects (Bradley and Gordon 1988). There are similar deposits from lakes such as Duddingston Loch in Edinburgh, and many other wet places. Previous explanations invoking casual loss in transit or battle must be rejected, and we must recognize a deliberate practice of ritual deposition. Items selected for such deposition were a carefully selected and unrepresentative sample of the available repertoire of bronze, and the meaning associated with individual forms was obviously very significant. The possible implications of such a practice of votive deposits are discussed in the next section.

The final type of bronze find to be considered are the hoards found on dry land. These appear to be deposited in a single act and therefore raise two separate questions: the reasons for assembling the collection and the reasons for depositing and not recovering it. Some of these hoards have been classified on the basis of their contents: 'personal hoards' are the ornaments owned by an individual, 'craftsmen's hoards' contain the tools of a specialist such as a carpenter or metalsmith, and 'merchants' hoards' include newly finished items awaiting distribution. Many hoards, as we have seen, contain scrap or axes representing an exchange commodity, and these were assembled as part of the process of recycling and redistributing bronze metal. Many of these hoards contain items on the periphery of their known distribution, and these hoards are particularly frequent in marginal locations such as the lower Thames Estuary. Like the French objects interrupted in transit by the Dover shipwreck, the items in these hoards may have been assembled for redistribution to another region, their value being more as a commodity for exchange than in their specific form.

This explanation does not fit every such hoard, nor will it explain all the regional and chronological patterns of variation in hoard composition. Above all, it does not address the question of why the hoards were deposited. Some appear to have been deposited within settlements, but many were not. The hiding of hoards for security at times of unrest or danger is a well-known practice; a certain proportion were inevitably never found again, and this may account for at least some of the later Bronze Age finds. Nevertheless, it does conjure up an extraordinary picture of a very disturbed period if so many such concealed hoards were never recovered, and other ideas need to be explored.

Although some items, especially small ones, may have been accidentally lost, and in other cases people may have been prevented from recovering deliberately concealed objects, we should perhaps think of the vast majority of bronze finds as the result of deliberate deposition with no intention of recovery. Whether found singly or in large collections, within settlements or isolated, in wet places or dry, these objects were deposited as part of a widespread and long-lasting practice of ritual deposition. We have already seen above some evidence for association with the abandonment of sites, but such acts of deposition may have been part of many different rituals.

These deposits show considerable regional and chronological variation, but some broad patterns emerge, especially in the selection of weaponry. In the south-east, many hoards include swords with a characteristic long tip (which is responsible for them being named carp's tongue swords), spearheads and associated items from belt fittings or even a sort of uniform; this set of equipment is also found in northern and western France. Elsewhere in southern England spears are the commonest weapons; in much of the Midlands region there are hoards containing a typical form of barbed spearhead, termed the Broadward type; and in the north hoards are dominated by swords.

LATER BRONZE AGE SOCIETY

The changes in economy, technology, material culture and ritual described above all add up to a major transformation of society in the later Bronze Age. The ritual monuments and burials which had formed such an important part of the archaeological record of the earlier Bronze Age, and were the prime focus for the playing out of social relationships and claims to authority at that time, had gone out of use, and in their place we find new sources of prestige and new social opportunities.

The earlier tradition of burial in a barrow died out, after a Middle Bronze Age phase of urned cremations frequently found as secondary deposits in or near barrows. Thereafter, there is little evidence for formal burial, though a growing number of cremations with or without urns is now being recognized, some placed within small kerb cairns (Brück 1995). This lack of a regularly recoverable burial rite does not mean that the dead were disposed of with any less respect, or that such ceremonies were no longer the occasion of elaborate rituals: it just means that, whatever they finally did with the remains of the dead, archaeologists cannot regularly find it. Whatever funerary rites were adopted, the ancestors no longer played the same central role as before, and the final disposal of the remains of the dead ceased to play such a central social role; instead, new forms of social activity, with their related material culture, were introduced. Four such themes can be recognized.

The most obvious is the conspicuous consumption of wealth through the ritual deposition of bronze. Such deposits were an indication of an individual's status, and in particular control over access to rare materials and technologies; whether as part of funeral ceremonies or as gifts to the gods, such deposits could be highly public statements about an individual's identity. To modern eyes such a practice may seem an inexplicable waste, but the value of bronze may have lain in the status conferred by the ability to acquire it, to possess it and to discard it, and its use in the demonstration of such status, as much as in any functional utility as a tool.

The second theme is warfare. The use of slashing swords and defensive armour suggests a new form of combat, and a new status for the fully armoured warrior. The edges of many swords show signs of use, but the shields and helmets appear too thin to have offered much protection in battle and may have been more for display, though one shield seems to have been pierced by a spear. The swords and armour were certainly some of the most elaborate products of the Bronze Age smiths, requiring many complex skills, and whether they were worn in real battles, in symbolic rituals of warfare or simply in showy parade, they were undoubtedly a very obvious symbol of power.

The third theme concerns feasting, the other main function for which sheet bronze was used. Cauldrons and their associated flesh-hooks represent the material evidence of the ritualized preparation and serving of meat, while finds of pottery and animal bones from some sites have also been interpreted in this way.

Finally, wheeled vehicles represented the most complex technological achievements of the Bronze Age, demanding high levels of skill in carpentry, metalwork, leatherwork and animal management.

The use to which such wagons were put is not clear. There may have been utilitarian versions, but others probably had a significant ritual role; wheeled vehicles have remained a favourite theme for lavish expenditure and symbolic display ever since. The recovery of a hoard of vehicle parts near the summit of Horsehope, Peeblesshire, indicates something of the possibilities.

These new areas of social activity show the relationship between prestige, material culture and technology; the demand for such items was a powerful stimulus to the development of technical skills by innovation and imitation. Control over access to such items and the skill to produce them were an important basis for prestige in later Bronze Age society and a means of demonstrating it. The importance of feasting links these ideas to the consumption of food, but the full articulation of the system of prestige goods to the agricultural economy is not clear. The intensification of agricultural production, the increasing signs of land division and the development of the salt industry all suggest that control over the production and distribution of food was also an important feature of later Bronze Age society.

The material evidence for these prestige activities assumes a high profile in the archaeological record, creating an inevitable emphasis on the hierarchical nature of later Bronze Age society, but it is not clear how extreme such inequalities were or how they were manifested in daily life. Nor are these relationships the only ones of interest, though they may be the most obvious. The emerging role of specialist craft producers has been discussed above, but relationships of age and gender may also have been changing at this time and may have been more meaningful for most people's lives, even if it is difficult to detect them; the changing nature of pottery produced in the later Bronze Age, at least in southern Britain, provides one possible insight and suggests that the domestic rituals of preparing, serving and consuming food were being ordered in new ways throughout society (Barrett 1989).

BRITAIN IN WIDER PERSPECTIVE

Britain was not isolated, and we have already seen some of the evidence for contacts in the form of boats and continental imports. The links ran much deeper, however, and can be seen in a wide range of stylistic, technological, economic and ritual developments, which affected many areas of temperate Europe at this time (Harding 2000). They are particularly clear in the material culture of the elite, and demonstrate the existence of social relationships through which knowledge of new styles and technologies could be transmitted, as well as facilitating the movement of people and objects.

New industries such as salt and textiles were matched by similar developments elsewhere in Europe, as were other changes in the agricultural economy: new crops, more emphasis on storage, increased evidence for territorial division and ultimately field systems are all seen throughout Europe, especially in the north and west, though the precise chronology is regionally very variable.

Close contacts with continental Europe can be seen in many features of Bronze Age material culture, most obviously in metalwork, where both style and technology show similar patterns of development (O'Connor 1980). The ornament styles of the Taunton phase link Britain particularly closely to northern Europe, but later connections are to western and central Europe; the bronze industries of southern Britain show especially close links with those of northern France, and the carp's tongue sword assemblage is distributed from south-eastern England along the Atlantic coast of Europe (Henderson 2007, 57–98). Some new styles are part of even more widespread networks of interaction: complex casting and sheet technologies were developed throughout much of Europe to provide objects for new forms of social prestige, especially vessels, arms and armour. Though the basic themes are standard, there is a high degree of regional variation: cauldrons and flesh-hooks are confined to the west and north-west, while buckets and cups are more common in central Europe; swords and sheet armour are found in most areas, but Britain has only swords, shields and helmets, not the breast-plates and greaves known elsewhere.

Britain can be seen as part of a wider north-west European zone in the later Bronze Age, including parts of northern France and the Low Countries. This zone was united not only by these shared technical and stylistic traditions, but also by common developments in ritual activity. Throughout the region the long-established Bronze Age burial tradition largely disappeared, and deposition in watery places became common. This north-western zone is sharply differentiated from another cultural province in central Europe, which extended as far west as central and southern France. There the later Bronze Age, though sharing many of the technical and stylistic innovations, is distinguished by the Urnfield tradition of crema-tion burials; many of the objects buried with these cremations are precisely the types that turn up in the watery deposits of the north-west.

CURRENT PROBLEMS

One of the main themes of this chapter has been the uncertainty of many of our current interpretations of the available evidence. We now have the framework for a reliable chro-nology and a better understanding is emerging of the nature of some parts of the surviving record. Nevertheless, the picture is very uncertain and the evidence very patchy.

In many areas very little is yet known about the nature of human occupation in the later Bronze Age. This is particularly true of large parts of western and northern Britain. It is precisely these areas that were most affected by the climatic and environmental changes of the late second millennium, and a major problem for the future is to investigate the nature of settlement in these areas and to assess the extent and speed of changes and the degree to which they can be attributed to external environmental factors rather than internal social forces.

Another problem needing investigation is the regional variability of settlement. Where detailed surveys have been carried out, one regular result has been the very fine-grained variation in the nature of settlement systems and their histories of long-term change. This makes it difficult to extrapolate from one set of evidence to a wider scale, but raises impor-tant questions about the social groupings which lie behind such patterns.

Although our understanding of some bronze finds, especially deposits in watery places, has improved enormously in recent years, there are still major problems with other find types, such as dry-land hoards, objects from settlements and the many so-called 'stray finds'. These make up a large part of the record, but are still little understood. There are also many questions still to be answered about the organization of bronze production.

Fundamental problems also remain for our understanding of the nature of the changes in later Bronze Age society. The emergence of new forms of ritual and new sources of prestige and authority, the connections between changes in agriculture and the elite activities of feasting and conspicuous consumption, and the nature of social relationships and differences of age, gender and status are some of the key problems that await more detailed examination.

Key texts

Barber, M., 2003. *Bronze and the Bronze Age: metalwork and society in Britain c.2500–800* BC. Stroud: Tempus.
Barrett, J. and Bradley, R. (eds) 1980. *Settlement and society in the British later Bronze Age.* Oxford: British Archaeological Reports British Series 83.
Bradley, R., 1998. *The passage of arms: an archaeological analysis of prehistoric hoards and votive deposits.* Oxford: Oxbow. 2 edn.
Brück, J. (ed.) 2001. *Bronze Age landscapes: tradition and transformation.* Oxford: Oxbow.
Pryor, F., 2001. *The Flag Fen Basin: archaeology and environment of a Fenland landscape.* Swindon: English Heritage.
Yates, D.T., 2007. *Land, power and prestige: Bronze Age field systems in southern England.* Oxford: Oxbow.

Bibliography

Barrett, J., 1980. 'The pottery of the later Bronze Age in lowland England', *Proceedings of the Prehistoric Society* 46, 297–319.
Barrett, J., 1989. 'Food, gender and metal: questions of social reproduction', in Sørensen, M.L. and Thomas, R. (eds) *The Bronze Age–Iron Age transition in Europe: aspects of continuity and change in European societies c1200 to 500* BC. Oxford: British Archaeological Reports International Series 483, 304–20.
Barrett, J., Bradley, R. and Green, M., 1991. *Landscape, monuments and society: the archaeology of Cranborne Chase.* Cambridge: Cambridge University Press.
Bond, D., 1988. *Excavation at the North Ring, Mucking, Essex.* Chelmsford: Archaeology Section, Essex County Council.
Bradley, R., Entwistle, R. and Raymond, F., 1994. *Prehistoric land divisions on Salisbury Plain: the work of the Wessex Linear Ditches Project.* London: English Heritage.
Bradley, R., Lobb, S., Richards, J. and Robinson, M., 1980. 'Two Late Bronze Age settlements on the Kennet gravels: excavations at Aldermaston Wharf and Knight's Farm, Burghfield, Berkshire', *Proceedings of the Prehistoric Society* 46, 217–95.
Bradley, R.J. and Gordon, K., 1988. 'Human skulls from the River Thames, their dating and significance', *Antiquity* 62, 503–09.
Brossler, A., Early, R. and Allen, C., 2004. *Green Park (Reading Business Park): Phase 2 Excavations – Neolithic and Bronze Age sites.* Oxford: Oxford Archaeology.

Brown, N., 1988. 'A Late Bronze Age enclosure at Lofts Farm, Essex', *Proceedings of the Prehistoric Society* 54, 249–302.

Brück, J., 1995. 'A place for the dead: the role of human remains in Late Bronze Age Britain', *Proceedings of the Prehistoric Society* 61, 245–77.

Brück, J., 2007. 'The character of Late Bronze Age settlement in southern Britain', in Haselgrove, C.C. and Pope, R. E. (eds) *The earlier Iron Age in Britain and the near continent*. Oxford: Oxbow, 24–38.

Buckley, D.G. and Hedges, J.D., 1987. *The Bronze Age and Saxon settlements at Springfield Lyons, Essex: an interim report*. Chelmsford: Essex County Council.

Buckley, V. (ed.) 1990. *Burnt offerings: international contributions to burnt mound archaeology*. Dublin: Wordwell.

Burgess, C.B., 1968. 'The later Bronze Age in the British Isles and northwestern France', *Archaeological Journal* 125, 1–45.

Clark, P. (ed.) 2004. *The Dover Bronze Age boat*. London: English Heritage.

Cowie, T.G. and Shepherd, I.A.G., 2003. 'The Bronze Age', in Edwards, K.J. and Ralston, I.B.M. (eds) *Scotland after the Ice Age*. Edinburgh: Edinburgh University Press, 151–68.

Drewett, P., 1982. 'Later Bronze Age downland economy and excavations at Black Patch, East Sussex', *Proceedings of the Prehistoric Society* 48, 321–400.

Ellison, A., 1981. 'Towards a socioeconomic model for the Middle Bronze Age in southern England', in Hodder, I., Isaac, G. and Hammond, N. (eds) *Pattern of the past: studies in honour of David Clarke*. Cambridge: Cambridge University Press, 413–38.

Fleming, A., 2008. *The Dartmoor Reaves: investigating prehistoric land divisions*. Oxford: Windgather. 2 edn.

Framework Archaeology, 2006. *Landscape evolution in the Middle Thames Valley: Heathrow Terminal 5 excavations Volume 1, Perry Oaks*. Oxford and Salisbury: Framework Archaeology.

Guttman, E.B. and Last, J., 2000. 'A Late Bronze Age landscape at Hornchurch, Greater London', *Proceedings of the Prehistoric Society* 66, 319–59.

Halstead, J., 2005. *Bronze Age settlement in the Welsh Marches*. Oxford: British Archaeological Reports British Series 384.

Harding, A.F., 2000. *European societies in the Bronze Age*. Cambridge: Cambridge University Press.

Hedges, J.W., 1975. 'Excavation of two burnt mounds at Liddle and Beaquoy', *Proceedings of the Society of Antiquaries of Scotland* 106, 39–98.

Henderson, J.C., 2007. *The Atlantic Iron Age: settlement and identity in the first millennium BC*. London: Routledge.

Lawson, A.J., 2000. *Potterne 1982–5: animal husbandry in later prehistoric Wiltshire*. Salisbury: Trust for Wessex Archaeology.

McCullagh, R.P.J. and Tipping, R., 1998. *The Lairg project 1988–1996. The evolution of an archaeological landscape in northern Scotland*. Edinburgh: Scottish Trust for Archaeological Research Monograph 3.

McOmish, D., 1996. 'East Chisenbury: ritual and rubbish in the British Bronze Age–Iron Age transition', *Antiquity* 70, 68–76.

Megaw, J.V.S. and Simpson, D.D.A. (eds) 1979. *Introduction to British prehistory: from the arrival of Homo sapiens to the Claudian invasion*. Leicester: Leicester University Press.

Moore, J. and Jennings, D., 1992. *Reading Business Park: a Bronze Age landscape*. Oxford: Oxford Archaeological Unit.

Musson, C.R., 1991. *The Breiddin hillfort: a later prehistoric settlement in the Welsh Marches*. London: Council for British Archaeology.

Needham, S.P., 1990. *The Petters Late Bronze Age metalwork: an analytical study of Thames Valley metalworking in its settlement context*. London: British Museum.

Needham, S.P., 1991. *Excavation and salvage at Runnymede Bridge, 1978: the Late Bronze Age waterfront site*. London: British Museum Press.

Needham, S.P., 1996. 'Chronology and periodisation in the British Bronze Age', *Acta Archaeologica* 67, 121–40.

Needham, S.P., 2007. '800 BC: the great divide', in Haselgrove, C.C. and Pope, R.E. (eds) *The earlier Iron Age in Britain and the near continent*. Oxford: Oxbow, 39–63.

Needham, S.P., Bronk Ramsey, C., Coombs, D., Cartwright, C. and Pettitt, P., 1997. 'An independent chronology for British Bronze Age metalwork: the results of the Oxford Radiocarbon Accelerator Programme', *Archaeological Journal* 154, 55–107.

Northover, J.P., 1982. 'The exploration of the long-distance movement of bronze in Bronze and early Iron Age Europe', *Bulletin of the University of London Institute of Archaeology* 19, 45–72.

O'Connor, B., 1980. *Cross-channel relations in the later Bronze Age*. Oxford: British Archaeological Reports International Series 91. 2 vols.

Pryor, F., 2001. *The Flag Fen Basin: archaeology and environment of a Fenland landscape*. Swindon: English Heritage.

Spratt, D.A., 1989. *Linear earthworks of the Tabular Hills, northeast Yorkshire*. Sheffield: John R. Collis Publications.

7

THE IRON AGE

Colin Haselgrove

INTRODUCTION

The Iron Age is usually taken as spanning the period from around 800 BC until the first century AD. No single archaeological horizon clearly marks the transition from the Late Bronze Age, however, while the Roman conquest took three generations to complete and affected only part of Britain. Many attributes once used to define the Iron Age – including the construction of hilltop enclosures and the development of a new repertoire of domestic pottery – can now be traced back into the Late Bronze Age. The adoption of iron technology was itself a lengthy process, difficult to follow in its earlier stages because of a lack of relevant evidence. Iron was already being worked at some sites as early as the tenth century BC, but the new metal initially had fairly limited impact and it was not until the later Iron Age that major social and economic changes occurred.

The Iron Age is above all characterized by its diverse and plentiful settlement evidence. Tens of thousands of settlements survive, many of them plough levelled, others still upstanding. These ranged from individual farmsteads occupied by a single household to hillforts containing communities of several hundred. The imposing drystone towers (brochs) of Atlantic Scotland are architecturally amongst the most sophisticated structures in Iron Age Europe, while the linear earthwork complexes ('territorial oppida') of south-east England are among the largest. Significant spatial and temporal variations exist; open settlements of village size are characteristic of eastern England, while large hillforts occur primarily in Wessex, the Welsh Marches and eastern Scotland. Many settlement forms in Atlantic Britain are extremely long-lived and cannot be considered characteristic solely of the Iron Age; these include small defended enclosures called raths, rounds and duns and artificial lake dwellings known as crannogs (Henderson 2007).

Iron Age landscapes also included field systems, trackways and linear boundaries. Unless directly associated with settlements, these are difficult to distinguish from their Bronze Age

149

and Roman counterparts. In the English–Scottish borders, extensive traces of upland cultivation, termed cord rig, have been recognized. Non-habitation sites are rare, but include a variety of ritual foci, as well as production sites for salt, shale and quernstones. Throughout the Iron Age, most of the dead were disposed of in ways that leave no archaeological traces; visible burial rites are restricted to a few regions.

The lack of burials, coupled with a sharp decline in hoarding from the eighth century BC, has greatly reduced the range of Iron Age material culture that survives, since diagnostic metalwork is only rarely found on settlements. Most such objects are isolated votive finds from east-flowing rivers like the Thames and Witham, or come from hoards of late date. Even small items like brooches (Figure 7.1) – useful for dating thanks to their affinities with the continental Hallstatt and La Tène cultures – do not become common until the end of the period. By default, pottery generally forms the basis of settlement chronology, but outside southern and eastern England and the Scottish islands, it, too, is scarce and shows little typological change over several centuries. Its place was presumably taken by organic containers, which only survive in exceptional conditions. Because of soil acidity, sizeable assemblages of animal bone are similarly missing from sites in northern and western Britain. A further contrast with the south and east is the near-total absence of grain storage pits, common in chalk and limestone areas, where they form a major source of artefactual and environmental data.

Based on changes in decorated pottery, the Iron Age south-east of a line drawn between the Bristol Channel and the Humber is often sub-divided into four phases, Earliest (*c.* 800–600 BC), Early (*c.* 600–400/300 BC), Middle (*c.* 400/300–100 BC) and Late (*c.* 100 BC–AD 43/84). To the north-west, the period is difficult to divide into meaningful phases, except at purely local level. Here it suffices to distinguish between an earlier Iron Age lasting to the fourth century BC, which shares many attributes with the later Bronze Age (Haselgrove and Pope

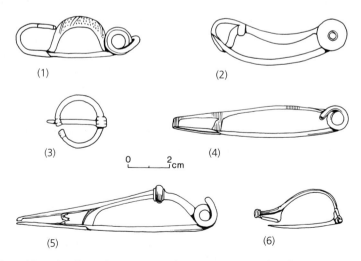

(1) (2) (3) (4) (5) (6)

0 2 cm

Figure 7.1 Selected Iron Age brooch types: 1. Early La Tène; 2. Involuted: 3. Penannular; 4. Nauheim; 5. Boss-on-bow; 6. Aucissa.

2007), and a later Iron Age from *c.* 350 BC, when insular societies entered a new period of transition. This reached its climax in the first century AD, after Julius Caesar's conquest of northern France and invasions of Britain had brought the South into direct contact with the Roman world (Haselgrove and Moore 2007).

THE RECENT DEVELOPMENT OF IRON AGE STUDIES

Until the 1960s, perceptions were still shaped by Fox's (1932) classic division of Britain into Highland and Lowland zones. With its poorer soils and wetter climate, the former was regarded as sparsely occupied by pastoralists, contrasting with a Lowland zone densely populated by mixed farmers. Nearer the Continent, this latter region was also seen as more open to externally induced cultural change, unlike the conservative Highland zone, where innovations were taken up at best gradually. This emphasis on continental influence accorded with Caesar's mention of Belgic immigrants from northern France, whom archaeologists like Hawkes (1960) saw as responsible for introducing coinage, cremation and wheel-made pottery in the first century BC (during Hawkes's Iron Age C). Earlier invaders were similarly credited with the introduction of iron and of hillforts (Iron Age A), and with the subsequent imposition of continental Early La Tène culture in certain regions (Iron Age B).

In the 1960s, this model was challenged as intellectual fashions changed. Hodson (1964) demonstrated that few of the supposed invasions were represented by clear-cut archaeological horizons. Instead, he pointed to long-term cultural continuities that distinguished Iron Age Britain from continental Europe, notably the preference for circular buildings and the lack of burials. With few exceptions, cross-Channel trade provided sufficient explanation for successive changes of artefact styles. Support came from radiocarbon dating, which freed north-western Britain from chronological dependence on sequences developed in areas nearer the Continent. Scottish and Welsh dates showed that Highland zone developments could be as early as in lowland Britain, if not more precocious. These included the occupation of defended hilltop settlements, now shown to have Late Bronze Age origins.

Current surveys of the period (e.g. Cunliffe 2004, 2005; James and Rigby 1997) tend to downplay externally induced cultural change, apart from the Late Iron Age, for which intensive contact between south-east England and the Roman world after 50 BC has taken over the role once accorded to Caesar's Belgic settlers. Emphasis has shifted to economic and social questions, prompted in part by Peacock's (1968) pioneering use of thin-sectioning to investigate pottery production. This pointed to the centralized manufacture of various fine decorated pottery styles originating in south-west England, implying that their distributions owed more to regional exchange networks than to cultural factors. Scientific analysis has also provided important insights into the composition and source of metal artefacts.

Cereal cultivation is now attested throughout the Highland zone, undermining the simple environmental dichotomy advanced by Fox. Mixed agriculture was evidently the preferred subsistence strategy for most communities, but local factors, such as altitude and soil type, were crucial in determining the exact balance between crops and livestock. Many areas show evidence of intensified woodland clearance during the later Iron Age, implying a significant increase in the amount of land under cultivation. Radiocarbon dating was vitally important in liberating Iron Age chronology from its dependence on diffusionist principles. As a result of the plateau in the calibration curve, dates are still rather imprecise between *c.* 800–400 cal. BC, but thanks to accelerator dating (allowing tiny samples of short-lived material like grain to be dated) and the application of Bayesian statistics, much tighter chronologies are gradually being constructed for the period (Haselgrove *et al.* 2001). The dating of the entire Wessex ceramic sequence is now underpinned by radiocarbon, whilst several wet sites have been precisely dated by dendrochronology, including the cult jetties at Fiskerton (Lincolnshire), the seasonal settlement at Goldcliff (Avon) and the marsh fort at Sutton Common (South Yorkshire).

Thanks to the pace and extent of modern development, the last 15 years have seen rapid advances in our knowledge of the period, with hundreds of new Iron Age sites being excavated all over Britain (e.g. Roberts *et al.* 2001). Widespread use of metal detectors has led to many other important finds, whilst approaches to interpretation have also changed radically, with topics like power and identity, regional differences and the organization of Iron Age societies all receiving detailed scrutiny (e.g. Bevan 1999; Creighton 2000; Gwilt and Haselgrove 1997; Hill 2006).

AGRICULTURE AND SETTLEMENT

Systematic investigation of Iron Age farming began with Bersu's (1940) excavations at Little Woodbury near Salisbury. His report was a model for its time, putting forward a convincing reconstruction of agricultural activities at such sites. As well as showing that the inhabitants lived in circular timber buildings, he identified a range of ancillary structures such as grain storage pits, working hollows, and two- or four-post settings, interpreted as drying racks and raised storage buildings. The sequence of palisaded enclosure later replaced by a banked and ditched compound has turned out to be common, although by no means universal, at Iron Age sites.

Cattle and sheep were the principal livestock, their relative importance varying with the local environment. Pig played a subsidiary role, and dog, small horses and domestic fowl were kept. Wild species were of negligible dietary importance, and fish was generally avoided, apart from shellfish at many northern coastal sites. During the first millennium BC, hulled barley superseded naked barley, and spelt wheat replaced emmer as the main cereal crops, although the timing of these transitions varied considerably (Cunliffe 2005). In north-east England, emmer remained the principal wheat on upland sites, long after lower-lying farms had switched to spelt. Bread wheat occurs occasionally at later Iron Age sites in areas including the south Midlands, north-east England and south-west Scotland, a development that may be linked to the colonization of heavy claylands. Other plant crops included beans, peas, and flax; wild plants such as chess were also exploited.

There are now very few areas of Britain where there have not been at least some large-scale excavations on Iron Age settlements, although outside Wessex and the Upper Thames Valley, evidence of earlier Iron Age occupation is often still fairly sparse. Most sites reveal traces of circular domestic buildings, generally between 6 and 15 m in diameter (Figure 7.2). Two main traditions exist: the double-ring and the single-ring forms, in which the main weight of the conical roof was taken respectively on an inner ring of posts and on the wall-head, with or without a central post. Methods of wall construction included stake- and post-rings; ring-grooves to accommodate closely set upright posts or planks; ring-plates; and dry-stone walls. Often only the drainage gullies around such structures remain to mark their positions.

Not all circular buildings were dwellings, some serving other purposes including as shrines. Various regional and temporal trends can be discerned. In southern Britain, very large round-houses are a feature of the earlier Iron Age, and the average size of buildings diminished markedly thereafter. Further north, substantial dwellings were constructed throughout the period (Hingley 1992). The imposing brochs of Atlantic Scotland and Cornish courtyard houses, both innovations of the later first millennium BC, represent variations on this theme. Rectangular buildings on sill-beams are found at many Late Iron Age sites in south-east England, but earlier examples also occur, like the well-preserved wattle- and plank-built structures at Goldcliff (Gwent). Another structural type found in south-west England and in Scotland is the souterrain: probably primarily for underground storage, these tunnel-like structures may also have had ritual functions.

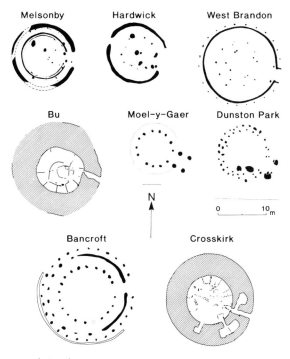

Figure 7.2 Different types of circular structures.

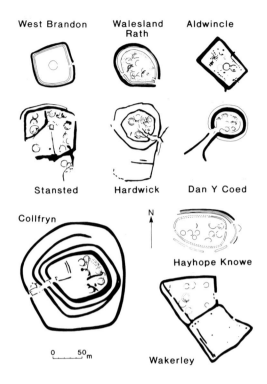

West Brandon   Walesland Rath   Aldwincle

Stansted   Hardwick   Dan Y Coed

Collfryn

N

Hayhope Knowe

0   50 m

Wakerley

Figure 7.3 Rectilinear and curvilinear settlement enclosures.

Enclosed farmsteads were probably the dominant settlement type throughout the Iron Age in many areas of Britain. These can be rectilinear, curvilinear or irregular in plan and enclose between 0.2 ha and more than 1 ha (Figure 7.3). In northern England, small sub-rectangular or D-shaped enclosures like West Brandon (Co. Durham) occupied by a single household are characteristic, whereas oval and curvilinear sites predominate in southern and eastern Scotland. Many Welsh and south-western settlements have widely spaced multiple embankments – as at Collfryn (Powys) – and some also have funnel entrances, a feature shared with the banjo enclosures of Wessex. Such arrangements might well relate to the needs of animal husbandry, but such details rarely show clear links to their inhabitants' subsistence base. The sub-rectangular enclosure at Fisherwick (Staffordshire) was set in a largely pastoral landscape: identical-looking sites elsewhere practised mixed farming.

Individual habitation sites often passed through both enclosed and open phases, including Bishopstone (Sussex) and Winnall Down (Hampshire), which oscillated between the two. At Dryburn Bridge in East Lothian, an earlier palisaded enclosure was succeeded by an unenclosed settlement; while at Thorpe Thewles (Cleveland), the enclosed farmstead was superseded by a larger open settlement during the later Iron Age (Figure 7.4). In some regions, unenclosed settlements were apparently the principal type, as in Scotland north of

154

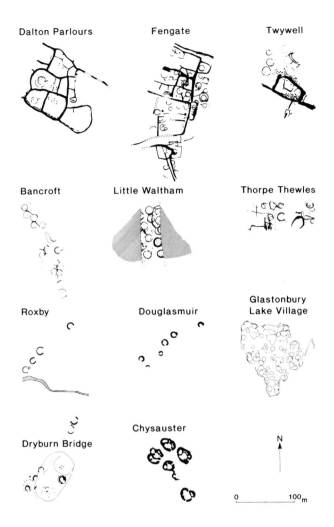

Figure 7.4 Plans of open and aggregated settlements.

the Forth, but even in areas where enclosures predominate, open settlements were probably far commoner than appears the case, thanks to the difficulties of recognizing them as crop-marks. Their size and form varied considerably: from individual houses scattered amongst fields like Kilphedir (Sutherland) – or rows of buildings as at Douglasmuir (Angus) and Roxby (North Yorkshire) – to looser aggregations of households each set within their own compound, such as Dalton Parlours (West Yorkshire) or Dragonby (Lincolnshire).

Aggregated settlements were common in eastern England during the later Iron Age. Such sites pose problems: How many buildings were standing at once? What proportion were resi-dential? What size of household inhabited each dwelling? At some sites like Little Waltham (Essex) frequent rebuilding has created a palimpsest of remains which may exaggerate the actual size of the community at any one time. At Fengate (Cambridgeshire), many buildings were probably ancillary structures and byres rather than houses, and the settlement probably contained no more than five households. A larger population has been suggested for the Glastonbury lake village (Somerset), reaching a maximum of 14 households in the early first century BC, before increasingly wet conditions led to contraction and abandonment (Coles and Minnitt 1995). A number of Roman small towns seem to originate in Late Iron Age aggregated settlements, as at Baldock (Hertfordshire).

In the Upper Thames Valley, different settlement types are seen on the upper and lower gravel terraces. The second terrace is dominated by aggregated settlements like Abingdon Ashville and Gravelly Guy, with separate areas for pit storage and domestic occupation (Cunliffe 2005). These farms may have operated communally, each with its strip of arable at the terrace edge, but sharing pasture away from the river. Smaller self-contained ditched or hedged enclosures with funnel entrances like Hardwick are found on the first terrace, reflecting an expansion of pastoral farming during the later Iron Age, whilst short-lived seasonally occupied sites were established on the floodplain to exploit summer grazing. Seasonal settlements also occur elsewhere, some linked to part-time craft specialization, as at Eldon's Seat (Dorset), where Kimmeridge Shale bracelets were manufactured. The wetland settlement at Meare (Somerset) is now interpreted as the site of a seasonal fair, whilst large midden sites like Potterne (Wiltshire) and Llanmaes (Glamorgan), where communities gathered periodically for feasting and exchange, were a particular feature of the Earliest Iron Age over much of southern Britain (Waddington 2008).The main period of hillfort building in southern England occurred during the sixth and fifth centuries BC. However, the defence of hilltops in Britain has a long, varied history, with construction peaking at different times in different regions. In north and central Wales, for example, the earliest hillforts like the Breiddin (Powys) succeeded Bronze Age enclosures, whereas in East Anglia and the Weald most hillforts were built in the later Iron Age. Southern Scottish sites like Eildon Hill North (Roxburghshire) and Traprain Law (East Lothian) were apparently abandoned as centres of habitation before the classic southern British hillforts were even built, although they were reoccupied during the Roman Iron Age and may have retained a ceremonial role during the intervening centuries. In southern England, the earliest hillforts occur from the Cotswolds along the chalk downs of north Wessex as far as the Chiltern scarp.

These early hillforts comprise two main categories: smaller, well-fortified sites with dense internal activity as at Crickley Hill (Gloucestershire) or Moel-y-Gaer (Powys); and larger hilltop enclosures like Bathampton Down (Avon), with scant evidence of any occupation. At this stage, the defences usually consisted of a single earth or stone rampart, often of box-framed or timber-laced construction, with a relatively simple entrance (Ralston 2006). After c. 350 BC, many early hillforts in Wessex and elsewhere were abandoned, while a smaller number, generally known as developed hillforts, were extended and often massively elaborated. These were usually protected by multiple glacis-style earthworks constructed so that the external face of each dump rampart formed a continuous profile with a V-shaped ditch, while entrances often consisted of long passages protected by complex outworks.

Good examples of developed hillforts include Cadbury Castle (Somerset); Croft Ambrey (Herefordshire); Danebury, (Hampshire); and Maiden Castle (Dorset).

Although neither Danebury – where more than half the interior has been excavated – nor Maiden Castle can be considered typical of British sites, between them they exemplify the main features of both early and developed hillforts, as well as illustrating the processes by which certain hillforts rose to dominate their locality between the fourth and second centuries BC (Cunliffe 2005). Their earlier phases were characterized by well-ordered layouts and by posses- sion of substantial food storage capacities. At Danebury (Figure 7.5), the northern interior was occupied by rows of four-post storage structures – later replaced by a mass of storage pits – while a limited number of circular buildings were constructed in its southern half and around the circumference. At this stage, finds apart from pottery were relatively sparse at either hillfort.

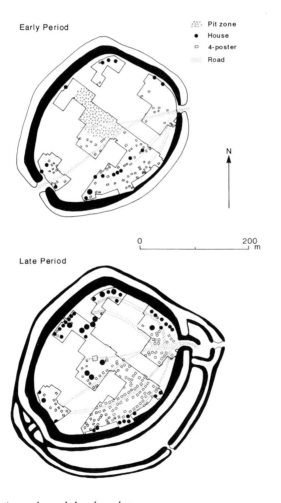

Figure 7.5 Danebury in its early and developed stages.
Source: Cunliffe, B.W., 1993. *Danebury*. London: Batsford / English Heritage

157

During their developed phases, the defences and entrances of both hillforts were repeatedly maintained and embellished, while the interiors show evidence of intensive occupation of a highly organized character. While the broad outlines of its plan remained unchanged, much of the southern half of Danebury was given over to large four- and six-post structures aligned in rows along internal roads, while circular buildings were now predominantly in the northern part. The centre was cleared and a group of larger rectangular structures, which may have been shrines, was erected. At both sites, the quantity of material deposited increased substantially, attesting a wide range of crafts and extensive external contacts.

The process by which Danebury and Maiden Castle developed into the dominant hillforts in their respective regions is now much clearer (Sharples 1991; Cunliffe 2005). Initially, this apparently involved the abandonment of weaker hillforts and farmsteads nearby, whose inhabitants moved into the fort. In time, the enlarged communities successfully overcame more distant rivals: these hillforts were demilitarized and their occupants were forced to live in undefended homesteads, leaving a minority of pre-eminent hillforts, each controlling a well-defined territory. Increasingly, the defences came to symbolize the prestige of individual hillfort communities, and defeated neighbours were probably made to labour on the earthworks, thereby reinforcing their dependent status.

Not all later southern British hillforts conform to this model. In Cambridgeshire, late ringworks like Arbury and Stonea Camps are almost devoid of occupation, suggesting use for occasional communal gatherings, or in periods of danger. The same is probably true of larger hilltop enclosures dating to the earlier Iron Age, while – despite the numerous hut circles visible in their interiors – it is difficult to believe that many hillforts at high altitude were ever occupied all year round.

In the second and first centuries BC, a new type of fortified site made its appearance in southern England. Generally known as 'enclosed oppida' (from the term Caesar used to describe fortified sites he encountered in Gaul), they are larger and more accessible than most hillforts. They range from plateau fortifications such as Bigbury (Kent) and Wheathampstead (Hertfordshire) to slope or valley-bottom enclosures like Oram's Arbour, Winchester, and Salmonsbury (Gloucestershire). Most had been abandoned by the Roman conquest. At some examples, including Braughing–Puckeridge (Hertfordshire) and Canterbury (which appears to succeed Bigbury), fortified enclosures form the nucleus of larger valley-bottom settlements.

In the later Iron Age, the Bronze Age practice of constructing linear earthworks and landscape boundaries resumed. Examples occur widely in southern Britain, from the Cotswolds to East Anglia and East Yorkshire. The 'territorial oppida' or 'royal sites' of southeast England – with their imposing but discontinuous earthworks defining large tracts of land around places of social and political importance – must be included in this phenomenon (Figure 7.6). They do not represent urban centres in any modern sense. At St Albans (*Verlamion*), much of the delimited area was occupied by individual settlements (both elite dwellings and ordinary farmsteads) and their fields, while other sectors were used for burial,

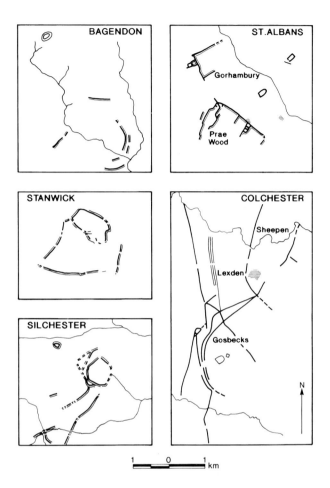

Figure 7.6 Plans of royal sites.

ritual and metalworking. The surrounding earthworks were probably constructed more for symbolic purposes than for defence. Only Silchester (*Calleva*; Hampshire), where a regular street plan was laid out in the late first century BC, has so far yielded evidence for a large nucleated settlement.

These territorial oppida themselves fall into two distinct groups, both of which have evidence of intensive contact with the Roman world. The first group, which includes Colchester (*Camulodunum*), Chichester, St Albans, Silchester and perhaps Leicester were founded a generation or two before the Claudian invasion, often by rulers who had obtained Roman backing and were client kings (Creighton 2000). The second group came to prominence after AD 43, when they found themselves on the frontiers of the newly established Roman province. Bagendon–North Cerney (Gloucestershire) and Stanwick (North Yorkshire) are examples. Many oppida are named on coins, emphasizing their political importance, and all of them seem to have been major cult centres. The latter should occasion

159

no surprise, given that the enactment of religious rituals and the reproduction of political power are linked in most traditional societies.

RELIGION AND BURIAL

Before the first century BC, domestic settlements provided the setting for ritual activity, including feasting and the sacrifice of domestic animals, household objects and sometimes people. Evidence comes in the form of remains periodically deposited in storage pits and at entrances or boundaries (Hill 1995). On smaller farms, such rituals took place once every few years, but at the hillforts which represented the main focus of communities, they were noticeably more frequent. These periodic rituals played an important social role, reaffirming the obligations between different sectors of the population. Religious beliefs were influential in the laying-out of sites: both roundhouse and enclosure entrances are often orientated directly towards either the equinox or the midwinter solstice.

During the Late Iron Age, recognizable shrines and sanctuaries appeared in southern Britain (Figure 7.7). These range from isolated sites like Harlow (Essex) and Hayling Island (Hampshire) – which with their associated offerings of brooches and coins resemble early Gallo-Roman temples – to rectangular buildings within settlements identified as shrines because they differ from normal domestic structures, as at Danebury, Heathrow (Middlesex)

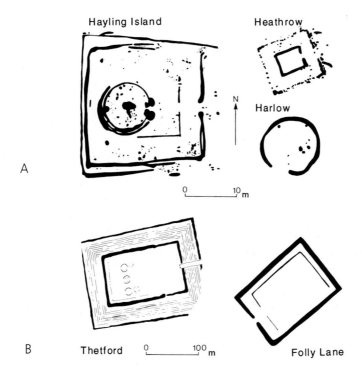

Figure 7.7 Plans of Iron Age shrines (A) and sacred enclosures (B).

and Stansted Airport (Essex). Many shrines within settlements probably remain unrecognized, because at the time of excavation such structures were not anticipated: examples have been claimed at Baldock and Kelvedon (Essex).

Many Iron Age shrines are identifiable primarily from the coins and other valuables deposited there as offerings. One of the most spectacular is Snettisham (Norfolk), where a group of early first century BC precious metal torc hoards amounting to over 30 kg of gold were found buried within a large polygonal enclosure. Other cult enclosures include Fison Way, Thetford (Norfolk); Gosbeck's, Colchester; and Folly Lane, St Albans – where a mass of burnt material including chain mail and horse harness was found in a pit beside a shaft at the centre of the enclosure. Important open-air shrines have been excavated near Market Harborough (Leicestershire) and Wanborough (Surrey). The amount of metalwork deposited in rivers, lakes and bogs also rose significantly during the later Iron Age, although for size and variety, the collection of weaponry, horse harness and vehicle fittings recovered from Llyn Cerrig Bach in Anglesey remains in a class of its own (Macdonald 2007).

The dead were mainly disposed of by excarnation or by scattering their cremated remains. The principal exceptions both have strong continental affinities. In the Arras tradition of East Yorkshire, inhumations were placed under small barrows defined by rectangular ditched enclosures, often grouped in large cemeteries like Burton Fleming–Rudston. A few high-status graves were accompanied by two-wheeled carts, as at Wetwang Slack (Figure 7.8). These traits were originally interpreted as evidence of Early La Tène immigrants from northern France, but differences from continental practice are apparent. A plausible alternative is to envisage a ruling group with far-flung contacts adopting exotic burial rites, particularly as chariot burials occasionally occur elsewhere in Britain, like the one found at Newbridge near Edinburgh. Although the earliest Arras burials could belong to the fourth century BC, the tradition peaked in the third and second centuries BC.

The Aylesford cremation rite, introduced into south-east England in the late second century BC, displays close affinities with burial practice in northern France. Burial grounds are typically small, but larger cemeteries are known at King Harry Lane, St Albans and Westhampnett, near Chichester (Cunliffe 2005). Most cremations were accompanied by at most two pottery vessels and occasionally items such as brooches or toilet sets. In some cases, the cremations lay within enclosures or clusters which suggest kin-groups. A few richer burials occur, mostly north of the Thames, as at Baldock and Welwyn Garden City (Hertfordshire). Their contents emphasize drinking and feasting: Italian wine amphorae and serving vessels as well as indigenous high-status items such as buckets, hearth furniture and gaming sets. Warrior equipment is absent from Aylesford burials, although it does occur in some of the East Yorkshire graves and in a few individual burials elsewhere. At Mill Hill, Deal (Kent), the grave of a young man dating to the late third century BC contained a sword, shield and bronze head-dress (Cunliffe 2005).

Other less prominent burial traditions occur in several regions. Later Iron Age cist-graves occur in Cornwall and eastern Scotland, while a tradition of crouched inhumation burial developed in Dorset during the first century BC Thanks to radiocarbon dating, we now know that

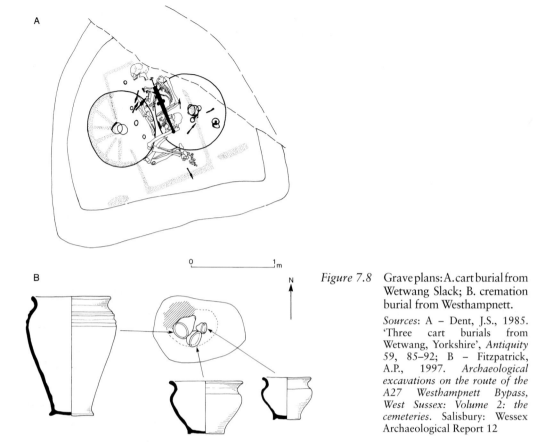

Figure 7.8 Grave plans: A. cart burial from Wetwang Slack; B. cremation burial from Westhampnett.

Sources: A – Dent, J.S., 1985. 'Three cart burials from Wetwang, Yorkshire', *Antiquity* 59, 85–92; B – Fitzpatrick, A.P., 1997. *Archaeological excavations on the route of the A27 Westhampnett Bypass, West Sussex: Volume 2: the cemeteries.* Salisbury: Wessex Archaeological Report 12

many unfurnished inhumation cemeteries and burials from counties as far apart as Cumbria, Hampshire, Norfolk, Oxfordshire and West Yorkshire belong to the period. Also plausibly of Iron Age date is Lindow Man (Cheshire) and some of the other bog body finds from north-west England, many of whom appear to have been ritually executed (Stead *et al.* 1986).

PRODUCTION AND EXCHANGE

The manufacture and exchange of finished goods became increasingly complex during the Iron Age (Morris 1994). Three levels of craft activity are identifiable: output to meet individual household or community needs; more specialized products for wider distribution; and luxury goods for the wealthiest sections of society. For most commodities, little evidence of production sites has survived, and the finished goods provide our main guide to the organization and scale of activity. Only a minority of craft workers are likely to have been full-time specialists; many activities, such as coastal salt production, metal ore extraction and pottery manufacture, could have been carried out by ordinary agricultural communities at slack times.

162

Significant technological advances during the Iron Age included the introduction of lathes for turning wooden and shale objects; the potter's wheel; and the ability to make glass beads and bracelets. In bronze-working, the use of lost-wax casting became widespread, and both gilding and tin-plating were introduced late in the period. Other important innovations included the development of the rotary quern for grinding grain and the introduction of iron-tipped ploughshares, which greatly facilitated the cultivation of heavier soils.

Successfully forging iron into durable artefacts required new skills and techniques and was extremely time-consuming. This helps to explain why, although communities were evidently experimenting with iron as early as the tenth century BC – as recent excavations at Hartshill Quarry (Berkshire) demonstrate (Collard *et al.* 2006) – iron artefacts do not become common until the later first millennium BC. Unlike bronze, iron could not be cast, because the available bowl furnaces were unable to achieve sufficiently high temperatures. On smelting, a spongy mass (bloom) collected in the furnace base and had to be repeatedly heated and hammered to remove slag and impurities. Since artefacts produced in this way were not inherently superior to bronze, the principal reasons why iron was adopted were presumably that most parts of Britain have access to iron ore and that wrought iron could be forged into shapes, which bronze could not. While the earliest iron artefacts – like the sword and sickle from the Llyn Fawr hoard (Glamorgan) – are simply bigger versions of existing bronze types, new tool types, better suited to the tensile properties of wrought iron, were gradually developed, including cutting discs, shafthole axes, shears and tongs. Many types of edge tools in use by the later Iron Age remained essentially unchanged until the Industrial Revolution (Figure 7.9).

Relatively few artefacts show evidence for advanced techniques like the deliberate use of steel, or even quenching and tempering, but smiths gradually learned enough about the properties of different ores to choose those best suited for particular tasks; thus implements like adzes and large sickles were generally manufactured from high-phosphorous ores, while high-carbon ores were used for chisels (Cunliffe 2005). As the period progressed, the best ores – from areas like Northamptonshire and the Forest of Dean – were increasingly exploited. By the third century BC at latest, good-quality iron was exchanged over considerable distances as standardized ingots. These were clearly of considerable value, frequently being hoarded or used as offerings. Three main forms are known: sword-shaped bars, spit-shaped bars and ploughshare bars; but detailed examination reveals over twenty types, each potentially indicating a different source. Stone weights found at many Iron Age settlements similarly imply an interest in standardization and equivalence in other spheres of exchange.

Most settlements yield some evidence of iron smithing – although this may simply indicate that metalworkers visited periodically to make and repair implements – but few have any traces of smelting, suggesting this was mostly undertaken away from the homestead. Exceptions include Hartshill Quarry, the Early Iron Age settlement at Brooklands (Surrey), where areas were set aside for smelting and for forging, and the later Iron Age defended site at Bryn y Castell (Gwynedd), where furnaces inside the enclosure were used for refining raw blooms and a more extensive iron-working area was located outside. At all these sites, however, output was probably only sufficient

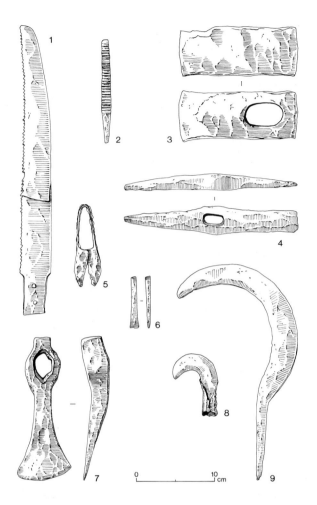

Figure 7.9 Selected iron tools. 1. saw; 2. file; 3. sledge-hammer; 4. pick; 5. shears; 6. chisel; 7. adze;
8. bill-hook; 9. scythe.

Sources: 1, 2, 6–8 – Cunliffe, B.W., 1984. *Danebury: an Iron Age hillfort in Hampshire. The excavations 1969–78*. London: CBA Research Report 52; 3 – Cunliffe, B.W., 1972. 'The late Iron Age metalwork from Bulbury, Dorset', *Antiquaries Journal* 52, 293–308; 4 – author; 5 – Stead, I.M. and Rigby, V., 1989. *Verulamium: the King Harry Lane site*. London: English Heritage Archaeology Report 12; 9 – Fox, C.F., 1946. *A find of the early Iron Age from Llyn Cerrig Bach, Anglesey*. Cardiff: National Museum of Wales

for local needs. As in the later Bronze Age, many craft activities are represented only by a few specialized tools. Combs, shuttles and needles made of bone and antler, and fired clay spindle-whorls and loom-weights attest to the ubiquity of textile production and leather-working, although the restricted distribution of loom-weights within some aggregated settlements could mean that here at least, particular households specialized in weaving. With the advent of iron tools, high-quality carpentry is evident in house and vehicle construction, while finds from wetland settlements indicate the range of domestic wooden equipment: stave-built, bent-wood, hand-carved and lathe-turned containers are present, as well as ladders, ladles, hurdles and mallets. Meare housed one of the few workshops for making glass beads known in Iron Age Europe.

The need for timber for construction, fuel and conversion to charcoal implies considerable woodland management. Another commodity in demand, for food storage and perhaps in cooking, was salt. Along the coasts of southern and eastern England, production sites abound. Produced by evaporation from sea water, salt was carried inland in standardized baked-clay (briquetage) containers. Production and distribution networks are known as far north as the Tweed Valley. Inland brine springs were also exploited. As early as the fifth century BC, salt from West Midlands sources was being distributed up to 50 km away, rising to over 100 km by the later Iron Age (Morris 1994). At Droitwich (Worcestershire), brine tanks, hearths and vast quantities of briquetage show that by the late first century BC salt production had become a large-scale industry.

Other important crafts included quern and pottery production and bronze-working. In southern England, the relatively standardized later Iron Age rotary querns from the greensand quarry at Lodsworth (West Sussex) were distributed over much greater areas than earlier saddle querns. The latter, variable in shape and size, suggest that an activity once undertaken by individual communities had become more centralized. In northern England, however, the changeover to rotary querns saw greater reliance on local sources, at the expense of high-quality products from further afield. Iron Age production thus does not conform to a simple model of increasing centralization through time.

The existing Late Bronze Age finewares set the tone for earlier Iron Age ceramic developments in southern Britain (Cunliffe 2005). Alongside coarsewares, most early assemblages contain a significant proportion of decorated forms such as situlate jars with finger-tip impressions, or furrowed bowls, often with a glossy red haematite coating, presumably intended to replicate the metal vessels from which they were copied (Figure 7.10). From the late sixth century BC, partly under continental influence, new forms appeared, including vessels with markedly angular profiles and pedestal bases. The Western Isles too developed distinctive decorated pottery, which was used for most of the later first millennium BC. While most wares were locally produced, a few finewares like the distinctive scratch-cordoned bowls of Wessex were exchanged more widely.

During the later Iron Age, the character of pottery production altered significantly. Over much of southern England, distinctive regional traditions dominated by new forms of decorated jars or bowls emerged, including a distinctive form known as 'saucepan pots'. In some areas, such as the Welsh Marches and south-west England, local workshops all but disappeared in favour of production concentrated at a few locations, whose wares were exchanged over considerable distances (Morris 1994). Wessex shows evidence for both local and regional distribution, although by the end of the period potters in the Wareham–Poole Harbour (Dorset) area were supplying highly standardized wares to most of the surrounding region. In much of Britain, however, localized manufacture remained the norm until the Roman conquest.

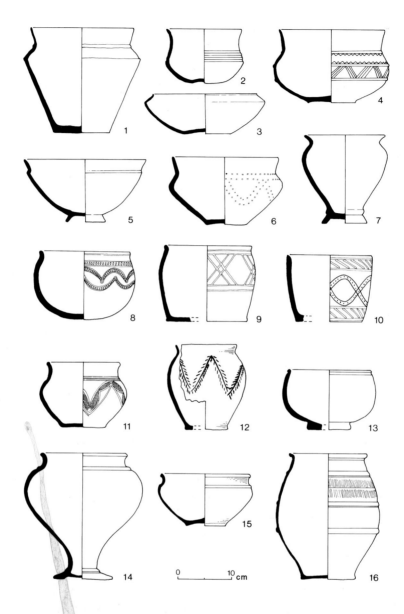

Figure 7.10 Selected Iron Age pottery: 1–3. Early Iron Age types; 4. scratch-cordoned bowl; 5–7. angular and pedestal forms; 8. Middle Iron Age decorated bowl; 9–10. saucepan pottery; 11. Glastonbury ware; 12. Western Isles jar; 13. Poole Harbour ware; 14–15. Late Iron Age forms; 16. Butt-beaker copy.

Sources: 1–10, 12 and 14 – Cunliffe 2005; 11 – Coles, J. M., 1987. *Meare Village East: the excavations of A. Bulleid and H. St George Gray 1932–56*. Exeter: Somerset Levels Papers 13; 13 – Cunliffe, B.W., 1987. *Hengistbury Head, Dorset*, vol. 1. Oxford: Oxford University Committee for Archaeology Monograph; 15 – Fitzpatrick, A.P., 1997. *Archaeological excavations on the route of the A27 Westhampnett Bypass, West Sussex: Volume 2: the cemeteries*. Salisbury: Wessex Archaeological Report 12; 16 – Stead, I.M. and Rigby, V., 1989. *Verulamium: the King Harry Lane site*. London: English Heritage Archaeology Report 12

The introduction of the fast potter's wheel in the late second century BC led to the appearance in eastern and southern England of curvaceous new vessel forms with horizontal grooves or raised cordons. Not all areas adopted the new technology, and traditional handmade fabrics often continued in use alongside finer, wheel-thrown forms. When Roman pottery began to be imported in quantity after *c.* 20 BC, the new shapes – beakers, cups, dishes, flagons, lids and platters – were quickly copied. Although domestic ovens are common on settlements, there is no firm evidence for pre-Roman pottery kilns in Britain, and even wheel-thrown vessels were probably fired in simple bonfire-clamps.

Bronze luxury goods were probably made by a small number of highly skilled and possibly itinerant metalworkers, adept in working both sheet and cast metal, and conversant with continental fashions. At Gussage All Saints (Dorset) a single pit yielded enough casting moulds for 50 sets of horse gear and vehicle fittings, although the context of this operation remains uncertain (Cunliffe 2005). Another relatively small settlement at Weelsby Avenue, Grimsby (Humberside), yielded debris, including failed castings, from the manufacture of horse harness, although here the evidence suggests a longer timespan for production. The main sources of copper, tin and lead seem to have been in the west and south-west, although some metal may have been imported. From the late first century BC onward, imported Roman brass (an alloy of copper and zinc) was often used for decorative metalwork in place of tin bronze.

The categories of decorative metalwork found reflect the same social and ritual preoccupations – feasting, warfare and driving vehicles – as in the later Bronze Age. Sheet bronze was employed for cauldrons, shields and scabbards, and to clad wooden objects like buckets and tankards, while lost-wax casting was used for chariot fittings and horse harness and to make components of composite artefacts like mirrors and torcs. A range of decorative techniques such as engraving and repoussé work, adding coloured ornament such as coral and enamel, and plating were all used. Based on the evolving form and decoration of the objects, Insular art is divided into five stages (I–V), starting in the fifth century BC and lasting to the early centuries AD, although the validity of this scheme has recently been challenged (Macdonald 2007).

Gold and silver objects were rare until the mid-second century BC, when imported Gallo-Belgic gold coinage began to circulate freely in south-east England, and hoards containing torcs were buried in some numbers. The presence at Snettisham of older torcs indicates that such objects may have been less uncommon in earlier centuries than the archaeological record now suggests. By the later first century BC, most areas of lowland Britain were striking gold and silver coinages. Copper-alloy coinage is however confined to south-east England, where struck types replaced cast issues at about this time. Most later coinages bear the name of the issuing ruler in Roman letters (Figure 7.11). Hardly any coin dies have yet been found, but most oppida have yielded baked-clay slab moulds, evidently used for minting or other forms of high-status metalworking.

Figure 7.11 Inscribed Iron Age coins: A. gold stater of Tasciovanus. The helmeted horseman on the reverse is brandishing a war trumpet; B. brass coin of Cunobelinus. Beneath the boar on the reverse is the name of his father, Tasciovanus, clearly inscribed; C. bronze coin of Cunobelinus, depicting a boat on the obverse and a winged Victory on the reverse.

ECONOMIC AND SOCIAL CHANGES

Between *c.* 800 and 600 BC, the climate became significantly colder and wetter, only recovering in the sixth century BC. An enforced retreat from upland areas and competition for land in favoured lowlands could well have been factors behind the construction of some early hillforts. The prominence of storage facilities confirms the importance of food supplies to such sites (Cunliffe 2005), many of which are in upland areas like the Welsh Marches, where resources would have come under pressure sooner than in predominantly lowland regions. The move to iron technology may also have been disruptive, undermining the elites who dominated later Bronze Age society through their control of long-distance exchange (Haselgrove and Pope 2007). In such conditions, larger communities coalesced and competed for the best agricultural land. The territorial control needed to support such communities itself became a significant means of achieving status and power. Given the regional differences in hillfort construction, it is, however, clear that no single explanation suffices and that diverse local factors were important.

After a brief return to wetter and colder conditions during the fourth century BC, the climate again improved and by the end of the Iron Age was probably similar to today's. This must have been significant for the agricultural changes of the later Iron Age, when many parts of Britain saw widespread expansion of settlement onto heavier, damper soils at the expense of forest and marginal land (Haselgrove and Moore 2007). Agricultural intensification is attested by greater use of manuring and crop rotation to maintain soil fertility; ditches for drainage; and by the switch to crops suitable for heavier soils. The dramatic increase in the number of later Iron Age settlements almost certainly indicates a rising population, although whether as a cause or a consequence of agricultural developments is unclear.

In Wessex, the developed hillforts exerted ever greater dominance over their surrounding territories. Elsewhere, widespread forest clearance and colonization of marginal environments suggest demographic pressure, other signs of which include episodes of hillfort construction in Essex and the Welsh Marches and increased settlement aggregation in eastern England. These pressures were gradually alleviated by rising agricultural production. In many cases, the colonization of new land was accompanied by the laying out of extensive field systems like the brickwork fields of Nottinghamshire and South Yorkshire (although their dating is contentious) and the co-axial field systems of East Anglia, or by a large-scale landscape reorganization, as in the Trent Valley.

This expansion into thinly settled areas can be linked with increasing specialization of production, seen in the first large-scale exploitation of iron resources in the Weald, the East Midlands and the Vale of York and in the growth of textile production, pottery manufacture and glass, metal and shale working in marginal areas like Holderness (East Yorkshire), the Isle of Purbeck (Dorset) and the Somerset Levels. By the Late Iron Age, many of these had become full-time specialist enterprises. Settlers in these agriculturally unpromising environments may have developed products for exchange to offset this disadvantage. Another possibility is that such activities were deliberately located on the peripheries of territories because the external contacts they engendered were regarded as a threat to the social order (Sharples 1991). Such groups frequently appear more innovative than others, possibly because they lacked the deep-rooted social relationships which characterized already-populous areas.

From 150 BC, southern Britain underwent a series of changes which mark a radical break from the preceding centuries, with Roman power and influence eventually assuming a key role. An early symptom was the circulation of imported Gallo-Belgic gold, and local cast bronze, coinage in south-east England. Around 100 BC, changes intensify significantly: cremation burial and wheel-thrown pottery appear, and widespread imitation of continental coinage and metalwork occurs. Limited immigration from Belgic Gaul may have fostered closer cross-Channel social and political ties. The Late Iron Age also witnessed the restructuring of settlement patterns in Wessex and south-east England. Many new farmsteads in the latter area were associated with agricultural innovations, and noticeably prospered after the Roman conquest compared to many long-established sites.

During the first century BC, a clearer separation between ritual and everyday life is reflected in the appearance of formal shrines and cemeteries (Hill 1995). A new emphasis on individual status and social ranking is evident in the increasingly differentiated burial rites – in which long-distance ties are often stressed in preference to local ones – and in the greater numbers of personal ornaments found. The conspicuous consumption of wealth through the ritual deposition of valuables in both wet and dry locations rose sharply (Gwilt and Haselgrove 1997). At the same time, coin legends and the founding of new royal sites like Colchester and St Albans reflect the greater centralization of political power. Growing Roman diplomatic and economic involvement in southern Britain – especially after 20 BC – was a major factor in these developments (Creighton 2000). In return for imported Roman luxuries, the writer Strabo lists corn, cattle, hunting dogs, slaves and metals among exported commodities.

Outside south-east England, the intensity of change during the later Iron Age varies. In many areas, a tendency towards even more massive enclosure is apparent initially, including parts of the East Midlands, Northumberland and south-east Scotland, the Severn Valley and the Vale of York, but by the first century AD these were largely replaced by open and aggregated settlements. Inevitably, the cultural changes in south-east England impinged on neighbouring areas like the Cotswolds, East Anglia and the East Midlands. Roman material culture appears, for example in occasional rich burials accompanied by mirrors. These areas probably suffered military and economic predation by their powerful south-eastern neighbours in search of booty and territory. In central-southern England, the organization of the remaining developed hillforts broke down, and most of their population dispersed to establish smaller enclosures and field systems, perhaps implying partitioning of land previously communally owned.

In western and northern Britain, the dominant picture is one of stability. Differences in social and political structures are implied by the failure of these regions to adopt coinage and in the virtual absence of Roman imports. Some areas like South Wales, however, exhibit a marked increase in the number of settlements, while elsewhere new settlement types developed, like the courtyard house clusters of Cornwall such as Carn Euny or Orcadian broch complexes like Gurness and Howe. This implies that some parts of northern and western Britain were experiencing processes of settlement aggregation similar to those which had occurred earlier in many lowland areas. The chronology of the more elaborate brochs remains tentative, not least because of difficulties in relating radiocarbon dates to their construction, but excavations at sites like Old Scatness (Shetland) and Crosskirk (Caithness) suggest that they probably began in the mid-first millennium BC (Harding 2004).

OVERSEAS CONTACTS AND THE WIDER EUROPEAN CONTEXT

Despite obvious differences, the rhythm of British Iron Age developments displays significant parallels with the near Continent. As in the later Bronze Age, metalwork types indicate close ties between leading elements of society on either side of the Channel, through which technical and stylistic innovations were transmitted. Some supposed differences are more apparent than real: recognizable Iron Age burial rites are absent or discontinuous in many continental areas.

The southern coastline and that of much of East Anglia face the Continent, linking these areas into wider European patterns by relatively short sea crossings. As the Fenland basin presented an obstacle to overland travel, an enduring pattern of maritime contact also developed up the eastern English coastline. The configuration of the western coast makes the Irish Sea one of its principal unifying features and creates a corridor for communication with coastal regions from Brittany to Galicia (Cunliffe 2004).

By the Late Iron Age, sea-going plank boats with sails – known from Caesar's description of Breton vessels and from representations on British coins – were in use around British shores; earlier in the Iron Age, hide craft were probably the dominant form. Substantial logboats like that from Hasholme (East Yorkshire), which could carry over 5 tonnes of cargo, plied inland waterways. Probable Iron Age ports with continental links include Hengistbury Head and Cleval Point in Dorset and Mount Batten on Plymouth Sound.

In temperate Europe, advanced iron technology came into common use during the Hallstatt C period (*c.* 800–625 BC). North-west Europe shares the sudden decline in the hoarding and ritual deposition of metalwork apparent in Britain. Insular Hallstatt C innovations are confined to new sword types (still of copper alloy) and the import of horse gear and objects such as razors. During Hallstatt D (*c.* 625–450 BC), southern British weaponry followed continental fashions, with daggers replacing the sword, while bow brooches began to be used for fastening clothes instead of ring-headed pins. With Belgium and northern France, southern Britain formed a zone which was occasionally penetrated by prestige goods from the Mediterranean, like the Etruscan beaked flagon from near Northampton and the Attic red-figure kylix recovered from the Thames near Reading. These exotica presumably arrived through gift exchange via southern Germany or eastern France.

The Early La Tène period (*c.* 450–325 BC) is marked by the reintroduction of long swords and the emergence of a new art style. A number of regions including East Yorkshire exhibit close continental links at this time. Contact between Brittany and south-west England is shown by pottery with stamped and rouletted ornamentation, and later with elaborate designs derived from Early La Tène metalwork (Cunliffe 2004). In south-east England, ceramic assemblages included angular tripartite bowls, some with low pedestal bases, which closely recall contemporary north French developments.

Continental influence diminished noticeably, but did not cease, during Middle La Tène (*c.* 325–150 BC). Innovations in sword technology and art styles indicate continuing contact. Increased regionalism is a feature of much of Europe at this period: most communities became less open to emulating outside fashions; Britain is no exception. Here, highly decorated regional pottery styles have no obvious external counterparts. British brooch types, including involuted and decorated forms, also diverged markedly from continental forms. Many of the masterpieces of Insular La Tène art, like the Witham and Wandsworth shields, date to this time.

A major feature of the Late La Tène period (*c.* 150–20 BC) was the arrival of the first Roman imports, principally Dressel 1 wine amphorae and metal drinking services. Initially, these goods were probably introduced through indigenous networks as cross-Channel contacts once again intensified rather than through direct exchange with the Roman world. From 20 BC, however, south-east England was increasingly exposed to cultural developments in the newly conquered provinces of Roman Gaul. Imported Roman-style brooch, coin and pottery types were widely copied, and the range of imports diversified. Differing attitudes to the body and changes in personal appearance are suggested by the use of toilet instruments, while the new vessel forms indicate differences in the way food and drink were prepared and served. A degree of literacy is implied by the use of Roman-style inscriptions on coins and by graffiti on pottery, although the latter could be the work of foreign traders.

CURRENT PROBLEMS AND PERCEPTIONS

Little is known for certain about how Iron Age societies were organized (Hill 2006). Until recently, this theme was usually approached by extrapolating from texts relating to the Celtic-speaking peoples of Gaul and (much later in time) Ireland. However, the archaeological record implies that the social and political organization of individual Celtic peoples differed significantly, while Classical authors consistently treat the Britons as distinct from the Gauls (Collis 2003). Modern excavation has shown that the surviving Iron Age material is much less straightforward to interpret than was previously realized, for the ritual deposits placed in many settlement contexts produce a distorted and selective picture of everyday life (Gwilt and Haselgrove 1997). We can no longer speak confidently of rich or poor inhabitants, or even of diet, without careful analysis of the formation processes of the archaeological record.

For the earlier and Middle Iron Age, the existence of socio-political hierarchies has come under scrutiny, since most excavated settlements yield little or no indication of the presence of elites (Hill 1995). Unless visible signs of ranking were deliberately suppressed, relatively low levels of social differentiation are probably indicated. The reduction in the number of occupied hillforts after 300 BC nonetheless suggests some concentration of power at this time. Archaeologists are also actively questioning whether the substantial houses found on Iron Age settlements in northern Britain represent high-status dwellings within a hierarchical social system or served to express the identity of individual households in more egalitarian structures (Hingley 1992). In practice, no single model can possibly account for the strong regional differences apparent, and answers will have to be sought at increasingly local levels.

The extent to which the period was dominated by endemic warfare is also being reassessed (Ralston 2006). Although particular groups of hillforts were quite possibly constructed in response to military crises and some sites show signs of actual conflict, this need not mean that the overall incidence of warfare in Iron Age Britain was any greater than in many other prehistoric societies. Evidence for wounding and violent death is not especially common in the surviving Iron Age burials, and the construction of some fortified enclosures appears to have been connected as much with identity and status as with defence. Many settlements become increasingly ostentatious with time, but the embellishments were often confined to their most conspicuous sectors, suggesting that military considerations were not always paramount.Debate continues over the relative importance of internal and external factors in the changes of the Late Iron Age (Haselgrove and Moore 2007). Was Roman imperialism the driving force behind the greater degree of social differentiation and political centralization evident in southern Britain at this period, or were these changes the culmination of indigenous processes which had been underway for centuries? The degree to which innovations like coinage or literacy are symptomatic of profound structural changes, such as the emergence of a market economy, is also contentious, since much of the evidence is ambiguous. Few coins can be convincingly interpreted as losses from commercial transaction, implying that they were primarily employed for political, social and religious purposes. The cultural significance of much Iron Age art is open to similar doubts and is being reassessed (Garrow *et al.* 2008). Another ongoing debate concerns the extent to which the tribal identities (*civitates*) recognized by the Roman administration in the first century AD reflect pre-existing political and cultural groupings or were essentially created by the conquerors.

Key texts

Cunliffe, B.W., 2005. *Iron Age communities in Britain*. London: Routledge. 4 edn.
Cunliffe, B.W., 2004. *Iron Age Britain*. London: English Heritage. 2 edn.
Harding, D.W., 2004. *The Iron Age in northern Britain*. London: Routledge
Haselgrove, C. and Moore, T. (eds) 2007. *The Later Iron Age in Britain and beyond*. Oxford: Oxbow.
Haselgrove, C. and Pope, R. (eds) 2007. *The Earlier Iron Age in Britain and the near Continent*. Oxford: Oxbow.

Bibliography

Bersu, G., 1940. 'Excavations at Little Woodbury, Wiltshire', *Proceedings of the Prehistoric Society* 6, 30–111.
Bevan B. (ed.) 1999. *Northern exposure: interpretative devolution and the Iron Ages in Britain*. Leicester: Leicester Archaeology Monograph 4.
Coles, J.M. and Minnitt, S., 1995. *Industrious and fairly civilised: the Glastonbury Lake Village*. Taunton: Somerset Levels Project.
Collard, M., Darvill, T. and Watts, M., 2006. 'Ironworking in the Bronze Age? Evidence from a 10th century BC settlement at Hartshill Copse, Upper Bucklebury, West Berkshire', *Proceedings of the Prehistoric Society* 72, 367–421.
Collis, J.R., 2003. *The Celts. Origins, myths, and inventions*. Stroud: Tempus.
Creighton, J., 2000. *Coins and power in late Iron Age Britain*. Cambridge: Cambridge University Press.
Fox, C.F., 1932. *The personality of Britain*. Cardiff: National Museum of Wales. 2 edn.
Garrow, D., Gosden, C. and Hill, J.D. (eds) 2008. *Rethinking Celtic art*. Oxford: Oxbow.
Gwilt, A. and Haselgrove, C.C. (eds.) 1997. *Reconstructing Iron Age societies: new approaches to the British Iron Age*. Oxford: Oxbow Monograph 71.
Haselgrove, C., Armit, I., Champion, T., Creighton, J., Gwilt, A., Hunter, F., Hill, J.D. and Woodward, A., 2001. *Understanding the British Iron Age – an agenda for action*. Salisbury: Trust for Wessex Archaeology / Prehistoric Society.
Hawkes, C.F.C., 1960. 'The British Iron Age', in Frere, S.S. (ed.) *Problems of the Iron Age in southern Britain*. London: Institute of Archaeology Occasional Paper 11, 1–16.
Henderson, J.C., 2007. *The Atlantic Iron Age*. London: Routledge.
Hill, J.D., 1995. *Ritual and rubbish in the Iron Age of Wessex*. Oxford: British Archaeological Reports British Series 242.
Hill, J.D., 2006. 'Are we any closer to understanding how later Iron Age societies worked (or did not work)?', in Haselgrove, C. (ed.) *Celtes et Gaulois: l'archéologie face à l'histoire: les mutations de la fin de l'âge du Fer*. Glux-en-Glenne: *Bibracte* 12.4, 169–79.

Hingley, R., 1992. 'Society in Scotland from 700 BC–AD 200', *Proceedings of the Society of Antiquaries of Scotland* 122, 7–53.

Hodson, F.R., 1964. 'Cultural groupings within the pre-Roman British Iron Age', *Proceedings of the Prehistoric Society* 30, 99–110.

James, S.T. and Rigby, V., 1997. *Britain and the Celtic Iron Age*. London: British Museum Press.

Macdonald, P., 2007. *Llyn Cerrig Bach. A study of the copper alloy artefacts from the Insular La Tène assemblage*. Cardiff: University of Wales Press.

Morris, E.L., 1994. 'Production and distribution of pottery and salt in Iron Age Britain: a review', *Proceedings of the Prehistoric Society* 60, 371–94.

Peacock, D.P.S., 1968. 'A contribution to the study of Glastonbury ware from south-west Britain', *Antiquaries Journal* 46, 41–61.

Ralston, I.B.M., 2006. *Celtic fortifications*. Stroud: Tempus.

Roberts, I., Burgess, A. and Burg, D., 2001. *A new link to the past. The archaeology of the M1–A1 link road*. Leeds: Yorkshire Archaeology 7.

Sharples, N.M., 1991. *Maiden Castle*. London: Batsford / English Heritage.

Stead, I.M., Bourke, J.B. and Brothwell, D., 1986. *Lindow Man. The body in the bog*. London: British Museum Press.

Waddington, K. 2008. 'Topographies of accumulation at Late Bronze Age Potterne', in Davies, O., Sharples, N. and Waddington, K. (eds) *Changing perspectives on the first millennium BC*. Oxford: Oxbow, 161–84.

8

ROMAN BRITAIN

The military dimension

W.S. Hanson

SETTING THE SCENE

The Roman army was one of the most successful in history, and the Roman acquisition of an empire was primarily a result of that success. Britain was one of the last additions to Roman territory, and the province has been one of the most intensively and extensively studied of the Empire.

It is not proposed in this chapter to provide a narrative of the military conquest and occupation of Britain. In the space available it could not provide anything but a superficial coverage, and such historical accounts are quite commonplace. For detailed discussion of that narrative the reader may turn to any one of several books (e.g. Mattingly 2006). The broad chronological outline, therefore, has been provided here in tabular form, indicating the prime sources of information for each chronological event (Table 8.1). This leaves the text free to concentrate more on particular issues and problems, and to demonstrate the way that archaeological evidence is both integrated into that account and facilitates its expansion in detail.

In chronological terms this chapter follows on from that on the Iron Age which precedes it, though with a certain amount of overlap, both chronologically and culturally, since the basic fabric of Iron Age society did not suddenly and ubiquitously become Roman. The chapter parallels, chronologically, that which succeeds it dealing with civil and rural society in Roman Britain, and links into the following chapters on the archaeology of the early historic period. As with all interfaces between periods defined by modern scholars, there is no clearly defined break, but elements of overlap and continuity, all the more so as some of the peoples who had been raiding the shores of the Roman province in the fourth century AD became settlers in the fifth.

Table 8.1 Events during the Roman conquest and occupation, with information on sources; a blank in this column means that the evidence is entirely archaeological.

Dates	Events	Literary/epigraphic/numismatic sources
AD 43	An invasion force of about 40,000 men under Aulus Plautius defeated the principal native opposition. Claudius personally led the army into *Camulodunum* (Colchester) and accepted the surrender of eleven British kings.	Dio Cassius, 60; Suetonius, *Claudius*, 17; Inscription, *CIL* V no. 920
AD 43–60	Successful campaigning continued in the south-west. Expansion continued into Wales, but was slowed by the guerrilla tactics of the natives and by revolts amongst the *Brigantes* and *Iceni*.	Suetonius, *Vespasian*, 4; Tacitus, *Annals*, 12 and 14
AD 60	The *Iceni* rebelled under the leadership of Queen Boudica. The towns of Colchester, London and *Verulamium* were destroyed.	Tacitus, *Annals*, 14
AD 69–74	The client kingdom of the *Brigantes* erupted into civil war. Eventually Rome intervened and conquered the area.	Tacitus, *Histories*, 3, 45 and *Agricola*, 17
AD 74–7	Expansion of the Roman province continued with the subjugation of most of Wales.	Tacitus, *Agricola*, 17
AD 77–9	Consolidation of north Wales and northern England was completed.	Tacitus, *Agricola*, 18 and 20
AD 80–3	Scotland was overrun. The Caledonians were defeated (*Mons Graupius*) and garrisons established as far as the Mounth after a brief halt on the Forth–Clyde isthmus. Britain was circumnavigated by the Roman fleet.	Tacitus, *Agricola*, 22–38
c. AD 87	Following the departure of troops to the Danube, the Romans withdrew from most of Scotland.	Inscription, *ILS* no. 2719
c. AD 105	The withdrawal from Scotland was completed and a frontier constructed across Tyne–Solway isthmus (the Stanegate).	
AD 122	The construction of Hadrian's Wall began shortly after Hadrian visited Britain.	SHA *Hadrian*, 5, 11
AD 139–42	Hadrian's Wall was given up and the Romans advanced back into Scotland, constructing a new wall between the Forth and the Clyde (the Antonine Wall).	SHA, *Antoninus Pius*, 5
c. AD 158/165	The Antonine Wall was abandoned and Hadrian's Wall reoccupied.	
AD 181/184	Unspecified northern tribes invaded the province but were repulsed.	Dio Cassius, 72; Coins, RIC 437, 440, 451
AD 196–7	Following his victory in the civil war, the Emperor Severus divided Britain into two provinces.	Herodian 3, 8
AD 197	The *Maeatae* and Caledonians in Scotland broke their treaty with Rome and waged war in the north. Peace was restored by the payment of subsidies.	Dio Cassius, 75, 5
AD 208–12	Following renewed troubles in northern Britain, Severus campaigned in Scotland in person. After initial successes he died at York. His sons, Geta and Caracalla, terminated the expedition and withdrew Roman forces from Scotland.	Dio Cassius, 76–7; Herodian, 3, 14–15

continued on next page

Table 8.1 continued

Dates	Events	Literary/epigraphic/ numismatic sources
AD 286–89	Carausius, appointed to protect the Channel coast from raiding, declared himself emperor.	Aurelius Victor, 39; Eutropius, 9, 21
AD 293	Carausius was assassinated by one of his ministers, Allectus, who was declared emperor in Britain and northern Gaul.	Eutropius, 9, 22
AD 296	Constantius Chlorus recovered control of Britain and Allectus was killed.	Panegyric of Constantius, 13–20
AD 305/306	Constantius Chlorus conducted a military campaign in northern Britain. While staying at York he died, and his son, Constantine, was declared emperor.	Anonymus Valesianus 2,4
AD 315	The Emperor Constantine celebrated a victory in Britain.	Coins, RIC 133–45
AD 342/343	A possible frontier problem prompted a winter visit to Britain by the Emperor Constans.	Libanius, *Orationes* 59
AD 360	Troops were sent to Britain to deal with the Picts and Scots.	Ammianus Marcellinus, 20, 1
AD 364	Barbarian raids by Picts, Scots and Saxons are recorded.	Ammianus Marcellinus, 26, 4
AD 367–8	Attacks on the frontiers take place from all directions. The situation was recovered by Count Theodosius after a major campaign.	Ammianus Marcellinus, 27, 8; 28, 3
AD 383–8	Magnus Maximus, an army commander in Britain, headed a successful revolt against the Emperor Gratian, gaining control of much of the western empire until he was defeated by Theodosius.	Zosimus, 4, 35, 37; Orosius, 7, 35
AD 396–9	The general Stilicho undertook an expedition against the barbarians in Britain, which successfully restored peace.	Claudian, *Stilicho*, 2, 247–255; Eutropius, 1, 391–3
AD 401/402	Troops were withdrawn by Stilicho to defend Italy.	Claudian, *Gothic War*, 416–18
AD 406–7	Three successive usurpers (Marcus, Gratian and Constantine III) took power in Britain.	Zosimus, 6, 2
AD 408–9	Britain was attacked by the Saxons. The Britons freed themselves and expelled their Roman governors.	Zosimus, 6, 5
AD 410	The Emperor Honorius turned down an appeal for help, ostensibly from Britain.	Zosimus, 6, 10

Regional strengths and weaknesses in the evidence

Because of the way in which the province developed and, in particular, the failure to complete the conquest of the whole island, the main geographical focus of any consideration of the military dimension of Roman Britain is on the frontier zone in the north and west. Because much of the area involved falls into the upland zone, which, historically, has been more sparsely occupied and less extensively developed, the state of preservation of many of the archaeological sites is relatively high. Furthermore, because the Roman conquest has been a subject of interest since the earliest days of the development of archaeology as a discipline, many of these sites have been excavated. By contrast, however, with the exception of some well-preserved late coastal defence sites (e.g. Maxfield 1989), the distribution of Roman military remains in the south and east of the country is less well understood and thus the archaeological evidence for the early stages of the conquest is rather weaker. Though this continues to be augmented by aerial photographic discoveries and excavation (e.g. Sauer 2000), the general pattern of a more limited (Figure 8.5) and certainly short-term military presence in the south-east is sufficiently consistent to support the argument that both the extent of native resistance and the Roman military response followed a different trajectory from that seen in the north and west.

Major and typical data types

Our understanding of the Roman conquest and occupation of Britain is based on several different sources of evidence. Britain did figure in the writings of Classical authors on those occasions when it entered the wider imperial stage, though rarely at any length or in any detail. Such evidence is at its fullest in the first century AD, mainly through the writings of the historian Tacitus. Occasional references in the surviving books of his *Histories* and *Annals*, covering the period from AD 14 to 96, are augmented by the biography of his father-in-law, Agricola, whose primary claim to fame was his conquest of north Britain (Hanson 1991). There is little literary evidence to elucidate the second-century history of Roman Britain, but slightly more when the province again features directly in the power politics of the early third century, particularly with the campaigns of Septimius Severus in Scotland. Finally, for a brief period in the later fourth century there is the excellent detailed account of Ammianus Marcellinus. An exciting and ongoing addition to the literary evidence for the military aspects of the province of Britain derives from the archaeological discovery of writing tablets, the most extensive collection of which comes from the fort of *Vindolanda* (Chesterholm) and includes elements of the fort's administrative archive as well as copies of private letters (Bowman 1994).

The Roman army was in the habit of commemorating events or making religious dedicatory inscriptions in monumental form, often in stone. Many of these inscriptions have survived, though not always in their complete state, and provide a valuable source of information (Collingwood and Wright 1965): military building inscriptions can provide accurate dates for the construction or reconstruction of forts and frontiers; religious altars can provide evidence of the range of cults to which the troops subscribed and indicate something of the underlying order of military life; while tombstones can indicate the origin of those troops, their life expectancy and family relationships (e.g. Figure 8.1). All three types of inscription can assist in the study of the movement of particular units or the careers of individuals (e.g. Birley 2005), which, in turn, can contribute to both refining the chronology and interpreting the significance of historical events.

The major contribution of archaeology is in the elucidation of military installations in terms of date and function. When on campaign in hostile territory, or simply operating away from

Figure 8.1 Tombstone of Tadius Exuperatus, Caerleon.
Source: by permission of the National Museum of Wales

home base, the Roman army constructed temporary defended enclosures, usually referred to as temporary camps, for overnight protection. More are known from Britain than from any other province of the Roman Empire (e.g. Davies and Jones 2006). They range in size dramatically, from less than 0.5 ha to 67 ha in area. The smaller examples are more likely to relate to the building activities of work parties involved in the construction or repair of military installations, but the larger camps can indicate the lines of march of troops on campaign, and are sometimes referred to as marching camps (Figure 8.2). Not infrequently such camps cluster at nodal points. For example, to the north of the fort at Ardoch (Perthshire) (1) (Figure 8.3), and partly overlapping its annexe (4), is a series of temporary camps (3, 5–7, 9), some elements of which are still visible on the ground. The largest camp, covering 52 ha (9), is the latest and replaces a 25.5 ha camp (7) which it partly overlies, though both probably relate to campaigning in the early third century by the Emperor Septimius Severus.

More permanent works which seem to be associated with campaigning are not infrequently attested, but their precise nature and function is much debated. Usually referred to as 'vexillation fortresses' and generally assumed to have, at least in part, a legionary garrison, they cover an area of some 8 ha (e.g. Frere and St Joseph 1974; Sauer 2000). The most extensively excavated example is at Red House, Corbridge (Northumberland), though its full size is unconfirmed. Internal timber buildings included a workshop, a large barrack block and several open-ended storage buildings (Hanson *et al.* 1979), while earlier work identified the remains of a large bath building close by (Figure 8.4b). Occupation of the site was short-lived and seems to have been associated with the campaigns of Agricola.

After its conquest had been achieved, control of an area was usually consolidated by a more permanent military presence, though the nature, extent and longevity of this process

Figure 8.2 Aerial photograph of the fort (f), annexe (A) and temporary camps (C) at Malling

Source: Crown Copyright: RCAHMS

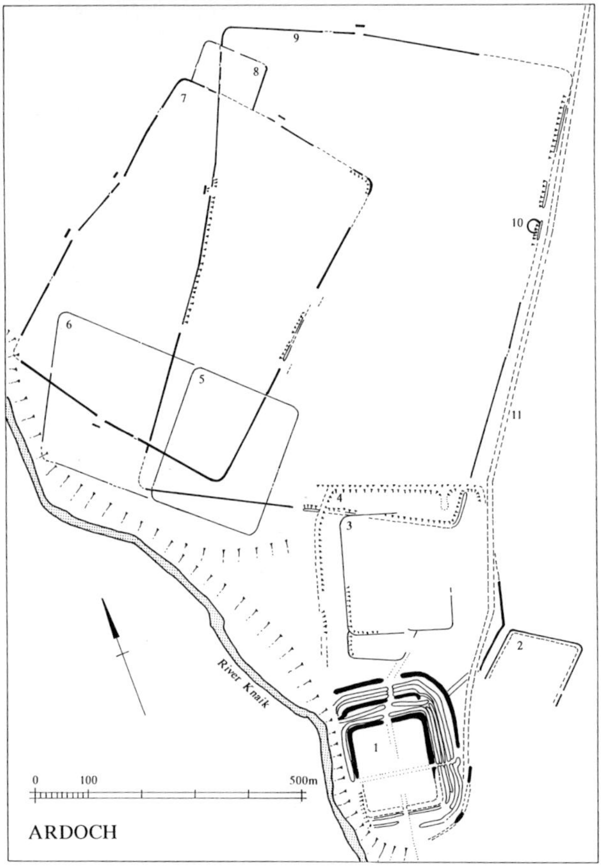

ARDOCH

Figure 8.3 Ardoch: fort (1, ?2), annexe (4), watchtower (10), temporary camps (3, 5-9) and road to Strageath (11).

vary according to the political geography of the area concerned. Close military control was usually manifested in the form of a network of forts and fortlets linked by a road system. This pattern is seen in Wales, northern England and Scotland in the first and second centuries AD, though such close supervision of conquered territory is not recorded in south-

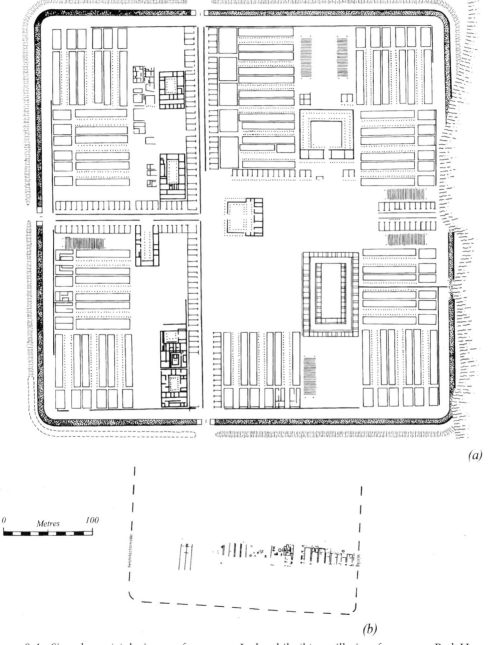

(a)

0   Metres   100

(b)

Figure 8.4 Site plans: (a) legionary fortress at Inchtuthil; (b) vexillation fortress at Red House, Corbridge.

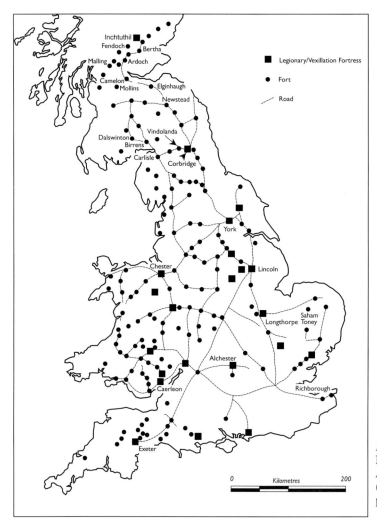

Figure 8.5
Distribution of first-century
AD Roman forts in Britain
(NB not all sites were occu-
pied contemporaneously).

eastern England (Figure 8.5). Here more sophisticated means of political control seem to have been applied immediately after the conquest, involving the use of diplomacy and the establishment of client or 'friendly' kings in an area where native political organization may have been more developed (see Chapter 7) and the opposition less intransigent, perhaps arising from longer-term political contact with Rome (Creighton 2000).

The Romans utilized a hierarchy of permanent military establishments. At its hub were the legionary fortresses, bases for some 5,000 citizen infantry who formed the core of the Roman army. The example with the most complete plan in Britain is that at Inchtuthil (Perthshire), which is both the most northerly and briefest-occupied of all the fortresses. It covered an area of some 20 ha and was clearly intended to house a full legion (Figure 8.4a) (Pitts and St Joseph 1985). All of the barrack blocks had been built, along with the headquarters building, hospital, workshop, some of the granaries and the houses for most of the junior officers, before the fortress was abandoned and dismantled as part of the Roman withdrawal from northern Scotland. Only four legions were used in the invasion of Britain and, by the mid-80s AD, only three remained in garrison. Legionary movements fluctuated considerably in the early years of campaigning and conquest, as indicated by the number of legionary bases recorded on Figure 8.5, eventually settling down in permanent fortresses at York, Caerleon and Chester.

The bulk of the military garrison, however, was made up of auxiliary troops, including cavalry, sub-divided into units nominally 500 or 1,000 strong. These were non-citizen soldiers, recruited from the provinces of the Empire, who formed the main front-line and garrison troops. They were housed in forts which varied considerably in size from 0.8 to 4 ha in internal area (Bidwell 2007). The most completely excavated example of a timber-built auxil-iary fort is that at Elginhaugh (Midlothian), occupied for less than a decade in the late first century (Hanson 2007). The 1.2 ha fort contained 11 accommodation blocks, mostly stable–barracks, suggesting part of a cavalry unit in garrison (Figure 8.6a). The stone-built auxiliary fort at Housesteads (Northumberland) attached to the rear of Hadrian's Wall is perhaps one of the most famous in Roman Britain (Figure 8.6b), though the apparently 'full' plan as often published is a composite of different periods derived from excavations at the end of the nine-teenth century. The fort, which covered an area of 2 ha, probably contained some 800–1,000 men and was occupied almost continuously from the reign of Hadrian through to the end of the fourth century or beginning of the fifth (Crow 1995). There is still much debate about the relationship between auxiliary fort sizes and the different types of unit known, though

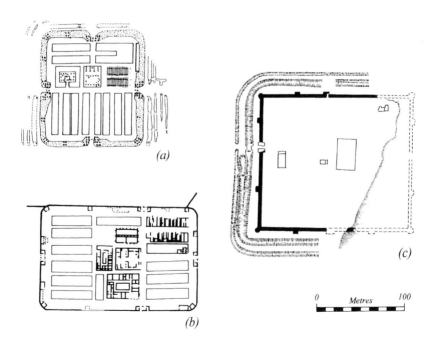

Figure 8.6 Site plans: forts: (a) Elginhaugh; (b) Housesteads; (c) Richborough.

it is becoming increasingly clear that there is no simple correlation between unit and fort, with units being split between different forts and/or different units occupying the same fort. However, the long debate concerning the housing of cavalry horses, whether outside or inside the fort, has now been resolved, with the identification of combined stable–barracks (e.g. Hodgson 2003, 71–86; Hanson 2007, 67–9 and 656–7). Removal of the need to identify separate stable blocks within forts also affects any calculations of garrison-type based on the number of accommodation blocks identified.

The splitting up of units is further attested by the frequent use of much smaller installations, known as fortlets, usually less than 0.5 ha in internal area and distinguished from small forts by the lack of central administrative buildings. The fortlet at Barburgh Mill (Dumfriesshire), the most completely excavated example of its type, enclosed an area of less than 0.1 ha and contained two small timber barrack blocks, sufficient to house a single century of infantry troops (Figure 8.7a) (Breeze 1974). Its occupation relates to the close control of south-west Scotland after the Antonine reconquest of the area.

The smallest permanent installations are watchtowers, simple timber or stone towers surrounded by a rampart and ditch, if free-standing, as at Westerton (Perthshire) (Figure 8.7b). Though individual examples do occur, they are usually associated with frontiers and are best known along Hadrian's Wall (the so-called turrets, which are built into the line of the Wall) and the Gask frontier in Perthshire (Figures. 8.9 and 8.10). They are not infrequently referred to as signal stations, though whether they were used to relay signals is much debated. Some

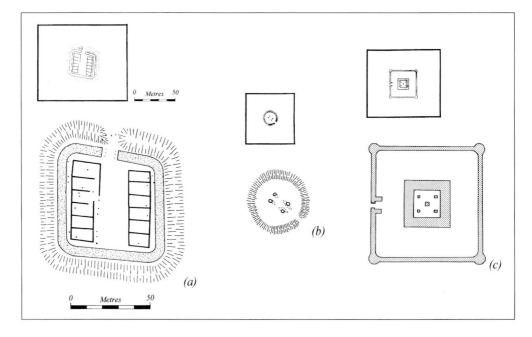

Figure 8.7 Site plans: fortlet and towers: (a) Barburgh Mill; (b) Westerton; (c) Filey. The plans in the boxed inserts are at the same scale as Figures 8.4 and 8.6 to facilitate comparison.

Figure 8.8
Aerial photograph of the fort and *vicus* at Old Carlisle, Cumbria.

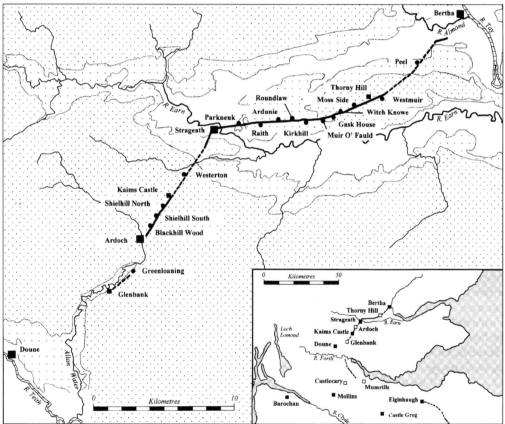

Figure 8.9   Plan of the Gask frontier.

capacity to pass on any information gained from look-outs would seem essential (Woolliscroft 2001), without necessarily implying the existence of a system for relaying complex messages.

Roman military architecture was remarkably consistent for long periods of time. However, some major changes become apparent from the late third century. New forts constructed at coastal locations around the south-east coast of England, the so-called Saxon Shore frontier (Figure 8.11) (Maxfield 1989), and in north and south Wales put greater emphasis on defence. They are provided with massive stone walls and projecting bastions, as at Richborough (Kent), where the walls were over 3 m thick and at least 7 m high (Figure 8.6c), though their internal buildings, where known, were of timber. Fourth-century AD watchtowers attested along the coast of North Yorkshire (Figure 8.11) show similar developments, as for example at Filey, where a massive stone tower situated on a coastal promontory was surrounded by a smaller stone wall with projecting corner bastions (Figure 8.7c) (Ottaway 1996). These towers acted as an early warning system against seaborne raiders.

Fort sites can often be quite closely dated. Knowledge of the overall historical framework provided by the literary account and the epigraphic sources usually allows a general context to be established. Refinement of that chronology derives from the associated material remains, particularly the coins, pottery and, to a lesser extent, glass and metalwork. Study of Roman pottery, particularly the fine tablewares, most notably the ubiquitous imported red glossware, known as samian, is so well developed as to allow quite close dating by that means alone in the first and second centuries AD. Occasionally circumstances permit even closer dating when waterlogged conditions preserve structural timbers which can be dated by dendrochronology, as for example at Carlisle and Alchester (Oxfordshire).

CHANGING PERCEPTIONS

The most substantive change in our perception of the military occupation of Britain since the last war has been brought about by aerial reconnaissance, which is the single most important method of discovering new archaeological sites. The combination of the morphological distinction of Roman military sites and the primary Roman period interest of some major aerial photographic practitioners has resulted in a massive increase in our knowledge of the number, type and distribution of both temporary and permanent military installations. This, in turn, has greatly enhanced our understanding of the process of conquest and consolidation. Some 45 per cent of all forts and fortlets in Scotland, for example, and the vast majority of all temporary camps in Britain have been discovered from the air since the Second World War (e.g. Figure 8.2).

Excavation techniques have developed significantly also, though their impact has been less dramatic and far-reaching. Military establishments were for long thought to be sufficiently regular in both form and layout to require only minimal examination. Thus, up to the 1970s, a process of small-scale sampling was deemed adequate to elucidate their history and development, as exemplified in the excavations at Fendoch (Perthshire), Birrens (Dumfriesshire) and Longthorpe near Peterborough (e.g. Frere and St Joseph 1974). It has since been realized that forts were less regular and standardized, and that their periods of occupation more complex. This requires more extensive investigation, as undertaken at, for example, Elginhaugh (Midlothian), South Shields and Wallsend (both in Tyne and Wear) (e.g. Hanson 2007). Similarly, many forts in Britain are provided with attached enclosures or annexes whose character is so under-researched that even their broad function in relation to military or civilian use is much debated. This situation is only slowly being remedied by a combination of geophysical survey and area excavation, which has tended to confirm their role as ancillary military enclosures for pack animals, wagons in transit or industrial activities (e.g. Hopewell 2005; Hanson 2007, 650–3).

These various developments have in turn contributed to an increasing emphasis being placed on archaeological evidence in its own right, more than simply as an adjunct to the literary sources which previously always took primacy. Such an approach is illustrated, for example, in the lengthy assessment of the role of Agricola in the conquest of the north (Hanson 1991) or the complex reassessment of the history of the Antonine Wall (Hodgson 1995).

While the development of radiocarbon dating, so important for prehistory, has had little or no effect on Roman archaeology because of its imprecision, dendrochronology has made some significant impact where excavation has recovered quantities of waterlogged timber. Dating by matching tree-ring patterns on oak timbers to a master sequence can give a chronological precision equal to the best historical or epigraphic dating. It has been responsible, for example, for confirming the early Claudian date of the 'vexillation fortress' at Alchester (Oxfordshire) and for pushing back the long-accepted date for the establishment of the fort at Carlisle, contributing to the reassessment of the chronology of the conquest of the north.

Other aspects of archaeological science are also proving significant. One of the most important has been the analysis of environmental evidence from excavations, both pollen and macro-fossil remains. These have made considerable contributions to our understanding of the impact of the Roman army on the local environment, particularly the extent to which it was responsible for deforestation, the diet of the troops and the logistics of their food supply (e.g. Hanson 2003). Similarly, geophysical survey is proving extremely useful in elucidating the layout of unexcavated forts and their immediate environs (e.g. Sauer 2000; Hopewell 2005); while metal detecting has greatly increased the recovery of Roman stray finds in the frontier zone (e.g. Hunter 2007, 12).

INTERRELATIONSHIPS

Though use of the term Romanization has come under considerable attack and various alternative terms have been proposed (e.g. Mattingly 2004), the two-way process of cultural interaction between the Roman invader and the indigenous population, resulting in the creation of a new social order characterized as Romano-British, remains central to the study of Roman Britain and is further highlighted in the next chapter. In the military context, the topic has three aspects:

- What was the impact of the Roman army on those areas which it occupied?
- What were the nature, extent and effect of contacts with peoples beyond the frontier once it had been established?
- What role did the army play in the process of Romanization?

The hypothesis that the Roman authorities sought to foster cultural assimilation to Roman 'norms', insofar as they can be identified, has been subject to considerable challenge. There is, however, sufficient evidence to suggest that the alternative view, which would explain the processes of interaction as entirely driven by the indigenous population, is extreme (*contra* Millett 1990). If the Roman authorities did indeed promote and assist the process of Romanization, then the military, as the primary arm of that administration, are likely to have been involved. It has long been argued, for example, that fort sites may have influenced the subsequent location of Roman towns, though this is likely to have been a passive rather than proactive process. It is also possible that direct military assistance was given to urban building projects, even though the evidence for this has been disputed (cf. Blagg 1984).

More certain, however, is the indirect military role in the general acculturation process. Once the army of garrison became relatively static, the process of inter-marriage and local recruitment will gradually have resulted in the army itself becoming increasingly Romano-British. Occasionally a tombstone can reveal something of this process, as for example that of Tadius Exuperatus from Caerleon (Gwent) (Collingwood and Wright 1965, no. 369) (Figure 8.1), who died while serving with the second legion on an expedition in Germany. He was commemorated beside the tomb of his father by his sister and mother, Tadia Vallaunius, whose *cognomen* (family name) is of Celtic origin. The fact that he took his mother's *nomen* (first name) probably indicates that he was the offspring of an illegal local liaison, since serving soldiers were not allowed to marry until the time of Septimius Severus. It is unfortunate, therefore, that relatively little is known about the nature, growth and development of civil settlements (*vici* and *cannabae*) outside Roman forts and fortresses, though on the northern frontier they appear to flourish during the lengthy period of peace through the third century which followed the Severan campaigns. Few have been extensively examined by excavation in recent years, though aerial reconnaissance has given some indication of the overall plan of several examples (e.g. Figure 8.8), and a recent programme of geophysical survey in both Wales and along Hadrian's Wall has made a substantial contribution to improving our understanding of the extent and complexity of these settlements (e.g. Hopewell 2005).

The military impact on Britain varies according to the area concerned. Because of the relatively short period of occupation involved, this impact is likely to have been very limited in the south-east and the extreme north. Whether the longer-term presence of the army stimulated the local economy by encouraging the production of a surplus to supply the military market, or depressed it by placing demands on the local system which it could not sustain, depends upon both the natural environment and the social and technological development of the area concerned. In north-western England, for example, the effect of the military presence seems to have been largely detrimental to the economic development of the indigenous population, whereas in south Wales and perhaps in south-eastern Scotland the opposite was the case. It is becoming increasingly clear, however, that the military impact on the local environment in the north, once thought to have been quite dramatic, is likely to have been relatively limited (Hanson 2003). Much of the forest seems to have been cleared as part of the long-term expansion of settlement and agriculture by the indigenous population, not to fulfil Roman building requirements; substantive disruption of the settlement pattern is not readily attested; and no major changes in agricultural production to cater for the Roman dietary preferences for beef and wheat are currently detectable.

The nature, extent and effect of contacts with peoples beyond the frontier are also much in debate (e.g. Hunter 2007). Apart from a few scant references in the Classical literature, the evidence is restricted to the relatively widespread distribution of Roman artefacts on native settlement sites, in votive deposits or as stray finds. Whether this material represents gifts received to cement diplomatic relations, booty from raiding or is the result of trading contacts is often difficult to determine, though there is increasing support for the first of these interpretations, as implied by the discovery at Birnie (Moray) of two separate late second-century hoards of silver *denarii* buried in native pots within an unenclosed Iron Age settlement. These and other coin hoards provide archaeological confirmation of the Roman policy of buying peace attested in the later Roman literary sources (Dio Cassius, 75.5.4). Two general trends are apparent in the character and distribution of Roman artefacts within contemporary native society. Firstly, there is a limited range of material found, indicating that it was being selectivity adopted to fit Iron Age social practices. Secondly, it is not evenly distributed either within or across that society, with strong regional and chronological variations and, in the main, greater access to Roman material amongst the upper social stratum of native society, suggesting that Rome may have targeted particular groups at certain times (Hunter 2007, 37).

CURRENT PERCEPTIONS AND OUTSTANDING PROBLEMS

Site of the invasion landing

One of the most heated debates of recent years has concerned whether the army of invasion in AD 43 landed in Kent or Sussex. The former is the traditional location because it represents the shortest sea crossing and there is some archaeological confirmation at Richborough (Kent), where an irregular temporary military enclosure was rapidly replaced by a major supply-base containing a large number of timber-built granaries. An association with the original conquest seems to have been reaffirmed by the construction of a monumental triumphal arch at the site in the Flavian period. An alternative view draws attention to the traces of early military activity at Fishbourne (Sussex), emphasizing the potential benefit of a landing in 'friendly' territory (e.g. Manley 2002). Whatever the solution, the subsequent focus of the invasion force was to cross the Thames and capture *Camulodunum* (Colchester, Essex), the capital of the *Catuvellauni*.

The search for a frontier

Whether it was the original intention to conquer the whole of the island of Britain is uncertain. The Romans were most familiar with the south-east because of Caesar's two expeditions in 55 and 54 BC and continued diplomatic and trading contacts thereafter, the former manifested archaeologically in the changes in Iron Age coin types (Creighton 2000); the latter in the distribution of Roman artefacts, particularly Dressel 1B wine amphorae (Peacock 1984). Such contacts also ensured that the conquest of AD 43 was achieved and maintained with relative ease in the south and east, since it was supported by certain factions within native society. The creation of three client or friendly kingdoms, the *Iceni* in Norfolk, the *Regni* in Sussex and the *Brigantes* in northern England, is an important feature of this early period. It underpinned Roman control of the province and freed troops to concentrate on areas of greater resistance.

It has been argued that it was intended to occupy only the south and east of England, but the identification of an early frontier along the Fosse Way, the Roman road from Exeter to Lincoln, is misconceived and not supported by the chronology of the sites involved (Jones and Mattingly 1991). Moreover, troop deployments, particularly the presence of legionary and vexillation fortresses along the periphery of the area under direct Roman control, indicate the intention to continue to advance, rather than simply to police the area overrun. In the context of the early consolidation of the Roman conquest, the idea of a frontier would have been psychologically unacceptable since it would, in effect, have implied that there was a definable limit to Roman expansion.

Continued conquest was slowed by less favourable terrain and increasing hostility from the indigenous tribes who had had no previous contact with Rome. It was further delayed by the Boudican rebellion of AD 60 and its aftermath, and a local uprising amongst the *Brigantes* in AD 69. Several of the limited number of forts known in south-eastern England, such as the second fort at Saham Toney (Norfolk), may have been established as a direct consequence of the Boudican rebellion, indicating the need to re-establish Roman control.

When conquest and concomitant expansion was resumed in AD 71 under a new imperial house, the Flavians, it progressed rapidly over the next 15 years under successive governors. Roman military occupation was extended north and west across northern England, Wales and Scotland (Figure 8.5). One current area of debate is the extent to which Petillius Cerialis, the first Flavian appointee as governor, may have penetrated north of the Tyne–Solway isthmus, given the dendrochronologically established felling date of AD 72 for timbers used in the construction of the auxiliary fort at Carlisle. Some even postulate that it was Cerialis and not Agricola who was primarily responsible for the conquest of Scotland, establishing bases beyond the Forth–Clyde isthmus and constructing the Gask frontier described below (Woolliscroft and Hoffman 2006, 175–202). However, such an interpretation flies in the face of both the detailed narrative of the eminent contemporary Roman historian Tacitus and a less selective consideration of the archaeological dating evidence (cf. Hanson 2007, 646–7).

The conquest of the whole island became a feasible proposition for Roman forces, though the possibility that they might fail to achieve such a goal may already have begun to be considered. Tacitus indicates (*Agricola*, 23) that a halt was made in the campaigns of conquest of his father-in-law, Agricola, and the line drawn across the most obvious geographical point, the Forth–Clyde isthmus. Supporting archaeological evidence remains problematic. It was once thought, for example, that Agricolan forts lay beneath many of the later fortifications along the Antonine Wall, but this belief can no longer be substantiated in most cases. Though several first-century forts are known across the isthmus, such as Mollins (Lanarkshire) and Camelon (Stirlingshire), both lying away from the later Wall line, not enough have been identified legitimately to confirm a frontier line.

However, following the road north of the isthmus as far as the Tay at Bertha (Perthshire), a series of forts, fortlets and timber watchtowers have been discovered, which have all the hallmarks of such a frontier. When the Romans were imposing close military control over an area, forts and fortlets tended to occur at regular intervals of 25–32 km, usually referred to as a day's march apart. When frontier lines begin to emerge, this spacing is reduced to half or less, often with fortlets interspersed between the forts, and closer supervision provided by the construction of watchtowers. The unusual survival of a number of these towers along the Gask Ridge in Perthshire was noted more than a century ago, and subsequently their extent has been augmented by aerial survey and tested by excavation, indicating that they stretch for some 40 km at intervals of between 800 and 1,500 m (Figure 8.9). There is still considerable disagreement about the chronological context and function of this system, some even suggesting that it was no more than a protected supply line (e.g. Pitts and St Joseph 1985, 278), but a link with Agricola's halt on the Forth–Clyde isthmus remains the most plausible explanation for these dispositions, which would make this the earliest artificially defined frontier in the Roman Empire.

Nonetheless, campaigning was soon resumed, probably as the result of a change of emperor, and the complete conquest of the island was clearly the intention. However, a serious military setback in Dacia resulted in the withdrawal of troops from Britain to the Danube frontier and the concomitant failure to consolidate the conquest of the north, reminding us that Britain was just one small, remote province in a huge empire, and that decisions which affected it were not necessarily always taken entirely with local considerations in mind.

For the next 130 years, the history of the northern frontier involves the search for a convenient limit to Roman occupation. On the Continent, the great rivers of the Rhine and Danube provided ready demarcators of Roman territory. In Britain, the geographical choice lay between the isthmuses of the Tyne–Solway and Forth–Clyde, though with variations on this theme. These variations give some clue to the Roman attitude towards frontiers and their function, though these subjects are still much debated.

The exact location of the frontier at the end of the first century is not absolutely clear. It does not appear at present that the Tyne–Solway isthmus became the frontier immediately after the withdrawal from Scotland in the late 80s AD. At least part of Lowland Scotland continued to be controlled by a network of forts, the most northerly of which were Newstead (Roxburghshire) in the east and Dalswinton (Dumfriesshire) in the west. Moreover, Roman control and influence seems to have extended beyond them, for the abandoned site of the auxiliary fort at

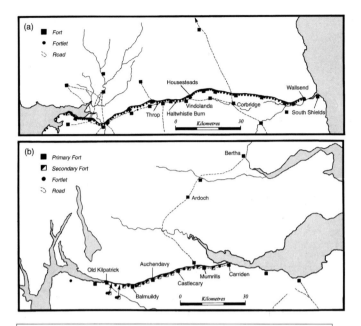

Figure 8.10 Frontiers across the Tyne–Solway and Forth–Clyde.

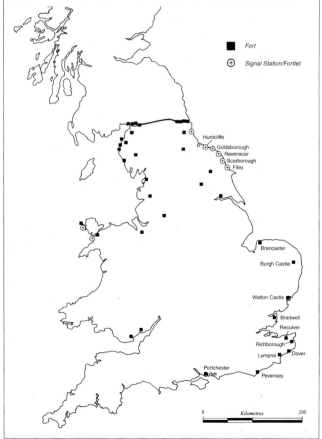

Figure 8.11 Distribution of Saxon Shore forts and late Roman coastal watchtowers.

Elginhaugh (Midlothian) was used by the Romans as a collection point for animals, presumably as part of the exaction of tribute from the area (Hanson 2007, 650–3). Within 20 years, however, these northern forts were abandoned, the withdrawal probably brought about by the demands of an extensive military commitment beyond the Danube in Dacia, as the Emperor Trajan sought the conquest of that area. In Britain we see the emergence of a frontier line across the Tyne–Solway isthmus, usually referred to as the Trajanic or Stanegate frontier (Breeze and Dobson 2000, 16–24) (Figure 8.10). The latter term derives from the medieval name for the Roman road which runs from east to west between Carlisle and Corbridge. This frontier is manifested archaeologically in a decrease in spacing between posts along that road. New forts were constructed, including two, Haltwhistle Burn and Throp (both in Northumberland), which, in terms of their size, lie halfway between fort and fortlet. As on the Gask frontier, the closer spacing seems to have been supplemented by the provision of watchtowers, though the system is still known only in embryo, best attested in the central sector.

These dispositions represent the first stages in the creation of a frontier across the Tyne–Solway isthmus which eventually culminated in the elaborate and extensively studied provisions of Hadrian's Wall (Breeze and Dobson 2000) (Figure 8.10). Nonetheless, there is still a good deal to discover of its earliest development. It is clear that the original Hadrianic plan was merely an augmentation of the pre-existing frontier along the Stanegate by the construction of a running barrier of stone or turf. This connected a series of watchtowers (usually now called 'turrets') at intervals of 500 m, with garrisoned gateways every 1.6 km (1 mile) in fortlets, generally now referred to as 'milecastles'. Thereafter, the plan underwent continuous modification until its abandonment when the Romans returned to occupy Scotland in 139 AD. The major change was the movement of forts up onto the line of the Wall, though only some of the forts to the rear were given up in the process. This was clearly recognition that the linear barrier not only served to exclude unwanted incursions from the north, but made it more difficult for the Romans to deploy troops rapidly beyond it.

Given that the army had just left one linear barrier which was still undergoing modification, it ought not to be surprising that they should choose to construct another, this time utilizing the shorter isthmus between Forth and Clyde, when the readvance into Scotland at the behest of the Emperor Antoninus Pius had been completed. As originally conceived, the Antonine Wall seems to have been modelled on Hadrian's Wall in its developed form, with forts attached to the barrier at intervals of approximately 13 km and fortlets 1.6 km apart between them, although the absence of a system of watchtowers, the equivalent of the turrets on Hadrian's Wall, remains a problem. But the Antonine Wall also underwent dramatic modification during its construction, with the addition of a series of smaller forts reducing the average spacing to some 3.5 km and resulting in a denser concentration of forces than on any other linear frontier in the Empire (Hanson and Maxwell 1986, 105–12) (Figure 8.10). Such a dramatic change can only have been in response to some perceived threat, though there is no direct evidence of it. However, occupation of the more northerly wall was relatively short-lived. By the early 160s AD the Romans had withdrawn to Hadrian's Wall, the previously assumed and much debated fluctuations in that process no longer accepted (Hodgson 1995). Apart from the brief period of the Severan campaigns, when completion of the conquest of Scotland was again a possibility, Hadrian's Wall remained the northern frontier of the province of Britain, though the distance over which control extended beyond it varies, as is indicated by the fluctuation in the occupation of outpost forts.

The function of frontiers

Hadrian's Wall is perhaps the best-known frontier in the whole of the Roman Empire, but it is far from typical of Roman frontiers. Most were not defined by linear barriers and, among those that were, the provision of a massive stone wall was not the norm. Even where obvious demarcation lines were provided, whether man-made or natural, such as rivers, they do not necessarily define the limit of Roman occupied territory and rarely do they define the full extent of the territory over which Roman control was exercised. The provision of outpost forts as a regular feature of both frontier walls in Britain indicates that military occupation normally extended approximately 8–40 km to the north of them. Moreover, it is quite clear that for most of the third and fourth centuries, patrols exercised Roman military control considerably further afield. Where no obvious line was demarcated, the definition of Roman territory can be even more difficult. Indeed, it remains a matter of debate whether there was ever a precisely defined legal limit to the Empire, even though this might seem a necessary prerequisite for administrative purposes.

Roman frontiers were built and operated by the army, and military defence was clearly one of their prime functions, but, at least until the early fourth century in Britain, the process was proactive as well as reactive. The Romans usually responded to threats to territory they occupied by undertaking a campaign against the aggressors, the principle best exemplified by the action of Agricola against the *Ordovices* in Wales immediately upon his arrival in the province as the new governor (Tacitus, *Agricola*, 18). Static defence from maintained positions was not normal Roman practice. When thoughts of completing the conquest of the island of Britain were given up and it was necessary to create a frontier, the Romans looked to natural features, such as the Forth–Clyde isthmus, for convenience of definition (Tacitus, *Agricola*, 23). Such features were at first augmented by a closer spacing of military garrisons than was the case when hostile territory was being controlled by a fort network, often utilizing smaller garrison posts, either small forts or fortlets. Other characteristic features were the provision of a system of watchtowers and of a lateral road connecting these various installations. This development can be seen on the Gask and Stanegate frontiers of late first- and early second-century date. Only later, after Hadrian's reign, do we see the addition of a linear barrier as part of the system.

This development sequence gives some indication of Rome's attitude to the function of frontiers. The provision of garrisons at closer intervals and of a regular system of watchtowers suggests a concern for the control of movement across the frontier, but there is no suggestion that a system of preclusive defence was intended. Even when linear barriers were added to the system, we see the provision of regular gateways at fortlets located every 1.6 km on both Hadrian's Wall and the Antonine Wall. If the primary function of frontiers was to exclude, such provision would have been both unnecessary and potentially disadvantageous, since gateways are a weak point in any defensive circuit. On the other hand, the provision of a linear barrier would be a logical step if concern was to increase the level of control and the intensity of security. Such action would serve to funnel all legitimate movement through the gateways under the watchful eyes of the Roman garrison, making the levying of customs dues more readily achieved, but would also effectively exclude small-scale illicit movement, such as border raiding. Linear barriers are of little use against major incursions, since external forces could be massed at a selected location, easily outnumbering any local troops, and could readily breach the wall before sufficient defensive reinforcements could be summoned to the spot.

Whether the wall line was ever intended to be defended as a barrier in the way that the perimeter of a fort would have been is much disputed, with the established view coming under challenge as a result of the discovery of additional defensive provision on the berm (the gap between rampart and ditch) along both Hadrian's Wall and the Antonine Wall (e.g. Bidwell 2005). Clearly, the original thickness of Hadrian's Wall (the so-called 'broad wall') could have accommodated a walkway, though there is no direct evidence that it was provided with the necessary parapet or crenellations. The reduction in the width of later sections of the wall to as little as 1.3 m, however, decreases the probability that it could have been used as a fighting platform. Evidence from the Antonine Wall is more difficult to assess since the details of the superstructure of the turf rampart are less certain. Analogy with the German frontier, however, where the barrier consisted of only a timber palisade, makes clear that the use of such barriers as elevated fighting platforms requires proof rather than being automatically assumed.

It has been further suggested that the provision of a linear barrier would provide greater protection to the local population within the province, thus encouraging and facilitating the process of Romanization (Hanson and Maxwell 1986, 163). However, whether this was the intended function rather than an incidental side-effect remains unproven.

Debate about the function of the Saxon Shore is more fundamental since its very identification as a frontier has been challenged. Thus, it has been suggested that the forts do not readily fit into any practical defensive strategy, but should better be seen as trans-shipment centres for the collection and distribution of state supplies (Cotterill 1993). However, various factors make it difficult to dismiss the current orthodoxy: the general distribution of the forts along the coast which faced the brunt of Saxon raiding (Figure 8.11); the way the forts seem to dominate access to important harbours or river mouths, a feature which is even more apparent against the background of the contemporary coastline where this is known (e.g. Maxfield 1989, 13–15); and the specific literary reference to defence against such attacks as the reason for the appointment of Carausius, under whose auspices most of the forts seem to have been built, to a command which spanned both sides of the Channel (Eutropius, 9, 21). Nonetheless, the absence of direct evidence of naval detachments at most of the forts remains a problem if their primary function was as defended strongholds for the fleet.

ROMAN BRITAIN IN ITS WIDER SETTING

Two distinctive approaches to the study of Roman Britain are apparent. The first emphasizes the distinctive nature of the island and the importance of local conditions in determining the extent, nature and course of that occupation. The second stresses Britain's position in the wider Empire, of which it was only a small part, and the impact of broader policy decisions and actions elsewhere on events in the province. Though the latter approach has become the orthodoxy in recent years, there is validity in both. Although, on the one hand, the physical and political geography will have varied from frontier to frontier, on the other hand, all the provinces were constituent parts of a wider imperial system whose personnel were frequently moving between provinces. Thus, though local circumstances must have influenced decisions taken about the strategy and tactics involved in the occupation, the personnel making those decisions will inevitably have been informed by their experiences in other parts of the Empire. Moreover, comparative frontier studies do reveal various consistent approaches to the exercising of control in frontier zones, such as the use of client or friendly monarchs or the levying of customs duties, as well as highlighting local differences, such as the absence of gateways along the German frontier palisade or the more restricted depth of military dispositions behind the frontiers along the Rhine and Danube.

The influence of the wider stage of imperial politics on events in Britain has already been hinted at above, when the resumption of advance in the Flavian period after the halt on the Forth–Clyde isthmus seems to coincide with the accession of a new emperor. There are, however, several more specific examples of this process. It is now widely accepted that the major stimulus for the invasion in AD 43 was the need of the new emperor, Claudius, for the prestige of a successful military conquest; while the same principle seems to underlie the reconquest of Scotland under Antoninus Pius. Similarly, attention has been drawn to the effect of circumstances in other parts of the Empire on determining the limits of Roman control in the north of Britain. In the late first century the transfer of troops to the Danube resulted in the withdrawal from northern Scotland; and in the early second century Trajan's concentration on wars of expansion in Dacia may have resulted in further retrenchment on the northern frontier.

Key texts

Bidwell, P., 2007. *Roman forts in Britain*. Stroud: Tempus.
Breeze, D.J. and Dobson, B., 2000. *Hadrian's Wall*. London: Penguin. 4 edn.
Hanson, W.S., 1991. *Agricola and the conquest of the north*. London: Batsford. 2 edn.
Hanson, W.S. and Maxwell, G.S., 1986. *Rome's north-west frontier: the Antonine Wall*. Edinburgh: Edinburgh University Press. 2 edn.
Jones, G.D.B. and Mattingly, D.J., 1991. *An atlas of Roman Britain*. Oxford: Blackwell.

Bibliography

Bidwell, P., 2005. 'The systems of obstacles on Hadrian's Wall: their extent, date and purpose', *Arbeia Journal* 8, 53–76.

Birley, A.R., 2005. *The Roman government of Britain*. Oxford: Oxford University Press.

Blagg, T.F.C., 1984. 'An examination of the connexions between military and civilian architecture', in Blagg, T.F.C and King, A.C. (eds) *Military and civilian in Roman Britain: cultural relationships in a frontier province*. Oxford: British Archaeological Reports British Series 136, 249–63.

Bowman, A.K., 1994. *Life and letters on the Roman frontier*. London: British Museum.

Breeze, D.J., 1974. 'The Roman fortlet at Barburgh Mill, Dumfriesshire', *Britannia* 5, 130–62.

Collingwood, R.G. and Wright, R.P., 1965. *Roman inscriptions of Britain*. Oxford: Clarendon Press.

Cotterill, J., 1993. 'Saxon raiding and the role of the late Roman coastal forts of Britain', *Britannia* 24, 227–39.

Creighton, J., 2000. *Coins and power in late Iron Age Britain*. Cambridge: Cambridge University Press.

Crow, J., 1995 *Book of Housesteads*. London: Batsford / English Heritage.

Davies, J.L. and Jones, R.H., 2006. *Roman camps in Wales and the Marches*. Cardiff: University of Wales Press.

Frere, S.S. and St Joseph, J.K.S., 1974. 'The Roman fortress of Longthorpe', *Britannia* 5, 1–129.

Hanson, W.S., 2003. 'The Roman presence: brief interludes', in Edwards, K.J. and Ralston, I.B.M. (eds) *Scotland after the ice age: environment, archaeology and history, 8000 BC–1000 AD*. Edinburgh: Edinburgh University Press, 195–216.

Hanson, W.S., 2007. *Elginhaugh: a Flavian auxiliary fort and its annexe*. London: Society for the Promotion of Roman Studies.

Hanson, W.S., Daniels, C.M., Dore, J.N. and Gillam, J.P., 1979. 'The Agricolan supply-base at Red House, Corbridge', *Archaeologia Aeliana* 7, 1–97.

Hodgson, N., 1995. 'Were there two Antonine occupations of Scotland?', *Britannia* 26, 29–49.

Hodgson, N. 2003. *The Roman fort at Wallsend (Segedunum): excavations 1997–98*. Newcastle-upon-Tyne: Tyne and Wear Museums.

Hopewell, D., 2005. 'Roman fort environs in north-west Wales', *Britannia* 36, 225–69.

Hunter, F., 2007. *Beyond the edge of empire – Caledonians, Picts and Romans*. Rosemarkie: Groam House Museum.

Manley, J., 2002. *AD 43 and the Roman invasion of Britain: a reassessment*. Stroud: Tempus.

Mattingly, D., 2004. 'Being Roman: expressing identity in a provincial setting', *Journal of Roman Archaeology* 17, 1–25.

Mattingly, D., 2006. *An imperial possession. Britain in the Roman empire, 55 BC–AD 409*. London: Allen Lane.

Maxfield, V.A. (ed.) 1989. *The Saxon Shore: a handbook*. Exeter: University of Exeter Press.

Millett, M., 1990. *The Romanization of Britain*. Cambridge: Cambridge University Press.

Ottaway, P., 1996. *Romans on the Yorkshire coast*. York: York Archaeological Trust.

Peacock, D.P.S., 1984. 'Amphorae in Iron Age Britain: a re-assessment', in Macready, S. and Thompson, F.H. (eds) *Cross-channel trade between Gaul and Britain in the pre-Roman Iron age*. London: Society of Antiquaries Occasional Papers NS IV, 37–42.

Pitts, L. and St Joseph, J.K.S., 1985. *Inchtuthil: the Roman legionary fortress*. London: Society for the Promotion of Roman Studies.

Sauer, E.W., 2000. 'Alchester, a Claudian "vexillation fortress" near the western boundary of the Catuvellauni: new light on the Roman invasion of Britain', *Archaeological Journal* 157, 1–78.

Woolliscroft, D.J., 2001. *Roman military signalling*. Stroud: Tempus.

Woolliscroft, D.J. and Hoffman, B., 2006 *Rome's first frontier. The Flavian occupation of northern Scotland*. Stroud: Tempus.

9

ROMAN BRITAIN

Civil and rural society

Simon Esmonde Cleary

SETTING THE SCENE

The Roman period, though one of the shortest in the archaeology of Britain (only some 400 years), is also one of the most recognizable, standing in marked contrast to the preceding and succeeding periods. In part this is because the incorporation of the southern part of the island into the Roman Empire led to the adoption of Roman-style social and cultural values and practices, resulting in a very distinctive archaeological record; in part it is because those values and practices entailed a hugely increased mobilization of agricultural, mineral and human resources that help to create a very visible archaeological record. The legacy of these values can be seen in such well-known phenomena as 'Roman roads' and Roman-style towns (resulting for the first time in a map that has recognizable similarities to that of modern England and Wales), or villas, temples and burials (Ordnance Survey 2001). As well as sites, there is a huge range and quantity of durable material culture, above all pottery, but also metalwork, glass and other materials. Because of the privileged place accorded to Roman culture, including visual culture, in Europe since the Enlightenment, much to do with Roman Britain can at first sight look familiar and therefore easily comprehensible: this is a temptation that must be resisted, for study of the archaeology of Roman Britain increasingly shows what a strange, not to say weird, place it would have been to our eyes.

In addition, because for nigh on 400 years *Britannia* was a province of the Roman Empire, there has been a long-standing dialectic in the approaches to the study of Britain which will be evident when we come to more detailed considerations of the evidence and the approaches to that evidence. On the one hand, the period can be approached from what might be labelled a 'Romanist' perspective, emphasizing viewpoints arising from the wider history, society, economy and culture of the empire; regarding Britain as a region within that empire and interpreting it through the prisms of 'grand narratives' for the wider Roman world. On the other hand, a 'nativist' perspective can be deployed, in which the period is seen as one within the continuum of insular archaeology, where an intrusive culture with highly distinctive manifestations is overlaid on longer-term processes within the island, a perspective which seeks to downplay the impact of Rome by regarding the period as a medium-term episode within the longer term of early Britain: in this reading it is the continuities of indigenous formations and their adoption and adaptation of Roman-style practices that were the more important trend. The interaction of the two traditions is seen in the common descriptor for the period 'Romano-British'. Acknowledging the impact of Rome but also showing that it cannot simply be seen (or written off) as 'Roman', it is a period defined by the response of the indigenous majority population to these Roman influences. Indeed, it is vital to remember that at all times the overwhelming majority of the people in Roman Britain were of British descent (Britons) rather than immigrants from abroad, least of all Romans from Rome.

Though the period is short relative to most other periods treated in this book (the historical sources give us apparently clear start and end dates of AD 43 and AD 410), it is nevertheless divided into two roughly equal chunks: an earlier period running from the middle of the first century AD to the first half of the third century, and a later period from the mid-third century into the first half of the fifth. As well as a broad chronological divide, there is a major regional divide: archaeologically, civil Roman Britain essentially consists of two culture-provinces, with the south and the east on the one hand and the north and the west on the other (Jones and Mattingly 1990). It is in the south and east that we find the expressions of 'classic' Roman provincial culture, with its major classes of site and material. These include: towns, with their accompanying categories of public buildings, private residences and artisan buildings; villas, the rural residences constructed to plans and in materials derived from Roman practice; temples and shrines of 'Romano-Celtic' type; burials, cremations and inhumations, sometimes with tombstones or grave-monuments; and associated with these abundant quantities of material culture such as pottery, coins and metalwork and sometimes more substantial markers of wealth and Classical culture such as mosaics. The north and west, by contrast, largely lack such a visible and distinctive archaeological record, especially outside the little islands of 'Roman-ness' represented by forts and their accompanying civil settlement. It has been seen as a landscape of absences; the absence of the towns, villas, etc. of the south and east. In fact it is more profitable to regard it as a landscape that has its own presences; ones such as settlement- and building-types which have clear links with those current before the Roman takeover and which also show continuities with pre-Roman traditions in such things as generally low levels (quantitatively, not necessarily qualitatively) of material culture, or in funerary traditions that leave little or no trace to the archaeologist. It should also be remembered that within the south and east there were major disparities by class, region and period. Villas, for instance, only ever housed a minority of the rural population; the majority lived in dispersed settlements of timber-built structures that owe little to Roman-style practice and used lesser quantities of coin or pottery. The incidence of villas was also highly variable by chronology (they were more common in the fourth than the second century) and by region (for instance the concentration in the Cotswolds by contrast with the neighbouring west midlands). The reasons for the gross disparities between the north and west as compared with the south and east is a major focus of discussion, and increasing recognition of regional, chronological and other variations is feeding into more nuanced analyses: it has become much more difficult to write generalizing narratives of 'Roman Britain'.

CHANGING PERCEPTIONS

For most of the twentieth century the dominant paradigm for the study of Roman Britain was 'The Romanization of Roman Britain' outlined by Haverfield in his 1909 book of that title. This sought to explain the changes visible in the archaeological record as the introduction by the Roman authorities of Roman-style civilization to the indigenous population and the more or less successful efforts of the latter to replicate it. The process was seen as essentially 'top-down', depending partly on the Roman historian Tacitus' account of how his father-in-law, the late first-century governor of Britain Cn. Iulius Agricola, encouraged the Britons to build Roman buildings, to adopt Roman habits and dress and to speak Latin (Tacitus, *Agricola*, 21). It also depended on the resonances this had for the classically educated elite of a modern European imperial power which felt that it too had a 'civilizing mission'. This view also chimed with the 'Romanist' perspective in the study of Britain, where texts and inscriptions (all in Latin) took precedence over the archaeology (of which there was still relatively little) and where the study of such classically Roman manifestations as the Roman army or Roman towns dominated other aspects of the province. With the rise of a generation of workers who had grown up after Britain's retreat from empire and who tended to be less trained in Classical languages and literature and to be more aware of issues such as gender or 'people without history' or post-colonial discourses, came a shift in perspective. 'Romanization' remained as the 'grand narrative' unifying the trends visible in the archaeology (by now much more abundant thanks to the boom in excavation from the 1960s onwards), but the agents for such change were now seen as the indigenous British, particularly the elite, selecting and adapting those elements of Roman custom and practice that suited their purposes: a shift in perspective crystallized in the hugely influential 1990 book by Millett, whose title *The Romanization of Britain* consciously echoed that of Haverfield's and demonstrated the persistence of 'Romanization' as process and explanation. In the succeeding 20 years the pace of the debate has increased considerably.

'Romanization' has fallen out of favour as an explanatory mechanism: in part this is because it is seen as too teleological, implying that the main driver of change was to 'become Roman'; in part it is because by concentrating on this one aspect others, equally or more important, such as status, age, gender, were downgraded. Instead, features of the post-modern (in archaeology often referred to as post-processual) critique have been adopted and currently form the foundation of the dominant paradigm. On the one hand there is the post-modern emphasis on identity, individual and group, in particular on the idea that most identity is neither innate nor immutable (gender largely being an exception); instead, identities, particularly social and ethnic identities, are 'constructed' and 'situational', that is they are malleable and can be adopted or altered as surrounding circumstances and structures suggest (Mattingly 2006). Moreover, both individual and group identities need to be expressed, and this is where the power of the debate over identity resides for archaeologists, since so much material culture, from building-plans to hair-ornaments, can be discussed in these terms (Todd 2004). This also fits well with debates in social theory, with 'structure' and 'agency' existing in a reflexive relationship whereby individuals operate within socially defined and accepted structures, but are also conscious agents in accepting, modifying or challenging those structures, resulting in feed-back which over time changes the structures. The applicability of such models to archaeology, particularly to the explanation of archaeological change, is readily apparent. The Roman period is one where such change is particularly evident and well attested in a wide range of archaeological evidence types. The construction and display of identity is a central concern in understanding the phases of rapid change at the beginning and end of that period when small groups of incomers (Romans, Anglo-Saxons) imposed themselves on the far more numerous indigenous populations.

'Romanization' was a useful 'grand narrative' for the earlier Roman period in Britain, where there were clearly considerable discrepancies between Roman and British social and cultural formations, discrepancies that progressively diminished as some Britons took on some aspects of Roman practice. But it is of little, if any, use for the later period, when Britons, particularly the elite, had become integrated into and agents within Roman structures and therefore such discrepancies as remain have more to do with regional variation and status/wealth gradients within the Western Empire than with lack of habituation to Roman ways. But the concept of 'Late Antiquity', a development in the study of the period since the Second World War, provides major themes that allow the British evidence to be contextualized. Late Antiquity sees the period c. AD 300–700 as a period in its own right, starting after the military and political 'crisis' of the empire in the third century, and continuing through the 'fall' of the Western Empire in the fifth century into the succeeding period in Europe of the construction of the 'successor states' often ruled by peoples of Germanic origin. Within this period there are other major themes such as the increasing military, political and fiscal demands of the Roman state, the creation of late antique elite culture, the spread of Christianity as the imperial religion and the replacement of the Western Empire by Germanic kingdoms in the course of the fifth century. In each of these Britain had its part to play, and their effects are visible in the archaeology of the later Roman period in the island. Since many of these themes, such as elite culture, Christianity, military status and Germanic ethnicity, are all matters of identity, the discourses of identity and their archaeological correlates continue to play a central part, down to and including the disappearance of Roman-style archaeologies and their replacement by others, principally Germanic, in the fifth century. A major consequence of the increasing emphasis on identity is that much more effort is now being expended in the field of material culture studies, since the manufacture, use and deposition of objects of a wide range of types was closely linked to identity, for instance in matters of dress and personal appearance or of houses or of funerary practices.

Dating

Compared with many other periods, the Roman is unusual in the tight date-brackets offered for sites and material. How this comes about needs some explanation and qualification. The Romans struck a tri-metallic coinage: gold; silver and bronze. The first two are seldom found as site-finds, though form a large proportion of hoards. Down to the mid-third century, base-metal coins are not that common as site-finds since they were only sporadically supplied to Britain and were of relatively high value. In the later third century and through the fourth this changed radically, with successive large-volume issues of base-metal, low-value coinage, very common as site-finds. Roman coins are datable (if legible) at least to the reign of an emperor, often more closely. But this is the year(s) of minting not deposition, and so can only yield a *terminus post quem*, a date *after which* the deposit containing the coin must have been created, since the coin did not exist earlier: this does not of course say how long after. The common association of pottery with coins has allowed a dating sequence to be established for changing centres of production, fabrics, forms and decorative styles, permitting relatively tight dating even on sites without coins (especially, for the first and second centuries, by the use of 'samian', a high-gloss, red-slipped pottery from Gaul, often decorated and/or stamped with the name of the potter). But it is important to bear in mind, first, the inherent problems of deriving dates from coins and, second, that a pottery 'date' is really the date-range when that type of pottery is most commonly *deposited* (not, unlike a coin, made), thus some pottery might be deposited 'too early' or 'too late'. As a rule of thumb, the fewer the coins and the less the pottery from a site, the more uncertain the dating. The apparent firm dating from artefacts in large part explains the relative neglect for the period of physical and other dating techniques, since, for radiocarbon dating especially, a calibrated date-range at one standard deviation is often wider than that derived from artefacts; but dendrochronology has made some important contributions, for instance in the study of the waterfront at London.

KEY DATA

Having outlined changing intellectual frameworks and preoccupations, it is time to look at major and distinctive classes of evidence that typify the Roman period, and also some of the debates over how these types of evidence should be interpreted. The section starts by looking at the types of site that most insistently proclaim the acceptance of Roman culture by the elites and certain others, particularly towns and villas. It then looks at the large sections of the population by geographical area and socio-economic groupings to whom such things were clearly of much less importance and whose acceptance of them was partial or almost absent. The impact of Rome on religion, ritual practice and burial is then reviewed.

Towns

The Roman Empire was an empire of towns and cities. They are distributed, albeit unevenly, all across the provinces, and in Europe there is nothing of this type beyond the frontiers. The Roman Empire could not function politically, legally, fiscally, economically or culturally without towns. They were the centres of civil administration, of the administration of justice, of the raising of taxes, of much commercial activity. But over and above these pragmatic functions they were also in the Graeco-Roman world the thing that, according to Aristotle, differentiated humans from animals and still give us positive vocabulary such as 'civilized' and 'urbane'. Their populations were the only group of people other than the Senate and the army to whom the emperor paid political attention. Their identities and aspirations were clothed in monumental forms deriving from Rome and Italy. Because of this, and because such towns were one of the features distinguishing the Roman period from what went before and after, the towns of Roman Britain have always served as a case-study for the whole Roman enterprise in Britain.

Major towns

Legally, there was a hierarchy of major towns in Britain: the *colonia* of legionary veterans (necessarily Roman citizens), in Britain founded by the end of the first century at Colchester, Gloucester and Lincoln with York and very probably London later promoted as a privilege; the *municipium* of non-citizens (*peregrini*), whose magistrates retired as Roman citizens, *Verulamium* may have been one such; the *civitas*-capital (a modern term for which there is no Latin equivalent), the principal town of a *civitas* (pl. *civitates*), which was an administrative area generally based on the lands of a pre-Roman people, towns such as Canterbury, Exeter, Leicester or Wroxeter. Though to the lawyer distinct, to the archaeologist they all look much the same. They were laid out on a regular street-grid and endowed with major public buildings such as the forum and basilica (administrative centre), public baths with water supply and drainage (not just for cleanliness, but through bathing, anointing, barbering and exercise to produce the 'Roman body'), possibly an amphitheatre or rarely a theatre (though what sorts of spectacles and performances went on in these we do not know), temples and in due course walls. The presence of the large 'town-houses' of the elite and of the simpler buildings housing artisans and traders attest to the towns both as a considerable nucleus of population largely not engaged in agriculture and as the focus for a range of commercial activity (Wacher 1995).

Although the account in Tacitus' *Agricola*, 21 of Agricola encouraging the Britons to build 'temples, forums, houses' was long held to show that towns were a deliberate creation at Roman behest, recent excavation and evaluation show a more complex picture. A number of Romano-British towns have evidence for important pre-Roman activity, particularly at towns such as Colchester and *Verulamium*, where the Roman town succeeds an *oppidum*, a major centre of Late Iron Age political, religious and economic activity, suggesting that the Roman-style town was a development out of and redefinition of an existing indigenous central place. At others such as Cirencester or Leicester there is increasing evidence for significant Late Iron Age use of the site, though of uncertain type. On the other hand, towns such as Exeter, Gloucester or London at present have no clear Late Iron Age antecedents.

Whereas most of these towns were later reoccupied, some were not, allowing larger-scale investigation of the site. One such is *Calleva*, Silchester (Hampshire), which has been the subject of two major campaigns of excavation, giving us our best example of a major Romano-British town (www.silchester.reading.ac.uk). The excavations at the end of the nineteenth century trenched all the area within the walls, yielding a plan (Figure 9.1) that instantly became a classic image of a Roman provincial town, articulated by a regular street-grid, with a central forum and basilica, baths in the south-eastern area and nearby a *mansio* (guest-house for important travellers and the messengers of the imperial message service, *cursus publicus*), to the north-east an amphitheatre outside the circuit of walls, many 'town-houses' and along the main through-streets commercial properties. The problem with this plan is that it largely lacks chronology as a result of the Victorian excavators concentrating on the latest surviving deposits: it is largely a plan of late Roman Silchester. Over the last 30 and more years a series of excavations has provided time-depth. Silchester originated as a major *oppidum*, presumably of the Atrebates people, and in the half-century before the Roman invasion was defined by major earthworks, had metalled streets, functioned as

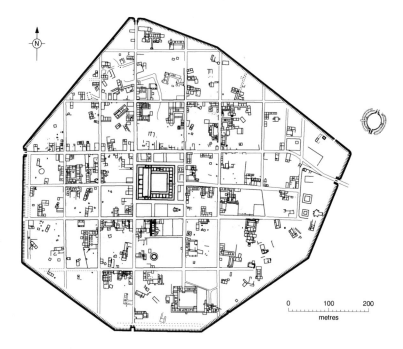

Figure 9.1 Plan of the *civitas*-capital at Silchester, Hampshire, showing the grid plan, defences, public and private buildings.

Source: Boon, G.C., 1974. *Silchester: the Roman town of Calleva*. Newton Abbott: David and Charles

a mint and was an important trading centre, including for prestige goods from the Roman Empire. So after the conquest we see not a new town, but a series of developments, such as the construction of a bath-house probably in the 60s, the laying-out of the street-grid only towards the end of the first century AD on an alignment different from the principal orientation of the Iron Age site and eventually in the first half of the second century the construction of the stone forum and basilica. In the late second century the town received a set of defences in earthworks enclosing *c*. 40 ha. (100 acres), with the front replaced in stone a century later: walls were a major civic monument as well as being defensive. The development of private buildings is as yet unclear, though it is evident that there remained buildings on the Iron Age alignment down at least into the second century. Certainly by the fourth century there were a number of large, complex 'town-houses', often equipped with mosaics. It seems likely that the disuse of the forum and basilica from the later third century may have been linked to the transfer of power from public buildings to the more controlled environment of the private sphere. The recent excavations have also shown that in the fourth century there were more artisan buildings than had been realized. Silchester remained occupied and active to the turn of the fourth and fifth centuries and probably for a time thereafter. Clearly the Romano-British town was always a 'work in progress' rather than something created once and for all according to a predetermined plan.

'Small' towns

Alongside the major, planned towns of Roman Britain there is a series of centres which are usually seen as urban (Burnham and Wacher 1990), though they lack the formal lay-out and public buildings of the major towns and have few if any large 'town-houses'. Some did have defences, and it is the areas enclosed within these, smaller than in the major towns, which has led to the appellation 'small' town, though some had considerable built-up areas outside the defences. The evidence suggests rather that they had important commercial functions and possibly religious and administrative ones also. They generally lie at important route-nodes, indicating the importance of communications. The main building type is the artisan shop/ workshop, and the evidence for the manufacture of goods and for the dispersal of goods from these sites into the surrounding countryside has long suggested that they performed functions analogous to the medieval market town for local commerce. In addition, some are known to have housed *mansiones* of the *cursus publicus*, and the site at Water Newton (Figure 9.2), well known through aerial photography, has evidence suggesting it may have been a *vicus* (a lower-order administrative site), both types of evidence arguing for an administrative role for some of these sites. The importance of temples at many of these sites suggests that they also discharged significant religious functions, perhaps as a centre for the town and its surrounding area. Though some, such as Water Newton, are green-field sites, they have never been accorded the same degree of attention as the major towns, probably in part because it was at the latter that 'Romanization' could most clearly be seen, whereas in the 'small' towns it was lacking.

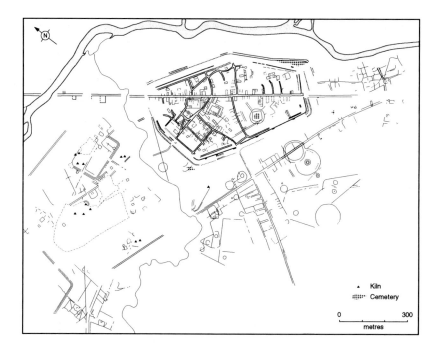

Figure 9.2   Plan of a 'small' town at Water Newton, Cambridgeshire, showing the defended nucleus, intramural building types, extra-mural occupation, and pottery kilns.
Source: Burnham and Wacher 1990

The countryside

The agrarian system

Despite important, Roman-inspired foci of population such as forts and towns, the population of Roman Britain remained overwhelmingly rural. Guesstimates of the population of the province have ranged from 1 to 5 million (at least giving an order of magnitude), and on the basis of estimates for elsewhere in the Roman Empire and for more recent pre-industrial societies, it is unlikely that more than about 10 per cent of the total (mainly the army and the urban population) were not agriculturalists of one sort or another. But the 'Romanization' agenda has also heavily skewed the study of rural archaeology in the Roman period, with one particular rural settlement type, the 'villa', consuming the lion's share of work on rural sites until quite recently. This was because it was held to demonstrate the impact of Roman culture in the countryside. Conscious efforts to rebalance the picture are now under way through increased attention to the agricultural economy and through much increased work on and thought about non-villa settlements and society.

By and large the Roman period in Britain does not seem to have been one of major agricultural innovation, certainly as far as staple crops and animal types were concerned (Fowler 2002). The main staple crop was spelt wheat, more dominant in the south, with a

206

higher proportion of emmer further north, and there was also a certain amount of bread-wheat, possibly associated with the military. Barley, rye and oats were also grown. This seems largely to be a development from existing Iron Age patterns. On the other hand, the Roman period did see considerable innovation in herbs and other plants and the introduction of several new species of fruit, presumably representing the uptake of 'Roman' styles of cuisine (Cool 2006). Likewise, the principal domesticated animals remained the same as in the Iron Age, the triad of cattle, sheep and pig. What may have altered in the Roman period is the balance between meat (along with the ways in which it was prepared) and secondary products such as leather or wool in the uses to which these animals were put. This raises the question of whether, even if the staples of arable and pastoral agriculture remained fairly constant, the socio-economic context within which agriculture was carried out had changed. At the beginning of this chapter it was argued that one of the defining features of the Roman period was the greatly increased mobilization of resources, agricultural included. Part of this was undoubtedly linked to the needs of the army, not just for foodstuffs (grain, meat) but also for animal raw materials, including leather and textiles as well as livestock as draught animals and mounts. After an initial stage of living off the land, the army would increasingly be able to demand what suited it; for example, this may partly account for the observable shift towards cattle in the bone assemblages from military sites, perhaps for meat, perhaps for leather, which will have fed back into the pastoral regimes of the island.

One of the ways in which such supplies were raised was through the taxation system, which in a heavily militarized province such as Britain would largely have been geared to army supply. In the earlier Roman period, when the province had a low level of monetization, this might have been largely in kind; in the later period, when there was more coinage, produced very much with taxation in mind, this may have altered, though the agrarian system would still have had to produce the surplus to gain the coin. Over and above supplies raised through taxation, the army, both units and individuals, could and did purchase supplies which could presumably have stimulated agrarian production since there was a return on it. In addition, the agriculturally idle mouths of the urban population would also need to be fed, another stimulus to production. If alongside grain and livestock one counts timber as an agricultural product, the huge quantities of timber consumed for buildings, furniture, means of transport, fuel for heating and for industrial processes, for the army and for everyone else, could have been a profitable, if long-term cash-crop. What is less knowable, but worth considering, is whether changes in the social relations of production also tended to increased output, if the social hierarchy became more pronounced and the mobilization of surpluses to satisfy the economic and cultural requirements of a developing *rentier* class also acted over the long term to stimulate the economy.

Villas

The rural manifestation of such a landowning class has always been held to be the 'villa', a Latin word signifying farm but appropriated by modern workers to indicate a farm with Roman-style characteristics in the overall layout and building plans (rectilinear), construction (stone, at least for the footings, brick, tile), amenities (e.g. baths) and decoration (e.g. mosaic) of at least the principal residential building, possibly other structures too. Earlier excavations on villas concentrated on the main residential building, where the more striking finds were likely to be and which also acted as an index of 'Romanization'. More recently greater attention has been paid to the agrarian buildings and the non-elite housing, but the picture remains very patchy overall. The earliest villas appear towards the end of the first century AD, most notably the spectacular and exceptional 'palace' at Fishbourne near Chichester, argued to be the residence of the pro-Roman British king Tiberius Claudius Togidubnus. More usual is a gradual development from modest beginnings at the turn of the first and second centuries, with increasing elaboration of the main residence and ancillary buildings over time. The villa at Gorhambury (Hertfordshire), close to *Verulamium*, is a good example of this (Figure 9.3), showing how little visible impact the Roman conquest of the mid-first century had at very

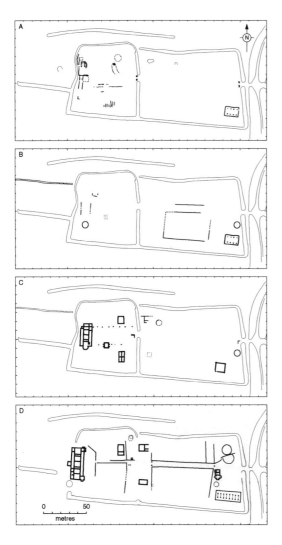

Figure 9.3 Gorhambury, Hertfordshire. (A) the Late Iron Age settlement; (B) the Early Roman period settlement; (C) the second-century villa; (D) the villa in the third century.

Source: Neal, D.S. *et al.*, 1990. *Excavation of the Iron Age, Roman and medieval settlement at Gorhambury, St Albans*. London: English Heritage Archaeological Report 14.

many sites. The main building at Gorhambury is of the classic 'winged-corridor façade' type, very common in Britain. More elaborate plans tended to have buildings grouped around one or more courtyards, with a growing distancing of the main residence from the agricultural dependencies. These tendencies reached their peak in the earlier part of the fourth century, which seems to have been the hey-day of the villa in Britain in terms both of the quantity of such sites and in their quality as expressed in the elaborateness of plans and decoration.

The social structures represented by these villa plans have been the subject of considerable recent debate (Perring 2002). The traditional assumption was that villas were the property of a male landowner who resided there with his nuclear family, his household and servants or slaves. This matched the patterns both as seen in Roman historical and agrarian writers and in the rural residences of the modern British aristocracy: the villa as proto-country house. More recently, attention has been drawn to the fact that many villas have evidence for more than one accommodation area, or for possible multiple groupings of accommodation in the same building, arguing that this suggests the shared residence of different branches of the same lineage operating a pattern of shared title over and inheritance of land. Other analyses have approached the plans of villas from the perspective of the evidence that Roman houses elsewhere were structured along axes of public/private and grand/simple. The importance in many societies of structuring by gender is an obvious avenue of investigation as is age or members of the household of low social status such as slaves. The problem is that ground-plans in themselves seldom yield diagnostic evidence of how a room was used, and few Romano-British villas have enough surviving decoration to enable us to differentiate between grander and humbler areas (save the presence of mosaics in what are presumably the main publicly accessible areas), and objects which can be securely related to particular genders or age-groups remain problematic because the place of final deposition may not be the place they were used. One area where comparative evidence is illuminating the significance of some areas of villas in Britain is that relating to the use of residences in displaying aristocratic identity in late Roman Britain. The plans of some reception rooms, their fixtures such as mosaics or sculpture and the references on mosaic or on silver plate to complex Graeco-Roman myths of the new imperial religion of Christianity clearly belong to the empire-wide culture of the educated aristocracy with links into the imperial service.

Landscapes without villas

The concentration on villas has had various unhelpful consequences for the study of the Romano-British countryside. It has meant that even in areas where villas are relatively common, work has focused on particular points in the wider physical and social landscape (the villas), downgrading the latter and thereby decontextualizing the villas. This has meant that the analytical developments brought about by the approaches characterized as 'landscape archaeology' have been hindered for the Roman period because of the emphasis on single sites rather than landscape complexes. In areas where there were few or no villas, other forms of rural settlement were not accorded the same level of interest, and since many

Figure 9.4 Settlement and landscape of the Roman period in the vicinity of Chalton, Hampshire.
Source: Cunliffe, B.W., 1976. 'A Romano-British village at Chalton, Hants', *Proceedings of the Hampshire Field Club* 33, 45–67

of these areas lay in the north and west, this neglect was accentuated by the traditional concentration on the exploration of Roman military sites (Taylor 2007).

This is yet another area of knowledge and research which has developed away from the traditional paradigms in important ways. On the one hand, survey work such as aerial photography has been undertaken much more systematically, resulting in the discovery of many new sites; the number of excavations on such sites has also risen enormously. Together these have increasingly given us landscapes (Dark and Dark 1997) rather than single points (Figure 9.4). On the other hand, much more consideration has been given to explaining why the north and west and much of the south and east demonstrate so little sign of traditional 'Romanization' (Hingley 1989). The north and west exhibit patterns of dispersed settlement, the sites commonly consisting of an enclosure containing one or more circular buildings ('round-houses') of the type common in Britain since at least the Bronze Age, suggesting that they housed either nuclear families or more extended kin-groups (Figure 9.5). These settlements are regularly associated

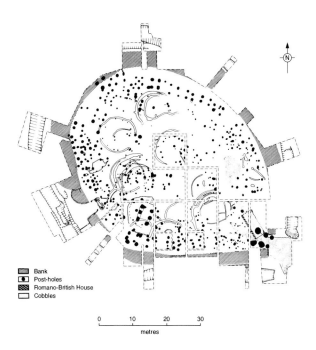

Bank
Post-holes
Romano-British House
Cobbles

0   10   20   30
metres

Figure 9.5   Walesland Rath, Pembrokeshire, a settlement with Iron Age-style layout and structures, but of the Roman period.
  Source: Wainwright, G.J., 1971. 'The excavation of a fortified settlement at Walesland Rath, Pembrokeshire', *Britannia* 2, 48–108

with field and enclosure systems and with trackways, sometimes leading to undivided uplands. Given the topography of much of the north and west, it can be argued that what is visible is an agrarian system with a strong pastoral element, possibly involving seasonal transhumance between the uplands and the richer lands of the river valleys and coastal plains. The demands of the Roman army stationed in these regions for meat, leather, wool and other animal products could well have stimulated surplus production, and there is some evidence for increasing numbers of these settlements during this period. Despite interacting with the Roman army as sources of produce, perhaps finished goods and probably recruits, the population shows little sign of interest in Roman-style building types or in material culture, to judge by the paucity even of pottery, let alone more distinctively Roman artefacts. Possible explanations for this have changed over time. Initially it was thought to be environmental determinism; these sites lie in the Highland zone, characterized by greater altitude and rainfall with poor soils, thus leading to little disposable surplus. But a comparison with the medieval period, when these regions could sustain elaborate built and material culture, shows that this can at best be only a partial answer. The 'Romanization' paradigm required explanations for those who 'failed' to take on Roman ways; this was sometimes seen as active resistance, an explanation that also accorded with post-colonial agendas. Another way of approaching this phenomenon may be that all provincials made choices about Roman-style practice: for some it could be interpreted in terms of their existing world-view and thus grafted onto it; for others it made much less sense and they therefore did not adopt it, preferring to maintain their traditional ways. It is noticeable for Britain that the 'adopter' regions were those that were largely of arable/mixed agriculture, whereas the 'non-adopter' regions were principally pastoral. Differences in the economic base may have entailed different social relations and cultural and religious formations, affecting the potential responses to new practice: 'innovator' or 'traditionalist'. Such an argument may also have uses in understanding why even in the villa-rich areas of the south and east, there were so many settlements that did not show the same receptiveness to Roman-style practice that characterized those who adopted, gradually and over time, the villa and its accompanying 'culture package'.

Religion

The preceding discussion invoked religion as an important element in indigenous responses to Rome. Archaeology has furnished considerable evidence for religious sites, for ritual practices and for objects used in rituals, but it has very little to tell us about the systems of belief that articulated these outward manifestations, comprehensible to the worshipper at the time but largely impenetrable from our very different mental world. This is a major stumbling-block to understanding the past, as of course in the ancient world religion was not just about worship. Religion structured the ways in which humans understood this world and placed it in relation to any divine world; divinities and demons explained natural occurrences from the seasons to illnesses; and it was the divine that dictated moral codes and legitimized political systems. Religion underpinned people's world-views and made sense of them in a way no longer common in the Western world. Without access to the belief-system, archaeology allows us only to see through a glass darkly; much that we now find incomprehensible would have made perfect sense at the time.

As in so much else, the archaeology of religion in Roman Britain shows a marked divide between the north and west as against the south and east (Henig 1984). The south and east holds the great majority of temples, shrines and burials, whereas the north and west is home to the great majority of inscriptions, tied very closely to the practices of military religion. The reluctance of the south and east to adopt the 'epigraphic habit', the practice of inscribing on stone, means that there is little evidence for the official religion of the Roman state, one of the political cements of the Roman Empire. Major deities such as Jupiter or Venus were worshipped, as a few inscriptions and rather more representations make clear (Henig 1995). The 'Imperial Cult', the worship of living and dead emperors and of personifications such as 'Roma', was also observed, above all at the huge Temple of Claudius at Colchester, site of the annual assembly of the Provincial Council drawn from the peoples of the province. But the bulk of the evidence from the south and east is for the worship of local deities. This generally took place at 'Romano-Celtic' temples, simple structures usually consisting of two concentric squares or rectangles (more rarely circles or polygons), the inner housing the divinity. These were small buildings, not intended for congregational

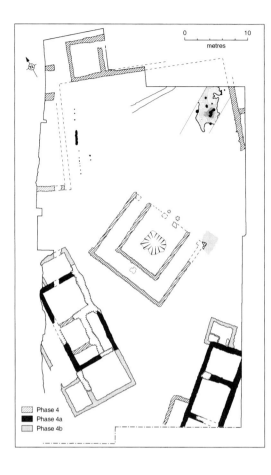

Figure 9.6 West Hill, Uley, Gloucestershire. The Romano-Celtic temple (centre) and ancillary buildings in the third/ fourth centuries.

Source: Woodward, A. and Leach, P., 1993. *The Uley Shrines: excavation of a ritual complex on West Hill, Uley, Gloucestershire: 1977–9*. London: English Heritage Archaeological Report 17

worship, though many stood in a precinct (*temenos*, pl. *temene*) where larger numbers could gather for festivals, and which sometimes, as at Uley (Glos.) (Figure 9.6), had subsidiary buildings around the main shrine. Uley is one of a number of Roman-period temples which clearly perpetuated sites sacred in the Iron Age. Perhaps the best example is Hayling Island (Hants), where an Iron Age shrine consisting of a circular structure within an enclosure was replaced in the Roman period by a more monumental Roman-style version in stone. On the other hand there are Roman-period temples which have no sign of Iron Age antecedents, so there was innovation as well as continuity in cult: indeed the very concept of masonry structures and features such as altars betrays the impact of Mediterranean-style ritual practice in an island which had previously had no equivalent. Another sign of this impact is the inscriptions which link a Roman with an indigenous deity, so-called *interpretatio romana*, where the choice of Roman deity presumably sheds some light on the nature of the indigenous one, for instance the pairing of Mars Camulos (note how the Roman deity usually takes precedence), with Mars as Roman god of war suggesting that Camulos was also a war god. There is a small amount of evidence for the importation to Britain of Mediterranean 'mystery' cults,

0   10   20   30

metres

Figure 9.7   Line drawing of the mid-fourth-century probable Christian mosaic from the villa at Hinton St Mary, Dorset.

Source: Toynbee, J., 1964. 'A new mosaic pavement found in Dorset', *Journal of Roman Studies* 54, 7–14

religions where the worship of a particular deity granted to initiates the promise of life in the hereafter. A temple of Mithras has been excavated in London, and since the Mithraic religion was popular with traders (and with the military, hence its more frequent appearance in the north) this is understandable. Otherwise, there is a small corpus of evidence (e.g. Figure 9.7) for the growing importance of Christianity in the south and east of fourth-century Britain, particularly at towns and villas (Petts 2003).

However, it is not easy to reconstruct much about religious belief or forms of worship simply from the ground-plans of buildings and some inscriptions, so these traditional sources for the study of religion in Roman Britain have somewhat fallen into abeyance. Instead, more attention is being paid to evidence for ritual practice, particularly through objects and the ways in which they are deposited, borrowing on concepts from prehistory such as 'structured deposition'. These approaches may be most revealing about areas of religion such as cosmology (the structure of the human and the divine, this world and any otherworld), studying how and where votive objects were placed looking at human and divine attributes such as gender or functions such as war or healing. But they do allow the archaeological evidence to speak on its own terms rather than follow agendas laid down by Mediterranean writers or by inscriptions. A good example of deposition is provided by the material from the Sacred Spring at Bath, including more than 12,000 coins and over 100 inscribed curse tablets in Latin calling down painful punishment on petty thieves. Clearly this hot, steamy water was some sort of point of contact with the divine world. The debate over the motivation behind the deposition of coin hoards reveals another example of possible ritual deposition; are these an index, as is commonly supposed, of threat of invasion, are they an index of monetary instability or could they be offerings to the gods? Equally, are the deposits of materials to be found in the backfill of wells simply to be seen as 'rubbish', or does the presence of items such as complete or partial human or animal carcasses suggest more purposeful and meaningful deposition?

Human burial, a very particular form of ritual deposition, has until recently been rather a poor relation in Romano-British studies (Philpott 1991), which is odd considering the number of Roman-period burials known and the importance of burial in other periods. Archaeologically visible burial was always very much a minority practice in the Iron Age, and to a great extent this continued in the Roman period, for all the impression that burial was common. In fact, in the Roman period archaeologically visible burials are essentially absent from the north and west, the few that there are being very much linked with military sites. Even in the south and east there is a clear bias towards urban sites, with comparatively few burials at villas and other rural sites. Osteological analysis of some urban cemeteries has shown a preponderance of males over females, and generally there is a marked absence of juveniles. So the burial record for Roman Britain is in fact much more patchy and skewed than might at first sight appear. In the early Roman period the predominant rite of disposal, as elsewhere in the Western Empire, was cremation, with Britain following the general trend towards inhumation from the end of the second century, with cremation little practised by the fourth century. But it is also becoming clear that there was a range of other places in which human remains might be deposited other than formal cemeteries, for instance ditches or wells, and that there were rites for the treatment of human bodies, such as decapitation or the separate deposition of body-parts and heads, which we find difficult to interpret and which serve as an example of how 'other' Roman Britain really was.

INTERRELATIONSHIPS

As stated at the outset, to the archaeologist perhaps the distinguishing feature of the Roman period in Britain is the huge increase in resource mobilization, along with the uses to which these resources were put. The impact of this on the agrarian systems of the Roman part of the island has already been considered; here the discussion centres on the exploitation of mineral resources. The island contained precious metals of interest to the Roman state, principally as the raw materials for the coinage; a small amount of gold was mined under military supervision at Dolaucothi (Dyfed), but of greater significance was silver. This was obtained from argentiferous lead (the lead being a much-used by-product), first in the

Mendips by the army, later in the Peak District worked by civilian contractors. The military was also involved in the exploitation of one of the main iron-mining areas, the Weald in modern East Sussex and Kent, where the winning and smelting of the ore was under the control of the *Classis Britannica*, the fleet, as numerous stamped tiles and other objects from the sites show. Other major iron-working areas included the Forest of Dean (Gloucestershire) and the area around the 'small town' of Water Newton (Cambridgeshire).

Copper from north Wales and tin from Cornwall were also mined to alloy into bronze, but as with iron the principal source of the metal was probably the melting-down and refashioning of existing objects. In addition to metals, other natural resources exploited included: stones for construction, architectural stonework and inscriptions, such as Bath stone and other freestones from the limestone belt; Kentish rag around the Thames estuary; specialist stones such as Purbeck 'marble' for inscriptions; shale, also from Dorset, for items of furniture and personal ornament; and jet from Whitby, again for personal adornment. An important resource, for its preservative properties, was salt from the brine springs at Droitwich (Worcestershire) and Middlewich and Wilderspool (Cheshire).

However, the most widespread and archaeologically useful exploitation of a natural resource was the working of clay into pottery, so prolific in the Roman period (Tyers 1996). Much used for dating, as noted earlier, it has also been a key resource for establishing contacts within Britain over longer and shorter distances, and is thus central to debates about the nature and functioning of the Romano-British economy.

Much Romano-British pottery can be tied to its place of manufacture, either because the kilns have been found or because petrological analysis permits the source area to be defined, the best-known instance of this being 'Black Burnished ware', containers found as far north as the Antonine Wall but which heavy-mineral analysis showed to come from Poole Harbour on the south coast. The great majority of pottery was utilitarian ('coarse wares') and was distributed locally, probably often through the urban network. Like so much manufacture in Roman Britain, it did not mark a step-change in technical terms, but rather the more intensive application of tried and tested but non-complex manufacturing methods. Some pottery was more specialized, such as the heavy food-preparation bowls, *mortaria*, or more carefully made and decorated ('fine wares'), and these could achieve regional distributions such as Hartshill/Mancetter *mortaria* in the second century or Oxfordshire fine wares in the fourth. Certain products, Black Burnished ware is an excellent example, achieved very long-distance distributions on the back of the supply network for the army in the north and west. What this shows is that there were varying levels of integration to the Romano-British economy. The bulk remained resolutely local, but some show much wider integration and may stand proxy for similar levels of trade in other, more perishable goods. In addition there was inter-provincial trade in certain prestige items such as glass or 'samian' ware as well as supplies for the army. So the Roman part of Britain was more economically active and integrated than in any preceding period and was not to be so again for several hundred years after the end of the period. To what extent this represented a 'market economy' is still up for debate. It is likely that much trade at local level could have remained 'embedded' in social relations, but the longer-distance movement of goods suggests economic rather than social gain. Moreover, the quantity of manufactured goods and their wide distribution on sites up and down the social hierarchy suggests that more people had greater access to a wider range of goods than before the conquest. How far this may have been lubricated by coinage is also by no means certain (Reece 2002). Perhaps not to a great extent for the first 200 years, but in the late third and fourth centuries, the large quantities of low-value coin, and the spates of counterfeiting in periods of low supply, suggest coin was much used, at least at certain sites, notably the towns. So whilst it would be going much too far to envisage a full market economy, goods and services did become much more widely available, especially to the better-off.

So if in the mid-fourth century there was a considerable degree of economic and other integration in the Roman-ruled areas of Britain expressed in a plentiful and visible archaeological record, how is it that only a hundred years later the situation had changed utterly?

THE END OF ROMAN BRITAIN

The end of the Roman period and the transition to the early medieval period involved what is probably the greatest collapse in the archaeological record in Britain, at least since the last retreat of the ice. Both archaeology and texts point to the first half of the fifth century as being the turning-point (Faulkner 2000). The archaeological sequence suggests that already in the second half of the fourth century 'Roman' archaeology was in steep numerical decline. This culminated in a major crisis in the early fifth century, with all the markers of 'Roman' culture in Britain such as towns, villas, temples, coins, pottery and other objects ceasing to be used or made. This lack of archaeological visibility meant that for a long time the master narrative was that apparently provided by the textual sources, which are actually a rag-bag of mainly much later compilations with different perceptions of the past they are describing, and so in no way a firm foundation for a narrative.

A major problem is dating. The last Roman coins to enter Britain were minted at the turn of the fourth and fifth centuries, but of course can only supply a *terminus post quem*. With no more coins, pottery can no longer be dated satisfactorily, so the period over which this major change took place is very difficult to define. What does seem to be the case is that it is the most visibly 'Roman' elements of the archaeology that collapse. The environmental evidence makes it clear that by and large the Roman part of the island must have remained peopled, since the landscape remained open and there was no major episode of reforestation: the land must have continued to be worked. In this case, we are not looking at any major population crisis (though very probably a drop in population levels). So what we are looking at is a crisis of the Roman system and its social, economic and cultural correlates. At one level, there seems to be a crisis of the elite, in that it is the archaeological manifestations of elite culture that are most seriously affected. The groupings that used towns and villas and the like were clearly those most catastrophically implicated in the collapse of Roman

SIMON ESMONDE CLEARY

political control and social and cultural formations in the early fifth century. At another level, the disappearance of the overarching political, economic and cultural formations that characterized Roman rule in the island led to a corresponding disintegration in what had been the Roman-ruled areas. Instead of widespread and relatively coherent expressions highly visible in the archaeology, we find an archaeology whose elements show instead a series of highly localized expressions suggesting groupings of relatively small numbers with simple structures and hierarchies, with little ability to mobilize resources and lacking much in the way of craft skills. Modern experience of 'failed states' suggests that precisely the sort of state collapse we see in Britain after AD 400 can entail massive economic, social and cultural dislocation and regression, with a transition to warlordism as small groupings fought to survive and to impose themselves on others. The sense of *Britannia* as a large-scale and highly complex entity which the Roman occupation had produced had given way to small-scale and simple groupings into which the Anglo-Saxons could fit and out of which more complex formations would re-emerge over the next hundred years and more.

Key texts

Jones. G.D.B. and Mattingly D.J., 1990. *An atlas of Roman Britain*. Oxford: Blackwell.

Mattingly, D.J., 2006. *An imperial possession: Britain in the Roman Empire, 54 BC–AD 409*. London: Penguin.

Millett, M.J., 1990. *The Romanization of Britain: an essay in archaeological interpretation*. Cambridge: Cambridge University Press.

Ordnance Survey, 2001. *Roman Britain: historical map and guide*. Ordnance Survey: Southampton.

Todd M. (ed.) 2004. *A companion to Roman Britain*. Oxford: Blackwell.

Bibliography

Burnham, B.C. and Wacher, J.S., 1990. *The 'small towns' of Roman Britain*. Batsford: London.

Cool, H.E.M., 2006. *Eating and drinking in Roman Britain*. Cambridge: Cambridge University Press.

Dark, K. and Dark, P., 1997. *The landscape of Roman Britain*. Stroud: Sutton Publishing.

Faulkner, N., 2000. *The decline and fall of Roman Britain*. Stroud: Tempus.

Fowler, P., 2002. *Farming in the first millennium A.D.: British agriculture between Julius Caesar and William the Conqueror*. Cambridge: Cambridge University Press.

Henig, M., 1984. *Religion in Roman Britain*. London: Batsford.

Henig, M., 1995. *Art in Roman Britain*. London: Batsford.

Hingley, R., 1989. *Rural settlement in Roman Britain*. London: Seaby.

Perring, D., 2002. *The Roman house in Britain*. London: Routledge.

Petts, D., 2003. *Christianity in Roman Britain*. Stroud: Tempus.

Philpott, R., 1991. *Roman burial practices in Britain: a survey of grave treatment and furnishing*. Oxford: British Archaeological Reports British Series 219.

Reece, R.M., 2002. *The coinage of Roman Britain*. Stroud: Tempus.

Taylor, J., 2007. *An atlas of Roman rural settlement in England*. York: Council for British Archaeology Research Report 151.

Tyers, P., 1996. *Pottery in Roman Britain*. London: Batsford.

Wacher, J.S., 1995. *The towns of Roman Britain*. London: Batsford.

10

EARLY HISTORIC BRITAIN

Catherine Hills

BACKGROUND

The second half of the first millennium AD saw the emergence of England, Scotland and Wales from what had been the Roman provinces of Britannia and the parts of modern Scotland that had remained outside the Empire. After the withdrawal of Roman authority in the early fifth century, Britain fell apart into numerous small warring groups led by chiefs of a variety of ancestries, both indigenous and invaders. However, by the seventh century, a number of larger kingdoms had emerged which formed the basis for the medieval kingdoms of Britain. The character of this developing society in the north and west of Britain is discussed in Chapter 11, but here, in England, the major kingdoms were Northumbria, Mercia, East Anglia, Kent and Wessex (Hill 1981; Yorke 1990; Figure 10.1). By the eighth century, it seemed that the Midlands kingdom of Mercia, under King Offa, would form the core of a consolidated England, but Mercia fell victim to the ninth-century Viking invasions, and it was instead the kings of Wessex, Alfred and his descendants, who first created a strong West Saxon kingdom south of the Thames and then, during the tenth century, conquered the rest of England to create the late Anglo-Saxon kingdom which was then in turn conquered by William of Normandy in 1066.

TERMINOLOGY

The history of this period has always been complicated by its role in national origin myths (Hills 2003) and it is difficult to find a name for it that does not betray a specific perspective. The popular name the 'Dark Ages' is a term that derives from the way in which people of the Renaissance saw the time between the Classical world and their own world, in which the glories of Greece and Rome were seen to have been 'reborn'. In between was a black hole of medieval superstition and ignorance. This contrast between antiquity and the Middle Ages

Figure 10.1 Map of kingdoms and tribal areas mentioned in text.

is now not so sharply drawn, and our ignorance of the early medieval world has lessened to the extent that the term 'Dark Ages' has almost disappeared from academic works. 'Arthurian' is another term more current in popular than academic literature; it implies the existence of a historical King Arthur or an 'Arthur-type figure' in the post-Roman period.

In England, 'the Anglo-Saxon period' is the term commonly used, taking its name from the dominant peoples amongst the fifth-century settlers. It is chronologically divided into 'Early' – roughly AD 450–650 – 'Middle' – AD 650–800 – and 'Late' – AD 800–1066. The division between 'Middle' and 'Late' is complicated by the arrival of Viking raiders and settlers (see Chapter 12). Alternative names given to the 'Early' period in Britain and Europe reflect the key role attributed to the movements of barbarian peoples into the former Roman Empire, hence 'the Migration period', or, alternatively, play down the break with Rome, hence 'late Antiquity'. Christianity can be seen as retrospectively defining the centuries before the arrival of the Augustinian mission in AD 597 as 'the Pagan period'. Attempts to find neutral descriptions include 'Early medieval' and 'Early Historic'. However, 'medieval' can still be understood as meaning 'after AD 1066', and 'Early Historic' suggests a very limited range of documentary sources, which is not true for the second half of the period covered in this chapter. Archaeological dating for this period is still largely dependent on artefact typology, metalwork and pottery throughout the period, with sculpture, architecture and manuscripts becoming important after the arrival of Christianity. Dendrochronology, used to great effect in this period in Scandinavia, depends on the survival of wood, which does not survive in great quantity in England. Radiocarbon dating is now more widely applied, and precision dating may soon allow more exact dating of burials (Scull and Bayliss 1999).

Historical sources underlie much archaeological dating, both indirectly, through coins and inscriptions, and directly. Historically derived dates are still the main basis for chronology, yet the significance of these dates is open to considerable doubt. We might begin in AD 410, the date when traditionally a beleaguered Emperor Honorius told Britain to look to its own defences; but had the withdrawal of troops begun much sooner? Did vestiges of Roman authority last much longer? Is this a reliably transmitted imperial letter? What impact did loss of imperial authority have on the inhabitants of Britain? Alternatively, we could start with the arrival of the Anglo-Saxons in AD 449, a date that Bede, writing centuries after the events, gives us as the best sense he could make of the records at his disposal. He was a careful scholar, but he could have been wrong, and much ink has been spilt in inconclusive discussion of both these dates. At the other end, 1066 is agreed by all as the date when William, Duke of Normandy defeated and replaced the Anglo-Saxon kings as ruler of England. However, this is a date which is not traceable in much of the evidence used by archaeologists. It can be seen in those places where the impact of an aggressive, intrusive, military aristocracy might be expected, most notably in the construction of castles, as well as in the scale of church building and in the localized destruction of ordinary houses, but in other respects there was no change: house types, burial practice, pottery and even coinage continued uninterrupted. Continuity from Anglo-Saxon to Norman and later medieval England can be traced in the evidence for everyday life, in the landscape, the pattern of villages, churches and towns and in the institutions which the new rulers did not invent, but exploited to their own profit.

SOURCES

Two major narrative sources survive from the earlier centuries, the *De Excidio Britanniae* by Gildas and the *Historia Ecclesiastica* by Bede (Lapidge *et al.* 1999). Both authors had messages to convey; neither was attempting to write 'objective' history and neither is easily verifiable outside their own writings, which themselves constitute the main sources for the periods about which (or during which) they wrote. For the fifth century, only one of them is really independent, since Bede drew heavily on Gildas for this period.

Gildas is usually described as a monk who wrote in the sixth century in south-western Britain, although this is not fully demonstrable. He was certainly an educated British Christian cleric, but his precise dates are not clear, although his life must have fallen within the second half of the fifth and the sixth centuries, and he probably lived in south-western Britain. The chapters of his work most often used today form only one part of a carefully constructed literary work, the main theme of which was a comparison of the Britons of his own day with the Israelites of the Bible. Gildas' account of the invasion of Britain by the Anglo-Saxons is presented within a framework of history in which assaults by barbarians were seen as punishments by God for the sins of the British. This had happened, he claimed, after the Romans had left (at a much-disputed date in the fifth century), and the wickedness of Gildas' contemporaries made it likely that it would happen again unless they mended their ways. From Gildas we learn that barbarians invaded Britain in the fifth century, that they caused great destruction and that they took control of parts of the country. However, much of the detailed history that has been constructed from *De Excidio* has gone far beyond what can legitimately be learnt from it.

Bede is better documented. He was a learned Christian monk who lived and wrote at the monastery of Jarrow in Northumbria. He died in AD 635, having completed the *Historia* in 631. In this work, he told the story of the Anglo-Saxons' conversion to Christianity. His main aim was not to write a narrative history of the creation of the Anglo-Saxon kingdoms, although the information he provides is our main source for that history. He wrote from an Anglo-Saxon perspective and had a negative view of the British, which he was able to support by reference to their own historian, Gildas.

Bede was not alone in his scholarship. From the later seventh century onwards, an increasing body of written documents of all kinds survives, both secular and religious in purpose, including poetry, chronicles, law codes, letters, charters and wills, gospel books, sermons, lives of saints and even collections of riddles (Lapidge *et al.* 1999). Late Anglo-Saxon England had a complex administration which used written records and which was taken over by the Normans. Domesday Book is an account of Anglo-Saxon England, although commanded by a Norman king. The Vikings have torn holes in our knowledge of the ninth century, but the eighth century, and the centuries immediately before the Norman Conquest, look as fully historical as those after it.

The archaeological evidence for the period is unevenly preserved in time and space, so that discussion of, for example, fifth-century Yorkshire will be based on different kinds of evidence from that of tenth-century Wessex and will need to be conducted on different terms. Cemeteries and the artefacts buried with the dead still provide the basis for research into the fifth to seventh centuries, although in recent decades settlement sites have been excavated more extensively, and considerable evidence for the Anglo-Saxon landscape and its settlements has been recovered from developer-funded excavation and from regional research projects (Hey 2004; Loveluck 2007). From the seventh century, most burials ceased to be elaborately furnished, while churches, sculpture and manuscripts emerge as an important class of evidence (Brown 2003; Webster and Backhouse 1991). At the same time, towns reappear for the first time since the Roman era, at first as coastal trading places but later as a network of administrative centres with, amongst other functions, that of mints for a re-established coinage.

CHANGING PERCEPTIONS

Because the history of the period has always been bound up with national identity, more significance has been attached to the differences between peoples than to their similarities. The Anglo-Saxons have been seen as arriving in force from northern Germany, displacing the Romano-Britons of eastern and southern Britain, so that the English were and are a distinct people from the Welsh and the Scots. This view suited not only the Anglo-Saxons but also the English of later centuries. In the sixteenth century, the Church of Bede was seen as ancestral to the reformed Anglican Church, predating and avoiding the errors of medieval Catholicism. We owe much of our knowledge of Anglo-Saxon England to this idea, because it was what led Queen Elizabeth's archbishop, Matthew Parker, to seek out, preserve and study Anglo-Saxon manuscripts (his collection remains to this day in the library of Corpus Christi, Cambridge, Parker's college). Seventeenth-century Parliamentarians saw the Anglo-Saxon *witan*, the council consulted by the king, as the model for constitutional monarchy from which the Stuarts had wrongly departed. They and others after them also believed in an ancestral, free, democratic Germanic society, which by the nineteenth century had become the basis for the thesis that the English were a peculiarly blessed nation, suited to rule others around the world and distinctly superior to their Celtic neighbours. The Victorians saw King Alfred as the model of a virtuous, wise and patriotic king (Figure 10.2). The twentieth century brought two wars with Germany and the end of empire, and it began to seem better to play down the role of the Anglo-Saxons and to stress both continuity from Roman to medieval and the kinship of all the inhabitants of Britain with each other, rather than with ancestors of the German enemy.

This approach is supported by an alternative version of the history of the fifth century in Britain which allows for the survival of an extensive part of Roman Britain under British rule, preferably the rule of King Arthur or someone like him. The existence of Arthur as a real person at all, let alone as a great king, has been much, and inconclusively, debated. The story became popular after the Norman Conquest, because it seemed to provide an alternative to the defeated Anglo-Saxons' view of the history of Britain. It was popularized most vigorously by Geoffrey of Monmouth, who wrote his *History of the kings of Britain* in the early twelfth century. At the end of the Middle Ages, Arthur was the name given by the Welsh Henry Tudor to his eldest son, and Arthur has persisted as a figure in myth and literature through the centuries. He had a brief vogue as an archaeological inspiration in the 1960s and early 1970s, with the excavation at South Cadbury ('Camelot'), and at other western British sites such as Glastonbury, Cadbury Congresbury and the Roman city of Wroxeter, near Shrewsbury. Occupation of these sites in the fifth or sixth centuries was seen as evidence for the existence of sub-Roman leaders and for survival of a partly Roman way of life, thus providing a factual basis for the later Arthurian stories. In part, this was the inspiration for a more widespread search for 'continuity' from Roman to Saxon on both urban and rural settlement sites. In towns, this search has been largely unsuccessful and has tended to confirm the traditional account of urban decline and destruction, although it has provided a more ambiguous and complex picture for the countryside (see below).

Figure 10.2 Perception of King Alfred.
Source: A.S. Esmonde Cleary

Under the influence of ideas partly derived from anthropology, developed by prehistorians from the 1960s onwards, social analysis became important in Anglo-Saxon archaeology (e.g. Arnold 1988; Hodges 1989), partly because it offers an alternative to the agenda set by historians, still focused largely on political history. Much research continues to be devoted to tracing population movements or regional variation through distributions of metalwork or place-names, or to the development of kingdoms from pottery and coins. New ideas about the mechanisms behind change in material culture have, however, encouraged criticism and reassessment of the traditional equation of different types of pottery and brooches with different ethnic groups. Interest has shifted to the detection of social complexity, whether in terms of hierarchical ranking and status or the roles of different people in society according to such factors as age, gender, occupation, family or religious affiliation (Lucy 2000; Lucy and Reynolds 2002). Attempts to understand the symbolism and ideology behind material culture, especially burial, have been the focus of recent research (Carver 1998, 2005; Williams 2006). A relatively peaceful late twentieth-century view of the 'Transformation of the Roman World' has been challenged in recent years, perhaps because we seem to be moving into a more uncertain world where catastrophe once again seems a convincing explanatory model.

Although some archaeologists would prefer to treat at least the earlier centuries as prehistoric, and although some historians would still prefer to disregard archaeology altogether, it is the existence of both kinds of evidence that is the greatest strength of the period. If the temptation to subordinate one kind of information to the other can be resisted, the combination of both allows each to provide different kinds of insight. Historical archaeology should be a key testing ground for both historians and archaeologists; the fact that instead it is often a poor relation is a result of the territoriality of academic disciplines, which should be continually challenged.

The question of the origin of the English has been revisited using new scientific techniques, especially genetics. Is it possible to demonstrate scientifically the extent to which the populations of Britain are descended from prehistoric colonists or from later immigrants? Extraction of DNA from ancient bone has become possible, but it remains difficult and has not yet contributed substantially to the debate. Another technique which uses direct evidence from ancient bones is that of isotopic analysis, mostly used to reconstruct diet, but also identifying individuals who had not grown up in the region where they were buried. However, an increasing database of modern DNA is available for research and, using this, geneticists have identified geographical patterning in modern genes. These patterns can be back-projected and used to reconstruct past population movements. This approach has met with some success in the identification of Norse populations in the north and west of the British Isles (see Chapter 12) but has proved more complicated in eastern England, which is why apparently contradictory conclusions have been published, especially in the popular media. One headline claims the Britons were wiped out by invading Frisians, while another suggests the majority of the population is descended from the Palaeolithic settlers who arrived after the last Ice Age. Distinguishing between fifth-century Anglo-Saxons and tenth-century Danish Vikings may not be possible, and the first millennium AD is only one period in the long history of human movement across and around the North Sea (Hills 2003). This is a new and fast-moving research area where clear results may soon become available, but at present (2009) it is still problematic.

KEY DATA

Landscapes

Environmental evidence (Dark 2000) has made it possible to approach the history of the landscape over the long term and to put recorded events into a longer and broader perspective. It is no longer possible to imagine the complete disappearance of the population of Roman Britain: survey and excavation have shown a density of occupation of lowland Britain during the Roman period that reached, or exceeded, that known for medieval England. A population of such size could not have completely disappeared, even in the face of prolonged war, famine and plague. It is true that the same evidence shows a less densely occupied land in the early medieval period, but not an empty one. The difference must partly derive from a genuine decline in population, but it is exaggerated by the difference between Roman and later people in terms of identifiable material culture. Romano-Britons appear to have created more rubbish than their successors, so that it is easier to find Roman sites than later ones. In the west and south-west it is difficult to identify early medieval sites, because pottery was not made or used in large quantities, and when it was, it was of poor quality, not durable and not easily identifiable. That is not, however, taken as evidence for complete depopulation of those regions. Even in eastern England, where many Anglo-Saxon sites have been identified, the majority are burials, so that when the practice of burying grave goods ends around AD 700, archaeological evidence for the Anglo-Saxons declines, at a time when we have no other reason to suppose that the population was itself in decline.

We know that the primeval forest in which it used to be imagined that Anglo-Saxon settlers hewed clearings for their newly founded settlements in an otherwise empty land had in fact been cleared millennia before they arrived. There may have been abandonment of some fields and a shift from arable to pasture, but no dramatic overall change in land use seems at present attributable to the middle of the first millennium AD (Dark 2000). Animal and plant species did not change at this point either, nor, as far as can be seen, did farming techniques (Fowler 2002). Even land divisions remained in use. Early maps show field boundaries, some still in existence, that underlie, and were therefore earlier than, Roman roads, but which must have continued in use through Anglo-Saxon, medieval and early modern centuries. If fields, plants and animals survived, so must some of the people.

Cemeteries

Anglo-Saxon cemeteries (Lucy 2000) are numerous, highly visible and apparently intrusive, because they do not appear to be a development from past indigenous practice but instead resemble burials found on the other side of the North Sea, where they form part of a long local tradition of burial ritual. This has always seemed to be evidence for the immigration of large numbers of Germanic peoples across the North Sea to Britain. However, it is not clear that native British burial practice was entirely different. Relatively few Iron Age burials have been excavated in Britain, and many of those appear to have belonged to the elite. Some excavated cremation cemeteries offer parallels to early Anglo-Saxon burials. Roman burial practice is still best known from urban cemeteries, where unfurnished inhumation became the norm by the fourth century (see previous chapter). The native rural population is still less apparent in the burial record, so it is difficult to see whether aspects of their burial practices survive into the Anglo-Saxon period. Burial clearly varied both before and during the Anglo-Saxon period according to many factors, including regional practice, social status, ethnicity and religious belief, and changed over time. Many Anglo-Saxon cemeteries are associated with prehistoric monuments such as Bronze Age barrows, which may represent newcomers laying claim to the ancestors of the lands they had taken over. The phenomenon may also represent a continuing veneration of monuments by people on lands they had always occupied themselves.

All the same, there are such similarities between English and continental burials that there must have been a close connection between the respective peoples involved, and migration cannot be discounted as a partial explanation. This need not mean that all the occupants of 'Anglo-Saxon' burials were of Germanic ancestry. Britons might have adopted foreign customs through social or political expediency or religious conversion. However, this would imply that Germanic culture was in the ascendancy, being current amongst an elite which believed itself to have continental origins.

In eastern England, the majority of the earliest burials were cremations. One of the largest cremation cemeteries excavated in England is Spong Hill, North Elmham, Norfolk, where more than 2,000 cremations and 57 inhumations were excavated from a cemetery used in the fifth and sixth centuries AD (Hills and Penn 1994; Figure 10.3). The bones were contained in hand-made pots, often elaborately decorated with incised, stamped or plastic decoration. Adults of both sexes and children had been buried there. Many of the graves also contained cremated animal bones, some of which might have been food offerings, but in many cases it seems that a whole animal, usually a horse, had been burnt on the pyre. The women buried had been laid out wearing their jewellery, glass beads and bronze brooches, the melted remains of which were then put in the pot with the bones. Men were not equipped with anything distinctive and were not accompanied by weapons. Also burnt were glass and bronze vessels, again representing the destruction of significant wealth, since they must all have been imported. There were also sets of miniature tweezers, razors and shears, often with full-size or miniature combs, usually unburnt and found in graves of all ages and both sexes.

Similar cemeteries have been found elsewhere in eastern England, for example at Sancton in Yorkshire, Loveden Hill and Cleatham in Lincolnshire. Comparison with the Continent shows a considerable overlap with finds from north Germany, in particular from Schleswig-Holstein and Lower Saxony. The grave goods are very similar, and much of the pottery has the same decoration. The main point of difference is that stamped pottery is very popular in England but not common in north Germany. Some of the stamps used on the Spong Hill pots include motifs such as animals, swastikas and runes, often carefully drawn, suggesting that, initially at least, stamped decoration had some meaning, although later it may have become purely ornamental. The similarities between Spong Hill and sites such as Issendorf, near Hamburg, relate not just to an initial settlement phase, but to much of the time that Spong Hill was in use. People did not get into their boats and sail to England, never to return. The communities on both sides of the North Sea remained in contact. The connections between them could have owed as much to the exchange of ideas and goods through trade, religion and political relationships as to migration.

In southern England, inhumation was always more popular, and it had superseded cremation everywhere by about AD 600 (although recently later ^{14}C dates have been published for cremations from Southampton). Late Roman burials had been mostly unfurnished inhumations, but the later fourth century saw the appearance in Britain and northern Gaul of inhumations accompanied by weapons and belt fittings. Although these have often been interpreted as the burials of Germanic mercenary soldiers, they need not be interpreted purely in ethnic terms, but rather as a fashion prevalent amongst a military elite, which

Figure 10.3 Cremation burials at Spong Hill.
Source: David Wicks, Field Archaeology Division, Norfolk Museums Service

included men of Germanic origin. These burials may have contributed to the development of the burial rite seen throughout western Europe and southern Britain between the fifth and seventh centuries. This was inhumation burial, often in large cemeteries arranged in rows, some bodies in coffins or stone sarcophagi. Men were buried with weapons, women with brooches and necklaces (Figure 10.4). In England these are attributed to Anglo-Saxons, in Gaul to the Franks, further south the Alemanni; but not all of those buried in this manner need have belonged to these ethnic groups.

Regional variation in England

According to Bede, the settlers came from three of the strongest tribes of Germany: the Angles, Saxons and Jutes. To some extent, regional patterning, in the distribution especially of dress fasteners, seems to reflect this tripartite division, which is also detectable in regional names (Hinton 2005). In East Anglia, the East Midlands and Yorkshire, women wore cruciform and annular brooches and fastened their sleeves with metal clasps. In southern England, in Sussex, Wessex and Essex, they preferred round brooches and did not use clasps. Most of the ornaments in these regions are made of copper alloy. Some of them are decorated with a distinctive form of animal ornament (Style I), where animals and humans are represented by disjointed limbs and heads. In Kent, allegedly settled by Jutes from Denmark, there was a greater use of gold and silver and some very elaborate ornaments, such as the

Figure 10.4 Anglo-Saxon grave from Kent.
Source: Canterbury Archaeological Trust

Kingston brooch, decorated with *cloisonné* garnets, glass and gold filigree. In Kent, the animal ornament used was often Style II, where the beasts had sinuous bodies like snakes or ribbons, tied in knots around each other. This style is also found in East Anglia, on some of the objects from Sutton Hoo (below). Some of the jewellery buried in Kentish graves had been imported from the Continent.

There is a tripartite regional division, but its explanation may not be straightforward. The north-east/south, 'Angle/Saxon' divide appears already in the fifth century in the distinction between those areas practising cremation and those favouring inhumation. This difference seems to reflect the situation at the end of the Roman period, when eastern England may have been overrun sooner and more completely than the south, which preserved more of its Romano-British culture. It may have been accentuated by Scandinavian contacts in the sixth century, and again by the division between Danelaw and Saxon England of the ninth and tenth centuries (see Chapter 12). The distinctive Kentish culture belongs to the sixth and seventh centuries, not to the initial migration period, and owes far more to contacts with Frankish culture than Danish. Bede was rationalizing distinctions that existed in his own time but which may have had complex origins.

SOCIAL ANALYSIS

Social analysis of Anglo-Saxon cemeteries has often focused on a few very elaborate, high-status burials. Most remarkable amongst these are those found at Sutton Hoo near Woodbridge on the coast of Suffolk (Carver 2005), where the burial mounds have attracted successive generations of investigators (Figure 10.5). Many were dug into and looted without record in the nineteenth

Figure 10.5 Sutton Hoo from the air.
  Source: C. Hoppit

century, three were opened in 1938 and 1939 and re-examined in the 1960s and a systematic exploration of the site in its wider context was carried out in the 1980s (Carver 1998). The most spectacular deposit was that from mound I, excavated in 1939. This contained the remains of a ship and a lavish deposit of grave goods including a helmet, sword, shield, gold buckle, gold and garnet fittings, bronze and silver bowls and a purse containing Merovingian coins. An even larger hoard of gold and garnet of similar quality and style has recently been found in a field in Staffordshire. Because most of these coins do not carry the names of kings, dating is not straight-forward, but the early seventh century seems most likely for the assemblage of the coins and also for the burial. The most popular contender for occupancy of mound I is King Redwald of East Anglia, known to us from Bede as a lapsed Christian king who died in the 620s. This may be correct, but, equally, mound I could have been the grave of a predecessor, one of the other mounds Redwald's grave. Another grave, excavated in 1991, contained a young man buried in a coffin with weapons, bronze and wooden vessels and horse harness. In a grave beside him lay his horse. The status of others buried at Sutton Hoo was less exalted. A series of graves was found in the recent excavation campaign that contained the remains of individuals who seemed to have been executed. Some of these were contemporary with the rich burials, others probably belong to a later Saxon use of the site as a place of execution (Carver 2005).

Attention has also been devoted to more subtle variations in status. Some graves contained sword, shield and spear, others spears only. Some had five brooches, others one or none. It is possible to use this variation to reconstruct pyramidal gradations of rank that compare well with those recorded in later law codes. However, some of the variation is regional or chronological, and some may be due to varying religious beliefs or the ancestral burial traditions of different families. It should also be remembered that the surviving fasteners and ornaments are only a small part of the original dress. Careful analysis of surviving traces of textile has allowed reconstruction of Anglo-Saxon dress (Walton-Rogers 2006), which would have given to contemporaries an immediate perception of the affiliation and status of the wearer.

Age and gender seem to structure some differences: the attribution of weapons to men and jewellery to women has been broadly confirmed by osteological sexing of the bones, and relatively few grave goods were buried with children. But not all men had weapons nor all women brooches, and each cemetery has practices different from its neighbour, displaying a wide variety of local preferences within a standard range, and making it very difficult to produce any but the most general patterns (Lucy 2000).

Settlements

Many settlements are known, although often only from air photographs, as scatters of pottery from field survey or from limited excavations. Several early Anglo-Saxon sites have been extensively excavated, including West Stow in Suffolk, Mucking in Essex and West Heslerton in Yorkshire. The visibility of Anglo-Saxon settlements is partly caused by a commonly found building type known as the *Grubenhaus*, or sunken featured building (Tipper 2004). The pit that characterizes this type of building usually produces occupation debris: pottery, artefacts and animal bones. Earlier interpretations of these pits suggested that the Anglo-Saxons lived in squalor in holes in the ground full of rubbish, but more recently, partly as a result of experimental reconstructions at West Stow, they have been explained as underfloor spaces, essentially cellars, for storage and insulation, underneath perfectly habitable thatched wooden houses. Much of the material found in the pits does not relate directly to the use of the building but represents later rubbish put there after the building had gone out of use and been demolished. *Grubenhäuser* were subsidiary buildings with a variety of domestic and industrial uses, while the most important buildings were larger rectangular 'halls' that did not have cellars.

Grubenhäuser appear on the Continent before they arrive in Britain. Like cremation burials, they are usually taken as an indication of Germanic immigrants, but it is not clear why this type of building was developed on the Continent, where it is found as early as the second century in the Netherlands. It may have had as much to do with changing climate and agricultural regimes as with population movements. The main house type in use in northern Europe was the longhouse, a narrow, aisled timber building that had accommodation for humans at one end and animal stalls at the other. The absence of this kind of building from early Anglo-Saxon settlements in England is one of the strongest arguments against a simple replacement of Briton by immigrant Saxon. The rectangular buildings that do occur on Anglo-Saxon sites have a distinctive plan: they are near to double-squares, with opposed doors in the middle of the long sides and a narrow partition at one end. Both

Romano-British and continental ancestry have been plausibly claimed for this building type (Hamerow 2002).

At Mucking and West Stow, it has been argued that the settlements consisted of groups of farms that shifted their locations over time, because there is some chronological variation in the distribution of the finds. Even Mucking, therefore, which looks quite large on the site plan, was no more than one (or two) villages, because the whole excavated area was not in use at any single point in time. At West Heslerton, however, it appears that the settlement was functionally zoned, with spatial separation of different activities. In some areas, industrial activities were carried out in or near *Grubenhäuser*, whereas in others there were only 'halls' and elsewhere animal pens. On this model, the whole site was in use during at least parts of its existence, with a planned layout that the excavator describes as closer to a town than a village.

The Anglo-Saxon occupation of West Heslerton is being investigated as part of research into the long-term use of the region. Geophysical survey on a large scale in the Vale of Pickering has produced a detailed picture of multi-phase occupation, amongst which the distinctive signatures of the *Grubenhäuser* show that Anglo-Saxon settlements existed approximately every two kilometres along the valley. Comparable settlement density for other regions is suggested from recent plots of metal-detector finds. The processes by which Roman, Saxon and medieval farms and villages succeeded each other are still in process of elucidation through detailed analysis, using projects such as that at Yarnton (Hey 2004) in the Thames valley, where several settlements with their associated landscapes were intensively investigated in advance of gravel quarrying.

Most excavated settlement sites have been found in arable land and produce only palimpsests of plans from different periods with few floors or occupation layers. At Flixborough in Lincolnshire, however, wind-blown sand covered a stratified sequence of buildings, dating from the seventh to the eleventh centuries AD (Loveluck 2007). Not only could phases of occupation be clearly distinguished stratigraphically, separated by spreads of rubbish, but the artefacts and animal bones from that rubbish allowed interpretation of the changing character of the settlement, including possibly monastic and aristocratic presences at different periods. Anglo-Saxon settlements need not have been static, single-function places, but variable and dynamic.

There is some regional variation amongst early settlement sites, in that *Grubenhäuser* are more numerous in eastern England, whereas south of the Thames, at sites such as Chalton in Hampshire, 'halls' predominate. This may be partly due to a difference in date, but this is difficult to demonstrate since sites that do not include *Grubenhäuser* produce fewer finds and are harder to date. The use of the building technique in which walls are constructed by setting upright posts in a narrow trench seems to be relatively later than the use of separate posts. However, both occur on the same site at Chalton and at Cowdery's Down, near Basingstoke, which could both be partly seventh century in date. This is also observable at the site of Yeavering in Northumbria.

Yeavering was discovered from aerial photographs that showed a complex of rectangular structures on a river terrace hill below the Iron Age hillfort of Yeavering Bell, near Wooler in Northumbria (Frodsham and O'Brien 2005). Excavation of this site in the 1950s produced a series of large, rectangular 'halls', some of massive construction, that had been burnt down at least twice. There was also a structure like a segment of an amphitheatre, burials and possibly both a temple and a church. Clearly this site had distinctive functions: the buildings required much wood, labour and skill, and the 'grandstand' suggests meetings and ceremonies. It has been identified as *Ad Gefrin*, which Bede tells us was a 'villa regalis', a residence of King Edwin of Northumbria which was visited by Bishop Paulinus in 626 when he came to preach Christianity to the Northumbrians. The buildings are consistent with such an interpretation, but there are very few finds, perhaps because the site was occupied only occasionally, or perhaps because the Anglo-Saxons, far from living in squalor, actually took pains to keep their houses, or indeed their royal residences, clean.

Yeavering has been interpreted as a 'palace' on historical grounds and because of the range and size of the buildings found there. Other 'royal' sites have been identified from aerial photographs, including several not far from Yeavering including Sprouston, in the Tweed Valley, and also in southern England (Welch 1992). At Cowdery's Down, the size of at least one of the buildings (22 m × 9 m) has allowed it to be added to the list of high-status sites. One late Saxon royal site, at Cheddar in Somerset, has been excavated (Reynolds 1999). Discussion of settlement hierarchy still rests on a limited sample of excavated sites, but the analysis of Flixborough shows how evidence such as animal bones can be used to detect status: evidence for conspicuous consumption including hunting indicates a phase of high-status activity in the tenth century which would not have been argued from the contemporary artefacts (Loveluck 2007).

Christianity

In the later fourth century, Britain, like the rest of the Roman Empire, was officially Christian. It is difficult to know the extent to which Christianity survived the end of Roman rule, but Gildas' account of the period was Christian, as were the rulers of south-western England and Wales whom he addressed. Ireland was converted from Britain, traditionally by St Patrick in the fifth century, and it was from Ireland that St Columba came to found a monastery on Iona in AD 563. This became one of the great centres of early Christian learning in Britain, and from Iona missionaries set out to convert the Picts and the Northumbrians. In 597, a mission led by Augustine, sent from Rome by Pope Gregory, reached England. Augustine had initial success in converting Ethelbert of Kent, but it was not until the middle decades of the seventh century that the other Anglo-Saxon kingdoms were converted, usually for reasons as much political as religious (Blair 2005).

Archaeological evidence for Christianity takes various forms, and the conversion was not a uniform process, and was driven by politics as often as by faith. Interaction with existing beliefs and practices produced a variety of initial responses, so that it is not easy to distinguish 'pagan' from 'Christian'. At first, furnished burial continued, and the impact of closer contact with the Mediterranean world appears in new styles of dress and ornament such as necklaces with pendants, a few in the shape of the cross, and decorated pins, some linked by chains, used to fasten cloaks and head-dresses (Webster and Backhouse 1991). Some prominent Christians were buried with objects; for example, St Cuthbert was interred with his pectoral cross, a portable altar and a comb. Kings and other landowners who endowed churches were buried in them, probably with elaborate clothing like that known from royal continental Christian burials, although comparable graves have not been found in Britain. Varied burial practice continued throughout the middle Saxon period, and it is only in the tenth century that it seems that the church had taken control of burial and a clear pattern emerges of uniform, unfurnished, east–west orientated inhumations in enclosed cemeteries beside churches in the middle of villages (Lucy and Reynolds 2002).

There was probably a tradition of wooden sculpture amongst the Anglo-Saxons, but only stone has survived. Anglo-Saxon England produced architectural sculpture, gravestones and free-standing stone crosses. The Mediterranean features of these crosses are clear: figures of Christ and the saints, vine scrolls, interlace and inscriptions in Roman letters; but the vines are inhabited by northern animals, and there are also inscriptions cut in runic letters (Webster and Backhouse 1991).

Churches

The building of churches may sometimes have meant no more than the dedication of an existing timber hall to Christian worship. Benedict Biscop, however, founder of Jarrow and Monkwearmouth, imported builders from France, because the crafts of building in stone, plastering, glazing windows and tiling roofs had disappeared from Britain. Timber, wattle and daub or dry-stone walls are the natural choice for northern builders, and the appearance of ashlar masonry and glazed windows would suggest strong continental influence, even if we had no documentation of the Conversion. Many churches from eastern and southern England can be shown to have been founded before the Norman Conquest and to preserve part of their original fabric. These churches have characteristic tall, narrow proportions, round arches, small windows and towers, sometimes decorated with applied strips like those at Earls Barton and Barnack. Most are not very large, but they were probably richly decorated with sculpture, painting and embroidered hangings. Early churches survive as excavated foundations or as parts of standing churches mostly in Kent and Northumbria, including St Augustine's, St Martin's and St Pancras at Canterbury, and Jarrow, Monkwearmouth and the crypts at Ripon and Hexham in Northumbria. The church at Brixworth, in Northamptonshire, shows the way in which Anglo-Saxon builders reused Roman materials, in this case tiles for the arches (Webster and Backhouse 1991; Blair 2005). Foundations of Anglo-Saxon cathedrals have been discovered at Winchester and at Canterbury, the latter nearly as large as its Norman successor, but not underneath York Minster. However, the great majority of identified Anglo-Saxon churches belong to the tenth and eleventh centuries.

Monasteries

Early monasteries do not present the classic plan of the later medieval Benedictine house, with its church, cloister and regular rectangular layout (see Chapter 14). Monastic houses seem to have been adaptations of contemporary secular building and settlement types and are therefore not always easily distinguishable from them. Identification as a monastery depends either on historical sources, or on peculiarities of plan or finds that are argued to be more monastic than secular in character.

The best-known of early Anglo-Saxon monasteries is Bede's Jarrow, where excavations showed long, narrow, rectangular buildings arranged in something that approximates to a cloister (Figure 10.6). Similar features were seen at the sister monastery at nearby Monk-wearmouth. Whitby, however, did not produce such clear evidence for a regular plan.

Other sites are less securely identified. Features that might be thought to rule out monasticism need not necessarily have done so. Cemeteries with men, women and children could be explained as belonging to double houses, with both monks and nuns and very young oblates or schoolchildren, and the graves of the sick, cared for in the monastery. Animal bones, evidence of meat eating, might reflect a less than complete observance of dietary

Figure 10.6 Model of the Anglo-Saxon monastery of St Paul, Jarrow, in the early eighth century. The appearance of the monastery is based on the results of excavation.

Source: South Tyneside Metropolitan Borough Council

rules. At Brandon in Suffolk, a settlement of Middle Saxon date consisted of rectangular buildings, one associated with burials and interpreted as a church. Finds included imported pottery, ornamented pins, precious metal and glass, both from vessels and windows, and a gold plaque, probably from a book cover, with the symbol of St John at Brandon (Figure 10.7). Flixborough in its eighth-century phase also produced rectangular buildings, possibly including a church, burials and evidence for literacy, which is normally associated with the Church, in the form of writing implements, styli and also an inscribed lead plaque and ring (Webster and Backhouse 1991; Loveluck 2007). Monasteries may have had significant economic functions, including playing a role in trade and the minting of coins, as the early *sceattas* carry images imbued with Christian symbolism (Gannon 2003).

It is in manuscript art that we can see most clearly the great achievement of the early Church in Britain in the fusion of three traditions: Mediterranean, Germanic and Celtic. The illuminated pages of the Lindisfarne Gospels (Brown 2003) show a dynamic combination of Classical figures, Germanic interlaced animals and Celtic patterns. The skills that had previously been devoted to the creation of jewellery were now deployed in the service of the Church. This art cannot be attributed to any one of the peoples of Britain: it is neither Anglo-Saxon nor

Figure 10.7 Gold plaque with symbol of St John from Brandon, Suffolk.
Source: R Carr, Suffolk County Council Archaeological Service

Celtic, and is often called 'Hiberno-Saxon', although that name does not allow for a Pictish contribution. The mobility of missionaries and craftsmen allowed the transmission of ideas from one secular or religious centre to another, so that it is often difficult to decide exactly where any one manuscript or artefact was created. The Lindisfarne Gospels are located by a written statement, but the Book of Kells has been attributed variously to Northumbria, Ireland and Iona. Manuscripts should not be studied in isolation from other art: book covers, reliquaries, chalices and other items of Church plate all demanded fine craftsmanship. Metalworking, painting, sculpture – either of stone or on the smaller scale of ivory – and embroidery all used similar designs and shared some techniques.

Towns and trade

Although urban centres do not fully emerge until towards the later part of the millennium (see Chapter 12), trade did not cease entirely in Britain between the early fifth and the late seventh centuries. Mediterranean pottery arrived in the west during the fifth and sixth centuries, presumably accompanying perishable goods such as wine or oil. Anglo-Saxon graves in East Anglia contained imported ivory, glass and bronze vessels, and Kent was in close contact with Frankish Gaul. Trade may not have been on a scale sufficient to demand permanent markets, and none has yet been identified in Britain for this period, but their existence should not be ruled out. In Denmark such a site has been found at Lundborg on Fyn which functioned from the second century to the seventh (Carver 1992). From the seventh century, local trade can be identified from the distribution of pottery, for example 'Ipswich' ware, which is found throughout East Anglia, around the east coast up the Thames to London. In the late Saxon period, it was succeeded by several wheel-thrown pottery types, including Thetford ware and Stamford ware, which was glazed.

Around AD 700, coastal trading places emerged all around the North Sea (Pestell and Ulmschneider 2003). Hedeby and Ribe in Denmark, Dorestad in the Netherlands and Quentovic in France are paralleled in England by Hamwic, near Southampton, and Ipswich. These were open, undefended sites, producing evidence for local manufacture and import of a wide range of goods. Similar sites have been identified outside the walls of Roman York and London (Figure 10.8). Because the place-name element -wic is common to many of them, they have sometimes been called by that name. They flourished in the eighth century and suffered from Viking raids in the ninth, after which decline set in and they either disappeared (like Quentovic), were relocated (like Hamwic and Hedeby) or retreated behind the old Roman walls (as at London and York). These places may have begun as seasonal fairs, but permanent structures and regular street plans appeared early in their history. The suggestion that they were deliberate foundations by rulers to control trade into their territories finds some support in the archaeological evidence, including the deliberate laying-out of streets and properties at one time, the restricted distribution of imported pottery and the limited diet suggested by the animal bones. Imported pottery may be a by-product of

Figure 10.8 Saxon London. A Middle Saxon road in the foreground with an alley leading away from the road, with the remnants of timber buildings on either side of the alley, found during excavations at the Royal Opera House.
Source: Museum of London Archaeology Service

the wine trade. Rhenish pottery is found in eastern England, while pottery from northern France reached southern England (Hodges 1989).

In Britain, coins went out of use at the end of the Roman period. Byzantine and Merovingian coins have been found in hoards, as stray finds and used as ornaments, and during the seventh century a limited gold coinage was struck in Kent. The history of Anglo-Saxon coins really begins with the silver currency, often called *sceattas*, small dumpy coins that were in use from the later seventh century until a new, larger, thin silver penny was created in the later eighth century. *Sceattas* are found in some quantity in the coastal trading places. They also occur on other inland sites, including some that have produced many artefacts, often through metal detecting. These 'productive sites' have not so far shown much evidence for permanent occupation and may perhaps have been seasonal fairs (Pestell and Ulmschneider 2003; Gannon 2003). Late Saxon coins were a carefully controlled part of West Saxon government, part of a centralized administration which manifested itself also in defended towns, administrative territorial divisions and judicial institutions (Reynolds 1999).

THE WIDER SETTING

After the end of Roman rule, Britain is sometimes seen as having been set adrift, cut off from Europe. It would be better to see it instead as belonging to interrelated maritime zones, centred on the North and Irish Seas, each with many lines of contact to the rest of Europe and beyond. In the east, around the North Sea, contact with north Germany and Scandinavia was continuous and intense. Germanic settlement in the fifth and sixth centuries and Viking raids and settlement in the ninth and tenth were followed by a brief period when England was part of a Danish empire. Contact with western Europe and the Mediterranean world never entirely ceased, and was dramatically renewed in the seventh century with the Christian mission. At the end of the period, England became, as it was to remain throughout the Middle Ages, closely connected to the politics of western Europe, especially to the area that was to become France.

By the time of the Norman Conquest, England was a centralized state with a complex system of government and administration, which was taken over and strengthened by the Normans. Just as the imposition of castles destroyed houses and changed parts of the plans of Anglo-Saxon towns, without ultimately replacing them, so Domesday Book records an Anglo-Saxon state under new lordship, changed but not replaced.

Key texts

Carver, M., 1998. *Sutton Hoo: burial place of kings*. London: British Museum.
Hills, C.M., 2003. *Origins of the English*. London: Duckworth.
Lapidge, M., Blair, J., Keynes, S. and Scragg, D. (eds.) 1999. *The Blackwell encyclopaedia of Anglo-Saxon England*. Oxford: Blackwell.
Lucy, S., 2000. *The Anglo-Saxon way of death*. Stroud: Sutton Publishing.
Reynolds, A., 1999. *Later Anglo-Saxon England*. Stroud: Tempus.
Welch, M., 1992. *Anglo-Saxon England*. London: Batsford / English Heritage.

Bibliography

Arnold, C.J., 1988. *An archaeology of the early Anglo-Saxon kingdoms*. London: Routledge.
Blair, J., 2005. *The church in Anglo-Saxon society*. Oxford: University Press.
Brown, M.P., 2003. *The Lindisfarne Gospels*. London: British Library.
Carver, M. (ed) 1992. *The age of Sutton Hoo*. Woodbridge: Boydell.
Carver, M., 2005. *Sutton Hoo: a seventh century princely burial ground*. London: British Museum.
Dark, P., 2000. *The environment of Britain in the first millennium* AD. London: Duckworth.
Fowler, P., 2002. *Farming in the first millennium* AD. Cambridge: University Press.
Frodsham, P. and O'Brien, C. (eds) 2005. *Yeavering: people, power and place*. Stroud: Tempus.
Gannon, A., 2003. *The iconography of early Anglo-Saxon coinage*. Oxford: Oxford University Press.
Hamerow, H., 2002. *Early medieval settlements*. Oxford: University Press.
Hey, G., 2004. *Yarnton: Saxon and medieval landscape*. Oxford: Oxford Archaeology.
Hill, D., 1981. *An atlas of Anglo-Saxon England*. Oxford: Blackwell.
Hills, C.M. and Penn, K.J., 1994. *Spong Hill part* V. Norwich: Norfolk Archaeological Unit East Anglian Archaeology Report 67.
Hinton, D., 2005. *Gold and gilt and pots and pins*. Oxford: Oxford University Press.

Hodges, R., 1989. *The Anglo-Saxon achievement*. London: Duckworth.

Loveluck, C., 2007. *Rural settlement, lifestyles and social change. Anglo-Saxon Flixborough in its wider context*. Oxford: Oxbow.

Lucy, S. and Reynolds, A. (eds) 2002. *Burial in early medieval England and Wales*. London: Society for Medieval Archaeology.

Pestell, T. and Ulmschneider, K., 2003. *Markets in early medieval Europe*. Macclesfield: Windgather.

Scull, C.J. and Bayliss, A., 1999. 'Dating burials of the 7th and 8th centuries: a case study from Ipswich, Suffolk', in Hines, J., Hoilund Nielsen, K. and Siegmund, F. (eds) *The pace of change: studies in early-medieval chronology*. Oxford: Oxbow, 80–8.

Tipper, J., 2004. *The Grubenhaus in Anglo-Saxon England*. Yedingham: Landscape Research Centre / English Heritage.

Walton-Rogers, P., 2006. *Cloth and clothing in early Anglo-Saxon England: AD 450-700*. York: CBA Research Report 145.

Webster, L. and Backhouse, J., 1991. *The making of England. Anglo-Saxon art and culture AD 600–900*. London: British Museum Publications.

Williams, H., 2006. *Death and memory in early medieval Britain*. Cambridge: Cambridge University Press.

Yorke, B., 1990. *Kings and kingdoms of early Anglo-Saxon England*. London: Seaby.

11

CELTIC BRITAIN IN THE EARLY HISTORIC PERIOD

Stephen T. Driscoll

SETTING THE SCENE

The collapse of the Roman province of Britannia liberated the native British peoples to build their own nations and created a vortex which drew Germanic migrants from across the English Channel and promoted stronger contacts with Gaels from across the Irish Sea. Although the social and political consequences of the collapse of imperial power were most conspicuous in southern and eastern Britain, where Roman culture was entrenched, the changes of the age were visible throughout the British Isles.

The arrival of Anglo-Saxon settlers initiated a period of struggle which ultimately led to a cultural and political fragmentation of Britain into regions where Celtic language and culture survived – the west and the north (Koch 2007) – and those where English language and culture came to dominate – principally the more Romanized south and east. These broad divisions present us with a unique area of study (e.g. Alcock 1971; Alcock 2003; Foster 1996; Laing 2006) and were sufficiently robust to have lasted throughout the medieval period.

The peoples who inhabited the western and northern regions of Britain shared a range of cultural traits, which have traditionally been described as Celtic, most notably a shared linguistic heritage (Figure 11.1). Although convenient, the term 'Celtic' is problematic, even with respect to language: Gaelic, Old Welsh (Brittonic) and Pictish are all in the Celtic language family but they are not mutually intelligible, and this common linguistic inheritance was not fully recognized until modern times. With respect to material culture, the evidence is even more heterogeneous, not least because of the diversity of environments found between Cornwall and Shetland. Thus while it is possible to identify common material-culture traditions, such as hillforts, stone crosses and penannular brooches, the specific architectural forms, preferred sculptural motifs and metalworking designs were regionally distinct, and in the case of portable artefacts the different designs may have been intended to signal local affiliations.

241

Figure 11.1 Map of areas and places mentioned in the text.
Source: Stephen T. Driscoll

One reason why such differences developed was that post-Roman Britain was politically fragmented. The centuries following the departure of the Roman legions were violent, as small war bands sought to carve out petty kingdoms. These new kingdoms, none of which appear to owe much to the Roman provincial structure, were constructed along ethno-linguistic lines and relied upon extended kinship networks for their stability. In this respect Celtic and Anglo-Saxon social organizations were similar: power was highly militarized and ethnic identities were constructed to create solidarity and differentiate new polities.

Although only a few of the kingdoms which emerged in the immediate post-Roman period survived for more than a few centuries, the basic distinctions drawn along ethnic and linguistic lines are still recognizable in contemporary Britain. The most fundamental distinctions have roots in the Roman period, the most enduring of which was the widespread adoption of Christianity. Paradoxically, Christianity was stronger in the western and northern regions, where the engagement with other aspects of Roman culture, such as urbanism and Latin speech, was less intense. Only in the far north did paganism survive and even here the Picts were converted by the end of the sixth century. This near-universal enthusiasm for Christianity contrasted with the migrant Anglo-Saxons, who remained resolutely pagan until well into the seventh century, thus creating fault lines which reinforced linguistic differences. The different paths to Christianity taken by the Anglo-Saxons and the Celts respectively survived for centuries in the parallel organizations of the Church, alternative devotional practices and dedications to different saintly cults.

CHRONOLOGICAL DIVISIONS AND DATING RESOURCES

The chronological challenges of this period are evident in the range of terminology used to describe it (see Chapter 10). Here it has become conventional to use the term Early Historic for AD 400–800, the end of which was marked by the arrival of the Vikings, and, although many of the sites, artefact types and historical sources continue, it is convenient to use 'Viking Age' to describe the changed political circumstances of the period AD 800–1050.

For the archaeologist and historian alike there are significant chronological problems presented when working in this period. The regeneration of literate society was a gradual process, and, more importantly, the institutional mechanisms for preserving documents were slow to develop. Consequently, the survival of texts is variable and the geographic coverage is uneven. So, for instance, it is impossible to corroborate the accounts by Gildas, the Welsh churchman writing in the 540s about the historicity of Arthur, because his is a lone voice.

Nevertheless there are some key texts which illuminate well specific places and times and provide an invaluable dating framework. For instance the foundation of the monastery of Iona by St Columba in AD 563 is recorded independently in the *Vita Columba*, the *Annals of Ulster* and Bede's *Ecclesiastical History*. But such instances of precision are unusual, and the majority of places remain historically dark throughout the Early Historic period even when they are illuminated by archaeological discoveries.

Material culture of the Early Historic period presents equally serious chronological limitations. Mass-produced Roman pottery, which had been so plentiful that it reached the most remote Scottish islands, ceased to be distributed after the fourth century. With respect to domestic pottery, the Celtic regions were largely aceramic – pottery was made for local consumption in Cornwall and the Hebrides, but is relatively coarse and of limited chronological value. Perhaps more significantly, the collapse of the Roman economy also saw the end of coinage. Given the usefulness of coins for dating this is a major problem. By the seventh century limited quantities of Anglo-Saxon coinage found their way on to sites in the north and west, but their rarity makes them of dubious value for dating. The situation only really improves when Viking coins start to circulate in the Irish Sea area in the ninth century, but in many northern areas coins do not become common until the twelfth century.

The end of the Roman Empire did not mean an end to the use of Latin, as can be seen in numerous memorial inscriptions erected in Wales and, more sparsely, in northern Britain (Figure 11.2). These monuments challenge the silence of the textual sources: not only do they indicate that Latin survived as a spoken language in some social circles, but the letter forms and formulae used in the inscriptions provide a way of calibrating the progress of Christianity in the north and west.

The most valuable artefacts from a dating perspective are pottery and glass vessels, which were imported from the Continent and the Mediterranean from the fifth to eighth centuries. The chronological and economic value of these vessels were recognized before their origins were identified and therefore they were initially given neutral labels (A-, B-, D- and E-wares), which are gradually being replaced as production areas are recognized (see below; also Campbell 2007). There are two broad groups of imports which represent two distinct trade networks. The earlier of these trade networks was a continuation of late Roman production and exchange systems centred on the Mediterranean. When in the mid-sixth century the Mediterranean connection dried up, it was replaced by trade from the near-Continent which continued until the end of the eighth century. The pottery which provides the archaeological signature for these networks was

Figure 11.2 Three crosses from Whithorn. On the right the oldest, the Latinus stone. Dating to the mid-5th century this monument to Latinus and his daughter is thought to be the oldest Christian monument in Scotland. This long, well-executed inscription reveals a deep familiarity with the epigraphic conventions of the late Roman Empire and a good command of Latin. In the middle a 10th century cross from the post-Viking revival of the site, and on the left the 7th century Petrus stone thought to have marked the boundary of the ecclesiastical precinct.

Source: Historic Scotland, Crown copyright.

accompanied by a range of glass vessels and beakers. Collectively these imports provide the most reliable artefact-based chronological controls, but they tend to be confined to high-status sites.

The Early Historic period was a creative period in the design and production of fine metalwork, which reached a creative peak in the years leading up to the Viking Age. The skills of the metal smith were utilized both for personal jewellery and on ecclesiastical objects for the adornment of the Church. A wide range of pins was developed as dress fasteners, particularly for use with the cloak, the main outer garment. The majority of the pins were simple, straight pins with limited scope for ornamentation and of restricted chronological value. From both a social and chronological perspective the most significant types of jewellery were penannular brooches. These consisted of a gapped hoop of metal to which a pin was fastened and was retained by an enlarged terminal at the gap.

Although high-quality jewellery is rarely discovered in archaeological excavations, the manufacturing debris has been recovered at a number of sites, most notably at Dunadd in Argyll. The manufacturing process involved clay moulds to cast the bronze, which were discarded after use. These moulds preserve the form of the object and reveal which types of object were being made and allow this activity to be tied into excavated archaeological sequences. Glass beads, another form of personal ornament, although not plentiful in the Celtic west, the more distinctive types can be closely dated. In addition they are rare evidence of participation in Anglo-Saxon trade networks.

As with other areas of archaeology the development of radiocarbon dating was of huge importance for Early Historic studies, because the rarity of coins and other closely datable objects placed a great reliance on metalwork typologies and the imports. As increasing number of radiocarbon dates have been obtained it has been possible to refine the chronologies of the material culture. Because metalwork and the imports are high-status objects, radiocarbon is additionally useful in providing dates for lower-status sites. Naturally where evidence allows, dendrochronology provides a desirable degree of precision: typically this is restricted to sites such as crannogs (artificial island sites, see Crone 2000), but occasionally soil conditions preserve suitable timbers on 'dry' sites as in the case of the Pictish hillfort of Dundurn.

REGIONAL VARIATIONS – KINGDOMS AND POWER CENTRES

It is traditional to address the archaeology of this period by reference to the modern nations – Scotland, Wales and, in England, Cumbria and Cornwall – but this is anachronistic and can be misleading, as the kingdoms of the Early Historic period were much more extensive than modern Scotland and Wales. A far more helpful way of approaching the regional variation is by the degree of Romanization. The most Romanized part of Britannia, where there had been towns and villas, broadly corresponds to the area occupied by the ancient Anglo-Saxon kingdoms. In those areas less influenced by Rome, traditional elements of Celtic society – language, place-names and social organization – were more enduring, although ironically it was also here that Latin as a spoken language survived longest and Christianity was most resilient. This observation is particularly helpful when looking at the foundations of the post-Roman kingdoms.

Within this western margin a series of small kingdoms can be identified: Dumnonia (Cornwall), Gwent, Glywysing and Dyfed (south Wales) and Gwynedd (north Wales). West of the Pennines we know of two kingdoms, Elmet (near Leeds) and Rheged, further north. Many of these did not long survive the expansion of the Anglo-Saxon kingdoms and, in the case of Rheged cannot even be located with certainty on the map. East of the Pennines the British kingdoms of Bernicia and Deira fared better and remained discernible within the Anglo-Saxon kingdom of Northumbria.

We know of several more kingdoms beyond the frontier marked by Hadrian's Wall, but the picture of the political geography is far from complete – in the Scottish Lowlands the kingdom of the Gododdin was centred around Edinburgh and was complemented by another kingdom founded on Dumbarton Rock (*Al Clut* in British) on the Clyde. Beyond these fixed points there were other kingdoms, such as Aeron in Ayrshire, but large gaps on the map reveal that there were other kingdoms which are now lost.

Amongst the early peoples of northern Britain the most enigmatic were the Picts, who created a unique pictographic script but left little in the way of historical texts. Until recently these inhabitants of the far north were regarded as peculiar and culturally removed from other native peoples of the British Isles, but current scholarship considers that the Picts were closely related to the northern Britons. The influence of the Roman frontier accounts for the cultural and linguistic differences exhibited by the Britons of the Clyde–Forth zone and the Picts who lived further north beyond regular contact with the Empire. The Grampian mountain massif divided them into northern and southern regions within which there were a number of smaller kingdoms.

The final group to mention are the Gaelic-speaking Scots who inhabited the western littoral of Scotland and the southern Hebrides in a kingdom known as Dál Riata which corresponds approximately to Argyll. In contrast to the native Britons between Cornwall and Orkney, including the Picts who spoke dialects of common British speech (ancestral to Welsh), the Scots spoke Gaelic, the language of Ireland. Given the geographical proximity of Ireland to Argyll it is not surprising that there should be shared cultural affinities, not least in the decorative arts, where the Insular art style spanned the Irish Sea (Youngs 1989; Redknap *et al.* 2001). How and when this linguistic fusion took place is more difficult to say. However, it is well to remember that the collapse of the Roman Empire simulated population movements all around Britain: the bilingual inscribed monuments in south Wales are unambiguous evidence of Irish settlers (Figure 11.3).

MAJOR DATA TYPES

Portable artefacts

The imported pottery and glass which provide the chronological structure to many sites, correspond to a sequence of trading relations, first from the Mediterranean and then from across the Channel in Gaul. The Mediterranean group includes fine tablewares in the *terra sigillata* tradition (A-wares) found predominantly in Cornwall and into south Wales, from material from western Turkey (Phocaean Red Slipware) and Carthage (African Red Slipware). This trade also included

Figure 11.3 Tavistock Class I stone, Tavistock (Buckland Monachorum), Devon 6th century. The bilingual inscription is in ogham and roman alphabets. Latin: *Dobunni fabri filii Enabarri* 'of Dobunnus, the smith, son of Enabarros'/ Ogham (on left edge): *Enabarri* 'of Enabarros'
Source: K. Forsyth.

a range of late Roman amphorae (B-ware), storage vessels used for the bulk transport of liquids such as wine and oil, manufactured across a similarly wide area. The various amphorae forms have long-lived typologies, but were probably imported into Britain as part of the trade which included the fine wares and have a fairly tight date range between AD 500–550.

The cross-Channel trade also included the tail end of the Roman fine-ware tradition as produced in western Gaul (probably around Bordeaux) known as *Dérivées sigillées paléochrétiennes* Atlantic group (DSPA) (formerly D-ware). This was not widely distributed and cannot be dated any more closely than to the sixth century on current evidence. The trade represented by DSPA material was in turn succeeded by E-ware. Like all the previous forms mentioned this is a well-made mass-produced pottery; it was not tableware but served more utilitarian functions and is of the greatest importance because it was the most widely imported (Figure 11.4). The precise source of E-ware is uncertain: it comes from either Rouen, the lower Loire or Saintonge. The bulk of the forms imported were storage jars and simple pots thought to have been used as containers for the transport of precious commodities, such as red madder dye. E-ware was imported from the late sixth to the late seventh century, with a floruit of AD 600–650.

In recent years, the chronological potential of imported glassware has been recognized, but it is less well studied and derives from more diverse sources. A range of vessels accompanied both

Figure 11.4 E-ware. A series of E-ware vessels from Dunadd.
    Source: E. Campbell.

the first groups of Mediterranean pottery, while distinctive conical beakers and other vessels accompanied the E-ware. The dating of these two traditions at present is linked to the pottery chronologies. In addition, a wide range of vessels in the Germanic tradition have been recognized. These have been discovered in small numbers and must have arrived in the west via different trade routes, probably up the east coast of Britain and overland across Anglo-Saxon England. Like the pots, drinking vessels were probably 'space fillers' for the main cargo commodities, such as wine, which was necessary for celebrating mass and desirable for secular feasting.

We have also noted how the debris from fine metalwork plays an important chronological role, but it is the objects themselves that were significant for the display of status and affiliation. The majority were fairly plain straight pins with a limited range of ornamentation. The most likely to survive in archaeological contexts were cast in bronze, but favourable soil conditions have preserved bone pins and they must have been ubiquitous. The distinc-

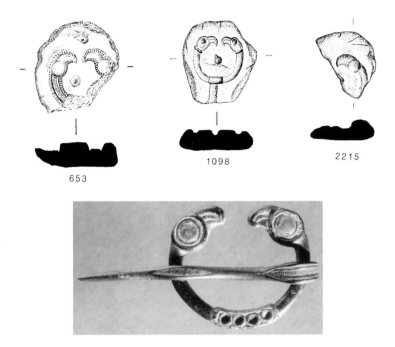

Figure 11.5 Moulds for making bird-headed penannular brooches from the Dunadd excavations and
an example of such a brooch from Clogh, Co. Antrim.
Source: Lane and Campbell 2000 (moulds) and British Museum (Brooch)

tive innovation was the development of the penannular brooch, a form which originated
in late Roman times (Figure 11.5). Over its period of use from the fifth to the eleventh
century it grew in size and decorative elaboration, which encouraged a number of regional
and chronological specific styles to evolve. Cast bronze was the most common medium,
but rare examples are known in silver. Initially decoration was confined to the terminals,
which were often zoomorphic, but over time the form evolved, the hoop and pin were flattened out to provide more space for embellishment and the range of materials expanded
to include enamel studs, amber, gem stones and gold filigree panels (Youngs 1989). These
brooches were worn by both men and women and can be seen on a number of sculptures
from Pictland and Ireland.

The artistic skills of the metalworker were also employed to adorn ecclesiastical objects used on
the altar, such as crosses, chalices and church plate. The covers of gospel books were embellished
with metalwork panels and relics were housed in small shrines fashioned from metal plates. We
know from examples that survive in Ireland that these were the greatest artistic achievements of the
age, and, from debris found at monastic sites, that they were also made in Britain, where the chief
surviving example is the Monymusk Reliquary, a church-shaped casket which once held the bones
of St Columba and brought victory to the Scots in battle. The chief way that this artistic tradition
has survived is in stone sculpture: many of the finest crosses, particularly in Scotland, appear to be
representations in stone of crosses covered with gold and jewels that once stood on altars.

Settlements

The characteristic form of elite settlement in Celtic-speaking Britain was the hillfort. Although sometimes built on the sites of Iron Age hillforts, the Early Historic hillfort was a new phenomenon. It tended to occupy a craggy knoll, rather than towering heights, and its elaborate masonry or earthwork ramparts enclosed relatively small areas suitable for the residence of the king and his extended household, but could not contain a large village. Although architecturally quite different from the later medieval castle, these fortified dwellings served a similar range of domestic, administrative and ceremonial functions (Ralston 2006).

The long-term political importance of these fortified sites is reflected in the rich legacy of place-names using a variation of the word for 'fort', such as Dumbarton, Dunbar, Dunadd (Figure 11.6) or Dinas Powys (see also Edwards and Lane 1988), some of which remain significant today. Contemporary references to secular power centres, such as hillforts, are few and fleeting, making it difficult to identify with certainty the vast majority of these sites or to link them with historical figures or events. Nevertheless, it is clear that they were politically crucial. When they are mentioned in contemporary sources it is most often because a battle was fought or a ruler died there. Where excavated these sites produce similar suites of evidence for the manufacturing of fine metalwork and the importation of pottery and glass.

During the Early Historic period rectangular domestic architecture began to be used at high-status sites such as South Cadbury, Tintagel and Dinas Powys. Whether this was influenced by Roman architecture, Anglo-Saxon practice or Church architecture is a matter of debate. Gradually the preference for corners and straight walls permeated all levels of society, and by the end of the millennium roundhouses ceased to be built in western Britain and on the Scottish mainland.

Figure 11.6 Aerial view of the hillfort of Dunadd.
Source: Copyright, Kilmartin House Museum.

Because of the slowness of this architectural transition it is more difficult to identify the settlements of the majority of the population. The houses of the lower orders were more ephemeral and are only rarely discovered archaeologically. Typically they are unenclosed or lightly defended with a timber palisade, and they can only be distinguished from Iron Age sites through radiocarbon dating. Nevertheless, the place-name evidence, provided for instance by the Pictish place-name element *Pit-*, 'portion', makes it plain that the population was dispersed widely across the countryside, with no towns or concentrations of population apart from monasteries.

In Atlantic Scotland, the Iron Age tradition of substantial roundhouse architecture persisted into the Early Historic period. In some cases brochs or duns, as they are known, continued to be occupied, and in some places even after abandonment the original structure served as the focal point for a developing settlement. As a consequence some scholars propose that a 'long Iron Age' lasted in the far north and west until the coming of the Vikings. This is problematic, as it consigns the islands to a timeless backwater and overlooks the clear signs of influences from the mainland: Pictish symbol stones were erected in the Northern and Western Isles (Figure 11.7), Christianity was adopted and there are clear signs of developing social complexity, particularly in Orkney.

Figure 11.7 Pictish Symbol Stone. The Aberlemno class I symbol stone characterizes the use of a natural boulder, perhaps reusing a prehistoric standing stone.

Source: Stephen T. Driscoll.

251

Churches and monasteries

In most Celtic areas the earliest evidence of Christianity is provided by memorial inscriptions, which were often erected in cemeteries. The preferred burial rite, inhumation with the head to the west, sometimes in a 'cist' of stone slabs, was practised in many of the Celtic regions, particularly in northern Britain. In the far north the Picts developed a distinctive form of burial under square and round cairns which began in the Later Iron Age and in places continued until the eighth century. It is thought that some of these early cemeteries enclosed by a circular boundary evolved into early churches, but the lack of church excavations and the fragility of early burials make it difficult to confirm this developmental sequence.

By comparison with the secular settlements ecclesiastical sites are better documented, but here too only the most significant churches and monasteries are mentioned in the historical record. For the rest, their Early Historic presence can be discerned only through the survival of a characteristic place-name element: *eccles*, from the Latin for 'church', which is considered to mark out the earliest church foundations, perhaps from the fifth or sixth century. This was subsequently superseded in the Gaelic areas by *kil*, from 'cell', as in Kilmarnock, and in the British speech areas by *Llan*, from 'enclosure', as in Llantwit Major. Of course in many cases, the original name has not survived, and frequently it is not even possible to know to which saint a church was dedicated. There are, however, physical characteristics which can be used to identify an early church site. Typically the ecclesiastical precinct was contained within a circular enclosure, sometimes described by the Latin word for 'wall', *vallum*. Locationally, early churches are often sited at the confluence of streams, and the presence of early sculpture is a good indication of their antiquity.

The upstanding remains of early churches are extremely rare. In their earliest phases they were probably built of timber, as the name of a number of early monasteries implies, for instance the Pictish monastery of Deer embodies the word for 'oak'. The early timber churches were subsequently replaced by stone-built structures, usually on the same site. The majority of churches were modest in scale and sufficient to serve the pastoral needs of a dispersed rural population (see Edwards and Lane 1992). At the major churches, often associated with monasteries, a number of small churches might proliferate to meet the needs of a large community of worshippers.

These great churches supported the only settlements in the region with urban characteristics. They attracted permanent populations and sustained significant centres of production and regional markets. Although they were fundamentally supported by agricultural production, the greatest monasteries housed large communities of monks and attracted a regular flow of merchants and pilgrims. It is a matter of debate whether such communities of scholars, craftsmen and labourers, sometimes described by the Latin word *civitas*, 'town', actually functioned as towns, but they were certainly the largest settlements, with residents perhaps numbering in the hundreds. They are of particular archaeological interest, not least because of their connections to the great secular powers. The most significant signs of these connections are the sculptured crosses and carved stone monuments which are such a distinctive feature of the early medieval Church in the west and north of Britain (Figure 11.8). The coastal

Figure 11.8 The Kildalton Cross, Islay, perhaps the finest cross to survive from the Iona School of sculpture.

Source: Stephen T. Driscoll.

location and the need to obtain wine and olive oil for liturgical purposes stimulated a degree of commerce with the wider world, and in due course attracted the attention of Viking raiders.

Monumental sculpture

Perhaps the most important and distinctive category of material culture for understanding the social and political characteristics of the native Celtic peoples were the carved stone monuments erected the length and breadth of Britain from the fifth to the twelfth centuries. Over the course of the period under consideration here the carved stone monuments evolved from the simple inscribed pillars erected to commemorate the dead into complex works of art intended to inspire religious devotion and glorify secular patrons. They provide evidence that the same aesthetic values found in the great illuminated manuscripts such as the Book of Kells and the Lindisfarne Gospels were present across the Celtic world. Over 3,000 such monuments are known, but even when they survive in a fragmentary and degraded state they reveal that a high level of technical accomplishment and intellectual sophistication was available across the region (Foster and Cross 2005). Although the monuments were not erected continuously or universally, they have the virtue of being relatively fixed in the landscape and

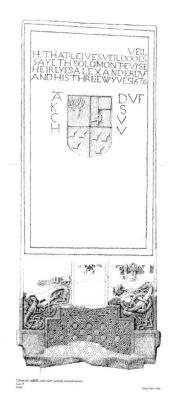

Figure 11.9 The Hilton of Cadboll (Easter Ross) cross-slab with Pictish symbols prominent at the top and a hunting scene featuring a woman wearing a penannular brooch riding side-saddle. Unfortunately the side which originally had the cross has been defaced to make a post-medieval burial monument.

Source: RCAHMS, crown copyright. Drawing by I. G. Scott

of expressing ideas about belief and ownership in the local artistic idiom (Figure 11.9).

Within the areas where Latin was the strongest, which included southern Scotland, the earliest monuments were in Latin, but beyond the Empire alternative scripts were invented. In Ireland a script based on clusters of lines inscribed on the corner of stone, known as *ogham*, was invented and exported to south Wales and to Scotland. In northern Scotland, the Picts invented their own pictographic symbolic language, which has no ready parallels in Europe. These images of animals and abstract symbols are most commonly found on pillars and boulders (so-called Class I symbols). It is not clear that these symbols developed in a pagan cultural environment, but some have argued this. However, what is clear is that these symbols had a great longevity and were incorporated into later, explicitly Christian monuments (so-called Class II symbols). These later monuments were dressed slabs of stone featuring complex imagery inspired by manuscript art and fine metalwork. The Pictish stones are a particularly valuable resource, because they include some of the most vivid and detailed representations of people from early medieval Europe. Most striking are the representations of secular figures, generally equipped for war or engaged in hunting.

The historical record

To some extent the sculpture can be used to fill the missing detail from the scanty historical records. Christianity, once established, required that books be produced, and a significant activity at the leading monasteries was the production of manuscripts. An incidental feature of the records required to keep track of the liturgical calendar was the compilation of short notes on the key events of a given year – the death of an abbot, a drought, a battle – which were collected into annual lists of events known as *annals*. These records are important because they are more or less contemporary and therefore generally reliable, but they are frustrating because they are brief and their coverage is uneven. The greatest part of the annalistic information survives in Irish compilations which include material from British sources, such as the lost annals of Iona and Dunkeld.

In contrast to the laconic annals, there are also poetic compositions composed in post-Roman Britain which are rich in contextual detail if short on concrete historical fact. The earliest and most significant is a body of praise poetry known as the *Gododdin* which survives in collections of medieval Welsh verse. This poetry describes the exploits and values of the warrior elite who inhabited what is now southern Scotland (the name Lothian evolved from the *Gododdin*). It reveals aspects of social contract between the warlord and his followers, material wealth, prestige and high living in exchange for unwavering military loyalty. It also describes some of the contemporary material culture of what has been described as a heroic society, but it is problematic in historical terms. It is difficult to determine its date of composition, although some would argue for an origin in the sixth century, and difficult to identify how it has been modified over time. The conventional reading is that it commemorated the men of the north who served King Mynythog in Din Eidyn (Edinburgh) and died fighting an unnamed enemy, presumed to be the Anglo-Saxons. This stanza in praise of Blaen gives a flavour of the work:

> First out of Eidyn's bright fort, he inspired
> Faithful warriors who'd follow him.
> Blaen, on down pillows, would pass around
> The drinking-horn in his opulent hall.
> The first brew of bragget was his.
> Blaen took delight in gold and purple;
> First pick of sleek steeds raced beneath him;
> At sound of battle his high heart earned them.
> First to raise the war-cry, gainful return,
> Bear in the path, ever slow to retreat.
> *The Gododdin*, stanza A16 (Clancy 1999, 50)

There is other early British poetry, which is equally remarkable for its detail and which is equally historically challenging, because this poetry survived only as part of a living bardic tradition and therefore was subject to modification over time. Perhaps as a conscious response to the poetic tradition the Church evolved a genre of literature to praise its own heroes, known as hagiography. The writing of lives of saints was intended to inspire devotion amongst the faithful and to promote the interests of the churches associated with particular saints. The most important of these was the *Vita Columba* composed by Adomnán abbot of Iona in the early seventh century. In recounting the biography of the saint, it provides considerable insight into the workings of an early monastery, the political influence of clerics and contemporary beliefs, as can be seen from this extract:

> Once, when the praiseworthy man [Columba] was living in the island of Hinba, he saw one night in a mental trance an angel of the Lord sent to him. He had in his hand a glass book of the ordination of kings, which St Columba received from him, and which at the angel's bidding he began to read. In the book the command was given to him that he should ordain Áedán as king …
>
> *Life of Columba*, III 5 (Sharpe 1995, 208)

The *Life of Columba* is exceptional because it was hugely popular and widely copied. It is also exceptional for its historical reliability; for instance we know from independent sources that this Áedán did indeed become king of Dál Riata. It confirms the intimate link between Iona and the royal house.

CHANGING PERCEPTIONS SINCE THE SECOND WORLD WAR

There have been two profound changes in the approach to the archaeology of Early Historic Britain since the middle of the twentieth century. Firstly, a new critical attitude was adopted towards the historical resources and the ability to identify the contemporary material remains in the archaeological record. These were reinforced by the second change, which saw the introduction of scientific dating methods and a general increasing rigour in the conduct of archaeological fieldwork.

The volume edited by Fredrick Wainwright, *The Problem of the Picts* (1955), included essays which typified the new multidisciplinary approach. This volume attempted to strip away the mystery and mythological nonsense which surrounded the Picts and replace it with empirical studies of field monuments, sculpture, linguistics and historical texts. Similar, less systematic efforts were being attempted in Northumbria, Wales and the West Country at about this time.

The first excavation to reveal the full potential of a historically informed approach to the archaeology was Leslie Alcock's work at Dinas Powys (1963), a small hillfort in south Wales which produced a wealth of evidence now seen to typify the period (Alcock 1963). There was an abundance of imported pottery and glass, debris from fine metalworking and animal remains which all contributed to a picture of elite consumption and hierarchical social organization. Although undertaken before the widespread use of radiocarbon dating, scientific analysis was applied to the glass and faunal remains. More importantly, the study of the pottery benefited from the pioneering work on the imported pottery by Charles Thomas and Bernard Wailes.

While the importance of the Dinas Powys work was acknowledged within the academic community, Alcock captured wider public interest in the archaeology of the post-Roman era when he began his search for Arthur. This was a deliberate ploy to attract media attention and funding for the large-scale excavations at the hillfort of South Cadbury in Somerset, a site identified with the legendary Camelot (Alcock *et al.*1995). The excavations were part of a larger project to rescue Arthur from his literary Anglo-French chivalric identity and restore him to his position as hero of the post-Roman Celts. The result of these efforts was the highly influential analytical survey *Arthur's Britain*, which faced up to the challenges of the ambiguous textual evidence for Arthur while synthesizing the archaeological evidence for the fifth to eighth centuries (Alcock 1971). It was notable for its efforts to integrate the historical and archaeological evidence and for considering both the Celtic and Anglo-Saxon inhabitants of Britain. Although criticized by some historians for encroaching on their scholarly turf, the book remains highly influential.

In *Arthur's Britain* attention is focused on the secular, the political and inevitably on the military conflict between native Britons and invading Saxons. Little attention was directed towards religion and the coming of Christianity, although the dichotomy between Christian Celt and pagan English was a fundamental part of the contemporary rhetoric of the conflict. This Christian identity is implicit in the monumental sculptural tradition, which utilized Christian formulae and occasionally symbols. The systematic archaeological exploration of the transition of Christianity from a marginal late Roman cult into the universal post-Roman religion is associated with Charles Thomas, whose surveys and excavations at early church sites dovetailed with Alcock's (Thomas 1971).

Although not promoted by Thomas, the notion of a Celtic Church which was monastic, decentralized and ruled by saintly abbots (rather than bishops) became commonplace. Partially inspired by the romantic island monasteries found in Ireland and Scotland, this view of a decentralized Church dominated by monasteries was sustained by C.A.R. Radford's influential interpretations of the Cornish coastal promontory fort of Tintagel as a monastery. It is only with the deconstruction of the notion of a universal Celtic Church by Wendy Davies and the re-excavation of Tintagel by Morris that the notion of an episcopal Church, characteristic of the rest of Europe, has been accepted (Barrowman *et al.* 2007).

The most distinctive aspect of the material culture – the sculpture – has been the slowest to be revitalized. In Scotland, the publication of a comprehensive corpus, Allen and Anderson's *Early Christian monuments of Scotland* (1903), stifled scholarship for a generation. R.B.K. Stevenson's art-historical studies of sculpture from Pictland and Dál Riata demonstrated the potential latent in this material (1955). The RCAHMS Inventories of Argyll begun in the late 1970s set new standards for the recording of the sculpture; these have remained a benchmark and have in recent years been extended to other areas of Scotland. However, the greatest interpretative advances in the imagery and symbolism of the Scottish material have been by Isabel Henderson, whose contribution to *Art of the Picts* (Henderson and Henderson 2004) is a *tour de force*. More sophisticated reading of the early inscriptions by Forsyth have rendered the northern inscriptions in Latin and ogham more intelligible (2005).

In Wales the great corpus by Nash Williams was published in 1950, so the need for revision was felt less acutely. Nevertheless steady improvements in epigraphical studies have been made, and in recent years Nancy Edwards and others have begun to produce a revised corpus (Edwards 2007).

Academic divisions still hamper study, and, despite the value of considering Celtic and Anglo-Saxon evidence together, few archaeologists and historians cross the ethnic divide. Martin Carver, excavator of Sutton Hoo and Portmahomack, is a rare exception. There remains much work to be done in deconstructing the received wisdom of medieval historical tradition, as can be seen by Ewan Campbell's reassessment of the evidence for the Gaelic migration from Ireland to western Scotland (2001). This suggests that the flow of material culture moved from east to west and that Gaelic may have been spoken on both sides of the North Channel of the Irish Sea long before the supposed arrival of the Gaels in Dál Riata.

KEY DATA

Secular sites

The Celtic kingdoms of the Early Historic period were ruled from imposing, rock-perched hillforts which have attracted considerable archaeological interest and consequently are the most familiar and best understood. Many carry names of ancient kings or royal associations, but few have more than one or two contemporary citations that demonstrate their royal status. Therefore a portfolio of evidence is required to make a royal identification, which includes imported pottery and glass, evidence for the manufacture of fine metalwork, weaponry, signs of feasting and conspicuous consumption and, ideally, contemporary historical notices. This list has been shaped by a small number of sites which possess some or all of these features.

One of the most evocative sites is Tintagel, a rocky headland on the Cornish coast, which is traditionally believed to be the birthplace of King Arthur. It has been subject to various excavations, including ones leading to the recognition of imported pottery in this period. Unfortunately, this material and other evidence were taken as signs that this was an early Christian monastery. More recent work has challenged this, and scholarly opinion is that this was a secular site that controlled the long-distance trade into south-western Britain (Barrowman *et al.* 2007).

South Cadbury, Somerset, was a major Iron Age hillfort, reoccupied in the Early Historic period and thought by some to be Arthur's residence of Camelot. In addition to large quantities of Mediterranean imports, the excavations produced evidence for a timber hall, which provides the clearest physical evidence of the feasting culture. In south Wales the small hillfort of Dinas Powys was reoccupied at a similar time (Alcock 1963); it was never a major power centre, perhaps occupied by a 'prince' rather than a king, but revealing a full range of evidence associated with high-status sites (see above). In Scotland the rocky site of Dunadd may have been the chief royal fortress of the Scots of Dál Riata. The fortification enclosed a metalworking area, marked by discarded moulds for brooches and other jewellery (Lane and Campbell 2000). It has also produced one of the largest assemblages of imported pottery and glass. Edinburgh Castle shows occupation dating back to *c.* 800 BC and a range of Roman goods attesting to a high-status settlement by the second to third centuries AD. This was possibly the seat of a great sixth-century king of the north Britons in the *Gododdin*, although the archaeological evidence is ambivalent (Driscoll and Yeoman 1997). Edinburgh's counterpart was probably Dumbarton, the political centre of the northern Britons in the west. Several seventh-century British kings are explicitly identified as kings of Clyde Rock, *Al Cluith*, in Irish annalistic sources, and excavation has produced imports from both Mediterranean and continental sources. The demise of Dumbarton can be dated precisely to AD 870, when it was sacked by a large force of Dublin Vikings. Evidence for the transition from a northern British stronghold to a Northumbrian one can be seen at Dunbar, a fortified port on the Lothian coast where excavation of the defences has revealed a series of structures from the seventh to the ninth centuries (Perry 2000). Historical evidence shows that Dunbar was held by a royal official for the Northumbrian king.

The Pictish fortification of Dundurn occupies a craggy hill overlooking one of the main land routes between southern Pictland and Dál Riata in a unique position adjacent to both Irish Sea and North Sea connections. Thanks to waterlogged conditions on the hilltop it provided exceptional evidence for timber architecture and other organic finds. The fortified headland of Burghead in the Moray Firth was probably a regional power centre, but has no contemporary historical references and has seen only limited excavations. The site is celebrated for the images of bulls carved on series of slabs in the Pictish animal style. Further north, in Orkney, the Brough of Birsay is a naturally defended tidal island where various excavations have discovered evidence for metal working, a Pictish symbol stone and an extensive Pictish settlement. The adjacent mainland may have provided the agricultural support system including the important Pictish farmhouse at Buckquoy before the area was commandeered by the Norse earls of Orkney, who made Birsay their principal residence (Morris 1989, 1996).

The Pictish royal site at Forteviot probably signals the decline of the hillfort tradition; it differs from these other high-status sites in being an undefended, open settlement. Probably the residence of Cináed mac Alpín ('Kenneth MacAlpine'), who died in a palace there in AD 858, the site has yielded an impressive collection of sculpture including a monolithic arch and the Dupplin Cross (with its inscription to King Constantín mac Firgusa (d. 820)), suggesting the presence of royal monastery which would foreshadow the preference for monastic palaces exhibited by later medieval Scottish monarchs. The truly remarkable aspect of Forteviot was revealed by aerial photographs showing an extensive Neolithic cropmark and a Pictish cemetery in the fields adjacent to the village (Figure 11.10).

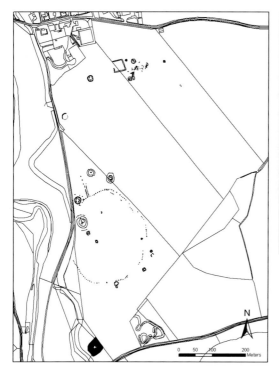

Figure 11.10 Transcription of aerial photographs of cropmarks at Forteviot. The cemetery including Pictish square and round barrows is located to the south-east of the village. The prehistoric ritual monuments concentrated around the circular timber enclosure lie to the south of the village. The photograph shows the henge monuments at the heart of the circular enclosure.

Source: RCAHMS, Crown copyright.

Church sites

Whithorn, in south-west Scotland, was home to St Ninian, who, according to Bede, was the greatest missionary to evangelize the north of Britain. An impressive collection of early medieval sculpture, including the Latinus Stone – the oldest inscription in Early Historic Scotland – would seem to support this view. However, evidence for an early church has eluded archaeologists, who have recovered the largest collection of imported glass drinking vessels in Britain (Hill 1997). To the north, the island monastery of Iona, founded by St Columba in AD 563, grew to become one of the greatest ecclesiastical centres in the British Isles, with a network of associated monasteries through northern Britain, Ireland and Northumbria. It also maintained extensive political links, not least with Dunkeld, the chief centre of the cult in Britain under the patronage of expanding Gaelic kings, and to where Columban relics were moved in response to Viking raids. In the north-east, Portmahomack occupies the headland of the Tarbat peninsula in Easter Ross, where recent excavations have exposed a sequence of churches extending back to the seventh century, part of a cemetery and a large area of workshops and agricultural buildings, including, uniquely in the British Isles, a workshop where vellum for manuscripts was prepared (Carver 2008). It seems likely that the exceptionally Pictish sculpture on the peninsula, including the Hilton of Cadboll cross-slab, was also produced at Portmahomack.

Sculpture of this kind is a major source of evidence, particularly in Scotland, where important collections are to be found at Iona, St Andrews, Meigle, St Vigeans and Whithorn (Fisher 2001). In Wales there are key groups around Llantwit Major, Glamorgan, and St Davids, Pembroke (Redknap and Lewis 2007). Stone sculpture is also a feature of Cornwall, but there are no great concentrations of sculpture. A remarkable monument to the expansion of the kingdom of Northumbria in southern Scotland is the Ruthwell Cross, arguably the finest piece of Anglo-Saxon sculpture in Britain. It was also an ecclesiastical site which yielded the most significant collection of native metalwork, the St Ninian's Isle hoard from Shetland (Small *et al.* 1973). The twelve silver penannular brooches, seven silver bowls and various other objects exhibit a high level of craftsmanship. They are thought to have been a collection of church treasures buried for safe keeping. Smaller hoards of Pictish silver are known from elsewhere, the most important of which comes from Norrie's Law in Fife.

SOCIAL AND POLITICAL INTERRELATIONSHIPS

Society

At the largest scale the most significant social feature was the increasingly state-like development of kingdoms such as Dál Riata, Fortriu and Northumbria. Warfare was the essential means of expanding petty kingdoms into regional hegemonies. At the start of this period military organization relied on personal bonds of loyalty and kinship obligations, but war bands assembled by charismatic leaders and maintained through the spoils of conquest were inherently unstable. Those kingdoms which lasted did so through the good fortune of having a sequence of strong kings and by expanding the governing class beyond the immediate kin group. The key development was the creation of landed estates and the formalization of the institutions of lordship. This was achieved by the granting of lands to individuals in exchange for rents in kind and services, particularly military services. It is likely that the early memorial stones and Pictish symbol stones were intended to fix claims to land through the erection of permanent monuments.

Although Christianity was well established in Britain by the end of the Roman era, at the time of the collapse of the Empire its institutional structure was weak and religious belief diffuse. In the early stages the Church's strength was locally grounded in the regional saints' cults which were closely linked to local kingdoms. As the Church matured and acquired more property it became increasingly politically influential. This interrelationship between secular and ecclesiastic power is most apparent in the Pictish cross-slabs with their combination of secular imagery and ecclesiastical symbolism.

Economy

The basis of the economy was overwhelmingly agricultural, and the crops and farming techniques were little altered from previous periods. However, the mechanism for managing production changed with the development of estates. Status was revealed in the nature of agricultural goods and services one received from social inferiors and in turn what one delivered to social superiors. In the absence of coinage cattle probably served as the main 'currency' and were used to measure wealth, settle debts and to cement relationships.

At the highest levels a prestige economy existed based upon imported goods – pottery, glass and, more importantly, non-durable commodities like wine and textiles. These goods were controlled by the ruling elite, who consumed them and distributed them through their fortified strongholds. The finds of imported pottery and glass are the residues of a culture of feasting and reward which underpinned the bonds of lordship, particularly those between warlords and their followers. The concentration of the production and distribution of fine metalworking found at the elite hillforts indicates that the brooches and other jewellery were utilized as part of this economy of lordship.

The Church operated a parallel system, as lands were granted to the Church they became landlords with tenants. The great churches, like the great secular leaders, were able to patronize the skilled craftsmen to adorn their altars, but they also supported a wider range of crafts including sculpture and manuscript art. In practice the need to extract an agricultural surplus may have been just as great for the leading churches as for the leading secular figures.

CURRENT PERCEPTIONS

The interrelated themes of nation-building and economic development are prominent archaeological interests. The process of nation-building amongst the Celtic peoples followed different paths from more Romanized and urbanized regions of Europe. How were Celtic cultural and religious traditions drawn upon in making these new kingdoms? To what extent were pre-existing regional identities manipulated to create ethnic distinctions?

It is becoming increasingly clear that in the absence of externally imposed practices of political organization, the native Britons relied upon existing mechanisms of political assembly. They looked to places that had been hallowed by ancient use, as can be seen in the wider archaeological context of Dunadd or Forteviot, where royal centres established links with the ancestral past as a means of enhancing their authority.

Northumbria was the only region in Britain with any significant evidence for cultural integration between Germanic incomers and natives. This raises the question of the extent to which the landscape and social organization of Northumbria was influenced by the British kingdoms of Bernicia and Deira. More generally, it is recognized that our understanding of the economic organization underpinning these emergent kingdoms is hampered by ignorance of the organization of the landscape and structure of the settlement pattern below the elite levels. Investigating these issues will require new strategies to locate the full spectrum of settlement activity and to elucidate the agricultural practices.

BRITISH EVIDENCE IN A WIDER SETTING

While the Celtic-speaking Britons were in some respects culturally introverted, there is ample evidence that they were aware of wider European cultural developments. The trade routes that brought imported goods to Britain also facilitated the transmission of ideas. The Irish Sea served as the main conduit by which the Britons and Gaels maintained contact with the continental Christian heirs to Rome and provided a direct route to the Mediterranean and the Continent, bypassing England. Native Britons and Gaels were fully engaged with the intellectual development of Christianity. The depth of their interest in the foundations of Christian belief is shown by the earliest-known guide to the Holy Land, which was written by Columba's biographer Adomnán of Iona drawing upon information from a visiting Gaulish bishop.

Ireland was the most important influence on Celtic Britain, and many of our ideas about Early Historic social organization have been shaped by the rich body of early Irish mythology, legal tracts and historical sources. The Irish Sea naturally facilitated regular contact with Ireland which penetrated far beyond the west-coast kingdom of Dál Riata to the Northern Isles, eastern Pictland, Northumbria and Wales.

Until the end of the eighth century, there was little or no contact with Scandinavia, but during the 790s Viking raids became increasingly common and the coastal monasteries were especially targeted. In the course of the next century the entire political map of Britain was redrawn as the Viking armies grew in size and ambition. All of the major kingdoms mentioned here succumbed to the Vikings, and in the ninth century were remade, often utilizing the institutional foundations laid in this period but generally having been renamed (for example the kingdom of Dumbarton became Strathclyde and the southern Pictish kingdom was renamed Alba), and were ruled by new dynasties. So with the coming of the Viking Age the social, political and spiritual world of Early Historic Britain came to an abrupt end.

Key texts

Alcock, A., 1971. *Arthur's Britain*. Harmondsworth: Penguin.
Alcock, A., 2003. *King and warriors, craftsmen and priests*. Edinburgh: Society of Antiquaries of Scotland.
Carver, M.O.H., 2008. *Portmahomack: monastery of the Picts*. Edinburgh: Edinburgh University Press.
Foster, S., 1996. *Picts, Gaels and Scots*. Edinburgh: Historic Scotland.
Laing, L., 2006. *The archaeology of Celtic Britain and Ireland c. AD 400–1200*. Cambridge: Cambridge University Press. 2 edn.

Bibliography

Alcock, L., 1963. *Dinas Powys: an Iron Age, Dark Age and early medieval settlement in Glamorgan.* Cardiff: University of Wales Press.

Alcock, L., with S.J. Stevenson and C.R. Musson, 1995. *Cadbury Castle Somerset: the early medieval archaeology.* Cardiff: University of Wales Press. Allen, J.R. and Anderson, J., 1903. *The early Christian monuments of Scotland.* Edinburgh: Society of Antiquaries of Scotland.

Allen, J.R. and Anderson, J., 1903. *The early Christian monuments of Scotland.* Edinburgh: Society of Antiquaries of Scotland.

Barrowman, R.C., Batey, C.E. and Morris, C.D., 2007. *Excavations at Tintagel Castle, Cornwall, 1990–1999.* London: Society of Antiquaries of London.

Campbell, E., 2001. 'Were the Scots Irish?', *Antiquity* 75, 285–92.

Campbell, E., 2007. *Continental and Mediterranean imports to Atlantic Britain and Ireland,* AD 400–800. York: Council for British Archaeology Research Report 157.

Clancy, T.O. (ed.) 1999. *The triumph tree: Scotland's earliest poetry* AD 550–1350. Edinburgh: Canongate.

Crone, A., 2000. *The history of a Scottish Lowland crannog: excavations at Buiston, Ayrshire, 1989–90.* Edinburgh: STAR Monographs.

Driscoll, S. and Yeoman, P.A., 1997. *Excavations within Edinburgh Castle 1988–91.* Edinburgh: Society of Antiquaries of Scotland Monograph 12.

Edwards, N., 2007. *A corpus of early medieval inscribed stones and stone sculpture in Wales,* vol. 2. Cardiff: University of Wales Press.

Edwards, N. and Lane, A. (eds) 1988. *Early medieval settlements in Wales* AD 400–1100. Bangor: UCNW Research Centre Wales; Cardiff: Department of Archaeology, University College.

Edwards, N. and Lane, A. (eds) 1992. *The early Church in Wales and the West.* Oxford: Oxbow.

Fisher, I., 2001. *Early medieval sculpture in the West Highlands and Islands.* Edinburgh: Royal Commission on the Ancient and Historical Monuments of Scotland.

Forsyth, K., 2005. 'HIC MEMORIA PERPETUA: the inscribed stones of sub-Roman southern Scotland', in Foster and Cross (eds), 113134.

Foster, S. and Cross, M. (eds) 2005. *Able minds and practised hands: Scotland's early medieval Sculpture in the 21st century.* Leeds: Society for Medieval Archaeology.

Henderson, I. and Henderson, G., 2004. *The art of the Picts.* London: Thames and Hudson.

Hill, P., 1997. *Whithorn and St Ninian: the excavation of a monastic town 1984-91.* Stroud: Sutton.

Koch, J., 2007. *An atlas for Celtic studies.* Oxford: Oxbow.

Lane, A. and Campbell, E., 2000. *Dunadd: an early Dalriadic capital.* Oxford: Oxbow.

Morris, C.D., 1989. *The Birsay Bay Project,* vol. 1. Durham: University of Durham.

Morris, C.D., 1996. *The Birsay Bay Project,* vol. 2. Durham: University of Durham.

Perry, D., 2000. *Castle Park, Dunbar: two thousand years on a fortified headland.* Edinburgh: Society of Antiquaries of Scotland.

Ralston, I.B.M., 2006. *Celtic fortifications.* Stroud: Tempus.

Redknap, M. and Lewis, J., 2007. *A corpus of early medieval inscribed stones and stone sculpture in Wales,* vol. 1. Cardiff: University of Wales Press.

Redknap, M., Edwards, N., Youngs, S., Lane, A. and Knight, J. (eds) 2001. *Pattern and purpose in Insular art.* Oxford: Oxbow.

Sharpe, R. (trans.) 1995. Adomnán of Iona, *The life of Columba.* Harmondsworth: Penguin Classics.

Small, A., Thomas, C. and Wilson, D.M., 1973. *St. Ninian's Isle and its treasure.* Aberdeen: University of Aberdeen Press.

Stevenson, R.B.K., 1955. 'Pictish art', in Wainwright (ed.), 97–128.

Thomas, C., 1971. *The early Christian archaeology of northern Britain.* Glasgow: University of Glasgow.

Wainwright, F.T. (ed.) 1955. *The problem of the Picts.* Edinburgh: Nelson. Reprinted 1980.

Youngs, S. (ed.) 1989. *The work of angels: masterpieces of Celtic metalwork, 6th–9th centuries* AD. London: British Museum.

12

THE SCANDINAVIAN PRESENCE

Julian D. Richards

BACKGROUND

For three centuries, beginning shortly before AD 800, the British Isles were subject to raids from Scandinavia. Initially these were hit-and-run affairs targeting vulnerable coastal sites, principally monasteries, such as Lindisfarne, Monkwearmouth and Iona. As the raiding parties gained in size and confidence, and as the need for reward increased, they seized land as well, although the rate at which raiding turned to settlement varied from area to area. Norse colonies were founded in the Northern and Western Isles of Scotland and on the Isle of Man. Documentary sources for these regions are scarce, and we are reliant on archaeological evidence. For England, however, the Anglo-Saxon Chronicle provides a near-contemporary, if one-sided, account of raids, annexations and Scandinavian invasions. It records the presence of a highly mobile Danish 'great army' in England from AD 865. Having captured York in AD 866, this army seized territory in Northumbria, Mercia and East Anglia. Within these areas, which became known as the Danelaw, many Scandinavians settled.

Despite living in a war zone, or perhaps because of it, this was a period of major social and economic change for the Anglo-Saxons. A network of fortified towns, or *burhs*, was founded in Mercia by King Offa and in Wessex by Alfred and his successors. As places of royal control and protection, these towns were centres of minting and taxation, and trade and industry were encouraged to develop within their ramparts. Rural craft production of precious items gave way to semi-industrialized mass production of standardized forms, often imitating Scandinavian artistic tastes. After some initial disruption and a shift to more easily defendable areas, the Middle Saxon *wics*, such as Hamwic (Southampton), London, Norwich, Ipswich and York, also prospered. Most burhs and wics continued beyond the Norman Conquest to expand into fully-fledged medieval towns (see Chapter 13). In the countryside, rural settlement was also reorganized. In many parts of England, Scandinavian settlement hastened the process of disintegration of those large estates that had been under direct royal or ecclesiastical control. Although some historians are reluctant to identify feudalism before the Norman Conquest, many agree that the laying out of villages in the tenth century represents the beginnings of a proto-manorial system (see Chapter 15). The contemporaneous boom in church building probably reflects the associated construction of private chapels attached to early manor sites (see Chapter 14).

TERMINOLOGY

The period commencing AD 800 is often described as the Viking Age, although some explanation of the term is needed. 'Viking' is an evocative word, but it was rarely used by contemporary chroniclers, who preferred to use 'Norse', 'Dane' or even 'heathen', often interchangeably. The term 'Viking' became widely used only in the nineteenth century, when translations of medieval Icelandic sagas captured the Victorian romantic imagination with tales of a heroic and mythical past. Some modern scholars go so far as to see the Vikings as inventions of the sagas, popularized by the Victorians and maintained by contemporary nationalism. Whilst there can be little doubt that Scandinavian warriors did go on sea-borne raids from at least AD 800, it is worth acknowledging that this was, to some extent, part of a continuing process of migration. For England, the end of the Viking Age is conveniently marked by the death of the last great Viking leader, Harald Hardraada, and the subsequent victory of William the Conqueror in 1066. The Western Isles of Scotland and the Isle of Man, however, remained under Scandinavian rule until 1266, and Orkney and Shetland belonged to Norway until 1469.

SOURCES

For archaeologists, the Scandinavian presence in the British Isles is recognizable by its distinctive material culture. In recent years metal-detector users have recovered large numbers of artefacts decorated in Scandinavian style from the ploughzone of eastern England. Burials accompanied by weaponry and jewellery in Scandinavian forms probably represent a first generation of pagan settlers, although their uneven distribution is also testimony to the extent of conversion amongst the settlers. In England, for example, where Christianized Danes formed the majority of the settlers, there are no more than 30 known burial sites, and most of these are solitary graves. On the northern and western fringes, by comparison, there are many more pagan burials per head of population. There are c. 130 Viking Age burials with grave goods in Scotland and 24 burials on the Isle of Man. This may partly reflect the Norse preponderance in these areas, although the overtly pagan nature of some of the burials suggests that they may have also emphasized their 'Vikingness' to stress their ethnic differences in this colonial context (Richards 2005). In some areas, especially Yorkshire and the Isle of Man, the following generation of settlers adopted stone burial markers and crosses which frequently combine pagan and Christian iconography. The Viking kingdom of York is also the centre of the distribution of the unique hogback stones, which appear to represent another distinctive colonial monument (Lang 1984).

Hoards of Viking silver are widely distributed throughout the British Isles, although their interpretation is far from straightforward. The largest, comprising over 40 kg of silver coins, bullion and arm rings, is that discovered in 1840 at Cuerdale, Lancashire, on the banks of the River Ribble (Figure 12.1); it has been interpreted as the pay chest of a Viking army, possibly recently arrived from Dublin in *c.* AD 905. Other smaller hoards from Scotland and the Isle of Man may represent the personal fortunes of Viking leaders, accumulated so that they could reward their followers and buy their allegiance through reciprocity. It has also been suggested that some hoards as well as river offerings of weapons continued the pagan Scandinavian tradition of making gifts to gods that were never intended to be recovered. Other hoards may simply represent personal wealth buried, but never recovered, under the threat of advance of a Viking raiding party (Graham-Campbell 1992).

In England there is little settlement evidence that can clearly be categorized as Scandinavian. Indeed, there is no reason why the buildings of Viking York should be any different from those of Saxon London, although the appearance in tenth-century York and Chester of town buildings with semi-sunken cellars, providing space for storage of traded and manufactured items, mirrors their occurrence in Danish towns. Similarly, the appearance of bow-sided halls, on high-status rural sites such as Sulgrave, Northamptonshire, and Goltho,

Figure 12.1 Cuerdale, Lancashire: part of the early tenth-century silver hoard.

Source: Trustees of the British Museum

267

Lincolnshire, matches the Trelleborg-style halls of Denmark. In the Northern Isles there are many diagnostic North-Atlantic-style longhouses with stone footings, central hearths and wall benches, at sites including Underhoull, Sandwick, and Jarlshof in Shetland and Tuquoy, Quoygrew, Beachview, Skaill and the Brough of Birsay in Orkney (Graham-Campbell and Batey 1998).

Linguistic evidence has also been widely employed to support the idea that there were a substantial number of immigrants. In the former East Riding of Yorkshire, for example, it has been calculated that 48 per cent of place-names are of Scandinavian influence; the English language also adopted a number of Old Norse words into everyday usage. In the Isle of Man, it has been argued that Gaelic was completely supplanted by Norse and was restored only at the end of Scandinavian rule. Scandinavian place-names blanket Shetland and Orkney and are also found in the Hebrides and on the Scottish mainland. A Scandinavian dialect, *Norn*, was spoken in the Northern Isles into the eighteenth century. However, such arguments beg the question of how many people are required to change a language, and linguistic studies have shown that a small but influential group can have an effect out of all proportion to their numbers. Similarly, arguments based on place-names often ignore the fact that they tell one only about who named the settlements, and sometimes about who collected the taxes, but not necessarily about who lived there. Certainly, the distribution of Scandinavian-type place-names corresponds fairly well with the areas of recorded Danish settlements in Yorkshire, Mercia and East Anglia and the Wirral, although there are also further concentrations, such as that in the Lake District, for which there is no historical documentation. It is perhaps intuitively unlikely that the newcomers arrived anywhere in the British Isles in such numbers, or replaced the local population to such an extent, as to form a majority of the population. Irrespective of its size, however, the fact remains that the Scandinavian presence had considerable influence throughout the British Isles.

CHANGING PERCEPTIONS

Since the Second World War, the saga-inspired view of horned-helmeted Norse raiders carrying off Anglo-Saxon treasure and women to their dragon-headed longships has gradually given way to a more positive image of the Scandinavian presence which owes more to IKEA than to Wagner. Urban archaeology within English towns has demonstrated the importance of the ninth and tenth centuries as a period of growth and industrialization, as reflected in the Jorvik interpretation centre in York.

In common with other periods, there has also been a tendency to downplay the extent and impact of invasion and migration. From the 1960s, revisionist historians, notably Peter Sawyer, have questioned the reliability of figures for the size of the Viking armies given in the Anglo-Saxon Chronicle and have suggested that these were generally small raiding forces (Sawyer 1971). Basil Megaw suggests that no more than 400 warriors may have formed the initial Viking settlement on the Isle of Man. They have also argued against simplistic interpretations of linguistic evidence to suggest that there was never a mass folk migration of Scandinavian settlers. Current archaeological and historical thinking emphasizes change at an elite level, but sees the vast majority of the population as unaffected by changes at the top. Trends in archaeological theory have also encouraged archaeologists to question whether artefact styles and cultural assemblages can be interpreted at face value. Certainly in York it seems that Anglo-Saxon-style disc brooches were decorated with Scandinavian Jellinge-style ornament, rather than Anglo-Saxon women adopting Scandinavian costume with the bow brooches needed to hold it in place. The debate has shifted to issues of ethnicity and has focused on the circumstances that led to the creation of hybrid Hiberno-Norse and Anglo-Scandinavian identities (see papers in Hadley and Richards 2000; Hadley 2006).

Advances in archaeological science have begun to impact on the study of the period. Stable isotope analysis of teeth from Viking Age burials has been used with some success to identify first-generation immigrants, particularly as the Norwegian geology means that the groundwater signature is very different from England. At Adwick-le-Street near Doncaster a woman buried with a pair of bow brooches and a copper alloy bowl at her feet was probably born in the Trondheim area of Norway (Speed and Walton Rogers 2004). Modern DNA studies are less convincing, as although they demonstrate genetic links between north-western Europe (including Denmark) and eastern England, and Norway and the Northern Isles, the results lack any chronological resolution and may reflect migration and population movement over a longer period. Where they have been tied to subsets of population which are likely to have been relatively static (by focusing on people with historically documented surnames for example) they may be more promising (Bowden *et al.* 2008). Nonetheless, despite scientific advances, the agenda is still largely that set by the documentary sources, which have determined the popular view of the Vikings as the outsiders; few British today would identify themselves with Viking ancestors. The Anglo-Saxons, under Alfred, are the ancestral English; the Vikings are still the invaders.

KEY DATA

Burials

It is rare to find archaeological evidence that appears to relate to a specific historical event, and dangerous to look for it, but investigations at Repton, Derbyshire, appear to support an entry in the Anglo-Saxon Chronicle that claims that the Viking army over-wintered there in AD 873–4. Excavations by Martin and Birthe Kjølbye-Biddle located a D-shaped enclosure constructed so that the River Trent formed the long side, whilst the rest of the site was surrounded by a bank and ditch into which the monastery church was incorporated as a gatehouse. Some 50 m west of the enclosure, an earthen mound had been built over a massive, two-roomed stone structure, which may originally have been intended as a mausoleum for the Mercian royal family. The mausoleum had been reused as a charnel house, in which the remains of some 250 individuals had been interred. The bones were disarticulated when they were buried, with longbones stacked together and skulls placed on top. This suggests that they had been exposed or buried elsewhere, allowing the flesh to come off, before being collected together for reburial. The mass burial is dated by a group of five pennies deposited sometime after AD 871. Analysis of the skeletal remains shows that 80 per cent were robust males who died aged 15–45, although they are just as likely to represent the inhabitants of the Mercian monastery as members of the Viking Great Army (Halsall 2000).

Further Scandinavian burials were found near the east end of the church at Repton, including that of a man aged 35–40, who had been killed by a massive cut to the top of his left leg. He wore a necklace of two glass beads and a Thor's hammer silver amulet. By his side was a sword in a fleece-lined scabbard, a folding knife and a key, whilst a boar's tusk and jackdaw bone had been placed between his legs. A substantial posthole at the east end of the grave suggests that it had been marked by a wooden post (Biddle and Kjølbye-Biddle 2001). Although the form of this burial is pagan it is significant that it was aligned east–west adjacent to the shrine of St Wigstan.

At Heath Wood, Ingleby, some 4 km south-east of Repton, fragmentary remains have been found of the only known Scandinavian cremation cemetery in England (Figure 12.2). The cemetery originally comprised 59 barrows in four groups. Excavations have revealed that some of the mounds contain spreads of charcoal and ash mixed with human and animal bone, representing cremation pyres; however, others appear to be empty, apart from token offerings. Richards (2004b) has argued that Heath Wood represents the war cemetery of a group of the Viking Great Army who had chosen to create an ostensibly pre-Christian rite, complete with animal sacrifice, unlike those other warriors who chose instead to be buried adjacent to the relics of St Wigstan at Repton.

Pagan symbolism is also evidenced amongst many of the burials of first-generation Viking settlers on the Isle of Man. The graves of these first landtakers were frequently marked by coastal

Figure 12.2 Heath Wood, Ingleby, Derbyshire: Viking burial mound under excavation.
Source: J.D. Richards

mounds that would have been visible from the sea. In the parish of Jurby, six out of eight of the quarterland farms (a quarterland was a unit of land division) on the coastal strip are distinguished by a prominently sited burial mound. At Balladoole (Figure 12.3), a stone cairn was erected forming the outline of a ship. The distribution of some 300 clench nails marks the location of an actual vessel, some 11 m in length. It appears that two corpses were buried in the boat, including a male accompanied by various personal items, a shield and riding equipment. The burial cairn was covered by a layer of cremated animal bones, including horse, ox, pig, sheep or goat, dog and cat. It had been cut into a Christian cist grave cemetery, some of whose occupants had been so recently buried that their limbs were still articulated. It is difficult to avoid the conclusion that such desecration was deliberate. At Ballateare, a circular mound covered a burial pit in which a young male had been placed. The body had been wrapped in a cloak held in place by a ringed pin. Various weapons had been placed outside the coffin, most of which showed evidence of deliberate mutilation. The sword had been broken in three pieces and replaced in its scabbard. A shield with two deep indentations to the boss had been placed on one side and two spears had been broken and thrown in the backfill. A thin layer of cremated animal bone had again been thrown over the mound, but this time it also included the skeleton of a young female killed by a slashing blow to

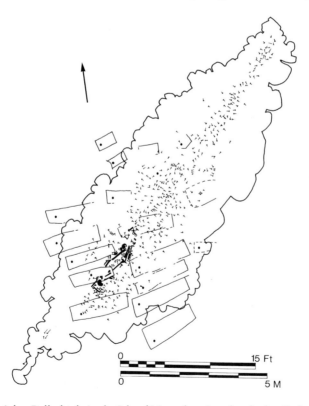

Figure 12.3 The burial at Balladoole in the Isle of Man, showing clenched nails from boat and outlines of earlier Christian graves.
Source: J.D. Richards

the top of her head. Most interpretations accept that this was a warrior accompanied to the after-world by various symbols or actual items of his property, including a slave girl (Wilson 2008).

Ship burials are also known from other areas of Norse settlement, including the Northern and Western Isles. At Scar on the island of Sanday in Orkney, a small rowing boat, about 6.3 m long, was discovered eroding out of a cliff in 1991. Despite the sea damage, it is one of the best-recorded Norse graves from Scotland. Buried in the boat were a man in his thirties, a woman in her seventies and a child. The age difference makes it unlikely that they were a typical family group, but both adults had rich personal grave goods, also making it unlikely that they were a master or mistress and slave. The man was armed with a sword and arrows and had a fine comb and a set of 22 gaming pieces. The woman was wearing a gilded brooch, and beside her were a whalebone plaque, a sickle, cooking spit, a small pair of shears and a steatite spindlewhorl (Owen and Dalland 1999).

The reappearance of pagan burial in the British Isles appears to have been a relatively short-lived phenomenon, representing the first generation of Scandinavian settlers. Their successors rapidly adopted local burial customs and become archaeologically indistinguishable from those given Christian burial. At Raunds, Northamptonshire, 368 Christian burials have been excavated in a tenth- and eleventh-century graveyard clustered around a church within a rectangular ditched enclosure. All the graves were aligned east–west with the head to the west; none was buried with grave goods. Most of the bodies were simply placed in holes in the ground, although slabs of limestone were used as pillow stones in about 60 per cent of the graves. There are indications of wooden coffins in some cases, and six elite burials were distinguished by being placed in lidded stone coffins. On the Isle of Man, over 300 Christian burials have been excavated in a cemetery to the north of St German's Cathedral, St Patrick's Isle, Peel. Most were in stone-lined cist graves, although the later ones simply have stone pillow slabs to protect the head, or are buried in wooden coffins. There are also at least seven Scandinavian burials of the tenth century, although only that of a high-status female was accompanied by grave goods, other than items of dress. The woman had been laid with a cushion to support her head and was accompanied by various items, including a cooking spit, a work box or bag with two needles, a pair of small shears, an antler comb and a curious 'mortar and pestle' amulet. Whilst of Scandinavian type the grave did not contain the brooches one would normally expect as part of female costume. All of the Peel burials share the same alignment and style of grave construction, suggesting no break in continuity at this site, unlike Balladoole (Wilson 2008).

In both the Danelaw and the Isle of Man, the Scandinavians also adopted the local custom of erecting stone crosses. This had previously been largely confined to monasteries and prestigious churches, but stone monuments now proliferated throughout northern and eastern England and on the Isle of Man. Some fragments depict Viking warriors with their weapons. One of the best examples is at Middleton, North Yorkshire (Figure 12.4); other examples include Levisham and Weston in North Yorkshire, and Sockburn, Co. Durham. These figures may well represent the new landlords, and the distribution of crosses may indicate the presence, if not the centres, of new landholdings (Bailey 1980).

The subjects chosen by the sculptors or their patrons are particularly striking; many emphasize the parallels between Christian and pagan stories. At Gosforth, Cumbria, a Crucifixion scene is paired with *Ragnarok*, the last great battle of Norse mythology; Thorwald's Cross at Kirk Andreas on the Isle of Man counterbalances the death of Odin at *Ragnarok* with the coming of Christ (Wilson 2008). The legend of Sigurd and his struggle with the dragon is another popular theme; the scene in which he roasts the heart of the dragon Fafnir and burns his thumb is found at Kirk Andreas and at Halton, Lancashire, and Ripon, North Yorkshire. At Nunburnholme, Humberside, there is a cross in which Sigurd has been recarved over a Eucharistic theme, drawing attention to the Sigurd feast as a pagan version of the Eucharist (Bailey 1980; Lang 1991).

Many of the graves of York's Viking Age elite discovered under York Minster are marked by recumbent grave slabs decorated with Scandinavian-style ornament; some have separate head and foot stones. These may be the predecessors of the distinctive so-called hogback stones, which were erected for a period of about 50 years from AD 920. Hogbacks are shaped like bow-sided buildings with ridged roofs and curved side walls, but their ends may be decorated with bearlike creatures, or sometimes wolves or dogs. They may also have been influenced by house-shaped shrines. Their distribution is concentrated in northern England but with outliers in Scotland, Wales and Cornwall. The best collection is in the church at Brompton, North Yorkshire, but the largest group is at Lythe, North Yorkshire (Lang 1984). Stocker (2000) associates them with the graves of a Hiberno-Norse mercantile elite.

Figure 12.4 The Middleton Cross, St Andrew's Church, Middleton, North Yorkshire.

Source: Department of Archaeology, University of Durham

Settlement

The stone monuments provide good evidence for an influential Scandinavian presence in the British Isles. In the ploughzone of lowland eastern England chance finds by metal-detector users of jewellery decorated with Scandinavian-style ornament provide the best evidence for extensive rural settlement to complement the place-name distribution. In many cases the artefacts reflect a hybrid Anglo-Scandinavian or Hiberno-Norse culture, with Scandinavian ornament on Anglo-Saxon disc-brooch forms. Such settlements rarely leave archaeological traces, but at Cottam, in East Yorkshire, a concentration of metal finds coincides with a series of cropmark enclosures. Excavations have revealed that a small eighth-/ninth-century Anglo-Saxon settlement – probably an outlying dependency of a multiple estate – was abandoned in the late ninth century to be replaced by a neighbouring farmstead with a grand timber gateway set within rectangular paddocks (Richards 1999). Judging by the Anglo-Scandinavian artefact types introduced, including a Borre-style buckle and so-called Norse bells, the new occupants may well have been Scandinavian colonists. They were no longer able to buy and sell with copper alloy coins, or *stycas*, as the Northumbrian mints had ceased production, but this did not prevent them trading west with York and south of the Humber to Lincolnshire, weighing out silver bullion to conduct their transactions. However, the new site was short-lived, before it was replaced in the tenth century by a planned settlement which developed into the medieval village.

In lowland England, it is becoming apparent that a number of villages were first established in the tenth century. At Furnells Manor, Raunds, Northamptonshire, a Middle Saxon settlement in a ditched enclosure was replaced by a large timber hall and an adjacent church in the early tenth century. At about the same time, the first regular tenements of peasant farmers were being laid out at Furnells and West Cotton in Northamptonshire and marked by ditched enclosures. At Goltho, an early ninth-century village was superseded by a fortified earthwork enclosing a bow-sided hall, a kitchen and weaving sheds. The manorial complex may have been founded by a member of the Saxon aristocracy, although the discovery of a Scandinavian-style bridle bit could be used to suggest that it was a late ninth-century Viking foundation. Bow-sided halls are associated particularly with Viking Age Denmark and are also found in most of the areas settled by Scandinavians. At Goltho, there was evidence that the hall, 24 m long by 6 m wide at the centre, was divided into three rooms, with a raised dais at one end and a cobbled hearth in the centre. During the late tenth and early eleventh centuries, the site underwent considerable expansion. The hall was replaced by an aisled version without internal partitions, and the bower was enlarged with a latrine attached at one end. After the Norman Conquest, it developed into a motte-and-bailey castle (Beresford 1987).

The upland farmstead at Ribblehead is frequently advanced as a Viking site but may be just an upland farmstead (Figure 12.5). It comprises the stone footings of a longhouse, bakery and smithy set in an enclosed farmyard with an associated field system (King 2004). At Doarlish Cashen, on the Isle of Man, a longhouse with wall benches was also discovered on marginal land at about 210 m above sea-level (Wilson 2008). Such settlements would undoubtedly have been familiar to Norse settlers, but they are also standard upland building forms.

In Orkney, Shetland and the Hebrides, it is easier to identify Norse settlements. Rectangular long-houses replace native houses based on oval or circular forms. Around the Bay of Birsay, Orkney, a likely seat of the Norse earls, are a number of Norse farmsteads. At the Point of Buckquoy at Birsay, a Norse farm had been built on top of the ruins of an earlier Pictish farm, and at first sight would appear to support a picture of conquest and replacement of the local population. However, the artefacts from the Norse occupation levels are not Scandinavian types but Pictish bone pins and decorated combs. These imply that the Viking newcomers were at least able to obtain equipment from a native population that had not been exterminated, and most probably inter-married with it. By contrast, the evidence from the Udal, North Uist, has been used to demolish the idea of social integration. Here the eighth-century native settlement was apparently replaced by an entirely Scandinavian culture. A short-lived defended enclosure was the first Viking Age structure; characteristic longhouses were then built amongst the ruins of five Pictish houses (Graham-Campbell and Batey 1998). Tenth- and eleventh-century longhouses with bowed walls and Scandinavian material culture have also been excavated at Bornish on South Uist (Sharples 2004).

At Jarlshof on Shetland, romantically named by Sir Walter Scott, a small Pictish community was replaced by a sequence of Norse longhouses in the ninth century. Houses over 20 m long by 5 m wide are known. The walls are built of stone rubble with a turf and earth core. Typically there are pairs of opposed doors placed in the long walls, stone-lined hearths and wall benches. At Jarlshof, the group of two or three houses and their outbuildings, perhaps representing an extended family unit, is unusual (Figure 12.6). In Scotland, the overall settlement pattern is dispersed, comprising individual farms. At Westness, Rousay, Orkney, excavations have revealed a fragment of a Viking

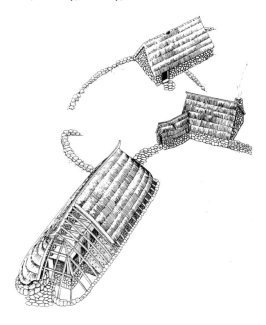

Figure 12.5 Ribblehead, North Yorkshire: an artist's reconstruction of the Viking Age farmstead.
Source: Yorkshire Museum

Age landscape. A coastal cemetery contained more than 30 graves, some pre-Norse, but with two small boat burials. Nearby was a farm consisting of a substantial longhouse and two byres, one interpreted as a cattle byre with space for about 18 animals, and the other for sheep. Beyond the cemetery was a boat-house, or *naust*, comprising a three-sided building, open to the sea (Graham-Campbell and Batey 1998). Late Viking Age settlements from the Northern and Western Isles therefore imply that society was explicitly Norse in the tenth to twelfth centuries.

Until recently there was little archaeological evidence from Wales, but excavations at Llanbedrgoch on Anglesey have revealed a fortified settlement on the coast which may have developed as an aristocratic estate centre. Scandinavian and Irish finds indicate wide trading connections and hack-silver reflects an active bullion economy. Five bodies, casually buried in the enclosure ditch, may indicate that Viking raiding led to the site's abandonment in the late tenth century (Redknap 2004).

Towns

In northern and western Britain, there are no towns during this period, but in England the Scandinavian presence coincided with a period of urban growth. In the East Midlands there are five towns, Derby, Leicester, Lincoln, Nottingham and Stamford, which are described in the Anglo-Saxon Chronicle as Five Boroughs; they were once thought to have been specially

Figure 12.6 Norse buildings at Jarlshof, Shetland.
Source: Historic Scotland

fortified towns, established by the Danes after the partition of the Danelaw and used by Alfred as a model for the burhs (below). However, they may not have become Danish strongholds until later, in which case they may have been modelled upon Alfred's foundations, rather than the other way round (Hall 1989).

There had been urban trading and manufacturing centres in England since the early eighth century. Sites such as Hamwic (Saxon Southampton), Eoforwic (York) and Lundenwic (London) developed under royal patronage around a waterfront where traders could beach their vessels and perhaps establish their booths in regulated plots. At most *wic* sites, however, the threat of attack in the Viking Age led the traders to seek protection within walled towns and may also have disrupted trade.

The site of Hamwic was depopulated by the late ninth century, and the focus of tenth-century occupation shifted to higher ground within the area that was to become the medieval walled town. In London, the exposed waterfront site along the Strand was abandoned and the area of the old Roman fortress was reoccupied in the tenth century, becoming known as Lundenburh. In York, a single coin of the 860s is the latest find from the Fishergate site, outside the confluence of the rivers Ouse and Foss, whilst activity commences in Coppergate at about this time. It is impossible to say, however, whether this starts before the Viking capture of York in AD 866 as a result of people seeking the protection of the walled town, or whether it is a consequence of the Viking settlement. It does appear that York's Viking rulers renovated its Roman defences and remodelled its street system. They constructed a new bridge across the Ouse and built houses along Micklegate, 'the great street', leading to the new crossing point. In Coppergate, excavations between 1976 and 1981 of an area of deep, oxygen-free organic soils have provided some of the best preserved evidence of Viking Age urban life in the Danelaw. The Viking Age street was established by AD 930, and possibly as early as AD 900, with the delineation of four tenements, each 5.5 m wide. Initially, a single line of buildings was constructed along the street frontage, narrow end facing the street (Figure 12.7). These first buildings comprised timber wall posts and roof supports with wattlework wall panels. Each was about 4.4 m wide and 8.2 m or more in length. They had central clay hearths that would have provided both heat and light. In some cases, traces of wall benches were preserved. The finds suggest that these buildings served both as houses and workshops. In the late tenth century they were pulled down and replaced by substantial semi-basement structures with planked walls. The new buildings were probably two-storey structures with living accommodation above and extra storage and workshop space below (Hall *et al.* 2004). The York examples are the best-preserved in the British Isles, but cellared buildings also occur in other major towns such as London, Chester, Oxford and Thetford. They seem to be a response to the increased pressure upon urban space and the need to store goods in transit and stock-in-trade.

Although some of the largest towns developed as trading sites, a much larger group of towns was established as defended forts or burhs, probably as a direct response to the Viking threat. The earliest examples were founded in Mercia *c.* AD 780–90 by King Offa, possibly

Figure 12.7 Excavated buildings at Coppergate, York.
Source: York Archaeological Trust

copying Carolingian practice. At Chester, the surviving walls of the Roman fort were refur-
bished and probably extended down to the River Dee by Ethelflaed in AD 907. A substantial
Hiberno-Norse trading community developed near the waterfront. At Lower Bridge Street, at
least five cellared timber buildings were erected in the tenth century (Mason 1985).

In Wessex, Alfred is credited with the establishment of a burghal system so that no part
of his kingdom was more than 32 km from a fortified burh. When Edward the Elder recon-
quered England in AD 911–19, he extended the network and fortified a number of new sites.
The Burghal Hidage, a tax assessment of *c.* 914–18, lists the Wessex burhs in the later years
of Edward's reign, and indicates the extent of their perimeters. In Bath, Chichester, Exeter,
Portchester (Hampshire), Southampton and Winchester, the burhs made use of Roman
stone walls and gates. At Cricklade (Gloucestershire), Oxford, Wallingford (Oxfordshire)
and Wareham (Dorset), new rectangular defences were erected on Roman models. The
ramparts were initially of clay and turfs with timber revetment and were probably crowned
with timber palisades. In the late tenth or early eleventh centuries, the timber palisade was
often replaced by a stone wall. At other sites, such as Lydford (Devon) or Malmesbury
(Wiltshire), natural defences such as promontories or peninsular sites were utilized; at South
Cadbury, the Iron Age hillfort was reoccupied. Within some of the larger burhs, a regular
street system was laid out, and whilst the temporary forts were abandoned after the decline
of the Viking threat, many of the larger burhs became permanent towns. They provided not
only a haven for industry but also an urban market for its products and for materials and
produce imported from the hinterland (Richards 2004a, 78–108).

Industry

In the towns, the Scandinavians provided one of the main catalysts for urban growth and helped create the conditions by which England experienced what Richard Hodges (1989) describes as the First Industrial Revolution. Pottery is a case in point. During the Middle Saxon period, most pottery was manufactured locally by hand. By the early ninth century, only Ipswich ware was produced on an industrial scale and traded widely. From the mid-ninth century, changes began to occur at a number of centres. In York, there were the first steps towards a specialized pottery industry with increased standardization of forms and fabrics. In East Anglia, the Ipswich potters began to use a wheel to make cooking pots in what is known as the Thetford tradition. By the tenth century, wheel-thrown pottery was manufactured over much of eastern England. This new pottery production was predominantly town-based: Northampton, Stamford, Stafford, Thetford and Winchester are all examples of new wares that take their names from towns in which kilns have been discovered. Stamford is notable for the introduction, in the late ninth century, of yellow or green glazing on spouted pitchers made in a fine, off-white fabric. The sudden appearance of glazing is coincidental with the Scandinavian presence in Stamford, but the technology appears to have been introduced from northern France or the Low Countries by potters who arrived in the wake of the Scandinavian takeover. Stamford ware was traded widely via coastal or riverine routes throughout the Danelaw; by the eleventh century it accounts for 25 per cent of all pottery in Lincoln and York. Its spread appears to have started with specialist industrial pottery; glazed crucibles are the first pottery to appear on tenth-century metalworking sites in Lincoln, Thetford and York.

Industrial-scale metalworking is also a feature of the new towns. The working of copper alloys and precious metals was hitherto restricted to high-status sites such as the royal palace at Cheddar, Somerset, and generally appears to have been carried out only under lordly or ecclesiastical patronage. By the tenth century, it had become an urban enterprise; at Coppergate, for example, two adjacent tenements were occupied by metalworkers and some 1,000 crucible fragments were found. The urban markets fuelled a large demand for mass-produced lead-alloy disc brooches decorated in a Scandinavian style. Iron working also spread to the towns, and whilst rural farmsteads still had their own smithies, it was in the towns that smiths experimented with new artefacts and new techniques. In York, for example, new types of knife were introduced and decoration proliferated (Hall *et al.* 2004).

The urban communities are also characterized by manufacture in bone and antler, leather and textiles. In each case, raw materials would have been available in the immediate rural hinterlands and the urban craftsmen produced goods on a large scale for local demand. To date, the relationship between towns and their hinterlands is best studied from the urban evidence, particularly that provided by environmental archaeology. In York, the Middle Saxon traders occupying the Fishergate site appear to have been dependent upon the ruling elite for most of their food supply and had little opportunity for trading with rural food-producers. The settlement at Fishergate seems to have had a narrow subsistence base. Cattle and sheep probably arrived in York on the hoof, although some pigs may have arrived as dressed carcasses. Minor animal components of the diet are very under-represented, and there are few wild mammals, birds and fish. In Viking Age York, by contrast, there was a great increase in the variety of foodstuffs available. Although there is little change in the staple meat species, there is a marked increase in those species identified as suitable for raising in backyards, such as pigs, geese and fowl. The fish bones show intensive exploitation of the river; plant remains, including moss, elder, blackberry, raspberry and sloe, reflect exploitation of local woodland resources. By the late tenth century, the exploitation pattern now has more in common with that seen in medieval York. Whereas the food supply of the Anglo-Saxon *wic* had been dependent upon a food rent system run by the elite, the Viking Age traders and craftsmen had greater freedom of operation than their controlled predecessors. Here we may see the emergence, therefore, of an independent mercantile urban class whose livelihood was based upon trade and exchange rather than redistribution (O'Connor 1994).

Commercial trade would have been dependent upon the development of a monetary economy. By the late tenth century, there were some 50–60 mints operating from burhs and major towns throughout England. The Isle of Man too began producing its own distinctive Hiberno-Manx coinage in the eleventh century, indicating that Man was linked into trading networks with England and Ireland. In the absence of towns trade must have been conducted via beachmarkets, such as that suspected at Ronaldsway. The process was much slower in Scotland, and Scottish hoards indicate that a monetary economy was not operating in the fringes of the British Isles until much later. Scottish hoards, such as that from Skaill, Orkney, contain not only imported silver coins but also hack-silver (i.e. fragments of silver objects that have been chopped up to use simply as bullion) and ring-money (i.e. plain silver arm rings, which were a convenient way of carrying measurable wealth). In England, imported silver was converted into the official coinage. At each mint, a number of private individuals, or moneyers, took responsibility for the coinage on behalf of royal authority. Whilst coins carried the name of the ruler on their obverse, on the reverse the name of the moneyer appeared. Chester, being the entry point from Dublin, became an important centre for coin production, and 24 moneyers worked there from AD 924–39. Although not all those with Scandinavian names may have been settlers, it is still significant that by the reign of Ethelred, 75 per cent of York's moneyers, and 50 per cent of Lincoln's, bore Scandinavian names.

The church

In the countryside, it seems that Scandinavian settlers presided over the fragmentation of great estates, establishing manorial centres and accelerating the market in the buying and selling of land. Alongside this we see a boom in the creation of rural parishes and parish churches, notably in the tenth and early eleventh centuries. By the time of Domesday Book, there were demonstrably over 2,600 local churches (Morris 1989). This explosion in church construction was a by-product of the quest for status of new landowners. The possession of a church was an important status symbol, as well as a source of income. Most of the manorial churches were new buildings, although some were adapted from existing minster or monastic sites. Many probably began as wooden buildings, but most were soon transformed into impressive stone buildings. The new churches generally started as simple, small, rectangular boxes to provide a nave, although chancels were often added later. At Wharram Percy, North Yorkshire, a small timber church was established in the tenth century, perhaps as a private chapel of an Anglo-Scandinavian lord. This was enlarged in the eleventh century by a small, two-celled church consisting of a nave and chancel. The church became a focus for burials of the early lords of the Percy manor, and later of the parish (Beresford and Hurst 1990). At Raunds, a small, rectangular, late ninth- or tenth-century church was erected on a stone foundation adjacent to the manorial enclosure. In the eleventh century, this building was replaced by a larger church, 15 m long, which by this time must have been serving the residents of the surrounding settlements who were buried in the graveyard.

Many of the new churches were founded by Scandinavian lords. The sequestration of monastic estates in the Danelaw may even have facilitated the creation of local churches, as some minsters lost control of their territories. At several Yorkshire sites, the lords chose to record their benefactions in a prominent position on the church sundial, for all to read. At Kirkdale, North Yorkshire, the inscription of AD 1055–65 commemorates a lord with a Norse name, Orm, who bought the redundant minster and erected a new church on its site. At Aldbrough, Yorkshire, a similar sundial records that 'Ulf ordered the church to be put up for himself and for Gunwaru's soul.'

THE WIDER SETTING

The Scandinavian presence in the British Isles needs to be set in the wider context of the Viking world. The geographical extent of Scandinavian cultural domination is one of the most striking aspects of the Viking Age. The Norse travelled westwards across the North Atlantic to the fringes of the known world, founding colonies in the Faroes, Iceland, Greenland and even reaching the coast of Newfoundland; in the east, Swedish Vikings had established trading ports down the major river routes into the heart of eastern Europe (Brink and Price 2008; Richards 2005). These provide valuable comparisons for the Scandinavian presence in Britain, allowing archaeologists to study the nature of contact and its effects upon the native peoples. In some cases, the Scandinavians were occupying virgin territory; in others, they were moving into already intensively settled and exploited lands. On the whole, it appears that the secret of their success lay in their ability to change and to adapt to local circumstances, enabling the incomers to blend, chameleon-like, into the background in some cases, such as in the Danelaw, or to emphasize and develop a distinctive Viking cultural identity in others.

Developments in Scandinavia are of particular relevance to Britain, as Scandinavian expansion overseas can be understood only in the context of state formation at home. Denmark, the first of the Scandinavian kingdoms to appear on the historical stage, must serve as an example. The date of the emergence of a kingdom that encompassed all of present-day Denmark is a vexed question, but it is at least accepted that by the reign of Harold Bluetooth in the late tenth century, most of Jutland plus the islands of Fyn, Sjælland and that southern portion of Sweden known as Skåne were under the control of the Danish king. At the royal burial site at Jelling, Harold erected a runestone monument on which he claimed responsibility for

JULIAN D. RICHARDS

the unification, as well as the conversion to Christianity, of Denmark. Harold established a system of ring forts, known after one of them as Trelleborg forts, in each part of his kingdom. At about the same time, we see the emergence of a class of warrior farmers who we presume made up the king's armies. This group might also have been the landholders at sites such as Vorbasse, with its bow-sided, Trelleborg-style halls. These sites have been termed magnate farms and, in parallel with Late Saxon England, are often interpreted as being farmed by tenant farmers on behalf of a lord to whom tribute and allegiance would be owed. This was the social and economic glue that bound the Viking raiding parties together.

The causes of Viking expansion have been much debated and have ranged from population pressure and a worsening climate at home to Viking skills at ship-building and navigation (Barrett 2008). Whilst these factors may have contributed, the most satisfactory explanation rests upon internal pressures caused by shortage of resources. Our understanding of pre-Viking Danish society suggests that the giving of prestige gifts both to others and to the gods was one of the key means by which chieftains maintained their status. If the internal supply of gifts were to dry up or fail to maintain pace with demand, the easiest solution would be to turn to external sources. During the initial stages of the Viking raids, Anglo-Saxon monastic treasures provided a ready means to reward one's war band. Later, as Denmark developed into a state society, the desire for portable wealth was supplemented by a desire for territorial control. Similarly, the giving of silver arm rings was augmented by the giving of rights to land. The division of the great estates of England was accelerated by the presence of Scandinavians, sharing land tenure between their followers in return for continued allegiance and support.

Key texts

Brink, S. and Price, N. (eds) 2008. *The Viking world*. London and New York: Routledge.
Graham-Campbell, J. and Batey, C.E., 1998. *Vikings in Scotland: an archaeological survey*. Edinburgh: University Press.
Hadley, D.M., 2006. *The Vikings in England: settlement, society and culture*. Manchester: Manchester University Press.
Hadley, D.M. and Richards, J.D. (eds) 2000. *Cultures in contact: Scandinavian settlement in England in the ninth and tenth centuries*. Turnhout: Brepols.
Hines, J., Lane, A. and Redknap, M. (eds) 2004. *Land, sea and home*. Leeds: Society for Medieval Archaeology Monograph 20.
Richards, J.D., 2004a. *Viking Age England*. Stroud: Tempus. Revised edn.
Richards, J.D., 2005. *The Vikings: a very short introduction*. Oxford: Oxford University Press

Bibliography

Bailey, R.N., 1980. *Viking Age sculpture in northern England*. London: Collins.
Barrett, J.H., 2008. 'What caused the Viking Age?', *Antiquity* 82, 671–85.
Beresford, G., 1987. *Goltho: the development of an early medieval manor c. 850–1150*. London: English Heritage Archaeological Report 4.
Beresford, M. and Hurst, J.G., 1990. *Wharram Percy: deserted medieval village*. London: Batsford/ English Heritage.

Biddle, M. and Kjølbye-Biddle, B., 2001. 'Repton and the "great heathen army", 873–4', in Graham-Campbell, J., Hall, R., Jesch, J. and Parsons, D. (eds) *Vikings and the Danelaw*. Oxford: Oxbow Books, 45–96.

Bowden G.R., Balaresque, P., King, T.E., Hansen, Z., Lee, A.C., Pergl-Wilson, G., Hurley, E., Roberts, S.J., Waite, P., Jesch, J., Jones, A.L., Thomas, M.G., Harding, S.E. and Jobling, M.A., 2008. 'Excavating past population structures by surname-based sampling: the genetic legacy of the Vikings in Northwest England', *Molecular Biology and Evolution* 25, 301–9.

Graham-Campbell, J. (ed.) 1992. *Viking treasure from the north-west: the Cuerdale hoard in its context*. Liverpool: National Museums and Galleries of Merseyside Occasional Papers 5.

Hall, R.A., 1989. 'The Five Boroughs of the Danelaw: a review of present knowledge', *Anglo-Saxon England* 18, 149–206.

Hall, R.A., Rollason, D.W., Blackburn, M., Parsons, D.N., Fellows-Jensen, G., Hall, A.R., Kenward, H.K., O'Connor, T.P., Tweddle, D., Mainman, A.J. and Rogers, N.S.H., 2004. *Aspects of Anglo-Scandinavian York*. York: Council for British Archaeology Archaeology of York 8/4.

Halsall, G., 2000. 'The Viking presence in Engand? The burial evidence reconsidered', in Hadley and Richards (eds), 259–76.

Hodges, R., 1989. *The Anglo-Saxon achievement*. London: Duckworth.

King, A., 2004. 'Post-Roman upland architecture in the Craven dales and the dating evidence', in Hines, Lane and Redknap (eds), 335–44.

Lang, J.T., 1984. 'The hogback: a Viking colonial monument', *Anglo-Saxon Studies in Archaeology and History* 3, 85–176.

Lang, J.T., 1991. *Corpus of Anglo-Saxon stone sculpture: volume 3. York and Eastern Yorkshire*. London: British Academy.

Mason, D.J.P., 1985. *Excavations at Chester: 26–42 Lower Bridge Street 1974–6: the Dark Age and Saxon periods*. Chester: Grosvenor Museum Archaeology, Excavation and Survey Reports 3.

Morris, R.K., 1989. *Churches in the landscape*. London: Dent.

O'Connor, T.P., 1994. '8th–11th century economy and environment in York', in Rackham, J. (ed.) *Environment and economy in Anglo-Saxon England*. London: CBA Research Report 89, 136–47.

Owen, O. and Dalland, M., 1999. *Scar: A Viking boat burial on Sanday, Orkney*. Phantassie: Tuckwell Press / Historic Scotland.

Redknap, M., 2004. 'Viking-age settlement in Wales and the evidence from Llanbedrgoch', in Hines, Lane and Redknap (eds), 139–75.

Richards, J.D., 1999. 'Cottam: an Anglian and Anglo-Scandinavian settlement on the Yorkshire Wolds', *Archaeological Journal* 156, 1–110.

Richards, J.D., 2004b. 'Excavations at the Viking barrow cemetery at Heath Wood, Ingleby, Derbyshire', *Antiquaries Journal* 84, 23–116.

Sawyer, P.H., 1971. *The age of the Vikings*. London: Edward Arnold.

Sharples, N., 2004. 'A find of Ringerike art from Bornais in the Outer Hebrides', in Hines, Lane and Redknap (eds), 255–72.

Speed, G. and Walton Rogers, P., 2004. 'A burial of a Viking woman at Adwick-le-Street, South Yorkshire', *Medieval Archaeology* 48, 51–90.

Stocker, D., 2000. 'Monuments and merchants: irregularities in the distribution of stone sculpture in Lincolnshire and Yorkshire in the 10th century', in Hadley and Richards (eds), 179–212.

Wilson, D.M., 2008. *The Vikings in the Isle of Man*. Aarhus: University Press.

13

LANDSCAPES OF THE MIDDLE AGES

Towns 1050–1500

John Schofield
(formerly Museum of London)

PRINCIPAL CHRONOLOGIES AND SUB-DIVISIONS

The period AD 1050–1500 in the British Isles is conventionally divided into three successive phases:

1   the development of towns and the countryside in a period of growth, 1050–1300;
2   the crises of the early and mid-fourteenth century, including the Black Death;
3   a long period of mixed fortunes from about 1350 to 1500, which comprised both decline for some towns and the rise of others, including in England the increasing dominance of London over a widening hinterland and a similar dominance in Scotland of Edinburgh (the national picture is provided in Palliser 2000).

In the eleventh century, there were already many towns in Britain, though the majority were in England, where Domesday Book records 112 places called boroughs in 1086. They were based on royal residences, trading settlements or the defended places of Saxons or Danes in the ninth and tenth centuries (Hinton 1990, 82–105). Some major centres such as London, Lincoln and York had longer histories, being Roman foundations of the first century AD.

In the towns, a period of comparative wealth and growth in the eleventh and twelfth centuries is illustrated by the range of civic and religious buildings that were constructed (Hinton 1990, 106–32; Platt 1978, 1–29). The great majority of urban defences in England and Wales, for instance, were built, or at least begun, before 1300. The Normans moved the seats of bishops to towns, which meant several new cathedrals, and established centres of secular authority. This usually meant the destruction of large areas of the Saxon towns to accommodate both cathedrals and castles (see Chapter 14). In the thirteenth century, the friars arrived in Britain seeking populous locations, and hospitals were founded in and around many urban places.

Weekly markets in the smaller towns are mentioned in the twelfth but especially in the thirteenth century; sometimes the grant of the market itself is recorded. The fair, on the other hand, was a wider kind of market, usually held once a year and lasting for at least three days and sometimes for as long as six weeks. As the market was the centre for exchange within the neighbourhood, so the fair was the centre for foreign wares, brought from outside the locality.

Between 1200 and 1500 about 2,800 grants of market were made by the English Crown, over half of them in the period 1200–75. Village markets and seasonal local fairs were augmented by weekly or bi-weekly markets held in centres of production, both existing towns and new towns. This was happening all over Europe, for instance in south-west France (the interface between the English and French kingdoms) and along the Baltic coast. Towns were valuable pieces of property, for the lord gained revenue from the court, tolls on merchandise and from the demands of the market, which benefited his own rural manors in the surrounding countryside (Platt 1978, 30–90). The main stimulus for economic growth in small towns may have been the needs of a local lord. Country landowners and religious houses acquired properties in the ports, where they could trade with the surplus of their own manors and farms and have access to the market in imported luxuries.

In this early phase, the merchants of many small British towns participated in overseas trade, and London's dominance was largely a thing of the future. Ships still came to the river-ports of York, Lincoln, Norwich, Gloucester and Chester. Wine from the English lands in Gascony (south-west France) came to Boston in Lincolnshire; wool exports through the town rivalled those of the capital. Along the eastern and southern coasts, small and medium-sized towns fed their regions with imports, and shipped out the local produce. By the twelfth century, however, London was the primary distribution centre for inland trade, and its size and wealth began to dominate south-east England.

In Wales, by 1135, a boundary zone of castles and nascent towns had been established along the Marches from Cardiff to Chester. Towns flourished particularly in south Wales during the eleventh and twelfth centuries: places like Monmouth, Cardiff, Abergavenny, Brecon (where the first civil town was laid out in the castle bailey, a pattern found elsewhere in the Welsh zone), Carmarthen and Pembroke. This southern group was complemented by a second wave of fortress towns added in the north and west by Edward I's campaigns in the 1270s; the many medieval cellars of Chester probably date from this period, as the town became a supply base for the royal army (Brown 1999).

In Scotland, by the eleventh century, there were also political and economic systems that could organize and support substantial centres of population, but urban history is obscure before the widespread introduction of the 'burgh' and its privileges by King David I (1124–53) and his successors. Some towns, like Edinburgh and Stirling, grew next to citadels, while others, such as Lanark, Selkirk and Dunfermline, are on unprotected sites.

In England, towards the end of the thirteenth century, there are signs of economic strain and social tensions, at least in the larger towns. The most important single industry was the making of cloth, but in the thirteenth century, in the face of the highly urbanized Flemish industry, England became an exporter of wool. Times were good, and many towns were established and prospered; the population rose in towns and in the countryside. Around 1300, however, fortunes changed. Crop failures and cattle disease caused widespread famines in 1315–25; a 50 per cent drop in production brought a 400 per cent increase in grain prices. England was at war with Scotland and from 1337 with France, which resulted in heavy taxes to pay for the king's campaigns. The Black Death of 1348, a Europe-wide epidemic of bubonic plague, was the *coup de grâce* to a country already weakened by political problems and natural disasters.

During the late fourteenth and fifteenth centuries, cloth went back to replacing wool as England's main export. By 1500, the bulk of the country's overseas trade was in English hands; so was the transformation of raw materials into finished products. Many towns, however, some sooner than others, went into decline. At Nottingham in 1376, houses were falling into decay; Bedford and Warwick similarly stagnated. At York around 1400, the textile industry was flourishing and the town's merchants engaged in overseas trade through the nearby port of Hull, but within 30 years, the textile industry had migrated to the countryside and wool exports had slumped. Hull could not compensate by more exports of cloth, for it faced Hanseatic opposition in the Baltic and London's interests in Flanders. Lincoln was declining more rapidly, initially from the effect of the plague and then from problems with its vital waterways, the Foss Dyke to the Trent and the Witham to Boston.

Other towns, however, succeeded. Gloucester and Coventry switched attention from wool to cloth production. Salisbury and Norwich did likewise, and whole regions came to specialize in cloth: notably the south-west (Totnes; Castle Combe), East Anglia (Lavenham; Hadleigh) and the former West Riding of Yorkshire (Halifax and Wakefield). Ports also fared better, as demonstrated by the fortunes of Bristol and London.

MAJOR AND TYPICAL DATA TYPES

Urban finds are of several kinds: ceramics (largely pottery); animal bones; human bones; buildings and loose building material; non-ceramic artefacts (in leather, wood and metals), and biological and botanical evidence. Buildings and streets are types of artefact, to be analysed in the same general ways as pottery or small finds. The town's archaeology is the result of a bundle of influences – climatic regimes, physical factors in the environment such as the influence of geology or gradual pollution, biological factors (e.g. dietary differences between people) and the ups and downs of the economic life of the place.

The archaeologist studying medieval British towns must use maps and documents as well as the trowel (Platt 1976; Schofield 1999; Schofield and Vince 2005). Medieval towns have, to varying degrees, the additional benefit of more records per square kilometre than rural places, or than towns in previous centuries. Archaeology gives more depth on individual

Figure 13.1 The thirteenth-century undercroft beneath the chapel on medieval London Bridge, revealed during demolition in 1832. Engravings like this are the earliest archaeological records of medieval towns; archaeologists should make frequent visits to local record offices.
Source: Guildhall Library, London

sites, while documentary study is wider and is effective at the level of larger units such as street or town. Engravings of prominent buildings and structures often survive to compare with the results of modern investigations (e.g. Figure 13.1).

CHANGING PERCEPTIONS SINCE THE SECOND WORLD WAR

In the first half of the twentieth century in Britain, urban history studies were dominated by a concern exclusively with constitutions and institutions; there was no attempt to think of towns as actual places. Urban archaeology in Britain began immediately after the last war in the bomb-damaged cellars of London, Canterbury and a small number of other towns, where medieval buildings and monuments had suffered destruction along with those of more recent centuries.

By the end of the 1960s, many archaeologists were concerned about the destruction of physical evidence for Britain's history in towns. This resulted in the survey *The Erosion of History* (Heighway 1972), which drew attention to the 'crisis in urban archaeology'. It argued that the most important English towns of all historical periods would be lost to archaeology in 20 years, if not before; half of the 906 historic towns remaining in mainland Britain were threatened with some sort of development, 159 of them seriously.

During the 1970s and early 1980s, archaeologists widened the debate and scope of their activities from being purely reactive to formulating strategic plans for individual towns. In the 1970s, the practice of asking every developer to pay for dealing with the archaeology of his site in an appropriate way spread from London and the larger cities to a more general use everywhere. Since 1990, government policy has been to insist on preservation of historic strata wherever possible, and rescue archaeology has diminished. At the same time, the urban archaeologists have been digesting the vast haul of information from the last 30 years of rescue work, and new perceptions of the medieval town and what went on in it are being formed.

KEY DATA: SITES AND ASSEMBLAGES

This chapter will briefly outline some of the recent thinking and discoveries concerning planned towns and planned parts of towns; urban defences; streets, markets and public buildings; suburbs and the waterfront areas of towns; houses and buildings on the domestic scale; evidence of manufacture and crafts, and the medieval urban environment. Castles, monasteries and churches in towns are dealt with in the following chapter.

Planned towns and planned parts of towns

From the modern street-plan of towns, or from maps showing their former state, we can identify certain layouts that were shared by new towns and by planned extensions to existing (pre-medieval) settlements. Three main variants have been identified. Firstly, in a small number of towns there is clear evidence of planning. A chequerboard pattern formed by at least four streets and nine squares is found rarely (Salisbury or Winchelsea) and must always have been exceptional. Ludlow, which now comprises a grid of streets, probably grew in a series of stages (Platt 1976, 38–44). A second grid-plan produced a ladder-like effect with two main streets in parallel (e.g. New Shoreham, Melcombe Regis). Thirdly, particularly in the years up to 1200, an urban castle might dominate the town plan to the extent of making it circular or D-shaped, following the castle's outer defences (Barnstaple; Pleshey).

A second group of apparently planned elements was more irregular, and concern the emphasis placed upon the market, especially as defensive considerations declined during the thirteenth century. Markets might be in the main street, causing its edges to bulge into a cigar-shape, or the meeting of two or three ways might produce a triangular space. These two market-forms are very common in towns, and one might ask what, if any, deliberate policy of planning they represent, apart from the initial decision to start the market.

Ideas of what may be termed medieval town planning are most evident in the new towns associated with Edward I. In the north at Berwick and in Wales at Flint, Conwy and Caernarvon, he hoped both to keep the peace by establishing garrison towns but also to encourage it by promoting ports and markets, incidentally ensuring effective markets to feed the garrisons. These towns were therefore military units in which castle and borough were designed as a single concept. The castles have survived well in these Welsh towns, but unfortunately there is little evidence at present for ordinary houses in these specialized places; we have to look to contemporary foundations in Gascony in France, where there are many English and French towns called 'bastides', in which the medieval fabric survives to be studied (Beresford 1988).

Many town plans were composed of a series of topographical units of different periods. The clearest examples are those towns of great age, such as Abergavenny, Doncaster, Godmanchester and Hereford, but the apparent homogeneity of planned towns should also be regarded with caution. New towns might have been laid out systematically at first, but soon spilled over and developed their own idiosyncrasies. In addition, as demonstrated in many 'planned' cases, the units of new settlement were based on field boundaries and ridges, as in the twelfth century at Stratford and Lichfield. In Scotland, cumulative phases of settlement from the twelfth to the fifteenth century and later are suggested at Perth by analysis of street-blocks and plot widths. The emphasis of wider European studies (Clarke and Simms 1985) has also been on the cumulative character of town plans, often with many stages from a Dark Age or Carolingian fortified centre, through markets, extensions and suburbs, to the fully expanded city of Renaissance times.

Urban defences

The best way to understand a town's topography is to start with the outer boundary (Bond 1987). Defences signified the town limits and the size or the intended size of the settlement. Extensions to circuits might therefore be caused by growth of population or expansion of building beyond original boundaries, as at Abergavenny, Bridgnorth and Southampton in the thirteenth century, or Cardiff and Pembroke in the fourteenth century. Only Bristol, Lincoln, Norwich and York developed extensions in several directions, which resemble the concentric rings of defences seen in continental cities, though there may be more examples to be identified. Rebuilding the defences to define a smaller area than before, which presumably reflects urban decay or retrenchment, is rare, but there are examples at New Winchelsea, where the defences in 1414–15 reduced the area of the town (Martin and Martin 2004), and at Berwick-on-Tweed, where the Elizabethan circuit covered only two-thirds of the area of the fourteenth-century town. Alternatively, city walls might be built, or lines of defence strengthened, by joining together existing lines of the walls of stone houses and blocking up openings such as doors and windows, as is documented at Southampton and Edinburgh.

Roman defensive circuits were reused by medieval towns on the same sites, for instance at Canterbury, Lincoln, London and York. The walls were of masonry, and the surviving Roman gates formidable structures, so that it was usual for medieval gates to occupy the same sites as their Roman predecessors. At other towns, a defensive circuit originally of Anglo-Saxon date was partly or wholly reused by the medieval town, as at Barnstaple, Bridgnorth, Oxford or Totnes.

New medieval circuits or extensions were substantially of masonry in the larger towns such as Berwick, Bristol, Edinburgh, London (Blackfriars), Newcastle, Norwich, Oxford,

Shrewsbury, Southampton, Stirling and Worcester. Gates of masonry were an essential part of these defences, and a good number survive, though some of the circuit walls have been lost. In a further group of towns, the gates were of masonry but the defences of earth and timber, giving both strength and prestige to the entry points into the town. This was the case, for instance, at Aberdeen, Coventry, Pontefract and Tewkesbury. At Banbury, there were four gates, but no walls; Glasgow also had gates across its streets, but no defences. Towards the end of the medieval period, town gates became increasingly ornamental and had little military significance. Similarly, few town walls in England or Wales were ever seriously tested in warfare; very few were ever rebuilt to take account of developments in the technology of warfare, such as the use of cannon from the late fourteenth century.

Defences performed many secondary functions besides protection of the town and exclusion of the outsider. Gates were used as accommodation for civic officers, as chapels, lock-ups and meeting-rooms. The defensive system included fishponds at Stafford and York and a lake at Edinburgh; at Hereford and other towns, water from the town ditch drove mills.

Streets, markets and public buildings

In some towns, the meeting of main roads, and the market, was to be found at the gate of the monastery or cathedral church, which took over the castle's role as epicentre of the place; this would have an effect on the neighbourhood round the new centre. Market life was also inextricably mixed with daily religious observance. Markets were held in or near churchyards, as at Llanelli or Haverfordwest; in many other places, churches lay in the middle of broad market streets.

The local ruler controlled the revenue of trade by establishing a market within a town, on only one site in the smaller and more typical towns. A central space, often near the main church, would be made available for stalls, which over time became permanent structures and buildings that in some cases survive today (as at Salisbury). By the late thirteenth century, covered specialized markets and civic warehouses for food, grain or cloth were to be found in larger towns. Archaeological work has, for instance, reconstructed the mid-fifteenth-century Leadenhall market in London. The complex comprised a large market space surrounded by arcades, with warehouses above; a chapel; and a grammar school, endowed by the rich mercer Simon Eyre. The larger places such as Bristol, Coventry and London had several specialized market places for different commodities.

The chief civic building would be the town hall or guildhall. This begins to appear in records in the twelfth and thirteenth centuries, when towns were straining towards self-government. During the fourteenth to sixteenth centuries, many were rebuilt in grander fashion, often in stone. Around the hall, used as a court and for assemblies, would be service buildings (especially kitchens for feasts) and rooms used for storing arms and keeping prisoners. Timber-framed public halls such those as at Canterbury, Coventry, Leicester and Lavenham were adaptations of house designs, but the larger towns in eastern England, during the fifteenth century, could afford guildhalls in stone that are comparable with those in continental towns (London (Bowsher *et al.* 2007), King's Lynn, Norwich, York). Along with the structures (real and symbolic) of civic organization, there was the infrastructure of justice, punishment and control. The larger prisons, such as the royal Fleet Prison in London and the jail at Lydford (Devon), looked like castles; the Fleet had been built in the late eleventh century on an island in the broad stream that ran down the side of the City of London to meet the Thames.

Suburbs and the waterfront

The actions of civic leaders in medieval towns can also be seen in the way in which the borders of towns, outside the line of the defences, were organized – the suburbs on land, and the waterfront zone along the town's river or its seafront.

Growth or decline in the suburbs of the town may be a reflection of its economic fortunes. The form of suburbs was usually dictated by existing approach roads and by the location of markets immediately outside the town gates, as illustrated most vividly by the space called St Giles outside the north gate of Oxford. During the eleventh and twelfth centuries, many of the older towns such as Canterbury, Winchester and York expanded their suburbs to reach their largest extent for several centuries. Prominent churches or bridges would be rebuilt as signs of prosperity. At Exeter, for instance, a suburb on Exe Island would have been promoted by the building of St Edmund's church and the contiguous Exe Bridge around 1200. Suburban expansion can be identified by areas of town called Newland, as at Banbury and Gloucester. After 1300, few if any towns expanded further, and many contracted in size. By the time of the earliest maps around 1600, great parts of their suburbs had reverted to fields.

Dangerous or obnoxious trades were often banned to the extramural areas. Blacksmiths, potters, tanners and fullers were found here, either excluded because of their smoke or noise, or taking advantage of the relatively open space (the bell-founders could dig for brickearth, the dyers stretch their cloths on frames called tenters). When the hospitals and friaries came in the twelfth and thirteenth centuries, they tended to form topographical obstacles rather than give encouragement to further growth (though there are exceptions: sometimes a friary would give a new tone to a suburb or neighbourhood, and richer houses would thereafter congregate around it).

Most suburbs were relatively poor, but some early developments were conspicuously wealthy, for instance in the western suburb of Winchester or outside the north gate at Gloucester. In a few cases, the town centre moved to what had previously been a suburb; at Hereford and Northampton, for example, the extramural market became the commercial centre of the town, and the later expansion of Leicester was around the East Gate.

The boundaries of suburbs, being the boundaries of the whole settlement, indicate the general prosperity or decline of the town, and suburbs often offer 'clean-slate' sites, where the occupation is easier to understand because it is on virgin soil. This occupation is often of an industrial character. A relative concentration of housing along certain streets identifies the major axis routes to the town, and if the date of this settlement can be established by archaeological and other means, the date of development of that route (a trading route out to the hinterland in a particular direction) can be explored. Two excavations of medieval suburban sites in recent years demonstrate these qualities: that of the Hamel, Oxford, and Alms Lane, Norwich (Atkin 1985). Alms Lane in particular shows a good suburban sequence. In the tenth century, it lay north of and outside the Saxon town, and until about 1275 was used as a refuse dump for the crafts of the town, as shown by the artefacts. Wetland plants and bones of frogs and toads indicate the environment. From the late thirteenth century, as demonstrated by archaeological and documentary evidence, the site was owned and used by workers in leather, skinning, bone-working and especially iron-working. In about 1375, however, the land was levelled and became the site of housing from the expanding city, and suburban industries were pushed out.

Besides spreading out along approach roads, the town often spread in a rather different manner into the adjacent river or sea. A waterfront zone often developed as a narrow strip of reclaimed land along the river bank or shore, modifying it to suit the needs both of landing and exporting goods, and in time for housing, warehouses and other buildings, even churches. Thus many towns actually increased their area – in the City of London, perhaps by as much as 15 per cent – over the medieval period by pushing out into the water.

Such reclaimed areas, though usually without churches, can be identified at British ports such as King's Lynn, London, Newcastle, Norwich and Hull, and in many continental ports (Good *et al.* 1991). The remarkable survival of archaeological strata and especially finds in a waterfront zone gives the area a general importance for greater understanding of a town's history in a number of significant ways, even in places which were not ports (e.g. Reading: Hawkes and Fasham 1997).

Firstly, the wealth of finds, especially of organic materials such as wood, leather and bone, is often accurately dated by a combination of dendrochronology (Figure 13.2) and coins. The finds often include trade waste (unfinished products) or industrial scrap. We know from documents that in many towns, rubbish heaps were not allowed to stand for more than a few

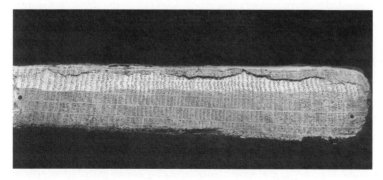

Figure 13.2 An oak board from a twelfth-century waterfront excavated at Seal House, Thames Street, London, in 1974. The tree from which it came was cut down around 1160.
Source: Museum of London Archaeology Service

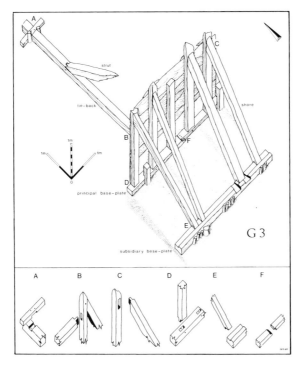

Figure 13.3 A revetment of 1270–90 excavated at Trig Lane, London, showing its repertoire of carpentry
joints. Sometimes timbers from medieval buildings formerly on land are found reused in the
waterfront constructions, enabling details of the lost townscape to be reconstructed.
Source: Museum of London Archaeology Service

days, and domestic and trade refuse was carted away. In the twelfth to fourteenth centuries,
especially, it was used to infill behind the reclamation units (e.g. Milne and Milne 1982). The
waterfront revetments (Figure 13.3) contain datable groups of medieval finds representative
of life in the wider city, since backfilling the revetments acted as private and civic rubbish
tips. The series of catalogues of medieval finds from excavations in London, nearly all from
waterfront sites, illustrates this most clearly (for example Crowfoot *et al.* 1992; Egan and
Pritchard 1991). The waterfront sites also provide the basis for the construction of pottery
chronologies on which so much other archaeological dating and inference depends.

Secondly, in many ports, the strip of land along the river has often been raised several times
against the rising river, and this action buried many medieval buildings, the fairly complete
plans of which may be recovered by excavation. At other ports, previous buildings are buried by
attempts to reach the water as the port silted up. In towns such as London and Hull, the buildings and the finds in and around them may be further illuminated by documentary study of their
owners and occupiers, including people of different social standing and of different trades.

Thirdly, overall, it is reasonable to suggest that the rate of reclamation in cubic metres is
indicative of activity and growth in the city at large; so that as our information increases from
a programme of excavations, we may be able to relate the volume of reclamation (measured by

archaeological contexts) with periods of growth in the city itself. This is one of the reasons for suggesting, from archaeological evidence, that the twelfth century was a time of urban growth. In London, the greatest amount of reclamation took place between about 1120 and 1220.

Houses and buildings on the domestic scale

The shape and size of individual buildings clearly contributed to the outline and definition of properties, particularly along street frontages; by 1150, in London, the frontages of streets such as Bow Lane and Milk Street were continuous rows of buildings. Equally, properties can be defined by the way in which rubbish pits were dug in groups or lines (Schofield *et al.* 1990). In some cases, the street frontage became indented or slightly curved, taking account of encroachments or obstacles formed by prominent buildings (as can still be seen in frontages in several medieval high streets, for instance at Canterbury). Some of these encroachments were buildings of stone, commonly with their gables against the street. The erection of a stone building by the street, often in the twelfth or thirteenth centuries (as for example also at Lincoln and Bury St Edmunds), would thereafter tend to anchor that part of the frontage for generations.

In Canterbury, London and Winchester, stone buildings near the street could occasionally be found by 1100; there are a number of twelfth-century examples, for instance in London at Well Court, also in Bow Lane, or on narrow waterfront properties immediately downstream of the medieval bridge site at New Fresh Wharf. In smaller but still important towns, the stone buildings tended to be in certain areas such as on or near the main street, or along the riverfront; some towns had areas where the small but economically significant Jewish community congregated, and they have been traditionally associated with stone houses. On the other hand, in towns such as Bury St Edmunds, there was a scattering of stone houses throughout, not in any one part (Schofield 2003 for the London evidence for this and the following paragraphs).

Many houses in both large and medium-sized towns belonged to a distant lord, whether lay or religious (a monastery or bishopric). There were two purposes for such a house: the provision of accommodation for those engaged in the everyday affairs of the house or the see, such as the selling of produce or the buying of goods, especially luxuries, and as the residence of the institution's head when in town. These urban depots of religious institutions from out of the town, whether based in another town or in the countryside, are found in many of the larger centres, such as York, or Edinburgh, where fifteenth-century ecclesiastical town houses have produced evidence of luxurious living, such as an unusual amount of imported German pottery; and in nascent county towns such as Shrewsbury.

In the majority of cases where their plans can be ascertained, the houses of religious and noble leaders were of courtyard plan. The hall of the property lay normally at the rear of a yard, though occasionally to the side on restricted sites, with a range of buildings (often separately let) fronting the street. Leaders of the merchant community in the larger towns, such as those who dealt in wine or some other aspect of royal service, also aspired to the style of house with a courtyard and an open hall of lofty proportions. Fourteenth- to sixteenth-century examples are known at Exeter, King's Lynn, London, Norwich and Oxford (Pantin 1963).

A smaller form of house, of three to six rooms in ground-floor plan, did not have a true courtyard with a formal gate to the street, though it might have a yard with buildings along one side, or an alley running the length of a long, narrow property. The latter arrangement is illustrated most clearly by properties on waterfront sites, such as in King's Lynn or south of Thames Street in London. Many had an alley down one side and, in consequence, buildings were usually arranged down the side of the plot behind the street-range which commonly comprised shops, sometimes let separately. Along, usually at the side of, most waterfront properties ran the access alley from the street to the river and the main water supply. This originated for the most part as a private thoroughfare, in some cases becoming public through time and custom. There were many variations on this long, narrow plan, and these houses do not conform easily to any type or standard design.

Smaller, and more uniform in its characteristics, was a house with two rooms on three or more floors. This type is known from documentary and archaeological evidence in London from the early fourteenth century; in several cases such houses form a strip, two rooms deep, fronting but separate from a larger property behind. Fourteenth-century examples are known from both excavation and from documents in London, and a block of three (originally five) still stand in

Figure 13.4 Medieval buildings survive in many British towns. Here, at the Cornmarket in Oxford, are three out of an original block of five houses that formed the street frontage of the New Inn. They were built, according to dendrochronology of the timbers, probably in 1386–7, and have been recently restored. Medieval buildings have much to contribute to the appearance of the city today.

Source: Julian Munby

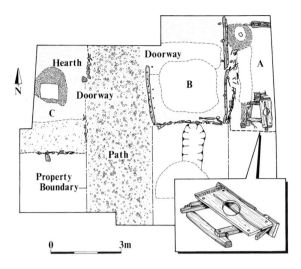

Figure 13.5 Three houses and a latrine in thirteenth-century Perth at Kirk Close.
Source: Scottish Urban Archaeological Trust, from Yeoman 1995

Cornmarket, Oxford; they are dated by dendrochronology to 1386–7 (Figure 13.4).

The houses of the medieval poor have largely been destroyed without trace in almost every town. By the time the depictions of towns in engravings became commonplace, these humble dwellings had largely disappeared; and as they commonly lay along street-frontages, archaeological excavation has not uncovered them because of later street-widening and the digging of cellars, especially in the nineteenth century. Sometimes the existence of buildings, probably forming continuous façades and one room deep, may be inferred from the absence of rubbish pits near the line of the street. One-room timber-framed houses of thirteenth- or early fourteenth-century date have been excavated at Lower Brook Street, Winchester, and more substantial examples in stone of the fifteenth century at St Peter's Street, Northampton. Work in Perth has uncovered graphic evidence of poor lifestyles, in single-room buildings with walls of posts and wattle which were probably both living and working space for cobblers and other artisans (Yeoman 1995; Figure 13.5). When several medieval properties are excavated at once, a detailed history of part of a street and its buildings over several centuries can be constructed, as at Coppergate, York (Hall and Hunter-Mann 2002).

Medieval towns, to varying degrees, had building regulations that sought to prevent fires and improve sanitation and drainage. Sometimes the observance or flouting of these regulations can be seen in the archaeological record: for instance, walls only 1 m wide dividing properties in London. Buildings of stone lasted longer and often formed links with former topographic arrangements among the comparatively restless mass of timber-framed buildings, which were easily taken down and reassembled, sometimes on a different site.

Evidence of manufacture and crafts

Today, in many towns, we can see a Butcher's Row or Ironmonger Lane. It is usual to think of the craft areas of medieval towns as being clearly demarcated one from another; but this is only part of a more complex picture.

Certainly, a common feature of twelfth-century and later urban industries is their nucleation. Not only do some industries occur in towns but not in the surrounding countryside, but there are distinct zones within towns. The existence of these quarters in the twelfth century can be demonstrated both by street names and also by the concentration of certain types of industrial waste, such as large, brass-melting crucibles and bronze-casting mould fragments from certain areas of the City of London. In Britain, as in France and Germany, such quarters seem to have been more prevalent in the twelfth and thirteenth centuries and significantly not later, when, after the plague, these local boundaries appear to have broken down.

Sometimes any zoning will be explicable in terms of the requirements of the industry. The fringes of a town will always be attractive to those industries that require large areas for storage or preparation, for example timber yards, pottery or tile kilns and tanneries. Most urban crafts, however, did not require distinctive workshops and many are therefore archaeologically almost invisible. We can study those industries that required the provision of heat, or abnormally high quantities of water or other unusual conditions. Medieval crafts that have left traces include the making of pottery and tiles, various stages in the manufacture of cloth, making salt, bells, tanning hides, burning lime for construction work and blacksmiths' workshops. The majority of the evidence is from finished or half-finished pieces or from manufacturing waste (Figure 13.6). Objects of fine workmanship fill our museums, and now we are beginning to understand how they were made (Biddle 1990; Blair and Ramsay 1991).

Were these industries efficient or innovative? We must be careful here, for these are modern terms. There is little evidence for technological innovations in British towns, though like all towns they probably acted as 'electrical transformers' (the phrase used by the French histo-

Figure 13.6 A piece of animal bone (a pig's jaw-bone) used for trying out artistic designs that were to be cut into leather or possibly metal objects. From an eleventh-century pit on the Milk Street site, London.

Source: Museum of London Archaeology Service

297

rian Fernand Braudel, for example in Braudel 1979) in transmitting and experimenting with new ideas from elsewhere in Europe and the Muslim world. Around 1200, increased sophistication in the production of pottery is apparent, and more complex joints in carpentry allowed the heightening of timber-framed buildings to two, three or more storeys to accommodate more people in towns (Milne 1992). Several luxury industries, such as the provision of marble tombs and brasses, were concentrated in the big cities. Literacy and schooling were always features of towns, and at the end of the period, printed books became more available. We would therefore expect new fashions in architecture, or dress, to be apparent in the archaeological record of towns before appearing in the countryside. It is also likely that technological or fashionable changes moved along lines of communication from town to town, bypassing areas of relatively backward countryside.

The medieval urban environment

Towns were small parts of larger rural landscapes, and very little food was grown within the walls. In medieval towns, we can study the way in which food was provided, the economic and therefore environmental relations between the town and its hinterland, and the lifestyle of the townsfolk as shown by their skeletons, and we can attempt to determine whether the quality of life in towns was different from – either better or worse than – that in the contemporary countryside.

A number of studies of animal bones from urban sites show that cattle, sheep and pigs were the main sources of meat. Cattle would often be slaughtered when their usefulness as dairy animals was over; similarly sheep were usually kept for their wool, and a large proportion of sheep bones in towns indicates an emphasis on sheep farming in the surrounding area. Pigs roamed the yards and streets of many towns and were tolerated as scavengers. Seeds of many plants also survive in dump deposits or in cesspits.

How good was the standard of living in medieval towns? Townspeople generally probably had a better diet than their neighbours in the countryside. If they had money, they could buy several kinds of bread, ale, wine, meat and fish. Fruit and vegetables came from town and suburban gardens. Over the period, there is some evidence that town dwellers ate more meat and less cereals or fish than their rural counterparts (Dyer 1989, 201–2).

Human skeletons from churchyards tell us about health and disease, but at present there are more questions than answers. Of vitamin deficiency diseases, only scurvy and rickets are detectable in skeletons. Scurvy (lack of vitamin C) is indicative of a restricted diet and was epidemic in medieval Europe in winter months, when fresh fruit and vegetables were unavailable. Rickets (lack of vitamin D) is a disease of children, enlarging the epiphyses (the ends) of growing bones; common among medieval skeletons, it was endemic in places that had little sunlight, and perhaps therefore it might be more prevalent in crowded parts of towns. The most common complaints suffered by excavated skeletons from medieval towns were osteoarthritis and problems with their teeth (Roberts and Cox 2003, 221–86).

Infectious diseases that might have been particularly rife in towns include leprosy, tuberculosis and syphilis. The first two in particular were common in the medieval period, though it has also been suggested that the spread of pulmonary tuberculosis led to the decline of leprosy in the post-medieval period, since the tubercle bacillus seems to have given some immunity from the bacterium that causes leprosy. So far few sites in Britain have produced examples of leprous bones, though the disease was common enough for there to be about 200 leper hospitals in thirteenth-century England (Steane 1985, 96–7). Five cases of tuberculosis and some possible cases of syphilis were noted at St Helen's in York. Other diseases known to have been virulent in medieval Europe include amoebic dysentery and smallpox.

CURRENT PERCEPTIONS AND OUTSTANDING PROBLEMS

Urban archaeology is good at establishing long sequences of layers that are often accurately dated by coins or dendrochronology, when timbers survive either in buried waterfront constructions or in standing buildings. We can quickly establish what was there, how it was built, what was left in each room or building, what date it was and what each object was made of. Beyond this, the wealth of information gathered from the last 30 years of work in towns points to exciting new possibilities that are only now being explored.

The medieval town is a place where we can study social organization, understand the role of women and children, and find out more about political centres and the boundaries of their influence. Buildings represent both these functions: the castle is a centre for warfare, feasting and political control; but it also reflects social divisions – it symbolizes the political and social elite in its height, manner of construction and location of the walls that both defended and constrained the town. From the sheer numbers of artefacts we can begin to study consumer demand for products, popular culture and fashion, for instance in dress (Egan and Pritchard 1991). Here archaeological work, particularly on the spectacular array of objects found in dated contexts on waterfront sites, is showing the popularity of shoddy, mass-produced items in base metals, especially after 1300, and allows researchers to identify the varied quality of products of the various traditions of manufacture mentioned in documents.

A second area to develop is that of the town as an economic unit. In distinction to the surrounding countryside, the economy of an urban place will be non-agricultural, will use coins or tokens (Figure 13.7) instead of barter or exchange, and, at least up to 1500, will not yet have the features of industrialization that were to follow. How much did kings and nobles use towns to control the redistribution of significant goods – not only luxuries, but necessities such as food? Although there were probably no factories in medieval British towns, we should study the history of technology and see if towns had any role in spreading innovation or new techniques of production. This will mean more emphasis on the medieval consumer than on production or manufacturing sites.

Third, archaeological investigation of medieval towns may bring to light evidence of medieval beliefs, superstitions and ritual (both religious and secular, for instance processions that brought together all the townsfolk) and may suggest how medieval people constructed their public and private worlds (Schofield and Vince 2005, 110–19). Sacred and profane spaces

299

Figure 13.7 Late thirteenth-century tokens found on the London waterfront near Billingsgate. They were probably used as fractions of pence, prior to the official issue of halfpence and farthings. They bridged the gap between official coins and the ancient practice of bartering and exchange of goods, and by their presence show the increasing commercialization of medieval towns and the demand for small coins or something like them.

Source: Museum of London Archaeology Service

can be recognized; the medieval concepts of 'clean' and 'dirty', 'male' and 'female' might be deduced from the internal arrangement of buildings or the distribution of artefacts.

Between 1100 and 1340, a new urban society came into being in British towns. Much of this development was in the twelfth century, as shown by the expansion of suburbs and waterfront areas, new stone houses and the birth of a consumer culture. At the same time, towns were largely driven by the institutions or noble power centres within them, which were large constructions – castles, monasteries and lords' houses. They used towns to get luxuries, particularly from faraway places within Britain and abroad. There were links with many European cities and states, but one strong link was with south-west France (Gascony), which was part of the English kingdom.

No more new towns were established after Queenborough in Kent (a special case, being a naval base) by Edward III in 1368. At the start of this chapter, the period of economic downturn in the early fourteenth century and the Black Death in 1348–9 was given separate status, and since urban archaeology can most easily chart change, the traumatic changes of this period should be apparent in the archaeological record. However, more fieldwork is required to test this picture or up-and-down graph of fortunes that we have been offered by documentary historians.

The third part of the Middle Ages, from 1350 to about 1500, is poorly understood by comparison with the earlier period, in towns as in the countryside. In contrast with the period before 1340, this is the time of growing power of the craft guilds and the lessening of power of the lords and religious magnates. In both large and small centres, the archaeological strata of this later period are thin; the waterfront zones are increasingly unhelpful, as stone walls take over from timber revetments and the dated groups of artefacts become far

Figure 13.8 Torksey, Lincolnshire: an aerial view of the shrunken medieval river port, in an angle of the River Trent (left) and the Foss Dyke (foreground). The town stretched from the Dyke to the later railway line 0.8 km away. In its heyday, it had three parish churches and two monasteries; now it is almost all fields.

Source: Cambridge University Committee for Aerial Photography; Crown copyright reserved

less frequent. It seems the case that after the Black Death, because there were considerably fewer people in towns, several processes took place. Shops disappeared from central streets; some houses became larger, while the unwanted margins of settlement crumbled, decayed and were covered with their own version of dark earth, the deposit normally associated with the Saxon centuries. Some towns, like Torksey in Lincolnshire, declined to almost nothing; now they are largely fields (Figure 13.8). But at the same time there was a broadening of the range of things to buy, and life improved for the reduced population. A similar pause in the rate of population growth and a concomitant rise in real wages occurred in the late seventeenth century, with similar results.

Archaeological and historical work is beginning to suggest that the period from 1350 to 1500 can be divided further. At first, up to about 1420, urban populations reproduced themselves and made up for the plague losses. Towns went through a period of self-selection, where one might decline, but a local rival rose (Wallingford overtaken by Reading, Torksey overtaken by Boston). The larger centres such as York, Norwich and King's Lynn went through a good period.

After 1420, more general decay set in, and even the larger towns declined. By the early sixteenth century, to take an extreme case, it was reported that a quarter of all the houses in Coventry were empty. At the same time, there was a fundamental change in the trading patterns around the south of Britain. The fifteenth century opened in a phase of prosperity for foreign commerce, which had slumped to less than half of its former value by the middle of the century and then rose to new heights. The area of trading swung away from Gascony and Normandy and withdrew from the Baltic, to a more concentrated North Sea axis centred on the Netherlands. These changes are evident in the character of imported objects on British sites. It was the port towns, some of them growing new functions for the first time, that survived in good shape into the sixteenth century – not only London and Bristol, but Newcastle, Colchester, Ipswich, Exeter and Chester. We are at present only dimly aware of all the factors at play here, and regional archaeological studies will show which areas retained vitality or exploited new markets. Even greater changes, to the topography of towns and to the lifestyles of townspeople, were about to follow in the 1530s with the dissolution of the monasteries and the religious changes collectively known as the Reformation (Gaimster and Gilchrist 2003). In many ways the upheavals of town life at the Dissolution and Reformation were a period of liberation for townspeople; and the sudden availability of large tracts of land in and around the towns must have facilitated the enormous amount of immigration into towns which then took place.

THE BRITISH EVIDENCE IN ITS WIDER SETTING

Although the rescue archaeology movement, in Britain and other European countries, has brought about the excavation and interpretation of sites of all periods from Palaeolithic to the modern, it has a special relevance for towns in Britain and for medieval archaeology. Urban archaeology as a discipline has grown up almost totally since 1945. Medieval archaeology as a subject has only a slightly longer history: in Britain, the first discussions of the concept date from about 1940. Rescue archaeology has also been active in medieval towns all over Europe (for examples of national reviews, see those for Germany (Fehring 1991) and France (Burnouf 2008)). Though archaeologists in European countries, like their British counterparts, are now digesting the evidence of the last five decades, some common questions and answers are appearing. A critical question concerns whether archaeologists in medieval towns should try to apply theoretical models to their results, and whether these models should be derived from historical sources and deal with historical problems, or should be constructed totally by archaeologists themselves.

Did medieval towns advance the economic development of Britain or Europe? Some scholars think that towns were irritants in the basically rural feudal system of life-control, and that towns were instrumental in the campaigns for individual rights (first for men, and later for women). Braudel (1979) distinguished between three sorts of town: the open town, which is still attached to its parent agricultural world; the subject town, which is shaped by an external political authority (a bishop, prince or king); and the closed town, where those within the town take over power for themselves. Western European economic growth is seen to be pushed forward by the attempts of some closed towns to increase and maintain their fortunes. This three-part grouping, which could be applied to British towns, underlines clearly that British towns are part of a larger European phenomenon. Though small towns in England, Wales or Scotland were largely the built expressions of local interests, they were part of a larger European picture with many regional variations.

This historical model (and there are several others) is, however, ultimately unsatisfactory. Towns refuse to be pinned down and categorized simply, and other scholars have argued that there is nothing special about towns, no independent city variable. Towns are sites where more general structures of power and struggles for power are dramatically expressed. It is true that the town can be profitably discussed as a social form in which larger systems of social relations are concentrated and intensified. What is fascinating is to see how this intensification brings out specialized forms of housing, ways of coping with density of settlement and its problems and the consequences of variety in occupations or ethnic groups.

Some archaeologists (Carver 1987; Schofield and Vince 2005) have begun to construct a model that starts with the mountain of data now dug up from British towns. Let the data speak; see what it has to say. The extraordinary value of waterfront archaeology, the most important product of post-war excavations in European towns, has revolutionized the study of material medieval culture. It has shown how archaeology, aided by spectacular preservation of artefacts and the development of dendrochronology, has constructed a whole new area of study and debate with historians, and on its own terms.

Note

This chapter is based on parts of Schofield and Vince 2005, with some further references.

Key texts

Dyer, C., 1989. *Standards of living in the later Middle Ages: social change in England c. 1200–1520.* Cambridge: Cambridge University Press.

Palliser, D.M. (ed) 2000. *The Cambridge urban history of Britain, I: 600–1540.* Cambridge: Cambridge University Press.

Platt, C., 1976. *The English medieval town.* London: Secker and Warburg.

Schofield, J. and Vince, A., 2005. *Medieval towns.* London: Equinox.

Steane, J.M., 1985. *The archaeology of medieval England and Wales.* Beckenham: Croom Helm.

Bibliography

Atkin, M., 1985. 'Excavations on Alms Lane', in Atkin, M., Carter, A. and Evans, D.H., *Excavations in Norwich 1971–78, part II.* Gressenhall: East Anglian Archaeology 26, 144–260.

Beresford, M., 1988. *New towns of the Middle Ages: town plantation in England, Wales and Gascony.* Gloucester: Alan Sutton. Rev. edn.

Biddle, M. (ed.) 1990. *Object and economy in medieval Winchester.* Oxford: Winchester Studies 7.ii.

Blair, J. and Ramsay, N. (eds) 1991. *English medieval industries.* London: Hambledon Press.

Bond, C.J. 1987. 'Urban defences: Anglo-Saxon and medieval', in Schofield and Leech (eds), 92–116.

Bowsher, D., Dyson, T., Holder, N. and Howell, I., 2007. *The London Guildhall: an archaeological history of a neighbourhood from early medieval to modern times.* London: Museum of London Archaeology Service Monograph 36.

Braudel, F., 1979. *Capitalism and material life 1400–1800*. London: Fontana.

Brown, A. (ed) 1999. *The Rows of Chester: the Chester Rows research project*. London: English Heritage Archaeological Report 16.

Burnouf, J., 2008. *Archéologie médiévale en France: le second Moyen Âge (XIIe–XVIe siècle)*. Paris: La Découverte.

Carver, M.O.H., 1987. 'The nature of urban deposits', in Schofield and Leech (eds), 9–26.

Clarke, H.B. and Simms, A. (eds) 1985. *The comparative history of urban origins in non-Roman Europe*. Oxford: British Archaeological Reports 255.

Crowfoot, E., Pritchard, F. and Staniland, K., 1992. *Textiles and clothing c. 1150–c. 1450*. London: HMSO (= Medieval finds from excavations in London 4).

Egan, G. and Pritchard, F., 1991. *Dress accessories*. London: HMSO (= Medieval finds from excavations in London 3).

Fehring, G.P., 1991. *The archaeology of medieval Germany*. London: Routledge.

Gaimster, D. and Gilchrist, R. (eds) 2003. *The archaeology of the Reformation 1480–1580*. Leeds: Maney Publishing (Society for Medieval Archaeology and Society for Post-Medieval Archaeology).

Good, G.L., Jones, R.H. and Ponsford, M.W. (eds) 1991. *Waterfront archaeology: proceedings of the third international conference, Bristol, 1988*. London: Council for British Archaeology Research Report 74.

Hall, R.A. and Hunter-Mann, K., 2002. *Medieval urbanism in Coppergate: refining a townscape*. York: Council for British Archaeology Archaeology of York 10.

Hawkes, J.W. and Fasham, P.J., 1997. *Excavations on Reading waterfront sites, 1979–1988*. Salisbury: Wessex Archaeology Report 5.

Heighway, C., 1972. *The erosion of history*. London: Council for British Archaeology.

Hinton, D.A., 1990. *Archaeology, economy and society: England from the fifth to the fifteenth century*. London: Seaby.

Martin, D. and Martin, B., 2004. *New Winchelsea Sussex: a medieval port town*. London: English Heritage and University College London Field Archaeology Unit.

Milne, G., 1992. *Timber building techniques in London c. 900–c. 1400*. London: London and Middlesex Archaeological Society Special Paper 15.

Milne, G. and Milne, C., 1982. *Medieval waterfront development at Trig Lane, London*. London: London and Middlesex Archaeological Society Special Paper 5.

Pantin, W.A., 1963. 'Medieval English town-house plans', *Medieval Archaeology* 6–7, 202–39.

Platt, C., 1978. *Medieval England: a social history and archaeology from the Conquest to 1600*. London: Routledge.

Roberts, C. and Cox, M., 2003. *Health and disease in Britain: from prehistory to the present day*. Stroud: Sutton.

Schofield, J., 1999. *The building of London from the Conquest to the Great Fire*. Stroud: Sutton. 3 edn.

Schofield, J., 2003. *Medieval London houses*. London: Yale University Press. 2 edn.

Schofield, J. and Leech, R. (eds) 1987. *Urban archaeology in Britain*. London: Council for British Archaeology Research Report 61.

Schofield, J., Allen, P. and Taylor, C., 1990. 'Medieval buildings and property development in the area of Cheapside', *Transactions of London and Middlesex Archaeological Society* 41, 39–238.

Yeoman, P., 1995. *Medieval Scotland*. London: Batsford.

14

LANDSCAPES OF
THE MIDDLE AGES

Churches, castles and monasteries

Roberta Gilchrist

BACKGROUND

Within a generation or so of the conversion to Christianity, each Anglo-Saxon kingdom was divided into large parishes (*parochiae*) administered by a minster church. These minsters (from the Latin *monasterium*) were instigated by episcopal or royal initiative, and their siting was frequently coincident with royal vills. These early minsters of the seventh to eighth centuries housed communities of priests or monks who lived a collegiate or monastic lifestyle and had pastoral responsibility for the inhabitants of the *parochia* (Blair 2005). Welsh churches, by contrast, were established in association with secular *llys* (courts); the processes behind the establishment of Scottish churches are less well known, but it is likely that bishops or laypeople founded mother-churches that had authority over local chapels. Between the tenth to twelfth centuries, these high-ranking churches were supplemented by the proliferation of private, or proprietary, churches, with a resident priest who served a local community. The emergence of the local church developed alongside the reorganization of settlement patterns that took place between the ninth and twelfth centuries, when large estates fragmented into smaller, self-contained local manors, and the development of the medieval village provided the social impetus for the local community church. These local churches, the ancestors of parish churches, did not immediately have full rights, such as baptism or burial. Between the eleventh and thirteenth centuries, the *parochiae* of the mother-churches across Britain were broken down into smaller territories of individual parishes, giving rise to the parochial system of the Middle Ages.

Churches subsequently became the focal point for ritual and social life in a medieval community. They were used as a place of worship and regular meeting, for religious and seasonal festivals, fairs and markets, baptism of infants, marriages and burial of the dead. Chapels, known as chapels-of-ease, were built to serve parishioners who lived some distance from the parish church, and palaces, castles and manor houses often had private chapels that served the resident family and retainers. Many thousands of churches and chapels of medieval date survive in Britain today as standing buildings, in addition to several hundred ruined churches and the countless sites of former churches that exist only as buried archaeological deposits. The expansion of towns in the tenth to eleventh centuries also resulted in the proliferation of parishes, some of which were carved from the territories of earlier minsters. Towns that expanded in the late Saxon period can be ranked according to the number of churches that they once possessed: London 100-plus, Norwich and Winchester 50-plus, York and Lincoln 40-plus and Exeter *c.* 20 (Morris 1989, 178).

The administration and character of the Church was reorganized to a considerable degree as a result of the Norman Conquest. Anglo-Saxon dioceses (the ecclesiastical territories under the jurisdiction of a bishop) were largely retained and new bishops' sees were added in the twelfth century, contemporaneous with the reorganization of the Church in Wales and Scotland under Anglo-Norman influence. The head of each diocese focused on an urban cathedral; these were a combination of two types of institution. Some were monastic cathedrals based around a community of monks headed by a prior, a form that had developed in Anglo-Saxon England, while others were secular cathedrals, in which a chapter of canons was led by a dean, an arrangement more common in Normandy and Brittany. Cathedral priories followed the rule of St Benedict, and their communities resembled the usual Benedictine arrangement (below), albeit on a much grander and larger scale. The secular cathedrals, in contrast, were staffed by prebends, priests who received a portion of the living. It became common to have a group of additional junior priests (vicars) who resided within the cathedral precinct: some lived in quasi-monastic dormitories (e.g. the Bedern at York, *c.* 1250; Lincoln from *c.* 1270), while others occupied individual houses and shared a common hall (Hall and Stocker 2005). The Vicars' Close at Wells was built in 1348 and survives today as a planned street or terrace of individual houses, each with a hall below and chamber above, with a common chapel and refectory at the ends of the street and a covered bridge providing direct access to the chapter house and cathedral church.

The medieval castle was the fortified residence of a lord. It served dual military and domestic functions, the latter including the accommodation of the lord's household and the administration of the estate. It also acted as a strategic point for gaining and maintaining control over a hostile territory. The castle was intimately linked with feudalism: a system of vassalage and land-holding that bound different strata of society together through bonds of loyalty. The king was the greatest overlord and landlord, and he rewarded his followers with lands, so that they owed him loyalty and became his vassals. They, in turn, secured the loyalty of a group of followers through a process of gift-giving. This system of reciprocity united medieval society and ensured that armies could be raised, while at the same time allowing the king to retain ultimate control over his people.

The first Norman castles to be built were strongholds along the progress of William the Conqueror, starting on 28 September 1066. By the 1070s to 1080s, the feudal system of military service was laid down and lands were transferred from Saxon thegns to Norman barons. By the time of Domesday Book in 1086, 20 per cent of land in England was held by the king,

50 per cent by the lay baronage and 30 per cent by the Church. The barons had been rewarded for their loyalty through gifts of land, and their status as lords entitled them to construct castles. The castle became symbolic of the office of lordship and the favour of the king, but conversely, a lord's castle could be destroyed or confiscated at the king's displeasure. Some 1,500 castles were built following the Conquest, although approximately half of these were small timber and earthwork constructions that had been abandoned by the early fourteenth century. Very few native Welsh castles were constructed in stone: the excavated example of Dryslwyn Castle (Carmarthenshire) was built in the thirteenth century and its waterlogged deposits yielded evidence of the food consumed by the Welsh lord Rhys ap Maredudd and his household *c.* 1280 (Caple 2007). Scottish kings were strategic in their support of castle-building: they established new lordships and associated castles where royal power was weakest, in the Highlands, Western Isles, Galloway, Lanarkshire, along the upper Clyde and over the north-east lowlands. Conversely, the royal stronghold of the south-east of Scotland saw few castles built.

The Normans also revitalized monastic life, introducing new continental orders and founding abbeys and priories in association with castles, town and rural manors. A monastery was an exceptional medieval community of celibate men or women who took religious vows to follow a set of strict rules that governed their lifestyle. The form and organization of the earlier medieval monasteries had been more fluid and diverse (seventh to ninth centuries), until a reform movement of the tenth century laid down rules to be observed in monasteries and nunneries (the *Regularis Concordia*), and more standard plans evolved that were based around the monastic cloister (Coppack 2006). The origins of this social movement can be traced back to the desert monasticism of fourth- and fifth-century Egypt, Palestine and Syria. Two basic forms of monastic life prevailed throughout the medieval world: the eremitic and the coenobitic. Eremitic monasticism (from *eremos* (Gk), the desert) followed the tradition of the hermit, in which an individual lived in isolation and sought a more challenging, ascetic spirituality, renouncing comfort and companionship. The more common, coenobitic, monasticism stems from the rule of St Benedict, written by Benedict of Nursia *c.* 525, at Monte Cassino in Italy. The Benedictine Rule emphasized communal living and laid down precise requirements for the structure and routine of the monastery. It was to be self-sufficient in all things, so that ties and obligations to the outside world could be minimized, and the monks were to worship together, sleep in a communal dormitory and eat in a common refectory.

By a conservative estimate, at least 2,000 monasteries and religious houses were founded in medieval England, Scotland and Wales, with particular orders coincident with certain chronological periods, associated variously with the town or countryside and committed to a broad range of religious and charitable purposes. Benedictine and Cluniac monasteries were founded by the Normans in England (*c.* 1067–1130) and were often used as a means of consolidating their royal or baronial authority over Anglo-Saxon areas. Monasteries following the rule of St Augustine were established for more pastoral and charitable functions. Houses of Augustinian canons were set up on a smaller scale and by lower-ranking patrons, in areas that required pastoral care (*c.* 1100–1260). The Cistercians sought isolated and remote places, particularly in Scotland and

Wales, Yorkshire and Cheshire, in order to follow their reformed version of the monastic life (*c.* 1125–1220). Initially the Cistercians were devoted to a life of simplicity; until the fourteenth century, they included lay-brothers in most of their monasteries, who were responsible for manual work and management of the estates and granges (farms). Orders of friars arrived in Britain *c.* 1225, including the Franciscans and Dominicans, with new foundations into the early fourteenth century, and aimed at preaching and educating the urban poor. In addition to the main orders for monks, canons and friars, there were corresponding houses for religious women, colleges, hospitals following monastic ordinances, preceptories of the Crusading Orders (the Templars and Hospitallers), Carthusian charterhouses (based on eremitic principles) and small hermitages (Coppack and Aston 2002; Gilchrist 1995). Most monasteries were established in the twelfth or thirteenth century, and continued in use for several hundred years, until the Dissolution of the monasteries in England and Wales under Henry VIII (1535–40), and in Scotland by Parliament in 1560, when monasteries were confiscated and their buildings and lands sold or redistributed.

KEY DATA

Churches

Early written sources are generally limited to references to church sites in wills, charters, saints' lives, monastic chronicles and law codes. Domesday Book, compiled in 1086, enumerated churches in England according to their financial value: approximately 2,700 were recorded, but many seem to have been omitted from the list, with accuracy varying according to the methods used by the compilers of the survey in each county. From the twelfth and especially the thirteenth century, a wider range of documentary sources was compiled, including bishops' registers, the records of church courts and, from the fourteenth century, churchwardens' accounts. By the fifteenth and sixteenth centuries, personal wills were regularly compiled that yield evidence of private bequests for building projects, the foundation of chantries and details of internal furnishings and fittings. Very occasionally, the foundation dates of churches can be recognized through the evidence of place-names or inscriptions.

The archaeological recording of churches has yielded new evidence on the nature of their design and construction. Material for the building of masonry churches of Anglo-Saxon date had been obtained by cannibalizing Roman sites for brick, tile and stone, until a more systematic industry of stone quarrying was stimulated by the eleventh- and twelfth-century expansion in church construction. The skills of the carpenter are evident in rubble-built parish churches well into the twelfth century. Stone was used to imitate wood by producing the appearance of lathe-turning, through pilaster stripwork that mimicked timber joints, for instance in the tower at Earls Barton, Northamptonshire, and in the wooden or basket-work windows and templates that were used, such as those at Hales and Framlingham Earl, Norfolk (Rodwell 2005). Regional building traditions resulted from the availability of stone types and building material, in addition to the conscious promotion of cultural preferences, such as the round towers of East Anglian churches.

Dating of extant medieval buildings has been carried out predominantly through stylistic or typological methods. Architectural style was regularly evolving from the late eleventh century to the fifteenth, so that it is possible to date certain diagnostic features to within 20–30 years, notably mouldings, capitals, window tracery and roofs. The dating of smaller parish churches can be more problematic in the earlier period (pre-1120) and from 1350–1500, when the date ranges achieved by means of stylistic methods can stretch from 50 to 100 years. An archaeological approach to the study of buildings, developed for particular application to Anglo-Saxon churches, is known as 'structural analysis': this consists of the close scrutiny of church fabric in order to discern the sequence in which constituent parts were added, modified or removed. This is a non-destructive approach that is based on the observation of vertical joints in walls, quoin types, fabric changes and blocked or inserted features (Rodwell 2005).

Scientific methods of absolute dating are used less frequently on medieval material, since after *c.* 1050, radiocarbon dates yield broader chronological ranges than those achieved through typological, stylistic or numismatic approaches. However, dendrochronology has been used to date roofs, bell-frames and remains of timber scaffolding, and has potential to establish firmer chronologies for transitional periods of architecture. Scientific dating is an essential tool for dating sequences of medieval burials: cemeteries attached to monasteries and parish churches were in regular use for hundreds of years, with the result that inhumations are often intercut and truncated. Radiocarbon dating has been used to phase medieval cemeteries more accurately, for example at St Mary Spital in London, while dendrochronology has been used to date preserved timber coffins at sites including Hull Augustinian Friary, where a group of 42 coffins was dated to the mid-fourteenth century (Gilchrist and Sloane 2005).

Where church sites have been extensively excavated, a primary phase has often been revealed to consist of a simple one- or two-cell church, sometimes constructed in timber. As churches evolved, these timber precursors were later either encased in a stone structure, or a stone successor was built adjacent to it (Rodwell 2005). Excavations at Raunds, Northamptonshire, showed the changes and variations that might occur: a single-cell church was established *c.* 875–925, which was later enlarged to two cells, rebuilt again and reorientated in the eleventh century and finally fell out of use *c.* 1200, when a church about 230 m away continued to function (Figure 14.1) (Boddington 1996).

The parish church and churchyard were closely integrated spatially and socially with the community (Blair 2005; Morris 1989; Turner 2006). The seigneurial associations (i.e. feudal relationship with a lord) of early churches were sometimes retained into the later Middle Ages, with churches situated adjacent to later medieval manor houses, moated sites or castles. Churches were often associated with villages: in cases of planned villages, placed close to a green or at the head of a street, forming the nucleus of the settlement. Where villages evolved from the coalescence of a number of settlements, multiple churches might result; in eastern England, cases of multiple lordship occasionally resulted in the sharing of a single churchyard by two or three parish churches, such as at Reepham, Norfolk. In regions of dispersed settlement, churches may have been founded in relative isolation, although

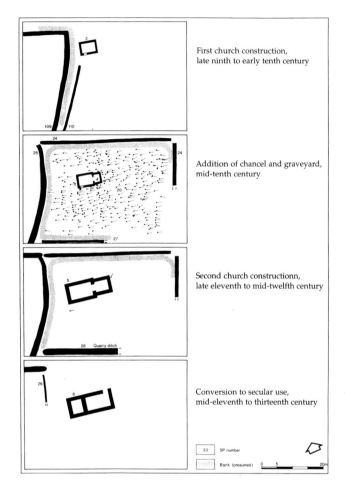

First church construction,
late ninth to early tenth century

Addition of chancel and graveyard,
mid-tenth century

Second church constructionn,
late eleventh to mid-twelfth century

Conversion to secular use,
mid-eleventh to thirteenth century

Figure 14.1 Sequence of church constructions at Raunds, Northamptonshire, late ninth to thirteenth centuries.
Source: Boddington 1996, Fig. 5

this appearance may sometimes be deceptive. Agricultural shifts, such as a transition from arable to pastoral farming, could cause the movement of settlement to areas of free grazing, such as greens and parish boundaries. In such cases, early village sites were deserted and churches that now appear to be isolated in the landscape were once in close proximity to their communities. Churches in towns were placed in order to encourage easy access: on street corners, on main thoroughfares, at markets, bridges and at gates in town walls, so that travellers and pilgrims could visit them easily when beginning or completing a journey.

Between 1050 and 1150, there was a massive rebuilding of churches, translating timber-built, local churches to the more substantial parish churches constructed in stone. Excavations have shown that these early stone churches were of fairly simple form, consisting of one or two cells, often incorporating an apsed eastern end: examples include All Saints, Barton Bendish, Norfolk; Barrow, Lincolnshire; St Paul-in-the-Bail, Lincoln; and St Benedict, Norwich. A small number of three-cell early churches are known, incorporating an axial, or central, tower, while others had towers attached to the western end of the church.

It has been suggested that such towers may have been reserved for the use of the lord who had built and owned the church, with the nave left open for public use (Morris 1989, 252–5); alternatively, it has been proposed that towers were added to pre-existing churches for the specific display of bells, connected with funeral services (Stocker and Everson 2006). The manorial residence of the lord seems to have been closely associated with the church: excavations at Barton-on-Humber, Humberside, which retains a highly embellished Anglo-Saxon tower, revealed that the church of *c.* 970–1030 was erected just west of a large bank and ditch, which defined a sub-circular enclosure that may have been the manor or residence of the lord (Figure 14.2) (Rodwell and Rodwell 1982).

From the twelfth or thirteenth century, aisles were added to the south and/or north side of the nave. This new construction sometimes involved the piercing of existing side walls with an arcade, a series of arches supported by piers and columns that would be screened to divide the envelope of the nave from the aisles. Aisles may have provided space for a growing population, but more likely reflect changes in the use of churches. Aisles and transepts were used to house separate chapels, or to provide special places for guilds and fraternities, groups linked by occupation or devotion to particular saints or feasts. During

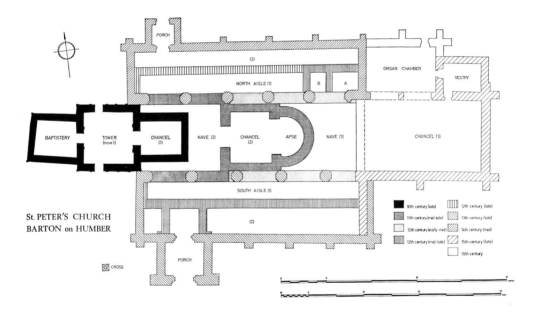

Figure 14.2 Composite ground-plan of St Peter's church, Barton-upon-Humber, Humberside. The original church was of three cells (AD 990±70). In the mid-eleventh century, the old chancel was demolished and replaced with a rectangular nave and apsidal chancel, with the former nave serving as the tower. This church was replaced by *c.* 1200 by a large, aisled building that involved the extension of the nave, the addition of a south aisle and two chambers to the north side of the nave that were incorporated subsequently into a north aisle. In the thirteenth and fourteenth centuries the aisles were widened, and in the fifteenth century the chancel was rebuilt.

Source: Rodwell and Rodwell 1982, Fig. 3

the fourteenth and fifteenth centuries, private family chapels and mausolea became common in the spaces of the aisles, particularly as chantry masses became more popular – prayers for the dead that were believed to hasten the passage of the soul through purgatory.

Before the twelfth century, burial was prohibited inside parish churches, with the exceptions of the graves of founders and priests. After this, important patrons and wealthy individuals were able to attain burial in the church interior. The first phases of the cemetery generally correspond with the foundation of the church, at least in eastern and southern England, while in places such as Winchester and Hereford the cathedral church retained the monopoly over burial of the dead until the later Middle Ages. Excavation of cemeteries has yielded important information on inhumation practices, zoning of burial according to age or sex and information from skeletons regarding demography, health and life-expectancy (Gilchrist and Sloane 2005). At Barton-on-Humber, a ninth-century cemetery pre-dated the church, and 29 burials were systematically cleared in order to begin its construction. The later Anglo-Saxon cemetery had interments concentrated along the south side and at the east end of the church, with possible clusters of family groups. Radiocarbon and dendrochronology dates have confirmed that use of timber coffins was the norm by the tenth century. These were oak coffins, lightly constructed with few nails or metal components and occasionally incorporating bases woven from wattles. By the fifteenth century, burial inside the church at Barton was taking place in front of the chancel and aisle screens, but interior burial was rare until the seventeenth century (Rodwell and Rodwell 1982; Waldron 2007). Osteological analysis of 687 burials from Wharram Percy (N. Yorkshire) showed a relatively low infant mortality rate and reasonable adult longevity: 15 per cent of the cemetery population consisted of infants and 40 per cent were aged 50 or over. Measurement of carbon and nitrogen isotopes of infant bones and teeth suggests that infants were weaned at around 18 months of age, indicating that common practices of child-rearing operated within the community (Mays 2007).

Castles

Archaeological excavation has enabled more rigorous study of the origins of the castle and has expanded our knowledge of early timber castles considerably, as for example at Hen Domen, Montgomeryshire (Figure 14.3). Documentary sources for the construction of the first Norman castles include the Anglo-Saxon Chronicle and Domesday Book, which record the destruction of Saxon settlement in the wake of castle construction (e.g. Wallingford, Norwich and Shrewsbury). It is generally agreed that castles – private fortified residences – did not exist in Anglo-Saxon England, but were stimulated by the process of conquest by the Normans. To some extent this conclusion rests on the definition of the castle, since the Saxon system of burhs included both fortified towns and the residences of thegns, where a bank and palisade protected the burgheat (e.g. Goltho, Lincolnshire). The Norman castle acted as a strategic point for gaining and maintaining control over a hostile territory; some measure of its success was due to the Norman use of cavalry, since the Saxons did not use horses for warfare. The earliest forms of the English castle had their origins in tenth-century France, where two essential components have been traced: the first-floor hall and the motte. However, in France and Germany, upper halls developed in the mid-tenth century for the purpose of defence. The classic site for discerning this evolution is Doué-la-Fontaine (Maine-et-Loire), where a ground-floor hall built *c.* 900 was converted into a fortified first-floor hall *c.* 950, with a first-floor entrance; an earthen mound was later piled up around its base in the eleventh century (De Meulemeester and O'Conor 2007, 331).

Castles have been classified into standard types that developed from the eleventh to the sixteenth centuries, although there is a wide degree of fluidity between types and variation between individual sites. Timber and masonry castles can be distinguished, the former consisting of ringwork and motte-and-bailey types, with the latter including a wide variety that developed chronologically from the tower-keep to the enclosure castle, concentric castle, quadrangular castle, courtyard house and tower house. In the later Middle Ages, forms of defensive structure were developed that no longer combined the dual features of residence and fortification that define the classic castle. From the later fourteenth century, block houses were built to house guns and protect gunners on inland waterways (such as the Cow Tower, Norwich, 1398). From the late fifteenth and particularly the sixteenth centuries, artillery castles were built mainly at coastal sites to house heavy guns, usually arranged as multiple tiers of concentric defences (e.g. Dartmouth Castle, Devon, 1481).

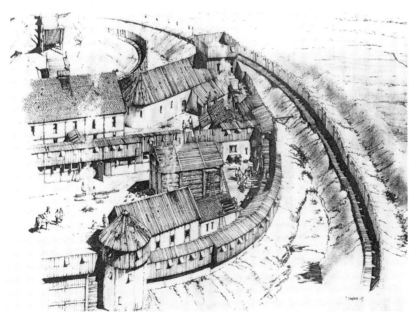

Figure 14.3 Reconstruction of defences and timber buildings at the castle of Hen Domen, Montgomeryshire, based on excavated structures dated to *c.* 1150.
Source: Higham and Barker 1992, Fig. 9.6

At the heart of the castle was the hall – used as a public eating and meeting place, for administration and for sleeping. Aisles were added to halls from *c.* 1100 to provide additional space for larger households. A bi-polar arrangement had emerged by the second half of the thirteenth century, in which the upper end of the hall was screened to provide a private chamber for the lord's household, while a lower end fulfilled the need for storage and services. From the thirteenth century, a castle might contain several different halls, each the focus of an individual household, in addition to the great hall, which was the centre of ceremonial and administrative life. Freestanding halls were generally located at the ground-floor level, open to the roof, sometimes with an associated two-storey chamber block to provide private chambers (e.g. Boothby Pagnell, Lincolnshire). Upper halls, located at first-floor level, were common in twelfth-century tower-keeps and proto-keeps (such as Chepstow, Gwent), and again in the fourteenth to fifteenth centuries, as at Nunney, Somerset.

Excavation has improved our understanding of the technology of castle construction. Traces of temporary workshops were uncovered at Sandal, West Yorkshire, and Portchester, Hampshire, the latter consisting of two lead-melting hearths set into the floor of a hall, with a temporary smithy erected in a courtyard. At Sandal, the conversion of the castle from timber to masonry required lead- and iron-working hearths and horse- and oxen-drawn carts to move supplies; tracks from these vehicles were traced during the excavations (Mayes and Butler 1983). Lime kilns are commonly found at castles, ranging from basic pits to stone-built kilns, such as a thirteenth-century example at Bedford. A kiln for the production of ridge-tiles, *c.* 1240, was excavated at Sandal, and additional evidence for roof furniture included tiles, slates and finials. Lead and stone tiles were also commonly used for roofing materials. Worked stone and fragments of decorated wall plaster have been recovered from excavated castles, together with window glass, although this was not common in non-royal castles until the later thirteenth century.

Along the coasts of Britain, naturally defensible sites were used for castle building, such as Corfe, Dorset. The earliest castles sometimes reused Roman forts and Saxon burhs, in order to take advantage of ready-made defences and good networks of roads. Royal castles were predominantly urban, associated with towns in order to dominate the largest concentrations of population and to ease the administration of a newly conquered land. The Norman barons held scattered parcels of land, rather than consolidated estates, and would build their castles at the centre of a concentration of lands, sited to take into account the availability of water, good communications and arable resources. Barnard Castle, Co. Durham, was sited on the boundary between woodland and grazing land, and its estate held a balanced range of land types and resources (Austin 2007). It was common to enhance the symbolism of lordship by twinning castles with parish churches or monasteries, especially Benedictine and Cluniac houses. Economic development was maximized by the Normans through foundations of new towns: up to one third of these grew up at the gates of castles. Grid-iron street plans developed at planned castle towns such as Castle Acre and New Buckenham, Norfolk.

Two major types of earthwork castles were constructed in Norman Britain: the motte and bailey and the ringwork. The motte and bailey outnumbered the ringwork by as much as four to one; it was built during the first century after the Conquest and during the civil war between King Stephen and Queen Matilda (1138–53). The motte was an artificial mound of earth, surrounded by a ditch, and frequently associated with one or more baileys, which were enclosures surrounded by earthen banks. A timber tower was placed within or on top of the motte. Excavations have shown that the tower was sometimes the primary feature, with the motte formed around it by heaping up earth from the encircling ditch. This method of construction is shown on the Bayeux Tapestry and has been confirmed by excavations at South Mimms, Hertfordshire, where a wooden tower 35 m square was set on a flint footing and surrounded by a motte with a low flint wall around its base. Entrance to the tower was gained via a tunnel through the motte, and the motte was revetted with timber shuttering. The ringwork castle, in contrast, was a simple enclosure comprising a bank and ditch. In some cases, ringworks were filled in with later mottes, as at Aldingham, Cumbria, while at Goltho, a motte was levelled in the twelfth century to serve as a raised platform for an aisled hall and domestic buildings. Timber buildings were placed within the bailey or ringwork: at Hen Domen, a motte and bailey castle first established c. 1070, there were 50 timber buildings of simple construction excavated in the bailey, which was encircled by a double bank and ditch (Figure 14.3) (Higham and Barker 1992).

The first castles to be built in stone were keeps or *donjons*: free-standing towers of at least two storeys with a highly fortified core. The earliest English tower-keep was the White Tower of London, built in 1075, and clearly symbolic of the authority of the new Norman king. The hall was located at first-storey level, with an off-centre cross-wall placed to allow the division of space into further suites of private rooms. Additional facilities included a kitchen, garderobes (latrines) and a chapel. In some cases houses may have evolved into keeps, as shown by the development of Castle Acre, Norfolk (Coad and Streeten 1982). Excavation on the site revealed a late eleventh-century stone structure surrounded by a weak ringwork. This was converted to a keep in the 1140 to 1150s, which involved doubling the thickness of the internal walls, raising the interior and blocking the main entrance and the door through the spinal wall. Only the northern half of the building was completed as a keep; the southern half became a courtyard. A masonry curtain wall was added to the bank of the ringwork (Figure 14.4). Shell keeps were built on mottes that could not support the full weight of a tower-keep. These shells were simply masonry walls built around the perimeter of the summit of a motte, replacing the timber palisade (e.g. Totnes, Devon).

By c. 1200, the emphasis of defence was shifting away from the highly fortified core of the castle to its outer, curtain walls, and at the same time the increasing degree of social stratification within castle communities demanded a change in the nature of accommodation. Innovation resulted in part from changes in warfare, including the use of the crossbow, mangonel and trébuchet (early siege machines that used rope tension and counterpoise systems, respectively). Enclosure castles such as Framlingham, Suffolk, rebuilt from 1190 to 1210, exhibit a range of new features. This change included the development of mural towers placed at intervals along the walls, the increasing importance of gatehouses for the defence of entrances and the introduction of new features such as barbicans (outworks protecting an entrance) and posterns (small, concealed gates in the curtain wall). The forti-

Figure 14.4 Castle Acre, Norfolk, a castle with inner and outer bailey connected by a bridge. The keep of the 1140 to 1150s was converted from a weakly defended house dating from the eleventh century; refortification included heightening the perimeter bank and adding a curtain wall.
Source: Derek A. Edwards, Norfolk Air Photographic Library, Norfolk Museums Service

fication of the curtain walls (*enceinte*) allowed the defence of a larger space, promoting an expansion in the size and facilities of castles. Enclosure castles provided accommodation for separate households, placed in buildings centred on free-standing, ground-floor halls or within stacking chambers in towers. By this date, a castle might have possessed several chapels, halls and kitchens, providing a number of foci for different social groups or households, defined by different social levels, gender or generations of the lord's family.

During the thirteenth century, building work at royal castles concentrated predominantly on the improvement of royal apartments and domestic residences. This frequently took the form of households sited in the bailey, as excavations have shown at Castle Rising, Norfolk, separate from the accommodation of the original keep. Between 1277 and 1304, a series of castles was built on the Welsh border by Edward I, during the period of the Welsh Wars. These concentric castles showed a renewed emphasis on the military considerations of castle design, while retaining the elements of comfort and privacy for the royal apartments. At Rhuddlan, Flintshire, for example, £10,000 was spent on the castle and town defences, beginning in 1277. The castle comprised an inner ward, which was a diamond-shaped courtyard containing the royal apartments, corner towers and two great gatehouses, and an outer ward that was wrapped around three sides of the inner one and surrounded by a broad, dry moat.

The relative prosperity of the fourteenth and fifteenth centuries promoted the construction of new castles by a greater social range of people, including lesser aristocracy, gentry and wealthy merchants. This period witnessed an increase in licences granted by the crown to crenellate,

316

perhaps indicating the pretensions of the lesser nobility who wished to achieve the appearance of a castle by fortifying their manor houses. During the last quarter of the fourteenth century, courtyard castles were built that elevated architectural display over the importance of defence. Their essential characteristics included ranges of stacking accommodation around a central courtyard, the use of decorative façades and an emphasis on symmetry that was absent in earlier buildings (Figure 14.5). On the Scottish borders, the need for defence continued to be balanced with the desire for improved accommodation. Tower houses were built by aristocratic and gentry landowners between 1350 and 1600. These consisted of a hall and cross-wing, with the wing raised in the form of a tower. The tower was often rectangular in plan and of three storeys, with vaulted basements, an entrance at ground level and a roof-walk with battlements. The hall and tower were surrounded by a courtyard that contained domestic offices.

Monasteries

Foundation dates for monasteries are usually provided by documentary sources (in particular charters and chronicles). The main monastic church and cloister often appear to be the best-preserved part of the monastery, frequently consisting of ruined buildings that were cleared for public display during the nineteenth century. However, in the case of rural monasteries, this central core may have made up only 20 per cent of the actual area of the precinct. The remaining 80 per cent was given over to non-religious purposes, including an

Figure 14.5 Bodiam Castle, Sussex, a quadrangular castle dating to the last quarter of the fourteenth century. The castle comprises a symmetrical courtyard placed within water defences; it is set within an early designed landscape, including viewing terraces.
Source: R. Gilchrist

inner and outer court that contained service buildings, industrial areas, fishponds and mills. The ideal rural monastery was situated in an isolated river valley, providing shelter, fresh water, timber and land for cultivation. In order to achieve this, it was not uncommon for monasteries to relocate existing villages, and to canalize rivers in order to shift their course to suit the requirements of the monastery for water (Bond 2004).

Norman foundations brought the fully developed monastic plan to Britain, which had evolved in Merovingian and Carolingian monasteries, and was depicted in the ninth-century plan of St Gall. This prototype for a monastery was probably drawn up for Haito, Bishop of Basle, in his *scriptorium* at Reichenau (Switzerland), around 825. The plan depicts the full range of facilities expected for a large, Benedictine monastery, including the domestic and industrial buildings, guest houses, an infirmary and school. The church and cloister continued to form the nucleus of most types of monastery throughout the Middle Ages, so that a familiar, repetitive plan can be recognized throughout Britain and western Europe (Figure 14.6). The cloister was normally to the south of the church, and consisted of a courtyard surrounded by covered walkways (the cloister alleys) that provided access to the three ranges of buildings that flanked the cloister. In the

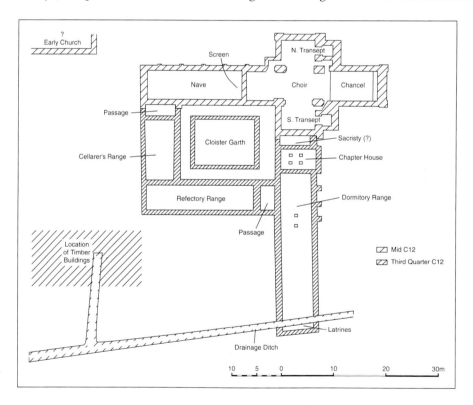

Figure 14.6 Norton Priory, Cheshire, an Augustinian monastery founded in 1134. The plan shows the location of the temporary timber buildings in relation to the monastic plan of the twelfth century, prior to substantial reordering in the thirteenth century.
Source: Greene 1989, Fig. 36

south range, opposite the church, was normally the refectory; to the west was the guest house or general offices and storage; to the east was the chapter house (where the community met daily), with the dormitory of the monks or nuns placed above it on the upper storey. Monastic churches were arranged on a cruciform ground-plan or a simple rectangle, the latter typical of many churches of canons and nuns. The church was divided into the presbytery in the east end, which contained the high altar; the choir, where the stalls of the monks or nuns were located, was in the vicinity of the crossing between the transepts; and the nave was situated to the west.

Excavations have shown that before permanent accommodation was built in stone, monasteries were in many cases provided with temporary timber buildings, for example at Fountains, North Yorkshire, and Sandwell, West Midlands. At Norton Priory, Cheshire, several phases of large timber buildings were excavated to the south-west of the cloisters (Figure 14.6). The actual cloister ranges themselves may have first been built in timber (Greene 1989). Construction of the stone buildings generally progressed starting with the church, built from east to west. Excavation at monasteries regularly reveals constructional evidence, including tile kilns, lime kilns, lead came and painted glass from windows, and bell-casting pits. Evidence can also be found for the destruction that followed the Dissolution, in particular the lead-melting pits for condensing lead stripped from roofs.

Monastic sites have yielded a wide range of material: artefacts excavated at Kirkstall Abbey, West Yorkshire, included those linked with domestic activity, such as bronze, glass and pewter vessels, building fittings, including door furniture, roof tiles, water pipes, glass and lead cames, and personal items such as belts and strap fittings, jewellery, toilet implements and coins and jettons (Moorhouse and Wrathmell 1987). Among the most commonly recovered artefacts are sherds of pottery, traditionally used to help assign dates to archaeological contexts. Larger monasteries for men housed *scriptoria* for copying manuscripts, and considerable archaeological evidence can be found for monastic literacy. For instance, styli, lead dry points, book plates and book clasps were all recovered from St Andrew's, York, and a number of sites have yielded evidence for pigments used in manuscript illumination, including the Carmelite friary at Linlithgow, West Lothian, mixed in oyster shells that served as convenient palettes. Fragments of glass vessels sometimes indicate the presence of monastic activities such as medical treatment (urinals used for diagnosis), literacy (ink wells) and perhaps even alchemy, a chemical procedure that was believed to turn base metals into gold. Concern with sanitation, in addition to ideas about spiritual purity, led to a strong emphasis in monasteries on provision of fresh water. The main requirements were three-fold: supply, distribution to buildings in the cloister and courts, and removal of waste. Especially in towns, it was necessary to transport water over long distances through lead or ceramic pipes, and to filter water from pollutants and contaminants by means of settling tanks.

The architecture of the church and some claustral buildings varied according to the filiation of the monastery, i.e. the monastic order to which it belonged. These variations included the ground-plan of the buildings and the nature of their architectural embellishment. For instance, the buildings of the Cluniacs were typically more highly ornamented than those of other orders (such as Much Wenlock, Shropshire), while those of the friars and the early phases of the Cistercians

Figure 14.7 Fountains Abbey, North Yorkshire, from the north-east. The Cistercian monastery was founded in 1132 and rebuilt on a massive scale by the 1150s. The square cloister projects from the south of the monastic church; the accommodation of the lay-brothers was contained in the extended west range (shown here with lead roof); adjacent is the monks' refectory, which projects at right angles from the cloister.
Source: R. Gilchrist

were simple, unadorned structures. The social composition of a monastery also affected its form. The inclusion of the lay-brothers in Cistercian monasteries required the provision of a second set of domestic accommodation. The west range of the monastery was therefore extended in scale to include the dormitory and refectory of the lay-brothers, with easy access to their space in the nave, as shown at Fountains (Figure 14.7). In order to serve the refectories of both the monks and the lay-brothers, a kitchen was placed in the angle between the west and south ranges. This required the monks' refectory to be turned at right angles in order to project from the cloister. A second complex was also required in the case of 'double houses', which were essentially nunneries that had a group of resident monks or canons attached. The ordering of space in the monastery was carefully arranged to divide social groups, separating monks from lay-brothers, canons from nuns, and all religious from secular (non-monastic) visitors. Even within the monastic choir and refectory, seating was carefully ordered according to seniority within the community.

Beyond the cloister, an inner court housed stables, store houses, laundries, gardens and ancillary structures. An outer court contained larger-scale industrial and storage buildings and work areas that were subject to frequent remodelling, including dovecotes, kilns, malt-houses, breweries and granaries, as shown by excavations at Thornholme, Lincolnshire. At Fountains, a masonry-built woolhouse has been excavated that underwent six phases of development, including conversion to a watermill for fulling and finishing cloth (Figure 14.8) (Coppack 1986). At Bordesley Abbey, Worcestershire, a series of timber-built mills

320

Figure 14.8 Fountains Abbey, North Yorkshire, reconstruction of the thirteenth-century woolhouse excavated in the outer court. Drawing by Simon Hayfield from research by Glyn Coppack. *Source*: Coppack 1986, Fig. 19

had hearths located near the wheel. Associated with this complex were metal off-cuts, but very little slag, indicative of water-powered metalworking (Astill *et al.* 2005). Fishponds were common on the outer edges of the precinct, and some sites included elaborate pond complexes for management of fish. Some orders, in particular the Cistercian, also held specialized farms (granges) located some distance from the monastery (Bond 2004). The plagues of the mid-fourteenth century caused a shortage of labour and recruits to serve as lay-brothers. As a result, such farms were increasingly leased out to tenant farmers.

The vocation of the friars to preach and educate the urban poor affected the form and location of their houses. Because they were relative latecomers to towns, they sometimes occupied the outer fringes, such as the Austin Friars at Leicester. Wherever possible, however, they would acquire a more central site, even if this meant moving when a new site could be purchased. The vocation to preach initiated the lofty preaching nave, a hall-like structure in which visibility and audibility were the priorities (e.g. the extant Dominican church at Norwich). The preaching nave was open to the public, and separated from the friars' choir in the eastern arm of the church by a screened space known as the 'walking place', which was often surmounted by a tower. Friaries followed the model of the cloister plan, but placed less emphasis on the regular ordering of space, requiring flexibility to fit their accommodation

Figure 14.9 Little Maplestead, Essex. Although now a parish church, this was the monastic church of a Hospitaller commandery, built *c.* 1245. The round nave was symbolic of the church of the Holy Sepulchre in Jerusalem.
Source: R. Gilchrist

into more cramped urban environments. A second, or 'little', cloister provided additional functions, including infirmaries, guest houses, industry or school rooms and almonries.

Monasteries of the military orders, the Templars and Hospitallers, are known as preceptories or commanderies. These acted principally as large agricultural holdings, amassing wealth to fund the Crusades to regain Jerusalem for the Christian West. The larger preceptories had churches with round naves, an unusual form of iconographic architecture that made a direct symbolic reference to the church of the Holy Sepulchre in Jerusalem (Figure 14.9). In Britain, preceptories seem to have been ordered more on the model of secular manors than on monasteries. Excavations at South Witham, Lincolnshire, showed that religious and agricultural buildings were contained in the same ditched enclosure, but were spatially separated. Domestic buildings in the south-eastern part of the site included halls and a chapel, while agricultural buildings were placed to the north and west, and fishponds were dug in the south-western corner (Mayes 2002).

Certain areas of the monastery were favoured for burial of the dead, including the chapter house, cloister garth (centre of the cloister courtyard), cloister alleys, the south transept and aisles of the nave. Place of burial was determined by social identity and status: the chapter house and eastern arm of the church were commonly reserved for abbots, priors or a monastery's founders or most significant patrons. Burial within the monastic precinct was not confined to religious personnel. Family groups were sometimes buried in chapels, such as those located in the transepts at Sandwell priory (Staffordshire), and occasionally special areas were given over to the burial of children, for example the western end of the chapter house at the Dominican Friary in Oxford (Gilchrist and Sloane 2005).

The long-term nature of occupation at monastic sites, together with their emphasis on the formalized use of space, can give the impression of static continuity and uniformity. Archaeology has in fact demonstrated a substantial diversity between different monastic orders, male and female houses and larger and smaller monasteries. A considerable degree of change can be observed particularly for the fifteenth and sixteenth centuries. At some monasteries, space became less strictly regulated, with buildings around the cloister being used for a variety of domestic activities, such as baking and brewing, and for storage of grain. The ideal of the communal life broke down as the concept of privacy evolved, and religious belief shifted towards the importance of the individual. In some monasteries, this is reflected in the partitioning of formerly communal dormitories and infirmary halls, and in extreme cases, such as the nunnery of Elstow, Bedfordshire, the withdrawal of small groups from the rest of the community to eat and live together in separate households. Evidence of animal bones suggests that prohibitions on diet were broken in all but the strictest of monasteries, while the recovery of personal artefacts and costly imported items suggests that earlier vows to eschew wealth and private property had been breached.

A SOCIAL ARCHAEOLOGY OF THE MIDDLE AGES

The last twenty years have seen a massive expansion in the application of archaeological science and data collection in medieval archaeology, especially where developer funding has fuelled urban excavations. This period has also seen the development of social and theoretical approaches to the Middle Ages: rather than using archaeological evidence to answer historical questions, medieval archaeologists have established research questions that complement historical study (Gerrard 2003). For example in relation to churches and rural settlement, the agenda has shifted towards the study of *agency*, the active strategies used by individuals or groups to transform their social contexts. Where previously it was assumed that local lords were responsible for the building of churches, recent studies have proposed that some local communities co-operated with non-resident lords to build churches on public spaces and greens (Stocker and Everson 2006). Social relationships can also be read in the developing plan and fittings of the local parish church, alongside changes in belief and liturgy (formalized religious practices). The ground-plans of the earliest excavated churches indicate that a simple plan was common by the eleventh century, consisting of a nave and chancel: the chancel contained the altar and officiating clergy, while the nave held the local people who stood in observation and worship. A division of responsibility emerged that reflected this usage, with the maintenance of the nave being the remit of the parishioners, and that of the chancel falling to the priest or patron. The altar seems to have been placed at the western end of the chancel at Raunds to allow easy visibility for those in the nave. The small scale of these churches implies an intimate setting and high degree of visibility and interaction between the priest and people. In contrast, during the thirteenth century, chancels were rebuilt in a more elongated form, increasing the distance between the altar and the nave, and reflecting the formalization of the liturgy at that time. The junction between the nave and chancel was marked by the rood screen, a decorated timber, or more rarely stone structure, that supported an image of the Crucifixion.

Pam Graves has argued that liturgy in parish churches became an area of tension between the church and secular patrons. By looking comparatively at churches in two regions, Norfolk and Devon, she suggests that we can perceive local intervention in the mass (Graves 2000). Devon and Norfolk were very different in the degree of centralized control that was exercised by the cathedral church: Exeter had a monopoly over burial of the dead within the city and a close hold on ritual practices within the churches of the diocese. She argues that centralized control of the liturgy in Devon can be seen in the treatment of the county's rood screens, which tended to be substantial structures that would deliberately obscure the ritual of the mass; in contrast, East Anglian screens were open structures to promote visibility of the mass. Few of the East Anglian screens have doors, which are common elsewhere and allowed the clergy to lock the chancel and control entry to it. Many of the East Anglian screens have donor inscriptions, suggesting that they were the product of local engagement with the church, rather than the result of centralized control. By the fifteenth or sixteenth century, sermons had become an important element of the service, and pulpits were sometimes placed at the eastern end of the nave. Benches and fixed seating also began to appear at this time, with their arrangement reflecting the social hierarchy of the community itself. Factors such as social status, gender and age influenced a parishioner's place in the church during life and death.

The study of medieval burial has been revitalized to challenge the standard assumption that death rituals had been removed from the family and community by the thirteenth century, and had become 'privatized' through the influence of priests and monks. The study of 8000 burials from excavated sites in Britain (c. 1050–1550) has revealed a great deal of variety in the funerary rites that were employed for the burial of religious personnel: abbots and bishops were interred in rich vestments with their staffs of office (crosiers); monks wore habits or hair-shirts, and nuns were provided with distinctive head-dresses; ordained priests were buried with copies of the sacramental chalice which was the symbol of their office. Practices employed for the burial of laypeople expanded between c. 1200–1300 to include clothed burial, an increased number of personal objects and jewellery, and the emergence of heart and viscera burials (the interment of individual body parts). By closely examining the sequence of medieval funerary rites it is possible to distinguish practices carried out in the home from those which took place in the church and cemetery. The pivotal point of transition between the family and the church seems to have been the funeral procession itself. Before this, the women of the family washed the corpse and dressed it in clothing or a shroud; once prepared, the body was displayed in the home on a bier or in a coffin. Certain items were placed in direct contact with the corpse, for example coins or stones placed in the mouth, crosses or bullae placed on the chest, and padlocks placed near the pelvis. These objects were deposited within the shroud during the preparation of the body in the home, and therefore reflect the agency of the deceased's family, rather than the formal rituals of the church. A number of regional practices have been discerned that also attest to the beliefs and interventions of local communities.

In Scotland and Wales it appears that earlier burial practices survived into the later Middle Ages, for example the inclusion of animal body parts and white pebbles in many graves excavated at Whithorn (Dumfries). In the south of England around the mid-fourteenth century, the practice developed of including bullae in burials (the lead seals from papal documents), and at some cemeteries hearth ash was deposited in the coffin (Gilchrist and Sloane 2005).

The interpretation of castles has undergone profound revision in the last decade, shifting from purely military perspectives to those which examine the social and symbolic functions of castles and aristocratic landscapes (e.g. Creighton 2002; Liddiard 2005). To some extent this transformation has resulted from landscape surveys carried out at castles such as Bodiam (Sussex) and Kenilworth (Warwickshire), which have been revealed to sit within 'designed landscapes'. These castles were approached by processional routes set out in the landscape, with viewing platforms positioned to accentuate their settings. Water was an essential tool in the designed landscape, used to reflect the castle, control approach routes, and to create a sense of theatre in jousts and tournaments (Johnson 2002). Other key components were features that carried the aristocratic associations of chivalry, hunting and religious patronage, such as gardens, dovecotes, rabbit warrens, fishponds, deer parks and churches, chapels and monasteries. Excavation has also played a role in shifting attention to everyday life in castles, for example at Barnard Castle emphasis was placed on the social zoning of the wards. Successive rebuildings of Barnard Castle reflect its changing meaning in the landscape – the fabric of the castle was crucial to the social process of embedding Anglo-Norman lordship in the north of England (Austin 2007).

THE WIDER VIEW

Castles developed in ninth-century Europe with the fragmentation of the Carolingian empire and the emergence of the social system of feudalism. It has been argued, however, that not all private, fortified residences were connected with the feudal order: castles also developed in kin-based societies such as Ireland (De Meulemeester and O'Conor 2007). In the tenth and eleventh centuries, castles were built exclusively by kings and members of the higher aristocracy, while lesser lords and knights constructed castles from the late eleventh century onwards. Fortified hill-top settlements, mottes, *donjons* (keeps) and *Bergfriede* (tall towers, not necessarily residential) appeared in France and Germany from the mid-tenth to the eleventh centuries, and towers on conical mounds were built at the same time in southern Germany and Italy. The motte and bailey form declined throughout north-western Europe by the twelfth to thirteenth centuries, when it began to flourish in southern and eastern Europe. The more defensive enclosure castle was developed in response to more effective siege-craft from *c.* 1200, in France, Ireland and England and Wales (e.g. Château Gaillard, Normandy). Designed landscapes may not have been typical in all regions of Europe, but they have been detected in England, France, Germany and Scandinavia.

Churches and monasteries developed in a similar manner throughout Christian Europe, with variations in the chronology and pace of Christianization. For example, Ireland was thoroughly Christianized in the seventh century, based on a monastic structure, whereas Scandinavia, Poland and Hungary were Christianized during the tenth century through the missionary activities of bishops; and in the thirteenth century, the Baltic region was forcibly converted by the crusades of the Teutonic Knights. Each region developed its own distinctive style of church architecture (O'Keeffe with Untermann 2007). In France and Germany, a 'westwork' was sometimes provided – a large, multi-storeyed building at the west end of the church (e.g. Corvey, *c.* 880); while in Ireland, tall, round towers were characteristic. Some regions developed unique styles based on earlier craft traditions and the availability of building materials, for example the elaborately carved, timber stave churches of Norway (e.g. Urnes, *c.* 1140). Burial traditions developed distinctly local variations: for example, the late conversion of the Baltic resulted in hybrid burial rites in parts of Estonia, Latvia and Lithuania, with ancient folk traditions persisting up to the post-medieval period. Estonian burials continued to include some grave goods that had been used in Late Iron Age cremations and inhumations: tools, jewellery, keys, coins and items of personal hygiene. Feasts and food offerings were made at the grave-site, including regular family meals held at the grave long after the interment. It should be noted that while Christianity was the major religion of Europe, Judaism was important in the regions of Sephardic (Iberian) and Ashkenazi Judaism (Rhineland), and there was a Jewish presence in England from the Norman Conquest until their expulsion in 1290. A significant number of medieval synagogues and mikva'ot (ritual baths) survive in Germany, and their archaeological evidence has been traced in London and Bristol, together with the excavation of a major Jewish cemetery in York. Islam was the major religion of al-Andalus (the Iberian Peninsula) under the dynasties of the Umayyads (756–1010) and the Almohads (1147–1248). Surviving examples of Friday mosques include those at Cordoba and Toledo, and smaller mosques attached to castles and villages (Stupecki and Valor 2007).

Key texts

Coppack, G., 2006. *Abbeys and priories*. Stroud: Tempus.
Creighton, O.H., 2002. *Castles and landscape*. London: Continuum.
Gilchrist, R. and Sloane, B., 2005. *Requiem. The medieval monastic cemetery in Britain*. London: Museum of London Archaeology Service Monograph.
Graham-Campbell, J. with Valor, M. (eds) 2007. *The archaeology of medieval Europe vol 1. Eighth to twelfth centuries* AD. Aarhus: Aarhus University Press.
Liddiard, R., 2005. *Castles in context. Power, symbolism and landscape, 1066–1500*. Oxford: Windgather Press.
Morris, R., 1989. *Churches in the landscape*. London: Dent.
Rodwell, W., 2005. *The archaeology of churches*. Stroud: Tempus.

Bibliography

Astill, G., Hirst, S. and Wright, S., 2005. 'The Bordesley abbey project reviewed', *Archaeological Journal* 161, 106–58.

Austin, D., 2007. *Acts of perception: a study of Barnard Castle in Teesdale. Vols 1 and 2*. The Architectural and Archaeological Society of Durham and Northumberland Research Report 6.

Blair, J., 2005. *The Church in Anglo-Saxon society*. Oxford: Oxford University Press.

Boddington, A., 1996. *Raunds Furnell. The Anglo-Saxon church and churchyard*. London: English Heritage.

Bond, C.J., 2004. *Monastic landscapes*. Stroud: Tempus.

Caple, C., 2007. *Excavations at Dryslwyn Castle 1980–1995*. Leeds: Society for Medieval Archaeology Monograph.

Coad, J.G. and Streeten, A.D.F., 1982. 'Excavations at Castle Acre Castle, Norfolk, 1972–77: country house and castle of the Norman earls of Surrey', *Archaeological Journal* 139, 138–301.

Coppack, G., 1986. 'The excavation of an outer court building, perhaps the woolhouse, at Fountains Abbey, North Yorkshire', *Medieval Archaeology* 30, 46–87.

Coppack, G. and Aston, M., 2002. *Christ's poor men: the Carthusians in England*. Stroud: Tempus.

De Meulemeester, J. and O'Conor, K., 2007. 'Fortifications', in Graham-Campbell with Valor (eds), 316–41.

Gerrard, C., 2003. *Medieval archaeology. Understanding traditions and contemporary approaches*. London: Routledge.

Gilchrist, R., 1995. *Contemplation and action. The other monasticism*. London: Leicester University Press.

Graves, C.P., 2000. *The form and fabric of belief: the archaeology of lay experience in medieval Norfolk and Devon*. Oxford: British Archaeological Reports 311.

Greene, J.P., 1989. *Norton Priory: the archaeology of a medieval religious house*. Cambridge: Cambridge University Press.

Hall, R. and Stocker, D. (ed.) 2005. *Cantate domino: the vicars choral at English cathedrals. History, architecture and archaeology*. Oxford: Oxbow.

Higham, R. and Barker, P., 1992. *Timber castles*. London: Leicester University Press.

Johnson, M.H., 2002. *Behind the castle gate: from medieval to renaissance*. London: Routledge.

Mayes, P. and Butler, L., 1983. *Sandal Castle excavations 1964–1973: a detailed archaeological report*. Wakefield: West Yorkshire Archaeology.

Mayes, P., 2002. *Excavations at a Templar preceptory: South Witham, Lincolnshire 1965–7*. Leeds: Society for Medieval Archaeology Monograph.

Mays, S., 2007. 'The human remains', in Mays, S., Harding, C. and Heighway, C. *The churchyard. Wharram: a study of settlement on the Yorkshire Wolds XI*. York: York University Archaeological Publications 13, 77–192.

Moorhouse, S. and Wrathmell, S., 1987. *Kirkstall Abbey volume 1. The 1950–64 excavations: a reassessment*. Wakefield: West Yorkshire Archaeology.

O'Keeffe, T. with Untermann, M., 2007. 'Religious buildings', in Graham-Campbell with Valor (eds), 398–419.

Rodwell, W. and Rodwell, K., 1982. 'St Peter's Church, Barton-upon-Humber: excavation and structural study, 1978–81', *Antiquaries Journal* 62, 283–315.

Stocker, D. and Everson, P., 2006. *Summoning St. Michael: early romanesque towers in Lincolnshire*. Oxbow: Oxford.

Stupecki, L. and Valor, M., 2007. 'Religions', in Graham-Campbell with Valor (eds), 366–97.

Turner, S., 2006. *Making a Christian landscape. The countryside in early medieval Cornwall, Devon and Wessex*. Exeter: Exeter University Press.

Waldron, T., 2007. *St Peter's Barton-upon-Humber, Lincolnshire. A parish church and its community. Volume 2. The human remains*. Oxbow: Oxford.

15

LANDSCAPES OF THE MIDDLE AGES

Rural settlement and manors

Paul Stamper

FRAMEWORKS

To most British archaeologists and historians, the Middle Ages (Middle, that is, between the Classical world and that of the Renaissance, when the term was first used) traditionally begins in 1066 with the Norman Conquest of England. While many would admit that this over-emphasizes the significance of what was essentially a political coup, the later eleventh century fell anyway in a period of significant changes sufficient by themselves to define a new age. At various times over the previous century or so, parish churches had proliferated, fully integrated manorial estates had evolved, nucleated settlements and open field systems had been established in most parts of lowland England and Romanesque (Norman) architecture had arrived. There is less agreement about when the Middle Ages ended, although historians generally take as their marker the Battle of Bosworth in 1485, which brought to a close the Wars of the Roses. Archaeologists, more attuned to the material world, tend to see the medieval world continuing until the 1540s, when the Dissolution of the monasteries not only brought down those key medieval institutions but also saw a redistribution of something like a third of the land of England, as monastic estates were sold off into lay (non-religious) ownership.

Those five centuries pivot about the mid-fourteenth century, and especially the first and most awful visitation in 1348–49 of bubonic plague, the Black Death, which killed a third of the country's population. This accelerated and accentuated changes that were already afoot. Labour, until then plentiful and cheap, was no longer so. More importantly, as the land of the dead was redistributed, far fewer families had to live at bare subsistence level and prey to starvation if their meagre acreage of crops failed. The greater availability of land similarly enabled the more enterprising peasants to start to put together larger holdings and to begin to take on the characteristics of the modern farmer (Platt 1978; Dyer 1989). Some see here the emergence of capitalism.

There is one other pivotal development that significantly affects the study of the Middle Ages, and this is the explosion in written record keeping that occurred in the thirteenth century. Within the space of a few decades around the middle of that century, title to land, estate accounts and legal proceedings all began routinely to be made in writing – a technology previously very restricted in its application. Before then, little was recorded in writing other than the doings of kings and their battles, but thereafter for many half-acres we know their full tenurial history and for many estates their productivity down to the last bushel of grain and piglet. Michael Clanchy (1993) has calculated that in the thirteenth century alone 8 million charters (deeds) may have been produced for England's peasants. The figure is incredible, and provides some measure of the scale of the transformation that he has characterized as the move from memory to written record.

This vast new dataset inevitably alters the role of archaeology in the study of the later Middle Ages, although opinion is divided in what way. Does archaeology become a tool to be used more selectively, given that documents tell us so much? Or does the availability, as it were, of written cross-checks open up the opportunity to have a far deeper and more critical understanding of, or dialogue with, the archaeological evidence? That such a fundamental question remains unresolved is a mark of the relative youth of the discipline of medieval archaeology, which, as will be seen, developed only after the Second World War. Prehistorians had banded together to found a national Prehistoric Society in 1935, but not until 1957, when the Society for Medieval Archaeology was established, was there an archaeological 'period' society and journal for the Middle Ages. That annual publication, *Medieval Archaeology*, remains the key periodical for the study of the archaeology of the Middle Ages in Britain and beyond.

The archaeological data available to the medievalist, both in range and quantity, is very similar to that which faces the Romanist. Although in some parts of the country little pottery was in use at the time of the Norman Conquest, by the twelfth century pottery was generally plentiful and, it would seem, cheap – certainly the coarser unglazed wares used for cooking and storage. In the thirteenth century, glazed vessels, especially jugs, became increasingly common and more spectacular in decoration, and scatters of sherds in the ploughsoil remain the best indicator in the countryside of the location of habitation sites. Excavation of such invariably recovers a wide range of manufactured goods – tools, fixtures and fittings and dress items – manufactured from stone, bone and all kinds of metal, although predominantly iron and bronze. Where soil conditions permit, as with the sites of any period, it will also yield a wide range of environmental remains, which can range from the bones of oxen and horses to charred, waterlogged or mineralized seeds. Little of this data can be securely dated on stylistic grounds, and even the most distinctive forms of glazed pottery can only be allocated, with any confidence, to a 50-year date band. The medievalist is therefore fortunate that the economy was quite heavily reliant on money, and that even peasants close to the bottom of the social spectrum routinely handled, and lost into what in time became archaeological deposits, datable small-denomination coinage.

The most precise dating available to the medieval archaeologist is dendrochronology (i.e. dating using tree-rings), although obviously that technique is applicable only where a structure with substantial original timbers is being studied (Figure 15.1), or where conditions have resulted

Figure 15.1 Pillar-and-stall coal mining exposed at Coleorton, Leicestershire, during modern opencast operations, dated by tree-ring analysis of pit props and shaft timbers to between 1450 and 1463. The workings are in a coal seam 3 m thick, which in the area shown is at a depth of 30 m. The long, thin 'pillars' of solid coal were left by the miners to support the roof. Access was gained to the seam not from the outcrop (although this was only 250 m to the left of the photo) but from carefully constructed timber-lined shafts sunk vertically from the surface.

Source: R.F. Hartley, Leicestershire Museums, Arts and Records Service

in the survival of waterlogged or charred timbers. In general, with the exception of geophysical prospection, scientific methods have had only a limited impact on medieval archaeology in the field, although undeniably, and as with sites of all periods, they assume a much greater importance in the laboratory when finds are subject to microscopic study and analysis. Techniques that are routinely used outdoors apart from 'geophys' include archaeomagnetic dating, where burnt clay features such as kilns, ovens and hearths are encountered, but rarely radiocarbon dating, because the very broad date brackets do not offer a 'tighter' date than that given by, say, pottery.

A medieval villager lived in a landscape of whose administrative complexity he was probably more aware than his modern-day equivalent. Each Sunday he would go to his parish church, the place where ultimately he would be buried. To that church he owed a tenth – a tithe – of all he produced on his holding, whether it be grain, hay or lambs. Once in a while, especially if doing duty as churchwarden, he might see the archdeacon, representative of the bishop and the greater Church beyond. During his life he would undoubtedly occasionally become aware of other systems of administration: of royal officials such as the county sheriff, tax collectors and travelling justices; of the county Quarter Sessions, where, from the later fourteenth century, Justices of the Peace dealt with matters including murder, assault and riot; of the county coroner to whom matters including suspicious deaths and discoveries of treasure had to be reported; of the Church's courts for those accused of moral and ecclesiastical offences; and of Forest courts, to which those who lived in the extensive areas deemed forest came if charged with poaching deer, damaging trees or bringing land into cultivation without permission.

The administrative unit most familiar to the villager, however, was the manor. Essentially this was the estate on which he lived and held his land. To its owner, the lord of the manor, in return for his holding he owed a money rent or labour services, that is a set number of days' work on the lord's own land. Although there were considerable variations both regionally and over time in the classes of peasantry and their obligations, by and large a distinction can be made between those who were 'free' – that is those, usually the minority, who owed only a money rent for their holding and in whose lives the lord had relatively little opportunity to interfere – and those servile tenants who were obliged to do labour services and who, at least in theory, often held their farm only during their own lifetime, after which it passed back to the lord to be reallotted. In many parts of the country, such men were called 'copyholders', that is they held their house and land according to an agreement made in the manor court of which they received a written copy. Such courts, termed 'courts baron', were held at regular intervals, perhaps monthly, and were at the heart of rural life. For here not only was the surrender and transfer of holdings dealt with but also the regulation of agricultural land and the appointment of officials. Those might include a hayward to look after fences and the manor's grazing land and, most importantly, a reeve, responsible for collecting any dues owed to the lord and acting as the main channel of communications between the lord and his tenants.

Parish and manor were therefore entirely separate: the first was the territory that supported a church through the payment of tithes, while the second was a lay estate comprising the land of the lord and that of his tenants. Both varied greatly in size and complexity, and many parishes, especially those established earlier rather than later in the era of parish formation in the later Saxon period, contained several manors. That having been said, it was perhaps commonest for parish and manor to be co-extensive – that is to have the same boundaries – reflecting the origin of so many parish churches as the private or estate chapel of a local lord.

Those frameworks, an appreciation of which is essential for the student of medieval society, have long been well understood; they survived little changed until the earlier nineteenth century and have been, and remain, the subject of intensive enquiry by historians. What then has archaeology to contribute to the study of rural settlement?

The first point that can be made is that before the mid-twentieth century few historians exhibited any interest whatsoever in material culture, whether it be the layout of a village's fields, the design of its houses or the range of their contents. That was especially so with regard to peasant society, which was assumed to be (in every sense) rude, crude and unworthy of scholarly investigation. In fairness to historians (and this is the second point), medieval documentary sources tend anyway to touch only indirectly on these matters. Even after the making of written records proliferated in the thirteenth century, narrative and descriptive passages of ordinary life are few and far between, and most documents are terse, factual memoranda: of the transfer of property, of misdemeanours and punishments and of grants of permissions. If these do mention, say, a house, a mill or a pig, it is rare for any descriptive gloss to be given.

Furthermore, although the mention or otherwise of items in documents may indicate the date of change – when large-scale goat-keeping declined (around the time of the Norman

Conquest) or when windmills first appeared (around 1180) – they rarely offer direct explanation. Archaeology's ultimate access to a much larger dataset, and to one with a degree of detail denied the historian, makes the investigation of explanation far more feasible.

That such an approach is now possible owes much to a small number of scholars who, between the early 1950s and the 1980s, not only established the techniques for studying the medieval countryside but also gathered much of the evidence and formed many of the interpretations that underpin our understanding of it (Gerrard 2003). Although as early as the 1840s John Wilson had excavated a medieval village, Woodperry, Oxfordshire, recording foundations, pottery and small finds, his lead was not followed up; only in the 1930s, when Martyn Jope excavated a peasant house at Great Beere, Devon, and Rupert Bruce-Mitford began to dig at the deserted village of Seacourt, Oxfordshire, was there a renewed interest in the possibilities such excavations offered. With survey, a similar pattern can be seen, of early landmarks not pursued. From the 1850s, Ordnance Survey surveyors were occasionally mapping in some detail medieval settlement remains, although these aroused little comment, while in 1924 O.G.S. Crawford published the first air photograph of a deserted medieval village, Gainsthorpe, Lincolnshire. In terms of more holistic landscape work, there was very little, although amateurs such as Ethel Rudkin in Lincolnshire, Helen O'Neil in Gloucestershire and Tony Brewster in Yorkshire used techniques including fieldwalking, air photography, experimental archaeology and excavation in pioneering individual studies.

Although it is to simplify matters, the publication of three books in the mid-1950s provided a vital catalyst for medieval landscape studies. In the 1940s, two economic historians, Maurice Beresford and William Hoskins, had independently begun to seek out on the ground and on air photos (which became far more widely available after the Second World War) medieval and later landscapes which they had encountered in documents and, in particular, on hand-drawn estate maps. Beresford's *Lost villages of England* appeared in 1954 and his *History on the ground* in 1957, and Hoskins's *Making of the English landscape* in 1955.

VILLAGES, HAMLETS AND HOUSES

Among the most important points those books established, despite the scepticism of some senior colleagues, was that not only were large numbers of villages deserted in the Middle Ages, but that their remains, readily identifiable as earthwork house platforms, hollow ways and banks and ditches, were to be seen in many parts of the country, sometimes in profusion. However, when the historians attempted to excavate individual houses, the results were disappointing, not least because of the primitive methods used. In one celebrated instance, Beresford searched for walls with a gargantuan coke shovel borrowed from the local railway stationmaster.

The defining moment in medieval rural archaeology came in 1952, when a Cambridge postgraduate, John Hurst, precociously engaged in the study of medieval pottery, visited one of Beresford's excavations, at Wharram Percy, in the high chalk landscape of the east Yorkshire Wolds (Beresford and Hurst 1990). Appalled by the historians' trenching, Hurst agreed to take over responsibility for the excavations, thus unwittingly launching not only one of the most celebrated partnerships of post-war archaeology but also what, over the whole course of its 40-year existence, was undoubtedly one of the most influential all-round projects in European archaeology. During that time, the project was the archaeological flagship of the Deserted Medieval Settlement Research Group, founded in the latter part of 1952, which was later to change its name as perceptions altered and interests broadened to the Medieval Village Research Group in 1971 and to the Medieval Settlement Research Group in 1986.

As excavations proper commenced at Wharram in 1953, Hurst abandoned the then 'industry standard' grid method made famous by Sir Mortimer Wheeler of digging a regular chequerboard of trenches separated by broad baulks whose sections recorded the vertical stratigraphy. Instead, and for the first time on a British medieval site, open-area excavation was adopted and the whole area of House 10 was opened up at once. Its excavation occupied summer seasons throughout the 1950s, as did a similar campaign on House 6 in the 1960s. The archaeology of both sites was complex, and its interpretation has changed radically over the years. That in itself is testimony to another innovation at Wharram, of meticulous recording: stone-by-stone planning and the noting of the position of every find, even pottery, in three dimensions. When the turf and the shattered chalk destruction rubble was removed and picked apart, what was exposed was apparently not the single-phase 30-m-long buildings that the earthworks had suggested but short, misaligned lengths of walling interpreted as evidence of the frequent rebuilding of what must therefore have been structurally flimsy buildings. Only in the 1980s, and following detailed work on the area's vernacular architecture, was Stuart Wrathmell able to reinterpret the same evidence and to demonstrate that these had been cruck-framed houses, sturdy and long-lived, standing for perhaps two centuries (Figure 15.2). What the excavators had found were the short lengths of walling between each timber cruck, walls that had no structural function (the roof being supported by the cruck frames) and which were replaced piecemeal as needs be.

The study of vernacular architecture – that is of ordinary houses and cottages constructed from locally available materials using traditional building techniques – has made a massive impact in general on the study of medieval housing, especially now that dendrochronology has supplied large numbers of precise dates. In Kent, for instance, admittedly a county where the tradition of timber-framed building was strong, it is now reckoned that there remain some 2,500 open-hall houses of late thirteenth- to late sixteenth-century date, most post-dating 1370, when rebuilding began with a vengeance after a 30-year gap following the Black Death. The sheer number strongly indicates that these represent not atypical structures, the survival of which can be explained by the use of exceptional materials or techniques, but the perfectly ordinary farmhouses of an emerging late medieval sub-gentry class (Pearson 1994). Documentary research has also played a part in advancing our understanding of peasant building, for although references to structural details are relatively infrequent, when collected together on a regional basis, significant patterns can emerge. In the West Midlands, for instance, the historical evidence enabled Dyer (1986) to characterize late medieval houses as well carpen-

Figure 15.2 Daily life in a late medieval cruck-built longhouse of the type excavated at Wharram Percy. One or more rooms provided living accommodation, the main room an open hall heated by an open fire on a central hearth. Lofts may have provided storage space, and perhaps a sleeping space for children. At the other end of the house, and divided from it by a cross-passage that ran between the house's main doors, was a byre where animals were stalled in the winter, and a central drain carrying slurry through a hole in the end wall. A screen along the cross-passage would normally have divided off the byre end.

Source: Beresford and Hurst 1990, 40. Drawing by Peter Dunn

tered, of two or three bays, erected around cruck principals and founded on low stone plinth walls. It is now clear that in many parts of the country the late medieval peasantry was living in well-built houses, many of which have survived to this day.

Returning to archaeology, from the mid-1960s, open-area excavation began on villages other than Wharram, both of single plots ('tofts') and more extensively (Gerrard 2003). Partly by design, and partly through the accidental pressures of rescue work, these were in many different parts of the country, and most usefully in areas with very different geophysical characteristics. Longhouses – structures with one or more living rooms, separated from a byre for animals by a cross-passage – were long thought to be the ubiquitous peasant house type, and certainly they were more widespread in the Middle Ages than later, when they came to be almost wholly associated with the upland farms of western and northern Britain. In lowland Britain, for instance, medieval examples have been found by excavation in Northamptonshire at Lyveden, in Gloucestershire at Upton, in Wiltshire at Gomeldon and in Sussex at Hangleton. Documentary evidence provides further occasional examples, for instance from Worcestershire, where in 1440 at Northfield a tenant agreed to build 'a hall … and a chamber at the front end of the hall with a byre at the rear end' (Dyer 1986, 25). In upland Britain sites include highland 'fermtouns', or hamlets (Figure 15.3), such as at Rosal in Sutherland and Lix in Perthshire, where survey combined with excavation identified a number of cruck-roofed longhouses (Yeoman 1991). Hound Tor, Devon, a granite-built hamlet sited high (335 m) on Dartmoor, was abandoned in the fourteenth century. Here the settlement latterly comprised an irregular group of farms, each with a longhouse at its centre and with substantial grain-drying

Figure 15.3 Home Farm, Wardhouse, Aberdeenshire. A Scottish fermtoun, or farming hamlet, surrounded by ridge and furrow, sometimes in Scotland called runrig.
Source: Aberdeen Archaeological Surveys

kilns among the associated structures. An equally inhospitable site was West Whelpington, Northumberland, sited on a dolerite outcrop 40 km north-west of Newcastle. This, however, was a large settlement, probably established as a planned village around a green *c.* 1100, and in the later thirteenth century with as many as 35 bondage (servile) tenancies, each with an average of 20 acres of land and 2 acres of meadow. At that time, the houses were of a type described by the excavators as 'protolonghouses', but after the village was burnt, probably by the Scots in the wake of Bannockburn in 1314, it was rebuilt with houses of a new type. Probably laid out through the initiative of the lord, these comprised four main terraces of long-houses, in all *c.* 28 dwellings, facing on to the green (Figure 15.4). Encroaching on the green were simpler, cottage dwellings and, added in the sixteenth century, a defensive pele tower. In Scotland, a terraced row of three cruck-built longhouses of the mid-thirteenth century, again argued by the excavator to represent seigneurial investment, was found at Springwood Park, about 35 miles south-east of Edinburgh (Yeoman 1995, 115) (Figure 15.5). Longhouses arranged end-to-end make the point that medieval building types do not fall conveniently into hard and fast types, and that the known range is likely to extend still further with excavations in the future. Terraced rows, although not of true longhouses, have also been found in village excavations at Thrislington, Durham, and Burton Dassett, Warwickshire.

A move away from longhouses in the later Middle Ages has sometimes been demonstrated by excavation. At Gomeldon, the twelfth-century longhouse was later replaced by a courtyard farm with separate buildings for people, animals and other farming activities. The same transition may also have been glimpsed at Hangleton, where, in the thirteenth century, both longhouses and farms were in use at the same time. Elsewhere, animals seem never to have been accommo-

Figure 15.4 The village of West Whelpington, with terraced rows facing on to the green, as it may have been in the early fifteenth century.
Source: Drawing by Howard Mason

dated in the main house, and during the later Middle Ages this tradition, of functionally discrete buildings set around a courtyard, seems to have become established even in areas where earlier longhouses may have been common. Within this general courtyard, layout differences reflected variations in local building materials and farming systems. In Hampshire, on the clay-with-flints soil at Popham, the fourteenth-century structures were built on flint sleeper walls, with the houses ranging in size from 7.2 m × 4.4 m to a three-roomed structure of 15 m × 5 m, with a

Figure 15.5 Thirteenth-century terraced longhouses at Springwood Park, Roxburghshire, each *c.* 4 m × 10 m.
Source: Drawing by Alan Braby

hearth in the central room. Most were aligned on the village street, with post-built barns and byres behind. At Greynston (or Grenstein), Norfolk clay lump (sun-dried clay and straw blocks) was used as the main building material in a farm complex of a house with two yards, both set about with barns, a cattle shed and outbuildings. Houses were also clay-walled in the villages of Goltho, Lincolnshire, and Barton Blount, Derbyshire, here the material being raised around a timber framework to create houses of two or three rooms. Outside, cattle were over-wintered in crewyards enclosed by the house, barn and any other agricultural buildings. Late medieval courtyard farms around crewyards have also been found in excavations at Wawne, Humberside, and can be recognized elsewhere as earthworks (at Towthorpe, for instance, another village in Wharram Percy parish), with the crewyards, lowered by successive annual scourings out of the winter's accumulated manure, appearing as distinct hollows.

Archaeology has also identified other aspects of farming regimes. On the Cotswolds, Dyer recognized the distinctive earthwork remains of sheepcotes, long sheds in which sheep were housed during bad weather and during lambing (Dyer 1995). Elsewhere in Britain, other ways in which farmers exploited the uplands are being revealed, many involving the summer grazing of animals (e.g. Winchester 2001) – simpler versions of what in mainland Europe is called transhumance. On village sites all manner of animal sheds and pens, although difficult to identify with certainty, have been claimed by excavators (Astill 1988, 58), such as the 1.5 m x 1 m animal cot found abutting a wall at Cosmeston, Glamorgan. Drains and sumps show the need to keep yards dry, to maintain water holes (some originating as quarry pits) and wells, and to collect and retain water, especially when stock was kept in. Grain-drying ovens, such as those found at Hound Tor, are common discoveries, if varying widely in form and capacity. Stack stands and rick ditches attest to the need to keep stored crops dry, as do structures interpreted as granaries (e.g. Burton Dassett). Astill has suggested that the average size of corn barns on peasant holdings may have risen in the fourteenth and fifteenth centuries, evidence of increasing prosperity and perhaps even of the retention of corn until the market price rose. Excavation has also begun to produce good samples, usually charred, of corn, peas and beans, which in some cases have allowed the agricultural regimes on individual sites to be characterized. At Cefn Graeanog, Gwynedd, for instance, charred macrofossils indicate that the arable effort in the twelfth and thirteenth centuries was directed towards the cultivation of oats (*Avena* sp.). Such a fact is often (as there) already known from the documentary evidence, and what is more exciting is the unique opportunity such finds present of assessing the *quality* of medieval crops (Bell 1989).

Manor houses themselves have been studied by archaeologists through excavation, by architectural historians who have looked at standing examples and by historians using documents, usually financial accounts of construction and repair. What these studies show is that, despite the huge variations in the details of manorial complexes – regionally, over time and in scale – the same elements tend to be ever present. At the heart of the complex would be a hall, scene of communal eating, with the lord and his retinue seated on a raised dais above socially inferior servants, tenants and guests, as well as other functions such as weekly or monthly manorial courts. From the 'high' dais end of the hall, there was usually direct access into the lord's private accommodation, formed of various chambers and usually including a solar or great chamber, a first-floor room that acted as the family's main living room and often the lord's bed chamber. Grouped in a rough courtyard arrangement would be other buildings: perhaps a chapel; the kitchen, generally a detached building in order to reduce the risk of fire; stables; barns; and other farm buildings. On bigger manors, the farm buildings were typically grouped in a separate court or courts, with gardens and orchards forming still further elements of the complex. Especially in the thirteenth and fourteenth centuries, a moat was often dug around the manorial complex; excavation has shown that most were only shallow, but with a thorn hedge on the inner bank this would have been enough to deter most would-be thieves. Crime was a serious problem in medieval society, especially when times were hard: Norfolk had a murder rate rivalling the more violent twentieth-century American cities.

Only a few common themes emerge from excavations of medieval rural houses. Most obvious is the change in the twelfth and thirteenth centuries from dwellings built wholly of wood to ones where at least the lowest parts of the walls, even if only a course or two, were built of stone. This can be seen, for instance, at Foxcotte, Hampshire, where a change from post-built structures to ones raised off unmortared flint sleeper walls took place in the late thirteenth or fourteenth century. At Goltho and Barton Blount, the change was almost resisted, although even here padstones began to be put under the posts in the later Middle Ages. The adoption of stone footings was definitely a fundamental technical advance that greatly lengthened the life of the structure by preventing its lower parts, and especially the bases of the main trusses or the sill beam, from rotting through being in direct contact with the ground. Initially this was seen as either a 'natural' progression or a response to the declining availability of structural timber as fields were enlarged at the expense of woods. Dyer, a historian, argued instead that this change marks the emergence, documented in the written record in about the thirteenth century, of professional carpenters. Each explanation relies on (and demands) a different explanation of the medieval economy and society; in the last case, for instance, that a specialized, market economy had filtered down to the base of rural society, and that there was sufficient money in circulation to support a range of professional specialists. Another common theme, picked up by Wrathmell (1989), appears to be the movement of the main hearth in the late Middle Ages from the centre of the living room to against the cross-passage wall. This was presumably to allow a firehood to be installed, although for what ultimate purpose is as yet unknown; whether it was to improve the living environment within the house by creating a fire with better (and safer) 'draw', or whether to allow the space above the living room to be converted into a loft. At Caldecotte, Hertfordshire, the next and final stage in the process was observed, with the insertion of wall chimneys before the settlement was deserted in the sixteenth century. It may also be the case that in the later Middle Ages the standard of fittings and fixtures improved, and at both Wharram and West Whelpington, lead-camed glass windows began to appear in the fifteenth century (Wrathmell 1989, 257).

One other development noted on a wide range of sites is the appearance of better-defined boundaries in the early Middle Ages. Hatch, near Basingstoke, Hampshire, was an 'open' settlement in the late Saxon period, largely without internal boundaries between properties, and remained so until the twelfth century, when ditches were dug to define the individual tenements. In a review of the evidence that demonstrated how widespread this trend towards ever more clearly defined boundaries was, especially in the late thirteenth and fourteenth centuries, Astill remarked that 'in chalk areas the tofts must have resembled stockades' and in general that 'the impression is that walking down the village street it would have been difficult to see into the individual tofts, for most of the banks, walls or hedges would have been at head height' (1988, 52–3). This clearer definition of individual ownership in villages mirrored developments in the wider countryside, as the rising population increased pressure on resources of all kinds. Woods, moors and heaths that had previously been inter-commoned, available for use by all the surrounding communities, came to be physically apportioned between them. Ditches and walls, or in woods linear clearings called trenches, were created to mark these new boundaries in what in many parts of Britain marked the last chapter in the allocation of the countryside into precisely defined territories.

Thus while it is possible to identify common themes in the vernacular buildings of medieval Britain, what emerges instead is an impression of great variety. Local, vernacular building styles, such as that identified by Austin in south-west England (Austin 1985), may have been just as marked in the early and high Middle Ages (the eleventh to later fourteenth centuries) as later. Those variations presumably reflect the availability (or otherwise) of local building materials and skilled carpenters, changing farming systems and differing levels of wealth and social status as well as innate local traditions.

As well as investigating variety in the plan and form of individual houses, archaeologists and geographers have also studied the settlements of which they formed a part. An ambitious attempt to define for the whole of England discrete areas of rural settlement types defined in a hierarchy of *settlement provinces*, *sub-provinces* and *local regions* (Roberts and Wrathmell 2000). Almost equally ambitious has been an attempt to map village types in the East Midlands and to investigate their relationship both to natural factors, such as soil type, and to historical ones, such as the influence of the Scandinavian settlements (Lewis *et al.* 1997). This was predominantly an area of *nucleated settlement* – one of large hamlets and villages. The other contrasting classification used by geographers is *dispersed settlement*, that is a countryside of hamlets and farmsteads. In the 1990s the Whittlewood Project looked at a landscape of this latter type on the Northamptonshire–Buckinghamshire border (Jones and Page 2006), again seeking the factors which led to the emergence of this settlement form. In the event, neither project (nor other smaller-scale ones) produced any clear evidence of correlations – cause and effect – and certainly not simple ones. But research goes on, and this – medieval settlement origins – remains a vibrant research theme (Gardiner and Rippon 2007).

Another major research project of the 1990s centred on a single village and its territory: Shapwick, a 1,284 ha parish in the centre of Somerset that runs up from the wetlands of the Somerset Levels to the Polden Hills 3 or 4 km away. The principal hypothesis that the project set out to test was that the present village and its medieval open-field system originated in the late Saxon period and replaced an earlier pattern of dispersed farmsteads each with its own individual fields. As with Wharram, the Shapwick Project was a largely voluntary exercise conducted by academics including Mick Aston and Chris Gerrard assisted by large numbers of specialists, students and voluntary helpers. A wide range of techniques was employed, some, like excavation, fieldwalking (on a heroic scale), earthwork survey, documentary research, air photography and hedgerow dating, well established, others quite innovative, certainly in a British medieval context. Shovel pit testing – the sieving of samples of topsoil where the landscape is predominantly pasture for pottery, flints and other finds – has proved remarkably effective in locating sites. Also tested was the possibility of locating aceramic settlements through geophysical and geochemical survey methods, including the identification of heavy metals in the soil (Gerrard and Aston 2007).

The continuing population growth seen in the twelfth and thirteenth centuries inevitably led to changes in the pattern of rural settlement and, as has already been indicated, intensification of land use is a recurrent theme at this time, from the individual holding to the wider countryside of fields and woods. Thus individual properties were sub-divided, most frequently to accommodate sons unable to find or afford their own land or to accommodate retired parents from whom the holding had been taken over. The 'newlands' found in some village plans indicate that, presumably at the initiative, or at least with the acquiescence of the lord, it was sometimes possible for a settlement to expand, although unless new arable land could be added to the village's fields, the result would be a reduction in average farm size. Especially in areas of dispersed settlement, secondary or 'daughter' settlements were sometimes established in areas until then considered as of only marginal use. In the Fenlands of East Anglia, for instance, linear villages were established along drove roads, and comparable developments can be seen in the Somerset Levels wetlands. The most developed studies of dispersed and secondary settlements, however, have been those undertaken in 'wood-pasture' areas, such as those of the Weald of Kent and the West Midlands. At Hanbury, Worcestershire, much of the parish was farmed in the early Middle Ages from houses clustered around hamlets called 'Ends', such as Morweysend and Brookend, tenanted by customary tenants required to do labour services for the lord. However, in the two centuries after the Norman Conquest, a large acreage of woodland was felled in the parish – some 1,000 acres, an eighth of its total area, in the thirteenth century alone – and brought into cultivation. Many of the new cultivators, it has been argued, stood apart from the older inhabitants of Hanbury both in being freemen and in that they lived in 'Green' hamlets such as Gallows Green and Mere Green.

For all this better understanding and more accurate description of settlement types, the most fundamental questions remain how, when and why villages emerged as perhaps the most quintessential (although not ubiquitous) element of the countryside. Archaeology has played a major part here, fieldwalking being used to establish, for instance, the very dispersed nature of settlement in the mid-Saxon period, even within areas later dominated by nucleated villages, and thereby establishing a *terminus post quem* for village formation. The Raunds Project included a series of excavations in and around a small Northampton-shire town and the field survey of 40 km² of the surrounding area. The excavations revealed how in the early and middle Saxon periods, the settlement was 'open' – without boundaries and apparently lacking planning (see also Chapter 10). A major change took place in the mid-tenth century, affecting all aspects of settlement, as rectilinear enclosures were laid out, probably (as at West Cotton nearby) to a standard width of 20 m, and a new building tech-nique was adopted using foundation trenches. One of the new buildings was much longer (37 m) than the rest and has been identified as a lord's hall, close to which a church was constructed a decade or two later (Audouy and Chapman 2008).

In fact it now seems likely that the replanning extended beyond the villages to encompass the whole landscape, and that the bringing together of estates' tenants from their previously dispersed farms and small hamlets into much larger settlements may have gone hand-in-hand with the creation of new, integrated, arable land-holding patterns, the great open-field systems of medieval England.

OPEN FIELDS

Across much of lowland medieval England, settlement land was divided up in such a way that while individuals grew and harvested their own crops, it was within a communal system. Each holding enjoyed, at least in theory, a fixed allocation of resources and rights: so much arable land, so much meadow, so many loads of wood and so on. The most important feature of the system was that much of the settlement's arable land was organized in a single rotation, with one third or one half left uncropped (fallow) each year. That fallow was used as communal grazing land, as was the remainder of the arable land once the crops were cut. This system is known variously as the three- or (if half the land was left untilled) two-course rotation, or the open-field system – the latter name because each of the 'open' fields would often have been entirely without visible internal boundaries: a prairie to rival anything in modern Norfolk. Another feature of arable farming in the Middle Ages, certainly in areas of heavier soils, was the ploughing of lands into ridges of between 5 m and 15 m in width. In a period without underdrainage, this was a deliberate technique to raise as much soil as possible into a relatively dry raised bed (ridge), separated from the next by a furrow that helped drain it. The technique produced whole landscapes of 'ridge and furrow' that in many parts of the countryside remained intact until the 1970s, when EEC policies encour-aged farmers to plough up land that had been down to grass since the end of the Middle Ages and, incidentally, to erase these most tangible remnants of the medieval countryside.

The mapping of ridge and furrow, and comparison of those results with detailed surveys and field books compiled while the systems were in use, has done much to elucidate the origins and operation of the open fields. Perhaps the most important work has been that of David Hall in Northamptonshire (Figure 15.6). This has shown how in the early Middle

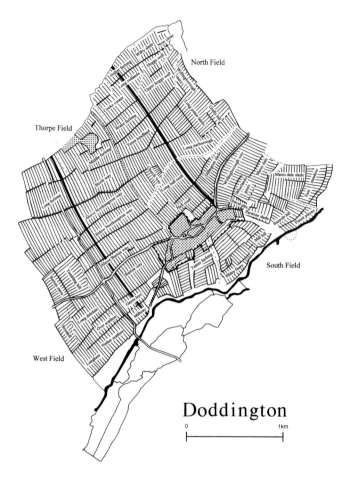

Figure 15.6 The open fields of Doddington, Northamptonshire, reconstructed by David Hall from earth-work survey combined with documentary evidence. The arable lands seem originally to have been almost 1.6 km long (as indicated by the two black-coloured examples); later they were divided into the much shorter, named, furlongs.
Source: David Hall

Ages, individuals' allotments of strips fell in a regular cycle (in other words, in a village of 32 households, every thirty-second strip belonged to the same tenant), and that those cycles can be related to eleventh-century fiscal returns. Another recent observation, made first in Yorkshire and later in the Midlands, is of evidence for what have been termed 'long lands'. These are individual strips that run for up to 2,000 m, sometimes right across townships, through and underneath what can be deduced to be later sub-divisions of the arable land into furlongs. These 'long lands' may represent the first stage of the great replanning of the countryside *c*. 900, and their discovery was very exciting.

To what extent this replanning of the countryside, embracing the creation of new villages and the reordering and reapportioning of large parts of the farming landscape (further reflected in the proliferation of charters with boundary clauses), required lordly coercion, rather than peasant cooperation or initiative, is unknown, although in a more hierarchical and frequently taxed society there may have been many advantages in a tenantry where each had an equal share of the resources and each the same obligations. Glenn Foard has gone so far as to suggest a precise context for the replanning: the imposition in the first half of the tenth century of a new local administrative organization following the reconquest of the Danelaw by Wessex. This established the hundred as the standard local unit of administration and the hide, nominally 48 ha, as the basic unit on which fiscal and military obligations were based. Newly divided up, the landscape then became 'a record in itself of dues; a regional imposition for national administrative purposes'. Whether this explanation is correct, and whether the process was rapid or more drawn out, this revelation of a great replanning of the midland countryside in the late Saxon period, at least equal to that which followed the enclosures of a millennium later, is one of the great discoveries of British archaeology of the later twentieth century.

Just as methodological advances have led to a better understanding of the lowland agricultural landscapes of the Middle Ages, so they are likewise beginning to unravel the stone-walled countryside of upland areas. At Roystone Grange, in the White Peak of Derbyshire, a multiperiod landscape criss-crossed with dry-stone walls of various prehistoric to post-medieval dates, careful examination of wall types, and of their relationship to each other and to dated features and sites, has allowed the reconstruction of the local countryside at different times. One phase of walling, for instance, seems to relate to the establishment of a Cistercian grange – a monastic farm – at Roystone in the later twelfth century, while a later one apparently dates from the enclosure of the moorland *c.* 1600 (Hodges 1991, ch. 2). Similarly, work in the Lakeland valleys for the National Trust has been equally successful in identifying several phases of walling, which has in turn led to the ascription of functions to the different zones of field. The most significant type of wall, the head dykes or ring garths that run continuously along the valleys, separating the cultivated land from the rough pastures above, is now seen as having been established here in the eleventh or twelfth century.

INDUSTRY

Over the last generation, a much better understanding of medieval industry has been arrived at, largely through the application of what may broadly be termed archaeological techniques, including, alongside excavation, the study of industrial landscapes and the scientific and technical studies of objects, by-products and residues (Blair and Ramsay 1991). With the iron industry, for instance, it can now be seen that by the twelfth century ore was having to be got via tunnels, trenches and bell pits, presumably because the easily available surface deposits had been worked out. While there were few changes in smelting techniques between the Romano-British period and the late Middle Ages, blast furnaces were introduced from abroad in the late fifteenth century. Newbridge, Sussex, is the earliest known; Henry VIII commissioned cast-iron ordnance from here in 1496, and within a short time the product range included domestic items such as firedogs, fire backs and tomb slabs. Water-powered forges, where a water wheel was used to drive bellows and hammers, appeared earlier, the first example being set up at Chingley, Kent, in the early fourteenth century. Archaeology has also shown, in excavations at Bordesley Abbey, Worcestershire, how water power was harnessed from the late twelfth century to provide power in a smithy housed in a mill equipped with wooden cogs and stone bearings (for milling in general see Watts 2002). While relatively few smithies have yet been excavated, the microscopic analysis of slags and hammer scales seems likely to enable a far fuller understanding both of the spatial organization within individual complexes and of the techniques employed there. The gradual advances in iron-working technologies were reflected in the ever-broader range of iron and steel goods manufactured, some advances at least being demand-led. The clergy, for instance, needed accurate time-keeping devices, and between 1280 and 1300 iron horologia begin to be mentioned; the earliest surviving example is that of 1386 in Salisbury Cathedral.

One of the most interesting studies published to date that demonstrates something of the complex interrelationships between different industries, natural resources and human controls has been that by Foard (1991) of the medieval pottery industries of Rockingham and Whittlewood forests, Northamptonshire. Here, in the twelfth and thirteenth centuries, what were two of the East Midlands' main pottery industries became concentrated in woodland villages, close to coppice woods that could supply fuel for the kilns. Not surprisingly, the distribution of the pottery industry in those forests broadly matches those of the similarly wood-dependent medieval iron- and charcoal-producing industries, in Rockingham concentrated around Stanion village and the Lyveden hamlets and in Whittlewood around the villages of Potterspury and Yardley Gobion (Figure 15.7). At a local level, however, distinct variations in the distribution can be seen. In Rockingham, it appears that the potters avoided (or were excluded from) those settlements where iron-working and charcoal-burning were large scale and well established – places such as Weldon, Fineshade and Corby – presumably because no coppice wood was available for a major new consumer. Foard has also observed that whereas the iron-working villages generally lay within the legally defined royal forest, the potters' villages lay outside, and that whereas iron production was centred primarily on royal manors, pottery manufacture generally took place on the lesser manors of other lords.

TRANSPORT

One of the popular images of medieval Britain is of a land with quagmire roads where communication was difficult. In fact, as documentary evidence of the movement of royal and other aristocratic households shows, that was not the case; Edward I's household, for instance, averaged 32 km a day when on the move between houses (Hindle 1982, 10). While for bulky and weighty goods such as stone and timber, transportation by water was clearly preferred, with rivers and minor waterways utilized far more than later (Blair 2008), study of the Lincolnshire limestone industry has demonstrated that carriage by road was perfectly feasible and the extra costs not prohibitive for major projects. Most essential to

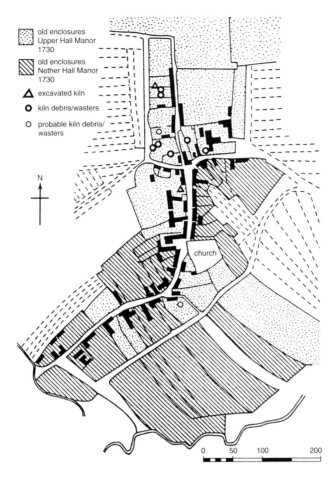

old enclosures
Upper Hall Manor
1730

old enclosures
Nether Hall Manor
1730

▲ excavated kiln

⦿ kiln debris/wasters

○ probable kiln debris/
wasters

N

church

0   50   100   200

Figure 15.7 Stanion, Northamptonshire, based on a map of 1730, showing how medieval industrial
activity concentrated on Upper Hall Manor.
Source: Foard 1991

the national transport network was the construction and maintenance of bridges at major
river crossings. Numerous stone examples still survive, of course, while in the early 1990s
dramatic evidence of bridge-building was found at Hemington, Leicestershire, where gravel
digging revealed three bridges that had successively spanned the Trent between the eleventh
and thirteenth centuries (Figure 15.8). Each was over 50 m long, the earlier two entirely of
timber and the last supported on massive stone plinths 9.6 m in length.

At a local level, the study of patterns of communication in the post-Roman period has
been used in a methodologically innovative study of the landscape around Yatesbury and
Avebury, Wiltshire. Topographical, cartographic, documentary and archaeological evidence
was used to dissect and date the pattern of Roman, Saxon and later roads, for once using
the study of communications to provide the chronological and spatial frameworks for a
broader study of the landscape, rather than as a dissociated or secondary venture.

345

Figure 15.8 The timber piers of the great bridge built in the 1090s across the Trent at Hemington, Leicestershire.
Source: Leicestershire Museums

OVERVIEW

Since the 1950s, excavation, fieldwork and documentary research – much, incidentally, undertaken by amateurs or by professionals in their holidays – has transformed our understanding of the medieval countryside. What has emerged is a picture not of a single countryside, fixed and unchanging, but of a landscape that was varied and dynamic, and at times highly sensitive to changing external circumstances. Population growth or contraction, expanding or declining market opportunities, climatic change, soil exhaustion, war, pestilence and famine, all at one time or another had an effect on housing and farming in Britain. Sometimes one of those things touched much, even if not all, of the country at the same time. At other times, the effect was more piecemeal, reflecting the wide variety of local farming and settlement regions that together made up medieval Britain. As work progresses, those regions will become more clearly defined and better understood; their characterization remains perhaps the principal challenge for the next generation of researchers (Rippon 2008).

Key texts

Astill, G. and Grant, A. (eds) 1988. *The countryside of medieval England*. Oxford: Basil Blackwell.
Dyer, C., 1989. *Standards of living in the Middle Ages: social change in England c. 1200–1520*. Cambridge: Cambridge University Press.
Gardiner, M. and Rippon, S., 2007. *Medieval landscapes: landscape history after Hoskins, volume 2*. Macclesfield: Windgather Press.

Gerrard, C., 2003. *Medieval archaeology: understanding traditions and contemporary approaches.* London: Routledge.

Platt, C., 1978. *Medieval England: a social history and archaeology from the Conquest to* AD *1600.* London: Routledge and Kegan Paul.

Bibliography

Astill, G., 1988. 'Rural settlement: the toft and the croft', in Astill and Grant (eds), 36–61.

Aston, M., Austin, D. and Dyer, C. (eds) 1989. *The rural settlements of medieval England.* Oxford: Basil Blackwell.

Audouy, M. and Chapman, A., 2008. *Raunds: the origins and growth of a medieval village,* AD *450–1500.* Oxford: Oxbow Books.

Austin, D., 1985. 'Dartmoor and the upland village of the south-west of England' in Hooke, D. (ed.) *Medieval villages: a review of current work.* Oxford: Oxford Monograph 5, 71–7.

Bell, M., 1989. 'Environmental archaeology as an index of continuity and change in the medieval landscape', in Aston, M., Austin, D. and Dyer, C, (eds), 269–86.

Beresford, M. and Hurst, J.G., 1990. *Wharram Percy: deserted medieval village.* London: Batsford.

Blair, J., 2008. *Waterways and canal-building in medieval England.* Oxford: Oxford University Press.

Blair, J. and Ramsay, N. (eds) 1991. *English medieval industries.* London: Hambledon Press.

Clanchy, M., 1993. *From memory to written record, 1066–1307.* Oxford: Basil Blackwell. 2 edn.

Dyer, C., 1986. 'English peasant buildings in the later Middle Ages', *Medieval Archaeology* 30, 19–45.

Dyer, C., 1995. 'Sheepcotes: evidence for medieval sheepfarming', *Medieval Archaeology* 39, 136–64.

Foard, G., 1991. 'The medieval pottery industry of Rockingham Forest, Northamptonshire', *Medieval Ceramics* 15, 13–20.

Gerrard, C. and Aston, M., 2007. *Shapwick project Somerset: a rural landscape explored.* London: Society for Medieval Archaeology.

Hindle, B.P., 1982. *Medieval roads.* Princes Richborough: Shire Books.

Hodges, R., 1991. *Wall-to-wall history. The story of Roystone Grange.* London: Duckworth.

Jones, R. and Page, M., 2006. *Medieval villages in a medieval landscape: beginnings and ends.* Macclesfield: Windgather Press.

Lewis, C., Mitchell-Fox, P. and Dyer, C., 1997. *Village, hamlet and field. Changing medieval settlements in central England.* Manchester: Manchester University Press.

Pearson, S., 1994. *The medieval houses of Kent: an historical analysis.* London: Royal Commission on the Historical Monuments of England.

Rippon, S., 2008. *Beyond the medieval village: the diversification of landscape character in southern England.* Oxford: Oxford University Press.

Roberts, B.K. and Wrathmell, S., 2000. *An atlas of rural settlement in England.* London: English Heritage.

Watts, M., 2002. *The archaeology of mills and milling.* Stroud: Tempus.

Winchester, A., 2001. *The harvest of the hills: rural life in northern England and the Scottish borders.* Edinburgh: Edinburgh University Press.

Wrathmell, S., 1989. 'Peasant houses, farmsteads and villages in north-east England', in Aston, M., Austin, D. and Dyer, C., (eds), 247–67.

Yeoman, P., 1991. 'Medieval rural settlement: the invisible centuries', in Hanson, W.S. and Slater, E.A. (eds) *Scottish archaeology: new perceptions.* Aberdeen: Aberdeen University Press, 112–28.

Yeoman, P., 1995. *Medieval Scotland.* London: Batsford / Historic Scotland.

16

BRITAIN FROM AD 1500

Landscape and townscape

Ian Whyte

BACKGROUND

This chapter covers the post-medieval period from *c.* 1500 until the start of the most rapid phase of industrialization around 1830. During this period, the British landscape was transformed dramatically: much of the landscape we see today was the product of this period (Everson and Williamson 1998). The most important background influences were the sustained growth of population following the post-medieval decline, along with growing prosperity for at least some social groups. Between the sixteenth and nineteenth centuries, the population of England and Wales trebled and in Scotland more than doubled. In the countryside, this encouraged commercialization of agriculture, with wide-ranging implications for the rural landscape. In the towns, it generated growth and structural changes. Major developments occurred in the technology and scale of many industries, leading to the creation of new industrial landscapes and regions. These changes influenced, and were in turn affected by, developments in transport. In 1500, society in England was predominantly rural with only *c.* 5 per cent of the population living in large towns. Wales and Scotland were even more lightly urbanized. By *c.* 1830, Britain was well on the way to becoming dominated by urban population and industry. The British landscape may be a palimpsest, but it is a palimpsest dominated by post-medieval features. It is impossible to present a comprehensive survey of such a complex period in a single chapter; attention will therefore focus on the main themes in landscape evolution, together with the approaches that have been adopted in studying them.

APPROACHES AND TECHNIQUES

The period since the publication of W.G. Hoskins's classic *The making of the English landscape* (1955) has seen considerable advances in our understanding of how the British countryside changed from the sixteenth to the nineteenth century. There has been an upsurge of interest in industrial archaeology and post-medieval archaeology in general (Barnwell and Palmer 2007; Crossley 1990; Rackham 1986; see also Chapters 17 and 18). The Society for Post-Medieval Archaeology was established in 1967, and the reviews of research in its journal demonstrate the range of current activity. The lack of research on the upland north of England compared with the lowland south has been partially addressed (Fleming 1998; Winchester 2000), while there has been renewed interest in the landscapes of post-medieval Scotland and Wales (Gibson 2007; Roberts 2006).

There has been a widespread belief that archaeological techniques, especially excavation, were inappropriate to a period for which historical sources were seemingly abundant and for which there were so many extant buildings and structures (Atkin and Howes 1993). Multiperiod landscape surveys still sometimes give the post-medieval period little attention, assuming that it can be studied from documentary sources. More recently, however, it has been appreciated that historical documents are silent on many aspects of society and economy after 1500. For instance, many industrial processes and the sites associated with them are not described in contemporary records and are only recoverable by field survey and excavation. Even as late as the eighteenth century, the volume and quality of surviving documentation diminishes as one moves from southern England northwards. Nevertheless, the late sixteenth century sees the start of detailed cartographic sources. Large-scale surveys become increasingly common, although full map coverage of the landscape was not achieved until the Ordnance Survey's 6-inch maps in the nineteenth century. In Scotland, however, estate plans are not common until the later eighteenth century (Gibson 2007).

Post-medieval archaeology has focused on field survey and the examination of surviving structures rather than excavation. This reflects lack of resources, but it also emphasizes that landscape remains from this period are often abundant and readily identifiable. However, a post-medieval dimension has been recognized in urban archaeology only relatively recently (Robertson 1990). Post-medieval layers have often suffered considerable damage from nineteenth-century cellars and more recent construction. The preponderance of rescue excavations on urban sites with limited time and resources as well as deep stratigraphy has often led to the use of the JCB rather than the trowel as a means of removing inconvenient post-medieval strata in order to reach medieval and Roman layers more quickly.

Until recently, the archaeology of the Industrial Revolution focused primarily on technology. Since the 1980s, there has been increasing interest in the broader social, economic and landscape effects of industrialization, such as the archaeology of navvy settlements associated with major construction projects (Morris 1994). Since the term 'industrial archaeology' was coined in 1955, the subject has remained largely a part-time amateur interest, away from mainstream archaeology (Palmer 1990). Definitions of the chronological scope of archaeology often stop short at the start of the era of industrialization, and it has been argued that industrial archaeology will be assured of a significant role only if, instead of being seen as a thematic topic, it is considered as a period discipline involving the archaeology of the industrial era and not just of industrial monuments.

RURAL SETTLEMENT

Approaches to the study of post-medieval settlement include the investigation of specific sites, the study of settlement landscapes and the analysis of broader aspects of settlement patterns. Settlement plans are sometimes treated as if they had evolved with only limited changes from their original form. The excavation of the deserted village at West Whelpington in Northumberland has demonstrated the change that could occur in settlement morphology (Evans and Jarrett 1987, 1988; Chapter 15). Change rather than stability may indeed be a characteristic feature of settlement layouts.

Settlement desertion has a range of underlying causes. Deserted villages have been recorded in every century from the twelfth to the twentieth. Cowlam is only one of many deserted settlements in the Yorkshire Wolds abandoned as a result of holding amalgamation (Brewster 1988). In Northumberland, the peak of desertions fell between 1660 and 1760, as older gentry families were bought out by wealthy merchants and lawyers keen to make a profit on their investment. The eighteenth century saw the addition of industrial villages – textile settlements like Styal in Cheshire, mining and quarrying settlements. Settlement change in post-medieval times was related to environmental changes as well as human activity, though interpretations of the chronology and causes of changes in settlement and cultivation limits have been debated (Parry 1977; Tipping 2002).

In Scotland, medieval or later rural settlements with their field systems form extensive landscapes in the upland fringes and, in parts of the Highlands, at low level. The Royal Commission has undertaken important field surveys backed up by limited excavation (e.g. RCAHMS 2001). This has allowed some regional and chronological variations in building types to be established. The extensive nature and complexity of these landscapes make them highly distinctive within a north-west European context. In the Western Highlands, Dodgshon (1993) has shown that the clachans (hamlet clusters) associated with runrig (open fields in fragmented occupation), which preceded the nineteenth-century crofting townships, were not the ancient settlement pattern that was once believed. They were preceded by earlier dispersed settlements associated with enclosed fields. The transition to runrig associated with clachans did not begin until late medieval times and was still incomplete in the eighteenth century.

Roberts and Wrathmell (2000) have mapped rural settlement characteristics for England based on the first edition of the 1-inch Ordnance Survey Map from the early and mid-nineteenth century. They have identified three broad settlement provinces: a central one with many nucleations; and two others to the south and east, and to the north and west with more dispersed settlements. These divisions fit broadly the champion/wood-pasture and ancient/planned countryside distinction that other landscape historians have identified. At a more local scale, Roberts has sub-divided each region on the basis of settlement, terrain and other variables.

In upland areas of the north and west, the practice of sending livestock to summer hill grazings, accompanied by part of the community who lived in temporary huts, survived into the seventeenth century or later. Shieling systems are recorded in Northumberland into the early seventeenth century, and the foundations of clusters of shieling huts can still be seen. In Wales, shielings in the Brecon Beacons may date from the same period. In the Scottish Highlands, shielings continued in widespread use until the later eighteenth century. Documentary sources and landscape evidence show that some shielings were converted to permanent settlements in the seventeenth and eighteenth centuries under pressure of population (Bil 1990). The use of shielings over much of the Highlands ended with the introduction of commercial sheep farming, but in areas like Lewis, unsuitable for sheep farming, shielings continued in use into the early twentieth century and still survive as upstanding structures (Figure 16.1).

BUILDINGS AND STRUCTURES

Excavation of deserted settlements from late and post-medieval times is beginning to show that, even in northern England, peasant dwellings were often substantially built and long-lived. Impressions gained from Wharram Percy that such peasant houses were flimsy affairs, built to last only a generation, may be misleading. The Tudor 'revolution' in housing was, in some cases at least, more one of layout rather than construction standards. At West Whelpington, a change from timber-walled houses to ones with stone walls to eaves level occurred in the fifteenth and sixteenth centuries, possibly because of a lack of timber (Evans and Jarrett 1988). Such dwellings were built to last for centuries. On other sites, 'rebuilding' may have involved only repairs to non-load-bearing walls with the crucks still in place. Such houses may have required more regular maintenance than their successors with mortared stone walls and slate roofs but were not necessarily less durable. They were demolished in the eighteenth and nineteenth centuries not because they were no longer usable but because they could not be readily converted to accommodate current fashions in housing and improvements in living standards.

Figure 16.1 Shieling huts, Lewis, Scotland, probably dating from the late nineteenth or early twentieth century.
Source: I. Whyte

Post-medieval housing styles first appear in southern England before 1500, generated by profits from production for the London market and rents that lagged behind rising prices. Medieval halls were floored over and chimneys and staircases installed to provide greater privacy, comfort and warmth. Brick began to replace wattle and daub with timber framing, while glass was used more extensively. Even within southern England there was a mosaic of rural economies, some of them less well integrated into the market than others, so that there can be distinct local variations in the timing of housing improvements. Regional variations in the evolution of peasant houses are still far from clear. In the North York moors, for example, a sizeable group of modified longhouses survives, but in the Yorkshire Pennines, if such houses were common in medieval times, few now exist. Longhouse layouts continued, with upgraded standards of comfort in parts of England, such as Devon, into the eighteenth century, while laithe houses, with farmhouse and outbuildings constructed as a continuous range but without a common entrance, were built in the Yorkshire Pennines and the Lancashire lowlands well into the nineteenth century.

Although Hoskins's theory of the 'Great Rebuilding' of Tudor England has been challenged (Johnson 2007), it is nevertheless clear that prosperity and improved housing construction spread slowly to many parts of northern England. In less prosperous areas, like Wales and especially Scotland, traditional housing styles and construction techniques remained in use through the eighteenth century and later. Many people continued to live with their animals in longhouses. Only gradually were such dwellings upgraded, with the byre being turned into storage accommodation. Upland Wales preserves many farmhouses that at their core have a converted longhouse. In Scotland, the change to better quality housing came only in the second half of the eighteenth century in the Lowlands, and the nineteenth century in the Highlands. In the Outer Hebrides, traditional 'black houses', typified by the surviving one at Arnol in Lewis, were occupied as late as the 1960s. Excavation is especially important in areas like northern England and Scotland, where housing standards were lower and ordinary domestic buildings from the sixteenth, seventeenth and early eighteenth centuries have virtually disappeared from the landscape.

With the end of private warfare under the growing power of the Tudors, country mansions began to replace medieval baronial castles. Excavation has played little part in the study of the evolution of English country houses, apart from vanished royal palaces like Nonsuch, Surrey, but, as with churches, there is much scope for the detailed survey of surviving structures. The shake-up in landholding with the Dissolution of the monasteries provided many gentry families with additional land and income. In some cases, the domestic buildings of monasteries were converted to secular uses; elsewhere they provided quarries for building stone. The country house and its surrounding parklands, emphasizing the control of great landowners over the countryside and its inhabitants, have come to epitomize the traditional English rural landscape (Figure 16.2). Distinctive, sometimes whimsical Tudor styles with exuberant decoration gave way to more sedate Jacobean and then to full classicism as the influence of Palladio spread. Inigo Jones, Surveyor of the King's Works from 1615, was the first architect to introduce the fully-fledged classical style to England. In the later seventeenth century, the taste for classical styles began to gather momentum, producing some monumental baroque houses like Blenheim, Oxfordshire. In the first half of the eighteenth century, a more restrained Palladianism spread throughout Britain. By the later eighteenth century, the Gothic style was becoming popular. The houses of the gentry changed more slowly than those of the aristocracy. Many medieval moated sites continued in use, while hall houses with screens passages were still being built in southern England in the sixteenth century.

In the far north of England and Lowland Scotland, fortified houses, ranging from baronial castles through tower houses to modest bastles, continued to be occupied and even constructed into the early seventeenth century. The study of late medieval Scottish castles has been dominated by architectural historians, and only recently have archaeologists started to make contributions. Excavations at sites like Smailholm, Borders, and Threave, Dumfries and Galloway, have established that the modern appearance of such structures is misleading. They were not isolated but were accompanied by halls and ranges of service buildings (Tabraham 1988). Fortified bastle houses went out of use in Cumberland and Northumberland following the pacification of the border after 1603. Recent surveys and excavations in upper Clydesdale have shown that such houses were more common in southern Scotland than has been supposed (Figure 16.3). The last Scottish tower house was completed as late as 1661. Some later Scottish

Figure 16.2 Montacute House, Somerset; a fine example of a Tudor country house.
Source: I. Whyte

Figure 16.3 Excavation of a sixteenth–seventeenth-century deserted bastle house and fermtoun site, Glenochar, upper Clydesdale.
Source: I. Whyte

fortified houses emphasized architectural embellishment as much as defence, adapting French chateau features to Scottish layouts in a distinctive style that reaches its apogee in castles like Crathes (Figure 16.4) and Craigievar, Aberdeenshire. Following the Restoration, Scottish landowners began to convert their castles, remodelling irregular façades and adding more spacious accommodation blocks, as at Traquair House, Peeblesshire. By the end of the seventeenth century, the first classical mansions were being built in Scotland by Sir William Bruce. By the later eighteenth century, Scottish architects like Robert Adam were influencing country-house styles south of the border. During the eighteenth century, the new trends spread to the Highlands, where the use of fortified houses continued until the Jacobite rebellion of 1745. From the 1740s, new-style mansions, such as Inveraray Castle, Argyll, began to appear.

Churches have been studied more for evidence of their origins and medieval development than for their post-medieval history. Relatively little attention has been given to studying how they adapted to population change after 1500. In parts of northern England, where medieval parishes were huge, rapid population growth in the sixteenth and seventeenth centuries led to the splitting of parishes and the establishment of new churches. In areas of rural depopulation churches declined: at Wharram Percy, there was a contraction of the church, with aisles and side chapels abandoned as the parish population dropped. From the late seventeenth century, there was a rapid increase in numbers of non-conformist chapels and meeting houses, a class of building that has only recently been the subject of serious research and which is particularly vulnerable to destruction and conversion.

Military architecture changed rapidly in the sixteenth and seventeenth centuries under the impact of artillery. Henry VIII's defences along the east and south coasts, begun in the late 1530s, were obsolete before they were finished, their round gun platforms (e.g. Camber

Figure 16.4 Crathes Castle, Aberdeenshire. A late sixteenth–early seventeenth-century Scottish fortified house.
Source: I. Whyte

Castle, Sussex) having been superseded by angled bastions. These were introduced in the earthwork forts constructed in Scotland during the campaigns of the late 1540s; the fort at Eyemouth, Berwickshire, is the best-preserved example. The new military technology was preserved more massively in the rebuilt defences of Berwick. Earthworks from the Civil War period, generally linked to sieges, have mostly been obliterated by urban expansion. Forts in the Scottish Highlands, designed to counter the Jacobite threat, have mostly disappeared. Only smaller outposts such as Ruthven Barracks and Glenelg, Highlands, survive in anything like their original form. The ease with which Fort Augustus and Fort George, Inverness-shire, were captured during the 1745 Rebellion prompted the construction of a much larger and more powerful Fort George east of Inverness. It survives intact as the best British example of an eighteenth-century artillery fortification.

LANDSCAPE

Approaches to the study of landscape have been largely empirical and qualitative, with explanations usually grounded in economic change. From the sixteenth century, with the advent of more detailed written surveys and estate plans, it becomes possible to quantify rates of landscape change, measuring changes in elements like boundaries, field and holding sizes, and different categories of land use: such approaches are still at a pioneer stage (Hunn 1994).

The pace of landscape change over much of England was continuous, though accelerating, from the sixteenth to the early nineteenth century. There were often sharp contrasts between adjacent parishes; some were enclosed in Tudor or Stuart times, while others remained in open field until the early nineteenth century. In Lowland Scotland, the medieval landscape of fermtouns and infield–outfield survived with only limited changes into the eighteenth century. Landscape change, beginning on the home farms of some estates in the later seventeenth century, continued through the first half of the eighteenth century but accelerated dramatically from the 1760s. The countryside in most parts of the Lowlands was transformed within two generations, leading to the observation that the Scottish rural landscape is one of revolution rather than evolution.

The greatest visual change in the British countryside between the sixteenth and the nineteenth centuries involved enclosure, with a shift from communal farming in open fields to individual decision-making (Butlin 1982). By the end of our period, only a few open-field systems were left, including the famous example at Laxton in Nottinghamshire. In the past, the emphasis of landscape change has been on parliamentary enclosure in the later eighteenth and early nineteenth centuries as part of a package of developments conventionally labelled the 'Agricultural Revolution'. More recently, it has been realized that enclosure in the sixteenth and seventeenth centuries, often piecemeal and poorly documented, was also important in changing the landscape in many areas. Unfortunately, while it is possible to estimate how much enclosure was accomplished before parliamentary enclosure, it is much harder to determine how much of this post-dated 1500.

Tudor enclosure brought population displacement and social problems to parts of lowland England. In other districts, such as Lancashire, Cumbria and the Welsh borders, many open-field systems, less extensive and less complex in their organization, were enclosed unobtrusively by private agreement (Porter 1980). Extensive areas in the Home Counties were enclosed early under the influence of the London market. In the later seventeenth and early eighteenth century, a similar process affected the country around the rapidly growing industrial area of Tyneside. The build-up of population during the sixteenth century encouraged the enclosure of land from waste by unauthorized squatting in some upland and wood-pasture areas, producing patterns of small, irregular enclosures similar to medieval assarts (intakes from the waste), often easy to identify in the landscape but frequently difficult to date.

In the early seventeenth century enclosure proceeded more commonly by agreement than by the dictates of individual landowners. The seventeenth century also witnessed substantial reclamation of land, particularly in the Fens, where some 142,000 ha were drained between the 1630s and 1670s. The Dutch engineers' work in digging a new channel for the Bedford River 21 m wide and 34 km long was a major engineering achievement. Shrinkage of the drying peat surface created drainage problems that were tackled by the construction of hundreds of windmills. There was also considerable reclamation of heathland and low-lying clay soils at this period. Another innovation, the floating of water meadows, has left many traces in the landscape of counties like Dorset, Hampshire and Wiltshire.

The final phase of enclosure in England and Wales occurred from the mid-eighteenth century to the mid-nineteenth, with four-fifths of the activity concentrated in the 1760s and 1770s and during the French wars from 1793 to 1815. As much as 8.4 million acres of England and Wales, 24 per cent of the area, was involved, 2.3 million acres of which was common pasture, a huge area that nevertheless emphasizes how much enclosure had already taken place. Parliamentary enclosure of upland waste changed the landscapes of many parts of northern and western England, with regular fields on the fellsides bounded by stone walls contrasting with the smaller, irregular earlier enclosures in the valleys. Although parliamentary enclosure was undertaken parish by parish with some variations over space and through time, standardized procedures for surveying the ground and planning the new allotments produced distinctive uniform landscapes with square and rectangular fields bounded by hawthorn hedges and wide, straight access roads. As new compact farms replaced fragmented, open-field holdings, farmsteads were moved from villages to the new compact holdings, while entire new farms were created on former upland commons (Whyte 2003). The landscape of thousands of parishes was transformed within five years or so. Sometimes, however, parliamentary enclosure followed the boundaries of the former open-field strips, preserving their gentle reverse-S shaped curves in the modern field pattern (Turner 1980).

Between 1660 and 1695, the Scottish parliament passed a series of acts encouraging estate improvement, particularly enclosure and the division of commonties, pastures in shared ownership between two or more landowners. In the eighteenth century the face of the Lowland countryside was transformed by the new, rational, planned landscapes. New farmsteads of superior design were built. Planned estate villages, acting as local market centres and foci for rural industry, were established in large numbers. The old farming system, even in the most fertile parts of Lowland Scotland, had included much uncultivated land. With improvement, much additional land was brought under cultivation, especially on the divided commonties, while reclamation of lowland peat bogs, as in the Carse of Stirling, also had a great impact on the landscape.

In the southern and eastern Highlands, agricultural improvement and landscape change began earlier in the eighteenth century and proceeded more gradually than further north, creating a balanced farming system with larger farms and smaller crofts. Surplus population readily found work in nearby Lowland towns. In the far north and west, however, change came later and more catastrophically. The traditional farming system began to intensify under the impact of population pressure from the sixteenth century, leading in some areas to the abandonment of plough cultivation in favour of hand tillage. The clearance of people from interior glens to make way for the new sheep farms led to the creation of planned crofting townships on the coast, frequently using land that had not previously been cultivated. Geometric crofting townships, sometimes involving the realignment of existing runrig touns but in other instances laid out fresh, are still a prominent feature in the landscape of the Hebrides and the Western Highlands (Whyte and Whyte 1991).

In the early nineteenth century, high grain prices encouraged an expansion of cultivation throughout Britain. Straight ridge and furrow in moorland and upland fringe areas often marks this phase of temporary, opportunist cropping. Much land remained in cultivation through to the mid-nineteenth century. During this period of 'high farming', there was tremendous investment in land improvement, including undersoil drainage, and the construction of new architect-designed steadings and improved farm workers' cottages on many estates. Agricultural depression from the late nineteenth century led to holding amalgamation and the abandonment of many farmsteads, a process which has been little studied.

From the sixteenth century to the nineteenth, there was an evolution in the appearance of the parks surrounding country houses (Currie and Locock 1993). Before the mid-sixteenth century, gardens had been small, often walled, incorporated into courtyard layouts or within defensive perimeters. From the reign of Henry VIII, these gave way to formal gardens on a grander scale (Figure 16.5), while parks began to be developed in more diverse ways than merely as deer sanctuaries. While many medieval parks disappeared and were converted to agricultural uses, new ones were laid out on some estates, often with profound consequences for the local population as well as the landscape. The creation of landscaped parks sometimes involved the removal and rebuilding of entire villages. In the later seventeenth century, British gardens were influenced by Versailles; by the early eighteenth century, French influences were considered unpatriotic. Less formal garden designs became fashionable, under the influence of picturesque landscape aesthetics, with temples, grottoes and statues. The work of Capability Brown represented a reaction against this fussiness with his use of grass, trees and water on a sweeping scale. Although his ideas dominated the second half of the eighteenth century, they gave way to a greater emphasis on the formal under Humphry Repton and the creation of more varied scenes with the introduction of exotic trees and plants. Aerial and ground survey as

Figure 16.5 Garden and landscaped park, Mellerstain, Scottish Borders.
Source: I. Whyte

well as excavation have identified a range of earthwork features associated with gardens (Daniels and Seymour 1990; Williamson 1998).

INDUSTRY

Although industry is traditionally considered separately from agriculture, it is important to appreciate that for much of the period under consideration the two were complementary elements in a predominantly rural landscape. In 1500, most industry was small in scale, operating at the level of the individual craftsman or workshop, and widely dispersed, although textile manufacture, mining and ironworking had more marked concentrations, and industries like lead mining had already been shaping the landscape of some areas for centuries. Population growth led to unrestricted squatting on waste land in many parts of northern England, with smallholders spinning and weaving cloth as an adjunct to subsistence agriculture. This produced the densely settled landscape of small farms and weavers' cottages of many parts of the southern Pennines, like the area around Haworth, West Yorkshire.

The iron industry, centred on the Weald, still used primitive bloomery forges in the early sixteenth century. The introduction of the blast furnace, used first in the Weald at the very end of the fifteenth century and only spreading to areas like South Wales and Shropshire by the 1560s, involved an increase in the scale of operations and required a more careful choice of site. As available charcoal resources, produced from carefully managed coppice woodlands, became inadequate to support further growth in the Weald, the industry moved to more remote areas like the West Midlands, the Forest of Dean, South Wales and Furness.

Mining for non-ferrous metals affected the landscape of many upland areas. In the sixteenth and early seventeenth centuries, mining technology was relatively simple, with veins being worked from shallow open stopes or short levels. Ore was crushed by hand. Much of this early working has been modified or obliterated by later developments. In addition, it can be difficult to distinguish early workings from later small-scale trials. Improved drainage equipment using horse and water power allowed deeper working during the seventeenth and eighteenth centuries, while these power sources were also applied to ore-crushing machinery. A feature of remote mining areas was the continued reliance on water power because of the expense of importing coal. Surviving waterwheels at Killhope in Weardale, the water-bucket pumping engine at Wanlockhead, Dumfries and Galloway, and the remains of complicated systems of sluices at Coniston, Cumbria, demonstrate the ingenuity of engineers in husbanding the limited water-power resources of these high-lying areas. Cornish tin mining began to be steam powered early in the eighteenth century because of the ease with which coal could be brought from South Wales. The chimneys and engine houses associated with Cornish tin mines remain an iconic image in the landscape today (Figure 16.6). Prospecting by hushing – constructing artificial reservoirs on hillsides and then releasing the water in a flood to strip off the topsoil and expose mineral veins – scarred many hillsides in upland mining areas, while the fumes from lead and copper smelters blighted the soil and killed vegetation. Later

Figure 16.6 Engine house of tin mine, Helston, Cornwall.
Source: I. Whyte

smelters were constructed with long flues leading to hilltop chimneys, carrying the poisonous fumes as far from settlements as possible. The peak of production in many upland mining areas occurred in the mid-nineteenth century, before a catastrophic fall in prices brought about by the opening up of large overseas ore deposits caused rapid contraction.

Coal mining also remained small scale and widely scattered until well into the nineteenth century, though deeper mining, requiring more sophisticated drainage, ventilation and winding technology, was being undertaken on some sites from the seventeenth century. Early mining by levels and shallow bell pits has mostly been obliterated in the main coalfields but is sometimes exposed in section with modern opencast extraction.

In the sixteenth and seventeenth centuries quarrying was a widespread, part-time, small-scale, poorly documented activity. As the demand for building stone became more special-ized, the industry became more localized. Rapid urban growth created a huge demand for building materials. Roofing slate from the Western Highlands, the Lake District and espe-cially North Wales came to dominate, with flagstones from the Pennines and Caithness. Portland stone was a prestige material for London builders. Granite, especially valued for heavy-duty structures like piers and lighthouses as well as for its ornamental value, was quarried on a large scale only from the nineteenth century, when steam-powered cutting equipment was developed. In Cornwall, the mining of china clay gave rise to one of the most distinctive landscapes associated with mineral extraction.

The lime industry also grew, with increasing demand not only for the building trade but for agricultural use. Simple clamp kilns covered in turf leaving rings of stones or low mounds have been shown to be much more common than previously supposed in areas like the Yorkshire Dales (Johnson 2002). These gave way to more sophisticated draw kilns, where coal and lime could be fed in continuously. In areas without limestone, boulders were sometimes washed out of glacial drift by the process of hushing. A later generation of small, square limekilns in field corners in areas like the Yorkshire Dales is associated with the enclosure of waste and the expansion of cultivation in the eighteenth and nineteenth centuries. The advent of canals and railways encouraged the development of larger lime-burning complexes (Johnson 2002).

The need of industries for water power continued to attract them to remote, sometimes upland, locations where suitable water resources were available. The eighteenth century saw important developments in the efficiency of water-powered machinery; late eighteenth-century county maps and early Ordnance Survey maps show the tremendous density of water-power sites in areas like the Pennine valleys and the southern Lake District, and the remains of many small mills with their weirs and lades may still be found on the ground. The first true factories, like Arkwright's mill at Cromford in Derbyshire (1771), were sited primarily for access to water power. Such remote communities had to be self-sufficient with shops and other facilities, while industrialists needed to provide good-quality housing at reasonable rents to attract and retain workers, creating 'model' communities like New Lanark, Lanarkshire, and Styal, Cheshire. Only gradually did steam power draw industry on to the coalfields and into the towns.

TRANSPORT

Transport developments were also a powerful force for landscape change. Road transport remained essentially medieval in character until the later seventeenth century and beyond, with roads mostly worn by use rather than deliberately constructed. The statute labour system, instituted in 1555, was largely ineffective. In upland areas, transport was mainly by pack horse. Cobbled pack-horse tracks were constructed in the Pennines, Lake District and Wales. Narrow pack-horse bridges with low parapets were built, while many medieval bridges remained in service.

The great era of turnpike (toll road) construction occurred in the later eighteenth and early nineteenth centuries. The roads that were improved or realigned at this time still form the basis of the modern A and B road network in most parts of Britain. Not every turnpike was well built or well maintained, but overall they were a tremendous improvement, allowing faster, easier and cheaper movement of people and goods, including bulky items like coal and lime, and generating a great increase in traffic. While the roads themselves have been upgraded, the milestones and toll houses, often with a characteristic 'house style' peculiar to individual turnpike trusts, are still prominent landscape features. Even more pronounced is the legacy of bridges from the eighteenth and nineteenth centuries, many still carrying today's traffic without alteration. The droving of cattle from Wales, northern

England and the Western Highlands to London and the industrial towns of England reached its peak in the late eighteenth and early nineteenth centuries. The drove roads that they used kept to high ground as far as possible. The stances where drovers rested their herds each night were often provided with alehouses, some of which survive today as remote Pennine inns. The droving trade declined rapidly in the 1840s with the establishment of a national railway network.

In the later eighteenth century, canals transformed the landscape even more profoundly than turnpikes (Ransom 1984). The earliest canals developed out of schemes to improve navigable rivers by dredging and installing locks to regulate and raise water levels. Canals like the Sankey Navigation, designed to supply coal to Liverpool, for which an Act was passed in 1755, had a specific purpose but soon became used by more general traffic. The scale of new engineering works associated with canal construction was first evident in the Bridgwater canal, completed in 1761, designed to bring coal from the third Duke of Bridgwater's mines at Worsley into Manchester. By the end of the century, trans-Pennine canals like the Huddersfield, Leeds–Liverpool and Rochdale canals were tackling gradients using flights of locks and tunnels, while elsewhere steam-powered inclined planes and vertical lifts were used.

Railways had seventeenth-century antecedents in colliery tramways on Tyneside. In the early nineteenth century, the extension of some of these tramways and a broadening of their role to include carrying general freight and passengers demonstrated that they could be competitive with other forms of transport even without steam locomotion (Ransom 1984). Extensive tramway systems were developed in the early nineteenth century in some areas like Brecon Forest, linking coal and iron deposits and encouraging agricultural improvement. However, the introduction of more effective steam locomotives in the later 1820s and 1830s encouraged the first true railways. The opening of the Liverpool–Manchester line in 1830, primarily to carry passengers, was a major landmark. By the end of the 1840s, a national railway network was taking shape, with almost every major town in England connected to the railway and two lines linking England and Scotland. The impact on the landscape, with cuttings, tunnels and bridges, was even more dramatic than that of the canals because of the much greater mileage involved. They created a number of new urban centres at important junctions such as Crewe and Swindon. They also caused profound changes in existing towns, as the construction of lines, sidings and stations with associated railway hotels required the demolition of huge areas of property including many historic buildings as well as large areas of slums.

Over the same period, marine transport was also transformed. Excavation has made only a limited contribution to the study of harbour developments. The growth of Britain's major ports has been well chronicled, but there is still much research to do into the history – and the physical remains – of a great many small ports (Jackson 1983; Figure 16.7). Sequences of harbour developments can be seen best on difficult estuaries like the Lune or the Tay, where growth of trade and increases in the size of vessels forced the construction of successive harbours further and further downstream (Bowler and Catchart 1994).

Figure 16.7 Mullion Cove, Cornwall, typical of many small British harbours from pre-industrial times.
Source: I. Whyte

TOWNSCAPES

Urban archaeology has made great advances in the last 30 years, but much of the effort has gone into the search for the Roman origins and medieval development of towns rather than their post-medieval features (Crossley 1990). Few excavations have been directed specifically at post-medieval sites and problems. The predominance of rescue excavations in urban archaeology has made it difficult to devise proper research strategies. Excavation has often been piecemeal, involving part of a building plot or even merely part of a building. Nineteenth-century cellars have sometimes destroyed all levels above the medieval ones. Excavation has tended to focus on the tails of burgage plots rather than on street frontages, and many finds have come from pits rather than from structures, their origins not easily attributed. In towns like Norwich, a change in the way in which rubbish was disposed from the mid-seventeenth century, with removal to the suburbs, has led to a paucity of artefacts in later levels (Ayres 1991).

As with the countryside, new sources become available from the sixteenth century for studying the evolution of townscapes. Bird's-eye views start to provide valuable information on townscapes from the later sixteenth century, while increasingly accurate and detailed town maps and plans were produced from the seventeenth century.

In 1500, towns throughout Britain were still suffering from the long period of decline and decay that had affected them throughout late medieval times. They remained small, within their medieval boundaries, often with ruined buildings and reduced populations testifying to their lack of trade and industry. In England, the sixteenth century saw the start of a massive phase of urbanization that was to transform towns and, on a wider scale, the entire countryside. In 1550, only 3.5 per cent of the population of England and Wales lived in towns of over 10,000 inhabitants. By 1600, this figure had risen to 5.8 per cent, by 1700 to 13.3 per cent and by 1800 to over 20 per cent. In Scotland, urban growth started from a lower baseline but had reached almost the same level as England by the early nineteenth century. The growth of large towns represents only the tip of the iceberg. Population growth also affected many medium-sized towns and smaller market centres. However, there was considerable variation when particular towns began to expand and change. Infilling of the existing built-up area was often gradual. York still retained a considerable amount of open space within its medieval walls into the nineteenth century.

The growth of urban population in the sixteenth and seventeenth centuries did not necessarily involve physical expansion. The bird's-eye views of English county towns drawn by John Speed *c.* 1610 show that there was plenty of space within the existing medieval limits. Most of London's huge population increase in the sixteenth and early seventeenth centuries was accommodated by intensified construction within the existing built-up area (Thompson *et al.* 1984). Urban growth occurred by the expansion of suburbs, the colonization of streets and market areas and the intensification of development on existing building plots. The increasingly tight packing of working-class housing into the tails of burgage plots behind street frontages led to severe overcrowding with problems of water supply and waste disposal, eventually producing some of the worst slum housing – court dwellings and back-to-backs – of the Industrial Revolution, bad enough in small towns, awful in larger ones like Manchester.

The Reformation often produced major townscape changes. In Gloucester, *c.* 16 per cent of the medieval town was occupied by friaries and the abbey. Following the Dissolution, their buildings were converted to residential and industrial uses, although Anglican cathedral closes developed as distinct enclaves in many towns. Almshouses, hospitals and other charitable foundations replaced the charity formerly provided by the Church, while increasing civic pride led to the construction or rebuilding of guild halls, town halls and market halls. The discovery and excavation of the Rose Theatre and part of Shakespeare's Globe has added a major new dimension to our understanding of Elizabethan theatre. The debate over the preservation of the remains of the Rose generated media attention and helped to give post-medieval urban archaeology a higher public profile (Orrell and Gurr 1989). At a later date, coaching inns, with their high arches and courtyards, were another addition to the urban scene.

The 'Great Rebuilding' in the English countryside had its urban counterpart. The evolution of urban housing styles closely paralleled those in the countryside, with modifications to allow for more cramped sites. In many English county and market towns, the later sixteenth and seventeenth centuries saw a move from timber frame with wattle and daub towards the use of brick and stone. This reflected growing prosperity but also in some cases rebuilding in more fireproof materials after major conflagrations. In Scotland, population pressure and shortage of space on a physically cramped site led to the replacement of timber-frame houses by stone tenements in Edinburgh during the early seventeenth century. Tenement housing was found in Glasgow and Dundee too at this period, while flatted housing was also a feature of St Andrews and other small Fife burghs, where pressure on space was less. It may reflect a different tradition with an acceptance, in a generally poorer country, of lower housing standards.

As with the post-medieval countryside, far more is known about the housing conditions of wealthier urban dwellers than those in the poorest social groups. In the sixteenth and seventeenth centuries, towns had distinctive social areas, with wealthier residents living in central locations and much of the poorer population living in peripheral areas. At a smaller scale, occupational groups were often located in distinct clusters. Urban housing continued in an essentially vernacular style well into the seventeenth century, with buildings designed individually rather than as part of larger schemes (Crossley 1990). Influences in urban planning began to reach England in the early seventeenth century. Inigo Jones's Covent Garden, a square with houses on three sides designed with uniform facades, the first true urban residential square in Britain, was built from 1630, the first of many such developments in London. New residential developments in the capital began to spread westwards in the later seventeenth century: the Earl of Southampton laid out Bloomsbury Square in 1661 and many others followed. Most of the late seventeenth- and early eighteenth-century squares in London were built piecemeal, although general building guidelines were imposed. Progress continued through the eighteenth century, with Bedford Square, *c.* 1775, being the best preserved of London's Georgian squares. Under the patronage of George IV, as regent and king, John Nash designed or refashioned parks, palaces, squares and streets into a brilliant sequence from Regent's Park to Buckingham Palace. Regent's Park itself was laid out as a garden suburb, dotted with isolated villas.

Similar developments spread to provincial towns, as landowners began to appreciate the profitability of releasing land for speculative building. If work transformed much of the British landscape in the eighteenth and nineteenth centuries, leisure also made its contribution. Spa centres such as Bath and Tunbridge Wells began to develop from the later seventeenth century, when continental ideas concerning the efficacy of taking spring water as a cure became popular, creating new centres and adding a new function to existing ones. In the early eighteenth century, Bath in particular became fashionable. The work of John Wood, father and son, from 1727 turned it into one of the finest towns in Europe. In Queen Square, started in 1729, the houses were treated on a monumental scale. Royal Circus, begun in 1754, was the first circular space in British town planning. Royal Crescent, from *c.* 1770, made striking use of a hillside site (Figure 16.8). In the later eighteenth and early nineteenth centuries, dozens of squares and crescents were built in other British towns, though rarely on the scale of Bath. The New Town of Edinburgh, begun in the 1750s, was an exception. The fragmented pattern of freeholds around many towns sometimes defeated grandiose schemes. The crescent at Buxton, Derbyshire, demonstrates the effect of new urban design on a smaller centre. Sea bathing also had its attractions: Scarborough developed from the early eighteenth century, and royal patronage encouraged the development of Brighton and Weymouth in the late eighteenth century, by which time Blackpool was just beginning to achieve local prominence as a summer resort.

The development of industrial towns in the late eighteenth and early nineteenth centuries was often, by contrast, unplanned and piecemeal. In areas like South Wales and Lancashire,

Figure 16.8 Royal Crescent, Bath: classical urban symmetry.
Source: I. Whyte

new towns mushroomed from nothing within a few years. Factory owners still often lived close to their workers, but only a few laid out planned housing developments for them, like Sir John Morris, the copper magnate, at Morriston near Swansea from *c.* 1793.

CONCLUSION

Despite limitations of space, it is hoped that this chapter has been able to convey the sheer range and vitality of the changes that occurred in landscapes and townscapes during a period that has often been written off as a mere appendage to the concerns of 'proper' archaeology. In future, the application of archaeological approaches and techniques to the remains of the early modern period and even the industrial era seems more assured. Increasing interest in Britain's industrial past, witnessed by heritage attractions and industrial museums, should help to place archaeology within this period on a firmer footing, a trend already evident in the work of many archaeological research and rescue units.

Key texts

Barnwell, P.S and Palmer, M., 2007. *Post-medieval landscapes*. Macclesfield: Windgather Press.
Crossley, D., 1990. *Post medieval archaeology in Britain*. Leicester: Leicester University Press.
Dodgshon, R.A. and Butlin, R.A. (eds) 1990. *An historical geography of England and Wales*. London: Academic Press. 2 edn.
Hoskins, W.G., 1955. *The making of the English landscape*. London: Hodder.
Rackham, O., 1986. *The history of the countryside*. London: Dent.
Whyte, I.D. and Whyte, K.A., 1991. *Scotland's changing landscape 1500–1800*. London: Routledge.

Bibliography

Atkin, M. and Howes, R., 1993. 'The use of archaeology and documentary sources in identifying the Civil War defences of Gloucester', *Post-Medieval Archaeology* 27, 15–42.

Ayres, B., 1991. 'Post medieval archaeology in Norwich: a review', *Post–Medieval Archaeology* 25, 1–24.

Bil, A., 1990. *The shieling 1600–1840. The case of the central Scottish Highlands*. Edinburgh: John Donald.

Bowler, D. and Catchart, R., 1994. 'Tay Street, Perth: the excavation of an early harbour site', *Proceedings of the Society of Antiquaries of Scotland* 124, 467–89.

Brewster, T.C.M., 1988. 'Cowlam deserted village: a case study of post medieval desertion', *Post–Medieval Archaeology* 27, 21–109.

Butlin, R.A., 1982. *The transformation of rural England c. 1580–1800*. Oxford: Oxford University Press.

Currie, C.K. and Locock, M., 1993. 'Excavations at Castle Bromwich Hall gardens', *Post-Medieval Archaeology* 27, 111–99.

Daniels, S. and Seymour, S., 1990. 'Landscape design and the idea of improvement 1730–1900', in Dodgshon and Butlin (eds), 487–520.

Dodgshon, R.A., 1993. 'West Highland and Hebridean settlement prior to crofting and the Clearances', *Proceedings of the Society of Antiquaries of Scotland* 123, 419–39.

Evans, D.H. and Jarrett, M.G., 1987. 'The deserted village of West Whelpington, Northumberland, part 1', *Archaeologia Aeliana* 15, 199–308.

Evans, D.H. and Jarrett, M.G., 1988. 'The deserted village of West Whelpington, Northumberland, part 2', *Archaeologia Aeliana* 16, 139–92.

Everson P. and Williamson, T., 1998. *The archaeology of landscape*. Manchester: Manchester University Press.

Fleming, A., 1998. *Swaledale: valley of the wild river*. Edinburgh: Edinburgh University Press.

Gibson, R., 2007. *The Scottish countryside. Its changing face, 1700–2000*. Edinburgh: John Donald.

Hunn, J.R., 1994. *Reconstruction and measurement of landscape change. A case study of six parishes in the St. Albans area*. Oxford: British Archaeological Reports 236.

Jackson, G., 1983. *The history and archaeology of ports*. London: World's Work.

Johnson, D., 2002. *Limestone industries of the Yorkshire Dales*. Stroud: Tempus.

Johnson, M., 2007. *Ideas of landscape*. Oxford: Blackwell.

Morris, S.M., 1994. 'Towards an archaeology of navvy huts and settlements', *Antiquity* 68, 573–84.

Orrell, J. and Gurr, A., 1989. 'What the Rose can tell us', *Antiquity* 63, 421–29.

Palmer, M., 1990. 'Industrial archaeology: a thematic or a period discipline?', *Antiquity* 64, 275–85.

Parry, M.L., 1977. *Climatic change, agriculture and settlement*. Folkestone: Dawson.

Porter, J., 1980. *The making of the central Pennines*, Ashbourne: Moorland.

Ransom, P.J.C., 1984. *The archaeology of the transport revolution 1750–1850*, London: World's Work.

Roberts, K., 2006. *Lost farmsteads: deserted rural settlements in Wales*. York: CBA Research Report 148.

Roberts, B.K. and Wrathmell, S., 2000. *An atlas of rural settlement in England*. London: English Heritage.

Robertson, J.C., 1990. 'Moving on from holes and corners: recent currents in urban archaeology', *Urban History* 20, 1–13.

RCAHMS (Royal Commission on the Ancient and Historical Monuments of Scotland), 2001. *'Well sheltered and watered'. Menstrie Glen, a farming landscape near Stirling*. Edinburgh: HMSO.

Tabraham, C.J., 1988. 'The Scottish medieval towerhouse as lordly residence in the light of recent excavations', *Proceedings of the Society of Antiquaries of Scotland* 118, 267–76.

Thompson, A., Grew, F. and Schofield, J., 1984. 'Excavations at Aldgate 1974', *Post-Medieval Archaeology* 18, 1–148.

Tipping, R., 2002. 'Climatic variability and "marginal" settlement in upland British landscapes', *Landscapes* 3.2, 10–28.

Turner, M., 1980. *English parliamentary enclosure*. Folkestone: Dawson.

Whyte, I.D., 2003. *Transforming fell and valley. Parliamentary enclosure and the landscape in north-west England*. Lancaster: Centre for NW Regional Studies.

Williamson, T., 1998. *Polite landscapes: gardens and society in eighteenth-century England*. Stroud: Sutton.

Winchester, A.J.L., 2000. *The harvest of the hills. Rural life in northern England and the Scottish Borders, 1400–1700*. Edinburgh: Edinburgh University Press.

17

THE WORKSHOP OF THE WORLD

The industrial revolution

Kate Clark and Eleanor Conlin Casella

THE INDUSTRIAL REVOLUTION AND INDUSTRIAL ARCHAEOLOGY

The industrial revolution, and its causes, is a topic engraved on the heart of every school-child. The great takeoff into sustained growth, during which Britain was transformed from a sleepy agricultural economy into the first industrial nation, has been a topic of endless fascination, not least to those economists interested in finding out how other nations might undergo a similar transformation, or how Britain might reverse its current decline. Studies of the industrial revolution have in general been dominated by economic historians, whose primary interest is large-scale, macro-economic transformations based on statistical measures of economic indices. Only recently have social historians and historical geographers begun to look more closely at the idea, asking not only whether or not a revolution took place, but also whether small-scale social, domestic or local sources of evidence might not be as useful a source as macro-economic indicators.

Archaeology, unfortunately, has played a relatively minor role in this debate, perhaps because the subject has traditionally been perceived as empirical and local and therefore unfashionable, or perhaps because in its early stages the archaeology of the industrial period, whose serious study is a very recent phenomenon, was initially more concerned with identifying sites than considering the wider historical implications of the data (Clark 1987). Nonetheless, as mainstream archaeology has increasingly focused on these later periods, this sub-field has offered valuable contributions to the wider study of the industrial revolution.

The nature of the industrial revolution

Few historians agree on the dating, origin, causes and nature of the industrial revolution, but most would accept that during the period between the middle of the eighteenth century and perhaps the second quarter of the nineteenth century, Britain underwent an economic and social transformation.

Agricultural output per hectare increased, as did the amount of land in cultivation; the first was as a result of changes in methods of husbandry and crop rotation, the latter following enclosure of the former open-field system. Coal replaced wood as a fuel, and steam replaced water as the predominant source of power for industry, making possible manufacturing on a much greater scale than had hitherto been viable. A 'wave of gadgets', as the historian T.S. Ashton has called it, swept Britain, with innovations in the manufacture of textiles, in the construction of canals, in iron smelting and puddling, in the use of iron in construction, the manufacture of porcelain and the introduction of the rotative engine. The factory system replaced more traditional forms of working, as people were brought together into single workplaces, and mechanical power systems replaced human labour as the basis of production. Towns grew as population moved from the countryside to work in the new factories, but also as the population itself increased. Real income per capita grew, as self-sufficiency diminished, and people relied more upon obtaining food and consumer goods from others.

Britain sought and exploited new overseas markets throughout Europe, Africa, America, Australasia and the Far East, becoming a major world trading power. Profits from this, and the notorious triangular trade between Britain, Africa and the Caribbean, provided capital for investment as well as new industrial opportunities for processing raw materials for re-export. London became the financial centre of the world, and capital was diverted into new industrial enterprises.

In Britain, the landscape was transformed by the pattern of enclosure and by massive increases in the exploitation of raw materials, leaving great scars across the countryside, whilst in towns, houses were built for the newly industrialized workforce, and factories, warehouses and other industrial buildings added whole new districts to what had been small market towns. The focus of settlement moved from the south and east, to the north and Midlands, and the population grew, perhaps as a result of changing marriage patterns or more likely falling death rates because of improved health. Transport of goods and people became easier as the roads were turnpiked and straightened, the navigable reaches of rivers were linked by a network of canals and the beginnings of the railway system were laid down (see Chapter 16).

Accompanying all this physical change were alterations in the financial and political institutions of Britain, in the role of the state, the nature of capital and banking and in the system of privileges and monopolies that had dominated trade. There is no single agreed date for either the beginning or the end of this process – the start of the process is variously placed in the mid-sixteenth century, in 1750 or in the early 1780s as the point at which statistical indicators move significantly upwards. At the other end, there is even less agreement on whether one cuts off in 1802, marking the end of a major watershed, or extends the process through the nineteenth century, when sectors such as brick-making were finally mechanized, or even the later twentieth century, when the rapid closure and loss of traditional industries has again transformed the nature of modern Britain.

Interpretative models of the industrial revolution

The following is a sweeping and fairly conventional version of a highly complex socio-economic process. Historians have many different views on why this transformation took place, and indeed whether it was quite such a transformation as the history books might suggest (Hudson 1992). Early nineteenth-century observers were aware of the way in which society was changing; whilst some were impressed by the ingenious machinery and the personalities of the great inventors, others were worried by working-class organization and the atmosphere of distrust between workers and capitalists that had grown out of the appalling living and working conditions that accompanied industrialization (Hobsbawm 1999). The idea of a 'revolution' came from French writers at the end of the eighteenth century, who themselves had seen extraordinary changes in their own society, and was perhaps best formalized in English history by Arnold Toynbee in his *Lectures on the Industrial Revolution* in 1884, outlining the basic model of economic transformation set out above.

This interpretation was questioned during the 1930s, when writers such as J.U. Nef, looking at the coal industry, saw a more evolutionary process at work, recognizing that it was necessary to look back into the sixteenth and seventeenth centuries in order to understand the changes of the eighteenth. Coal was already replacing wood as fuel in a range of manufactures in the sixteenth century, and the transport systems, mining techniques and capital formation that accompanied the growth in coal production were essential preconditions for later industrialization. Others writing during the Depression saw the industrial revolution as one wave in a pattern of economic cycles, whereas in the more optimistic 1950s, writers such as Rostow identified the preconditions for growth that he hoped might be applied to the economies of other developing nations. Against this view, others saw industrialization as something that was a product of exploitation, with Britain succeeding only at the expense of the economies of dependent states (Hobsbawm 1999). Subsequently, dynamic entrepreneurs, technological innovation and capital formation have all been identified as prime movers in precipitating change. Underlying all of this was a search for the causes of the industrial revolution.

In contrast with this approach, social historians have looked at small-scale, local changes, and feminists such as Maxine Berg have paid more attention to the role of domestic organization and women's working patterns. In a period of industrial decline, more pessimistic historians have seen the industrial revolution as a 'limited, restricted piecemeal phenomenon in which various things did not happen or where they did, they had far less effect than was previously supposed', although the information revolution has brought a new fascination with the impact of technological change (Hudson 1992, 37). Historical geographers have borrowed heavily from social theory when looking at industrialization, moving from positivist, environmentally determinist approaches to structural and symbolic ones as they debate the role of humans versus environments in shaping industry.

What unites almost all of the traditional historical views of the period is the lack of reference to industrial archaeology or indeed, with the exception of some historical geographers, any adequate use of physical evidence for the period in general.

INDUSTRIAL ARCHAEOLOGY

Origins and development

The origins of industrial archaeology lie in the nineteenth-century fascination with technology. The enthusiasm for travelling to industrial areas was shared between foreign spies seeking technical information, fellow industrialists, artists, writers and those seeking the curious and unusual. Many eighteenth-century writers left descriptions of the way in which the landscapes and towns of Britain were changing, the origins of the physical remains that they saw and the impact of the new industries on society. The Great Exhibition of 1851 celebrated the industrial achievements of some of Britain's best-known firms and became a showcase for their products. Items were collected that represented outstanding contributions to the development of engineering and technology, such as early locomotives, and became the nucleus of museum collections which remain important, but neglected, sources for industrial archaeology. The founding of the Newcomen Society in 1919 provided a forum for the study of all aspects of technology, as well as creating a new awareness of the importance of industrial monuments and their conservation.

Industrial archaeology as a branch of archaeology rather than a tradition of technical history dates only to the 1950s, however, when evening classes and local societies sprang up, devoted to the study of industrial remains. Those who took part in the classes often did fieldwork of their own, and one of the key themes in the work of this period is identification and cataloguing of sites. There are a good number of excellent regional and national accounts of industrial remains in Britain (e.g. Falconer 1980; Cossons 1987; Trinder 1994; the David and Charles regional industrial archaeology series and the county guides published by the Association for Industrial Archaeology). Additionally, a growing number of edited volumes have presented thematic case studies to illuminate how this material legacy reflected complex dynamics of social *and* technological change (Barker and Cranstone 2004; Casella and Symonds 2005; Gwyn and Palmer 2005). National bodies such as the Royal Commissions in Scotland and Wales (and the former Royal Commission in England) have taken particular interest in recording industrial remains either regionally or thematically, and a formal Industrial Monuments Survey is now housed with the RCHME in Swindon. The Council for British Archaeology also took an early initiative by establishing an Industrial Archaeology Research Committee to look at listing and protecting industrial sites, and today the Association for Industrial Archaeology promotes the subject and publishes a journal devoted to the subject. Interest in industrial archaeology cannot be separated from the broader conservation agenda, and Historic Scotland, CADW and English Heritage as well as the National Trust are all active in the field (Palmer and Neaverson 1998).

The scope of industrial archaeology has never been clearly defined: it may refer on the one hand to the archaeology of industry of all periods, whether prehistoric or modern, and on the other, to all of the archaeology of the period of the industrial revolution, whether it be country houses, industrial sites, railway locomotives or the growth of cities (Figure 17.1). The

Figure 17.1 Study of industrial archaeology is often associated with museums. The entrance to Beamish Museum.
Source: Kate Clark

term 'historical archaeology' is widely accepted abroad but not commonly used in Britain, as it is often argued that archaeology of all of the past 2,000 years is to some extent dependent upon written sources. In this chapter, the term 'industrial archaeology' is used to refer to the archaeology of the late second millennium AD – of the period during and after Britain's industrial transformation. No end-date has been chosen, and even the archaeology of the twentieth century is a growing period of concern to scholars and heritage managers (see Chapter 18).

Current perceptions and outstanding problems

If archaeology is seen in terms of explicitly archaeological field methods, i.e. the use of stratigraphy and the rigorous analysis of physical evidence in time and space, then one attempt to meet this ideal might be cited. A survey of the Ironbridge Gorge, Shropshire (Alfrey and Clark 1993), set out to explore the use of archaeology in understanding a complex landscape over several hundred years. The survey brought evidence for buildings of all types – vernacular, polite, industrial and commercial – together with the archaeology of the landscape in which they were set, and used methods of landscape analysis to show the way in which the area changed from the medieval period to the present day, and to provide a context for some of the best-known developments in the industrial period. The strength of the methodology was that it was possible to go beyond the traditional concept of the site to look at landscape as an entity; the weakness of the work has been cited as the resource implications of such intensive study. One of the themes that emerged from the work was that even in an area said to be the 'cradle of the industrial revolution', adaptation and reuse of sites, the approach of make do and mend, predominated throughout its history. Innovations such as the first iron bridge (Figure 17.2) have to be seen in the context of a pre-existing landscape and not as isolated events.

Industrial archaeology also shows that there are some types of historical question that physical evidence can address, and some that are best left to documentary historians. Industrial archaeologists can rarely see the work of individuals or the large-scale changes in economic output cited by economic historians. However, field evidence does demonstrate processes such as the take-up of innovations or the decisions made by industrialists in siting industries. It shows how industrial complexes changed through time and stresses the importance of links not only between different industries but between different aspects of the economy, such as settlement and industry, or transport and urbanization. Further, through the excavation of both workplaces and households, archaeology can expand our appreciation of the conditions of daily life, the impact of consumer goods and the changing nature of labour that characterized the industrial era. Ultimately, it is through the integration of empirical and theoretical approaches that a dynamic research framework has begun to emerge for industrial archaeology.

Figure 17.2 The Iron Bridge, Shropshire: the first iron bridge in the world.
Source: Ben Osborne

THE ARCHAEOLOGY OF THE INDUSTRIAL REVOLUTION

Pre-industrial landscape of Britain

Archaeology suggests that the changes in British industry in the latter half of the eighteenth century were neither sudden nor particularly revolutionary. However, they did take place on a large scale, and in order to understand precisely what happened, it is necessary to look first at the archaeology of Britain in the years before 1750. As Trinder notes, Britain presented a 'busy, thriving, trading and manufacturing nation' (Trinder 1987, 51), with a variety of industries scattered about the countryside. Pottery and glass-making, woollen textiles production, ironworking and non-ferrous metals were all well established, some in expanding market towns and ports serving overseas trade, whilst other industries, such as fulling in the countryside, made use of water power. The overall pattern was not, however, one that was very different from other European countries, and it was only after 1750 that the face of Britain began to change visibly.

Raw materials

The development of the British coal industry in the years prior to 1750 was to have a significant impact on the wider process of industrialization. The expansion of the coal industry not only enabled industries to move from dependency on timber or charcoal but also created much of the transport, capital and settlement infrastructure on which later industrialization was based. This infrastructure is very apparent in the archaeological record.

In order to understand the development of coal production, it is important to realize that there are different types of coal in Britain – domestic coals, coking coal that can be used in furnaces, steam coal and anthracite. The earliest coals to be exploited were the low-sulphur domestic coals, which could be burnt comfortably in a grate without emitting noxious fumes. This coal was also used for industrial purposes on a large scale from the sixteenth century onwards for burning lime, malting, glass-making and baking. The demand for coking coals grew considerably during the late eighteenth century, following the discovery of ways in which to use such coal in iron-making.

Early coal mines consisted of adits, or short tunnels into the seam where it outcropped near the surface, but little evidence for these survives on the surface. In areas such as the Clee Hills in Shropshire, or Rudland Rigg in North Yorkshire, regular patterns of circular spoil mounds are surface evidence for the short shafts or bell pits dug from the surface down into the coal below. One of the biggest problems with any evidence for mining is the difficulty of dating surface evidence such as this without some access to below-ground works; the large open-cast coal mines dug in recent years have often exposed, and destroyed, archaeological evidence for the techniques used in early coal mines. In 1991, a timber pit prop from Lounge colliery in Leicestershire dating to between 1450 and 1463 provided one of the earliest accurately dated coal-mining finds in Britain and showed that pillar and stall workings dated to the late fifteenth century.

Mines provide only a tiny fraction of the evidence for coal mining. Coal was bulky and road transport difficult, and hence one of the earliest solutions was the use of wooden wagons or railways pioneered in Newcastle early in the seventeenth century. Elsewhere, historic tramways survive in the landscape as old routes or footpaths and occasionally as large pieces of engineering, as at the Causey Arch near Durham – a huge masonry tramway bridge that demonstrates the sophistication of, and level of investment in, many of these early tramway routes. Coal mining also created a new demand for labour that could not always be satisfied from by-employment amongst traditional agricultural villages near the coalfields. From the seventeenth century onwards, new communities are found in coal-mining areas and can be evidenced from scattered plots of land. Many, such as those in the Forest of Dean, the Potteries and the Black Country, became the nuclei of later industrial areas.

Iron

One of the great breakthroughs in industrialization was the increasing use of iron as a material in construction, in engineering and even in ship-building. Wrought iron had been produced in small quantities since prehistoric times in bloomeries, but it was only with the introduction of the charcoal blast furnace in *c*. 1500 that iron was produced in large quantities, both as cast iron straight from the furnace or converted into the more flexible wrought iron at the finery forge.

Archaeological survey and excavation of charcoal furnaces in the ore-bearing areas of Sussex, Kent and Surrey, such as that at a sixteenth-century furnace at Chingley in Kent (Cleere and Crossley 1985), have shown how such furnaces developed and operated in the area where they were first introduced from Europe. It has been demonstrated that the use of blast furnaces spread from there to the Midlands, to Wales in the seventeenth century and only much later into the Forest of Dean, where bloomeries persisted until *c*. 1700. This is a pattern that illustrates a very common phenomenon in the industrial period – namely that the adoption of new technology within an industry is rarely automatic, nor is the spread of technology to new places a steady or straightforward process.

The transition from charcoal smelting to coke smelting, often held to be one of the major factors behind increased iron production during the eighteenth century, is an equally complex process. In 1709, Abraham Darby began to smelt iron using coke rather than charcoal at an old charcoal furnace at Coalbrookdale in Shropshire that he adapted for the purpose (Clark 1993). However, it is important to note that the iron Darby produced was suitable for castings, but could not be converted into the more flexible wrought iron. It was not until much later that a means of using coke to produce iron that could be converted to wrought iron was discovered, and coke production began to expand rapidly. The transition is illustrated in archaeological excavations at Rockley in Yorkshire, where the site of a seventeenth-century water-powered bloomery was reopened and used with coke in the late eighteenth century. In some areas, such as Furness in Cumbria, coppicewood for charcoal production was plentiful, and charcoal iron smelting persisted until 1867.

A number of charcoal or coke iron furnaces survive across Britain, but the furnace was only one element in a working industrial complex that would have included casting houses, blacking mills, grinding mills for cleaning off castings, pattern-making shops and offices, almost all of which have now disappeared. One of the best-preserved charcoal iron complexes is that at Bonawe, Argyll, where buildings for storing charcoal and ore survive, as well as the furnace and associated water power system (Figure 17.3). Archaeological excavations over a large area at Newdale in Shropshire illustrated the extent of a works devoted to remelting iron for castings – the site included back-to-back workers' cottages, air furnaces, a casting building and forge, all without any form of water power.

Steel was essential for producing sharp blades. Most steel was imported until the introduction in the seventeenth century of a German method of cementation that has since been identified from excavations at Derwentcote in Co. Durham. Crucible steel production (where metal is heated in pots) can be seen at Abbeydale Forge in Sheffield, but steel was produced only on a very large scale, and thus cheaply, after the introduction of the Bessemer converter in 1856.

Non-ferrous metals

As with iron, the exploitation of non-ferrous metals expanded greatly during the eighteenth and nineteenth centuries. Copper, tin and lead had been worked on a small scale for centuries, but new demands were created by, for example, ship building, tin plating or the metal trades of Birmingham or the need for engines. In the Derbyshire Pennines, for example, lead occurs as veins in the limestone, and early mining can be traced where it follows the ore in long rakes that criss-cross the landscape; at Charterhouse in Somerset, continuity in mining is suggested from

Figure 17.3 Ironworks at Bonawe, Argyll.
Source: Kate Clark

the Roman period until the nineteenth century. In order to process lead ore, it has first to be crushed and then washed, and associated with such rakes are often found remains of stamp mills and buddles, used to wash the ore, such as the complex excavated at Killhope, Co. Durham.

Copper mining on a large scale began in 1568, and continued until largely superseded by imported ores at the end of the nineteenth century. Copper occurred in workable quantities in Cornwall, Devon, Anglesey and the Lake District, and perhaps one of the best surviving landscapes is at Red Dell Beck in the Lake District, where crushing and stamping works, adits, shafts and waste heaps survive. The spectacular landscape of Parys Mountain, Anglesey, is all that remains of what was once the largest copper working in Europe, where working continued until 1815, with a few subsequent revivals (Figure 17.4). The nearby harbour at Amlwch developed in the eighteenth century as a port for shipping the copper ore out to smelters sited closer to sources of coal.

Such sites also demonstrate the general principle that the final smelting of minerals such as iron, lead or copper rarely took place in areas where they were mined. Field evidence suggests that fuel, or easy access to fuel via a good transport network, was a more important determinant of location. Relatively little copper smelting took place in Cornwall; most of it occurred in areas such as Swansea in South Wales, where there were plentiful supplies of cheap coal (Hughes 2000).

At Gawton in West Devon, archaeological survey of a quay, copper mine, lime kilns and arsenic works shows how copper mining operated together with a variety of other activities at a site that had the advantages of both raw materials and transport. Another complex associated with copper mining is Aberdulais Falls in West Glamorgan, where ironworking and tinplate manufacturing were also found. Such sites are very common and illustrate how difficult it is archaeologically to isolate the evidence for single industries from their contexts.

Figure 17.4 Landscape at Parys Mountain, Anglesey, showing the legacy of copper working.
Source: Kate Clark

Power systems

The processing of minerals in any quantity depended upon a ready supply of power, as indeed did the functioning of many other industries. The move from water power to steam power is one of the factors commonly cited as being responsible for the large increases in output in British manufacturing in the latter part of the eighteenth century. Archaeological evidence, nevertheless, suggests that water power remained important for industrial purposes until well into the nineteenth century, and well after the steam engine had become firmly established (Cossons 1987; Rynne 2006).

Waterwheels were cheap, easy to install and could drive rotative machinery well before steam engines could; only after the 1840s were steam engines built that were more powerful. The technology of the waterwheel was well established by the sixteenth century and, by the early eighteenth century, simple undershot wheels were common. Key technical developments in waterwheel technology through the eighteenth and early nineteenth century include improvements to the buckets and more elaborate means of driving wheels to take advantage of different conditions. The water turbine was developed after 1820 by Benoit Fourneyron in France to take advantage of low heads of water, and the technology spread, perhaps illicitly, to Northern Ireland, where they were manufactured by the MacAdam brothers of Belfast in the 1840s. Water turbines remain in use today for the generation of hydro-electricity.

Many waterwheels survive in Britain, and at many sites field survey of the associated leats, sluices and tailraces and analysis of the relevant falls is often the only source of evidence for the precise way in which the system worked. At Quarry Bank Mill, Styal in Cheshire, more explicitly archaeological techniques have been used to untangle the sequence of use of water, steam and gas as sources of power at a large textile mill complex. Although a steam engine was installed at the site in 1810, waterwheels remained in use there until 1889, when water turbines were installed, demonstrating that various sources of power often coexisted. Archaeological analysis has also been used at Bordesley, Worcestershire, where remains of a water-powered needle mill were identified. Through time, many industrialized valleys developed extremely complex water power systems, often with steam engines being used not to drive the machinery directly (although such technology was available) but to pump water back up, so it could be recycled back around the earlier dams and waterwheels. Indeed, Cossons (1987) argues that the decline in water power may have had more to do with the diversion of water by land-drainage schemes, or for urban domestic consumption, than the inefficiency of water power itself.

Whilst water power remained common in rural areas until the nineteenth century, and indeed survived in some places until the twentieth century, in urban areas the take-up of steam was more widespread. This illustrates the ultimate advantage that steam had over water power – it was a flexible, movable source of power that could be set up where required. Despite the importance of water power (and its greater legibility in the archaeological record), the application of steam engines to industrial uses from mining and mineral production through to textiles, manufacturing and transport undoubtedly made possible much higher levels of productivity, and ultimately freed many areas of manufacturing from dependency upon human and horse power.

Newcomen engines remained in use for pumping coal mines, where fuel was relatively cheap and where vertical motion was the main requirement. However, the improvements in steam engines created by Watt's patents of the late eighteenth century resulted in engines that used less fuel and thus were cheaper and could turn as well as lift. Textile mills, forges, metal works, glass-making, breweries and water works all found ready uses for such engines, and by 1800 nearly 500 had been built. Steam engine development did not stop with Boulton and Watt, and throughout the nineteenth century a series of patents resulted in smaller, more powerful and yet more portable engines. Reciprocating steam engines were used for electricity production in the 1880s, but only began to become redundant with the patenting of the steam turbine in 1884, which was immediately useful for electricity generation.

The portability of steam engines is illustrated by the earliest surviving engine, a Newcomen engine that today stands in Dartmouth. It was moved there, having been used successively at Griff Colliery in Warwickshire, at Measham in Leicestershire and at Hawkesbury Junction on the Coventry canal. Such portability makes it very difficult to interpret the archaeological evidence for steam engines on the basis of site remains alone. The vast majority of engines do not survive *in situ*, and those engine bases that do survive may have been modified either as their engines were adapted, or replaced, and as engines became smaller and less dependent upon built features such as engine houses.

By contrast, engine houses do tend to survive. The Cornish pumping engine was a higher-pressure, single-acting engine developed specifically for mining. An archaeological survey of such engine houses in Cornwall has produced a methodology for classifying them as a single building type within the wider context of crushers, waste heaps and mines that survive in the Cornish landscape (Figure 17.5). Cornish mining technology was very distinctive and was exported to other parts of the world in the nineteenth century, including South Australia, where Cornish-style engine houses may still be seen today.

In contrast to steam, remains of the gas and electricity industries survive somewhat better, although they are increasingly under threat, and should also be seen as relevant to the study of the industrial revolution. The way in which the Ironbridge power stations, opened respectively in 1932 and 1969, were designed, built and altered through time and the associated impact on the local landscape, which already had a long history of industrialization, are explored by Stratton (1994). The application of power to industrial processes provides a context for the development of the factory system whereby production became highly organized, and labour specialized.

Textiles

The most potent symbol of the factory system is the multi-storey textile mill, with its steam engine or waterwheel powering several floors of spinning machinery. The spinning and weaving of woollen cloth and the production of lace and hosiery were common amongst the textile industries in Britain in the early part of the eighteenth century. However, major innovations in textile machinery for spinning yarn, culminating in spinning mules of over

Figure 17.5 Engine house, Cornwall.
Source: Kate Clark

1,000 spindles, revolutionized the scale of yarn production. Weaving remained hand operated, often in association with spinning mills, until the development of an effective power
loom in the early nineteenth century. It was the displacement of once highly skilled hand-
loom workers that generated the Luddite machine smashing, exacerbated by the depression
following the Napoleonic Wars. Many of these developments applied to cotton, but were
extended to woollen production, hosiery and lace.

   The textile mill buildings provide a graphic illustration of the changing nature of textile
production and stand as one of the most visible reminders of the industrial revolution. Early
production took place in the home, assisted by factors who purchased materials in bulk, and
'put out' work. Large windows on the top storeys of buildings in many small towns, such as
Newtown, Powys, indicate that lofts were used for weaving. The earliest purpose-built mills,
such as Lombe's factory in Derby, were well lit, five storeys high, long and narrow, with line
shafting to carry power from an engine, and lots of repetitive spaces supported by brick or
cast-iron columns. Because they were vulnerable to fire, most of the earliest mills have now
been burnt down or altered almost beyond recognition. Most were simple, brick structures,
and although largely functional, the use of classical detailing such as pediments and clock
towers became common. Such buildings were generally located on streams and thus concentrated in areas where water power was available. In the 1780s a form of fireproof construc-

tion, involving cast-iron beams and shallow brick jack arches, was developed. This was used at Stanley Mill in Gloucestershire, a 'fireproof' woollen mill, where the use of Palladian windows and decorative cast iron also illustrates the architectural pretension of the mill complex.

Steam was applied to spinning in 1785, making possible factory buildings in towns, close to sources of labour and materials. The mill buildings of the Ancoats area in Manchester exemplify the way in which urban areas became transformed by concentrations of multi-storey textile complexes (Miller and Wild 2007; Nevell 2008), although there is plentiful evidence to show that 'out-working' persisted as a mode of operation (by the mid-nine-teenth century only half the textile workers operated in factories). A survey of Yorkshire textile mills places rural water-powered mills in their landscape context and demonstrates the importance of looking at where and how mills were built as well as studying the build-ings themselves (Giles and Goodall 1992).

It is easy to forget that mills were usually only one element in a large industrial complex that might include single-storey weaving sheds, dye houses, engine houses, carding build-ings, offices and a multitude of other small structures needed for the factory's operation. In Manchester and Liverpool, the huge warehouses represent the role of shipping, marketing and distribution in the textile industry (Taylor *et al.* 2002; Giles and Hawkins 2004). At Saltaire in Bradford, West Yorkshire, the mill became part of a social experiment where the mill owner, Titus Salt, built rows of houses for employees, adding a church, hospital, baths and schools. Such structures are usually very vulnerable, and archaeology can play a role in ensuring that the more obvious structures are placed in their context (Hughes 2000).

Building technology

Textile mills are only one of a wide range of new building types that began to appear in the late eighteenth century as a result of industrialization. Some categories were very specific and a direct reflection of the process they housed, such as iron furnaces or gas holders, whilst other build-ings depended upon a vocabulary of features that were designed to provide light, shelter, access, fireproofing and perhaps power for industrial processes. Building technology evolved rapidly, as early building types were found to be unsuitable for industrial processes and often burnt down or were shaken to bits. The introduction of iron to support buildings, fireproofing, and new construction techniques involving the use of concrete and rolled steel, zig-zag north light roofs to bring in more light and the use of steel framing all created extraordinarily innovative buildings. It should not be assumed that all such buildings were purely functional and without pretension. The earliest eighteenth-century factories made use of the Palladian idiom in their deployment of pediments and ornate roofs, and the industrial buildings of the Victorian period – such as the Egyptian-style Temple Mill – illustrate all of the major themes in the architecture of the period. By the early twentieth century, new forms of building materials proliferated, with concrete, aluminium, asbestos, plastics and rubber increasingly transforming the built environ-ment of both workplaces and residential sites (Stratton and Trinder 2000; Cooper 2008).

Workers' housing

Industries depended upon people, and many historians have commented upon the population changes in Britain during the period of industrialization. As the overall population grew, traditional settlement patterns transformed dramatically. In some cases, urban centres rapidly expanded as specific industries came to dominate the region; in others, new forms of residence emerged from the pre-existing agricultural landscape. Thus, the study of industrial housing can provide details on the crucial transformation of domestic life, community networks and residential patterns from the eighteenth century onwards.

Prior to the development of mass transport, few people lived far from their place of work, and most industrial areas are characterized by workers' housing. Early urban dwellings seem to have been small, single-storey cottages, perhaps with lofts, built of local materials. Rural industries frequently adapted their housing stock from pre-existing agricultural structures (Casella and Croucher 2010). Some were self-built by workers who squatted on former common or waste land; others were thrown up by speculators or investors, including the companies themselves (Hughes 2000; Nevell 2008). By the nineteenth century, the terrace house came to characterize industrial housing, with a variety of internal layouts developed in response to increasing regulation over urban planning (Newman and Newman 2008). A study of workers' housing in West Yorkshire uses surviving buildings to show these different building processes at work, illustrating how the unbridled and chaotic development of industrial housing influenced the utopian designs of reformers such as Salt and the later council-built housing of the twentieth century (Caffyn 1986).

Uncontrolled development and overcrowding, particularly in towns, soon led to health problems such as the great cholera epidemics of the mid-nineteenth century. Reform was slow, but did come eventually in the form of national legislation and planning regulations to ensure sanitation in towns, and also the provision of services such as gas, water, drains and transport.

Transport

The changing pattern of settlement is intimately bound up with the development of new transport networks in the latter part of the eighteenth century. Canals, roads, railways, ports and harbours were all upgraded in order to cope with increased movement in goods and people. With the communication came new termini and often new towns, such as Swindon, Wiltshire, on the Great Western Railway.

At the end of the seventeenth century, the only really efficient form of transport for bulky industrial goods such as coal was by coastal route and along navigable parts of the river network. Some rivers were made more navigable by the introduction of locks, and a canal was built near Exeter in 1566, but the big boom in canal-building occurred during the late eighteenth century, when, for example, Brindley's canal over the River Irwell in Manchester linked mines with the Mersey. Canal mania developed between 1789 and 1793, resulting in the estuaries of the Thames, Severn, Humber and Mersey being linked, the Pennines traversed and London linked with the Midlands and the north. Nigel Crowe's surveys of the buildings of Britain's canal network demonstrate the variety of structures that were needed to support this enterprise (Crowe 1994).

Ingenious devices were constructed to cope with the differences in height on canals. In many cases, flights of locks were used, but in some cases, inclined planes powered by water or by steam engines lifted boats bodily up and down sloping railway tracks. The Anderton boat lift near Northwich, Cheshire, built in 1865, was a similar device that lifted boats physically, using hydraulic rams and later electricity (Figure 17.6).

Roads were heavily rutted and impassable at many times of the year. Private trusts had been set up to build turnpike roads in the early nineteenth century, but their great period of geographical expansion was between 1750 and 1780. Real improvements came only after the introduction of new techniques for road construction – the use of tar and crushed stones and Telford's road improvements (Cooper 2008). Today mileposts, toll-houses and the occasional buried surface encountered during road improvement are reminders of the turnpiking process.

Wooden railways had been in use since the early seventeenth century for transporting coal. In 1767, iron rails were adopted, laid on top of wooden frameworks, and were themselves superseded by 'L'-shaped tracks from the 1780s. Horse-drawn tramways were built extensively well into the 1830s, in association with canals and collieries, and occasionally for public use (Figure 17.7). The earliest experiments in using steam locomotion were undertaken by Richard Trevithick in 1802, but it was only in 1829 with George Stephenson's use of steam that the fortunes of the locomotive began to turn.

Canals, roads and indeed railways all faced the problem of crossing rivers or valleys while remaining level. Bridge and aqueduct technology was another area of innovation during the late eighteenth century, when engineers devised new methods, including the use of cast iron on the first iron bridge at Ironbridge in Shropshire. The history of these and many of the

Figure 17.6
Anderton boat lift, Cheshire.
Source: Kate Clark

Figure 17.7 Reconstruction of a coal wagon on a wooden wagon way, Causey, Durham.
Source: Kate Clark

other great iron structures tends to be dominated by the great engineers who built them: John Rennie (1761–1821), Thomas Telford (1757–1834) and John Smeaton (1724–92). However, it is important to remember the role of the firms they worked with: William Hazeldine, the Coalbrookdale Company and, in the nineteenth century, the Butterley Company and others whose day-to-day experience in using cast iron was likely to have been equally important in creating practical designs.

Agriculture

Two major changes transformed the agricultural landscape between the middle of the eighteenth century and the end of the nineteenth century. The first was the process of enclosure of the former open fields as a result of privately sponsored parliamentary Acts (placed in the wider context of rural changes in the previous chapter); the second was the industrialization of agriculture itself. Both are clearly visible in the archaeological record. The increased productivity of the land was needed to feed the growing industrial populations.

In the late eighteenth century, consolidated holdings and capital investment, as well as an interest in improving farming, seem to have resulted in fine model farms. This was particularly the case in Scotland, where sweeping changes after the Jacobite rising of 1745 and the systematic enclosure by large estates led to a programme of farm improvement. George Meikle, from East Lothian, experimented with applying horse power to threshing; steam was introduced early in areas such as East Lothian and Yorkshire where coal was cheap.

One way of increasing productivity was through the application of fertilizer, and much of the industrial archaeology of agriculture can be seen to relate to fertilizer production and distribution. Lime was very important as a source of fertilizer, and the kilns at Calke Abbey, Derbyshire, illustrate the importance of lime as part of the workings of a large estate. During the 1850s, a boom in agricultural prices and new research into the science of farming created an optimism that is translated in some extraordinary groups of buildings. Cattle were brought in and fed for much of the year on new feed compounds, their manure collected and taken to the fields. At Leighton, Powys, during the 1850s, John Naylor erected cattle sheds, circular piggeries, a root house, engine houses and other buildings. Manure was collected from the stockhouses, mixed with bone meal ground on the site, and pumped up to an enormous slurry tank where it was then fed on to the fields. There was a funicular railway, a decorative poultry house, a saw mill, gas works and brickworks and a broad-gauge railway taking ricks directly into the huge barn (Figure 17.8). Archaeological investigation shows the way in which the systems were designed to work together on the steep hillside, and also suggests that the scheme was very short-lived (Wade Martins 1991).

The elaborate tramways of the Brecon Beacons also relate to this period of high agricultural optimism. Archaeological survey has shown how a network was originally constructed to bring lime to the uplands as part of a large scheme of agricultural development. Nonetheless, the enterprise failed, and the tramways were subsequently adapted in order to serve the industrial areas of the Swansea valley (Hughes 2000).

Consumer goods

Probate inventories, compiled when people died, were lists of possessions that are often used by historians to explore changes in material culture. Archaeology, however, can also provide

Figure 17.8 The great barn at Leighton, Powys, constructed in the 1850s and designed so that hay ricks could be brought in on a broad-gauge railway.
Source: Kate Clark

Figure 17.9 Kilns at Gladstone Pottery Museum, Stoke-on-Trent.
Source: Kate Clark

an alternative source of information for how people lived, and the influence of consumer goods within industrial households offers a necessary material direction for this scholarship (Casella and Croucher 2009; Beauchamp and Unwin 2002; Trinder 1993). Eighteenth- and nineteenth-century ceramics, for example, are often the subject of research by collectors and art historians, anxious to establish firm attributions for individual pieces. The archaeological study of ceramics for the industrial period, however, has concentrated much more on methods of production (Barker 1991) (Figure 17.9) – there have, for example, been many excavations of kilns in major ceramic-producing areas such as Stoke-on-Trent in the Midlands. Only recently have traditional excavation reports begun to deal seriously with post-eighteenth-century ceramics (Figure 17.10).

The production of tin-glazed wares, stonewares and domestic earthenwares was established in Britain by the end of the seventeenth century (Barker and Majewski 2006). Pottery production was transformed, however, in the latter half of the eighteenth century, when the new fashions for drinking tea, coffee and chocolate were being initially satisfied by the importation of blue and white porcelains from China. Local manufacturers were desperate to recreate these and started making white stonewares with incised blue decoration. Firms in Worcester, and later at Caughley and Coalport in Shropshire, in Liverpool and in Nantgarw, Gwent, experimented with, and finally succeeded in making, hard- and soft-paste porcelains

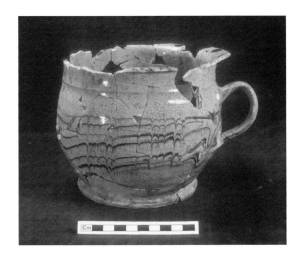

Figure 17.10 Slip-glazed chamber-pot: an example of the ordinary domestic ceramics that became important in the second half of the eighteenth century.
Source: Kate Clark

in Britain, applying hand-painted and later transfer-printed blue designs in imitation of the Chinese wares. These were, however, specialist wares. The first successful mass production of ceramics was undertaken by Josiah Wedgwood, who developed and patented a cream-coloured earthenware that was cheap to produce and could be coloured. 'Queensware', as it was called, was successfully marketed throughout Britain, and the predominance of creamwares in archaeological assemblages throughout the parts of the world with which Britain had trading contacts is particularly notable.

INDUSTRIAL AND HISTORICAL ARCHAEOLOGY

In compiling this brief survey, it has not always been easy to show how distinctively archaeology is contributing to our understanding of the period. The problem is not lack of application – much hard work has been done in the field and in the library, and many good inventories compiled – but one of defining how archaeology might best be utilized and which approaches should be taken.

The theoretical basis for the archaeology of the past two centuries is much better developed in countries outside Britain such as the United States of America, South Africa, Canada and Australia, where it has long been recognized that the study of historical industries requires an appreciation of socially oriented questions of labour relations, settlement patterns, technological diffusion, colonial innovation, production and consumption, power and status and social identities. In such countries, industrial archaeology is frequently approached as a sub-focus within the broader field of historical archaeology.

It is to these overseas contexts that the archaeologist interested in the material culture of the eighteenth and nineteenth century – in those mass-produced consumer goods manufactured and distributed through British industrialization – should turn, because within this literature sequences of artefacts tend to be better published and better dated. More recent American studies are dominated by themes such as consumer behaviour, ethnicity, gender roles, labour relations and urbanization, and it is argued, for example, that struggles between different groups in society, be they women and men, slaves and planters, capitalists and workers, may all be communicated through the use of pottery, glass bottles or metal food containers, through town planning or through the basic design of buildings. In an age that has seen a new fascination with the impact of information technology, the relationship between people and technology, or the way in which innovations are adopted, has also gained a new relevance.

The other factor that has shaped industrial archaeology has been the need to consider, rank, research, defend and care for industrial monuments as part of the wider spectrum of heritage conservation. Within Europe, major conservation initiatives in France, Ireland and in the Ruhr in Germany have generated a renewed interest in the remains of the period; in Britain, the systematic surveys of English Heritage's Monuments Protection Programme have greatly enhanced our understanding of the range of sites that remain. Perhaps the emphasis on the 'industrial' aspects of historical archaeology is particularly strong in Britain because, as Cossons argues, it was an epoch when Britain 'for a brief period of perhaps five generations, held the centre of the world stage as the first industrial nation, birthplace of the Industrial Revolution' (1987, 10).

The subject matter for industrial archaeology is vast, and the contribution of archaeology is limited only by the number of archaeologists who are prepared to tackle it. The impact of the new technologies of the nineteenth and twentieth centuries has barely been touched upon. Emerging topics of interest include the rise of the leisure industry (see Chapter 18), the role of British technological innovations and manufactured goods within the colonial world and the impact of recent deindustrialization on Britain's heritage landscape. Yet if archaeologists are to make an impact on the understanding of the history of the past two centuries, two things are vital: firstly that we go beyond catalogues and begin to interpret our evidence; and secondly that we are more rigorous about our archaeological methods and have the courage to be more openly critical of our own data.

Key texts

Barker, D. and Cranstone, D., 2004. *The archaeology of industrialization*. Leeds: Maney Publishing.

Casella, E.C. and Symonds, J., 2005. *Industrial archaeology: future directions*. New York: Springer.

Gwyn, D. and Palmer, M., 2005. 'Understanding the workplace: a research framework for industrial archaeology in Britain', *Industrial Archaeology Review* 27.1, 5–183.

Palmer, M. and Neaverson, P., 1998. *Industrial archaeology: principles and practice*. London: Routledge.

Trinder, B., 1994. *The Blackwell encyclopedia of industrial archaeology*. Oxford: Blackwell.

Bibliography

Alfrey, J. and Clark, C., 1993. *The landscape of industry. Patterns of change in the Ironbridge Gorge*. London: Routledge.

Barker, D., 1991. *Potworks: the industrial architecture of the Staffordshire potteries*. London: RCHME.

Barker, D. and Majewski, T., 2006. 'Ceramic studies in historical archaeology', in Hicks, D. and Beaudry, M. (eds) *The Cambridge companion to historical archaeology*. Cambridge: Cambridge University Press, 205–31.

Beauchamp, V. and Unwin, J., 2002. *The historical archaeology of the Sheffield cutlery and tableware industry, 1750–1900*. Sheffield: ARCUS.

Casella, E.C. and Croucher, S., 2009. *The Alderley Sandhills Project: an archaeology of community life in (post)industrial England*. Manchester: Manchester University Press.

Caffyn, L., 1986. *Workers' housing in West Yorkshire 1750–1920*. Wakefield: RCHME and West Yorkshire Metropolitan Council.

Clark, C., 1993. *English Heritage book of the Ironbridge Gorge*. London: Batsford.

Clark, C.M., 1987. 'Trouble at t'mill: industrial archaeology in the 1980s', *Antiquity* 61, 169–79.

Cleere, H.F. and Crossley, D.W., 1985. *The iron industry in the Weald*. Leicester: Leicester University Press.

Cooper, T., 2008. *Laying the foundations: a history and archaeology of the Trent Valley sand and gravel industry*. York: Council for British Archaeology Research Report 159.

Cossons, N., 1987. *BP book of industrial archaeology*. Newton Abbott: David and Charles (3 edn 1996).

Crowe, N., 1994. *The English Heritage book of canals*. London: Batsford.

Falconer, K., 1980. *Guide to England's industrial heritage*. London: Batsford.

Giles, C. and Goodall, I.H., 1992. *Yorkshire textile mills 1770–1930*. London: RCHME.

Giles, C. and Hawkins, B., 2004. *Storehouses of empire: Liverpool's historic warehouses*. London: English Heritage.

Hobsbawm, E., 1999. *Industry and empire: the birth of the industrial revolution*. New York: The New Press.

Hudson, P., 1992. *The industrial revolution*. London: Edward Arnold.

Hughes, S., 2000. *Copperopolis: landscapes of the early industrial period in Swansea*. Aberystwyth: RCAHMW.

Miller, I. and Wild, C., 2007. *A & G Murray and the cotton mills of Ancoats*. Lancaster: Oxford Archaeology North Lancaster Imprints 13.

Nevell, M., 2008. *Manchester: the hidden history*. Stroud: The History Press.

Newman, C. and Newman, R., 2008. 'Housing the workforce in 19th-century east Lancashire: past processes, enduring perceptions and contemporary meanings', *Post-Medieval Archaeology* 42.1, 181–200.

Rynne, C., 2006. *Industrial Ireland, 1750–1930: an archaeology*. Wilton: The Collins Press.

Stratton, M., 1994. *Ironbridge and the electric revolution*. London: John Murray.

Stratton, M. and Trinder, B., 2000. *Twentieth century industrial archaeology*. London: E. & F.N. Spon.

Taylor, S., Cooper, M. and Barnwell, P.S., 2002. *Manchester: the warehouse legacy*. London: English Heritage.

Trinder, B., 1987. *The making of the industrial landscape*. Stroud: Alan Sutton.

Trinder, B., 1993. 'The archaeology of the British food industry 1660–1966: a preliminary survey', *Industrial Archaeology Review* 15.2, 119–39.

Wade Martins, S., 1991. *Historic farm buildings*. London: Batsford.

18

THE MODERN AGE

John Schofield
(English Heritage)

SETTING THE SCENE

There is a fascination for me in the archaeology of the modern age (or the 'supermodern', Gonzalez-Ruibal 2008): a direct connection to my life and those of others I know; there is a strong sense of ownership and belonging and of the familiar. By definition the deeper past is a long way from such personal experiences and memory. It is still important that we understand this deeper past, how it shaped us as a society and as individuals within it, and how in the past we responded to challenges such as climate change and food shortages. But for me the modern age has greater interest and appeal. It is where I think the value of archaeology to society can be most keenly felt.

I was introduced to modern material culture as a prehistorian, studying the deeper past at a time when Binford's (e.g. 1983) and other ethnographers' writings were in vogue. I was encouraged in a forward-thinking department to recognize the value and merit of studying the recent past, something that didn't always sit comfortably in an academe where traditional views of archaeology were prevalent. Personally I was enthralled by the idea of archaeologists studying places that remained in occupation, and where one could watch people occupying and using a space, talk with them about it and record the material remains they left behind. Anthropology and ethnography were thus drawn into an explicitly archaeological context, the difference between this and other ethnographic lines of enquiry being one of emphasis and outcome. This was 'ethnoarchaeology': studying the modern world for what it might teach us about human behaviour of the deeper past. The difference now is that we study modern material culture for what it can tell us about ourselves: as a critique of modern life (Graves-Brown 2000), something that challenges certain 'taken for granteds' of the modern world (Buchli and Lucas 2001a). Perhaps it is this connection with ethnoarchaeology that explains why so many archaeologists initially specialized in earlier prehistoric periods before switching or extending to the modern.

In this overview of twentieth- and twenty-first-century (hereafter referred to as 'contemporary') archaeology in Britain I begin by considering why the chapter has been called for now, but was not included in the first edition. I describe some of the methods used in archaeological projects that explore the contemporary world. The main part of the chapter then provides a rapid overview, describing Britain's contemporary archaeology under the headings of various categories of landscape. These headings represent the highest point of a hierarchical scheme that lists these activities before dividing them into monument, landscape and building types. It represents the beginnings of a thesaurus, if such is a useful way to think about and compartmentalize the considerable range and diversity of contemporary archaeology.

CHANGING PERCEPTIONS

Archaeologists study the past, and convention dictates that the deeper past should be our focus, our *raison d'être*. So when, and how, did we find it acceptable to extend our interest into the modern period, a period which arguably holds greater relevance in other disciplines such as social anthropology, history, architectural history and cultural geography? Why, as archaeologists, do we need to get involved, and why now?

It seems that archaeologists entering new territory will examine it in a very particular way. Whether it is the early days of Roman or medieval archaeology, post-medieval or modern, attention typically focuses first on its military remains, before extending to religious sites and architecture for earlier periods and industrial legacies for later ones, then 'big' monuments and finally the more mundane and ordinary things. And this is exactly how it was for the twentieth century, with attention focused firmly at first on military remains, including English Heritage's Monuments Protection and Thematic Listing Programmes of the 1990s (Dobinson *et al.* 1997; Cocroft and Thomas 2003; Schofield 2009b; see Dobinson 2001 for an example of the thematic studies undertaken).

But conscious that we tend always to begin with military and industrial before extending into other areas of life, English Heritage and others now also pay close attention to 'the rest'. There are two contexts to this: one philosophical and one methodological, though these are closely connected. The philosophical point relates to the broader view of archaeology and the extended scope and breadth of enquiry amongst archaeologists. If one follows Ian Hodder's view that archaeology has extended its reach from 'the study of the past through its material remains' several decades ago to a more contemporary view of archaeology as 'a mode of enquiry into the relationship between people and their material pasts' (2003, 2), then embracing modern material culture alongside earlier remains becomes perfectly reasonable and justifiable. Some say (presumably implying criticism) that it is hard now to distinguish archaeological projects on the contemporary past from those that have a basis in anthropology or cultural geography. Funding bodies and councils often ask in which disciplinary category applicants wish their applications for research funding to be considered, and it may be that some of my own applications have suffered from my insistence that the basis is archaeology. I feel quite strongly about this. Whatever the methods I intend using, and whatever the material culture I will investigate, material culture is always central to my research. This alone should render the study primarily an archaeological one. There is also the argument that I am an archaeologist, so my work is archaeo*logical*, inevitably. English Heritage's activities, alongside those of other agencies, trusts and local authorities, raise some of the same issues, but are archaeological for the same reasons. As archaeologists we are interested in the physical traces of human activity, and that, typically, is where our enquiries begin, just as they do for sites and landscapes of earlier date. The difference is that in prehistory the physical remains are the only source; for the modern they are one of many. But the physical remains still represent our starting point.

The methodological point concerns a new approach to this material evidence and the benefits of a broader view: landscape characterization. Rather than focus only on particular types of places (e.g. military, industrial or religious sites) historic landscape characterization (HLC) takes as its material evidence the entire landscape – everything that we see in the landscape today. HLC will examine green lanes and fields as they exist now but representing boundaries that are millennia old. The view therefore is predominantly one of the *modern* landscape, and to my eyes at least it is an archaeological view that I am seeing. I deliberately personalize this point, as the reading of landscape is personal and will be conditioned by who we are, where we come from and what we know. As the European Landscape Convention (2008) usefully puts it: '"Landscape" means an area, as perceived by people, whose character is the result of the action and interaction of natural and/or human factors.'

Everyone's view of landscape will be different and everyone's view should count. In today's increasingly democratic and participatory world, this is important, and it is why contemporary archaeology can have particular importance to people. Many people will not take much interest in a Bronze Age burial mound preserved by the state for their benefit, but an old factory where they or their father used to work, or a working men's club now closed, or a shop, a music venue, or a pub, a school or one's former home – these places often will matter, a lot. In my view these types of places are archaeological, in the sense that they consist of material remains which can lend themselves to archaeological enquiry. I have spent time in countries where a '50-year rule' prevents anything younger than 50 years old being considered as heritage or as archaeological. Thank goodness no such rule exists in Britain. It ensures that much valuable and interesting work can take place, and that – where necessary or appropriate, and often amidst great controversy – modern buildings and places can be afforded statutory protection, whether the cruise missile shelters at Greenham Common, post-war prefab housing or iconic architecture. Many twentieth-century sites are also now included routinely on local authority historic environment records. This too is important. The past was not discontinuous in time or space. The past remains with us, and we continue to create, curate and reshape it in our everyday lives and social practices. This chapter will reflect the complexity of this relationship. But we begin with working methods. How do we 'do' contemporary archaeology? Is it any different from doing the archaeology of earlier periods?

WORKING METHODS

Hardly anyone, if anyone at all, in fact, has been trained specifically in contemporary archaeology, those of us now 'specializing' in this area having come to it from earlier periods, typically from studies in prehistory. Yet many practitioners have embraced this modern archaeology with great enthusiasm and alacrity. Whether they work for agencies, local authorities
or commercial units, many people have discovered the archaeology of the modern age and
found it to be a worthwhile and captivating endeavour. Projects that explore this modern
period are popular, and increasingly so, it seems. Here I review briefly some of the methods
for investigating archaeological sites, artefacts and landscapes of the modern age, asking the
question: is this archaeology of the very recent past so different from that of earlier periods?
Is it simply a matter of transferring skills from the more familiar grounds of the deeper past?
I believe that to large extent it is, though recognizing the heightened degree to which our
diverse cultural backgrounds will influence the way we think about and interpret material
remains that are often very familiar. Here I refer only to artefact study and archaeological
survey, as well as commenting briefly on documents and oral historical sources.

Let us begin with artefacts. As has already been suggested, the types and categories of artefacts that exist today are broadly the same as they have always been: there is a predominance of
domestic assemblages and the traces of industry, religious activity and militarism, for example.
But there is also commercial activity and leisure and pleasure, making modern assemblages
more diverse than those of earlier periods. Equally, we now have a more wasteful society and
of course a consumer society. We love to shop, and ultimately we throw away much of what
we buy. In very recent years recycling has become important and popular, first through charity
shops and the second-hand market, then car boot sales and now the Internet and eBay. But
nevertheless, much still gets discarded for archaeologists now and in the future.

Studying these artefacts can be fascinating. Taking a biographical view of almost any
modern object can draw out a life history of extraordinary scale and complexity. This situation is represented in the parts and objects from a Ford Transit van excavated in 2006. Maps
showing the points of origin and destiny of van parts betray certain symmetries (Bailey *et
al*. 2009). These maps centred on Avonmouth (north Somerset) from where shredded raw
materials are exported to the Far East for car manufacture and to which newly manufactured cars are again imported. Avonmouth, like other similar places around the world, is a
conduit: a place through which many of our most familiar objects pass and repass.

Identifying artefacts has benefits for site interpretation and dating, even for sites of such
recent date. A Smith's crisp packet recovered from the peace camps at Greenham Common
was dated to 1983 by its advertising of the James Bond film *Octopussy*, released late that year.
The camp at which this item was found opened in 1983 (Schofield 2009a). Often with modern
artefacts it is not scientific analyses that are needed, but simple Internet research ('googling'),
or the identification of items in catalogues and through archives and templates held by the
original manufacturer. Nails and screws, for example, can be tightly defined to type and function, if not approximate date (e.g. Bailey *et al*. 2009), and meaningful analyses can certainly

be conducted for modern and familiar material items, as Shanks and Tilley have demonstrated in their study of British and Swedish beer cans (1992, ch. 8). This study was partly in response to the criticism levelled at many early forays into contemporary archaeology, that such studies had, 'failed to realize the potential of the study of modern material culture as a critical intervention in contemporary society, an intervention with transformative intent' (ibid., 172).

What about the archaeological sites on which these artefacts are found? Are they just as archaeological as Stone Age settlements and Roman forts? Certainly, sites of modern date can be investigated using the same techniques as for earlier periods. Aerial photography has been used, for example, to map and assess Second World War sites as built and as they survive. A study of anti-invasion coastal defences in Suffolk has created elaborate maps displaying the scale and complexity of Britain's coastal defences, constructed to repel enemy invasion in summer 1940 (Hegarty and Newsome 2007; Figure 18.1). Aerial photography is also used to record the changing landscape as it exists today. Many of the images in English Heritage's *Conservation Bulletin: Modern Times* (EH 2007), and in *Images of change* (Penrose 2007) are aerial views, while the popular television series *Britain from above* has succeeded in giving this perspective popular appeal. Indeed aerial photography and the aerial perspective are almost exclusively a twentieth-century construction. Online resources such as live local and Google Earth provide additional possibilities for researching the modern landscape.

Field survey is now applied routinely to modern sites and landscapes (Figure 18.2), with much of English Heritage's work in this area seeking specifically to relate physical remains with their technological and political contexts. There is no reason to suppose that documents always provide an accurate representation of what exists on the ground or of what was originally built. Design drawings will typically portray what was intended. But sometimes what was built was not quite the same; subsequent changes involving removal or alteration create divergence from what is depicted. Furthermore, many sites are not designed at all, but just 'appear'. Examples are the numerous peace camps at Greenham Common (Schofield 2009a), and the protest camp at Nine Ladies stone circle, Derbyshire (below). Within sites one can also see the value of archaeological survey for interpreting artefact distributions. Studies have investigated the depositional phases and actions as well as post-depositional distortion in the back of a Transit van (Bailey *et al.* 2009) (Figure 18.8), the evidence of occupation in an abandoned council flat (Buchli and Lucas 2001b) and the archaeology of artistic genius at Francis Bacon's studio (Cappock 2005) (Figure 18.3).

Many of the same rules apply in the marine environment. Take the example of HMS/m *A1*, the first British-designed and -built submarine used by the Royal Navy. Built by Vickers in 1902 the *A1* sank twice in her career, the first time in 1904 (when all of her crew died) and again in 1911 off Selsey Bill. The site has been inspected, mapped and surveyed using multi-beam technology (Figure 18.4), just as one might survey an earlier wreck. Also, as with other earlier wrecks, the submarine is under threat from unscrupulous divers (see EH 2008).

Photography and film-making are well suited to documenting contemporary sites, buildings and landscapes (e.g. Boulton 2006). Photographic characterization has been completed at the

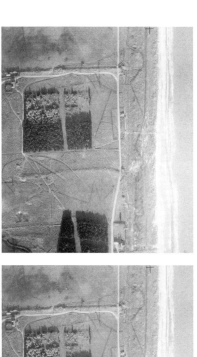
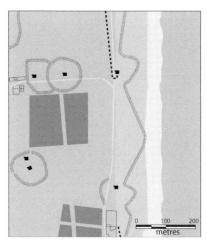
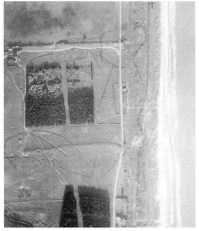
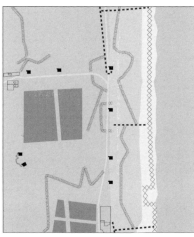

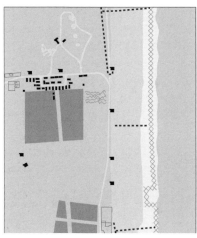

Figure 18.1
Sizewell in Suffolk: 1940 anti-invasion defences, consisting mainly of barbed wire and pillboxes, typified the development of the coastal crust following the German invasion of France (top). By the end of 1941 things have changed (middle). Beach scaffolding now runs along the shore, connecting with new anti-tank cubes. Spaces between new, camouflaged pillboxes are filled with complex interlinking barbed wire entanglements. These defences were maintained until 1944, by which time the threat from Hitler's flying bombs surpassed that of invasion. By November 1944 a diver battery and its camp had been established, remodelling the area's defences to face this new threat (bottom).
Source: after Hegarty and Newsome 2007, 60–2

Figure 18.2 Surveying Cold War structures at Orford Ness, Suffolk.

Source: English Heritage

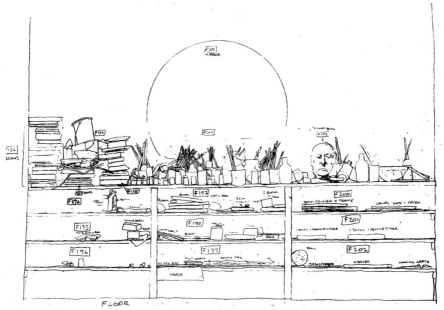

Figure 18.3 The elevation of a bookcase, part of the archaeological survey of Francis Bacon's studio.

Source: copyright Edmond O'Donovan Collection: *Dublin City Gallery, The Hugh Lane*

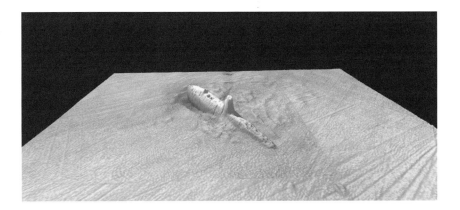

Figure 18.4 Multibeam scan of the *A1* submarine.
      Source: data acquired by ADUS and processed by Wessex Archaeology; image made by Wessex Archaeology

former RAF station at Coltishall (Norfolk). Here the aim was to record the base and its buildings whilst they remained occupied and in use, but also to record the process of draw-down and closure, and ultimately the site in its abandoned state. Hence photographers conversant with historic buildings recording undertook a photographic survey, whilst artists were also invited to create their own record of the changing landscape, unencumbered by the conventions of heritage recording. Similarly, photographic recording has been used to document the Maze prison, Belfast, alongside archaeological studies of the site (McAtackney 2005). The watch-towers of Northern Ireland were similarly recorded prior to decommissioning. Much of this work has been done by artists, who, as I have argued elsewhere (Schofield 2006), can contribute in a helpful and interesting way to our documentation of the contemporary past. Far from being nervous or suspicious of their involvement, we should welcome this particular trans-disciplinary collaboration.

Beyond these similarities, can contemporary archaeology also differ from that of earlier periods in the availability of oral historical sources and the frequency and diversity of documentary records, for example? Is there also a heightened sense of reflexivity, of historiographic perspective – histories of the history, which can be equally enlightening, telling us how events and attitudes were documented and interpreted at different times? Oral historical sources give colour to the often grey architecture of the modern period; they tell us what things were like, again adding detail and personal perspectives to the official records and instructions issued to staff and personnel. Greenham Common has been subject to numerous oral history projects and initiatives. The Imperial War Museum gathered the accounts of peace women present there to oppose cruise missiles in the 1980s and 1990s, while the consultants CgMS obtained further information from former base personnel. The Internet has made the gathering of oral historical information much easier. Often, conventional archaeological methods such as buildings recording are helpfully enhanced by the introduction of social anthropological practices, such as 'bimbling' described by Jon Anderson (2004) as interviews conducted in and through a place, to generate a collage of collaborative knowledge and giving people the opportunity to re-experience their connections with landscape and reminisce, prompting 'other life-course memories associated with that individual's relationship with place' (ibid., 258).

All of these approaches and methods are valid measures for examining the twentieth and twenty-first centuries through their material traces. And in most cases (excepting oral accounts and, to large extent, archives – which feature in some of the examples below) these are just as relevant for the recent as for the deeper past. The precise emphasis may be different, but in essence the approaches are the same for archaeologies of all periods and in all places. Sitting astride all of this is the wider view of landscape, as seen already in applications of online aerial photographic mapping and investigation and HLC, which uses GIS applications to take a wider landscape view. In English Heritage's *Modern Times* (EH 2007) and *Images of change* (Penrose 2007), for example, the ubiquitous 'big sheds' are described as a characteristic of later twentieth-century industrial expansion, alongside motorways and airfields, and post-war suburban development. The wider view recognizes the significance and impact of such places and the degree to which they have become characteristic. These may be ordinary, mundane sorts of places, but that is perhaps what makes them important. These are people's familiar landscapes; the places often representing home, or the homely. Paul Graves-Brown's (2007) study of an out-of-town retail park at Trostre (South Wales) encapsulates this sense of social significance, as well as being a perfectly valid landscape archaeological study. I return to this example below.

Milton Keynes illustrates how HLC and the benefits of GIS enable the broader landscape view to then be 'excavated' into its various layers or phases, as in the physical act of excavating urban stratigraphy. Figure 18.5 highlights the twentieth-century landscape character of Milton Keynes. Surprising here may be the extent of areas where twentieth-century character prevails; but equally maybe those areas where it does not, where the prevailing character is that of an earlier period. In numerous places around Milton Keynes, and in particular in the built-up areas, the well-preserved earthwork remains of medieval settlements and field systems survive, often by virtue of their having been designated as scheduled monuments prior to the main building phase of the new town in the 1970s and 80s. Of course these preserved medieval sites, surrounded by late twentieth-century houses and designed landscapes of retail and leisure, have also now become twentieth-century landscapes of conservation and the desire to protect and preserve for the future. The irony now is that the shopping centre at Milton Keynes has also been designated as a building of special historic interest. Both the old and the new have thus become monuments of (or to) modernity.

LANDSCAPES, SITES AND ASSEMBLAGES

Political landscapes

As we saw earlier, much of the focus on contemporary archaeology began with work on Second World War sites and landscapes. The Defence of Britain Project, much of English Heritage's National Mapping Programme (e.g. Hegarty and Newsome 2007; Figure 18.1), the work of English Heritage survey teams previously part of the Royal Commission on the Historical Monuments of England (RCHME) (e.g. Cocroft and Thomas 2003) and work

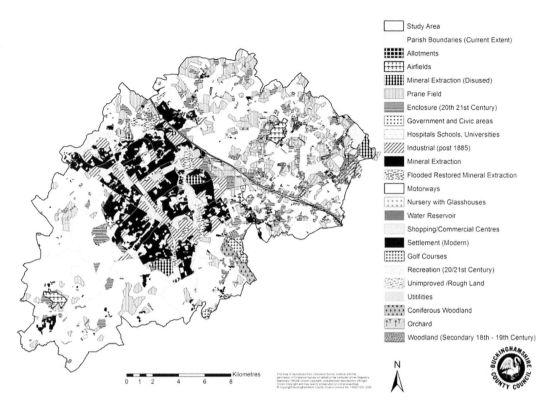

Study Area
Parish Boundaries (Current Extent)
Allotments
Airfields
Mineral Extraction (Disused)
Prarie Field
Enclosure (20th 21st Century)
Government and Civic areas
Hospitals Schools, Universities
Industrial (post 1885)
Mineral Extraction
Flooded Restored Mineral Extraction
Motorways
Nursery with Glasshouses
Water Reservoir
Shopping/Commercial Centres
Settlement (Modern)
Golf Courses
Recreation (20/21st Century)
Unimproved /Rough Land
Utitilities
Coniferous Woodland
Orchard
Woodland (Secondary 18th - 19th Century)

Figure 18.5 Historic Landscape Characterization map showing twentieth-century impact on the Milton Keynes landscape.
Source: Buckinghamshire County Council

commissioned by the Monuments Protection Programme and the Listing Team in 1995–2002 (e.g. Dobinson 2001) provide examples of the potential for different approaches and applications. English Heritage's thematic studies reveal the extent to which a combination of documentary and aerial photographic sources can enhance our understanding of what survives today. Uniquely, given the accuracy of comprehensive documentary records, direct comparison can be made between what remains and what was originally built. We know how rare surviving sites are, despite their comparatively recent date and their structural solidity. For example, some 1,000 heavy anti-aircraft gun sites were built in the Second World War. These were robust and extensive sites, with gun emplacements, radar, domestic accommodation, access roads, etc. Only a very small percentage of these sites survive in a form that is legible to visitors, the majority having been lost through post-war urban expansion (Dobinson 2001). Within this research project, national archives provided information on precisely what was built, where, why and when. A combination of 1946 and modern aerial photographs then enabled a rapid assessment of which documented sites survived, and in what condition. Similar studies have been completed for bombing decoys of the

Second World War, radar sites, prisoner of war camps and coastal batteries, and for sites in Scotland, Wales and Northern Ireland.

For the Cold War, detailed field survey of key sites has provided information on construction, form and layout not currently available in documentary sources. At Spadeadam, Cumbria, for example, the monumental architecture of test stands has been surveyed, a process that was also the subject of artistic intervention (Cocroft and Wilson 2006). The earthwork remains of the beginnings of an excavation for a missile silo were revealed (Figure 18.6). Treasury documents reveal spending for this, but no technical plans or drawings are known to survive. The study also surveyed features associated with the site's construction, such as builders' yards and navvy camps, representing aspects of the history of the Cold War not previously discussed. War art, including signage and graffiti, can also provide information about military sites and culture that is unavailable through other official sources. These paintings and signs provide information on the way space was used and demarcated and its separation into private and public spheres for example. They also illuminate the way art was used to generate *esprit de corps*, simply to improve living conditions and to entertain and enliven (Cocroft *et al.* 2006).

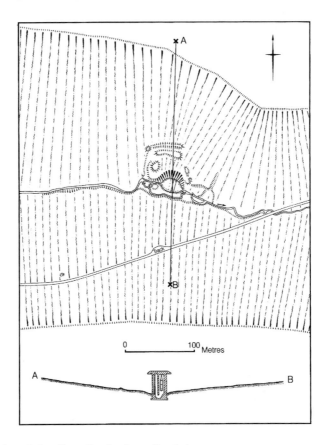

Figure 18.6 Drawing of the silo at Spadeadam, Cumbria.
Source: English Heritage. Drawing by Deborah Cunliffe

Another less monumental form of archaeological site that equates closely with the traditional camp-sites of prehistory are peace and protest camps, increasingly now the subject of archaeological attention. Here, archaeological survey is often the most appropriate form of investigation, with its systematic and detailed recording methods and the reflexivity that often now characterizes archaeological investigations of the contemporary past. Survey has been used to record the Stanton Moor protest camp, established in 1999 within the Peak District National Park to protest (successfully as it turned out) against the proposed reopening of Stanton Lees and Endcliffe quarries under the terms of a 1952 planning permission (Badcock and Johnston 2009). The archaeology of the camp, and the survey conducted by archaeologists reflects the prehistoric archaeology of the local area, including the iconic Nine Ladies stone circle. These components are both equally part of this area's archaeological record, and it is now hard to fully appreciate one without the other. The survey methodology was a conventional one: structures and other camp features were mapped and photographed (Figure 18.7), including houses/benders, tree-houses, tree platforms, aerial rope walkways, defensive structures, signs, washing facilities, latrine pits, artworks and garden plots. Camp residents were asked to annotate copies of the survey with place names in addition to including anecdotes and memories. This is landscape archaeology in its traditional sense, though highly socially relevant, and controversial in the way it challenges conventional views of what would otherwise be a landscape only of prehistoric remains and post-medieval and modern industry. As at Greenham, this is significant also in representing an archaeology of the subaltern, whose visibility is notoriously hard to establish, even for the modern period.

Figure 18.7 Surveying the Stanton Moor protest camp.
Source: Anna Badcock and Bob Johnston, ARCUS

Social landscapes

One of the great impressions on the English landscape over the course of the twentieth century has been the road network and the influence of the motor car. Most people now own one, and people's lives are dominated by the car and the speed at which it can deliver us from A to B, for work, school, shopping and so on. And the physical traces associated with this dramatic transformation are everywhere and are widely studied, often by archaeologists. The production line has been investigated, often at the point at which factories are closed and redeveloped, as the geography of the industry has shifted from its traditional heartland. Between 1986 and 1993 an archaeological survey was undertaken of every one of the c. 1,500 sites in the UK where cars were manufactured. The study revealed the scale and geographical spread of the industry and the character of its archaeological remains (after Collins 2002, 169). Key findings included the fact that the industry was based largely in Greater London and the West Midlands; that 62 firms were making cars before 1900 and 33 continued to do so afterwards; and that 430 new firms entered the industry between 1900 and 1910, and 221 in the 1920s. Of the c. 1,500 sites, 224 had extant remains at the time of the survey. Equally, no two car factories were alike, with each built in response to a unique series of events and circumstances. Even stripped of their production technology, most car-factory buildings retain ample and interpretive evidence of their former use (ibid., 172).

The material culture of the car extends also to roadside and ownership ephemera, garages, trunk roads, often straightened to create lay-bys from former bends, and the cars themselves. Diana Smith (2002) has researched the 'Dodge-tide', a metaphorical play on the idea of a tide that remains static for an unusually long period. In Australia rural watercourses often become sites for the collective disarray of mechanical flotsam, and the Dodge truck is frequently present in these assemblages (ibid., 161). Cars and other mechanical equipment accumulate in Britain, too, on farms as well as on waste ground and urban fallow. And as we have seen, cars (Bailey *et al.* 2009; Stauffer and Bonfanti 2006), like aeroplanes (Morris 2006), can reveal much about their former use (Figure 18.8). Whether we consider them sites, buildings or artefacts seems irrelevant. Their potential to reveal much about the conditions of use, and their users, is immense.

One of the attractions of archaeology of the modern period, and one of the reasons it is often so controversial and challenging, is the close proximity that often exists between our own lives and the places we study. One might almost say it is a unique characteristic of modern archaeology, not shared by archaeological research of earlier periods. In 2005 and 2006 ARCUS was commissioned by Bovis Lend Lease to undertake a programme of archaeological recording at the University of Sheffield's student halls of residence in Endcliffe and Ranmoor. Features of archaeological and historic interest were recorded and a report produced (Dawson and Jessop 2007). At one level, this study detaches itself from the students that occupied the halls of residence, describing Building I (Ranmoor House), for example, as being 'designed by architects Hadfield, Cawkwell and Davidson, and built in 1968. It is of four storeys linked by covered walkways and bridges to the other buildings of Ranmoor

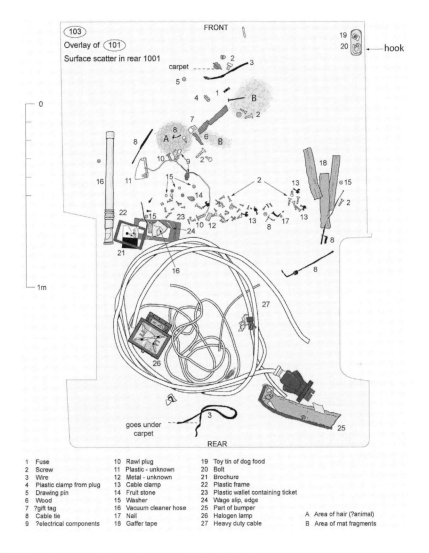

103
Overlay of 101
Surface scatter in rear 1001

FRONT

19
20 ———hook

carpet

goes under
carpet

REAR

1	Fuse	10	Rawl plug	19	Toy tin of dog food	
2	Screw	11	Plastic - unknown	20	Bolt	
3	Wire	12	Metal - unknown	21	Brochure	
4	Plastic clamp from plug	13	Cable clamp	22	Plastic frame	
5	Drawing pin	14	Fruit stone	23	Plastic wallet containing ticket	
6	Wood	15	Washer	24	Wage slip, edge	
7	?gift tag	16	Vacuum cleaner hose	25	Part of bumper	A Area of hair (?animal)
8	Cable tie	17	Nail	26	Halogen lamp	B Area of mat fragments
9	?electrical components	18	Gaffer tape	27	Heavy duty cable	

Figure 18.8 Artefact-spread from the rear of a Ford Transit.
    Source: drawing by Anne Leaver

Hall.' A description of Building II also details the form of construction and the materials used, yet makes specific mention of students' study-bedrooms, which of course represent the hall's *raison d'être*. Photographs include images of the study-bedrooms (e.g. Figure 18.9). Overall the report is a record of the building, completed purely for recording purposes, prior to the site's demolition and under the terms of national planning policy guidance. The report is also implicitly an assessment of the buildings and their cultural significance. An archaeologist involved with this study had been an occupant of Ranmoor when a student at Sheffield. For him there was proximity here and a social significance which gave the study added weight and meaning. Dan Ratcliffe said the following about the project:

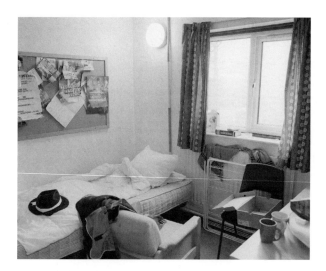

Figure 18.9 Archaeological record of a typical student study-bedroom, Woodvale Flats, University of Sheffield.
Source: Simon Jessop, ARCUS

The strangest thing was taking my children to see where Daddy had lived getting blown up! [http://webcam.cpanel.shef.ac.uk/sorby/] I don't know if they ever recorded my room (F29) although it was informally asked of ARCUS. Nearly all the rooms were the same, although I think the hall tutors may have had en suites.

It was strange as an archaeologist to see somewhere I'd lived be surveyed in this way. It's the ranging rod in the pictures that seems strangest to me – especially in the pictures of the wardens' residences. There is a slightly 'clinical' feel about it which reminds me of 'scenes of crime' officers, or surveillance camera images.

On the other hand it is good to know that there is a record of what was a very transitory, but probably quite significant home to many people as they made the leap to independent living.

So says an archaeologist, commenting on an archaeological survey of a place where he lived while training to become an archaeologist!

This unlikely situation is reminiscent also of 'The office', a rapid archaeological survey of the place where I once worked, and the artefacts and other traces that remained after English Heritage abandoned it in 2005 (Schofield 2008).

Profitable landscapes

One of the more distinctive later twentieth- and twenty-first-century landscapes is the retail park, often on the outskirts of towns and cities and close to major road or motorway junctions. Some, like Cribbs Causeway (Bristol), have taken on the significance almost of shrines, special places in the landscape where people congregate at certain times of the year to participate in the annual rituals of Christmas shopping and the January sales. In the social context of Danny Miller's (1998) seminal study of shopping, Paul Graves-Brown examined the landscape archaeology of the Trostre Park retail centre on the outskirts of Llanelli, South Wales. This the author describes as a landscape/observational study, 'treating the site as if it were an historic or prehistoric landscape' (Graves-Brown 2007, 75). This is a place Graves-Brown likens to a concrete island, surrounded by busy roads, farmland and industry; a focus of consumer activity surrounded by no-man's-land anonymity. It is a place people travel to by road; to reach it on foot is virtually impossible. What is interesting here is the way the plan has been circumvented because of the inconvenience that it has created amongst its visitors. An informal use of space can be seen at Trostre in the form of paths which cut across planted areas. The intention is not so much to confront authority as to circumvent the shortcomings of a planned environment:

> In wishing to get from A to B people appropriate what their environment affords. Normally speaking we tacitly accept the many boundaries and non-spaces that are created in the urban landscape, but when the sanction of these barriers becomes inconvenient we overcome our tendency to conform. (Graves-Brown 2007, 79).

Such places and paths are never formally mapped, but simply 'become'. And it is interesting in a world where so much is planned, and so much is concrete, that the highly ephemeral can often prevail, holding particular value in the society whose subversive actions have created these landscapes in the face of authority.

Another contemporary landscape containing characteristically twentieth-century building types is Swindon, Wiltshire, the archetypal nineteenth-century railway town that has witnessed huge transformation since the Second World War. Until 1960 Swindon was a railway town but experienced drawdown of the industry after the last locomotive was built there. Yet its late twentieth-century legacy has not merely been one of post-industrial decline, as was the case elsewhere, but rather one of urban and industrial renaissance, notably through the production of cars and the electrical and electronics industries. And with an archaeological gaze we can view this on two particular scales: at landscape scale, through the changing shape, size and character of the urban area and sprawl along the M4 corridor; and in the architecture, the particular building types associated with these new industries and the new, post-1960s housing to accommodate workers. The landscape and its material remains were transformed concomitant with the town's fortunes. Swindon is also now home to what is reputedly the largest heritage campus anywhere, with English Heritage, the National Trust and the Steam Museum sharing a reinvigorated landscape of former railway workshops and offices.

Archaeological survey has recently been concluded for the Trent Valley sand and gravel industry, representing a thematic and regional survey of aggregates, arguably the quintessential industry of the twentieth century, which literally shaped the world we now inhabit (Cooper 2008). At landscape scale we see various stages of a process: 'working landscapes' and 'worked-out landscapes', which often then later become 'reclaimed' (one reclamation scheme currently in the news involves a plan to reshape the landscape in the form of a vast reclining female figure). The monuments and sites of the industry occur widely across the region and beyond, relating to preparation, extraction, transportation, processing and use of aggregates. It is extraordinary in the scale of its impact and the diversity of surviving structures. As is often the case with this modern archaeology, there are also interesting relations with more conventional archaeological remains and conservation. The Aggregates Levy Sustainability Fund has for some years funded research where archaeological remains are affected by gravel extraction (including this survey of the industry), and the published review covers examples of this. The relationship between archaeology as traditionally defined and the archaeology of processes that have caused its destruction is an ambiguous one, but fascinating nonetheless and certainly no reason to ignore the archaeology of our own lives and the destructive processes (sometimes even through archaeological practices) that can cause the removal of what came before. Archaeology is concerned primarily with processes of change, after all.

Leisure landscapes

The archaeology of leisure takes in a diversity of activities characteristic of the twentieth and twenty-first centuries. It is concerned with distinctive monument and building types and material culture: the seaside resort, for example, sport and conservation, and includes the creation of national parks for public benefit and enjoyment. Here, though, I will describe briefly an example that combines the material with the immaterial or intangible elements of cultural heritage that also merit the attention of archaeologists studying this modern period: the archaeology of popular culture, and popular music in particular. In 2000 I wrote about this (Schofield 2000), with three case studies intended to demonstrate the range of site types and material culture and their potential for archaeological research: the field archaeology of festival sites, akin almost to medieval fairs; the material culture of musical style-tribes or sub-cultural groups, notably punks and their propensity for reversing meaning, transgressing an object's proper place in society; and then the intangible element, the music itself. My main point here was the degree to which music is representative of the place as well as the people who created it, through lyrics, of course, but also the wider soundscape that is created – the band Joy Division, for example, capturing the essential character of Manchester in the late 1970s, described as the 'alienated, terrible glee of a decayed city' (cited in Cohen 1994, 123). This archaeology incorporates materiality, therefore, but also immateriality, and it is the two elements together with their wider social context that make this relevant and interesting.

An example of the gradual acceptance of this particular archaeology of leisure is English Heritage's National Monuments Record (NMR), a representative inventory of England's cultural heritage, which now increasingly incorporates modern sites, including clubs and other venues for popular music, mainly from the 1950s and 60s. This desk-based project focused initially on London but has expanded to include regional examples in Liverpool associated with The Beatles and Merseybeat. Entries have included the Cavern and the Casbah Club, the latter including murals by individual Beatles, and sites relating to the rare 1960s and 70s phenomenon of Northern Soul including the Wigan Casino. But the main focus has been Soho of the late 1960s. Examples include the seminal mod haunt, the Scene Club (now a car park), the Flamingo, where the all-nighter was pioneered, and La Discothèque, one of the first true discothèques in Britain.

406

A recent study in Liverpool has investigated the city's popular cultural associations, investigating the social context of music-making in the city, documenting what people describe as their influences and how the music created in the city reflects these. But it is also about the places where music is made, produced, performed and sold. The study, by the Institute of Popular Music (University of Liverpool) in association with National Museums Liverpool and English Heritage, examines the city streets where buskers perform for passers-by, the venues large and small where musicians perform for paying audiences and the recording studios and record shops. Asking musicians to produce maps that illustrate the physical extent of their influence has produced some fascinating insight. Young MCs, for example, appear to focus more on neighbourhood (the 'hood') and the cribs (homes) within it; while others draw greater influence from some of the city's landmarks and historic venues (Schofield *et al.* 2010). The main product of music-making (the music itself) is intangible, as increasingly is the medium through which it is distributed and heard (as records and CDs are replaced by downloads); but the physical places – as we saw from the NMR records mentioned above – remain and are increasingly important to the communities for whom Liverpool's diverse musical heritage holds significance, a significance that continues after the places are abandoned but where they remain 'thickly woven into local leisure practices' (Edensor 2005, 50).

CONCLUSIONS

In addition to this rapid overview, this chapter has sought to outline the extent to which archaeology of the twentieth and twenty-first centuries bears close comparison with archaeologies of earlier periods. This contemporary archaeology is not, to my mind, a separate discipline, or even necessarily a sub-discipline, with different ground-rules and emphases, or one which makes use of a different suite of techniques and theoretical frameworks. Of course there are differences in emphasis, and some sources may be more relevant than others. Essentially, though, it is the same thing. The issues are different, it is (arguably) a more familiar past that we are investigating, and there will certainly be close personal connections to what we do. But because we are interested primarily in material culture, and material culture specifically in the pursuit of understanding, it is archaeology that this chapter describes.

When I was approached to write this chapter, the focus was intended to be militarism. But as I have become more involved with investigating the application of archaeology to the twentieth and twenty-first centuries I have increasingly realized just how unhelpful the division is, between 'military' or 'militarism' and 'everything else'. Just as one cannot really separate out 'warfare' from 'social context' in prehistory, one cannot, or should not, introduce similar boundaries if an overview of the modern period is to have coherence or unity. I have used subheadings here to divide 'politics', 'social', 'profit' and 'leisure', but I hope that in these examples the connections between these thematic areas are obvious to the reader. Military archaeology, alongside industrial archaeology, has set us on the path of using archaeological approaches to investigate the twentieth and twenty-first centuries. But now, at the time of writing, the breadth of contemporary archaeology has expanded hugely, and it is appropriate therefore to provide a broader view.

Some purists may not like the idea that the examples presented here are archaeological. But that, for me, is their loss. Originally a prehistorian, I have never been so challenged, so enlightened and so fascinated as I am in this area of work. To question the validity of archaeological research on the basis that we know it all already, from other sources, seems unhelpful. While to simply say 'it is too recent' is equally nonsensical. What some consider 'familiar' is actually perhaps the least familiar of all the periods we study. The archaeology of the twentieth and twenty-first centuries is diverse, broad, revealing and above all has the potential to hold a relevance to society that simply does not exist for earlier periods. That does not mean that archaeology of earlier periods is not socially relevant – it is, for all sorts of reasons. It is just that the archaeology of the twentieth and twenty-first centuries has the potential to serve society in new and helpful ways, especially in difficult times, when people increasingly value the closely familiar things and places around them; that is why, with knife crime, credit crunch and oil crises on our minds, the lure of the local, and of the familiar past, is rapidly gaining acceptance.

Key texts

Buchli, V. and Lucas, G. (eds) 2001a. *Archaeologies of the contemporary past*. London and New York: Routledge.
Cocroft, W.D. and Thomas, R.J.C., 2003. *Cold War: building for nuclear confrontation, 1946–1989*. London: English Heritage.
Graves-Brown, P. (ed) 2000. *Matter, materiality and modern culture*. London: Routledge.
Penrose, S., with contributors, 2007. *Images of change: an archaeology of England's contemporary landscape*. Swindon: English Heritage.
Schofield, J., 2009b. *Aftermath: readings in the archaeology of recent conflict*. New York: Springer.

Bibliography

Anderson, J., 2004. 'Talking whilst walking: a geographical archaeology of knowledge', *Area* 36.3, 254–61.
Badcock, A. and Johnston, R., 2009. Placemaking through protest: an archaeology of the Lees Cross and Endcliffe Protest Camp, Derbyshire, England. *Archaeologies* 5 (2), 306-322.
Bailey, G., Newland, C., Nilsson, A. and Schofield, J., 2009. 'Transit, transition: Excavating J641 VUJ', *Cambridge Archaeological Journal* 19, 1–27.
Binford, L.R., 1983. *In pursuit of the past: decoding the archaeological record*. London: Thames and Hudson.
Boulton, A., 2006. 'Film making and photography as record and interpretation', in Schofield, J., Klausmeier, A. and Purbrick, L. (eds) *Re-mapping the field: new approaches in conflict archaeology*. Berlin: Westkreuz-Verlag, 35–8.
Buchli, V. and Lucas, G., 2001b. 'The archaeology of alienation: a late twentieth-century British council house', in Buchli and Lucas (eds), 158–67.
Cappock, M., 2005. *Francis Bacon's studio*. London and New York: Merrell.
Cocroft, W.D. and Wilson, L.K., 2006. 'Archaeology and art at Spadeadam Rocket Establishment (Cumbria)', in Schofield, J., Klausmeier, A. and Purbrick, L. (eds) *Re-mapping the field: new approaches in conflict archaeology*. Berlin: Westkreuz-Verlag, 15–21.
Cocroft, W.D., Devlin, D., Schofield, J. and Thomas, R.J.C., 2006. *War art: murals and graffiti – military life, power and subversion*. York: Council for British Archaeology.

Cohen, S., 1994. 'Identity, place and the "Liverpool sound"', in Stokes, M. (ed.) *Ethnicity, identity and music: the musical construction of place*. Oxford and Providence, RI: Berg, 117–34.

Collins, P., 2002. 'British car factories since 1896 – lessons learned from the first complete survey of the remains of a 20th century industry in the United Kingdom', in Jones, D. (ed) *20th century heritage: our recent cultural legacy. Proceedings of the Australia ICOMOS national conference 2001*. Adelaide: School of Architecture, Landscape Architecture & Urban Design, University of Adelaide; Burwood, Vic.: Australia ICOMOS Secretariat, 166–75.

Cooper, T., 2008. *Laying the foundations: a history and archaeology of the Trent Valley sand and gravel industry*. York: Council for British Archaeology Research Report 159.

Dawson, L. and Jessop, O., 2007. *Archaeological building recording of student residences, Fulwood Road, Endcliffe Crescent, Endcliffe Vale Road and Oakholme Road, Sheffield, South Yorkshire*. Sheffield: ARCUS, University of Sheffield. Unpublished report.

Dobinson, C., 2001. *AA command: Britain's anti-aircraft defences of the Second World War*. London: Methuen.

Dobinson, C., Lake, J. and Schofield, J., 1997. 'Monuments of war: defining England's 20th-century defence heritage', *Antiquity* 71, 288–99.

Edensor, T., 2005. *Industrial ruins: space, aesthetics and materiality*. Oxford and New York: Berg.

EH (= English Heritage), 2007. *Conservation Bulletin: Modern Times* 56.

EH, 2008. 'HMS/m *A1*', available online at www.english-heritage.org.uk/server/show/conWebDoc.7475 (accessed 3 November 2008).

European Landscape Convention, 2008 [2000]. 'European Landscape Convention: An extract', in Fairclough, G., Harrison, R., Jameson, Jr., J. and Schofield, J. (eds) *The heritage reader*. London: Routledge, 405–7.

Gonzalez-Ruibal, A., 2008. 'Time to destroy: an archaeology of supermodernity', *Current Anthropology* 49.2, 247–79.

Graves-Brown, P., 2007. 'Concrete islands', in McAtackney, L., Palus, M. and Piccini, A. (eds) *Contemporary and historical archaeology in theory: papers from the 2003 and 2004 CHAT conferences*. Oxford: Archaeopress BAR International Series 1677, 75–81.

Hegarty, C. and Newsome, S., 2007. *Suffolk's defended shore: coastal fortifications from the air*. Swindon: English Heritage.

Hodder, I., 2003. *Archaeology beyond dialogue*. Salt Lake City: University of Utah Press.

McAtackney, L., 2005. 'Long Kesh/Maze: an archaeological opportunity', *British Archaeology* 84, 10–15.

Miller, D., 1998. *A theory of shopping*. Ithaca, NY: Cornell University Press.

Morris, D., 2006. *Corsair KD431: the time-capsule fighter*. London: The History Press Ltd.

Schofield, J., 2000. 'Never mind the relevance: popular culture for archaeologists', in Graves-Brown (ed), 131–55.

Schofield, J., 2006. *Constructing place: when artists and archaeologists meet*. ebook published by Proboscis, available online at http://diffusion.org.uk/?tag=art. Also in Shofield 2009 b.

Schofield, J., 2008. 'The office: heritage and archaeology at Fortress House', *British Archaeology* 100, 58–64.

Schofield, J., 2009a. 'Peace site: an archaeology of protest at Greenham Common', *British Archaeology* 104, 44–9.

Schofield, J., Kiddey, R. and Lashua, B., 2010. 'People and landscape', in Carman, J., McDavid, C. and Skeates, R. (eds) *The Oxford companion to public archaeology*. Oxford: Oxford University Press.

Shanks. M. and Tilley, C., 1992. *Re-constructing archaeology: theory and practice*. London: Routledge. 2 edn.

Smith, D., 2002. 'Dodge-tide: a rusting rural legacy', in Jones, D. (ed) *20th century heritage: our recent cultural legacy. Proceedings of the Australia ICOMOS national conference 2001*. Adelaide: School of Architecture, Landscape Architecture & Urban Design, University of Adelaide; Burwood, Vic.: Australia ICOMOS Secretariat, 161–5.

Stauffer, E. and Bonfanti, M., 2006. *Forensic investigation of stolen-recovered and other crime-related vehicles*. London: Academic Press.

19

REELING IN THE YEARS

The past in the present

Timothy Darvill

INTRODUCTION

Fragments of the past are all around us, components of our modern world that, by chance or design, have survived to become part of the fabric of everyday life and provide a historic dimension to our environment. As earlier chapters in this book illustrate, archaeological remains provide the raw materials from which each successive generation of archaeologists constructs an understanding of the past; but archaeological remains are much more than this. Britain is an old country that has been continuously occupied for over 10,000 years. Thousands of archaeological sites in Britain are still in use, in some cases perpetuating the purposes for which they were originally built. Ancient churches are probably the most obvious and widespread examples, but they head a long list that also includes houses, mills, bridges, roads, tracks and many kinds of boundary. Tens of thousands of sites have fallen out of use yet remain to be seen in the countryside, in villages and in towns (Darvill 1987), and every day archaeological remains are brought back into the light of day after hundreds or thousands of years of lying hidden or forgotten in the ground.

Archaeological remains are real things that can be seen, encountered, experienced, explored, touched and engaged with in all sorts of ways (Figure 19.1). Yet the historic environment as a whole is wider still and harder to pin down. It is the habitat that people have created for themselves through conflict and co-operation over thousands of years; the product of human interaction with nature; something we inhabit both physically and imaginatively; our experiences based on the emotional and aesthetic responses triggered by participation, engagement, memory, history and association with our tangible and intangible heritage (English Heritage 2000). Because of this, the historic environment has a contemporary social context that gives it political, economic and ideological meanings, while at the same time making it susceptible to control, manipulation and negotiation.

Figure 19.1 Ancient monuments in the countryside: a Bronze Age round barrow cemetery on King Barrow Ridge, Amesbury, Wiltshire.
Source: Timothy Darvill

This chapter considers how archaeological strands within the historic environment are treated in Britain today, especially in relation to the social context and competing demands placed upon the material itself. The philosophies, theoretical perspectives, practices and professional skills discussed here are collectively known as archaeological resource management.

BACKGROUND

Archaeological resource management is a relatively new branch of archaeology (Harrison 1994; Hunter and Ralston 2006), although its roots penetrate deep into the history of the discipline as a whole. As long ago as AD 1533, Henry VIII appointed John Leland as the first, and as it turned out only, 'King's Antiquary'. He was commissioned to search England and Wales for surviving antiquities and monuments, which he did between 1534 and 1543, although he never published the results. Leland died insane in 1552, but the idea of cataloguing, recording and trying to preserve archaeological remains endured. In the seventeenth, eighteenth and nineteenth centuries, interest in the preservation and care of monuments can be glimpsed in the writings of antiquaries such as William Camden (1561–1623), John Aubrey (1626–97), William Stukeley (1687–1765) and James Douglas (1753–1819). All, however, were operating in the intellectual traditions of the Age of Enlightenment and the political climate of conservatism. It was not until the scientific revolution, positivist thinking and Liberal political reforms of the late nineteenth century that things started to change.

In 1870, John Lubbock, later Lord Avebury, introduced into parliament a Bill that later became the first piece of ancient monuments legislation, the Ancient Monuments Protection

Act 1882. Although limited in its coverage and powers, it established precedents for state control over the destiny of important archaeological sites. On 1 January 1883, General Pitt Rivers, a well-known and well-established archaeologist, took up the post of the first Inspector of Ancient Monuments, a role he continued in until his death in 1900.

Massive devastation of historic cities such as London, Bristol, Winchester, Exeter and Southampton during the Second World War prompted substantial archaeological provision during redevelopment. Indeed, the need had been recognized even before the end of the war when, in March 1944, the Council for British Archaeology was founded to promote British archaeology in all its aspects. The principle that became established in Britain was what later became known as 'rescue archaeology' – the rapid recording of archaeological sites immediately in advance of their destruction. This is all that could be done in a political climate and legal framework that promoted a presumption in favour of development.

During the 1950s and early 1960s, a substantial group of itinerant rescue archaeologists moved from site to site, excavating and recording remains, often in difficult and frustrating conditions (Rahtz 1974). In a few areas, permanent excavation 'units' were established, Winchester being among the first in 1961, soon followed by Southampton, Oxford, Lincoln, Colchester and others; but this was not enough. In 1960, the Royal Commission on Historical Monuments sounded a warning bell about the destruction of archaeological sites in the English countryside through the publication of a book entitled *A matter of time*, but its message was never really acted upon. The pace of construction and reconstruction continued unabated into the 1970s, and new threats came into play, for example the development of the motorway system, expanded mineral extraction and the extensification of forestry.

In America, similar problems were being encountered, sometimes on an alarming scale. In the 10-year period to 1972, for example, it was estimated that 25 per cent of all known archaeological sites in Arkansas had been destroyed (McGimsey 1972, 3). 'Salvage archaeology', as it is called in the US, was commonplace and widespread, but even by the early 1970s there was disenchantment with the approach. As McGimsey put it: 'The archaeologist cannot afford to continue to let the engineer, the farmer, and the urban developer determine where he is to utilize the limited resources at his command' (ibid., 18). What emerged instead was 'cultural resource management', an approach that advocated preservation and protection as the primary objective, followed by the controlled and carefully reasoned exploitation of archaeological remains (Fowler 1986). In this view, archaeological remains were seen as existing not primarily for archaeological research as and when archaeologists felt like it, but rather as something rather more valuable that was a community resource for which there was shared responsibility (Cleere and Fowler 1976). It was the translation of these principles across the Atlantic into Britain during the 1980s, mixed with Britain's own traditions of rescue archaeology and a primary concern for the care of ancient monuments, that provides the basis of modern archaeological resource management in what can now be seen as the post-rescue era (Thomas 1977).

Archaeology and politics have always been closely connected, and during the 1980s archaeological resource management embraced and developed responses to two politically charged ways of thinking. First was *cultural relativism* and the recognition that what is sometimes called the Western Gaze provided a very distorted view of the past by perpetuating an essentially imperialist view of heritage in which there was just one view on how it should be looked after and what it all meant (Smith 2006). David Lowenthal memorably referred to the 'past as a foreign country' in his book of the same name, arguing forcefully that the past had ceased to be a sanction for inherited power or privilege, but rather had become a focus for personal and national identity and a bulwark against distressing change (Lowenthal 1985). Second was the idea of *sustainability*, a perspective that originated in the Western world and which has been evangelically promoted across the planet and linked closely with the 'green debate' (Macinnes and Wickham-Jones 1992). In an archaeological context it effectively means making good use of resources for the needs of today without compromising the ability of future generations to do the same.

Responding to these challenging new ways of thinking had a big impact on archaeological resource management, but both cultural relativism and sustainability were in a sense middle-range theories that mediated high-level political philosophy with low-level solutions to the day-to-day problems of actually dealing with the heritage in terms of land use, visitor management, education programmes, access and infrastructure. As the first decade of the twenty-first century unfolds there is a new challenge to heritage thinking, at least within the centre-left political systems now widespread in Europe and North America. The old high-level political philosophy of *monetarism* so influential through the 1970s, 1980s and 1990s has been overtaken by an approach known as *instrumentalism*: the promotion of actions or activities not because they are useful or interesting in their own right but because they are tools or instruments in the attainment of wider ambitions in the realm of human experience. Such experiences are not simply a sensory state of 'happiness' but an aesthetic dimension of life in which the individual citizen optimizes their individual potential as a member of a global society in an environment that is stable, just, secure and sustainable.

At the European level such thinking harmonizes with deeply embedded principles of democratization, subsidiarity of decision-making and cultural identity enunciated in the Maastricht Treaty on European Union (Art. 128). It can also be seen in debates initiated by English Heritage on the future of the historic environment, its role in people's lives and its contribution to the cultural and economic well-being of the nation (English Heritage 2000), and is core to the idea of culturally led regeneration (Jowell 2005).

The orientation of archaeological resource management towards people and the greater well-being of individuals is already beginning to manifest itself in practical terms that can be summed up as a cycle of understanding, valuing, caring and enjoying (Figure 19.2). Structuring those relations are a series of evolving principles and ideals (English Heritage 2008, with additions):

- The historic environment is a shared resource.
- Everyone should be able to participate in sustaining the historic environment so that a representative sample is available for future generations to utilize.

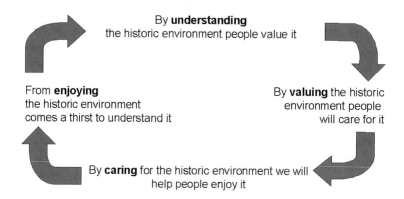

Figure 19.2 Diagram showing the heritage cycle.
Source: Based on English Heritage 2008

- Understanding the significance of places and things is vital to the management process.
- Decisions about change must be reasonable, transparent and consistent.
- Plurality of endeavour is encouraged so that there is a balance between the preservation of material for the future through conservation and protection, and exploitation for the present through investigation and research.
- Decision-makers should be well informed about the relative importance of known dimensions of the historic environment, usually through some kind of structured assessment or evaluation process.
- Documenting and learning from decisions is essential.

The majority of archaeologists working in Britain are employed in the field of archaeological resource management. A survey of the profession by the Institute for Archaeologists in 2007–8 revealed that there were nearly 7,000 professional archaeologists working in the UK: about 51 per cent with organizations engaged in field research and investigation in the private sector; 17 per cent worked in local government mainly in the administration of the planning system and providing archaeological advice; 15 per cent were based in universities; 10 per cent worked for national government agencies; and 8 per cent worked for other kinds of archaeological organizations (Aitchison and Edwards 2008). Archaeology in Britain has become a highly professionalized discipline, and within archaeological resource management there are clearly defined role-sets including: *curators*, who are responsible for the overall well-being of the resource; *contractors*, who carry out archaeological investigations and surveys; and *consultants*, who advise and guide individuals and organizations on archaeological matters.

What unites everyone, however, is a concern for the raw material of archaeology, the stuff of the discipline that is in, on or under the ground, and which has come to be understood as the archaeological resource.

WHAT IS THE ARCHAEOLOGICAL RESOURCE?

Defining what constitutes the archaeological resource as a strand of the historic environment is far from easy, and offers both intellectual and practical considerations. At a theoretical level, what is of interest to archaeologists largely depends on the interpretative frameworks within which they work. In Britain, as in other Western societies, archaeology is distanced from the societies that created the things that are studied. Archaeological remains are examined with detachment and from numerous viewpoints. Thus within the processual perspectives of the 'New Archaeology' common from the 1960s through into the late 1980s, the archaeological resource was the material against which theories were tested. In the post-processual archaeologies widely practised since the mid-1980s, it is not so much the individual elements that are important as the totality, the materials and their context from which broadly based narratives can be constructed.

In practical terms, there are problems and issues too. The core is easy, as things like Palaeolithic hand-axes, Neolithic long barrows, Roman villas, deserted medieval villages and shipwrecks are widely recognized as being within the archaeologist's domain. But where does it stop? What about hedgerows and boundaries that are still in use but which were first built in prehistoric or Saxon times? Is a historic building or ancient church archaeological? And what about a peat-bog, a Second World War airfield, the folklore attached to a remote cross-roads or the songs, dances and traditions of those harvesting crops in nineteenth-century fields? The problem is that, operationally, much of what is interesting to archaeologists is also of interest to others. The boundaries of the subject are blurred, and archaeological interests overlap with history, sociology, landscape geography, anthropology, ethnology, architectural history, folklore studies and many others beside. Peter Fowler once argued that the whole of Britain should be seen as one enormous archaeological site, and in a sense he was right. Since earliest times, people have lived, worked and been buried within a space that, in social terms, is infinite because it stretches outwards in all directions from the focus of an individual's existence: their home or home territory. While space is socially infinite it is, however, physically constrained. There is only so much of it, and the distribution of activities within space is uneven and discrete. What the archaeologist normally finds are hot-spots or nodes where evidence of the activities that took place is rich enough, or substantial enough, or well-preserved enough to be visible, recognizable and recordable. This is the archaeological resource, but there is no neat embracing definition of it; it is effectively whatever archaeologists recognize as relevant to their work at any given point in time. In this sense, the intellectual or theoretical constitution of archaeological work drives and defines its practical application.

While the exact definition of what the archaeological resource comprises evolves and develops, a number of common characteristics can be recognized:

• Finite: there is only so much of it, even though we do not know exactly how much.
• Immovable: context and relationships are critical to understanding and appreciating

415

archaeological material. While individual objects and sometimes whole sites have been moved, doing so destroys their authenticity, setting and context.

- Non-renewable: archaeological material does not regenerate itself. Once destroyed it has gone for ever. It could be argued that because the social process continues, more archaeology is being formed all the time, but this is an extension to the record, not a replacement or replenishment of it.
- Fragile and vulnerable: archaeological remains are easily toppled and broken, buried remains can be segmented or the environments that surround them inadvertently changed.
- Integrity is consequent upon completeness of survival: the value of the resource lies partly in our ability to interpret it and read it. Legibility is therefore important and the more complete the surviving pieces the more that can be done with them.
- Each element has spatial, temporal and socially determined relationships with other elements. The material that comprises the resource was created as part of a set of social processes that were not confined to single sites or places.
- Attributed meaning: archaeological objects do not have inherent meaning; people and society give them meaning.
- Includes both tangible and intangible elements that are sometimes connected.
- What is represented is a unique record of human achievement over the whole duration of human existence.

Within these common characteristics, it is recognized that for practical purposes three main kinds of archaeological deposits and situations can be identified, partly as a result of conditions of survival and partly because of the intrinsic nature of the material itself. These provide useful pragmatic categories for dealing with remains but are not intended to be all-embracing:

- Single monuments: the most familiar items that archaeologists are concerned with, including relatively discrete structures such as round barrows, long barrows, Roman villas, deserted villages, mines, shipwrecks or glasshouses.
- Urban deposits: composite deposits created in heavily occupied areas from Roman times through to the present day. Especially important is the way in which they build up within a restricted area and become reworked, over and over again.
- Relict landscapes: potentially the most important kind of data for archaeology, especially for earlier periods, relict landscapes comprise groups of related monuments and structures bound together as though in some form of articulation (natural or man-made), even though the archaeological deposits may not themselves be continuous. Historic Landscape Characterization (HLC) has become an important tool in defining and describing areas of relict landscape (Clark *et al.* 2004).

One major problem with all three forms is the extent to which we know what we have. No one is ever able to see the complete picture, and there is no way of really knowing how much archaeology there is to find. For this reason, the resource has to be conceptualized and

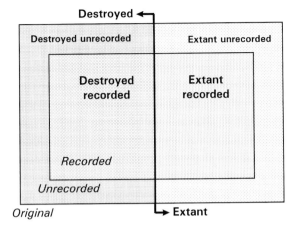

Figure 19.3 Diagram showing the main components of the archaeological resource.

quantified in a carefully structured way. Figure 19.3 shows a diagram representing the main elements. The outer box represents what, within any particular definition of archaeology, there is to know about the 'original resource'. Part of that material is recorded in various ways. Britain is very fortunate to have numerous and long-standing lists and inventories of ancient monuments held at national and local level by government agencies and local authorities. This can be referred to as the 'recorded resource'. In England, for example, the recorded resource is currently estimated at about 900,000 items, including stray finds, place-name records and many other relatively ephemeral pieces of information. About 600,000 items refer to what could be called archaeological monuments of one sort or another: sites and structures (including ancient buildings) that contain archaeological deposits (Darvill and Fulton 1998).

Part of the original resource and the recorded resource remains extant and is therefore able to be investigated or experienced. That part of the original resource that is extant but not yet recorded is the target for surveys and studies whose objectives involve the discovery of new sites. That part of the original resource that has been destroyed but was recorded before being lost is now known only through the records themselves, which range in quality from the very comprehensive to the almost incomprehensible. The resource destroyed without record will never be known about and is now completely lost. In large measure, how we see the archaeological resource and how it will expand in future comes down to its importance and how it is valued by society today.

WHY DO WE VALUE ARCHAEOLOGICAL REMAINS?

Importance and value are two rather different things. The former applies differentially to particular elements of the archaeological resource, in the sense that some things are regarded as more important than others. In determining whether remains are of sufficient importance to merit designation under the prevailing national legislation (see below), remains are judged against defined criteria: survival/condition, period, rarity, fragility/vulnerability, diversity, documentation, group value and potential, which can be systematically applied (Darvill *et al.* 1987). More general measures of importance have also been suggested, for example the idea of 'legibility' in the case of urban deposits (Carver 1996).

Value, however, is rather different as it relates to broad, socially defined perceptions of what is good, right and acceptable. It applies not so much to individual sites or monuments, but rather to the resource as a whole and the way it is publically perceived. Many attempts have been made to articulate and understand the way in which society values its heritage (Mathers *et al.* 2005; Clark 2006). In most the idea of 'value' is conceived in its sociological sense, a set of standards against which things are compared and placed on a gradient between extremes such as desirable or undesirable, appropriate or inappropriate, worthwhile or pointless.

In a ground-breaking review of archaeological value systems, William Lipe (1984) considered four types of value: Economic, Aesthetic, Associative and Informational. These he linked to a range of interests within society, recognizing that archaeological value is embedded in wider issues, although retaining the notion that cultural materials from the past function as resources in the present.

A second approach is to look at value in terms of what we do with archaeological remains in relation to three kinds of future, the short, medium and long term (Darvill 1995). For the short term the idea of *use values* focuses on the immediate consumption of the historic environment, recognizing that the act of consumption is also creative, through such activities as: research; art; education; recreation and tourism; symbolic representation; the legitimization of action; social solidarity; and monetary and economic gain (Figure 19.4). For the medium term *option values* direct attention towards the deferred use the heritage not only in fulfilment of the conservation

Figure 19.4 Visitors at Stonehenge, Wiltshire.
   Source: Timothy Darvill

ethic of preservation but also the realization that not all possible uses are currently definable. Axiomatic to this value system is the physical preservation of things in order to achieve the notional preservation of options, an idea at the heart of the 'green debate'. Finally, for the long term, *existence values* are related to emotional attachments to things that cannot be directly experienced: the sense of well-being, contentment and satisfaction – the so-called 'feel-good' factor. Thus at one end of the value gradient is the elation of knowing that all is well because everything is safe, that viability and diversity are being maintained and that existence is assured. At the other end is despondency because the resource is under great threat, viability and integrity are marginal, diversity is low and continued existence endangered.

More recently, developing the instrumentalist agenda, news ways of examining and documenting value have emerged. In particular, Robert Hewison and John Holden (Clark 2006, 14–18) propose three opposing dimensions to value that can be conceived as pulling against each other. First is the *intrinsic value* of heritage itself in terms of an individual's experience of heritage intellectually, emotionally and spiritually. Second is *instrumental value*, referring explicitly to the ancillary effects of heritage used to achieve a social or economic purpose. Third is *institutional value*, which refers to the processes and techniques that organizations adopt in creating something for the public good.

Running through all these approaches is the idea that values are supported by a constructive tension between different modes of thought in the minds of individuals. This carries through into the demands placed upon archaeological materials. John Barrett has argued that the proper role for archaeologists is the construction of histories (1995), and in many ways this is the most widely recognized and obvious element of archaeological work, the things that archaeologists find are the props and scenery for such stories. But is archaeology just a form of history? What archaeologists make may be a kind of history, but what they actually see through their excavations, surveys and technical studies is something else. In his inaugural lecture as Professor of European Archaeology in the Institute of Archaeology, University of London, in 1946, Gordon Childe argued that archaeology was a social science, in effect the recording of the longest-lived, non-repeatable survey of social change ever. Certainly what archaeologists record are glimpses of the behaviour and actions of individuals and groups in the past, but what they make is best described as 'knowledge', including, for example, narrative knowledge, strategic knowledge, contemplative knowledge and indigenous knowledge (Darvill 2008).

THE CONCEPT OF 'MANAGEMENT' IN ARCHAEOLOGY

The fact that archaeological remains are recognized and given value by society means that choices have to be made about what to do with ancient sites, structures and finds. The contemporary world is full of competing demands; change is the natural state of things and provides the engine that drives society forward. Change is the process by which archaeological deposits are both created and destroyed, and the context in which choices, sometimes very difficult choices, have to be made: do we keep this Roman villa or construct a new wing for the local hospital?

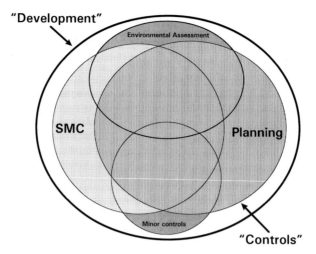

Figure 19.5 Diagram showing the relationship of different controls over developments impacting on archaeological deposits. SMC = Scheduled Monument Consent procedure.
Source: Timothy Darvill

It would be nice to think that everything can be preserved, but that is utopian. The concept of management in archaeology is all about controlling change – the contrived regulation of situations for the fulfilment of defined objectives. These objectives flow from the general guiding principles of archaeological resource management already noted and can be summarized as follows:

- To retain the rich diversity of archaeological remains that is known to exist in the landscape.
- To make the archaeological heritage satisfy the demands made upon it by society as a whole.
- To reconcile conflict and competition for the use of land containing ancient monuments.

In addition to its intellectual context, archaeological resource management must also fit within the legislative frameworks that relate both to its practice and to the materials with which it is concerned. As already noted, the scope and range of legislative controls is itself a reflection of society's interest in and concern for the past (Figure 19.5). Today, legislative controls for archaeology fall into two main spheres: firstly, spatial planning and environmental legislation; and, secondly, ancient monuments legislation. All find expression at three main levels – international, national and local.

Spatial planning and environmental legislation

The key concept here is that of 'development', which in Britain is taken to mean: 'the carrying out of building, engineering, mining or other operations in, on, over or under land, or the making of any material change in the use of any buildings or other land' (*Town and Country Planning Act 1990* S55(1)). All development is regulated in two main ways, through strategic planning and development control.

Strategic spatial planning takes place at a regional and local level through the construction, debate and agreement of development plans for specific administrative areas. The confirmed plans, which are intended to produce a vision for the future of places and identify how positive social, economic and environmental outcomes will be delivered, provide frameworks for decision-making and development control. Amongst the topics covered by strategic plans are the expected impact of proposals on archaeological remains and how such impacts can be minimized. All parts of the UK are covered by high-level regional strategies which in turn inform development plans produced by individual local planning authorities (variously County, District, Unitary or National Park) and should include guidance on archaeology and heritage. Since 2001 all extensive spatial plans are subject to Strategic Environmental Assessment (SEA) as established by a *European Commission Directive on the Assessment of the Effects of Certain Plans and Programmes on the Environment*. The aim of SEA is to better inform decision-makers about the sustainability of the strategies and plan and ensure that the full impact of delivery schemes on all aspects of the environment is understood.

Development control relates to the decision-making process as it applies to particular schemes and is undertaken at regional and local level through the granting of planning permission by local planning authorities. In determining applications these authorities must give consideration to a wide range of factors. Since 1985 this has included the results of Environmental Impact Assessment (EIA) carried out under the European Directive on Environmental Assessment, implemented in the United Kingdom through various Statutory Implements. EIA provides for the full review of large and potentially damaging schemes, including an assessment of potential impacts on archaeological remains.

National guidance notes set out the parameters within which decisions can be taken, and in England PPG16 on 'Archaeology and Planning' and PPG15 on 'Planning and the Historic Environment' set out the main considerations (similar guidance is provided for Scotland and Wales in separate documents but it should be noted that at the time of writing there is much discussion about the revision and/or consolidation of all these guidance notes and in late 2009 draft replacement documents were issued for consultation. In particular, the desirability of preserving nationally important sites *in situ* is made a material consideration, and rescue archaeology is identified as a second-best option where preservation *in situ* is not possible. In granting planning permission, the local planning authority has the power to impose planning conditions that provide for an agreed programme of archaeological works (a mitigation strategy) to be carried out prior to the development taking place. Such works would normally be undertaken at the developer's expense.

In England, approximately 595,000 planning applications were submitted to local planning authorities in 2008, of which about 88 per cent were approved outright or subject to conditions. Processing all these amounts to a very considerable volume of work, especially when it is recognized that nearly 2 per cent of applications had archaeological implications, with perhaps a little less than 1 per cent having direct archaeological impacts on recorded remains (Darvill and Russell 2002). Of course, the definition of development is not all-embracing, and many things that are archaeologically damaging fall outside the definition or are excluded from it by other pieces of special-purpose legislation (e.g. works carried out by public utility companies). Equally, there is provision for the preservation or investigation of archaeological remains within other legislation, for example as part of the designation of National Parks, and, most recently, for England and Wales, through the reporting of stray finds as set out in the *Treasure Act 1997*.

Ancient monuments legislation

At an international level there are four main pieces of guiding legislation, two from UNESCO and two from the Council of Europe. The oldest is the *Convention Concerning the Protection of the World Cultural and Natural Heritage*, better known as the World Heritage Convention, adopted by UNESCO's General Conference in Paris on 16 November 1972 and ratified by the UK government in 1984. By 2008 there were 22 cultural World Heritage Sites within the UK, including Stonehenge and Avebury, Canterbury Cathedral and St Augustine's Abbey, the City of Bath, Edinburgh, the Tower of London, Blenheim Palace and Hadrian's Wall and the Antonine Wall as part of a transnational 'Frontiers of the Roman Empire' site. The primary aim of the convention is to identify sites considered to be of such exceptional interest and such universal value that their protection is the responsibility of all mankind, although the direct responsibility for managing sites on the World Heritage list rests firmly with the government of the state in which the designated site lies.

A second important UNESCO Convention is concerned with 'Safeguarding of the Intangible Cultural Heritage'. It was opened for signature in October 2003 but has not yet been ratified by the UK government. A relatively new concept in archaeological resource management, the intangible heritage is taken to mean: 'the practices, representations, expressions, knowledge, skills – as well as the instruments, objects, artefacts and cultural spaces associated therewith – that communities, groups and, in some cases, individuals recognize as part of their cultural heritage' manifest in such domains as 'oral traditions and expressions, language, performing arts, social practices, rituals, festive events, traditional craftsmanship, and knowledge and practices concerning nature and the universe' (Article 2).

At a European level, the *Convention on the Protection of the Archaeological Heritage*, better known as the Malta Convention, was opened for signature in January 1992 in Valletta, Malta, by the Council of Europe; it was ratified by the UK government in September 2000. The definition of archaeological sites in the convention is broad, including structures, constructions, groups of buildings, developed sites, movable objects and monuments of other kinds whether situated on land or under water (Article 1). Emphasis is placed on the need to maintain proper inventories of recorded sites; the information is subsequently used in the planning process to ensure well-balanced strategies for the protection, conservation and enhancement of sites of archaeological interest.

Also at a European level is the *Framework Convention on the Value of Cultural Heritage for Society* opened for signature in Faro on 27 October 2005 but not yet ratified by the UK government. In it, the cultural heritage is recognized as 'a group of resources inherited from the past which people identify, independently of ownership, as a reflection and expression of their constantly evolving values, beliefs, knowledge and traditions. It includes all aspects of the environment resulting from the interaction between people and places through time.' The aim of this convention is to provide a sound and all-embracing structure in order to ensure cultural heritage of its rightful place at the centre of a new vision for sustainable development.

At a national level, the main legislation is the *Ancient Monuments and Archaeological Areas Act 1979*, amended for England by the *National Heritage Act 1984*. However, between 2000 and 2007 a thorough review of the heritage legislation was undertaken in order to consolidate diverse existing provisions and make it fit for the twenty-first century. In consequence, a *Draft Heritage Protection Bill* was published in April 2008, but at the time of writing it is understood that this will not be put before parliament in the foreseeable future.

Under the prevailing legislation sites or monuments that are explicitly recognized as being of national importance are given special protection. Three such classes of monument are defined: Scheduled Monuments, of which there are currently about 16,000 in England, 5,300 in Scotland and 2,700 in Wales; Guardianship Monuments, of which there about 440 in England, 330 in Scotland and 125 in Wales; and Areas of Archaeological Importance, which are confined to five historic towns in England (Canterbury, Chester, Exeter, Hereford and York). Apart from Guardianship, where the objective of direct management is total preservation of the site, the other designations focus on methods of controlling change as a means of achieving preservation. In the case of Scheduled Monuments, control is achieved through a Scheduled Monument Consent procedure, whereby permission is needed to undertake any kind of works likely to damage the monument. Such permissions may be subject to conditions, including the full archaeological investigation and recording of remains prior to works commencing.

Dealing with all these legal and advisory frameworks, together with numerous policy statements issued by public bodies and interested parties, the process of decision-making has become highly complicated. Moreover, one of the fundamental principles of archaeological resource management is that decision-making should be properly informed. Accordingly, what has become known as the 'management cycle' has developed as an informed, consolidated, repeatable and widely applicable system to guide the acquisition of information and the decision-making process (Darvill and Gerrard 1994, 157; Clark 2001). Figure 19.6 shows the management cycle in schematic form with eight main stages:

- Appraisal: define the problem or issue. In the case of a development programme, this would first involve the definition of the development site boundaries and the nature and scale of what was to be done.
- Assessment. This represents the first substantial piece of work in the management cycle, usually desk-based, and will most likely be undertaken according to a project design or specification established at the appraisal stage.

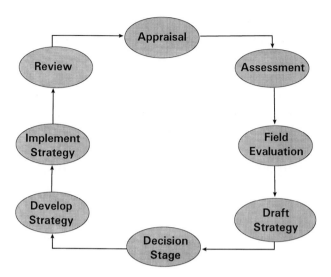

Figure 19.6 Schematic representation of the management cycle applied to archaeological situations.
Source: Timothy Darvill

- Field evaluation. This stage involves the close examination of the archaeological resource, sometimes through excavation, to determine, as far as practicable, the principal physical characteristics of the quality, extent, survival, condition and fragility of the deposits, as well as details of form, interpretation, date and archaeological potential.
- Strategy formulation. This stage involves the construction of an archaeological management or mitigation strategy or detailed project design of some kind, based on the information and conclusions documented by the field evaluation.
- Decision. Here a competent authority will decide whether the strategy as formulated should proceed or not. In the context of a development proposal, this stage will primarily be through the planning system, although where Scheduled Monuments are involved, the decision will also be through the scheduled monument consent system. In the case of research programmes, the project design will probably be the basis of funding approvals.
- Strategy development. Using comments and information from the decision phase, the strategy itself can be developed and expanded, with more detail added if necessary.
- Strategy implementation. In archaeological terms, this is the most visible element of the work, as it involves what most people would regard as the real business of archaeology: excavations, surveys, technical studies and so on. In the case of a development scheme, this often happens in three phases:
  1 *Pre-construction works*: preparatory works for the preservation or conservation of deposits, and the total or selective excavation of areas before groundworks get under way.

2 *Intra-construction works*: small-scale excavations, watching briefs and recorded observations undertaken in parallel with groundworks and the activities of construction contractors on the site.

3 *Post-construction works*: archaeological operations carried out after the development is complete, including on-site operations such as the establishment and maintenance of long-term conservation or preservation measures, and off-site operations such as the analysis of finds and records from earlier phases of archaeological work, the conservation of fragile finds, the preparation of general and academic reports and accounts of the work, and the deposition of the archive and finds in an appropriate museum.

For research programmes, the implementation stage will comprise the execution in series or in parallel of the various pieces of data-collection, followed by an analysis and reporting stage.

• Review. The final stage in the cycle is a review of what has been done and whether it has achieved what was intended. In some cases, this stage may last several years, with regular monitoring to see that aspects of the scheme are working.

In all these stages, professionalism is increasingly important. Since its creation in 1982, the Institute of Field Archaeologists, since 2008 known as the Institute for Archaeologists, has been concerned with the promotion and raising of professional standards. Its membership, which represents over one third of all professional archaeologists in the UK, works to an agreed set of 'standards' for archaeological projects. However, what no legislation, policy, guidance or standards can deal with are the political and emotional aspects of the process. Both are surprisingly important. In the case of planning decisions, it is not the professional advisers who make the decisions but elected representatives as council members who sit on planning committees. It is these groups who ultimately decide whether archaeological considerations must give way to social, economic or ideological pressures, or vice versa; and the general public have an increasingly strong voice in these discussions, as the case of the Rose Theatre in London illustrated very clearly (Biddle 1989; Wainwright 1989).

Even where the proper procedures have been followed to the letter there are no easy answers to satisfy everyone. An important element of archaeological resource management has become the skill of finding ways of satisfying more than one demand at a time, of balancing competing interests. The tools available to do this comprise what are called 'management options'. These can be deployed either in series or in parallel for maximum effect, the full range of such options being very considerable, and expanding. Broadly, however, they fall into three groups: protection, conservation and exploitation.

• Protection. This involves minimizing or guarding against the adverse effects of some kind of identifiable threat to the archaeological resource. The main source of such threats

Figure 19.7 Protecting monuments: wooden barriers in place around a section of Iron Age rampart at Badbury Rings, Dorset.
Source: Timothy Darvill

comes from disturbance of the ground in which ancient structures and deposits lie.

In urban areas, construction works such as the excavation of basements, foundations, soak-aways, drains and lift-shafts are all common causes of such disturbance, as too is the laying of pipelines or groundworks connected with the creation of level surfaces for car-parks and playing fields. These can be anticipated and a balance achieved between the economical construction of buildings and the constraints (archaeological and otherwise) of the site. There are a number of ways in which the preservation of archaeological deposits can be achieved, many of which require an engineered solution to the problem of supporting large structures on small but strong foundations.

In the countryside, the main threats are from agriculture and extensive land use such as forestry. Here protection can be provided by creating local micro-environments for recognized monuments, for example by taking them out of cultivation or by fencing and marking them (Figure 19.7). Intensive threats in the countryside, from quarrying, mineral extraction and road construction, for example, require similar protective measures to those used in urban areas, and here again engineers are becoming increasingly imaginative in what can be achieved.

- Conservation. This, by contrast, is a dynamic response and involves establishing a positive relationship between processes of change and the maintenance of the archaeological resource. Typically this involves the adoption of land-management regimes that promote the stability of buried or upstanding archaeological deposits, and keeping in check any events that might cause the accelerated decay of such remains (Figure 19.8). Conservation requires constant vigilance and the availability of skills not only to recognize signs reflecting the onset of accelerated decay but also to do something about it. In the case of small-scale effects, the process is straightforward. Visitor erosion where footpaths cross archaeological sites is one of the most widespread examples, where the opportunity to move the main path slightly or divert users to allow the regeneration of vegetation cover may be all that is needed. Bigger problems are more difficult, among the worst being tree-throw in strong winds and coastal erosion. The National Trust in particular is at the forefront of developing new approaches to these kinds of problems in the countryside, and much innovative research is carried out on their properties.

- Exploitation. Many demands are placed upon the archaeological resource by today's society. These range from access to ancient monuments for educational and recreational use, promotion of the archaeological heritage as a tourist attraction and visitor facility and the exploration of the past through research and study. All represent perfectly legitimate claims and need to be taken into account when considering the long-term future of the resource. Intensive exploitation of the archaeological resource through excavation or restoration for public display can be as destructive as developing the land for a completely non-archaeological objective.

Making accessible some of the more tangible remains of the past often finds public support. Within the development process, and in countryside management, there are numerous opportunities to make aspects of the local archaeological resource accessible. Nor need presentational work always be archaeologically destructive. There is often enough visible already to allow the creation of a 'heritage trail', whether as a self-guided facility or as part of a more

Figure 19.8 Conservation in action: restoration and consolidation in progress at Lulworth Castle, Dorset.
Source: Timothy Darvill

structured experience. In almost any development there is scope to mark the positions of earlier buildings in coloured brick, or perpetuate historic alignments or reconstruct important features. Sociologically, such things serve to strengthen the 'existence' value of the historic elements of cultural heritage, but other values are important too. A poll by MORI of 3,000 people in England in 2000 found that 88 per cent thought the historic environment was important in creating jobs and boosting the economy, 87 per cent thought the historic environment played an important part in the cultural life of the country, while 76 per cent thought their own lives were richer for having the opportunity to visit it or see it.

The number of publicly accessible archaeological sites, museums, heritage centres and historic attractions has risen dramatically in recent decades, and with increases in available leisure time within the population as a whole, historic sites and displays are important destinations for trips and visits. Whether in public or private hands, there is a range of attractions that run from the almost untouched site opened up for visitors with very little razzmatazz, through to the intensively marketed 'heritage attraction' where 'the past comes alive' in a way that is more theatre than exhibition (Figure 19.9). Across this spectrum there is also a visible shift from the authentic at one end to the fabricated at the other. Motivation and purpose are important considerations when judging these kinds of facility. Some wholly fabricated reconstructions, like Butser Hill Iron Age farm in Hampshire or Bede's World in Jarrow, Tyne and Wear, are serious scientific experiments, carefully researched and packaged

Figure 19.9 Heritage at work: the Morwellham Quay Heritage centre, Devon.

Source: Timothy Darvill

in a way that maintains their integrity as well as providing a good visitor experience. The highly popular Jorvik Centre in York comes close to this too, being a reconstruction based on, and situated exactly over, the excavated remains of one small part of the Viking city.

Simple structures and monuments in the countryside are hard to present to the public to everyone's satisfaction, and raise many interesting issues of interpretation. To what extent should the things presented be authentic? Do the visiting public discern between what is real and what is not? Again the picture is far from simple, with progression from the wholly authentic, through the restored, to the reconstructed (Figure 19.10), and on again to the totally fabricated. At Guardianship properties managed by English Heritage, the policy is to consolidate as found, in other words not to add anything or take anything away but simply to make safe whatever is there when they take the site over. Even this can be misleading, however, because the Victorians in particular were great restorers and some of what is visible at well-known monuments today is little more than 100 years old. Moreover, painstaking research is often needed to spot the additions. The Rollright Stones in Oxfordshire provide a good example (Lambrick 1988). This well-known and much-visited stone circle today comprises about 73 upright stones in what appears to be an almost perfect ring. Studies by the Oxford Archaeological Unit, however, revealed that at least a third of the stones had been repositioned in AD 1882, and that another third of them were leaning or displaced at this time. Two stones were probably added. Of the stones visible today, only about one third are in the same positions they occupied in the seventeenth century AD.

Social, political and ethical issues are also important, as Stonehenge, Wiltshire, demonstrates time and again (Darvill 2006, 267–82). While for most of the twentieth century the main stone

Figure 19.10 Reconstructing archaeological remains: Roman gatehouse at South Shields, Tyne and Wear.
Source: Timothy Darvill

circle was accessible to the public, it was closed off in 1983 when visitor numbers rose to over 800,000 per year. The site had become a victim of its own success in the sense that the experience everyone came to see was clouded by the sheer weight of numbers. Interest in the site at the summer solstice followed a similar course. Until the early 1980s, various groups including latter-day druids, hippies, travellers and many others gathered to witness the sunrise and make festival. Between 1985 and 2001 the Stonehenge area was inaccessible to the public over the solstice, much to the dismay of almost everyone (Chippindale 1986). Its reopening has certainly proved popular and most years since have seen around 20,000 people in and around the stones at sunrise on the summer solstice. Numerous plans for the conservation and management of Stonehenge and its surroundings, including the closure of the road that runs past the site, the removal of existing visitor facilities at the stones, the creation of an archaeological park containing not only Stonehenge but also many associated monuments, and the resiting of visitor facilities on the edge of the World Heritage Site have been proposed and several consultations held (Wainwright 1996; Darvill 2006, 277–8).

As an essentially academic subject, archaeology is driven forward by the results of research and new discoveries (Figure 19.11). There has been much debate about what constitutes research in this sense, who should do it and who should be setting the agenda; but much of the discussion misses the point that all archaeological work that involves the investigation or examination of original data is research in one sense or another. To try to sub-divide and partition archaeological research rigidly into discrete elements is futile, but two very broad and by no means mutually exclusive groupings can be recognized: problem-orientated research and development-prompted research.

Figure 19.11 Archaeological excavations at Silchester, Hampshire.
  Source: Timothy Darvill

Problem-orientated research arises from the definition of a potentially interesting problem and a methodology that allows it to be explored. The work may involve the application of particular methodologies, including perhaps excavation, at a local or regional level, depending on the nature of the problem under investigation. Funding for this kind of work usually comes from public sources through government agencies, local authorities, charitable trusts or universities. Naturally there is considerable competition for the relatively limited sums available.

Development-prompted research arises from the need to investigate deposits that in the normal course of events will be destroyed. This is usually because the preservation of a monument, or part of it, is not feasible or is deemed to be of secondary importance to the benefits of the works that will replace it. Superficially, this is 'rescue excavation', at one time rather euphemistically called 'preservation by record'; but to compare modern rescue excavation with that undertaken in the 1960s and early 1970s is unfair. Much earlier work was literally rescuing what could be salvaged; nowadays the skill of the archaeological curator specifying the work and the archaeological contractor carrying out the work lies in getting the best information possible from the opportunity available, being selective within defined research parameters.

CONCLUSION

The past gets out of date very quickly, not so much because of new discoveries (although these are always important) but because of new ideas, new models and new explanations. How long the explanations and accounts presented in this book will stand up remains to be seen, but alongside a continuing concern for explanation there is, as this chapter seeks to show, considerable interest in the raw data on which explanations are built. Society continually steals bits of its past to shape its future, sometimes to construct knowledge and create history, at other times out of an interest in physical remains providing the focus for a day out.

Key texts

Darvill, T., 1987. *Ancient monuments in the countryside*. Historic Buildings and Monuments Commission for England Archaeological Report 5. London: English Heritage.
Harrison, R. (ed.) 1994. *Manual of heritage management*. Oxford: Butterworth Heinemann.
Hunter, J.R. and Ralston, I.B.M. (eds) 2006. *Archaeological resource management in the UK: an introduction*. Stroud: Sutton Publishing. 2 edn.
Lowenthal, D., 1985. *The past is a foreign country*. Cambridge: Cambridge University Press.
Smith, L., 2006. *Uses of heritage*. London: Routledge.

Bibliography

Aitchison, K., and Edwards, R., 2008. *Archaeology labour market intelligence: profiling the profession 2007/08*. Reading: Institute for Archaeologists.
Barrett, J.C., 1995. *Some challenges in contemporary archaeology*. Oxford: Oxbow Books.
Biddle, M., 1989. 'The Rose reviewed: a comedy (?) of errors', *Antiquity* 63, 753–60.
Carver, M., 1996. 'On archaeological value', *Antiquity* 70, 45–56.

Chippindale, C., 1986. 'Stoned Henge: events and issues at the summer solstice 1985', *World Archaeology* 18, 38–58.

Clark, K., 2001. *Informed conservation*. London: English Heritage.

Clark, K. (ed.) 2006. *Capturing the public value of heritage*. London: English Heritage. Available online at www.hlf.org.uk/English/PublicationsAndInfo/AccessingPublications/Capturing.htm.

Clark, J., Darlington, J. and Fairclough, G., 2004. *Using historic landscape characterization*. London and Lancaster: English Heritage and Lancashire County Council.

Cleere, H. and Fowler, P., 1976. 'US archaeology through British eyes', *Antiquity* 50, 230–2.

Darvill, T., 1995. 'Value systems in archaeology', in Cooper, M.A., Firth, A., Carman, J. and Wheatley, D. (eds) *Managing archaeology*. London: Routledge, 40–50.

Darvill, T., 2006. *Stonehenge: the biography of a landscape*. Stroud: Tempus.

Darvill, T., 2008. 'Research frameworks for World Heritage Sites and the conceptualization of archaeological knowledge', *World Archaeology* 39.3, 436–57.

Darvill, T. and Fulton, A., 1998. *MARS: the monuments at risk survey of England, 1995. Main report*. Bournemouth and London: Bournemouth University and English Heritage.

Darvill, T. and Gerrard, C., 1994. *Cirencester: town and landscape*. Cirencester: Cotswold Archaeological Trust.

Darvill, T. and Russell, B., 2002. *Archaeology after PPG16: archaeological investigations in England 1990–1999*. Bournemouth: Bournemouth University School of Conservation Sciences Research Report 10. Available online at http://csweb.bournemouth.ac.uk/aip/ppg16/index.htm.

Darvill, T., Saunders, A. and Startin, B., 1987. 'A question of national importance: approaches to the evaluation of ancient monuments for the Monuments Protection Programme in England', *Antiquity* 61, 393–408.

English Heritage, 2000. *The power of place*. London: English Heritage. Available online at http://www.english-heritage.org.uk/server/show/nav.1447.

English Heritage, 2008. *Conservation principles. Policies and guidance for the sustainable management of the historic environment*. London: English Heritage. Available online at www.english-heritage.org.uk/server/show/nav.9181.

Fowler, D., 1986. 'Conserving American archaeological resources', in Meltzer, D.J., Fowler, D.D. and Sabloff, J.A. (eds) *American archaeology past and future*. Washington, DC: Smithsonian Institution, 135–62.

Jowell, T., 2005. *Better places to live: government, identity and the value of the historic and built environment*. London: Department for Culture, Media and Sport. Available online at www.culture.gov.uk/reference_library/publications/3695.aspx.

Lambrick, G., 1988. *The Rollright Stones: megaliths, monuments, and settlement in the prehistoric landscape*. Historic Buildings and Monuments Commission for England Archaeological Report 6. London: English Heritage.

Lipe, W.D., 1984. 'Value and meaning in cultural resources', in Cleere, H. (ed) *Approaches to the archaeological heritage*. Cambridge: Cambridge University Press, 1–11.

McGimsey, C.R., 1972. *Public archaeology*. New York and London: Seminar Press.

Macinnes, L. and Wickham-Jones, C.R. (eds) 1992. *All natural things. Archaeology and the green debate*. Oxford: Oxbow Monograph 21.

Mathers, C., Darvill, T. and Little, B. (eds) 2005. *Heritage of value, archaeology of renown*. Gainesville: University Press of Florida.

Rahtz, P.A. (ed.) 1974. *Rescue archaeology*. Harmondsworth: Penguin.

Thomas, C., 1977. *After RESCUE, what next?* London: Council for British Archaeology (first de Cardi lecture).

Wainwright, G.J., 1989. 'Saving the Rose', *Antiquity* 63, 430–5.

Wainwright, G.J., 1996. 'Stonehenge saved?', *Antiquity* 70, 9–12.

INDEX

eBooks

eBooks – at www.eBookstore.tandf.co.uk

A library at your fingertips!

eBooks are electronic versions of printed books. You can store them on your PC/laptop or browse them online.

They have advantages for anyone needing rapid access to a wide variety of published, copyright information.

eBooks can help your research by enabling you to bookmark chapters, annotate text and use instant searches to find specific words or phrases. Several eBook files would fit on even a small laptop or PDA.

NEW: Save money by eSubscribing: cheap, online access to any eBook for as long as you need it.

Annual subscription packages

We now offer special low-cost bulk subscriptions to packages of eBooks in certain subject areas. These are available to libraries or to individuals.

For more information please contact webmaster.ebooks@tandf.co.uk

We're continually developing the eBook concept, so keep up to date by visiting the website.

www.eBookstore.tandf.co.uk

Related titles from Routledge

PREHISTORIC BRITAIN
Second Edition

Timothy Darvill

Britain has been inhabited by humans for over half a million years, during which time there were a great many changes in lifestyles and in the surrounding landscape. This book, now in its second edition, examines the development of human societies in Britain from earliest times to the Roman conquest of AD 43, as revealed by archaeological evidence. Special attention is given to six themes which are traced through prehistory: subsistence, technology, ritual, trade, society, and population.

Prehistoric Britain begins by introducing the background to prehistoric studies in Britain, presenting it in terms of the development of interest in the subject and the changes wrought by new techniques such as radiocarbon dating, and new theories, such as the emphasis on social archaeology. The central sections trace the development of society from the hunter-gatherer groups of the last Ice Age, through the adoption of farming, the introduction of metalworking, and on to the rise of highly organized societies living on the fringes of the mighty Roman Empire in the 1st century AD. Throughout, emphasis is given to documenting and explaining changes within these prehistoric communities, and to exploring the regional variations found in Britain. In this way the wealth of evidence that can be seen in the countryside and in our museums is placed firmly in its proper context. It concludes with a review of the effects of prehistoric communities on life today.

With over 120 illustrations, this is a unique review of Britain's ancient past as revealed by modern archaeology. The revisions and updates to Prehistoric Britain ensure that this will continue to be the most comprehensive and authoritative account of British prehistory for those students and interested readers studying the subject.

Timothy Darvill is Professor of Archaeology and Director of the Centre for Archaeology, Anthropology and Heritage in the School of Conservation Sciences, Bournemouth University. His research interests focus on the prehistory of northwest Europe and he has excavated at Stonehenge, Wiltshire, as well as in other parts of England, Wales, the Isle of Man, Greece, and Russia. Among his many publications is The Concise Oxford *Dictionary of Archaeology* (2008) and *Stonehenge: the biography of a landscape* (2006).

Hb: 978-0-415-49026-9
Pb: 978-0-415-49027-6

Available at all good bookshops
For ordering and further information please visit:
www.routledge.com